1980

Peter A. French

EXPLORING PHILOSOPHY

Revised Edition

SCHENKMAN PUBLISHING COMPANY, INC.

Cambridge, Massachusetts 02138

to Sandra

Schenkman books are distributed by
General Learning Press
250 James Street
Morristown, New Jersey

PRINTED IN THE UNITED STATES OF AMERICA

Library of Congress Catalog Card Number: 75–118573

CONTENTS

PREFACE

INTRODUCTORY students often view philosophy as a series of difficult-to-read opinions, without knowing the problems or questions with which philosophers deal. For such students introductory philosophy becomes a kind of academic archeology. This book is an attempt to alter that misconception of a dynamic subject. It is designed to aid the student in his exploration of certain problems in philosophy.

Each chapter begins with non-philosophic readings chosen because of their provocative nature. There follows an inquiry to the philosophic problem which arises out of the introductory readings with guidelines for examining the ideas of well-respected philosophers on the problem. No attempt has been made to present a historical account of the problems nor to structure the readings in a historical pattern. The majority of the selections are from contemporary sources. But if the student or the instructor wishes to examine the problems within their historical context, the book provides suggestions for such an analysis.

In each of the chapter inquiries several questions are posed in order to stimulate a discussion of the problem. Frequently the student is called upon to stop his reading and attempt to find answers to questions, imagine circumstances, or to construct examples relative to the problem. The intention is to involve the student and instructor in a probing intellectual activity which will reveal the complexities of the issues under examination. Philosophy cannot just be read. The participants in its activity must constantly re-evaluate the issues and themselves. At the discretion of the instructor some of the questions raised in the introductions may be emphasized, others ignored.

The brief headnotes to each philosophical selection serve a number of purposes. Most of them give a concise, though obviously incomplete, statement of that particular philosopher's general position and clues concerning what to look for in the reading. Also included in the headnotes are some questions not raised in the chapter introductions, questions which might lead to discussion of related issues or to cross-referencing other articles. Wherever possible philosophical jargon has been avoided. Where it has been necessary to use technical terms, they have been parenthetically defined.

The traditional philosophical areas of epistemology (theory of knowledge), metaphysics (theory of reality), history of philosophy, logic, and value theory (axiology) are involved in the issues dealt with in the chapters, although they are not used as a means of organizing the book. Parts I–III deal with problems related to our social lives, problems of which our newspapers and televisions make us painfully aware. The next Parts, IV and V, concern the individual, his identity and his idea of death (and mind/body dualism). We then turn in Parts VI–VIII to issues which arise in areas of three of our most important pursuits: religion, art, and science.

This book is the result of the recognition, by my fellow professors of philosophy and myself, of the need to involve the introductory student of philosophy in a dynamic and relevant way, to make his experience in philosophy an on-going activity, not a passive memorization of antiquity.

I must express my gratitude to those members of my profession who have encouraged and criticized this book in its various forms. I am especially indebted to my colleagues Professors Lancelot M. Dent and Robert G. Krantzler, to Professor Charles Ledbetter of Thorton Junior College, Professor Phillip Wagand of MaComb County Community College, and Professor Dwight Young of San Diego City College for their thoughtful suggestions on the introductions as well as on the selections to be included. I must express my thanks for generous comments to Professor H. H. Price, Professor William Werkmeister, and Professor H. D. Lewis. The book has also benefited from my association with Professor Richard C. Hall, Professor Jere Jones, Professor Norman Richardson, Professor Chan Coulter, Professor William O'Neill, and Professor James W. Oliver. Their suggestions and inspiration, I hope, have found their way through my style.

P. A. F.

TO THE STUDENT

PHILOSOPHY is an activity; it is done, not read or watched. You can have no real appreciation of the philosophic enterprise unless you do it. Unless you are a participant in its explorations and inquiries, all descriptions of philosophy are rather like word games. This book is designed to involve you in the exploration of certain philosophical problems which are relevant to our daily lives.

One of the characteristics of philosophical problems is that most all of us have answers to them, even if we have not considered the reasons behind our answers. They are problems that occur in living, problems related to "my responsibilities in social situations, my idea of God, my concept of death, my reaction to student activism," etc. Philosophy is much more than the study of highly technical and complex questions of logic. Doing philosophy forces you to engage in one of the most difficult of human tasks: trying "to think, really honestly, about your life and other people's lives," as philosopher Ludwig Wittgenstein wrote to Norman Malcolm. He added, Malcolm reports, "And the trouble is that thinking about these things is *not thrilling* but often downright nasty. And when it's nasty then it's most important." Philosophy is a serious endeavor!

What constitutes philosophical problems? They are not the kind of problems that science can solve or even provide much aid in solving. They are embedded in our language, our feelings, our way of life. They are the sort of problems which the adding of new information fails to alter. They lie just below the surface of our activities, deeply involved in most of what we do. The solutions we accept for these problems are of more concern to us than any in mathematics or the sciences. Often we are called upon to die for them.

Exploring Philosophy is an attempt to bring into the open the causes of these problems. Philosophers attempt to clarify the confusions and misunderstandings into which we often fall. They examine the complexities of problems which seem at first to be so simple. They attempt to help us understand the depths of our commitments and theories about our society, ourselves, our religion, our art, our science.

Wittgenstein characterized a philosophical problem as having the form, "I don't know my way about." We get tangled up in our language and our theorizing on the issues of our day and on the way we think about ourselves. Perhaps we even lose sight of the very questions we are trying to answer. *Exploring Philosophy* is a way of putting before you many of the alternative viewpoints and perspectives on these issues, and it is a way of examining the depths of our concerns relieved of the demands of prejudice. The exploration of philosophical problems has a kind of therapeutic effect. Your goal when doing philosophy ought to be a clear view of the problem, how it arises, and how it is seen by others as well as yourself. Only then will you be in a position to make meaningful evaluations and suggestions relative to it. In fact, in the process of clarifying the intricacies of the problem it may cease to be a problem.

Another Twentieth Century philosopher, Alfred North Whitehead, reminded us that "The pursuit of philosophy is the one avocation denied to omniscience." Philosophy is something a god, an all-knowing divinity, cannot do. No one philosophical position can claim to be any more philosophic than any other position. "No one truth, thoroughly understood in all of the infinitude of its bearings, is more or less philosophical than any other truth." Philosophy is our task, if only because it deals with the uncertainties of being a man. We must live with ourselves.

Each Part of this book confronts you first with philosophical problems as they arise in literature or life itself. The more subtle aspects of the problems are then outlined in the chapter Inquiries. Many questions are raised which you should investigate within your own frame of reference. Then you are ready to explore the ways in which some outstanding philosophers have dealt with the problems.

You cannot expect to create a complete and systematic philosophical position which will provide a suitable answer to all of the questions raised in this book. As an introductory student first you must become aware of what philosophical problems are and why they are so important in our lives. This book is designed for that purpose.

PART I

DUTY AND RESPONSIBILITY

INTRODUCTORY READINGS

Martin Gansberg

William Golding

INQUIRY

SELECTED SOURCES

Kant

Bradley

Sartre

Werkmeister

Strang

Austin

Martin Gansberg

38 Who Saw Murder Didn't Call Police*

FOR MORE THAN HALF AN HOUR 38 RESPECTABLE, LAW-ABIDING CITIZENS in Queens watched a killer stalk and stab a woman in three separate attacks in Kew Gardens.

Twice their chatter and the sudden glow of their bedroom lights interrupted him and frightened him off. Each time he returned, sought her out, and stabbed her again. Not one person telephoned the police during the assault; one witness called after the woman was dead.

That was two weeks ago today.

Still shocked is Assistant Chief Inspector Frederick M. Lussen, in charge of the borough's detectives and a veteran of 25 years of homicide investigations. He can give a matter-of-fact recitation on many murders. But the Kew Gardens slaying baffles him—not because it is a murder, but because the "good people" failed to call the police.

"As we have reconstructed the crime," he said, "the assailant had three chances to kill this woman during a 35-minute period. He returned twice to complete the job. If we had been called when he first attacked, the woman might not be dead now."

This is what the police say happened beginning at 3.20 A.M. in the staid, middle-class, tree-lined Austin Street area:

Twenty-eight-year-old Catherine Genovese, who was called Kitty by almost everyone in the neighborhood, was returning home from her job as manager of a bar in Hollis. She parked her red Fiat in a lot adjacent to the Kew Gardens Long Island Rail Road Station, facing Mowbray Place. Like many residents of the neighborhood, she had parked there day after day since her ar-

* From *The New York Times* (Friday, March 27, 1964).

rival from Connecticut a year ago, although the railroad frowns on the practice.

She turned off the lights of her car, locked the door, and started to walk the 100 feet to the entrance of her apartment at 82–70 Austin Street, which is in a Tudor building, with stores on the first floor and apartments on the second.

The entrance to the apartment is in the rear of the building because the front is rented to retail stores. At night the quiet neighborhood is shrouded in the slumbering darkness that marks most residential areas.

Miss Genovese noticed a man at the far end of the lot, near a seven-story apartment house at 82–40 Austin Street. She halted. Then, nervously, she headed up Austin Street toward Lefferts Boulevard, where there is a call box to the 102nd Police Precinct in nearby Richmond Hill.

She got as far as a street light in front of a bookstore before the man grabbed her. She screamed. Lights went on in the 10-story apartment house at 82–67 Austin Street, which faces the bookstore. Windows slid open and voices punctuated the early-morning stillness.

Miss Genovese screamed: "Oh, my God, he stabbed me! Please help me! Please help me!"

From one of the upper windows in the apartment house, a man called down: "Let that girl alone!"

The assailant looked up at him, shrugged, and walked down Austin Street toward a white sedan parked a short distance away. Miss Genovese struggled to her feet.

Lights went out. The killer returned to Miss Genovese, now trying to make her way around the side of the building by the parking lot to get to her apartment. The assailant stabbed her again.

"I'm dying!" she shrieked. "I'm dying!"

Windows were opened again, and lights went on in many apartments. The assailant got into his car and drove away. Miss Genovese staggered to her feet. A city bus, 0–10, the Lefferts Boulevard line to Kennedy International Airport, passed. It was 3:35 A.M.

The assailant returned. By then, Miss Genovese had crawled to the back of the building, where the freshly painted brown doors to the apartment house held out hope for safety. The killer tried the first door; she wasn't there. At the second door, 82–62 Austin Street, he saw her slumped on the floor at the foot of the stairs. He stabbed her a third time—fatally.

It was 3:50 by the time the police received their first call, from a man who was a neighbor of Miss Genovese. In two minutes they were at the scene. The neighbor, a 70-year-old woman, and another woman were the only persons on the street. Nobody else came forward.

The man explained that he had called the police after much deliberation. He had phoned a friend in Nassau County for advice and then he had crossed the roof of the building to the apartment of the elderly woman to get her to make the call.

"I didn't want to get involved," he sheepishly told the police.

Six days later, the police arrested Winston Moseley, a 29-year-old business-machine operator, and charged him with the homocide. Moseley had no previous record. He is married, has two children and owns a home at 133–19 Sutter Avenue, South Ozone Park, Queens. On Wednesday, a court committed him to Kings County Hospital for psychiatric observation.

When questioned by the police, Moseley also said that he had slain Mrs. Annie May Johnson, 24, of 146–12 133d Avenue, Jamaica, on Feb. 29 and Barbara Kralik, 15, of 174–17 140th Avenue, Springfield Gardens, last July. In the Kralik case, the police are holding Alvin L. Mitchell, who is said to have confessed that slaying.

The police stressed how simple it would have been to have gotten in touch with them. "A phone call," said one of the detectives, "would have done it." The police may be reached by dialing "O" for operator or SPring 7–3100.

Today witnesses from the neighborhood, which is made up of one-family homes in the $35,000 to $60,000 range with the exception of the two apartment houses near the railroad station, find it difficult to explain why they didn't call the police.

A housewife, knowingly if quite casual, said, "We thought it was a lover's quarrel." A husband and wife both said, "Frankly, we were afraid." They seemed aware of the fact that events might have been different. A distraught woman, wiping her hands in her apron, said, "I didn't want my husband to get involved."

One couple, now willing to talk about that night, said they heard the first screams. The husband looked thoughtfully at the bookstore where the killer first grabbed Miss Genovese.

"We went to the window to see what was happening," he said, "but the light from our bedroom made it difficult to see the street." The wife, still apprehensive, added: "I put out the light and we were able to see better."

Asked why they hadn't called the police, she shrugged and replied: "I don't know."

A man peeked out from a slight opening in the doorway to his apartment and rattled off an account of the killer's second attack. Why hadn't he called the police at the time? "I was tired," he said without emotion. "I went back to bed."

It was 4:25 A.M. when the ambulance arrived to take the body of Miss Genovese. It drove off. "Then," a solemn police detective said, "the people came out."

William Golding

The Killing of Simon*

THE BOYS RANGED THEMSELVES IN ROWS ON THE GRASS BEFORE HIM but Ralph and Piggy stayed a foot lower, standing on the soft sand. Jack ignored them for the moment, turned his mask down to the seated boys and pointed at them with the spear.

"Who is going to join my tribe?"

Ralph made a sudden movement that became a stumble. Some of the boys turned towards him.

"I gave you food," said Jack, "and my hunters will protect you from the beast. Who will join my tribe?"

"I'm chief," said Ralph, "because you chose me. And we were going to keep the fire going. Now you run after food——"

"You ran yourself!" shouted Jack. "Look at that bone in your hands!"

Ralph went crimson.

"I said you were hunters. That was your job."

Jack ignored him again.

"Who'll join my tribe and have fun?"

"I'm chief," said Ralph tremulously. "And what about the fire? And I've got the conch——"

"You haven't got it with you," said Jack, sneering. "You left it behind. See, clever? And the conch doesn't count at this end of the island——"

All at once the thunder struck. Instead of the dull boom there was a point of impact in the explosion.

"The conch counts here too," said Ralph, "and all over the island."

* William Golding, *Lord of the Flies* (New York: Capricorn Books, 1959), pp. 185–195. Reprinted by permission of Coward-McCann, Inc. from *Lord of the Flies* by William Golding. Copyright © 1954 by William Gerald Golding.

"What are you going to do about it then?"

Ralph examined the ranks of boys. There was no help in them and he looked away, confused and sweating. Piggy whispered.

"The fire—rescue."

"Who'll join my tribe?"

"I will."

"Me."

"I will."

"I'll blow the conch," said Ralph breathlessly, "and call an assembly."

"We shan't hear it."

Piggy touched Ralph's wrist.

"Come away. There's going to be trouble. And we've had our meat."

There was a blink of bright light beyond the forest and the thunder exploded again so that a littlun started to whine. Big drops of rain fell among them making individual sounds when they struck.

"Going to be a storm," said Ralph, "and you'll have rain like when we dropped here. Who's clever now? Where are your shelters? What are you going to do about that?"

The hunters were looking uneasily at the sky, flinching from the stroke of the drops. A wave of restlessness set the boys swaying and moving aimlessly. The flickering light became brighter and the blows of the thunder were only just bearable. The littluns began to run about, screaming.

Jack leapt on to the sand.

"Do our dance! Come on! Dance!"

He ran stumbling through the thick sand to the open space of rock beyond the fire. Between the flashes of lightning the air was dark and terrible; and the boys followed him, clamorously. Roger became the pig, grunting and charging at Jack, who side-stepped. The hunters took their spears, the cooks took spits, and the rest clubs of fire-wood. A circling movement developed and a chant. While Roger mimed the terror of the pig, the littluns ran and jumped on the outside of the circle. Piggy and Ralph, under the threat of the sky, found themselves eager to take a place in this demented but partly secure society. They were glad to touch the brown backs of the fence that hemmed in the terror and made it governable.

"Kill the beast! Cut his throat! Spill his blood!"

The movement became regular while the chant lost its first superficial excitement and began to beat like a steady pulse. Roger ceased to be a pig and became a hunter, so that the centre of the ring yawned emptily. Some of the littluns started a ring on their own; and the complementary circles went round and round as though repetition would achieve safety of itself. There was the throb and stamp of a single organism.

The dark sky was shattered by a blue-white scar. An instant later the noise was on them like the blow of a gigantic whip. The chant rose a tone in agony.

"Kill the beast! Cut his throat! Spill his blood!"

Now out of the terror rose another desire, thick, urgent, blind.

"Kill the beast! Cut his throat! Spill his blood!"

Again the blue-white scar jagged above them and the sulphurous explosion beat down. The littluns screamed and blundered about, fleeing from the edge of the forest, and one of them broke the ring of biguns in his terror.

"Him! Him!"

The circle became a horseshoe. A thing was crawling out of the forest. It came darkly, uncertainly. The shrill screaming that rose before the beast was like a pain. The beast stumbled into the horseshoe.

"Kill the beast! Cut his throat! Spill his blood!"

The blue-white scar was constant, the noise unendurable. Simon was crying out something about a dead man on a hill.

"Kill the beast! Cut his throat! Spill his blood! Do him in!"

The sticks fell and the mouth of the new circle crunched and screamed. The beast was on its knees in the centre, its arms folded over its face. It was crying out against the abominable noise something about a body on the hill. The beast struggled forward, broke the ring and fell over the steep edge of the rock to the sand by the water. At once the crowd surged after it, poured down the rock, leapt on to the beast, screamed, struck, bit, tore. There were no words, and no movements but the tearing of teeth and claws.

Then the clouds opened and let down the rain like a waterfall. The water bounded from the mountain-top, tore leaves and branches from the trees, poured like a cold shower over the struggling heap on the sand. Presently the heap broke up and figures staggered away. Only the beast lay still, a few yards from the sea. Even in the rain they could see how small a beast it was; and already its blood was staining the sand.

Now a great wind blew the rain sideways, cascading the water from the forest trees. On the mountain-top the parachute filled and moved; the figure slid, rose to its feet, spun, swayed down through a vastness of wet air and trod with ungainly feet the tops of the high trees; falling, still falling, it sank towards the beach and the boys rushed screaming into the darkness. The parachute took the figure forward, furrowing the lagoon, and bumped it over the reef and out to sea.

Towards midnight the rain ceased and the clouds drifted away, so that the sky was scattered once more with the incredible lamps of stars. Then the breeze died too and there was no noise save the drip and trickle of water that ran out of clefts and spilled down, leaf by leaf, to the brown earth of the island. The air was cool, moist, and clear; and presently even the sound of the water was still. The beast lay huddled on the pale beach and the stains spread, inch by inch.

The edge of the lagoon became a streak of phosphorescence which advanced minutely, as the great wave of the tide flowed. The clear water mirrored the clear sky and the angular bright constellations. The line of phosphorescence bulged about the sand grains and little pebbles; it held them each in a dimple of tension, then suddenly accepted them with an inaudible syllable and moved on.

Along the shoreward edge of the shallows the advancing clearness was full of strange, moonbeam-bodied creatures with fiery eyes. Here and there a larger pebble clung to its own air and was covered with a coat of pearls. The tide swelled in over the rain-pitted sand and smoothed everything with a layer of silver. Now it touched the first of the stains that seeped from the broken body and the creatures made a moving patch of light as they gathered at the edge. The water rose further and dressed Simon's coarse hair with brightness. The line of his cheek silvered and the turn of his shoulder became sculptured marble. The strange, attendant creatures, with their fiery eyes and trailing vapours, busied themselves round his head. The body lifted a fraction of an inch from the sand and a bubble of air escaped from the mouth with a wet plop. Then it turned gently in the water.

Somewhere over the darkened curve of the world the sun and moon were pulling; and the film of water on the earth planet was held, bulging slightly on one side while the solid core turned. The great wave of the tide moved further along the island and the water lifted. Softly, surrounded by a fringe of inquisitive bright creatures, itself a silver shape beneath the steadfast constellations, Simon's dead body moved out towards the open sea.

Piggy eyed the advancing figure carefully. Nowadays he sometimes found that he saw more clearly if he removed his glasses and shifted the one lens to the other eye; but even through the good eye, after what had happened, Ralph remained unmistakably Ralph. He came now out of the coco-nut trees, limping, dirty, with dead leaves hanging from his shock of yellow hair. One eye was a slit in his puffy cheek and a great scab had formed on his right knee. He paused for a moment and peered at the figure on the platform.

"Piggy? Are you the only one left?"

"There's some littluns."
"They don't count. No biguns?"
"Oh—Samneric. They're collecting wood."
"Nobody else?"
"Not that I know of."
Ralph climbed on to the platform carefully. The coarse grass was still worn away where the assembly used to sit; the fragile white conch still gleamed by the polished seat. Ralph sat down in the grass facing the Chief's seat and the conch. Piggy knelt at his left, and for a long minute there was silence.
At last Ralph cleared his throat and whispered something.
Piggy whispered back.
"What you say?"
Ralph spoke up.
"Simon."
Piggy said nothing but nodded, solemnly. They continued to sit, gazing with impaired sight at the chief's seat and the glittering lagoon. The green light and the glossy patches of sunshine played over their befouled bodies.
At length Ralph got up and went to the conch. He took the shell caressingly with both hands and knelt, leaning against the trunk.
"Piggy."
"Uh?"
"What we going to do?"
Piggy nodded at the conch.
"You could——"
"Call an assembly?"
Ralph laughed sharply as he said the word and Piggy frowned.
"You're still Chief."
Ralph laughed again.
"You are. Over us."
"I got the conch."
"Ralph! Stop laughing like that. Look there ain't no need, Ralph! What's the others going to think?"
At last Ralph stopped. He was shivering.
"Piggy."
"Uh?"
"That was Simon."
"You said that before."
"Piggy."
"Uh?"
"That was murder."
"You stop it!" said Piggy, shrilly. "What good're you doing talking like that?"

He jumped to his feet and stood over Ralph.

"It was dark. There was that—that bloody dance. There was lightning and thunder and rain. We was scared!"

"I wasn't scared," said Ralph slowly, "I was—I don't know what I was."

"We was scared!" said Piggy excitedly. "Anything might have happened. It wasn't—what you said."

He was gesticulating, searching for a formula.

"Oh Piggy!"

Ralph's voice, low and stricken, stopped Piggy's gestures. He bent down and waited. Ralph, cradling the conch, rocked himself to and fro.

"Don't you understand, Piggy? The things we did——"

"He may still be——"

"No."

"P'raps he was only pretending——"

Piggy's voice tailed off at the sight of Ralph's face.

"You were outside. Outside the circle. You never really came in. Didn't you see what we—what they did?"

There was loathing, and at the same time a kind of feverish excitement in his voice.

"Didn't you see, Piggy?"

"Not all that well. I only got one eye now. You ought to know that, Ralph."

Ralph continued to rock to and fro.

"It was an accident," said Piggy suddenly, "that's what it was. An accident." His voice shrilled again. "Coming in the dark—he hadn't no business crawling like that out of the dark. He was batty. He asked for it." He gesticulated widely again. "It was an accident."

"You didn't see what they did——"

"Look, Ralph. We got to forget this. We can't do no good thinking about it, see?"

"I'm frightened. Of us. I want to go home. O God I want to go home."

"It was an accident," said Piggy stubbornly, "and that's that."

He touched Ralph's bare shoulder and Ralph shuddered at the human contact.

"And look, Ralph," Piggy glanced round quickly, then leaned close—"don't let on we was in that dance. Not to Samneric."

"But we were! All of us!"

Piggy shook his head.

"Not us till last. They never noticed in the dark. Anyway you said I was only on the outside——"

"So was I," muttered Ralph, "I was on the outside too."

Piggy nodded eagerly.

"That's right. We was on the outside. We never done nothing, we never seen nothing."

Piggy paused, then went on.

"We'll live on our own, the four of us——"

"Four of us. We aren't enough to keep the fire burning."

"We'll try. See? I lit it."

Samneric came dragging a great log out of the forest. They dumped it by the fire and turned to the pool. Ralph jumped to his feet.

"Hi! You two!"

The twins checked a moment, then walked on.

"They're going to bathe, Ralph."

"Better get it over."

The twins were very surprised to see Ralph. They flushed and looked past him into the air.

"Hullo. Fancy meeting you, Ralph."

"We just been in the forest——"

"—to get wood for the fire——"

"—we got lost last night."

Ralph examined his toes.

"You got lost after the . . ."

Piggy cleaned his lens.

"After the feast," said Sam in a stifled voice. Eric nodded. "Yes, after the feast."

"We left early," said Piggy quickly, "because we were tired."

"So did we——"

"—very early——"

"—we were very tired."

Sam touched a scratch on his forehead and then hurriedly took his hand away. Eric fingered his split lip.

"Yes. We were very tired," repeated Sam, "so we left early. Was it a good——"

The air was heavy with unspoken knowledge. Sam twisted and the obscene word shot out of him. "—dance?"

Memory of the dance that none of them had attended shook all four boys convulsively.

"We left early."

INQUIRY

A man said to the universe:
"Sir, I exist!"
"However," replied the universe,
"The fact has not created in me
A sense of obligation."

STEPHEN CRANE

ARE you shocked that upper middle-class Americans watched the murder of Kitty Genovese and did nothing, even though they could have prevented it? You are certain that you would have done better. Indignantly you say such things as, "Didn't these people recognize their duty to a fellow human being in trouble? Are they irresponsible people? Are they inhuman? Have they no social conscience?" You might even add, "Just what is our society coming to?" This moral outcry, which followed the Kew Gardens case and echoed as far as the halls of Congress, involved all of these reactions. The murderer was seldom mentioned in the general abuse heaped upon the residents of Kew Gardens. Some people even suggested that the residents of Kew Gardens were accessories to the murder, that they were, in fact, responsible for it.

Our concern in this chapter is with the meaning of the terms "duty" and "responsibility" and how we apply those terms to concrete social situations. Think back on how you came to formulate your sense of responsibility or duty. When you say that you have a conscience, do you mean only that you know the difference between right and wrong? Or does knowing what is right carry with it the obligation to do what is right? Have you ever felt compelled to do something other than what you know to be right? Can you decide that some course of action is right and yet feel no compulsion to do it or suffer no guilt feelings when you do otherwise? Is that what is meant by "conscience"?

Suppose that you want to teach a child of five or six years of age about obligations. You cannot hope to catalogue for him all of the things thought to be right and wrong, have him memorize the list and then act accordingly. Such a method is not likely to produce success. The child would have little if any concrete behavior to which he could apply the "rights" and "wrongs." Is it enough to teach him only what is socially acceptable? Soon you will discover that your method of teaching will depend mostly upon him, upon the things he does and does not do. Attempts to anticipate all situations in which he will be called upon to distinguish between proper and improper behavior can only be futile.

At what point in the training would you be satisfied that the child has a conscience, that he is morally responsible for the things he does, that he has developed a sense of obligation? Let us say that one day he borrows another child's toy and unintentionally breaks it. That night, appearing rather contrite, he tells you what happened and claims that he feels badly about it all. You have succeeded, a conscience is born! But then he tells you that he hopes his friend will not miss the toy and that he really feels badly because he is worried that the friend may not invite him to his forthcoming birthday party. The necessity of continuing the lessons is apparent: right emotion, wrong reason. You follow with a lecture on accepting responsibility and the consequences of one's actions.

Now suppose that throughout his childhood he never is involved in a situation in which his help is needed by someone in trouble. He is not a particularly brave or reckless individual. Would you expect that it would occur to him during his adult life that he ought to go to the aid of someone in distress?

You might think that men are naturally moral animals, basically good and honest, and that our ethical standards are derived from human nature. But recent ethnological theorists have reached far less ideal concepts of men in nature, concepts closer to the ideas of Seventeenth Century philosopher Thomas Hobbes. He wrote that "the life of man (in nature) is solitary, poor, nasty, brutish, and short." Contemporary scientists claim that man is a mediocre biological success and that he should be classed with the world's most aggressive animals.* Fundamentally, men enjoy the torturing and the killing not only of other animals but of fellow men. Urges to murder, homosexuality, and sexual promiscuity, we are told, are more basic drives of man than social and family concerns. If all this is so, thinking about good, bad, right, and wrong must be related to the development of standards of acceptable social behavior. Human actions concerned with the idea of "ought" in social relations are not a part of our nature but are learned or acquired behavioral patterns. The weight of scientific evidence and theory seems to topple any notion that man is a naturally moral being.

In the history of moral philosophy we find a number of significant attempts to formulate or examine standards of right conduct. When the terms "duty" and "responsibility" arise, we most often expect ethical theories based on the notion that men ought to perform or to refrain from performing certain acts regardless of personal gain. Certain kinds of behavior are deemed right or wrong

* *Time* (January 17, 1969), pp. 42–43.

regardless of the peculiar circumstances in which men may find themselves. That certain actions contribute to the greatest good or happiness in one's society is often taken as secondary to the fact that they have been commanded—by God ("Thou Shalt Not Kill"), by the state, or even by a promise.

"Having an Obligation" and "Being Obliged"

Consider the obligations that arise when you promise to do or not to do something. Your promises are freely given, but you can be held accountable for them at some future date. Someone expects it of you; someone has the right to expect it of you. You promised it. Ought you to do what you promise to do? Perhaps, if the reasons you had for making the promise remain the same when you are called upon to fulfill it. Maybe you ought to keep only those promises which, when the time comes, still are in your self-interest. What would happen to the making of promises if personal considerations, after the promise is made, allow the maker to keep or not to keep the promise at his pleasure? Should I keep my promises even if I don't expect others to do so? Circumstances might arise to prevent one from accomplishing what has been promised, but would that relieve one of the obligation created by the promise? I promise to buy a lunch for a friend at a famous restaurant. He arrives at the agreed time, takes a table, and waits; but I fail to appear. Later that day we meet and he with restraint asks where I had been at lunch. I tell him that my car had a flat tire and that by the time I fixed it I realized that I had to rush to make an afternoon business engagement. He says he understands; but as he leaves, he says, "You still owe me a lunch there."

The responsibilities in promising are part of the nature of a promise itself. If I were to make promises without thinking that I was obligated to keep them, then I need a lesson in language, on how to use the word "promise" properly, not a lesson about values. Notice the difference in our use of the words "obliged" and "obligation." The former is a kind of psychological statement. When a thief orders you at gunpoint to hand over your wallet you certainly are obliged to do so. That is, in retrospect you would describe your actions to the police in terms of a felt need to comply in order to avoid some greater discomfort or even death. Saying "I was obliged to do X" is just saying that you had certain feelings, motives, or beliefs about the circumstances, i.e. the thief would kill you. On the other hand, when we say of someone (or ourselves) "he was obligated to do something" or "he had an obligation to do something," reference to psychological considerations are irrelevant. Moral or legal rules are involved. Our language shifts from talk of feelings to statements of a normative nature. "He ought to have done something. It is proper to do such and such." If you were obliged to do something (give a gunman your wallet) and by a stroke of luck you escape the circumstances, you are no longer obliged. But in regard to the Kew Gardens residents, we say that the fact that they did not do what they ought to have done has no bearing on the obligation to help a fellow human being in distress. The word "obligation" is one of the important terms in our vocabulary of rule behavior. We need to examine carefully our use of it.

Kant's Moral Principles

One of the most famous ethical philosophers, Immanuel Kant, claimed that a formal moral criterion could be established by reference to the nature of human reason alone. Kant derived his principle of duty by requiring us, as rational beings, to will the maxims of our actions to be universal for all men. In other words, according to Kant, we should only act in ways we would be willing to allow all others to act. He called this principle the "categorical imperative." It commands men to do what is right without external enticements or punishments. According to Kant, we should do right because it is right to do so.

For Kant, morality is always a matter of conscious choice. Men cannot be accidentally moral, doing right by chance. The alternatives to the chosen behavior must be actively considered. Inclinations serve as no criterion of right conduct. In fact, Kant tells us that moral goodness is often to be found in acting counter to inclination. Also, according to Kant's thinking, the motive is of prime importance, not the accomplishment. You cannot tell if a man is moral simply by observing his behavior.

What do most men mean when they make judgments of moral worth? Kant is not concerned with distinguishing moral from immoral behavior. We are normally able to do that with little difficulty. But there are many different reasons that motivate men to do good deeds, or seeming good deeds. Notice that we seem to reserve our highest respect for men who act neither from self-centered motives nor from natural dispositions to do good, but for men who realize they must do something despite their personal concerns and inhibitions.

Imagine you are interviewing a wealthy businessman who has just given a large sum of money for a park to benefit ghetto children. On the surface the act seems morally commendable. Men ought to help those less fortunate whenever possible. You ask the businessman why he did so, and he tells you that it makes him feel very good when he gives to the poor. What is his motive? To make himself feel good. This cannot be a moral motive, Kant argues. If it were, then only those people with certain natural dispositions would be capable of moral actions, and all other people would have to be excused from doing what is morally right. Only if an act is done from a consideration of duty for its own sake can it have moral worth.

Kant stresses the importance of treating human beings always as ends, worthy of dignity and respect, and never as means only. Imagine what a society would be like if the rule were that men had no absolute worth and could at all times treat other men as means.

You could use and abuse other men at will as long as you were able to impress them into your service. The concept of duty to another human being in trouble would disappear. You would watch the death of another man with a kind of clinical interest. Imagine treating people like an automobile. Yet do we always treat men as if they had absolute worth without concern for their stations or status in the community? When we criticize the residents of Kew Gardens, we imply that their aid was called for regardless of who the victim was. Notice that when the average man makes a moral judgment, he does it unconditionally: "That was wrong." Such judgments, Kant points out, are never conditional.

In contrast to Kant's position, it might be argued that our moral duties are derived from the kind of people we are, the kind of jobs we do, the social positions we occupy, and the social tradition into which we were born. "Out of the ordinary" events, like the murder of Kitty Genovese, do not call us to action because the required responses are not a part of our normal behavior. It is enough to be responsible for our services to the society. To a degree this kind of reasoning about duty and responsibility is used by Stanley Milgram and Paul Hollander who, in attempting to explain the actions of the residents of Kew Gardens, maintain that in our highly specialized society it is taken for granted that certain functions such as the control of criminals will be assumed by specially trained people. Furthermore, they argue that a "calculated and strategic indifference is an unavoidable part of life in our cities."* Carried a step further, we might add that one is doing his duty when he is meeting the requirements birth and society place upon him and that he ought not concern himself, or at least he ought not be deemed immoral for not concerning himself, with events that fall outside of his normal sphere of activity.

"What if Everyone Did That?" as a Moral Argument

What if everybody acted as the citizens of Kew Gardens? Imagine the result in your own neighborhood. Try to extend the "what if everyone . . . " argument to form a basis for morality. "You must not resist the armed services' draft," a mother recently cautioned her son, "because if everyone did that, no one would protect our country from its enemies." The son replied, "But everyone will not resist the draft, so the fact that I do is immaterial to the country's protection." Suppose you were one of the Kew Gardens residents; might you not use this type of argument to excuse your inaction? "I can't get involved. It could bring me more trouble than it's worth. But everybody certainly will not think my way. Someone will help the woman. Someone will call the police."

Colin Strang examines the uses and validity of the "what if everyone did that?" argument. If the consequences of everyone doing what you are doing are disastrous to the community welfare, should

* *The Nation* (June 15, 1964).

that make what you are doing immoral, even if you are the only person engaged in the activity? It might well be argued that if it can be shown that disastrous results would occur, then freedom to do what you are doing ought to be limited. If everyone refuses to help another human being in danger, and such behavior undermines the basic solidarity of the community with fear, then refusing to help ought to be made illegal and personal moral considerations ought to be removed from the issue. But then, "If everyone did that," far from being an argument for duty or morality, would be only an argument for law.

Consider the selection from *Lord of the Flies*. The killing of Simon during a tribal ritual and the following encounter of Ralph and Piggy provide us with further insights into the concepts of duty and responsibility. All of the boys participated in the murder; even Ralph and Piggy were drawn into the circle of the hunters by its promise of a partial security that "hemmed in the terror and made it governable." (Notice the place of ritual in learning moral behavior). Simon came to understand that the beast the boys feared, against which their society had been restructured, is part of the nature of man and not something they can hunt or affect through legislation. Simon put himself outside of the community by exposing its myths. He became the beast himself—that which would disrupt the society. He was the enemy.

We, like the boys on the island, seldom refer to the enemy as "men" or "women." (War casuality reports list "enemy killed," not "men murdered" or even "men killed." A recent correspondent's television report referred to the number of "South Vietnamese women murdered" and also to the number of "female Viet Cong killed.") We do not call them "beasts," but the names we adopt serve the same purposes. They delimit the extension of our moral inhibitions; that is, these names set boundaries on how far we need follow our codes of conduct, in this case in relation to murder. We certainly ought not to kill a fellow member of our society, but killing for our society is sanctioned. We seem to be saying that "Thou shalt not kill" does not mean that killing is always wrong.

Examine the attitudes of Ralph and Piggy on the day after the killing of Simon. We should expect them to be relieved, perhaps even in a mood of celebration. The little beast is dead. Yet they are conscience-stricken. Piggy refuses to admit his participation in the act, and Ralph calls the deed "murder." Murder is immoral. Yet in this case, the whole society has sanctioned the act, in fact, participated in it.

Can an act be criminal or immoral if it is not outlawed by the society in which it occurs? Ralph appears to have a concept of morality which does not adjust to changes in social values. Ralph feels guilty. By calling his actions "murder" he accepts the responsibility for them. But should he? Piggy disclaims responsibility for the act. He maintains that he was on the outside of the circle. It was a social movement, it was a crowd reaction, it was an accident. It cannot be called murder because no one is responsible for what everyone did. Piggy even blames Simon, the victim: "He hadn't no business crawling like that out of the dark."

Responsibility and Existentialism

Ask yourself where your responsibility for your actions begins and at what point you are no longer responsible. Are you responsible for everything you do? Are there times when you are only following someone else's orders? Are there cases of doing your duty when you are not responsible?

The existentialists, and especially Jean-Paul Sartre, claim that there are no events in which you participate for which you can disclaim responsibility. Ultimately no one but you is responsible for what you do; and, to the existentialist viewpoint, what you do is what you are. You are what you make yourself by your choices to act or not to act. The existentialists see man as an undetermined being, creating himself in the image he deems best by committing himself to various courses of action. Sartre says, "In war there are no innocent victims," and "We have the war we deserve." His point is that while a man is involved or caught up in the events of war, he cannot send the responsibility that he bears for his actions and his life on holiday and "just follow orders." Men in war have chosen not to desert or commit suicide; they have therefore accepted the responsibility for *everything* that takes place in the war. The war only exists for them because they choose to recognize it. They are the war. Responsibility, for Sartre, is the key to being a man. It is not a sometime thing.

Excuses as a Key

The Kew Gardens affair is not an isolated incident. Similar cases have occurred throughout the United States. There is generally one common denominator: a desire on the part of witnesses to supply excuses for their inaction. J. L. Austin claims that by closely investigating our use of excuses we learn a great deal about proper moral conduct. When excuses are used we know immediately that some abnormality or failure in conduct has taken place. "I'm sorry, please forgive me, I thought . . . " is language appropriate only when something has gone wrong. The way in which we frame our excuses points to the manner of our failure. Distinguish between incidents in which you might say: "I didn't know . . . , It was a mistake . . . , It was an accident . . . , I wasn't aware . . ." Compare the excuses of the Kew Gardens residents with those of Piggy, Ralph, and Samneric.

Is the way something was done more important than the fact that it was done? There are various ways of doing immoral things. Certainly our ideas of "accident," "mistake" and "intention" are involved in moral judgments. Did Ralph and Piggy kill Simon by accident? Were they intending something different? We would not say that the inaction of the Kew Gardens residents was an accident. Perhaps it was a mistake. But no, neither the people of Kew Gardens nor the boys on the island were trying to do something else and mistakenly did what they did. Might we not even say that both did what they did deliberately, on purpose? Their excuses seem to tell us that. Perhaps our ideas of compulsion mitigates against moral censure. Then we might not blame the boys, but we still would blame the Kew Gardens residents, who were certainly under no compulsion. On the other hand, we cannot ignore Ralph's use of "murder." Can murder be committed unintentionally, without purpose, not deliberately? Is an "accident" or "mistake" of this type a justification of such conduct?

1

IMMANUEL KANT
(1724–1804)

*The Categorical Imperative**

Kant's theory of ethics is based on the concept that man is a rational being. Moral conduct is action performed from respect for duty. Kant tells us that the only thing which is good without qualification is a good will. By that he means that the motives by which men act, and not merely the results they accomplish, are important to questions of duty. It is not enough to appear to other men to be doing your duty. If actions are not motivated by a sense of duty, they are not moral. Reason dictates what is necessary, what is one's duty in particular circumstances of daily life. Kant calls the moral law of duty the "categorical imperative." "Categorical" means universal, and an imperative is a command. The categorical imperative is to act only in such a way that you could will that the maxim of your action become a universal law of nature for all men. Kant also formulates the law of duty in another way: act always so as to treat all humanity, yourself and others, always as ends and never as means only. Compare this to the Golden Rule of Christian ethics. Kant never specifically tells men what they ought to do. Instead he provides a structure or a plan by which men can discover for themselves what their moral obligations are. Kant's analysis of morality, of course, presupposes that men are free to make moral choices, and he gives no rewards for acting morally. Duty is to be done for its own sake and for the sake of reason, not in the hope of better crops, heaven, social cohesion, nor from fear.

* Immanuel Kant, *Fundamental Principles of the Metaphysics of Morals*, T. K. Abbott, trans. (New York: Longmans, Green & Co., 1909), Sections 1 and 2.

Transition from the Common Rational Knowledge of Morality to Philosophical Knowledge

NOTHING can possibly be conceived in the world, or even out of it, which can be called good without qualification, except a *good will.* Intelligence, wit, judgment, and other *talents* of the mind, however they may be named, or courage, resolution, perseverance, as qualities of temperament, are undoubtedly good and desirable in many respects; but these gifts of nature may also become extremely bad and mischievous if the will which is to make use of them, and which, therefore, constitutes what is called *character,* is not good. It is the same with the *gifts of fortune.* Power, riches, honor, even health, and the general well-being and contentment with one's condition which is called *hap-*

piness, inspire pride, and often presumption, if there is not a good will to correct the influence of these on the mind, and with this also to rectify the whole principle of acting, and adapt it to its end. The sight of a being who is not adorned with a single feature of a pure and good will, enjoying unbroken prosperity, can never give pleasure to an impartial rational spectator. Thus a good will appears to constitute the indispensable condition even of being worthy of happiness.

There are even some qualities which are of service to this good will itself, and may facilitate its action, yet which have no intrinsic unconditional value, but always presuppose a good will, and this qualifies the esteem that we justly have for them, and does not permit us to regard them as absolutely good. Moderation in the affections and passions, self-control, and calm deliberation are not only good in many respects, but even seem to constitute part of the intrinsic worth of the person; but they are far from deserving to be called good without qualification, although they have been so unconditionally praised by the ancients. For without the principles of a good will, they may become extremely bad; and the coolness of a villain not only makes him far more dangerous, but also directly makes him more abominable in our eyes than he would have been without it.

A Will is Good by Virtue of What It Wills

A good will is good not because of what it performs or effects, not by its aptness for the attainment of some proposed end, but simply by virtue of the volition—that is, it is good in itself, and considered by itself is to be esteemed much higher than all that can be brought about by it in favor of any inclination, nay, even of the sum-total of all inclinations. Even if it should happen that, owing to special disfavor of fortune, or the niggardly provision of a step-motherly nature, this will should wholly lack power to accomplish its purpose, if with its greatest efforts it should yet achieve nothing, and there should remain only the good will (not, to be sure, a mere wish, but the summoning of all means in our power), then, like a jewel, it would still shine by its own light, as a thing which has its whole value in itself. Its usefulness or fruitlessness can neither add to nor take away anything from this value. It would be, as it were, only the setting to enable us to handle it the more conveniently in common commerce, or to attract to it the attention of those who are not yet connoisseurs, but not to recommend it to true connoisseurs, or to determine its value. . . .

We have then to develop the notion of a will which deserves to be highly esteemed for itself, and is good without a view to anything further, a notion which exists already in the sound natural understanding, requiring rather to be cleared up than to be taught, and which in estimating the value of our actions always takes the first place and constitutes the condition of all the rest. In order to do this, we will take the notion of duty, which includes that of a good will, although implying certain subjective restrictions and hindrances. These, however, far from concealing it or rendering it unrecognizable, rather bring it out by contrast and make it shine forth so much the brighter.

Evaluation of Actions Done from Duty

I omit here all actions which are already recognized as inconsistent with duty, although they may be useful for this or that purpose, for with these the question whether they are done *from duty* cannot arise at all, since they even conflict with it. I also set aside those actions which really conform to duty, but to which men have *no* direct *inclination,* performing them because they are impelled thereto by some other inclination. For in this case we can readily distinguish whether the action which agrees with duty is done *from duty* or from a selfish view. It is much harder to make this distinction when the action accords with duty, and the subject has besides a *direct* inclination to it. For example, it is always a matter of duty that a dealer should not over-charge an inexperienced purchaser; and wherever there is much commerce the prudent tradesman does not overcharge, but keeps a fixed price for everyone, so that a child buys of him as well as any other. Men are thus *honestly* served; but this is not enough to make us believe that the tradesman has so acted from duty and from principles of honesty; his own advantage required it; it is out of the question in this case to suppose that he might besides have a direct inclination in favor of the buyers, so that, as it were, from love he should give no advantage to one over another. Accordingly the action was done neither from duty nor from direct inclination, but merely with a selfish view.

On the other hand, it is a duty to maintain one's life; and, in addition, everyone has also a direct inclination to do so. But on this account the often anxious care which most men take for it has no intrinsic worth, and their maxim has no moral import. They preserve their life as *duty requires,* no doubt, but not *because duty requires.* On the other hand, if adversity and hopeless sorrow have completely taken away the relish for life, if the unfortunate one, strong in mind, indignant at his fate rather than desponding or dejected, wishes for death, and yet preserves his life without loving it—not from inclination or fear, but from duty—then his maxim has a moral worth.

To be beneficent when we can is a duty; and besides this, there are many minds so sympathetically constituted that, without any other motive of vanity or self-interest, they find a pleasure in spreading joy around them, and can take delight in the satisfaction of others so far as it is their own work. But I maintain that in such a case an action of this kind, however proper, however amiable it may be, has nevertheless no true moral worth, but is on a level with other inclinations, for example, the inclination to honor, which, if it is happily directed to that which is in fact of public utility and accordant with duty, and consequently honorable, deserves praise and encouragement, but not esteem. For the maxim lacks the moral import, namely, that such actions be done *from duty,* not from inclination. Put the case that the mind of that philanthropist was clouded by sorrow of his own, extinguishing all sympathy with the lot of others, and that while he still has the power to benefit others in distress, he is not touched by their trouble because he is absorbed with his own; and now suppose that he tears himself out of this dead insensibility and performs the action without any inclination to it, but simply from duty, then first has his action its genuine moral worth. Further still, if nature has put little sympathy in the heart of this or that man, if he, supposed to be an upright man, is by temperament cold and indifferent to the sufferings of others, perhaps because in respect of his own he is provided with the special gift of patience and fortitude, and supposes, or even requires, that others should have the same—and such a man would certainly not be the meanest product of nature—but if nature had not specially framed him for a philanthropist, would he not still find in himself a source from whence to give himself a far higher worth than that of a good-natured temperament could be? Unquestionably. It is just in this that the moral worth of the character is brought out which is incomparably the highest of all, namely, that he is beneficient, not from inclination, but from duty.

To secure one's own happiness is a duty, at least indirectly; for discontent with one's condition, under a pressure of many anxieties and amidst unsatisfied wants, might easily become a great *temptation to transgression of duty*. But here again, without looking to duty, all men have already the strongest and most intimate inclination to happiness, because it is just in this idea that all inclinations are combined in one total. But the precept of happiness is often of such a sort that it greatly interferes with some inclinations, and yet a man cannot form any definite and certain conception of the sum of satisfaction of all of them which is called happiness. It is not then to be wondered at that a single inclination, definite both as to what it promises and as to the time within which it can be gratified, is often able to overcome such a fluctuating idea, and that a gouty patient, for instance, can choose to enjoy what he likes, and to suffer what he may, since, according to his calculation, on this occasion at least, he has [only] not sacrificed the enjoyment of the present moment to a possibly mistaken expectation of a happiness which is supposed to be found in health. But even in this case, if the general desire for happiness did not influence his will, and supposing that in his particular case health was not a necessary element in this calculation, there yet remains in this, as in all other cases, this law—namely, that he should promote his happiness not from inclination but from duty, and by this would his conduct first acquire true moral worth.

It is in this manner, undoubtedly, that we are to understand those passages of Scripture also in which we are commanded to love our neighbor, even our enemy. For love, as an affection, cannot be commanded, but beneficence for duty's sake may, even though we are not impelled to it by any inclination—nay, are even repelled by a natural and unconquerable aversion. This is *practical* love, and not *pathological*—a love which is seated in the will, and not in the propensions of sense—in principles of action and not of tender sympathy; and it is this love alone which can be commanded.

Moral Worth Derived from the Maxim of Actions

The second* proposition is: That an action done from duty derives its moral worth, *not from the purpose* which is to be attained by it, but from the maxim by which it is determined, and therefore does not

* The first proposition was that to have moral worth an action must be done from duty. Translator's footnote.

depend on the realization of the object of the action, but merely on the *principle of volition* by which the action has taken place, without regard to any object of desire. It is clear from what precedes that the purposes which we may have in view in our actions, or their effects regarded as ends and springs of the will, cannot give to actions any unconditional or moral worth. In what, then, can their worth lie if it is not to consist in the will and in reference to its expected effect? It cannot lie anywhere but in the *principle of the will* without regard to the ends which can be attained by the action. For the will stands between its *a priori* principle, which is formal, and its *a posteriori* spring, which is material, as between two roads, and as it must be determined by something, it follows that it must be determined by the formal principle of volition when an action is done from duty, in which case every material principle has been withdrawn from it.

Duty as the Necessity of Acting from Respect for the Law

The third proposition, which is a consequence of the two preceding, I would express thus: *Duty is the necessity of acting from respect for the law.* I may have *inclination* for an object as the effect of my proposed action, but I cannot have *respect* for it just for this reason that it is an effect and not an energy of will. Similarly, I cannot have respect for inclination, whether my own or another's; I can at most, if my own, approve it; if another's, sometimes even love it, that is, look on it as favorable to my own interest. It is only what is connected with my will as a principle, by no means as an effect—what does not subserve my inclination, but overpowers it, or at least in case of choice excludes it from its calculation—in other words, simply the law of itself, which can be an object of respect, and hence a command. Now an action done from duty must wholly exclude the influence of inclination, and with it every object of the will, so that nothing remains which can determine the will except objectively the *law*, and subjectively *pure respect* for this practical law, and consequently the maxim that I should follow this law even to the thwarting of all my inclinations.

Thus the moral worth of an action does not lie in the effect expected from it, nor in any principle of action which requires to borrow its motive from this expected effect. For all these effects—agreeableness of one's condition, and even the promotion of the happiness of others—could have been also brought about by other causes, so that for this there would have been no need of the will of a rational being; whereas it is in this alone that the supreme and unconditional good can be found. The pre-eminent good which we call moral can therefore consist in nothing else than *the conception of law* in itself, *which certainly is only possible in a rational being,* in so far as this conception, and not the expected effect, determines the will. This is a good which is already present in the person who acts accordingly, and we have not to wait for it to appear first in the result.

But what sort of law can that be the conception of which must determine the will, even without paying any regard to the effect expected from it, in order that this will may be called good absolutely and without qualification? As I have deprived the will of every impulse which could arise to it from obedience to any law, there remains nothing but the universal conformity of its actions to law in general, which alone is to serve the will as a principle, that is, I am never to act otherwise than so *that I could also will that my maxim should become a universal law.* Here, now, it is the simple conformity to law in general, without assuming any particular law applicable to certain actions, that serves the will as its principle, and must so serve it if duty is not to be a vain delusion and a chimerical notion. The common reason of men in its practical judgments perfectly coincides with this, and always has in view the principle here suggested. Let the question be, for example: May I when in distress make a promise with the intention not to keep it? I readily distinguish here between the two significations which the question may have: whether it is prudent or whether it is right to make a false promise? The former may undoubtedly often be the case. I see clearly indeed that it is not enough to extricate myself from a present difficulty by means of this subterfuge, but it must be well considered whether there may not hereafter spring from this lie much greater inconvenience than that from which I now free myself, and as, with all my supposed *cunning,* the consequences cannot be so easily foreseen but that credit once lost may be much more injurious to me than any mischief which I seek to avoid at present, it should be considered whether it would not be more *prudent* to act herein according to a universal maxim, and to make it a habit to promise nothing except with the intention of keeping it. But it is soon clear to me that such a maxim will still only be based on the fear of consequences. Now it is a wholly different thing to be truthful from duty, and to be so from apprehension of injurious consequences. In the first case, the very notion of the action already implies a law for me; in the second case, I must first look about elsewhere to see what results may be combined with it which would affect myself. For to deviate from the principle of duty is beyond all doubt wicked; but to be unfaithful to my maxim of prudence may often be very advantageous to me, although to abide by it is certainly safer. The shortest way, however, and an unerring one, to discover the answer to this question whether a lying promise is consistent with duty, is to ask myself, Should I be content that my maxim (to extricate myself from difficulty by a false promise) should hold good as a universal law, for myself as well as for others; and should I be able to say to myself, "Every one may make a deceitful promise when he finds himself in a difficulty from which he cannot otherwise extricate himself"? Then I presently become aware that, while I can will the lie, I can by no means will that lying should be a universal law. For with such a law there would be no promises at all, since it would be in vain to allege my intention in regard to my future actions to those who would not believe this allegation, or if they over-hastily did so, would pay me back in my own coin. Hence my maxim, as soon as it should be made a universal law, would necessarily destroy itself.

I do not, therefore, need any far-reaching penetration to discern what I have to do in order that my will may be morally good. Inexperienced in the course of the world, incapable of being prepared for all its

contingencies, I only ask myself: Canst thou also will that thy maxim should be a universal law? If not, then it must be rejected, and that not because of a disadvantage accruing from it to myself or even to others, but because it cannot enter as a principle into a possible universal legislation, and reason extorts from me immediate respect for such legislation. I do not indeed as yet *discern* on what this respect is based (this the philosopher may inquire), but at least I understand this—that it is an estimation of the worth which far outweighs all worth of what is recommended by inclination, and that the necessity of acting from *pure* respect for the practical law is what constitutes duty, to which every other motive must give place because it is the condition of a will being good *in itself,* and the worth of such a will is above everything. . . .

Transition from Popular Moral Philosophy to the Metaphysic of Morals

Everything in nature works according to laws. Rational beings alone have the faculty of acting according *to the conception* of laws—that is, according to principles, that is, have a *will.* Since the deduction of actions from principles requires *reason,* the will is nothing but practical reason. If reason infallibly determines the will, then the actions of such a being which are recognized as objectively necessary are subjectively necessary also, that is, the will is a faculty to choose *that only* which reason independent of inclination recognizes as practically necessary, that is, as good. But if reason of itself does not sufficiently determine the will, if the latter is subject also to subjective conditions (particular impulses) which do not always coincide with the objective conditions, in a word, if the will does not *in itself* completely accord with reason (which is actually the case with men), then the actions which objectively are recognized as necessary are subjectively contingent, and the determination of such a will according to objective laws is *obligation,* that is to say, the relation of the objective laws to a will that is not thoroughly good is conceived as the determination of the will of a rational being by principles of reason, but which the will from its nature does not of necessity follow.

The conception of an objective principle, in so far as it is obligatory for a will, is called a command (of reason), and the formula of the command is called an Imperative.

All imperatives are expressed by the word *ought* [or *shall*], and thereby indicate the relation of an objective law of reason to a will which from its subjective constitution is not necessarily determined by it (an obligation). They say that something would be good to do or to forbear, but they say it to a will which does not always do a thing because it is conceived to be good to do it. That is practically *good,* however, which determines the will by means of the conceptions of reason, and consequently not from subjective causes, but objectively, that is, on principles which are valid for every rational being as such. It is distinguished from the *pleasant* as that which influences the will only by means of sensation from merely subjective causes, valid only for the sense of this or that one, and not as a principle of reason which holds for every one.

A perfectly good will would therefore be equally subject to objective laws (viz., laws of good), but could not be conceived as *obliged* thereby to act lawfully, because of itself from its subjective constitution it can only be determined by the conception of good. Therefore no imperatives hold for the Divine will, or in general for a *holy* will; *ought* is here out of place because the volition is already of itself necessarily in unison with the law. Therefore imperatives are only formulae to express the relation of objective laws of all volition to the subjective imperfection of the will of this or that rational being, for example, the human will.

Imperatives

Now all *imperatives* command either *hypothetically* or *categorically*. The former represent the practical necessity of a possible action as means to something else that is willed (or at least which one might possibly will). The categorical imperative would be that which represented an action as necessary of itself without reference to another end, that is, as objectively necessary.

Since every practical law represents a possible action as good, and on this account, for a subject who is practically determinable by reason as necessary, all imperatives are formulae determining an action which is necessary according to the principle of a will good in some respects. If now the action is good only as a means *to something else*, then the imperative is *hypothetical;* if it is conceived as good *in itself* and consequently as being necessarily the principle of a will which of itself conforms to reason, then it is *categorical.*

Thus the imperative declares what action possible by me would be good, and presents the practical rule in relation to a will which does not forthwith perform an action simply because it is good, whether because the subject does not always know that it is good, or because, even if it know this, yet its maxims might be opposed to the objective principles of practical reason.

Accordingly the hypothetical imperative only says that the action is good for some purpose, *possible* or *actual.* In the first case it is a *problematical,* in the second an *assertorial* practical principle. The categorical imperative which declares an action to be objectively necessary in itself without reference to any purpose, that is, without any other end, is valid as an *apodictic* (practical) principle.

Whatever is possible only by the power of some rational being may also be conceived as a possible purpose of some will; and therefore the principles of action as regards the means necessary to attain some possible purpose are in fact infinitely numerous. All sciences have a practical part consisting of problems expressing that some end is possible for us, and of imperatives directing how it may be attained. These may, therefore, be called in general imperatives of *skill.* Here there is no question whether the end is rational and good, but only what one must do in order to attain it. The precepts for the physician to make his patient thoroughly healthy, and for a poisoner to ensure certain death, are of equal value in this respect, that each serves to effect its purpose perfectly. Since in early youth it cannot be known what ends

are likely to occur to us in the course of life, parents seek to have their children taught a *great many things,* and provide for their *skill* in the use of means for all sorts of arbitrary ends, of none of which can they determine whether it may not perhaps hereafter be an object to their pupil, but which it is at all events *possible* that he might aim at; and this anxiety is so great that they commonly neglect to form and correct their judgment on the value of the things which may be chosen as ends.

There is *one* end, however, which may be assumed to be actually such to all rational beings (so far as imperatives apply to them, viz., as dependent beings), and, therefore, one purpose which they not merely *may* have, but which we may with certainty assume that they all actually *have* by a natural necessity, and this is *happiness.* The hypothetical imperative which expresses the practical necessity of an action as means to the advancement of happiness is *assertorial.* We are not to present it as necessary for an uncertain and merely possible purpose, but for a purpose which we may presuppose with certainty and *a priori* in every man, because it belongs to his being. Now skill in the choice of means to his own greatest well-being may be called *prudence,* in the narrowest sense. And thus the imperative which refers to the choice of means to one's own happiness, that is, the precept of prudence, is still always *hypothetical;* the action is not commanded absolutely, but only as means to another purpose.

Finally, there is an imperative which commands a certain conduct immediately, without having as its condition any other purpose to be attained by it. This imperative is *categorical.* It concerns not the matter of the action, or its intended result, but its form and the principle of which it is itself a result; and what is essentially good in it consists in the mental disposition, let the consequence be what it may. This imperative may be called that of *morality.* . . .

The Categorical Imperative

When I conceive a hypothetical imperative, in general I do not know beforehand what it will contain until I am given the condition. But when I conceive a categorical imperative, I know at once what it contains. For as the imperative contains besides the law only the necessity that the maxims* shall conform to this law, while the law contains no conditions restricting it, there remains nothing but the general statement that the maxim of the action should conform to a universal law, and it is this conformity alone that the imperative properly represents as necessary.

There is therefore but one categorical imperative, namely, this: *Act only on that maxim whereby thou canst at the same time will that it should become a universal law.*

Now if all imperatives of duty can be deduced from this one im-

* A "maxim" is a subjective principle of action, and must be distinguished from the *objective principle,* namely, practical law. The former contains the practical rule set by reason according to the conditions of the subject (often its ignorance or its inclinations), so that it is the principle on which the subject *acts;* but the law is the objective principle valid for every rational being, and is the principle on which it *ought to act*—that is an imperative.

perative as from their principle, then, although it should remain undecided whether what is called duty is not merely a vain notion, yet at least we shall be able to show what we understand by it and what this notion means.

Since the universality of the law according to which effects are produced constitutes what is properly called *nature* in the most general sense (as to form)—that is, the existence of things so far as it is determined by general laws—the imperative of duty may be expressed thus: *Act as if the maxim of thy action were to become by thy will a universal law of nature.*

We will now enumerate a few duties, adopting the usual division of them into duties to ourselves and to others, and into perfect and imperfect duties.

1. A man reduced to despair by a series of misfortunes feels wearied of life, but is still so far in possession of his reason that he can ask himself whether it would not be contrary to his duty to himself to take his own life. Now he inquires whether the maxim of his action could become a universal law of nature. His maxim is: From self-love I adopt it as a principle to shorten my life when its longer duration is likely to bring more evil than satisfaction. It is asked then simply whether this principle founded on self-love can become a universal law of nature. Now we see at once that a system of nature of which it should be a law to destroy life by means of the very feeling whose special nature it is to impel to the improvement of life would contradict itself, and therefore could not exist as a system of nature; hence that maxim cannot possibly exist as a universal law of nature, and consequently would be wholly inconsistent with the supreme principle of all duty.

2. Another finds himself forced by necessity to borrow money. He knows that he will not be able to repay it, but sees also that nothing will be lent to him unless he promises stoutly to repay it in a definite time. He desires to make this promise, but he has still so much conscience as to ask himself: Is it not unlawful and inconsistent with duty to get out of a difficulty in this way? Suppose, however, that he resolves to do so, then the maxim of his action would be expressed thus: When I think myself in want of money, I will borrow money and promise to repay it, although I know that I never can do so. Now this principle of self-love or of one's own advantage may perhaps be consistent with my whole future welfare; but the question now is, Is it right? I change then the suggestion of self-love into a universal law, and state the question thus: How would it be if my maxim were a universal law? Then I see at once that it could never hold as a universal law of nature, but would necessarily contradict itself. For supposing it to be a universal law that everyone when he thinks himself in a difficulty should be able to promise whatever he pleases, with the purpose of not keeping his promise, the promise itself would become impossible, as well as the end that one might have in view in it, since no one would consider that anything was promised to him, but would ridicule all such statements as vain pretenses.

3. A third finds in himself a talent which with the help of some culture might make him a useful man in many respects. But he finds

himself in comfortable circumstances and prefers to indulge in pleasure rather than to take pains in enlarging and improving his happy natural capacities. He asks, however, whether his maxim of neglect of his natural gifts, besides agreeing with his inclination to indulgence, agrees also with what is called duty. He sees then that a system of nature could indeed subsist with such a universal law, although men (like the South Sea islanders) should let their talents rest and resolve to devote their lives merely to idleness, amusement, and propagation of their species—in a word, to enjoyment: but he cannot possibly *will* that this should be a universal law of nature, or be implanted in us as such by a natural instinct. For, as a rational being, he necessarily wills that his faculties be developed, since they serve him, and have been given him, for all sorts of possible purposes.

4. A fourth, who is in prosperity, while he sees that others have to contend with great wretchedness and that he could help them, thinks: What concern is it of mine? Let everyone be as happy as Heaven pleases, or as he can make himself; I will take nothing from him nor even envy him, only I do not wish to contribute anything to his welfare or to his assistance in distress! Now no doubt, if such a mode of thinking were a universal law, the human race might very well subsist, and doubtless even better than in a state in which everyone talks of sympathy and good-will, or even takes care occasionally to put it into practice, but, on the other side, also cheats when he can, betrays the rights of men, or otherwise violates them. But although it is possible that a universal law of nature might exist in accordance with that maxim, it is impossible to *will* that such a principle should have the universal validity of a law of nature. For a will which resolved this would contradict itself, inasmuch as many cases might occur in which one would have need of the love and sympathy of others, and in which, by such a law of nature, sprung from his own will, he would deprive himself of all hope of the aid he desires.

These are a few of the many actual duties, or at least what we regard as such, which obviously fall into two classes on the one principle that we have laid down. We must be *able to will* that a maxim of our action should be a universal law. This is the canon of the moral appreciation of the action generally. Some actions are of such a character that their maxim cannot without contradiction be even *conceived* as a universal law of nature, far from it being possible that we should *will* that it *should* be so. In others, this intrinsic impossibility is not found, but still it is impossible to *will* that their maxim should be raised to the universality of a law of nature, since such a will would contradict itself. It is easily seen that the former violate strict or rigorous (inflexible) duty; the latter only laxer (meritorious) duty. Thus it has been completely shown by these examples how all duties depend as regards the nature of the obligation (not the object of the action) on the same principle.

If now we attend to ourselves on occasion of any transgression of duty, we shall find that we in fact do not will that our maxim should be a universal law, for that is impossible for us; on the contrary, we will that the opposite should remain a universal law, only we assume the liberty of making an *exception* in our own favor or (just for this time only) in favor of our inclination. Consequently, if we considered all cases from one and the same point of view, namely, that of reason, we should find a contradiction in our own will, namely, that a certain principle should be objectively necessary as a universal law, and yet subjectively should not be universal, but admit of exceptions. As, however, we at one moment regard our action from the point of view of a will wholly conformed to reason, and then again look at the same action from the point of view of a will affected by inclination, there is not really any contradiction, but an antagonism of inclination to the precept of reason, whereby the universality of the principle is changed into a mere generality, so that the practical principle of reason shall meet the maxim half way. Now, although this cannot be justified in our own impartial judgment, yet it proves that we do really recognize the validity of the categorical imperative and (with all respect for it) only allow ourselves a few exceptions which we think unimportant and forced from us. . . .

The Second Formulation of the Categorical Imperative

The will is conceived as a faculty of determining oneself to action *in accordance with the conception of certain laws.* And such a faculty can be found only in rational beings. Now that which serves the will as the objective ground of its self-determination is the *end,* and if this is assigned by reason alone, it must hold for all rational beings. On the other hand, that which merely contains the ground of possibility of the action of which the effect is the end, this is called the *means.* The subjective ground of the desire is the *spring,* the objective ground of the volition is the *motive;* hence the distinction between subjective ends which rest on springs, and objective ends which depend on motives valid for every rational being. Practical principles are *formal* when they abstract from all subjective ends; they are *material* when they assume these, and therefore particular, springs of action. The ends which a rational being proposes to himself at pleasure as *effects* of his actions (material ends) are all only relative, for it is only their relation to the particular desires of the subject that gives them their worth, which therefore cannot furnish principles universal and necessary for all rational beings and for every volition, that is to say, practical laws. Hence all these relative ends can give rise only to hypothetical imperatives.

Supposing, however, that there were something *whose existence* has *in itself* an absolute worth, something which, being *an end in itself,* could be a source of definite laws, then in this and this alone would lie the source of a possible categorical imperative, that is, a practical law.

Now I say: man and generally any rational being *exists* as an end in himself, *not merely as a means* to be arbitrarily used by this or that will, but in all his actions, whether they concern himself or other rational beings, must be always regarded at the same time as an end. All objects of the inclinations have only a conditional worth; for if the inclinations and the wants founded on them did not exist, then their object would be without value. But the inclinations themselves, being sources of want, are so far from having an absolute worth for which they should be desired that, on the contrary, it must be the universal wish of every rational being to be wholly free from them. Thus the worth of any object which is *to be acquired* by our action is always conditional. Beings whose existence depends not on our will but on nature's, have nevertheless, if they are not rational beings, only a relative value as means, and are therefore called *things;* rational beings, on the contrary, are called *persons,* because their very nature points them out as ends in themselves, that is, as something which must not be used merely as means, and so far therefore restricts freedom of action (and is an object of respect). These, therefore, are not merely subjective ends whose existence has a worth *for us* as an effect of our action, but *objective ends,* that is, things whose existence is an end in itself—an end, moreover, for which no other can be substituted, which they should subserve *merely* as means, for otherwise nothing whatever would possess *absolute worth;* but if all worth were conditioned and therefore contingent, then there would be no supreme practical principle of reason whatever.

If then there is a supreme practical principle or, in respect of the human will, a categorical imperative, it must be one which, being drawn from the conception of that which is necessarily an end for everyone because it is *an end in itself,* constitutes an *objective* principle of will, and can therefore serve as a universal practical law. The foundation of this principle is: *rational nature exists as an end in itself.* Man necessarily conceives his own existence as being so; so far then this is a *subjective* principle of human actions. But every other rational being regards its existence similarly, just on the same rational principle that holds for me; so that it is at the same time an objective principle from which as a supreme practical law all laws of the will must be capable of being deduced. Accordingly the practical imperative will be as follows: *So act as to treat humanity, whether in thine own person or in that of any other, in every case as an end withal, never as means only.* We will now inquire whether this can be practically carried out.

To abide by the previous examples:

First, under the head of necessary duty to oneself: He who contemplates suicide should ask himself whether his action can be consistent with the idea of humanity *as an end in itself.* If he destroys himself in order to escape from painful circumstances, he uses a person merely as *a mean* to maintain a tolerable condition up to the end of life. But a man is not a thing, that is to say, something which can be used merely as means, but must in all his actions be always considered as an end in himself. I cannot, therefore, dispose in any way of a man in my own person so as to mutilate him, to damage or kill him. (It belongs to ethics proper to define this principle more precisely, so as to avoid all misunderstanding, for example, as to the amputation of the limbs in order to preserve myself; as to exposing my life to danger with a view to preserve it, etc. This question is therefore omitted here.)

Secondly, as regards necessary duties, or those of strict obligation, towards others: He who is thinking of making a lying promise to others will see at once that he would be using another man *merely as a mean,* without the latter containing at the same time the end in himself. For he whom I propose by such a promise to use for my own purposes cannot possibly assent to my mode of acting towards him, and therefore cannot himself contain the end of this action. This violation of the principle of humanity in other men is more obvious if we take in examples of attacks on the freedom and property of others. For then it is clear that he who transgresses the rights of men intends to use the person of others merely as means, without considering that as rational beings they ought always to be esteemed also as ends, that is, as beings who must be capable of containing in themselves the end of the very same action.

Thirdly, as regards contingent (meritorious) duties to oneself: It is not enough that the action does not violate humanity in our own person as an end in itself, it must also *harmonize with it.* Now there are in humanity capacities of greater perfection which belong to the end that nature has in view in regard to humanity in ourselves as the subject; to neglect these might perhaps be consistent with the *maintenance* of humanity as an end in itself, but not with the *advancement* of this end.

Fourthly, as regards meritorious duties towards others: The natural end which all men have is their own happiness. Now humanity might indeed subsist although no one should contribute anything to the happiness of others, provided he did not intentionally withdraw anything from it; but after all, this would only harmonize negatively, not positively, with *humanity as an end in itself,* if everyone does not also endeavor, as far as in him lies, to forward the ends of others. For the ends of any subject which is an end in himself ought as far as possible to be *my* ends also, if that conception is to have its *full* effect with me.

This principle that humanity and generally every rational nature is *an end in itself* (which is the supreme limiting condition of every man's freedom of action), is not borrowed from experience, *first,* because it is universal, applying as it does to all rational beings whatever, and experience is not capable of determining anything about them; *secondly,* because it does not present humanity as an end to men (subjectively), that is, as an object which men do of themselves actually adopt as an end; but as an objective end which must as a law constitute the supreme limiting condition of all our subjective ends, let them be what we will; it must therefore spring from pure reason. In fact the objective principle of all practical legislation lies (according to the first principle) in *the rule* and its form of universality which makes it capable of being a law (say, for example, a law of nature); but the *subjective* principle is in the *end;* now by the second principle, the subject of all ends is each rational being inasmuch as it is an end in itself. Hence follows the third practical principle of the will, which is the ultimate condition of its harmony with the universal practical reason, viz., the idea of *the will of every rational being as a universally legislative will.*

On this principle all maxims are rejected which are inconsistent with the will being itself universal legislator. Thus the will is not subject to the law, but so subject that it must be regarded *as itself giving the law,* and on this ground only subject to the law (of which it can regard itself as the author).

In the previous imperatives, namely, that based on the conception of the conformity of actions to general laws, as in a *physical system of nature,* and that based on the universal *prerogative* of rational beings as *ends* in themselves—these imperatives just because they were conceived as categorical excluded from any share in their authority all admixture of any interest as a spring of action, they were, however, only *assumed* to be categorical, because such an assumption was necessary to explain the conception of duty. But we could not prove independently that there are practical propositions which command categorically, nor can it be proved in this section; one thing, however, could be done, namely, to indicate in the imperative itself, by some determinate expression, that in the case of volition from duty all interest is renounced, which is the specific criterion of categorical as distinguished from hypothetical imperatives. This is done in the present (third) formula of the principle, namely, in the idea of the will of every rational being as a *universally legislating will.*

For although a will *which is subject to laws* may be attached to this law by means of an interest, yet a will which is itself a supreme lawgiver, so far as it is such, cannot possibly depend on any interest, since a will so dependent would itself still need another law restricting the interest of its self-love by the condition that it should be valid as universal law.

Thus the *principle* that every human will is *a will which in all its maxims gives universal laws,** provided it be otherwise justified, would be very *well adapted* to be the categorical imperative, in this respect, namely, that just because of the idea of universal legislation it is *not based on any interest,* and therefore it alone among all possible imperatives can be *unconditional.* Or still better, converting the proposition, if there is a categorical imperative (that is, a law for the will of every rational being), it can only command that everything be done from maxims of one's will regarded as a will which could at the same time will that it should itself give universal laws, for in that case only the practical principle and the imperative which it obeys are unconditional, since they cannot be based on any interest. . . .

The Kingdom of Ends

The conception of every rational being as one which must consider itself as giving in all the maxims of its will universal laws, so as to judge itself and its actions from this point of view—this conception leads to another which depends on it and is very fruitful, namely, that of a *kingdom of ends.*

By a "kingdom" I understand the union of different rational beings in a system by common laws. Now since it is by laws that ends are determined as regards their universal validity, hence, if we abstract

* I may be excused from adducing examples to elucidate this principle, as those which have already been used to elucidate the categorical imperative and its formula would all serve for the like purpose here.

from the personal differences of rational beings, and likewise from all the content of their private ends, we shall be able to conceive all ends combined in a systematic whole (including both rational beings as ends in themselves, and also the special ends which each may propose to himself), that is to say, we can conceive a kingdom of ends, which on the preceding principles is possible.

For all rational beings come under the *law* that each of them must treat itself and all others *never merely as means*, but in every case *at the same time as ends in themselves.* Hence results a systematic union of rational beings by common objective laws, that is, a kingdom which may be called a kingdom of ends, since what these laws have in view is just the relation of these beings to one another as ends and means. It is certainly only an ideal.

A rational being belongs as a *member* to the kingdom of ends when, although giving universal laws in it, he is also himself subject to these laws. He belongs to it *as sovereign* when, while giving laws, he is not subject to the will of any other.

A rational being must always regard himself as giving laws either as member or as sovereign in a kingdom of ends which is rendered possible by the freedom of will. He cannot, however, maintain the latter position merely by the maxims of his will, but only in case he is a completely independent being without wants and with unrestricted power adequate to his will.

Morality consists then in the reference of all action to the legislation which alone can render a kingdom of ends possible. This legislation must be capable of existing in every rational being, and of emanating from his will, so that the principle of this will is never to act on any maxim which could not without contradition be also a universal law, and accordingly always so to act *that the will could at the same time regard itself as giving in its maxims universal laws.* If now the maxims of rational beings are not by their own nature coincident with this objective principle, then the necessity of acting on it is called practical necessitation that is, *duty.* Duty does not apply to the sovereign in the kingdom of ends, but it does to every member of it and to all in the same degree.

The practical necessity of acting on this principle, that is, duty, does not rest at all on feelings, impulses, or inclinations, but solely on the relation of rational beings to one another, a relation in which the will of a rational being must always be regarded as *legislative,* since otherwise it could not be conceived as *an end in itself.* Reason then refers every maxim of the will, regarding it as legislating universally, to every other will and also to every action towards oneself: and this not on account of any other practical motive or any future advantage, but from the idea of the *dignity* of a rational being, obeying no law but that which he himself also gives.

In the kingdom of ends everything has either *value* or *dignity.* Whatever has a value can be replaced by something else which is *equivalent;* whatever, on the other hand, is above all value, and therefore admits of no equivalent, has a dignity.

Whatever has reference to the general inclinations and wants of mankind has a *market value;* whatever, without presupposing a want, corresponds to a certain taste, that is, to a satisfaction in the mere purposeless play of our faculties, has a *fancy value;* but that which constitutes the condition under which alone anything can be an end in itself, this has not merely a relative worth, that is, value, but an intrinsic worth, that is, *dignity*.

2

F. H. BRADLEY

(1846–1924)

*My Station and Its Duties**

This famous essay on duty is Bradley's answer to Kant's ethical philosophy. For Bradley, no member of the community can find his function or his duty apart from his involvement with the community. Each man is "but as a 'heart-beat in its system'." There are no individual men for Bradley. Men are what they are because of the community. Each man is simply a particularization of what is common to all men. To know what a man is, is to know his position in society, his relationship to others. Duties arise because of the station a man occupies. Bradley claims that knowledge of right and wrong is based on intuition. A man has feelings of the rightness or wrongness of possible courses of action when he has identified his will with the moral spirit of the community. He begins to feel what is expected of him in his station.

* F. H. Bradley, *Ethical Studies* (Oxford: Oxford Press, 1876), Essay V, with omissions.

WE are not going to enter on a metaphysical question to which we are not equal; we meet the metaphysical assertion of the "individualist" with a mere denial and, turning to facts, we will try to show that they lead us in another direction. To the assertion, then, that selves are "individual" in the sense of exclusive of other selves, we oppose the (equally justified) assertion that this is a mere fancy. We say that, out of theory, no such individual men exist; and we will try to show from fact that, in fact, what we call an individual man is what he is because of and by virtue of community, and that communities are thus not mere names but something real, and can be regarded (if we mean to keep to facts) only as the one in the many.

And to confine the subject and to keep to what is familiar, we will not call to our aid the life of animals, nor early societies, nor the course of history, but we will take men as they are now; we will take ourselves and endeavor to keep wholly to the teaching of experience.

The "Individual" Man

Let us take a man, an Englishman as he is now, and try to point out that apart from what he has in common with others, apart from his sameness with others, he is not an Englishman—nor a man at all; that if you take him as something by himself, he is not what he is. Of course we do not mean to say that he cannot go out of England without disappearing, nor, even if all the rest of the nation perished that he would not survive. What we mean to say is that he is what he is because he is a born and educated social being, and a member of an individual social organism; that if you make abstraction of all this, which is the same in him and in others, what you have left is not an Englishman, nor a man, but some I know not what residuum, which never has existed by itself and does not so exist. If we suppose the world of relations, in which he was born and bred, never to have been, then we suppose the very essence of him not to be; if we take that away, we have taken him away; and hence he now is not an individual, in the sense of owing nothing to the sphere of relations in which he finds himself, but does contain those relations within himself as belonging to his very being; he is what he is, in brief, so far as he is what others also are. . . .

The "individual" man, the man into whose essence his community with others does not enter, who does not include relation to others in his very being, is, we say, a fiction, and in the light of facts we have to examine him. Let us take him in the shape of an English child as soon as he is born; for I suppose we ought not to go further back. Let us take him as soon as he is separated from his mother and occupies a space clear and exclusive of all other human beings. At this time, education and custom will, I imagine, be allowed to have not as yet operated on him or lessened his "individuality." But is he now a mere "individual," in the sense of not implying in his being identity with others? We cannot say that if we hold to the teaching of modern physiology. Physiology would tell us, in one language or another, that even now the child's mind is no passive "tabula rasa"; he has an inner, a yet undeveloped nature, which must largely determine his future individuality. What is this inner nature? Is it particular to himself? Certainly not all of it, will have to be the answer. The child is not fallen from heaven. He is born of certain parents who come of certain families, and he has in him the qualities of his parents, and, as breeders would say, of the strains from both sides. Much of it we can see and more we believe to be latent and, given certain (possible or impossible) conditions, ready to come to light. On the descent of mental qualities modern investigation and popular experience, as expressed in uneducated vulgar opinion, altogether, I believe, support one another, and we need not linger here. But if the intellectual and active qualities do descend from ancestors, is it not, I would ask, quite clear that a man may have in him the same that his father and mother had, the same that his brothers and sisters have? And if anyone objects to the word "same," I would put this to him. If, concerning two dogs allied in blood, I were to ask a man, "Is that of the same strain or stock as this?" and were answered, "No, not the same, but similar," should I not think one of these things, that the man either meant to deceive me, or was a "thinker," or a fool?

But the child is not merely the member of a family; he is born into other spheres, and (passing over the subordinate wholes which nevertheless do in many cases qualify him) he is born a member of the English nation. It is, I believe, a matter of fact that at birth the child of one race is not the same as the child of another; that in the children of the one race there is a certain identity, a developed or undeveloped national type which may be hard to recognize, or which at present may even be unrecognizable, but which nevertheless in some form will appear. If that be the fact, then again we must say that one English child is in some points, though perhaps it does not as yet show itself, the same as another. His being is so far common to him with others; he is not a mere "individual."

We see the child has been born at a certain time of parents of a certain race, and that means also of a certain degree of culture. It is the opinion of those best qualified to speak on the subject that civilization is to some not inconsiderable extent hereditary; that aptitudes are developed, and are latent in the child at birth; and that it is a very different thing, even apart from education, to be born of civilized and of uncivilized ancestors. These "civilized tendencies," if we may use the phrase, are part of the essence of the child. He would only partly (if at all) be himself without them; he owes them to his ancestors, and his ancestors owe them to society. The ancestors were made what they were by the society they lived in. If in answer it be replied, "Yes, but individual ancestors were prior to their society," then that, to say the least of it, is a hazardous and unproved assertion, since man, so far as history can trace him back, is social; and if Mr. Darwin's conjecture as to the development of man from a social animal be received, we must say that man has never been anything but social, and society never was made by individual men. Nor, if the (baseless) assertion of the priority of individual men were allowed, would that destroy our case, for certainly our more immediate ancestors were social; and, whether society was manufactured previously by individuals or not, yet in their case it certainly was not so. They at all events have been so qualified by the common possessions of social mankind that, as members in the organism, they have become relative to the whole. If we suppose then that the results of the social life of the race are present in a latent and potential form in the child, can we deny that they are common property? Can we assert that they are not an element of sameness in all? Can we say that the individual is this individual because he is exclusive, when, if we deduct from him what he includes, he loses characteristics which make him himself, and when again he does include what the others include, and therefore does (how can we escape the consequence?) include in some sense the others also, just as they include him? By himself, then, what are we to call him? I confess I do not know unless we name him a theoretical attempt to isolate what cannot be isolated, and that, I suppose, has, out of our heads, no existence. But what he is really, and not in mere theory, can be described only as the specification or particularization of that which is common, which is the same amid diversity, and without which the "individual" would be so other than he is that we could not call him the same.

Thus the child is at birth; and he is born not into a desert, but into a living world, a whole which has a true individuality of its own, and into a system and order which it is difficult to look at as anything else than an organism, and which, even in England, we are now beginning to call by that name. And I fear that the "individuality" (the particularness) which the child brought into the light with him now stands but a poor chance, and that there is no help for him until he is old enough to become a "philosopher." We have seen that already he has in him inherited habits, or what will of themselves appear as such; but, in addition to this, he is not for one moment left alone, but continually tampered with; and the habituation which is applied from the outside is the more insidious that it answers to this inborn disposition. Who can resist it? Nay, who but a "thinker" could wish to have resisted it? And yet the tender care that receives and guides him is impressing on him habits, habits, alas, not particular to himself, and the "icy chains" of universal custom are hardening themselves round his cradled life. As the poet tells us, he has not yet thought of himself; his earliest notions come mixed to him of things and persons, not distinct from one another, nor divided from the feeling of his own existence. The need that he cannot understand moves him to foolish, but not futile, cries for what only another can give him; and the breast of his mother, and the soft warmth and touches and tones of his nurse, are made one with the feeling of his own pleasure and pain; nor is he yet a moralist to beware of such illusion and to see in them mere means to an end without them in his separate self. For he does not even think of his separate self; he grows with his world, his mind fills and orders itself; and when he can separate himself from that world, and know himself apart from it, then by that time his self, the object of his self-consciousness, is penetrated, infected, characterized by the existence of others. Its content implies in every fiber relations of community. He learns, or already perhaps has learned, to speak, and here he appropriates the common heritage of his race; the tongue that he makes his own is his country's language, it is (or it should be) the same that others speak, and it carries into his mind the ideas and sentiments of the race (over this I need not stay), and stamps them in indelibly. He grows up in an atmosphere of example and general custom, his life widens out from one little world to other and higher worlds, and he apprehends through successive stations the whole in which he lives, and in which he has lived. Is he now to try and develop his "individuality," his self which is not the same as other selves? Where is it? What is it? Where can he find it? The soul within him is saturated, is filled, is qualified by, it has assimilated, has got its substance, has built itself up from, it *is* one and the same life with the universal life, and if he turns against this he turns against himself; if he thrusts it from him, he tears his own vitals; if he attacks it, he sets his weapon against his own heart. He has found his life in the life of the whole, he lives that in himself, "he is a pulse-beat of the whole system, and himself the whole system."

The Individual Finds his Life in the Life of the Whole

"The child, in his character of the form of the possibility of a moral individual, is something subjective or negative; his growing to manhood is the ceasing to be of this form, and his education is the discipline or the compulsion thereof. The positive side and the essence is that he is suckled at the breast of the universal Ethos, lives in its absolute intuition, as in that of a foreign being first, then comprehends it more and more, and so passes over into the universal mind." The writer proceeds to draw the weighty conclusion that virtue "is not a troubling oneself about a peculiar and isolated morality of one's own, that the striving for a positive morality of one's own is futile, and in its very nature impossible of attainment; that in respect of morality the saying of the wisest men of antiquity is the only one which is true, that to be moral is to live in accordance with the moral tradition of one's country; and in respect of education the one true answer is that which a Pythagorean gave to him who asked what was the best education for his son, If you make him the citizen of a people with good institutions."*

But this is to anticipate. So far, I think, without aid from metaphysics, we have seen that the "individual" apart from the community is an abstraction. It is not anything real and hence not anything that we can realize, however much we may wish to do so. We have seen that I am myself by sharing with others, by including in my essence relations to them, the relations of the social state. If I wish to realize my true being I must therefore realize something beyond my being as a mere this or that, for my true being has in it a life which is not the life of any mere particular, and so must be called a universal life.

Realization of "My Station and Its Duties"

What is it then that I am to realize? We have said it in "my station and its duties." To know what a man is (as we have seen) you must not take him in isolation. He is one of a people, he was born in a family, he lives in a certain society, in a certain state. What he has to do depends on what his place is, what his function is, and that all comes from his station in the organism. Are there then such organisms in which he lives, and if so, what is their nature? Here we come to questions which must be answered in full by any complete system of Ethics, but which we cannot enter on. We must content ourselves by pointing out that there are such facts as the family, then in a middle position a man's own profession and society, and, over all, the larger community of the state. Leaving out of sight the question of a society wider than the state, we must say that a man's life with its moral duties is in the main filled up by his station in that system of wholes which the state is, and that this, partly by its laws and institutions and still more by its spirit, gives him the life which he does live and ought to live. That objective institutions exist is of course an obvious fact; and it is a fact which every day is becoming plainer that these institutions are organic, and further, that they are moral. The assertion that communities have been manufactured by the addition of exclusive units is, as we have seen, a mere fable; and if, within the state, we take that which seems wholly to depend on individual caprice, *e. g.*, marriage, yet even here we find that a man does give up his self so far as it excludes others; he does bring himself under a unity which is superior to the particular person and the impulses that belong to his single existence, and which makes him fully as much as he makes it. In short, man is a social being; he is real only because he is social, and can realize himself only because it is as social that he

* Hegel, *Philosophische Abhandlungen*, I, 389.

realizes himself. The mere individual is a delusion of theory; and the attempt to realize it in practice is the starvation and mutilation of human nature, with total sterility or the production of monstrosities. . . .

[In] "my station and its duties," I realize myself morally, so that not only what ought to be in the world is, but I am what I ought to be, and find so my contentment and satisfaction. If this were not the case, when we consider that the ordinary moral man is self-contented and happy, we should be forced to accuse him of immorality, and we do not do this; we say he most likely might be better, but we do not say that he is bad, or need consider himself so. Why is this? It is because "my station and its duties" teaches us to identify others and ourselves with the station we fill; to consider that as good, and by virtue of that to consider others and ourselves good too. It teaches us that a man who does his work in the world is good, notwithstanding his faults, if his faults do not prevent him from fulfilling his station. It tells us that the heart is an idle abstraction; we are not to think of it, nor must we look at our insides, but at our work and our life, and say to ourselves, Am I fulfilling my appointed function or not? Fulfill it we can, if we will. What we have to do is not so much better than the world that we cannot do it; the world is there waiting for it; my duties are my rights. On the one hand, I am not likely to be much better than the world asks me to be; on the other hand, if I can take my place in the world I ought not to be discontented. Here we must not be misunderstood; we do not say that the false self, the habits and desires opposed to the good will, are extinguished. Though negated, they never are all of them entirely suppressed, and cannot be. Hence we must not say that any man really does fill his station to the full height of his capacity; nor must we say of any man that he cannot perform his function better than he does, for we all can do so, and should try to do so. We do not wish to deny what are plain moral facts, nor in any way to slur them over.

Identification with the Good

How then does the contradiction disappear? It disappears by my identifying myself with the good will that I realize in the world, by my refusing to identify myself with the bad will of my private self. So far as I am one with the good will, living as a member in the moral organism, I am to consider myself real and I am not to consider the false self real. That cannot be attributed to me in my character of member in the organism. Even in me the false existence of it has been partly suppressed by that organism; and, so far as the organism is concerned, it is wholly suppressed because contradicted in its results, and allowed no reality. Hence, not existing for the organism, it does not exist for me as a member thereof; and only as a member thereof do I hold myself to be real. And yet this is not justification by faith, for we not only trust, but see, that despite our faults the moral world stands fast, and we in and by it. It is like faith, however, in this, that not merely by thinking ourselves, but by willing ourselves as such, can we look on ourselves as organs in a good whole, and so ourselves good. And further, the knowledge that as members of the system we are real, and not otherwise, encourages us more and more to identify ourselves with that system; to make ourselves better, and so more real, since we see that the good is real, and that nothing else is.

Or, to repeat it, in education my self by habituation has been growing into one with the good self around me, and by my free acceptance of my lot hereafter I consciously make myself one with the good, so that, though bad habits cling to and even arise in me, yet I cannot but be aware of myself as the reality of the good will. That is my essential side; my imperfections are not, and practically they do not matter. The good will in the world realizes itself by and in imperfect instruments, and in spite of them. The work is done, and so long as I will my part of the work and do it (as I do), I feel that, if I perform the function, I *am* the organ, and that my faults, if they do not matter to my station, do not matter to me. My heart I am not to think of, except to tell by my work whether it is in my work, and one with the moral whole; and if that is so, I have the consciousness of absolute reality in the good because of any by myself, and in myself because of and through the good; and with that I am satisfied, and have no right to be dissatisfied.

The individual's consciousness of himself is inseparable from the knowing himself as an organ of the whole; and the residuum falls more and more into the background, so that he thinks of it, if at all, not as himself, but as an idle appendage. For his nature now is not distinct from his "artificial self." He is related to the living moral system not as to a foreign body; his relation to it is "too inward even for faith," since faith implies a certain separation. It is no other-world that he cannot see but must trust to: he feels himself in it, and it in him; in a word, the self-consciousness of himself *is* the self-consciousness of the whole in him, and his will is the will which sees in him its accomplishment by him; it is the free will which knows itself as the free will, and as this beholds its realization and is more than content. . . .

The next point we come to is the question, How do I get to know in particular what is right and wrong? . . .

We know what is right in a particular case by what we may call an immediate judgment, or an intuitive subsumption. These phrases are perhaps not very luminous, and the matter of the "intuitive understanding" in general is doubtless difficult, and the special character or moral judgments not easy to define; and I do not say that I am in a position to explain these subjects at all, nor, I think, could anyone do so, except at considerable length. But the point that I do wish to establish here is, I think, not at all obscure. The reader has first to recognize that moral judgments are not discursive; next, that nevertheless they do start from and rest on a certain basis; and then if he puts the two together, he will see that they involve what he may call the "intuitive understanding," or any other name, so long as he keeps in sight the two elements and holds them together.

On the head that moral judgments are not discursive, no one, I think, will wish me to stay long. If the reader attends to the facts he will not want anything else; and if he does not, I confess I cannot prove my point. In practical morality, no doubt, we *may* reflect on our principles, but I think it is not too much to say that we *never* do so, except where we have come upon a difficulty of particular application. If anyone thinks that a man's *ordinary* judgment, "this is right or wrong," comes from the having a rule *before* the mind and bringing the particular case under it, he may be right, and I cannot try to show that he is wrong. I can only leave it to the reader to judge for himself. We say we "see" and we "feel" in these cases, not we "conclude." . . .

Moral Judgments are Not Isolated

Taking for granted then that our ordinary way of judging in morals is not by reflection and explicit reasoning, we have now to point to the other side of the fact, viz., that these judgments are not mere isolated impressions, but stand in an intimate and vital relation to a certain system, which is their basis. Here again we must ask the reader to pause, if in doubt, and consider the facts for himself. Different men, who have lived in different times and countries, judge a fresh case in morals differently. Why is this? There is probably no "why" before the mind of either when he judges; but *we* perhaps can say, "I know why A said so and B so," because we find some general rule or principle different in each, and in each the basis of the judgment. Different people in the same society may judge points differently, and we sometimes know why. It is because A is struck by one aspect of the case, B by another; and one principle is (not *before,* but) *in* A's mind when he judges, and another in B's. Each has subsumed, but under a different head; the one perhaps justice, the other gratitude. Every man has the morality he has made his own in his mind, and he "sees" or "feels" or "judges" accordingly, though he does not reason explicitly from data to a conclusion. . . .

If a man is to know what is right, he should have imbibed by precept, and still more by example, the spirit of his community, its general and special beliefs as to right and wrong, and, with this whole embodied in his mind should particularize it in any new case, not by a reflective deduction, but by an intuitive subsumption, which does not know that it is a subsumption, by a carrying out of the self into a new case, wherein what is before the mind is the case and not the self to be carried out, and where it is indeed the whole that feels and sees, but all that is seen is seen in the form of *this* case, *this* point, *this* instance. Precept is good, but example is better; for by a series of particulars (as such forgotten) we get the general spirit, we identify ourselves both on the side of will and judgment with the basis, which basis (be it remembered) has not got to be explicit.

There are a number of questions which invite considerations here, but we cannot stop. We wished to point out briefly the character of our common moral judgments. This (on the intellectual side) is the way in which they are ordinarily made; and, in the main, there is not much practical difficulty. What is moral *in any particular given case* is seldom doubtful. Society pronounces beforehand; or, after some one course has been taken, it can say whether it was right or not; though society cannot generalize much, and, if asked to reflect, is helpless and becomes incoherent. But I do not say there are no cases where the morally minded man has to doubt; most certainly such do arise, though not so many as some people think, far fewer than some would be glad to think. A very large number arise from reflection, which wants to act from an explicit principle, and so begins to abstract and divide, and, thus becoming one-sided, makes the relative absolute. Apart from this, however, collisions must take place, and here there is no guide whatever but the intuitive judgment of oneself or others.*

This intuition must not be confounded with what is sometimes miscalled "conscience." It is not mere individual opinion or caprice. It presupposes the morality of the community as its basis, and is subject to the approval thereof. Here, if anywhere, the idea of universal and impersonal morality is realized. For the final arbiters are the *φρόνιμοι*, persons with a will to do right, and not full of reflections and theories. If they fail you, you must judge for yourself, but practically they seldom do fail you. Their private peculiarities neutralize each other, and the result is an intuition which does not belong merely to this or that man or collection of men. "Conscience" is the antipodes of this. It wants you to have no law but yourself, and to be better than the world. But this tells you that, if you could be as good as your world, you would be better than most likely you are, and that to wish to be better than the world is to be already on the threshold of immorality.

* I may remark on this (after Erdmann, and I suppose Plato) that collisions of duties are avoided mostly by each man keeping to his own immediate duties, and not trying to see from the point of view of other stations than his own.

3

JEAN-PAUL SARTRE

(1905–   )

*Freedom and Responsibility**

Sartre attacks the problems of responsibility from the existentialist point of view. Briefly, existentialism is the philosophy based on the theory that "existence precedes essence" in man. By that phrase, Sartre and other existentialists mean that man first simply is, and then through his actions he determines what he is to be. "Essence" in philosophy has meant "the reality of a thing," what something really is behind what it appears to be. Many philosophers and religious thinkers believe that man has an essence, a human nature, created by God or endowed by Nature, which gives meaning to human life. The existentialists deny these ideas and claim instead that men are what, and only what, they make of themselves. There are no efforts to explain the activities of men. We are "condemned to be free," says Sartre: "Condemned" because our births were not our choices, "free" because there are no traditional excuses to restrict us. A man is no more than what he does; what we do with our lives is our own fault. Existential life begins, Sartre claims in his play The Flies, *when people come to realize that they must act without hope of external reward. "Human life begins on the far side of despair." When all ways of avoiding responsibility are taken away, every act becomes significant. Each of us by living his own life participates in the process of creation, creating a man. Responsibility is the acceptance of our condition, realizing that each of us is the only one on whom blame or praise for his actions can be placed.*

* Jean-Paul Sartre, Being and Nothingness, Hazel Barnes, trans. (New York: Philosophical Library, 1953), Pt. IV, Chap. 1, iii, pp. 52–60. Used by permission of the publishers, Philosophical Library, Inc.

ALTHOUGH the considerations which are about to follow are of interest primarily to the ethicist, it may nevertheless be worthwhile after these descriptions and arguments to return to the freedom of the for-itself and to try to understand what the fact of this freedom represents for human destiny.

The essential consequence of our earlier remarks is that man being condemned to be free carries the weight of the whole world on his shoulders; he is responsible for the world and for himself as a way of being. We are taking the word "responsibility" in its ordinary sense as "consciousness (of) being the incontestable author of an event or of an object." In this sense the responsibility of the for-itself is overwhelming since he* is the one by whom it happens that *there is* a world; since he is also the one who makes himself be, then whatever may be the situation in which he finds himself, the for-itself must wholly assume this situation with its peculiar coefficient of adversity, even though it be insupportable. He must assume the situation with the proud consciousness of being the author of it, for the very worst disadvantages or the worst threats which can endanger my person have meaning only in and through my project; and it is on the ground of the engagement which I am that they appear. It is therefore senseless to think of complaining since nothing foreign has decided what we feel, what we live, or what we are.

Absolute Responsibility is the Logical Requirement of the Consequences of our Freedom

Furthermore this absolute responsibility is not resignation; it is simply the logical requirement of the consequences of our freedom. What happens to me happens through me, and I can neither affect myself with it nor revolt against it nor resign myself to it. Moreover everything which happens to me is *mine*. By this we must understand first of all that I am always equal to what happens to me *qua* man, for what happens to a man through other men and through himself can be only human. The most terrible situations of war, the worst tortures do not create a non-human state of things; there is no non-human situation. It is only through fear, flight, and recourse to magical types of conduct that I shall decide on the non-human, but this decision is human, and I shall carry the entire responsibility for it. But in addition the situation is *mine* because it is the image of my free choice of myself, and everything which it presents to me is *mine* in that this represents me and symbolizes me. Is it not I who decide the coefficient of adversity in things and even their unpredictability by deciding myself?

Thus there are no *accidents* in a life; a community event which suddenly bursts forth and involves me in it does not come from the outside. If I am mobilized in a war, this war is *my* war; it is in my image and I deserve it. I deserve it first because I could always get out of it by suicide or by desertion; these ultimate possibles are those which must always be present for us when there is a question of envisaging a situation. For lack of getting out of it, I have *chosen* it. This can be due to inertia, to cowardice in the face of public opinion, or because I prefer certain other values to the value of the refusal to join in the war (the good opinion of my relatives, the honor of my family, *etc.*). Anyway you look at it, it is a matter of a choice. This choice will be repeated later on again and again without a break until the end of the war. Therefore we must agree with the statement by J. Romains, "In war there are no innocent victims."† If therefore I have preferred war to death or to dishonor, everything takes place as if I bore the

* I am shifting to the personal pronoun here since Sartre is describing the for-itself in concrete personal terms rather than as a metaphysical entity. Strictly speaking, of course, this is his position throughout, and the French "*il*" is indifferently "he" or "it." Tr.

† J. Romains: *Les hommes de bonne volonte;* "Prélude à Verdun."

entire responsibility for this war. Of course others have declared it, and one might be tempted perhaps to consider me as a simple accomplice. But this notion of complicity has only a juridical sense, and it does not hold here. For it depended on me that for me and by me this war should not exist, and I have decided that it does exist. There was no compulsion here, for the compulsion could have got no hold on a freedom. I did not have any excuse; for as we have said repeatedly in this book, the peculiar character of human-reality is that it is without excuse. Therefore it remains for me only to lay claim to this war.

Human-Reality is Without Excuse

But in addition the war is *mine* because by the sole fact that it arises in a situation which I cause to be and that I can discover it there only by engaging myself for or against it, I can no longer distinguish at present the choice which I make of myself from the choice which I make of the war. To live this war is to choose myself through it and to choose it through my choice of myself. There can be no question of considering it as "four years of vacation" or as a "reprieve," as a "recess," the essential part of my responsibilities being elsewhere in my married, family, or professional life. In this war which I have chosen I choose myself from day to day, and I make it mine by making myself. If it is going to be four empty years, then it is I who bear the responsibility for this.

Finally, as we pointed out earlier, each person is an absolute choice of self from the standpoint of a world of knowledges and of techniques which this choice both assumes and illumines; each person is an absolute upsurge at an absolute date and is perfectly unthinkable at another date. It is therefore a waste of time to ask what I should have been if this war had not broken out, for I have chosen myself as one of the possible meanings of the epoch which imperceptibly led to war. I am not distinct from this same epoch; I could not be transported to another epoch without contradiction. Thus *I am* this war which restricts and limits and makes comprehensible the period which preceded it. In this sense we may define more precisely the responsibility of the for-itself if to the earlier quoted statement, "There are no innocent victims," we add the words, "We have the war we deserve." Thus, totally free, undistinguishable from the period for which I have chosen to be the meaning, as profoundly responsible for the war as if I had myself declared it, unable to live without integrating it in *my* situation, engaging myself in it wholly and stamping it with my seal, I must be without remorse or regrets as I am without excuse; for from the instant of my upsurge into being, I carry the weight of the world by myself alone without anything or any person being able to lighten it.

Yet this responsibility is of a very particular type. Someone will say, "I did not ask to be born." This is a naive way of throwing greater emphasis on our facticity. I am responsible for everything, in fact, except for my very responsibility, for I am not the foundation of my being. Therefore everything takes place as if I were compelled to be responsible. I am *abandoned* in the world, not in the sense that I might remain abandoned and passive in a hostile universe like a board floating on the water, but rather in the sense that I find myself suddenly alone and without help, engaged in a world for which I bear the whole responsibility without being able, whatever I do, to tear myself away from this responsibility for an instant. For I am responsible for my very desire of fleeing responsibilities. To make myself passive in the world, to refuse to act upon things and upon Others is still to choose myself, and suicide is one mode among others of being-in-the-world. Yet I find an absolute responsibility for the fact that my facticity (here the fact of my birth) is directly inapprehensible and even inconceivable, for this fact of my birth never appears as a brute fact but always across a projective reconstruction of my for-itself. I am ashamed of being born or I am astonished at it or I rejoice over it, or in attempting to get rid of my life I affirm that I live and I assume this life as bad. Thus in a certain sense I *choose* being born. This choice itself is integrally affected with facticity since I am not able not to choose, but this facticity in turn will appear only in so far as I surpass it toward my ends. Thus facticity is everywhere but inapprehensible; I never encounter anything except my responsibility. That is why I can not ask, "*Why* was I born?" or curse the day of my birth or declare that I did not ask to be born, for these various attitudes toward my birth—*i.e.*, toward the *fact* that I realize a presence in the world—are absolutely nothing else but ways of assuming this birth in full responsibility and of making it *mine*. Here again I encounter only myself and my projects so that finally my abandonment—*i.e.*, my facticity—consists simply in the fact that I am condemned to be wholly responsible for myself. I am the being which *is* in such a way that in its being its being is in question. And this "is" of my being *is* as present and inapprehensible.

Under these conditions since every event in the world can be revealed to me only as an *opportunity* (an opportunity made use of, lacked, neglected, *etc.*), or better yet since everything which happens to us can be considered as a *chance* (*i.e.*, can appear to us only as a way of realizing this being which is in question in our being) and since others as transcendences-transcended are themselves only *opportunities* and *chances,* the responsibility of the for-itself extends to the entire world as a peopled-world. It is precisely thus that the for-itself apprehends itself in anguish; that is, as a being which is neither the foundation of its own being nor of the Other's being nor of the in-itselfs which form the world, but a being which is compelled to decide the meaning of being—within it and everywhere outside of it. The one who realizes in anguish his condition as *being* thrown into a responsibility which extends to his very abandonment has no longer either remorse or regret or excuse; he is no longer anything but a freedom which perfectly reveals itself and whose being resides in this very revelation. But as we pointed out at the beginning of this work, most of the time we flee anguish in bad faith.

4

WILLIAM WERKMEISTER

(1901–)

*Value Theory and the Problem of Moral Obligation**

Werkmeister's major concern in philosophy is theories of values. He maintains that our concept of moral obligation can best be understood by examining the practice of promising. Notice how a simple promise creates an obligation for the promiser and a right for the person promised. Werkmeister's theory is that a promise is a commitment, and commitments entail obligations and bestow rights and are therefore the basis of moral philosophy. Obviously there are a great number and type of commitments and various levels of commitments; this leads us into conflicts of commitments, which are at the root of our moral choices. Kant's interest lay with those conflicts between inclination and duty; Werkmeister stresses conflicts of obligation: the common situation where more than one obligation is involved. How do we resolve such conflicts? Werkmeister's answer is that we must justify our choice in terms of our higher value theory.

* From *The Personalist*, Vol. XLV (1964) pp. 354–361. Used by kind permission of Professor Werkmeister and the editors of *The Personalist.*

IN recent years there has been an upsurge in Western philosophy in the discussion of problems of value theory and ethics. It is possible that the challenges to traditional views so forcefully presented by logical positivists and by existentialists have contributed notably to this development. The culmination of the positivistic arguments was the formulation of the emotive theory of value and obligation; and the contribution of at least some of the existentialists was the outright denial of rationally grounded standards. But the radicalism of these two divergent positions has forced philosophers everywhere to re-examine —and to re-examine most carefully and most critically—the whole complexus of problems pertaining to values and obligations. The result has been not only a renewed and vigorous activity in value theory and theoretical ethics, but a remarkable clarification of basic categories and their interrelations. It is my purpose here to contribute to this development by pointing up briefly what appear to be possible solutions to some of the crucial problems.

Let us begin with the fact that, traditionally, two radically different answers have been given to the question, What ought I to do? One philosophical tradition, going back to the Greek classics but finding renowned spokesmen at all times, accepts as key categories the terms 'good' and 'bad.' The other tradition, first formulated in the Mosaic Code but, since the days of Kant, finding increasing philosophical recognition, accepts as basic category the terms 'obligation' and 'right.' That both sets of categories have at all times been recognized as important and that they are unquestionably interrelated in some manner does not alter the fact that one of the sets is basic in one philosophical tradition and the other is equally basic in another tradition. I shall here argue that an interpretation of moral matters in terms of 'obligation' and 'right' is most fruitful and that it is basic; but that, even so, it must find its ultimate "vindication" in terms of value. The specific interrelation of obligation and value is, however, a special problem.

Promises and Commitments

The best way of approaching the several issues involved in our over-all problem, it seems to me, is to consider the nature of a *promise*. If I promise Mr. Smith to meet him tomorrow at a certain time and place, then I have obligated myself to meet him as promised, and I have given him a right to expect that I do so. There is nothing mysterious about this; nor does it assume the existence of an agency which can enforce the promise. The obligation is self-imposed and the right freely granted by the very act of promising. It is clear, also, that if the "promise" was extracted under duress, neither the obligation nor the right exists. Obligating oneself by making a promise presupposes freedom of choice and of action. Moreover, it is evident that a promise can be assumed to be binding only when it was made in full understanding of all circumstances essential to it. In my terminology, therefore, a promise freely given—and given with a full understanding of what is involved—entails an obligation which I call *moral.* And this same promise, by placing me under an obligation, also bestows a right upon the person to whom the promise is made—the right, namely, to expect that I act as promised.

Now, a promise is a commitment; and my thesis is that any commitment entails an obligation and bestows a right in the same sense in which a promise does so. Thus, taking the marriage vow or the oath of allegiance to a particular country is to make a commitment which entails moral obligations, on the one hand, and the right to expect fulfilment of the obligations, on the other. To be sure, in the case of marriage and in that of citizenship, there are also legal obligations which arise out of the commitment and which society can and does enforce. This does not alter the fact, however, that the basic obligations (and the corresponding rights) are moral, and that the entailed legal obligations are but society's explicit recognition and codification of at least some of the obligations and rights entailed by the commitment.

It is also evident from the example of citizenship that not all our commitments need be explicitly formulated. Two different situations may, in fact, be distinguished. The first is this: If I leave the country of my birth and become a citizen of some other country, I must and do take an oath of allegiance; and in so doing I make an explicit commitment which entails all the obligations of citizenship. But if I remain in my native land, it may be the case that I never have to take an oath of allegiance; for it is taken for granted that, as long as I remain a resident, I am also a citizen, having all the obligations and rights appertaining to citizenship. In this case, my commitment is and remains implicit only: it is implied in my remaining a resident of my native land. But the obligations arising out of an implicit commitment are as binding as are obligations entailed by an explicit commitment.

The second type of implicit commitment stems from the fact that, at the moment of explicit commitment, I may not explicitly affirm all the details of implied obligations. Thus, when taking the oath of allegiance, I may not explicitly promise to pay taxes; yet the obligation to do so, whether specifically recognized or not, is entailed by my basic commitment. In making the basic commitment, either explicitly or implicitly, I have implicitly committed myself to whatever it entails. It is because of such implicit commitments, incidentally, that I may at times reconsider and change my basic commitment. So long, however, as my basic commitments remain unaltered, obligations which they entail—even when not explicitly formulated—remain binding.

Commitment to an Ideal

Up to this point I have argued as if my thesis required at all times a commitment—be it explicit or implicit—to an actually existing individual or a social group. I must now amend this line of argument; for the commitment may also be made to a "projected" or "ideal" society. Thus, I may commit myself to membership in that "ancient and honorable society of scholars" so often referred to in the United States when the doctor's degree is being conferred at graduation from the university. Or, to bring my argument at once to its conclusion, I may commit myself to an ideal of a human society *as human;* I may commit myself to an ideal humanity—to St. Augustine's "City of God," to Kant's "Kingdom of Ends," to Royce's "Beloved Community," to the "Brotherhood of Man." Out of such commitments, also, obligations and rights arise. And it may well be the case that the obligations entailed by the ideal to which I stand committed impose upon me the duty to work toward a change in the actual human situation so as to bring actuality into closer harmony with the ideal. As a human being I cannot avoid this commitment to humanity—this commitment to an ideal; or I can do so only at the price of my own humanity.

But if this is the case, it is clear also, I believe, that (1) I can make a commitment to an ideal hitherto not envisioned by man: "Ye have heard that it was said to them of old time . . . but I say unto you . . ."; that (2) I can make a commitment for myself only and without other witnesses; and that (3) I am under obligation to evaluate actual situations in the light of my ideal commitments. My ideal commitments, incidentally, insofar as they become my habitual attitude, are the "voice of conscience" within me.

It is true, however, that human relations—the social group, the "community of scholars," the ideal humanity—be they actual or ideal, can and do exist only by virtue of certain rules and broad principles which guide men's actions; that, in fact, the principles and rules are constitutive of the social group itself and that, therefore, commitment to a group is, in its very essence, commitment to the principles and rules which are constitutive of that group. The obligations arising out of commitments are thus obligations to live by certain principles and rules—by principles and rules, that is, which, being constitutive of the community to which we are committed, may themselves be regarded as moral principles and moral rules. And these same commitments entail the right of our fellow human beings to expect fulfilment of our obligations.

Conflicts among Commitments

It is clear from our discussion so far that there are various levels of commitment, ranging from the level of casual promises in concrete and actual situations to that of deepest personal and metaphysical involvement, and commitments to our highest ideals. But where the possibility of such a variety of commitments exists, there exists, of necessity, also the possibility of conflict in our commitments. Making use of ideas introduced earlier, I now hold that conflicts of commitments—and, therefore, of obligations—exist wherever the principles or rules to which we stand committed are mutually contradictory. The conflicts arise, in other words, not only where commitments oblige us to act contrary to impulse or desire, but also—and, from a moral point of view, more importantly—where obligation stands against obligation. Human existence involves us in both kinds of conflict.

For our purposes it will be sufficient to examine the type of conflict in which one obligation contradicts another; for the solution here will also be a solution for the other type. The obvious remedy in the case of mutually contradictory obligations seems to be to avoid contradictory commitments, or (what amounts to the same thing) to avoid commitments involving mutually contradictory principles and rules. Non-contradiction is, thus, at least a minimum requirement of harmony in our commitments. In itself, however, this principle of non-contradiction is not adequate because the logical problem of establishing non-contradiction cannot be solved in the case of unrelated or independent principles or rules. Non-contradiction alone provides a criterion only when our choice lies between two directions of actions—one affirmative, the other negative—with respect to one and the same obligation; or when, because of the practical limitations inherent in every human situation, we cannot actually live up to our contradictory commitments.

The case is quite different, however, when we accept as our criterion, not mere non-contradiction, but systematic integration; when the specific principles and rules upon which we act are entailed by an integrative and, therefore, a more comprehensive commitment.

In order to make my point quite clear, I shall briefly refer to an analogy from the history of science. Galileo's "law of falling bodies" and Kepler's three "laws of planetary motion," as originally conceived, were independent laws. In their logical independence they were non-contradictory, to be sure. But it was only in Newton's law of gravitation that the more specific laws of Galileo and Kepler found systematic integration which not only revealed the absence of contradictions but brought the laws together as indispensable elements in a more comprehensive law. By analogy, so I shall maintain, the real test of non-contradiction in moral principles—and, therefore, in moral obligations—is the integrative harmony achieved by our highest commitment. But if this is so, then we have a criterion which will enable us to resolve conflicts in moral obligations—without abandoning the thesis that every commitment entails an obligation. In any actual situation of conflict we have but to ask, What is our highest commitment? And what obligations does it entail? Given a clear conception of this commitment, we can determine the harmony and integrative consistency of all entailed commitments and, therefore, of our obligations and of the rights we bestow upon others.

Justification of Commitments

But now a further question arises: On what grounds do we justify our commitments? It is at this point that a comprehensive value theory must supplement our interpretation of obligation and of rights bestowed.

A promise or commitment, so we have seen, entails an obligation and bestows a right. The logic here is clear and compelling. The entailment is purely analytical. But why should I promise something or make a commitment? Let us recognize, first of all, that it is of the essence of a promise or commitment that it be a free and deliberate act—an act of our own choosing. And if this is so, then we must have a reason for making the commitment. This reason is not fully reducible to mere facts in the case but inevitably pertains to values. Thus, when I promise to have lunch with you tomorrow, I may do so, for example, because I enjoy your company, or because I find it an opportune time to transact some business. But "to enjoy someone's company" or "to find it an opportune time for business transactions" are value considerations. My promise, therefore, is value-motivated. We must be clear on one point, however: *making the promise* is value-motivated, but the *obligation* I am under to keep my promise (and the right you have to expect that I will do so) derives from the nature of the promise as promise, not from the value consideration which induced me to make it. Similarly, when I take the oath of allegiance, my obligations as a citizen are entailed by that commitment, but pledging my allegiance and thus committing myself is justifiable only in terms of values. And if, beyond the state in its actuality, I envision an ideal humanity, then valuations embodied in that ideal are again justification of a commitment entailing particular obligations and bestowing certain rights.

Let it be noted, however, that our ultimate commitment, too, must be freely made and must be personal. This much at any rate is the truth of existentialism: In our ultimate commitments we ourselves are at stake as a person. What is not true in existentialism is the thesis that we have nothing to guide us in making our ultimate decision; that we commit ourselves blindly. The fact of the matter is that our species-specific and our individual potentialities provide a framework for development in value-accented directions, and that culture-patterns of the societies in which we live and the whole history of the human race add perspective and further weight to certain dominant trends. Within the historical and cultural perspectives of all times we find valuations and value projections which point up certain ideals to which we may commit ourselves or beyond which we may envision still higher ideals. Despite all vicissitudes of the moment, the ideal of a free humanity emerges ever more clearly in the long course of history; and commitment to this ideal—justificable in terms of the values involved—entails moral obligations (and rights) which we cannot deny or conveniently forget.

The ideal of a free humanity, for example, first envisioned by prophets and thinkers of various regions and times, has of late found expression in the Charter of the United Nations and a Universal Bill of Rights. Here are the first embodiments of a projection based upon value considerations and valuations. And if we fulfill the obligations entailed by our commitment to these values—or to an ideal which even transcends these actual projections—then mankind itself will take a gigantic step forward in the realization of an ideal that gives substance and meaning to our commitments. The highest moral obligations which we have as members of the human race derive from our commitment to the highest ideal of a free humanity. The ideal itself is perhaps not yet fully defined. In fact, a certain "openness" ought always to be preserved in view of changing perspectives and a better understanding of the nature and potentialities of being a person. But whatever the ideal, it must ultimately find its justification in terms of values—and in terms of human values at that. Only a value theory can thus provide a dependable basis for our commitments and our obligations, and for the rights which our commitments bestow.

5

COLIN STRANG

(1922–)

*What If Everyone Did That?**

In this selection Strang attempts to deal with the common moral argument that takes the form, "Do you think you ought to do that; have you considered what it would be like if everyone did it?" Strang constructs a dialogue between a defaulter (on income tax and military service) and a moralist in order to examine the validity of the "What if everyone did that?" argument for doing one's duty. Consider the arguments Strang's defaulter provides which the people of Kew Gardens might have used to justify their inaction in the Genovese murder. Notice also how some of Piggy's arguments find restatement in the defaulter's position. Compare Strang's analysis of military duty and responsibility to Sartre's. Strang's moralist concludes that an argument for duty can be drawn by reference to the social situation, the universality of moral behavior, and an idea of fairness. Basically, his argument is that unless certain things are done at certain times within society, the consequences will be disastrous, and the burden of doing these tasks falls equally on particular classes of people within each society. Every member of one of those classes therefore bears the duty of at least attempting to do what is called for. By "classes" Strang might refer to young able-bodied males, or neighbors, or relatives, etc., as the situation demands.

* From *The Durham University Journal,* Vol. LIII, No. 1 (December, 1960), pp. 5–10. Used by kind permission of M. E. James, Editor of *The Durham University Journal.*

I WANT to discuss the force and validity of the familiar type of ethical argument epitomized in my title. A typical example of it would be: 'If everyone refrained from voting the result would be disastrous, therefore *you* ought to vote.' Now since the argument is addressed to the person concerned simply *qua* member of the class of people entitled to vote, it could be addressed with equal force to any member or all members of that class indifferently: so the conclusion might just as validly be: 'therefore *everyone* ought to vote.'

There is no doubt that this argument has some force. People *are* sometimes impressed by it. But it is not nearly so obvious that it is a valid one, i.e. that they *ought* to be impressed by it.

One way of not being impressed by it is to reply: 'Yes, but everyone *won't* refrain from voting, so there will be no disaster, so it's all right for me not to vote.' But this reply is beside the point. The argument never claimed that this one abstention would lead to disaster, nor did it claim that universal abstention (which *would* be disastrous) would occur; indeed it implied, on each point, the very opposite. This brings out the important fact that the argument does not appeal to the consequences of the action it condemns and so is not of a utilitarian type, but that it is applicable, if anywhere, just where utilitarian arguments do *not* apply.

The objector, who remains unimpressed, will continue: 'Granted that my first objection is beside the point, I still can't see how you get from your premiss to your conclusion. Your premiss is, roughly: "Everyone's non-voting is to be deplored," and your conclusion is: "Everyone's voting is obligatory." Why should it be irrational to accept the premiss but deny the conclusion? In any case the validity of the argument cannot depend on its form alone. Plenty of arguments of the very same form are plainly invalid. For instance; if everyone switched on their electric fires at 9 a.m. sharp there would be a power breakdown, therefore no one should; furthermore, this argument applies not only to 9 a.m. but to all times, so no one should ever switch on an electric fire. Again, if everyone taught philosophy whole-time we should all starve, so no one should; or if everyone built houses or did anything else whatever (bar farming) whole-time, we should all starve; and if everyone farmed we would be without clothes or shelter and would die of exposure in winter, so no one should farm. It rather looks, on your kind of argument, as if every whole-time activity is forbidden to everyone. Conversely, if no one farmed we would all starve, so everyone should farm; if no one made clothes we would all die of exposure, so everyone ought to make clothes—and so on. So it also looks, on your kind of argument, as if all sorts of part-time activity are obligatory on everybody. You surely do not mean to commit yourself to enjoining self-sufficiency and condemning specialization? What I want to know is why some arguments of this form are valid (as you claim) while others are not (as you must admit).'

In face of this kind of objection the obvious move is to place certain restrictions on the use of arguments of this form, and to show that only those satisfying certain conditions are valid while the rest are not. This is in fact the move adopted in two recent treatments of this problem: one is by A. C. Ewing (*Philosophy,* January 1953), and the other by M. G. Singer (*Mind,* July 1955). These two are independent, since Singer makes no mention of Ewing; and Ewing, incidentally, regards himself as doing pioneer work in the subject, being able to quote only one previous treatment of it (C. D. Broad, *International Journal of Ethics,* 1915–16). But the restrictions these two wish to impose on the argument seem to me *ad hoc;* they fail to explain why the argument is valid in the remaining cases, and it is just this that I aim to discover.

Why me? Compare the voting case with this one: 'If everyone here refuses to dig a latrine the camp will be insanitary, therefore everyone ought to dig one.' Surely the conclusion we want is, rather: 'therefore *someone* ought to dig one.' In the voting case, on the other hand, given the premiss 'If everyone refused to vote there would be no government,' the conclusion 'therefore someone ought to vote' clearly will not do; and even the conclusion 'therefore everyone ought to vote' is hardly cogent on the reasonable assumption that a 10% abstention will do no harm. If the argument is to be at all cogent it must make some reference to the percentage vote (say n%) needed, thus: 'If more than (100—n)% of the electorate abstained there would be no government'; this allows us to draw an acceptable conclusion, i.e. 'therefore n% must vote to avert anarchy and one must dig to avert disease. But our argument has gained in cogency and precision (being now of a simple utilitarian kind) only at the expense of being no longer effective, or even seemingly so, against the defaulter. He will reply: 'All right, so n% ought to vote (someone ought to dig), but why me?' However, there is hope yet for the moralist. To the retort 'Why me?' the argument may not suggest any obvious reply; but the retort itself does suggest the counter-retort 'Why not you?', to which again there is no obvious reply. An impasse is thus reached in which the moralist cannot say why the defaulter should vote or dig, and the defaulter cannot say why he should not. Evidently it was a mistake to amend the original argument, and yet there seemed to be something wrong with it as it stood; and yet, as it stood, it still seemed to be giving an answer, however obscurely, to the baffling question 'Why me?': 'Because if *everyone* did that . . .'

To return to the camp: certainly it is agreed by all members of the party that some digging ought to be done, and it is also agreed that the duty does not lie on anyone outside the party. But just where it lies within the party is hard to say. It does not lie on everyone, nor on anyone in particular. Where then? Whatever the answer to that apparently pressing question may be, we all know what would in fact happen. Someone would volunteer, or a leader would allot duties, or the whole party would cast lots. Or, if the thing to be done were not a once-and-for-all job like digging latrines but a daily routine like washing up, they might take it in turns.

Although various acceptable answers to the question how the duties are to be allotted are readily listed, they leave us quite in the dark as to just *who* ought to dig, wash up, etc. That question hardly seems to arise. In the absence of an argumentative defaulter there is no call to think up reasons why I or you should do this or that or reasons why I or you should not, and we are left with the defaulter's 'Why me?' and the moralist's 'Why not you?' unanswered.

Our enquiry has made little progress, but the fog is beginning to lift from the territory ahead. We are evidently concerned with communities of people and with things that must be done, or not done, if the community is to be saved from damage or destruction; and we want to know whose duty it is to do, or not to do, these things. The complexity of the problem is no longer in doubt. (1) There are some things that need doing once, some that need doing at regular intervals, and some that need doing all the time. (2) Some things need doing by one person, some by a number of people which can be roughly estimated, and some by as many as possible. (3) In practice, who shall do what (though not who *ought* to do what) is determined by economic factors, or by statutory direction (e.g. service with the armed forces in war, paying income tax), or merely by people's inclinations generally, i.e. when enough people are inclined to do the thing anyway.

A Dialogue Between a Defaulter and a Moralist

Somewhere in this territory our quarry has its lair. The following dialogue between defaulter and moralist on the evasion of income tax and military service begins the hunt. Our first steps are taken on already familiar ground:

Defaulter: £ 100 is a drop in the ocean to the exchequer. No one will suffer from their loss of £ 100, but it means a good deal to me.

Moralist: But what if everyone did that and offered the same excuse?

Defaulter: But the vast majority won't, so no one will suffer.

Moralist: Still, would you say it was *in order* for anyone whatever to evade tax and excuse himself on the same grounds as you do?

Defaulter: Certainly.

Moralist: So it would be quite in order for *everyone* to do the same and offer the same excuse?

Defaulter: Yes.

Moralist: Even though disaster would ensue for the exchequer and for everyone?

Defaulter: Yes. The exchequer would no more miss my £ 100 if *everyone* evaded than they would if only I evaded. They wouldn't miss anyone's individual evasion. What they would miss would be the aggregate £ 1,000,000,000 or so, and that isn't my default or yours or anyone's. So even if everyone evades it is still all right for me to evade; and if it's all right for me to evade it's all right for everyone to evade.

Moralist: You seem now to be in the paradoxical position of saying that if everyone evaded it would be disastrous, and yet no one would be to blame.

Defaulter: Paradoxical, perhaps, but instructive. I am not alarmed. Let me recur to one of your previous questions: you asked whether it would be in order for all to evade and give the same excuse. I now want to reply: No, it would not be in order, but only in the sense that it would be disastrous; but it *would* be in order in the sense that each person's grounds for evasion would still be as valid as they would have been if he had been the *only* evader and no disaster had ensued. In other words, none of the defaulters would be to blame for the disaster —and certainly not one of them would blame himself: on the contrary, each one would argue that had he paid he would have been the only one to pay and thus lost his £ 100 without doing himself or anyone else any good. He would have been a mug to pay.

Moralist: But surely there can't be a disaster of this kind for which no one is to blame.

Defaulter: If anyone is to blame it is the person whose job it is to circumvent evasion. If too few people vote, then it should be made illegal not to vote. If too few people volunteer, then you must introduce conscription. If too many people evade taxes, then you must tighten up your system of enforcement. My answer to your 'If everyone did that' is 'Then someone had jolly well better see to it that they don't; it doesn't impress me as a reason why *I* should, however many people do or don't.

Moralist: But surely you are being inconsistent here. Take the case of evading military service.

Defaulter: You mean not volunteering in time of crisis, there being no conscription? I do that too.

Moralist: Good. As I was saying, aren't you being inconsistent? You think *both* that it is all right not to volunteer even if too few other people volunteer (because one soldier more or less could make no difference), *and* think that you ought to be conscripted.

Defaulter: But that is not at all inconsistent. Look: the enemy threatens, a mere handful volunteer, and the writing is on the wall; my volunteering will not affect the outcome, but conscript me with the rest to stay the deluge and I will come without a murmur. In short, no good will come of my volunteering, but a great good will come of a general conscription which gathers me in with the rest. There is no inconsistency. I should add that my volunteering would in fact do positive harm; all who resist and survive are to be executed forthwith. There will be one or two heroes, but I did not think you were requiring me to be heroic.

Moralist: I confirm that I was not, and I concede that your position is not inconsistent, however unedifying. As I see it, the nub of your position is this: Given the premiss 'if everyone did that the result would be disastrous' you cannot conclude 'therefore *you* oughtn't' but only 'therefore someone ought to see to it that they don't.' If you are right, the 'if everyone did' argument, as usually taken, is invalid. But then we are left with the question: Whence does it derive its apparent force?

Defaulter: Whence, indeed?

(*interval*)

Moralist: Suppose when you give your justification for evading ('no one will miss *my* contribution') I reply: But don't you think it *unfair* that other people should bear the burden which you shirk and from the bearing of which by others you derive benefit for yourself?

Defaulter: Well, yes, it is rather unfair. Indeed you make me feel a little ashamed; but I wasn't prepared, and I'm still not, to let your pet argument by without a fight. Just where does fairness come into it?

Moralist: I think I can see. Let me begin by pushing two or three counters from different points on the periphery of the problem with the hope that they will meet at the centre. First, then: if someone is morally obliged (or permitted or forbidden) to do some particular thing, then there is a reason why he is so obliged. Further, if someone is obliged to do something for a particular reason, then anyone else whatever is equally obliged provided the reason applies to him also. The reason why a particular person is obliged to do something will be expressible in general terms, and could be expressed by describing some class to which he belongs. My principle then reads as follows: If someone is obliged to do something *just because* he is a member of a certain class, then any other member of that class will be equally obliged to do that thing. You yourself argued, remember, that any member of the class of people whose contribution would not be missed (here I allude to your reason for evasion) was no less entitled to evade than you.

Defaulter: Agreed.

Moralist: My second counter now comes into play. 'Fairness,' you will agree, is a moral term like 'rightness.' An act is unfair if it results in someone getting a greater or lesser share of something (whether pleasant or unpleasant) than he ought to get—more or less than his fair share, as we say.

Now there are a number of things, burdensome or otherwise, which need to be done if the community is not to suffer. But who precisely is to do them? Why me? Why not me? You will also agree, I hope, to the wide principle that where the thing to be done is burdensome the burden should be fairly distributed?

Defaulter: Certainly. I seldom dispute a truism. But in what does a fair distribution consist?

The Fairness Principle and the Universalization Principle

Moralist: In other words: given two people and a burden, how much of it ought each to bear? I say: *unless there is some reason why one should bear more or less of it than the other, they should both bear the same amount.* This is my Fairness Principle. It concerns both the fair allocation of the burden to some class of community members and the fair distribution of it within that class (and this may mean dividing the class into sub-classes of 'isophoric' members): there must always be a *reason* for treating people differently. For instance, people who are unfit or above or below a certain age are exempted or excluded from military service, and for good reasons; women are exempted or excluded from certain kinds of military service, for what Plato regarded as bad reasons; those with more income pay more tax, while those with more children pay less, and for good reasons—and so on. You will have noticed that the typical complaint about unfair dealing begins with a 'why': 'Why did they charge me more than him?' (unfair distribution), or 'Why should married couples be liable for so much surtax?' (unfair allocation). The maxim governing differential treatment, i.e. which is behind the reasons given for it, seems to be: From each according to his resources, to each according to his need. You might argue that my principle about equal burdens is no more than a special case of this maxim. But that principle is all I need for my argument and all I insist on; I shall not stick my neck out further than necessary.

Defaulter: It is not, thus far, too dangerously exposed, I think.

Moralist: Good. We are now ready to move a little nearer to the core of the problem. But first compare the two principles I have advanced. The first was: if a thing is obligatory etc. for one person, then it is obligatory etc. for anyone in the same class (i.e. the class relevant to the reason given). This is a license to argue from one member of a class to all its members; we will call it the Universalization Principle (U-Principle). The second, which is my Fairness Principle, is: A burden laid on a particular class is to be shared equally by all its members, unless there is reason to the contrary. This, in contrast to the first, is a license to argue from the class itself to each of its members. I take it, by the way, that these two principles are independent, that neither follows from the other.

Defaulter: Granted, granted. I am impatient to know what light all this throws on your 'if everyone did' argument.

Why not You?

Moralist: I am coming to that. You will remember that you used the U-Principle yourself to argue that if it's all right for you to evade it's all right for everyone else. But it was no use to me in pressing my case, and we can now see why: it argues from one to all, and there was no *one* to argue from. Nor, of course, could I argue from the consequences of your act. 'Why me?' you asked, and I had then no reply. But I did at least have a retort: 'Why not you?'. Now it seems to me that it is just my Fairness principle that lies behind the effectiveness of this retort, for by it you can be shown to have a duty in cases like this unless you can show that you have not. You would have to show, in the military service example, that you were not a member of the class on which the duty of military service is normally (and we will assume, fairly) regarded as lying. But you cannot show this: you cannot claim to be under age or over age or blind or lame. All you claim is that you have a certain property, the property of being one whose contribution won't be missed, which is shared by every other member of the military class; and this claim, so far from being a good reason for not volunteering, now stands revealed as no reason at all.

Defaulter: Still, you didn't dispute my point that the blame for a disaster following upon wholesale evasion lay upon those whose duty it was, or in whose power it lay, to prevent such evasion.

Moralist: You certainly had a point, but I can see now that you made too much of it. I concede that the authorities failed in their duty, but then the military class as a whole failed in theirs too. The duty of both was ultimately the same, to ensure the safety of the state, just as the duty of wicket-keeper and long-stop is the same, to save byes. To confine the blame to the authorities is like saying that it's all right to burn the house down so long as it's insured or that the mere existence of a police force constitutes a general license to rob banks. As for the individual defaulter, you wanted to absolve him from all blame—a claim which seemed at once plausible and paradoxical: plausible because he was not, as you rightly pointed out, to blame for the disaster (it was not his duty to prevent that, since it was not in his power to do so); paradoxical because he was surely to blame for *something*, and we now know what for: failure to bear his share of the burden allotted to his class.

Defaulter: Maybe, but it still seems to me that if I volunteer and others don't I shall be taking on an unfair share of it, and *that* can't be fair. Then again if I don't volunteer I shall be doing less than my share, and *that* can't be fair either. Whichever I do, there's something wrong. And that can't be right.

Moralist: There are two mistakes here. Whichever you do there's something wrong, but nothing unfair; the only wrong is people failing in their duty. Fairness is an attribute of distributions, and whether you volunteer or not neither you nor anyone else are distributing anything. Nor, for that matter, are fate or circumstances, for they are not persons. That is your first mistake. Your second is this: you talk as if the lone volunteer will necessarily do more than his fair share. He may, but he needn't. If he does, that is his own look out: *volenti non fit iniuria.*

Defaulter: It's more dangerous to fight alone than as one among many. How can he ration the danger?

Moralist: He can surrender or run away. Look, he isn't expected to be heroic or to do, or even attempt, the impossible. If two are needed to launch and man the lifeboat, the lone volunteer can only stand and wait: *he also* serves. The least a man can do is offer and hold himself ready, though sometimes it is also the most he can do.

Defaulter: Let it be so. But I am still in trouble about one thing: suppose I grant all you say about fairness and the defaulter, I'm still not clear why you choose to make your point against him in just the mysterious way you do, i.e. by fixing him with your glittering eye and beginning 'If everyone did that.'

Moralist: It is a little puzzling, isn't it? But not all that puzzling. After all, the premiss states and implies a good deal: (1) It states that wholesale evasion will have such and such results; (2) it states or implies that the results will be bad; (3) it implies strongly that a duty to prevent them must lie *somewhere;* (4) it implies that the duty does not lie solely on the person addressed (otherwise a quite different kind of argument would apply); (5) it implies, rather weakly, that nevertheless the person addressed has no better excuse for doing nothing about it than anyone else has. The conclusion is then stated that he ought to do something about it. A gap remains, to be sure; but it can't be a very big one, or people wouldn't, as they sometimes do, feel the force of the argument, however obscurely. The 'Why me?' retort brings out implication (4), while the 'Why not you?' counter-retort brings out implication (5); and we didn't really have very far to go from there.

The argument is clearly elliptical and needs filling out with some explicit reference to the Fairness principle. I would formalize it as follows:

Unless such and such is done, undesirable consequences X will ensue;
the burden of preventing X lies upon class Y as a whole;
each member of class Y has a *prima facie* duty to bear an equal share of the burden by doing Z;
you are a member of class Y;
therefore you have a *prima facie* duty to do Z.

I have introduced the notion of a *prima facie* duty at this late stage to cover those cases where only a few members of class Y are required to do Z and it would be silly to put them all to work. In the latrine case only one person needs to dig, and in America only a small proportion of fit persons are required for short-term military service. In such cases it is considered fair to select the requisite number by lot. Until the lot is cast I must hold myself ready; if I am selected my *prima facie* duty becomes an actual duty; if I am spared, it lapses. Why selection by lot should be a fair method I leave you to work out for yourself.

Notice that the argument only holds if the thing to be done is burdensome. Voting isn't really very burdensome; indeed a lot of people seem to enjoy it, and this accounts for the weakness of the argument in this application. If the thing to be done were positively enjoyable one might even have to invoke the Fairness principle against over-indulgence.

Notice, finally, that the argument doesn't apply unless there is a fairly readily isolable class to which a burden can be allotted. This rules out the farming and such like cases. You can't lay it down that the burden of providing food for the nation (if it *is* a burden) lies on the farmers (i.e. the class that provides food for the nation), for that is a tautology, or perhaps it implies the curious proposition that everyone *ought* to be doing the job he *is* doing. Might one say instead that *everyone* has a *prima facie* duty to farm, but that the duty lapses when inclination, ability and economic reward conspire to select a sufficient farming force? Far-fetched, I think. The matter might be pursued, but only at the risk of tedium. Well, are you satisfied?

Defaulter: Up to a point. Your hypothesis obviously calls for a lot more testing yet. But I have carried the burden a good deal further than my fair share of the distance; let others take it from here.

6

J. L. AUSTIN

(1911–1960)

*A Plea for Excuses**

Austin and Wittgenstein have been the two most influential philosophers of the English ordinary language school. Austin's approach is far more methodical than Wittgenstein's. In "A Plea for Excuses" he tells us his general views on the enterprise of philosophy. He recommends our examination of what we would say in certain instances, what language is appropriate when certain things occur. Using ordinary language as our guide, we discover the ways to treat problems of responsibility; we study the propensity we have to make certain excuses in certain situations. Austin suggests two major sources for the study of responsibility, the dictionary and the law. Commenting on "A Plea for Excuses" in another paper, "Three Ways of Spilling Ink," Austin writes: "The point of what I had to say there was that there isn't much point to discussing it (responsibility) in general terms. . . . Briefly it is the idea . . . that questions of whether a person was responsible for this or that are prior to questions of freedom . . . to discover whether someone acted freely or not, we must discover whether this, that, or the other plea will pass—for example, duress, or mistake, or accident, or so forth."

* J. L. Austin, "The Presidential Address to the Aristotelian Society, 1956," *Proceedings of the Aristotleian Society, 1956–1957,* Vol. LVII (1957). Used by courtesy of the Editor of the Aristotelian Society, copyright 1957, The Aristotelian Society.

THE subject of this paper, *Excuses,* is one not to be treated, but only to be introduced, within such limits. It is, or might be, the name of a whole branch, even a ramiculated branch, of philosophy, or at least of one fashion of philosophy. I shall try, therefore, first to state *what* the subject is, *why* it is worth studying, and *how* it may be studied, all this at a regrettably lofty level: and then I shall illustrate, in more congenial but desultory detail, some of the methods to be used, together with their limitations, and some of the unexpected results to be expected and lessons to be learned. Much, of course, of the amusement, and of the instruction, comes in drawing the coverts of the microglot, in hounding down the minutiae, and to this I can do no more here than incite you. But I owe it to the subject to say, that it has long afforded me what philosophy is so often thought, and made, barren of—the fun of discovery, the pleasures of cooperation, and the satisfaction of reaching agreement.

What, then, is the subject? I am here using the word "excuses" *for a title,* but it would be unwise to freeze too fast to this one noun and its partner verb: indeed for some time I used to use "extenuation" instead. Still, on the whole "excuses" is probably the most central and embracing term in the field, although this includes others of importance —"plea," "defense," "justification," and so on. When, then, do we "excuse" conduct, our own or somebody else's? When are "excuses" proffered?

In general, the situation is one where someone is *accused* of having done something, or (if that will keep it any cleaner) where someone is *said* to have done something which is bad, wrong, inept, unwelcome, or in some other of the numerous possible ways untoward. Thereupon he, or someone on his behalf, will try to defend his conduct or to get him out of it.

One way of going about this is to admit flatly that he, X, did do that very thing, A, but to argue that it was a good thing, or the right or sensible thing, or a permissible thing to do, either in general or at least in the special circumstances of the occasion. To take this line is to *justify* the action, to give reasons for doing it: not to say, to brazen it out, to glory in it, or the like.

A different way of going about it is to admit that it wasn't a good thing to have done, but to argue that it is not quite fair or correct to say *baldly* "X did A." We may say it isn't fair just to say X did it; perhaps he was under somebody's influence, or was nudged. Or, it isn't fair to say baldly he *did* A; it may have been partly accidental, or an unintentional slip. Or, it isn't fair to say he did simply A—he was really doing something quite different and A was only incidental, or he was looking at the whole thing quite differently. Naturally these arguments can be combined or overlap or run into each other.

In the one defense, briefly, we accept responsibility but deny that it was bad: in the other, we admit that it was bad but don't accept full, or even any, responsibility.

The Confusion Between Excuses and Justifications

By and large, justifications can be kept distinct from excuses, and I shall not be so anxious to talk about them because they have enjoyed more than their fair share of philosophical attention. But the two certainly can be confused, and can *seem* to go very near to each other, even if they do not perhaps actually do so. You dropped the tea tray: Certainly, but an emotional storm was about to break out: or, Yes, but there was a wasp. In each case the defense, very soundly, insists on a fuller description of the event in its context; but the first is a justification, the second an excuse. Again, if the objection is to the use of such a dyslogistic verb as "murdered," this may be on the ground that the killing was done in battle (justification) or on the ground that it was only accidental if reckless (excuse). It is arguable that we do not use the terms "justification" and "excuse" as carefully as we might; a miscellany of even less-clear terms, such as "extenuation," "palliation," "mitigation," hovers uneasily between partial justification and partial excuse; and when we plead, say, provocation, there is genuine uncertainty or ambiguity as to what we mean—is *he* partly responsible, because he roused a violent impulse or passion in me, so that it wasn't truly or merely me acting "of my own accord" (excuse)? Or is it rather that, he having done me such injury, I was entitled to retaliate (justification)? Such doubts merely make it the more urgent to clear up the usage of these various terms. But that the defenses I have for convenience labeled "justification" and "excuse" are in principle distinct can scarcely be doubted.

This then is the sort of situation we have to consider under "excuses." I will only further point out how very wide a field it covers. We have, of course, to bring in the opposite numbers of excuses—the expressions that *aggravate*, such as "deliberately," "on purpose," and so on, if only for the reason that an excuse often takes the form of a rebuttal of one of these. But we have also to bring in a large number of expressions which at first blush look not so much like excuses as like accusations—"clumsiness," "tactlessness," "thoughtlessness," and the like. Because it has always to be remembered that few excuses get us out of it *completely:* the average excuse, in a poor situation, gets us only out of the fire into the frying-pan—but still, of course, any frying-pan in a fire. If I have broken your dish or your romance, maybe the best defense I can find will be clumsiness.

Why, if this is what "excuses" are, should we trouble to investigate them? It might be thought reason enough that their production has always bulked so large among human activities. But to moral philosophy in particular a study of them will contribute in special ways, both positively towards the development of a cautious, latter-day version of conduct, and negatively towards the correction of older and hastier theories.

The Meaning of Doing an Action

In ethics we study, I suppose, the good and the bad, the right and the wrong, and this must be for the most part in some connection with conduct or the doing of actions. Yet before we consider what actions are good or bad, right or wrong, it is proper to consider first what is meant by, and what not, and what is included under, and what not, the expression "doing an action" or "doing something." These are expressions still too little examined on their own account and merits, just as the general notion of "saying something" is still too lightly passed over in logic. There is indeed a vague and comforting idea in the background that, after all, in the last analysis, doing an action must come down to the making of physical movements with parts of the body; but this is about as true as that saying something must, in the last analysis, come down to making movements of the tongue.

The beginning of sense, not to say wisdom, is to realize that "doing an action," as used in philosophy,* is a highly abstract expression—it is a stand-in used in the place of any (or almost any?) verb with a personal subject, in the same sort of way that "thing" is a stand-in for

* This use has little to do with the more down-to-earth occurrences of "action" in ordinary speech.

any (or when we remember, almost any) noun substantive, and "quality" a stand-in for the adjective. Nobody, to be sure, relies on such dummies quite implicitly quite indefinitely. Yet notoriously it is possible to arrive at, or to derive the idea for, an oversimplified metaphysics from the obsession with "things" and their "qualities." In a similar way, less commonly recognized even in these semi-sophisticated times, we fall for the myth of the verb. We treat the expression "doing an action" no longer as a stand-in for a verb with a personal subject, as which it has no doubt some uses, and might have more if the range of verbs were not left unspecified, but as a self-explanatory, ground-level description, one which brings adequately into the open the essential features of everything that comes, by simple inspection, under it. We scarcely notice even the most patent exceptions or difficulties (is to think something, or to say something, or to try to do something, to do an action?), any more than we fret, in the *ivresse des grandes profondeurs*, as to whether flames are things or events. So we come easily to think of our behavior over any time, and of a life as a whole, as consisting in doing now action A, next action B, then action C, and so on, just as elsewhere we come to think of the world as consisting of this, that, and the other substance or material thing, each with its properties. All "actions" are, as actions (meaning what?), equal, composing a quarrel with striking a match, winning a war with sneezing: worse still, we assimilate them one and all to the supposedly most obvious and easy cases, such as posting letters or moving fingers, just as we assimilate all "things" to horses or beds.

If we are to continue to use this expression in sober philosophy, we need to ask such questions as: Is to sneeze to do an action? Or is to breathe, or to see, or to checkmate, or each one of countless others? In short, for what range of verbs, as used on what occasions, is "doing an action" a stand-in? What have they in common, and what do those excluded severally lack? Again we need to ask how we decide what is the correct name for "the" action that somebody did—and what, indeed, are the rules for the use of "the" action, "an" action, "one" action, a "part" or "phase" of an action and the like. Further, we need to realize that even the "simplest" named actions are not so simple—certainly are not the mere makings of physical movements, and to ask what more, then, comes in (intentions? conventions?) and what does not (motives?), and what is the detail of the complicated internal machinery we use in "acting"—the receipt of intelligence, the appreciation of the situation, the invocation of principles, the planning, the control of execution and the rest.

In two main ways the study of excuses can throw light on these fundamental matters. First, to examine excuses is to examine cases where there has been some abnormality or failure: and as so often, the abnormal will throw light on the normal, will help us to penetrate the blinding veil of ease and obviousness that hides the mechanisms of the natural successful act. It rapidly becomes plain that the breakdowns signalized by the various excuses are of radically different kinds, affecting different parts or stages of the machinery, which the excuses consequently pick out and sort out for us. Further, it emerges that not *every* slip-up occurs in connection with *everything* that could be called an "action," that not every excuse is apt with every verb—far indeed from it: and this provides us with one means of introducing some classification into the vast miscellany of "actions." If we classify them according to the particular selection of breakdowns to which each is liable, this should assign them their places in some family group or groups of actions, or in some model of the machinery of acting.

A Classification of Actions

In this sort of way, the philosophical study of conduct can get off to a positive fresh start. But by the way, and more negatively, a number of traditional cruces or mistakes in this field can be resolved or removed. First among these comes the problem of Freedom. While it has been the tradition to present this as the "positive" term requiring elucidation, there is little doubt that to say we acted "freely" (in the philosopher's use, which is only faintly related to the everyday use) is to say only that we acted *not* unfreely, in one or another of the many heterogeneous ways of so acting (under duress, or what not). Like "real," "free" is only used to rule out the suggestion of some or all of its recognized antitheses. As "truth" is not a name for a characteristic of assertions, so "freedom" is not a name for a characteristic of actions, but the name of a dimension in which actions are assessed. In examining all the ways in which each action may not be "free," i.e., the cases in which it will not do to say simply "X did A," we may hope to dispose of the problem of Freedom. Aristotle has often been chidden for talking about excuses or pleas and overlooking "the real problem": in my own case, it was when I began to see the injustice of this charge that I first became interested in excuses.

There is much to be said for the view that, philosophical tradition apart, Responsibility would be a better candidate for the role here assigned to Freedom. If ordinary language is to be our guide, it is to evade responsibility, or full responsibility, that we most often make excuses, and I have used the word myself in this way above. But in fact "responsibility" too seems not really apt in all cases: I do not exactly evade responsibility when I plead clumsiness or tactlessness, nor, often, when I plead that I only did it unwillingly or reluctantly, and still less if I plead that I had in the circumstances no choice: here I was constrained and have an excuse (or justification), yet may accept responsibility. It may be, then, that at least two key terms, Freedom and Responsibility, are needed: the relation between them is not clear, and it may be hoped that the investigation of excuses will contribute towards its clarification.*

* Another well-flogged horse in these same stakes is Blame. At least two things seem confused together under this term. Sometimes when I blame X for doing A, say for breaking the vase, it is a question simply or mainly of my disapproval of A, breaking the vase, which unquestionably X did: but sometimes it is, rather, a question simply or mainly of how far I think X responsible for A, which unquestionably was bad. Hence if somebody says he blames me for something, I may answer by giving a *justification,* so that he will cease to disapprove of what I did, or else by giving an *excuse,* so that he will cease to hold me, at least entirely and in every way, responsible for doing it.

So much, then, for ways in which the study of excuses may throw light on ethics. But there are also reasons why it is an attractive subject methodologically, at least if we are to proceed from "ordinary language," that is, by examining *what we should say when*, and so why and what we should mean by it. Perhaps this method, at least as *one* philosophical method, scarcely requires justification at present—too evidently, there is gold in them thar hills: more opportune would be a warning about the care and thoroughness needed if it is not to fall into disrepute. I will, however, justify it very briefly.

Words are Tools

First, words are our tools, and, as a minimum, we should use clean tools: we should know what we mean and what we do not, and we must forearm ourselves against the traps that language sets us. Secondly, words are not (except in their own little corner) facts or things: we need therefore to prize them off the world, to hold them apart from and against it, so that we can realize their inadequacies and arbitrariness, and can relook at the world without blinkers. Thirdly, and more hopefully, our common stock of words embodies all the distinctions men have found worth drawing, and the connections they have found worth marking, in the lifetimes of many generations: these surely are likely to be more numerous, more sound, since they have stood up to the long test of the survival of the fittest, and more subtle, at least in all ordinary and reasonably practical matters, than any that you or I are likely to think up in our armchairs of an afternoon—the most favored alternative method.

In view of the prevalence of the slogan "ordinary language," and of such names as "linguistic" or "analytic" philosophy or "the analysis of language," one thing needs specially emphasizing to counter misunderstandings. When we examine what we should say when, what words we should use in what situations, we are looking again not *merely* at words (or "meanings," whatever they may be) but also at the realities we use the words to talk about: we are using a sharpened awareness of words to sharpen our perception of, though not as the final arbiter of, the phenomena. For this reason I think it might be better to use, for this way of doing philosophy, some less misleading name than those given above—for instance, "linguistic phenomenology," only that is rather a mouthful.

Using, then, such a method, it is plainly preferable to investigate a field where ordinary language is rich and subtle, as it is in the pressingly practical matter of Excuses, but certainly is not in the matter, say, of Time. At the same time we should prefer a field which is not too much trodden into bogs or tracks by traditional philosophy, for in that case even "ordinary" language will often have become infected with the jargon of extinct theories, and our own prejudices too, as the upholders or imbibers of theoretical views, will be too readily, and often insensibly, engaged. Here too, Excuses form an admirable topic; we can discuss at least clumsiness, or absence of mind, or inconsiderateness, even spontaneousness, without remembering what Kant thought, and so progress by degrees even to discussing deliberation without for once remembering Aristotle or self-control without Plato. Granted that our subject is, as already claimed for it, neighboring, analogous, or germane in some way to some notorious center of philosophical trouble, then, with these two further requirements satisfied, we should be certain of what we are after: a good site for *field work* in philosophy. Here at last we should be able to unfreeze, to loosen up and get going on agreeing about discoveries, however small, and on agreeing about how to reach agreement.* How much it is to be wished that similar field work will soon be undertaken in, say, aesthetics; if only we could forget for a while about the beautiful and get down instead to the dainty and the dumpy.

Loose Usage

There are, I know, or are supposed to be, snags in "linguistic" philosophy, which those not very familiar with it find, sometimes not without glee or relief, daunting. But with snags, as with nettles, the thing to do is to grasp them—and to climb above them. I will mention two in particular, over which the study of excuses may help to encourage us. The first is the snag of Loose (or Divergent or Alternative) Usage; and the second the crux of the Last Word. Do we all say the same, and only the same, things in the same situations? Don't usages differ? And, Why should what we all ordinarily say be the only or the best or final way of putting it? Why should it even be true?

Well, people's usages do vary, and we do talk loosely, and we do say different things apparently indifferently. But first, not nearly as much as one would think. When we come down to cases, it transpires in the very great majority that what we had thought was our wanting to say different things of and in *the same* situation was really not so—we had simply imagined the situation *slightly* differently: which is all too easy to do, because of course no situation (and we are dealing with *imagined* situations) is ever "completely" described. The more we imagine the situation in detail, with a background of story—and it is worth employing the most idiosyncratic or, sometimes, boring means to stimulate and to discipline our wretched imaginations—the less we find we disagree about what we should say. Nevertheless, *sometimes* we do ultimately disagree: sometimes we must allow a usage to be, though appalling, yet actual; sometimes we should genuinely use either or both of two different descriptions. But why should this daunt us? All that is happening is entirely explicable. If our usages disagree, then you use "X" where I use "Y," or more probably (and more intriguingly) your conceptual system is different from mine, though very likely it is at least equally consistent and serviceable: in short, we can find *why* we disagree—you choose to classify in one way, I in another. If the usage is loose, we can understand the temptation that leads to it, and the distinctions that it blurs: if there are "alternative" descriptions, then the situation can be described or can be "structured" in two ways, or perhaps it is one where, for current purposes, the two alternatives come

* All of which was seen and claimed by Socrates, when he first betook himself to the way of Words.

down to the same. A disagreement as to what we should say is not to be shied off, but to be pounced upon: for the explanation of it can hardly fail to be illuminating. If we light on an electron that rotates the wrong way, that is a discovery, a portent to be followed up, not a reason for chucking physics: and by the same token, a genuinely loose or eccentric talker is a rare specimen to be prized.

As practice in learning to handle this bogey, in learning the essential *rubrics,* we could scarcely hope for a more promising exercise than the study of excuses. Here, surely, is just the sort of situation where people will say "almost anything," because they are so flurried, or so anxious to get off. "It was a mistake," "It was an accident"—how readily these can *appear* indifferent, and even be used together. Yet, a story or two, and everybody will not merely agree that they are completely different, but even discover for himself what the difference is and what each means.*

The Last Word

Then, for the Last Word. Certainly ordinary language has no claim to be the last word, if there is such a thing. It embodies, indeed, something better than the metaphysics of the Stone Age, namely, as was said, the inherited experience and acumen of many generations of men. But then, that acumen has been concentrated primarily upon the practical business of life. If a distinction works well for practical purposes in ordinary life (no mean feat, for even ordinary life is full of hard cases), then there is sure to be something in it, it will not mark nothing: yet this is likely enough to be not the best way of arranging things if our interests are more extensive or intellectual than the ordinary. And again, that experience has been derived only from the sources available to ordinary men throughout most of civilized history: it has not been fed from the resources of the microscope and its successors. And it must be added too, that superstition and error and fantasy of all kinds do become incorporated in ordinary language and even sometimes stand up to the survival test (only, when they do, why should we not detect it?). Certainly, then, ordinary language is *not* the last word: in principle it can everywhere be supplemented and improved upon and superseded. Only remember, it *is* the *first* word.†

For this problem too the field of Excuses is a fruitful one. Here is matter both contentious and practically important for everybody, so that ordinary language is on its toes: yet also, on its back it has long had a bigger flea to bite it, in the shape of the Law, and both again have lately attracted the attentions of yet another, and at least a

* You have a donkey, so have I, and they graze in the same field. The day comes when I conceive a dislike for mine. I go to shoot it, draw a bead on it, fire: the brute falls in its tracks. I inspect the victim, and find to my horror that it is *your* donkey. I appear on your doorstep with the remains and say—what? "I say, old sport, I'm awfully sorry, etc., I've shot your donkey *by accident*"? Or *"by mistake"*? Then again, I go to shoot my donkey as before, draw a bead on it, fire—but as I do so, the beasts move, and to my horror yours falls. Again the scene on the doorstep—what do I say? "By mistake"? Or "by accident"?

† And forget, for once and for a while, that other curious question "Is it true?" May we?

healthily growing, flea, in the shape of psychology. In the law a constant stream of actual cases, more novel and more tortuous than the mere imagination could contrive, are brought up *for decision*—that is, formulas for docketing them must somehow be found. Hence it is necessary first to be careful with, but also to be brutal with, to torture, to fake, and to override, ordinary language: we cannot here evade or forget the whole affair. (In ordinary life we dismiss the puzzles that crop up about time, but we cannot do that indefinitely in physics.) Psychology likewise produces novel cases, but it also produces new methods for bringing phenomena under observation and study: moreover, unlike the law, it has an unbiased interest in the totality of them and is unpressed for decision. Hence its own special and constant need to supplement, to revise and to supersede the classifications of both ordinary life and the law. We have, then, ample material for practice in learning to handle the bogey of the Last Word, however it should be handled.

Methods and Resources used to Investigate Excuses

Suppose, then, that we set out to investigate excuses, what are the methods and resources initially available? Our object is to imagine the varieties of situation in which we make excuses, and to examine the expressions used in making them. If we have a lively imagination, together perhaps with an ample experience of dereliction, we shall go far, only we need system: I do not know how many of you keep a list of the kinds of fool you make of yourselves. It is advisable to use systematic aids, of which there would appear to be three at least. I list them here in order of availability to the layman.

First we may use the dictionary—quite a concise one will do, but the use must be *thorough*. Two methods suggest themselves, both a little tedious, but repaying. One is to read the book through, listing all the words that seem relevant; this does not take as long as many suppose. The other is to start with a widish selection of obviously relevant terms, and to consult the dictionary under each: it will be found that, in the explanations of the various meanings of each, a surprising number of other terms occur, which are germane though of course not often synonymous. We then look up each of *these*, bringing in more for our bag from the "definitions" given in each case; and when we have continued for a little, it will generally be found that the family circle begins to close, until ultimately it is complete and we come only upon repetitions. This method has the advantage of grouping the terms into convenient clusters—but of course a good deal will depend upon the comprehensiveness of our initial selection.

Working the dictionary, it is interesting to find that a high percentage of the terms connected with excuses prove to be *adverbs*, a type of word which has not enjoyed so large a share of the philosophical limelight as the noun, substantive or adjective, and the verb: this is natural because, as was said, the tenor of so many excuses is that I did it but only *in a way*, not just flatly like that—i.e., the verb needs modifying. Besides adverbs, however, there are other words of all kinds, including numerous abstract nouns, "misconception," "accident," "purpose," and the like, and a few verbs too, which often hold key positions for the grouping of excuses into classes at a high level ("couldn't help," "didn't mean to," "didn't realize," or again "intend," and "attempt"). In connection with the nouns another neglected class of words is prominent, namely, prepositions. Not merely does it matter considerably which preposition, often of several, is being used with a given substantive, but further the prepositions deserve study on their own account. For the question suggests itself, Why are the nouns in one group governed by "under," in another by "on," in yet another by "by" or "through" or "from" or "for" or "with," and so on? It will be disappointing if there prove to be no good reasons for such groupings.

Our second sourcebook will naturally be the law. This will provide us with an immense miscellany of untoward cases, and also with a useful list of recognized pleas, together with a good deal of acute analysis of both. No one who tries this resource will long be in doubt, I think, that the common law, and in particular the law of tort, is the richest storehouse; crime and contract contribute some special additions of their own, but tort is altogether more comprehensive and more flexible. But even here, and still more with so old and hardened a branch of the law as crime, much caution is needed with the arguments of counsel and the dicta or decisions of judges: acute though these are, it has always to be remembered that, in legal cases, (1) there is the overriding requirement that a decision be reached, and a relatively black or white decision—guilty or not guilty—for the plaintiff or for the defendant; (2) there is the general requirement that the charge or action and the pleadings be brought under one or another of the heads and procedures that have come in the course of history to be accepted by the courts (These, though fairly numerous, are still few and stereotyped in comparison with the accusations and defenses of daily life. Moreover contentions of many kinds are beneath the law, as too trivial, or outside it, as too purely moral—for example, inconsiderateness); (3) there is the general requirement that we argue from and abide by precedents (The value of this in the law is unquestionable, but it can certainly lead to distortions of ordinary beliefs and expressions). For such reasons as these, obviously closely connected and stemming from the nature and function of the law, practicing lawyers and jurists are by no means so careful as they might be to give to our ordinary expressions their ordinary meanings and applications. There is special pleading and evasion, stretching and strait-jacketing, besides the invention of technical terms, or technical senses for common terms. Nevertheless, it is a perpetual and salutary surprise to discover how much is to be learned from the law; and it is to be added that if a distinction drawn is a sound one, even though not yet recognized in law, a lawyer can be relied upon to take note of it, for it may be dangerous not to—if he does not, his opponent may.

Finally, the third sourcebook is psychology, with which I include such studies as anthropology and animal behavior. Here I speak with even more trepidation than about the Law. But this at least is clear, that some varieties of behavior, some ways of acting or explanations of the doing of actions, are here noticed and classified which have not been observed or named by ordinary men and hallowed by ordinary language, though perhaps they often might have been so if they had been of more practical importance. There is real danger in contempt for the "jargon" of psychology, at least when it sets out to supplement, and at least sometimes when it sets out to supplant, the language of ordinary life.

With these sources, and with the aid of the imagination, it will go hard if we cannot arrive at the meanings of large numbers of expressions and at the understanding and classification of large numbers of "actions." Then we shall comprehend clearly much that, before, we only made use of *ad hoc*. Definition, I would add, explanatory definition, should stand high among our aims: it is not enough to show how clever we are by showing how obscure everything is. Clarity, too, I know, has been said to be not enough: but perhaps it will be time to go into that when we are within measurable distance of achieving clarity on some matter.

So much for the cackle. It remains to make a few remarks, not, I am afraid, in any very coherent order, about the types of significant result to be obtained and the more general lessons to be learned from the study of Excuses.

Significant Results and General Lessons

1. *No modification without aberration.* When it is stated that X did A, there is a temptation to suppose that given some, indeed perhaps *any*, expression modifying the verb we shall be entitled to insert either it or its opposite or negation in our statement: that is, we shall be entitled to ask, typically, "Did X do A Mly or not Mly?" (e.g., "Did X murder Y voluntarily or involuntarily?"), and to answer one or the other. Or as a minimum it is supposed that if X did A there must be at least *one* modifying expression that we could, justifiably and informatively, insert with the verb. In the great majority of cases of the use of the great majority of verbs ("murder" perhaps is not one of the majority) such suppositions are quite unjustified. The natural economy of language dictates that for the *standard* case covered by any normal verb—not, perhaps, a verb of omen such as "murder," but a verb like "eat" or "kick" or "croquet"—no modifying expression is required or even permissible. Only if we do the action named in some *special* way or circumstances, different from those in which such an act is naturally done (and of course both the normal and the abnormal differ according to what verb in particular is in question), is a modifying expression called for, or even in order. I sit in my chair, in the usual way—I am not in a daze or influenced by threats or the like: here, it will not do to say either that I sat in it intentionally or that I did not sit in it intentionally,* nor yet that I sat in it automatically or from habit or what you will. It is bedtime, I am alone, I yawn: but I do not yawn invol-

* Caveat or hedge: of course we can say "I did *not* sit in it 'intentionally'" as a way simply of repudiating the suggestion that I sat in it intentionally.

untarily (or voluntarily!), nor yet deliberately. To yawn in any such peculiar way is just not to just yawn.

2. *Limitation of application.* Expressions modifying verbs, typically adverbs, have limited ranges of application. That is, given any adverb of excuse, such as "unwittingly" or "spontaneously" or "impulsively," it will not be found that it makes good sense to attach it to any and every verb of "action" in any and every context: indeed, it will often apply only to a comparatively narrow range of such verbs. Something in the lad's upturned face appealed to him, he threw a brick at it—"spontaneously"? The interest then is to discover why some actions can be excused in a particular way but not others, particularly perhaps the latter.* This will largely elucidate the meaning of the excuse, and at the same time will illuminate the characteristics typical of the group of "actions" it picks out: very often too it will throw light on some detail of the machinery of "action" in general (see 4), or on our standards of acceptable conduct (see 5). It is specially important in the case of some of the terms most favored by philosophers or jurists to realize that at least in ordinary speech (disregarding backseepage of jargon) they are not used so universally or so dichotomistically. For example, take "voluntarily" and "involuntarily": we may join the army or make a gift voluntarily, we may hiccough or make a small gesture involuntarily, and the more we consider further actions which we might naturally be said to do in either of these ways, the more circumscribed and unlike each other do the two classes become, until we even doubt whether there is *any* verb with which both adverbs are equally in place. Perhaps there are some such; but at least sometimes when we may think we have found one it is an illusion, an apparent exception that really does prove the rule. I can perhaps "break a cup" voluntarily, *if* that is done, say, as an act of self-impoverishment: and I can perhaps break another involuntarily, *if*, say, I make an involuntary movement which breaks it. Here, plainly, the two acts described each as "breaking a cup" are really very different, and the one is similar to acts typical of the "voluntary" class, the other to acts typical of the "involuntary" class.

3. *The importance of Negations and Opposites.* "Voluntarily" and "involuntarily," then, are not opposed in the obvious sort of way that they are made to be in philosophy or jurisprudence. The "opposite," or rather "opposites," of "voluntarily" might be "under constraint" of some sort, duress or obligation or influence;† the opposite of "involuntarily" might be "deliberately" or "on purpose" or the like. Such divergences in opposites indicate that "voluntarily" and "involuntarily," in spite of their apparent connection, are fish from very different kettles. In general, it will pay us to take nothing for granted or as obvious about negations and opposites. It does not pay to assume that a word must have an opposite, or one opposite, whether it is a "positive" word

* For we are sometimes not so good at observing what we *can't* say as what we can, yet the first is pretty regularly the more revealing.

† But remember, when I sign a check in the normal way, I do *not* do so *either* "voluntarily" *or* "under constraint."

like "wilfully" or a "negative" word like "inadvertently." Rather, we should be asking ourselves such questions as why there is no use for the adverb "advertently." For above all it will not do to assume that the "positive" word must be around to wear the trousers; commonly enough the "negative" (looking) word marks the (positive) abnormality, while the "positive" word, *if* it exists, merely serves to rule out the suggestion of that abnormality. It is natural enough, in view of what was said in (1) above, for the "positive" word not to be found at all in some cases. I do an act A_1 (say, crush a snail) *inadvertently* if, in the course of executing by means of movements of my bodily parts some other act A_2 (say, in walking down the public path), I fail to exercise such meticulous supervision over the courses of those movements as would have been needed to ensure that they did not bring about the untoward event (here, the impact on the snail).* By claiming that A_1 was inadvertent we place it, where we imply it belongs, on this special level, in a class of incidental happenings which must occur in the doing of any physical act. To lift the act out of this class, we need and possess the expression "not . . . inadvertently": "advertently," if used for this purpose, would suggest that, if the act was not done inadvertently, then it must have been done noticing what I was doing, which is far from necessarily the case (e.g., if I did it absent-mindedly), or at least that there is *something* in common to the ways of doing all acts not done inadvertently, which is not the case. Again, there is no use for "advertently" at the *same* level as "inadvertently": in passing the butter I do not knock over the cream-jug, though I do (inadvertently) knock over the teacup—yet I do not by-pass the cream-jug *advertently:* for at this level, below supervision in detail, *anything* that we do is, if you like, inadvertent, though we only call it so, and indeed only call it something we have done, if there is something untoward about it.

A further point of interest in studying so-called "negative" terms is the manner of their formation. Why are the words in one group formed with *un-* or *in-*, those in another with *-less* ("aimless," "reckless," "heedless," etc.), and those in another with *mis-* ("mistake," "misconception," "misjudgment," etc.)? Why care*less*ly but *in*attentively? Perhaps care and attention, so often linked, are rather different. Here are remunerative exercises.

4. *The machinery of action.* Not merely do adverbial expressions pick out classes of actions, they also pick out the internal detail of the machinery of doing actions, or the departments into which the business of doing actions is organized. There is for example the stage at which we have actually to *carry out* some action upon which we embark—perhaps we have to make certain bodily movements or to make a

* Or analogously: I do an act A_1 (say, divulge my age, or imply you are a liar) *inadvertently* if, in the course of executing by the use of some medium of communication some other act A_2 (say, reminiscing about my war service), I fail to exercise such meticulous supervision over the choice and arrangement of the signs as would have been needed to ensure that. . . . It is interesting to note how such adverbs lead parallel lives, one in connection with physical actions ("doing") and the other in connection with acts of communication ("saying"), or sometimes also in connection with acts of "thinking" ("inadvertently assumed").

speech. In the course of actually *doing* these things (getting weaving) we have to pay (some) attention to what we are doing and to take (some) care to guard against (likely) dangers: we may need to use judgment or tact: we must exercise sufficient control over our bodily parts: and so on. Inattention, carelessness, errors of judgment, tactlessness, clumsiness, all these and others are ills (with attendant excuses) which affect one specific stage in the machinery of action, the *executive* stage, the stage where we *muff* it. But there are many other departments in the business too, each of which is to be traced and mapped through its cluster of appropriate verbs and adverbs. Obviously there are departments of intelligence and planning, of decision and resolve, and so on: but I shall mention one in particular, too often overlooked, where troubles and excuses abound. It happens to us, in military life, to be in receipt of excellent intelligence, to be also in self-conscious possession of excellent principles (the five golden rules for winning victories), and yet to hit upon a plan of action which leads to disaster. One way in which this can happen is through failure at the stage of *appreciation* of the situation, that is at the stage where we are required to cast our excellent intelligence into such a form, under such heads and with such weights attached, that our equally excellent principles can be brought to bear on it properly, in a way to yield the right answer.* So too in real, or rather civilian, life, in moral or practical affairs, we can know the facts and yet look at them mistakenly or perversely, or not fully realize or appreciate something, or even be under a total misconception. Many expressions of excuse indicate failure at this particularly tricky stage: even thoughtlessness, inconsiderateness, lack of imagination, are perhaps less matters of failure in intelligence or planning than might be supposed, and more matters of failure to appreciate the situation. A course of E. M. Forster and we see things differently: yet perhaps we know no more and are no cleverer.

5. *Standards of the unacceptable.* It is characteristic of excuses to be "unacceptable": given, I suppose, almost any excuse, there will be cases of such a kind or of such gravity that "we will not accept" it. It is interesting to detect the standards and codes we thus invoke. The extent of the supervision we exercise over the execution of any act can never be quite unlimited, and usually is expected to fall within fairly definite limits ("due care and attention") in the case of acts of some general kind, though of course we set very different limits in different cases. We may plead that we trod on the snail inadvertently: but not on a baby —you ought to look where you are putting your great feet. Of course it *was* (*really*), if you like, inadvertence: but that word constitutes a plea, which is not going to be allowed, because of standards. And if you try it on, you will be subscribing to such dreadful standards that your last state will be worse than your first. Or again, we set different standards, and will accept different excuses, in the case of acts which are rule-governed, like spelling, and which we are expected absolutely to get right, from those we set and accept for less stereotyped actions: a

* We know all about how to do quadratics: we know all the needful facts about pipes, cisterns, hours and plumbers: yet we reach the answer "3¾ men." We have failed to cast our facts correctly into mathematical form.

wrong spelling may be a slip, but hardly an accident, a winged beater may be an accident, but hardly a slip.

6. *Combination, dissociation, and complication.* A belief in opposites and dichotomies encourages, among other things, a blindness to the combinations and dissociations of adverbs that are possible, even to such obvious facts as that we can act at once on impulse and intentionally, or that we can do an action intentionally yet for all that not deliberately, still less on purpose. We walk along the cliff, and I feel a sudden impulse to push you over, which I promptly do: I acted on impulse, yet I certainly intended to push you over, and may even have devised a little ruse to achieve it: yet even then I did not act deliberately, for I did not (stop to) ask myself whether to do it or not.

It is worth bearing in mind, too, the general rule that we must not expect to find simple labels for complicated cases. If a mistake results in an accident, it will not do to ask whether "it" was an accident or a mistake, or to demand some briefer description of "it." Here the natural economy of language operates: if the words already available for simple cases suffice in combination to describe a complicated case, there will be need for special reasons before a special new word is invented for the complication. Besides, however well-equipped our language, it can never be forearmed against all possible cases that may arise and call for description: fact is richer than diction.

7. *Regina* v. *Finney.* Often the complexity and difficulty of a case is considerable. I will quote the case of *Regina* v. *Finney.**

Shrewsbury Assizes. 1874. 12 Cox 625.

Prisoner was indicted for the manslaughter of Thomas Watkins.

The Prisoner was an attendant at a lunatic asylum. Being in charge of a lunatic, who was bathing, he turned on hot water into the bath, and thereby scalded him to death. The facts appeared to be truly set forth in the statement of the prisoner made before the committing magistrate, as follows: "I had bathed Watkins, and had loosed the bath out. *I intended putting in a clean bath,* and asked Watkins if he would get out. At this time *my attention was drawn* to the next bath by the new attendant, who was asking me a question; and *my attention was taken from the bath* where Watkins was. I put my hand down to turn water on in the bath where Thomas Watkins was. *I did not intend to turn the hot water,* and *I made a mistake in the tap. I did not know what I had done until* I heard Thomas Watkins shout out; and *I did not find my mistake out till* I saw the steam from the water. You cannot get water in this bath when they are drawing water at the other bath; but at other times it shoots out like a water gun when the other baths are not in use. . . ."

(It was proved that the lunatic had such possession of his faculties as would enable him to understand what was said to him, and to get out of the bath.)

A. Young (for Prisoner). The death *resulted from accident.* There was no such *culpable negligence* on the part of the prisoner as will support this indictment. A *culpable mistake,* or some degree of *culpable negligence,*

* A somewhat distressing favorite in the class that Hart used to conduct with me in the years soon after the war. The italics are mine.

causing death, will not support a charge of manslaughter; unless the *negligence* be so gross as to be *reckless.* (*R.* v. *Noakes.*)

Lush, J. To render a person liable for *neglect of duty* there must be such a degree of culpability as to amount to *gross negligence* on his part. If you accept the prisoner's own statement, you find no such amount of *negligence* as would come within this definition. It is not every little *trip or mistake* that will make a man so liable. It was the duty of the attendant not to let hot water into the bath while the patient was therein. According to the prisoner's own account, *he did not believe that* he was letting the hot water in while the deceased remained there. The lunatic was, we have heard, a man capable of getting out by himself and of understanding what was said to him. He was told to get out. A new attendant who had come on this day, was at an adjoining bath and he *took off the prisoner's attention.* Now, if the prisoner, knowing that the man was in the bath, had turned on the tap, and turned on the hot instead of the cold water, I should have said there was gross negligence; for he ought to have looked to see. But from his own account he had told the deceased to get out, and *thought he had got out.* If you think that indicates gross *carelessness,* then you should find the prisoner guilty of manslaughter. But if you think it *inadvertence* not amounting to culpability—i.e., what is properly termed an *accident*—then the prisoner is not liable.

Verdict, Not guilty.

In this case there are two morals that I will point. (1) Both counsel and judge make very free use of a large number of terms of excuse, using several as though they were, and even stating them to be, indifferent or equivalent when they are not, and presenting as alternatives those that are not. (2) It is constantly difficult to be sure *what* act it is that counsel or judge is suggesting might be qualified by what expression of excuse. The learned judge's concluding direction is a paradigm of these faults.* Finney, by contrast, stands out as an evident master of the Queen's English. He is explicit as to each of his acts and states, mental and physical: he uses different, and the correct, adverbs in connection with each: and he makes no attempt to boil down.

8. *Small distinctions, and big too.* It should go without saying that terms of excuse are not equivalent, and that it matters which we use: we need to distinguish inadvertence not merely from (save the mark) such things as mistake and accident, but from such nearer neighbors as, say, aberration and absence of mind. By imagining cases with vividness and fullness we should be able to decide in which precise terms to describe, say, Miss Plimsoll's action in writing, so carefully, "DAIRY" on her fine new book: we should be able to distinguish between sheer, mere, pure, and simple mistake or inadvertence. Yet unfortunately, at least when in the grip of thought, we fail not merely at these stiffer hurdles. We equate even—I have seen it done—"inadvertently" with

* Not but what he probably manages to convey his meaning somehow or other. Judges seem to acquire a knack of conveying meaning, and even carrying conviction, through the use of a pithy Anglo-Saxon which sometimes has literally no meaning at all. Wishing to distinguish the case of shooting at a post in the belief that it was an enemy, as *not* an "attempt," from the case of picking an empty pocket in the belief that money was in it, which *is* an "attempt," the judge explains that in shooting at the post "the man is never on the thing at all."

"automatically": as though to say I trod on your toe inadvertently means to say I trod on it automatically. Or we collapse succumbing to temptation into losing control of ourselves—a bad patch, this, for telescoping.*

All this is not so much a *lesson* from the study of excuses as the very object of it.

9. *The exact phrase and its place in the sentence.* It is not enough, either, to attend simply to the "key" word: notice must also be taken of the full and exact form of the expression used. In considering mistakes, we have to consider seriatim "by mistake," "owing to a mistake," "mistakenly," "it was a mistake to," "to make a mistake in or over or about," "to be mistaken about," and so on: in considering purpose, we have to consider "on," "with the," "for the," etc., besides "purposeful," "purposeless," and the like. These varying expressions may function quite differently—and usually do, or why should we burden ourselves with more than one of them?

Care must be taken too to observe the precise position of an adverbial expression in the sentence. This should of course indicate what verb it is being used to modify: but more than that, the position can also affect the *sense* of the expression, i.e., the way in which it modifies that verb. Compare, for example:

a_1 He clumsily trod on the snail.
a_2 Clumsily he trod on the snail.
b_1 He trod clumsily on the snail.
b_2 He trod on the snail clumsily.

Here, in a_1 and a_2 we describe his treading on the creature at all as a piece of clumsiness, incidental, we imply, to his performance of some other action: but with b_1 and b_2 to tread on it is, very likely, his aim or policy, what we criticize is his execution of the feat.† Many adverbs, though far from all (not, for example, "purposely") are used in these two typically different ways.

10. *The style of performance.* With some adverbs the distinction between the two senses referred to in the last paragraph is carried a stage further. "He ate his soup deliberately" may mean, like "He deliberately ate his soup," that his eating his soup was a deliberate act, one perhaps that he thought would annoy somebody, as it would more commonly if he deliberately ate *my* soup, and which he decided to do:

* Plato, I suppose, and after him Aristotle, fastened this confusion upon us, as bad in its day and way as the later, grotesque, confusion of moral weakness with weakness of will. I am very partial to ice cream, and a bombe is served divided into segments corresponding one to one with the persons at High Table: I am tempted to help myself to two segments and do so, thus succumbing to temptation and even conceivably (but why necessarily?) going against my principles. But do I lose control of myself? Do I raven, do I snatch the morsels from the dish and wolf them down, impervious to the consternation of my colleagues? Not a bit of it. We often succumb to temptation with calm and even with finesse.

† As a matter of fact, most of these examples *can* be understood the other way, especially if we allow ourselves inflections of the voice, or commas, or contexts. a_2 might be a poetic inversion for b_2: b_1, perhaps with commas round the "clumsily," might be used for a_1: and so on. Still, the two senses are clearly enough distinguishable.

but it will often mean that he went through the performance of eating his soup in a noteworthy manner or *style*—pause after each mouthful, careful choice of point of entry for the spoon, sucking of moustaches, and so on. That is, it will mean that he ate *with* deliberation rather than *after* deliberation. The style of the performance, slow and unhurried, is understandably called "deliberate" because each movement *has the typical look* of a deliberate act: but it is scarcely being said that the making of each motion *is* a deliberate act or that he is "literally" deliberating. This case, then, is more extreme than that of "clumsily," which does in both uses describe literally a manner of performing.

It is worth watching out for this secondary use when scrutinizing any particular adverbial expression: when it definitely does not exist, the reason is worth inquiring into. Sometimes it is very hard to be sure whether it does exist or does not: it does, one would think, with "carelessly," it does not with "inadvertently," but does it or does it not with "absent-mindedly" or "aimlessly"? In some cases a word akin to but distinct from the primary adverb is used for this special role of describing a style of performance: we use "purposefully" in this way, but never "purposely."

11. *What modifies what?* The judge in *Regina* v. *Finney* does not make clear what event is being excused in what way. "If you think that indicates gross carelessness, then. . . . But if you think it inadvertence not amounting to culpability—i.e., what is properly called an accident—then. . . ." Apparently he means that Finney may have *turned on the hot tap* inadvertently:* does he mean also that the tap may have been turned accidentally, or rather that *Watkins may have been scalded* and killed accidentally? And was the carelessness in turning the tap or in thinking Watkins had got out? Many disputes as to what excuse we should properly use arise because we will not trouble to state explicitly *what* is being excused.

To do so is all the more vital because it is in principle always open to us, along various lines, to describe or refer to "what I did" in so many different ways. This is altogether too large a theme to elaborate here. Apart from the more general and obvious problems of the use of "tendentious" descriptive terms, there are many special problems in the particular case of "actions." Should we say, are we saying, that he took her money, or that he robbed her? That he knocked a ball into a hole, or that he sank a putt? That he said "Done," or that he accepted an offer? How far, that is, are motives, intentions, and conventions to be part of the description of actions? And more especially here, what is *an* or *one* or *the* action? For we can generally split up what might be

* What Finney says is different: he says he "made a mistake in the tap." This is the basic use of "mistake," where we simply, and not necessarily accountably, take the wrong one. Finney here attempts to account for his mistake, by saying that his attention was distracted. But suppose the order is "Right turn" and I turn left: no doubt the sergeant will insinuate that my attention was distracted, or that I cannot distinguish my right from my left—but it was not and I can; this was a simple, pure mistake. As often happens. Neither I nor the sergeant will suggest that there was any accident, or any inadvertence either. If Finney had turned the hot tap inadvertently, then it would have been knocked, say, in reaching for the cold tap: a different story.

named as one action in several distinct ways, into different *stretches* or *phases* or *stages*. Stages have already been mentioned: we can dismantle the machinery of the act, and describe (and excuse) separately the intelligence, the appreciation, the planning, the decision, the execution, and so forth. Phases are rather different: we can say that he painted a picture or fought a campaign, or else we can say that first he laid on this stroke of paint and then that, first he fought this action and then that. Stretches are different again: a single term descriptive of what he did may be made to cover either a smaller or a larger stretch of events, those excluded by the narrower description being then called "consequences" or "results" or "effects" or the like of his act. So here we can describe Finney's act *either* as turning on the hot tap, which he did by mistake, with the result that Watkins was scalded, *or* as scalding Watkins, which he did *not* do by mistake.

It is very evident that the problems of excuses and those of the different descriptions of actions are throughout bound up with each other.

12. *Trailing clouds of etymology.* It is these considerations that bring us up so forcibly against some of the most difficult words in the whole story of Excuses, such words as "result," "effect," and "consequence," or again as "intention," "purpose," and "motive." I will mention two points of method which are, experience has convinced me, indispensable aids at these levels.

One is that a word never—well, hardly ever—shakes off its etymology and its formation. In spite of all changes in and extensions of and additions to its meanings, and indeed rather pervading and governing these, there will still persist the old idea. In an *accident* something befalls: by *mistake* you take the wrong one: in *error* you stray: when you act *deliberately* you act after weighing it up (*not* after thinking out ways and means). It is worth asking ourselves whether we know the etymology of "result" or of "spontaneously," and worth remembering that "unwillingly" and "involuntarily" come from very different sources.

And the second point is connected with this. Going back into the history of a word, very often into Latin, we come back pretty commonly to pictures or *models* of how things happen or are done. These models may be fairly sophisticated and recent, as is perhaps the case with "motive" or "impulse," but one of the commonest and most primitive types of model is one which is apt to baffle us through its very naturalness and simplicity. We take *some very simple action,* like shoving a stone, usually as done by and viewed by oneself, and use *this,* with the features distinguishable in it, as our model in terms of which to talk about other actions and events: and we continue to do so, scarcely realizing it, even when these other actions are pretty remote and perhaps much more interesting to us in their own right than the acts originally used in constructing the model ever were, and even when the model is really distorting the facts rather than helping us to observe them. In primitive cases we may get to see clearly the differences between, say, "results," "effects," and "consequences," and yet discover that these differences are no longer clear, and the terms themselves no longer of real service to us, in the more complicated cases where we had been bandying them about most freely. A model must be recognized for what it is. "Causing," I suppose, was a notion taken from a man's own experience of doing simple actions, and by primitive man every event was construed in terms of this model: every event has a cause, that is, every event is an action done by somebody—if not by a man, then by a quasi-man, a spirit. When, later, events which are *not* actions are realized to be such, we still say that they must be "caused," and the word snares us: we are struggling to ascribe to it a new, unanthropomorphic meaning, yet constantly, in searching for its analysis, we unearth and incorporate the lineaments of the ancient model. As happened even to Hume, and consequently to Kant. Examining such a word historically, we may well find that it has been extended to cases that have by now too tenuous a relation to the model case, that it is a source of confusion and superstition.

There is too another danger in words that invoke models, half-forgotten or not. It must be remembered that there is no necessity whatsoever that the various models used in creating our vocabulary, primitive or recent, should all fit together neatly as parts into one single, total model or scheme of, for instance, the doing of actions. It is possible, and indeed highly likely, that our assortment of models will include some, or many, that are overlapping, conflicting, or more generally simply *disparate.**

13. In spite of the wide and acute observation of the phenomena of action embodied in ordinary speech, modern scientists have been able, it seems to me, to reveal its inadequacy at numerous points, if only because they have had access to more comprehensive data and have studied them with more catholic and dispassionate interest than the ordinary man, or even the lawyer, has had occasion to do. I will conclude with two examples.

Observation of animal behavior shows that regularly, when an animal is embarked on some recognizable pattern of behavior but meets in the course of it with an insuperable obstacle, it will betake itself to energetic, but quite unrelated, activity of some wild kind, such as standing on its head. This phenomenon is called "displacement behavior" and is well identifiable. If now, in the light of this, we look back at ordinary human life, we see that displacement behavior bulks quite large in it: yet we have apparently no word, or at least no clear and simple word, for it. If, when thwarted, we stand on our heads or wiggle our toes, then we are not exactly *just* standing on our heads, don't you know, in the ordinary way, yet is there any convenient adverbial expression we can insert to do the trick? "In desperation"?

* This is by way of a general warning in philosophy. It seems to be too readily assumed that if we can only discover the true meanings of each of a cluster of key terms, usually historic terms, that we use in some particular field (as, for example, "right," "good," and the rest in morals), then it must without question transpire that each will fit into place in some single, interlocking, consistent, conceptual scheme. Not only is there no reason to assume this, but all historical probability is against it, especially in the case of a language derived from such various civilizations as ours. We may cheerfully use, and with weight, terms which are not so much head-on incompatible as simply disparate, which just do not fit in or even on. Just as we cheerfully subscribe to, or have the grace to be torn between, simply disparate ideals—why *must* there be a conceivable amalgam, the Good Life for Man?

Take, again, "compulsive" behavior, however exactly psychologists define it, compulsive washing for example. There are of course hints in ordinary speech that we do things in this way—"just feel I have to," "shouldn't feel comfortable unless I did," and the like: but there is no adverbial expression satisfactorily pre-empted for it, as "compulsively" is. This is understandable enough, since compulsive behavior, like displacement behavior, is not in general going to be of great practical importance.

Here I leave and commend the subject to you.

Further Reading

Aristotle. *Ethics*. New York: Dutton, 1963.

Collins, James. *The Existentialists*. Chicago: Henry Regnery Company, 1952.

Duncan, A. R. C. *Practical Reason and Morality*. London: Thomas Nelson and Sons, 1957.

Ewing, A. C. *Ethics*. New York: Free Press, 1953.

Hare, R. M. *The Language of Morals*. Oxford: Clarendon Press, 1952.

Stevenson, C. L. *Ethics and Language*. New Haven: Yale University Press, 1944.

Thomson, J. J. and Dworkin, Gerald. *Ethics*. New York: Harper & Row, 1968.

Von Wright, Georg Henrik. *Norm and Action*. London: Routledge and Kegan Paul, 1963.

Werkmeister, William. *Theories of Ethics*. Lincoln: Johnsen Publishing, 1961.

87 DUTY AND RESPONSIBILITY

PART II

JUSTICE, LAW, AND MORALITY

INTRODUCTORY READING

Shaw v. Director of Public Prosecutions

INQUIRY

SELECTED SOURCES

Plato

Locke

Rousseau

Wolfenden

Mill

Devlin

Shaw V. Director of Public Prosecutions

FREDERICK CHARLES SHAW, A BRITISH SUBJECT, HAD PUBLISHED A magazine, *The Ladies' Directory*, giving the names, addresses, and telephone numbers of female prostitutes, and indicating, in code, their sexual specialities. The magazine, which included a number of nude photographs, made it quite clear that the women listed in the magazine were making themselves available for sexual intercourse and, when called for, sexual exhibitions of various kinds. In 1961, Shaw was brought to trial, charged with the following three offenses:

1. Conspiracy to corrupt public morals. Particulars of Offence. . . . conspired with certain persons who inserted advertisements in issues of a magazine entitled Ladies' Directory numbered 7, 7 revised, 8, 9, 10 and a supplement thereto, and with certain other persons whose names are unknown, by means of the said magazine and the said advertisements to induce readers thereof to resort to the said advertisers for the purposes of fornication and of taking part in or witnessing other disgusting and immoral acts and exhibitions, with intent thereby to debauch and corrupt the morals as well of youth as of divers other liege subjects of Our Lady The Queen and to raise and create in their minds inordinate and lustful desires.
2. Living on the earnings of prostitution, contrary to section 30 of the Sexual Offences Act, 1956.
3. Publishing an obscene article, the Ladies' Directory, contrary to section 2 of the Obscene Publications Act, 1959.

The jury found Mr. Shaw guilty of having committed all three offenses and he was given a nine-month prison sentence—which

° Shaw v. Director of Public Prosecutions; 2 All English Reports 446; (1962) Appeal Cases 220.

he immediately appealed. His first appeal, to the Court of Criminal Appeal, was rejected; however, he was granted permission to appeal to the House of Lords. In May of 1961, the House of Lords (by a vote of four to one) upheld the jury's verdict.

The following is an excerpt from the speech given before the House of Lords by Viscount Simonds in which he urges that the jury's findings be upheld:

. . . My Lords, as I have already said, the first count in the indictment is "conspiracy to corrupt public morals," and the particulars of offence will have sufficiently appeared. I am concerned only to assert what was vigorously denied by counsel for the appellant, that such an offence is known to the common law, and that it was open to the jury to find on the facts of this case that the appellant was guilty of such an offence. I must say categorically that, if it were not so, Her Majesty's courts would strangely have failed in their duty as servants and guardians of the common law. Need I say, my Lords, that I am no advocate of the right of the judges to create new criminal offences? I will repeat well-known words: "Amongst many other points of happiness and freedom which your Majesty's subjects have enjoyed there is none which they have accounted more dear and precious than this, to be guided and governed by certain rules of law which giveth both to the head and members that which of right belongeth to them and not by any arbitrary or uncertain form of government." These words are as true today as they were in the seventeenth century and command the allegiance of us all. But I am at a loss to understand how it can be said either that the law does not recognise a conspiracy to corrupt public morals or that, though there may not be an exact precedent for such a conspiracy as this case reveals, it does not fall fairly within the general words by which it is described. I do not propose to examine all the relevant authorities. That will be done by my noble and learned friend. The fallacy in the argument that was addressed to us lay in the attempt to exclude from the scope of general words acts well calculated to corrupt public morals just because they had not been committed or had not been brought to the notice of the court before. It is not thus that the common law has developed. We are perhaps more accustomed to hear this matter discussed upon the question whether such and such a transaction is contrary to public policy. At once the controversy arises. On the one hand it is said that it is not possible in the twentieth century for the court to create a new head of public policy, on the other it is said that this is but a new example of a well-established head. In the sphere of criminal law I entertain no doubt that there remains in the courts of law a residual power to enforce the supreme and fundamental purpose of the law, to conserve not only the safety and order but also the moral welfare of the State, and that it is their duty to guard it against attacks which may be the more insidious because they are novel and unprepared for. That is the broad head (call it public policy if you wish) within which the present indictment falls. It matters little what label is given to the offending act. To one of your Lordships it may appear an affront to public decency, to another considering that it may succeed in its obvious intention of provoking libidinous desires it will seem a corruption of public morals. Yet others may deem it aptly described as the creation of a public mischief or the undermining of moral conduct. The same act will not in all ages be regarded in the same way. The law must be related to the changing standards of life, not yielding to every shifting impulse of the popular will but having regard to fundamental assessments of human values and the purposes of society. Today a denial of the fundamental Christian doctrine, which in past centuries would have been regarded by the ecclesiastical courts as heresy and by the common law as blasphemy, will no longer be an offence if the decencies of controversy are observed. When Lord Mansfield, speaking long after the Star Chamber had been abolished, said that the Court of King's Bench was the custos morum of the people and had the superintendency of offences contra bonos mores, he was asserting, as I now assert, that there is in that court a residual power, where no statute has yet intervened to supersede the common law, to superintend those offences which are prejudicial to the public welfare. Such occasions will be rare, for Parliament has not been slow to legislate when attention has been sufficiently aroused. But gaps remain and will always remain since no one can foresee every way in which the wickedness of man may disrupt the order of society. Let me take a single instance to which my noble and learned friend Lord Tucker refers. Let it be supposed that at some future, perhaps early, date homosexual practices between adult consenting males are no longer a crime. Would it not be an offence if even without obscenity, such practices were publicly advocated and encouraged by pamphlet and advertisement? Or must we wait until Parliament finds time to deal with such conduct? I say, my Lords, that if the common law is powerless in such an event, then we should no longer do her reverence. But I say that her hand is still powerful and that it is for Her Majesty's judges to play the part which Lord Mansfield pointed out to them.

I have so far paid little regard to the fact that the charge here is of conspiracy. But, if I have correctly described the conduct of the appellant, it is an irresistible inference that a conspiracy between him and others to do such acts is indictable. It is irrelevant to this charge that section 2 (4) of the Obscene Publications Act, 1959, might bar proceedings against him if no conspiracy were alleged. It may be thought superfluous, where that Act can be invoked, to bring a charge also of conspiracy to corrupt public morals, but I can well understand the desirability of doing so where a doubt exists whether obscenity within the meaning of the Act can be proved.

I will say a final word upon an aspect of the case which was urged by counsel. No one doubts—and I have put it in the forefront of this opinion—that certainty is a most desirable attribute of the criminal and civil law alike. Nevertheless there are matters which must ultimately depend on the opinion of a jury. In the civil law I will take an example which comes perhaps nearest to the criminal law—the tort of negligence. It is for a jury to decide not only whether the defendant has committed the act complained of but whether in doing it he has fallen short of the standard of care which the circumstances require. Till their verdict is given it is uncertain what the law requires. The same branch of the civil law supplies another interesting analogy. For, though in the Factory Acts and the regulations made under them, the measure of care required of an employer is defined in the greatest detail, no one supposes that he may not be guilty of negligence in a manner unforeseen and unprovided for. That will be a matter for the jury to decide. There are still, as has recently been said, "unravished remnants of the common law."

So in the case of a charge of conspiracy to corrupt public morals the uncertainty that necessarily arises from the vagueness of general words can only be resolved by the opinion of twelve chosen men and women. I am content to leave it to them.

The appeal on both counts should, in my opinion, be dismissed.

INQUIRY

"If the law supposes that," said Mr. Bumble, . . . "the law is an ass, an idiot."

CHARLES DICKENS
Oliver Twist

WHAT is the best form of government? In order to tackle such a complex question we need to have some idea why there are societies and not roving individual human beings. Is social living an unnatural, forced union of normally self-interested human beings? Or is man by nature dependent upon his fellows and is society a natural outgrowth of this interdependence?

Forms of Society

Let us attempt to construct an example for study. Suppose that each one of ten cavemen discovers, more or less simultaneously, while on his independent hunting expedition, that the other nine live within a relatively short distance of his home cave. Assuming that each has some notion of self-identity and can see a resemblance between himself and the other nine, what do you think would most likely happen? Here are some possibilities.

1. All ten cavemen see each other as imminent threats to their own survival. They cannot trust each other, and fights constantly break out until one or none is left. No social union is founded.

2. The strongest caveman forces the others to join him, perhaps by first brutally killing one of the nine as a warning to any who object. The others set out together as a team to hunt game for the leader, who of course receives the largest portion. The eight or nine others at first follow from fear, but soon they realize that, despite the fact that they no longer select the time and place for the hunt, they are eating better and feeling less worried at night about the wild beasts prowling near by. Eventually they loyally defend to the death their leader and his right to the largest portion.

3. The ten come to realize that their lives demand a variety of

skills to be successfully performed and that none of them is able to do all tasks to perfection. Each man, however, tends to excel in some necessary facet of their collective lives. One is an expert at tracking game, another has a talent for sharpening stones, and a third is able to prepare and cook meat with all the skill of a primitive gourmet. It occurs to each that to adjust his life style to do for the group the task he performs best is both reasonable and rewarding. Each begins to "sell" his service for the benefits of the others. Their specializations create their interdependence.

4. A common enemy is discovered. A vicious beast has been robbing their caves and has killed one or two of them. None is particularly brave. They realize that alone each is impotent and that if they do not unite they will lose whatever they have. They decide to join together against the killer, yet resolve to set out in divergent directions. It takes only a few steps for them to realize that they are in no better position if each in his own way attempts to accomplish the group purpose, than if each attempts to accomplish his own purpose. It is clear that they must go as a group, but which way will they go? After preliminary haggling over "my rights," "my ideas," "my property," "my life," they choose a leader to organize their strategy and agree to abide by his decisions.

Do any of these possibilities strike you as likely? When would we say the cavemen have become a community? How does our notion of community serve to distinguish our social life from that of apes or other animals such as the ants? Perhaps it might help to imagine what you would do if in one moment all existing governmental controls and enforcements were lifted from your community.

The Origin of Law

Consider a further possibility. Caveman A kills Caveman B in a fight over a piece of meat. Caveman C, who had befriended B, in turn kills A. Eight cavemen are left. Is it plausible to assume that one of the remaining cavemen might suggest that this sort of thing must stop or soon there will be no more cavemen? Construct the dialogue which might occur between the cavemen about this suggestion. Would it revolve around appeals for control, rights for protection, the necessity of enforcement? What objections might be raised in the discussion? Some questions undoubtedly would involve concepts of order, justice, law, and restraint. Someone would raise questions about dissolving the union under certain circumstances. Would personal protection be the sole basis of their legal system?

If we take men to be naturally social animals (Plato's conception) then we should conclude that society is inevitable and that the ideas of justice, law and government simply arise out of the general composition of society. In other words, if men are not born self-sufficient, then an organized society to provide for their wants is natural. We would suspect that social awareness is a part of man's very nature. Justice and legality no doubt would be defined in terms of maintaining the balance of interdependence between men, what Plato calls leaving each to his business.

Does Law Produce Justice?

We are taught that at the root of our social system is "liberty and justice for all." Is "justice" then a thing we can take for granted? Does the law insure justice? We say, after a criminal has been convicted, that justice has been served. Are the facts of each case alone sufficient in determining what will be just in that case?

Famous lawyers have denied that our legal system is designed to produce justice. They claim instead that ours is an adversary system, not too unlike a game played between the opposing lawyers, who represent the interests of their clients or the state. The method of courtroom play is more a matter of the deliberate introduction of confusion into the case than a search for truth. In other words, despite the Perry Mason clichés, if something we call "justice" results from the legal system, it is not necessarily due to the structure of that system. In fact, our particular system is less than consistent regarding its own aims.

Must an Individual Obey the Law?

Each individual member of society is bound to live by the laws of society, regardless of how his obligation arises. One of the commitments a naturalized citizen or one inducted into the armed services is specifically required to make is to abide by and enforce the laws of the land. It is understood that native-born citizens, because they do not expatriate themselves, accept a similar commitment. In fact, for similar reasons Socrates refused to escape his execution, telling Crito that he was born, nurtured, and educated by the state and enjoyed the security and entertainments of the state, and therefore he had agreed to be governed according to the laws of the state and must suffer his punishment under that law, despite the fact he felt that he had been unjustly treated. He thought of himself as a victim of men, not of law.

If a citizen considers a particular law to be unjust, ought he nonetheless to obey it? And what rights should he have in relation to changing it? It has been maintained that the citizens of Nazi Germany ought not to have obeyed the laws of their state. The German people must have known that the laws concerning genocide were wrong; they should not have obeyed them. Similar arguments have been used by Vietnam War protesters urging draft evasion and the revelation of secret documents. Henry David Thoreau in his essay "Civil Disobedience" (Part III) lays the groundwork for much of our thinking along these lines.

But, on the other hand, is it not possible that one of the basic human tendencies is to obey an established authority without questioning the rightness or wrongness of what is demanded? Psychologist Stanley Milgram's study* demonstrates that the obedient tendencies in men are far stronger than even the best learned moral inhibitions against hurting or killing another human being. Perhaps

* Stanley Milgram, "A Behavioral Study of Obedience," *Journal of Abnormal and Social Psychology* (1963), pp. 371–378.

those who would seek to weaken the power of the law to command obedience are "abnormal." Do we not enjoy our servitude because it tends to free us from responsibility? Rousseau comments: "Man is born free, and everywhere he is in chains."

On what grounds can we call laws wrong? Some laws might be shown to be "illegal," that is, inconsistent with the accepted legal system; but draft laws, for example, have withstood that test. Would you argue that to obey some laws is to violate a natural or spiritual law? This argument seems to play a role in Daniel Ellsberg's justification of his turning secret documents over to the press. Can we identify a natural law of human conduct? On what authority are moral principles given precedence over the laws of the land?

Often we hear talk of the rights of man, civil rights, the right to dissent; but questions of rights only appear to arise in social situations. Do men have natural rights, or are my rights, your rights, our rights established through the process of government and clarified in its legal system? Locke and Rousseau discuss these issues. Is it not reasonable to assume that if the rights of men are totally determined and protected by the existence of a particular government, then that government has the right to suspend or revoke the rights of its citizens at will? Is the ultimate governmental principle "might makes right?"

There have been times, usually during international stress, when governments deemed it necessary to suspend indefinitely the rights of citizens. If the government were to suspend all the rights of its citizens, would they lose the right to change that government? Who is in the best position to judge whether the actions of a political system warrant the general revolt of the people and the total overthrow of government? Certainly the government is in no position to judge its own behavior. But the citizens who think themselves tyrannized also are prejudiced. Can you offer guidelines to serve in measuring acceptable command against total tyranny?

The Relation between Law and Morality

What ought to be the basis for the laws of society that control the behavior of adult individuals? It has been suggested by some lawyers and philosophers that there is a distinction to be drawn between law and morality; that these are two separate and unrelated concerns. The restraints of morality should not be codified into legal prohibitions on the activities of individuals.

Ask yourself what the real function of laws is. Should laws be designed to mirror moral teachings and to impress the moral views of the majority upon the actions of the members of society as a whole, insuring the continuance of standards the majority thinks good? Or should our laws function entirely outside of moral concern; that is, should they only establish limits on the freedoms of individuals where the lack of a limit would lead to injury of another individual or group? Should law simply keep order? Should law be neutral on moral questions? We may say, when we observe behavior which is offensive to us. "There ought to be a law against that." A rather popular cartoon strip takes that as its premise. But consider seriously just which acts found to be offensive ought to be illegal.

Many people are offended by anyone who constantly takes the name of God in vain. Should there be a law against cursing? Adultery is considered immoral by most Western ethical codes, but should adulterers be made to wear the letter "A" for the rest of their lives or thrown in jail? What reasons were and are given for laws prohibiting the sale of alcoholic beverages and the use of narcotics? In other words, consider what "moral wrongs" ought to be crimes. Murder is certainly both morally wrong and, usually, legally wrong. But some men argue that the same cannot be said of fornication and other private sexual behavior among consenting adults, that law must not impose a particular pattern of moral behavior upon its subjects because we have no objective criterion on morals. Should the law be involved in cases like that of Shaw and *The Ladies' Directory?*

Perhaps we create undue criminality. Consider a statement by Sir Herbert Read: "Pornography is a social problem; it is a commodity brought into existence by certain characteristics of a highly developed civilization." Ought there be laws against pornography? Assume you are in the position of limiting personal liberty through law. If you choose to do so in certain cases, use of narcotics for example, whom are you protecting from what? What is your rule for deciding how far to go? In most of the United States, gambling, the use of narcotics, and prostitution are illegal. No one is forced to gamble, use drugs, or contract for the services of a prostitute. Can an act be illegal when the "victim" consents? The existence of these laws suggests that there is more than the idea of an offended individual involved in the philosophy at the basis of our legal system.

The Wolfenden Committee in the United Kingdom examined the problems of governmental intervention in the private lives of citizens and concluded that private behavior is no business of the law. However, many legal philosophers (most vocally, Lord Devlin) attacked the Committee's report on the grounds that laws must be designed to maintain the existence of society and that society, after all, is only a collection of moral attitudes. Therefore, society not only has the right but the obligation to legislate against the deviate moral behavior of individuals, public or private. Such behavior, it is maintained, cannot be allowed to continue or society will crumble from an internal decay of the principles upon which it was founded.

1

PLATO
(427–347 B.C.)

*The Formation of a Community**

Plato's Republic *is one of the most influential works in all philosophy. In the dialogue Socrates is discussing the virtues of a perfect state and the character training of the men who would live in such a state. Justice must be the practiced virtue, but how does justice arise in the state? Socrates reasons that one must first understand the way in which a state develops before one can understand how justice works. Plato's theory is that men by nature are social creatures, creatures who are interdependent. By practicing their talents men sustain each other. The state is a natural outgrowth of our interrelationships. What is justice in this state? Plato tells us it is doing one's own business.*

* Plato, *The Republic,* 3rd ed., B. Jowett, trans. (Oxford: The Clarendon Press, 1892), excerpts from Bk. II and Bk. IV.

I WILL tell you, I replied; justice, which is the subject of our inquiry, is, as you know, sometimes spoken of as the virtue of an individual, and sometimes as the virtue of a State.

True, he replied.

And is not a State larger than an individual?

It is.

Then in the larger the quantity of justice is likely to be larger and more easily discernible. I propose therefore that we inquire into the nature of justice and injustice, first as they appear in the State, and secondly in the individual, proceeding from the greater to the lesser and comparing them.

That, he said, is an excellent proposal.

And if we imagine the State in process of creation, we shall see the justice and injustice of the State in process of creation also.

I dare say.

When the State is completed there may be a hope that the object of our search will be more easily discovered.

How a State is Formed

Yes, far more easily.

But ought we to attempt to construct one? I said; for to do so, as I am inclined to think, will be a very serious task. Reflect therefore.

I have reflected, said Adeimantus, and am anxious that you should proceed.

A State, I said, arises, as I conceive, out of the needs of mankind; no one is self-sufficing, but all of us have many wants. Can any other origin of a State be imagined?

There can be no other.

Then, as we have many wants, and many persons are needed to supply them, one takes a helper for one purpose and another for another; and when these partners and helpers are gathered together in one habitation the body of inhabitants is termed a State.

True, he said.

And they exchange with one another, and one gives, and another receives, under the idea that the exchange will be for their good.

Very true.

Then, I said, let us begin and create in idea a State; and yet the true creator is necessity, who is the mother of our invention.

Of course, he replied.

Now the first and greatest of necessities is food, which is the condition of life and existence.

Certainly.

The second is a dwelling, and the third clothing and the like.

True.

And now let us see how our city will be able to supply this great demand: We may suppose that one man is a husbandman, another a builder, some one else a weaver—shall we add to them a shoemaker, or perhaps some other purveyor to our bodily wants?

Quite right.

The barest notion of a State must include four or five men.

Clearly.

And how will they proceed? Will each bring the result of his labours into a common stock?—the individual husbandman, for example, producing for four, and labouring four times as long and as much as he need in the provision of food with which he supplies others as well as himself; or will he have nothing to do with others and not be at the trouble of producing for them, but provide for himself alone a fourth of the food in a fourth of the time, and in the remaining three-fourths of his time be employed in making a house or a coat or a pair of shoes, having no partnership with others, but supplying himself all his own wants?

Adeimantus thought that he should aim at producing food only and not at producing everything.

Probably, I replied, that would be the better way; and when I hear you say this, I am myself reminded that we are not all alike; there are diversities of natures among us which are adapted to different occupations.

Very true.

And will you have a work better done when the workman has many occupations, or when he has only one?

When he has only one.

Further, there can be no doubt that a work is spoilt when not done at the right time?

No doubt.

For business is not disposed to wait until the doer of the business is at leisure; but the doer must follow up what he is doing, and make the business his first object.

He must.

And if so, we must infer that all things are produced more plentifully and easily and of a better quality when one man does one thing which is natural to him and does it at the right time, and leaves other things.

Undoubtedly.

Then more than four citizens will be required; for the husbandman will not make his own plough or mattock, or other implements of agriculture, if they are to be good for anything. Neither will the builder make his tools—and he too needs many; and in like manner the weaver and shoemaker.

True.

Then carpenters and smiths, and many other artisans, will be sharers in our little State, which is already beginning to grow?

True.

Yet even if we add neatherds, shepherds, and other herdsmen, in order that our husbandmen may have oxen to plough with, and builders as well as husbandmen may have draught cattle, and curriers and weavers fleeces and hides, —still our State will not be very large.

That is true; yet neither will it be a very small State which contains all these.

Then, again, there is the situation of the city—to find a place where nothing need be imported is wellnigh impossible.

Then there must be another class of citizens who will bring the required supply from another city?

There must.

But if the trader goes empty-handed, having nothing which they require who would supply his need, he will come back empty-handed.

That is certain.

And therefore what they produce at home must be not only enough for themselves, but such both in quantity and quality as to accommodate those from whom their wants are supplied.

Very true.

Then more husbandmen and more artisans will be required?

They will.

Not to mention the importers and exporters, who are called merchants?

Yes.

Then we shall want merchants?

We shall.

And if merchandise is to be carried over the sea, skilful sailors will also be needed, and in considerable numbers?

Yes, in considerable numbers.

Then, again, within the city, how will they exchange their productions? To secure such an exchange was, as you will remember, one of our principal objects when we formed them into a society and constituted a State.

Clearly they will buy and sell.

Then they will need a market-place, and a money-token for purposes of exchange.

Certainly.

Suppose now that a husbandman, or an artisan, brings some production to market, and he comes at a time when there is no one to exchange with him,—is he to leave his calling and sit idle in the market-place?

Not at all; he will find people there who, seeing the want, undertake the office of salesmen. In well-ordered States they are commonly those who are the weakest in bodily strength, and therefore of little use for any other purpose; their duty is to be in the market, and to give money in exchange for goods to those who desire to sell and to take money from those who desire to buy.

This want, then, creates a class of retail-traders in our State. Is not 'retailer' the term which is applied to those who sit in the market-place engaged in buying and selling, while those who wander from one city to another are called merchants?

Yes, he said.

And there is another class of servants, who are intellectually hardly on the level of companionship; still they have plenty of bodily strength for labour, which accordingly they sell, and are called, if I do not mistake, hirelings, hire being the name which is given to the price of their labour.

True.

Then hirelings will help to make up our population?

Yes.

And now, Adeimantus, is our State matured and perfected?

I think so.

Where, then, is justice and where is injustice, and in what part of the State did they spring up?

Probably in the dealings of these citizens with one another. I cannot imagine that they are more likely to be found anywhere else.

I dare say that you are right in your suggestion, I said; we had better think the matter out, and not shrink from the inquiry.

. . .

Justice in the State

Well then, tell me, I said, whether I am right or not: You remember the original principle which we were always laying down at the foundation of the State, that one man should practise one thing only, the thing to which his nature was best adapted;—now justice is this principle or a part of it.

Yes, we often said that one man should do one thing only.

Further, we affirmed that justice was doing one's own business, and not being a busybody; we said so again and again, and many others have said the same to us.

Yes, we said so.

Then to do one's own business in a certain way may be assumed to be justice. Can you tell me whence I derive this inference?

I cannot, but I should like to be told.

Because I think that this is the only virtue which remains in the State when the other virtues of temperance and courage and wisdom are abstracted; and, that this is the ultimate cause and condition of the existence of all of them, and while remaining in them is also their preservative; and we were saying that if the three were discovered by us, justice would be the fourth or remaining one.

That follows of necessity.

If we are asked to determine which of these four qualities by its presence contributes most to the excellence of the State, whether the agreement of rulers and subjects, or the preservation in the soldiers of the opinion which the law ordains about the true nature of dangers, or wisdom and watchfulness in the rulers, or whether this other which I am mentioning, and which is found in children and women, slave and freeman, artisan, ruler, subject,—the quality, I mean, of every one doing his own work, and not being a busybody, would claim the palm—the question is not so easily answered.

Certainly, he replied, there would be a difficulty in saying which.

Then the power of each individual in the State to do his own work appears to compete with the other political virtues, wisdom, temperance, courage.

Yes, he said.

And the virtue which enters into this competition is justice?

Exactly.

Let us look at the question from another point of view: Are not the rulers in a State those to whom you would entrust the office of determining suits at law?

Certainly.

And are suits decided on any other ground but that a man may neither take what is another's, nor be deprived of what is his own?

Yes; that is their principle.

Which is a just principle?

Yes.

Then on this view also justice will be admitted to be the having and doing what is a man's own, and belongs to him?

Very true.

Think, now, and say whether you agree with me or not. Suppose a carpenter to be doing the business of a cobbler, or a cobbler of a carpenter; and suppose them to exchange their implements or their duties, or the same person to be doing the work of both, or whatever be the change; do you think that any great harm would result to the State?

Not much.

But when the cobbler or any other man whom nature designed to be a trader, having his heart lifted up by wealth or strength or the number of his followers, or any like advantage, attempts to force his way into the class of warriors, or a warrior into that of legislators and guardians, for which he is unfitted, and either to take the implements or the duties of the other; or when one man is trader, legislator, and warrior all in one, then I think you will agree with me in saying that this interchange and this meddling of one with another is the ruin of the State.

Most true.

Seeing then, I said, that there are three distinct classes, any meddling of one with another, or the change of one into another, is the greatest harm to the State, and may be most justly termed evil-doing?

Precisely.

And the greatest degree of evil-doing to one's own city would be termed by you injustice?

Certainly.

This then is injustice; and on the other hand when the trader, the auxiliary, and the guardian each do their own business, that is justice, and will make the city just.

PLATO
(427–347 B.C.)

*The Crito**

The Crito *is set in prison. Socrates is awaiting execution and Crito, one of his students, urges him to escape. Socrates refuses to leave. He explains his reasons to Crito in terms of an imagined conversation between himself and the law. Socrates maintains that loyalty is due the state because it raised and educated him. When punishment is meted out by the exercise of its laws, to seek to escape from such punishment is to do a greater injustice to the state. You would be breaking the implied promise between yourself, your friends and your country. It is better to suffer at the hands of men than to do injury to the state and the law.*

* Plato, *The Crito,* 3rd ed., B. Jowett, trans. (Oxford: The Clarendon Press, 1892).

PERSONS OF THE DIALOGUE

SOCRATES **CRITO**

SCENE:—The Prison of Socrates

Socrates. Why have you come at this hour, Crito? It must be quite early?

Crito. Yes, certainly.

Socrates. What is the exact time?

Crito. The dawn is breaking.

Socrates. I wonder that the keeper of the prison would let you in.

Crito. He knows me, because I often come, Socrates; moreover, I have done him a kindness.

Socrates. And are you only just arrived?

Crito. No, I came some time ago.

Socrates. Then why did you sit and say nothing, instead of at once awakening me?

Crito. I should not have liked myself, Socrates, to be in such great trouble and unrest as you are—indeed I should not: I have been watching with amazement your peaceful slumbers; and for that reason I did not awake you, because I wished to minimize the pain. I have always thought you to be of a happy disposition; but never did I see anything like the easy, tranquil manner in which you bear this calamity.

Socrates. Why, Crito, when a man has reached my age he ought not to be repining at the approach of death.

Crito. And yet other old men find themselves in similar misfortunes, and age does not prevent them from repining.

Socrates. That is true. But you have not told me why you come at this early hour.

Crito. I come to bring you a message which is sad and painful; not, as I believe, to yourself, but to all of us who are your friends, and saddest of all to me.

Socrates. What? Has the ship come from Delos, on the arrival of which I am to die?

Crito. No, the ship has not actually arrived, but she will probably be here to-day, as persons who have come from Sunium tell me that they left her there; and therefore to-morrow, Socrates, will be the last day of your life.

Socrates. Very well, Crito; if such is the will of God, I am willing; but my belief is that there will be a delay of a day.

Crito. Why do you think so?

Socrates. I will tell you. I am to die on the day after the arrival of the ship.

Crito. Yes; that is what the authorities say.

Socrates. But I do not think that the ship will be here until to-morrow; this I infer from a vision which I had last night, or rather only just now, when you fortunately allowed me to sleep.

Crito. And what was the nature of the vision?

Socrates. There appeared to me the likeness of a woman, fair and comely, clothed in bright raiment, who called to me and said: O Socrates,

'The third day hence to fertile Phthia shalt thou go.'*

Crito. What a singular dream, Socrates!

Socrates. There can be no doubt about the meaning, Crito, I think.

Crito Again Asks Socrates to Escape

Crito. Yes; the meaning is only too clear. But, oh! my beloved Socrates, let me entreat you once more to take my advice and escape. For if you die I shall not only lose a friend who can never be replaced, but there is another evil: people who do not know you and me will believe that I might have saved you if I had been willing to give money, but that I did not care. Now, can there be a worse disgrace than this—that I should be thought to value money more than the life of a friend? For the many will not be persuaded that I wanted you to escape, and that you refused.

Socrates. But why, my dear Crito, should we care about the opinion of the many? Good men, and they are the only persons who are worth considering, will think of these things truly as they occurred.

Crito. But you see, Socrates, that the opinion of the many must be regarded, for what is now happening shows that they can do the greatest evil to any one who has lost their good opinion.

* Homer, *Il* ix. 363.

Socrates. I only wish it were so, Crito; and that the many could do the greatest evil; for then they would also be able to do the greatest good—and what a fine thing this would be! But in reality they can do neither; for they cannot make a man either wise or foolish; and whatever they do is the result of chance.

Crito. Well, I will not dispute with you; but please to tell me, Socrates, whether you are not acting out of regard to me and your other friends: are you not afraid that if you escape from prison we may get into trouble with the informers for having stolen you away, and lose either the whole or a great part of our property; or that even a worse evil may happen to us? Now, if you fear on our account, be at ease; for in order to save you, we ought surely to run this, or even a greater risk; be persuaded, then, and do as I say.

Socrates. Yes, Crito, that is one fear which you mention, but by no means the only one.

Crito. Fear not—there are persons who are willing to get you out of prison at no great cost; and as for the informers, they are far from being exorbitant in their demands—a little money will satisfy them. My means, which are certainly ample, are at your service, and if you have a scruple about spending all mine, here are strangers who will give you the use of theirs; and one of them, Simmias the Theban, has brought a large sum of money for this very purpose; and Cebes and many others are prepared to spend their money in helping you to escape. I say, therefore, do not hesitate on our account, and do not say, as you did in the court, that you will have a difficulty in knowing what to do with yourself anywhere else. For men will love you in other places to which you may go, and not in Athens only; there are friends of mine in Thessaly, if you like to go to them, who will value and protect you, and no Thessalian will give you any trouble. Nor can I think that you are at all justified, Socrates, in betraying your own life when you might be saved; in acting thus you are playing into the hands of your enemies, who are hurrying on your destruction. And further I should say that you are deserting your own children; for you might bring them up and educate them; instead of which you go away and leave them, and they will have to take their chance; and if they do not meet with the usual fate of orphans, there will be small thanks to you. No man should bring children into the world who is unwilling to persevere to the end in their nurture and education. But you appear to be choosing the easier part, not the better and manlier, which would have been more becoming in one who professes to care for virtue in all his actions, like yourself. And indeed, I am ashamed not only of you, but of us who are your friends, when I reflect that the whole business will be attributed entirely to our want of courage. The trial need never have come on, or might have been managed differently; and this last act, or crowning folly, will seem to have occurred through our negligence and cowardice, who might have saved you, if we had been good for anything; and you might have saved yourself, for there was no difficulty at all. See now, Socrates, how sad and discreditable are the consequences, both to us and you. Make up your mind then, or rather have your mind already made up, for the time of deliberation is over, and there is only one thing to be done, which must be done this very night, and if we delay at all will be no longer practicable or possible; I beseech you therefore, Socrates, be persuaded by me, and do as I say.

Whose Opinion is to be Regarded?

Socrates. Dear Crito, your zeal is invaluable, if a right one; but if wrong, the greater the zeal the greater the danger; and therefore we ought to consider whether I shall or shall not do as you say. For I am and always have been one of those natures who must be guided by reason, whatever the reason may be which upon reflection appears to me to be the best; and now that this chance has befallen me, I cannot repudiate my own words: the principles which I have hitherto honoured and revered I still honour, and unless we can at once find other and better principles, I am certain not to agree with you; no, not even if the power of the multitude could inflict many more imprisonments, confiscations, deaths, frightening us like children with hobgoblin terrors. What will be the fairest way of considering the question? Shall I return to your old argument about the opinions of men?—we were saying that some of them are to be regarded, and others not. Now were we right in maintaining this before I was condemned? And has the argument which was once good now proved to be talk for the sake of talking—mere childish nonsense? That is what I want to consider with your help, Crito:—whether, under my present circumstances, the argument appears to be in any way different or not; and is to be allowed by me or disallowed. That argument, which, as I believe, is maintained by many persons of authority, was to the effect, as I was saying, that the opinions of some men are to be regarded, and of other men not to be regarded. Now you, Crito, are not going to die to-morrow—at least, there is no human probability of this—and therefore you are disinterested and not liable to be deceived by the circumstances in which you are placed. Tell me then, whether I am right in saying that some opinions, and the opinions of some men only, are to be valued, and that other opinions, and the opinions of other men, are not to be valued. I ask you whether I was right in maintaining this?

Crito. Certainly.

Socrates. The good are to be regarded, and not the bad?

Crito. Yes.

Socrates. And the opinions of the wise are good, and the opinions of the unwise are evil?

Crito. Certainly.

Socrates. And what was said about another matter? Is the pupil who devotes himself to the practice of gymnastics supposed to attend to the praise and blame and opinion of every man, or of one man only—his physician or trainer, whoever he may be?

Crito. Of one man only.

Socrates. And he ought to fear the censure and welcome the praise of that one only, and not of the many?

Crito. Clearly so.

Socrates. And he ought to act and train, and eat and drink in the way which seems good to his single master who has understanding, rather than according to the opinion of all other men put together?

Crito. True.

Socrates. And if he disobeys and disregards the opinion and approval of the one, and regards the opinion of the many who have no understanding, will he not suffer evil?

Crito. Certainly he will.

Socrates. And what will the evil be, whither tending and what affecting, in the disobedient person?

Crito. Clearly, affecting the body; that is what is destroyed by the evil.

Socrates. Very good; and is not this true, Crito, of other things which we need not separately enumerate? In questions of just and unjust, fair and foul, good and evil, which are the subjects of our present consultation, ought we to follow the opinion of the many and to fear them; or the opinion of the one man who has understanding? ought we not to fear and reverence him more than all the rest of the world: and if we desert him shall we not destroy and injure that principle in us which may be assumed to be improved by justice and deteriorated by injustice;—there is such a principle?

Crito. Certainly there is, Socrates.

Socrates. Take a parallel instance:—if, acting under the advice of those who have no understanding, we destroy that which is improved by health and is deteriorated by disease, would life be worth having? And that which has been destroyed is—the body?

Crito. Yes.

Socrates. Could we live, having an evil and corrupted body?

Crito. Certainly not.

Socrates. And will life be worth having, if that higher part of man be destroyed, which is improved by justice and depraved by injustice? Do we suppose that principle, whatever it may be in man, which has to do with justice and injustice, to be inferior to the body?

Crito. Certainly not.

Socrates. More honourable than the body?

Crito. Far more.

Socrates. Then, my friend, we must not regard what the many say of us: but what he, the one man who has understanding of just and unjust, will say, and what the truth will say. And therefore you begin in error when you advise that we should regard the opinion of the many about just and unjust, good and evil, honourable and dishonourable.—'Well,' some one will say, 'but the many can kill us.'

Crito. Yes, Socrates; that will clearly be the answer.

Socrates. And it is true: but still I find with surprise that the old argument is unshaken as ever. And I should like to know whether I may say the same of another proposition—that not life, but a good life, is to be chiefly valued?

Crito. Yes, that also remains unshaken.

Socrates. And a good life is equivalent to a just and honourable one —that holds also?

Crito. Yes, it does.

Would it be Right to Escape?

Socrates. From these premisses I proceed to argue the question whether I ought or ought not to try and escape without the consent of the Athenians: and if I am clearly right in escaping, then I will make the attempt; but if not, I will abstain. The other considerations which you mention, of money and loss of character and the duty of educating one's children, are, I fear, only the doctrines of the multitude, who would be as ready to restore people to life, if they were able, as they are to put them to death—and with as little reason. But now, since the argument has thus far prevailed, the only question which remains to be considered is, whether we shall do rightly either in escaping or in suffering others to aid in our escape and paying them in money and thanks, or whether in reality we shall not do rightly; and if the latter, then death or any other calamity which may ensue on my remaining here must not be allowed to enter into the calculation.

Crito. I think that you are right, Socrates; how then shall we proceed?

Socrates. Let us consider the matter together, and do you either refute me if you can, and I will be convinced; or else cease, my dear friend, from repeating to me that I ought to escape against the wishes of the Athenians: for I highly value your attempts to persuade me to do so, but I may not be persuaded against my own better judgment. And now please to consider my first position, and try how you can best answer me.

Crito. I will.

Socrates. Are we to say that we are never intentionally to do wrong, or that in one way we ought and in another way we ought not to do wrong, or is doing wrong always evil and dishonourable, as I was just now saying, and as has been already acknowledged by us? Are all our former admissions which were made within a few days to be thrown away? And have we, at our age, been earnestly discoursing with one another all our life long only to discover that we are no better than children? Or, in spite of the opinion of the many, and in spite of consequences whether better or worse, shall we insist on the truth of what was then said, that injustice is always an evil and dishonour to him who acts unjustly? Shall we say so or not?

Crito. Yes.

Socrates. Then we must do no wrong?

Crito. Certainly not.

Socrates. Nor when injured injure in return, as the many imagine; for we must injure no one at all?

Crito. Clearly not.

Socrates. Again, Crito, may we do evil?

Crito. Surely not, Socrates.

Socrates. And what of doing evil in return for evil, which is the morality of the many—is that just or not?

Crito. Not just.

Socrates. For doing evil to another is the same as injuring him?

Crito. Very true.

Socrates. Then we ought not to retaliate or render evil for evil to any one, whatever evil we may have suffered from him. But I would have you consider, Crito, whether you really mean what you are saying.

For this opinion has never been held, and never will be held, by any considerable number of persons; and those who are agreed and those who are not agreed upon this point have no common ground, and can only despise one another when they see how widely they differ. Tell me, then, whether you agree with and assent to my first principle, that neither injury nor retaliation nor warding off evil by evil is ever right. And shall that be the premiss of our argument? Or do you decline and dissent from this? For so I have ever thought, and continue to think; but, if you are of another opinion, let me hear what you have to say. If, however, you remain of the same mind as formerly, I will proceed to the next step.

Crito. You may proceed, for I have not changed my mind.

Socrates. Then I will go on to the next point, which may be put in the form of a question:—Ought a man to do what he admits to be right, or ought he to betray the right?

Crito. He ought to do what he thinks right.

Socrates. But if this is true, what is the application? In leaving the prison against the will of the Athenians, do I wrong any? or rather do I not wrong those whom I ought least to wrong? Do I not desert the principles which were acknowledged by us to be just—what do you say?

Crito. I cannot tell, Socrates; for I do not know.

The Necessity of Obedience to the Laws of the State

Socrates. Then consider the matter in this way:—Imagine that I am about to play truant (you may call the proceeding by any name which you like), and the laws and the government come and interrogate me: 'Tell us, Socrates,' they say; 'what are you about? are you not going by an act of yours to overturn us—the laws, and the whole state, as far as in you lies? Do you imagine that a state can subsist and not be overthrown, in which the decisions of law have no power, but are set aside and trampled upon by individuals?' What will be our answer, Crito, to these and the like words? Any one, and especially a rhetorician, will have a good deal to say on behalf of the law which requires a sentence to be carried out. He will argue that this law should not be set aside; and shall we reply, 'Yes; but the state has injured us and given an unjust sentence.' Suppose I say that?

Crito. Very good, Socrates.

Socrates. 'And was that our agreement with you?' the law would answer; 'or were you to abide by the sentence of the state?' And if I were to express my astonishment at their words, the law would probably add: 'Answer, Socrates, instead of opening your eyes—you are in the habit of asking and answering questions. Tell us,—What complaint have you to make against us which justifies you in attempting to destroy us and the state? In the first place did we not bring you into existence? Your father married your mother by our aid and begat you. Say whether you have any objection to urge against those of us who regulate marriage?' None, I should reply. 'Or against those of us who after birth regulate the nurture and education of children, in which you also were trained? Were not the laws, which have the charge of education, right in commanding your father to train you in music and gymnastics?' Right, I should reply. 'Well then, since you were brought into the world and nurtured and educated by us, can you deny in the first place that you are our child and slave, as your fathers were before you? And if this is true you are not on equal terms with us; nor can you think that you have a right to do to us what we are doing to you. Would you have any right to strike or revile or do any other evil to your father or your master, if you had one, because you have been struck or reviled by him, or received some other evil at his hands?—you would not say this? And because we think right to destroy you, do you think that you have any right to destroy us in return, and your country as far as in you lies? Will you, O professor of true virtue, pretend that you are justified in this? Has a philosopher like you failed to discover that our country is more to be valued and higher and holier far than mother or father or any ancestor, and more to be regarded in the eyes of the gods and of men of understanding? also to be soothed, and gently and reverently entreated when angry, even more than a father, and either to be persuaded, or if not persuaded, to be obeyed? And when we are punished by her, whether with imprisonment or stripes, the punishment is to be endured in silence; and if she lead us to wounds or death in battle, thither we follow as is right; neither may any one yield or retreat or leave his rank, but whether in battle or in a court of law, or in any other place, he must do what his city and his country order him; or he must change their view of what is just: and if he may do no violence to his father or mother, much less may he do violence to his country.' What answer shall we make to this, Crito? Do the laws speak truly, or do they not?

Crito. I think that they do.

Socrates. Then the laws will say; 'Consider, Socrates, if we are speaking truly that in your present attempt you are going to do us an injury. For, having brought you into the world, and nurtured and educated you, and given you and every other citizen a share in every good which we had to give, we further proclaim to any Athenian by the liberty which we allow him, that if he does not like us when he has become of age and has seen the ways of the city, and made our acquaintance, he may go where he pleases and take his goods with him. None of us laws will forbid him or interfere with him. Any one who does not like us and the city, and who wants to emigrate to a colony or to any other city, may go where he likes, retaining his property. But he who has experience of the manner in which we order justice and administer the state, and still remains, has entered into an implied contract that he will do as we command him. And he who disobeys us is, as we maintain, thrice wrong; first, because in disobeying us he is disobeying his parents; secondly, because we are the authors of his education; thirdly, because he has made an agreement with us that he will duly obey our command; and he neither obeys them nor convinces us that our commands are unjust; and we do not rudely impose them, but give him the alternative of obeying or convincing us;—that is what we offer, and he does neither.

'These are the sort of accusations to which, as we were saying, you, Socrates, will be exposed if you accomplish your intentions; you, above all other Athenians.' Suppose now I ask, why I rather than anybody else? they will justly retort upon me that I above all other men have acknowledged the agreement. 'There is clear proof,' they will say, 'Socrates, that we and the city were not displeasing to you. Of all Athenians you have been the most constant resident in the city, which, as you never leave, you may be supposed to love. For you never went out of the city either to see the games, except once when you went to the Isthmus, or to any other place unless when you were on military service; nor did you travel as other men do. Nor had you any curiosity to know other states or their laws: your affections did not go beyond us and our state; we were your special favourites, and you acquiesced in our government of you; and here in this city you begat your children, which is a proof of your satisfaction. Moreover, you might in the course of the trial, if you had liked, have fixed the penalty at banishment; the state which refuses to let you go now would have let you go then. But you pretended that you preferred death to exile, and that you were not unwilling to die. And now you have forgotten these fine sentiments, and pay no respect to us the laws, of whom you are the destroyer; and are doing what only a miserable slave would do, running away and turning your back upon the compacts and agreements which you made as a citizen. And first of all answer this very question: Are we right in saying that you agreed to be governed according to us in deed, and not in word only? Is that true or not?' How shall we answer, Crito? Must we not assent?

Crito. We cannot help it, Socrates.

The Alternative of Going to Another State

Socrates. Then will they not say: 'You, Socrates, are breaking the covenants and agreements which you made with us at your leisure, not in any haste or under any compulsion or deception, but after you have had seventy years to think of them, during which time you were at liberty to leave the city, if we were not to your mind, or if our covenants appeared to you to be unfair. You had your choice, and might have gone either to Lacedaemon or Crete, both which states are often praised by you for their good government, or to some other Hellenic or foreign state. Whereas you, above all other Athenians, seemed to be so fond of the state, or, in other words, of us her laws (and who would care about a state which has no laws?), that you never stirred out of her; the halt, the blind, the maimed were not more stationary in her than you were. And now you run away and forsake your agreements. Not so, Socrates, if you will take our advice; do not make yourself ridiculous by escaping out of the city.

'For just consider, if you transgress and err in this sort of way, what good will you do either to yourself or to your friends? That your friends will be driven into exile and deprived of citizenship, or will lose their property, is tolerably certain; and you yourself, if you fly to one of the neighbouring cities, as, for example, Thebes or Megara, both of which are well governed, will come to them as an enemy, Socrates, and their government will be against you, and all patriotic citizens will cast an evil eye upon you as a subverter of the laws, and you will confirm in the minds of the judges the justice of their own condemnation of you. For he who is a corrupter of the laws is more than likely to be a corrupter of the young and foolish portion of mankind. Will you then flee from well-ordered cities and virtuous men? and is existence worth having on these terms? Or will you go to them without shame, and talk to them, Socrates? And what will you say to them? What you say here about virtue and justice and institutions and laws being the best things among men? Would that be decent of you? Surely not. But if you go away from well-governed states to Crito's friends in Thessaly, where there is great disorder and licence, they will be charmed to hear the tale of your escape from prison, set off with ludicrous particulars of the manner in which you were wrapped in a goatskin or some other disguise, and metamorphosed as the manner is of runaways; but will there be no one to remind you that in your old age you were not ashamed to violate the most sacred laws from a miserable desire of a little more life? Perhaps not, if you keep them in a good temper; but if they are out of temper you will hear many degrading things; you will live, but how?—as the flatterer of all men, and the servant of all men; and doing what?—eating and drinking in Thessaly, having gone abroad in order that you may get a dinner. And where will be your fine sentiments about justice and virtue? Say that you wish to live for the sake of your children—you want to bring them up and educate them—will you take them into Thessaly and deprive them of Athenian citizenship? Is this the benefit which you will confer upon them? Or are you under the impression that they will be better cared for and educated here if you are still alive, although absent from them; for your friends will take care of them? Do you fancy that if you are an inhabitant of Thessaly they will take care of them, and if you are an inhabitant of the other world that they will not take care of them? Nay; but if they who call themselves friends are good for anything, they will—to be sure they will.

'Listen, then, Socrates, to us who have brought you up. Think not of life and children first, and of justice afterwards, but of justice first, that you may be justified before the princes of the world below. For neither will you nor any that belong to you be happier or holier or juster in this life, or happier in another, if you do as Crito bids. Now you depart in innocence, a sufferer and not a doer of evil; a victim, not of the laws but of men. But if you go forth, returning evil for evil, and injury for injury, breaking the covenants and agreements which you have made with us, and wronging those whom you ought least of all to wrong, that is to say, yourself, your friends, your country, and us, we shall be angry with you while you live, and our brethren, the laws in the world below, will receive you as an enemy; for they will know that you have done your best to destroy us. Listen, then, to us and not to Crito.'

This, dear Crito, is the voice which I seem to hear murmuring in my ears, like the sound of the flute in the ears of the mystic; that voice, I say, is humming in my ears, and prevents me from hearing any other.

And I know that anything more which you may say will be vain. Yet speak, if you have anything to say.

Crito. I have nothing to say, Socrates.

Socrates. Leave me then, Crito, to fulfil the will of God, and to follow whither he leads.

2

JOHN LOCKE

(1632–1704)

*Second Treatise of Government**

Locke's political theory has played a major role in the philosophical foundations of our form of government. For Locke men in a state of nature are equally endowed with certain rights, such as life, liberty and property. The state of nature, in fact, would be an ideal situation, but some men are always tempted to intrude upon the rights of others and warfare results. The majority of men, while attempting to preserve their rights, band together for protection and place some of their rights in the hands of the government. Government must be founded on the consent of the governed. If a government exceeds its established authority and threatens the personal rights of its citizens, then it must be overthrown. But Locke does not counsel hasty revolution. Acts of a tyrannical government must span a number of years to warrant the turmoil of revolt.

* John Locke, *Two Treatises of Government* (1764), selections from "The Second Treatise." You might also refer to *Two Treatises of Government* (London: Thomas Tegg, 1823), Vol. V.

Of the State of Nature

TO understand political power right, and derive it from its original, we must consider what state all men are naturally in, and that is, a state of perfect freedom to order their actions and dispose of their possessions and persons, as they think fit, within the bounds of the law of nature; without asking leave, or depending upon the will of any other man.

A state also of equality, wherein all the power and jurisdiction is reciprocal, no one having more than another; there being nothing more evident than that creatures of the same species and rank, promiscuously born to all the same advantages of nature, and the use of the same faculties, would also be equal one amongst another without subordination or subjection; unless the Lord and Master of them all should, by any manifest declaration of his will, set one above another, and confer on him, by an evident and clear appointment, an undoubted right to dominion and sovereignty.

. . .

Men being, as has been said, by nature all free, equal, and independent, no one can be put out of this estate and subjected to the political power of another without his own consent. The only way whereby any one divests himself of his natural liberty and puts on the bonds of civil society is by agreeing with other men to join and unite into a community for their comfortable, safe, and peaceable living one amongst another, in a secure enjoyment of their properties and a greater security against any that are not of it. This any number of men may do, because it injures not the freedom of the rest; they are left as they were in the liberty of the state of nature. When any number of men have so consented to make one community or government, they are thereby presently incorporated and make one body politic wherein the majority have a right to act and conclude the rest.

For when any number of men have, by the consent of every individual, made a community, they have thereby made that community one body, with a power to act as one body, which is only by the will and determination of the majority; for that which acts any community being only the consent of the individuals of it, and it being necessary to that which is one body to move one way, it is necessary the body should move that way whither the greater force carries it, which is the consent of the majority; or else it is impossible it should act or continue one body, one community, which the consent of every individual that united into it agreed that it should; and so every one is bound by that consent to be concluded by the majority. And therefore we see that in assemblies impowered to act by positive laws, where no number is set by that positive law which impowers them, the act of the majority passes for the act of the whole and, of course, determines, as having by the law of nature and reason the power of the whole.

And thus every man, by consenting with others to make one body politic under one government, puts himself under an obligation to every one of that society to submit to the determination of the majority and to be concluded by it; or else this original compact, whereby he with others incorporates into one society, would signify nothing, and be no compact, if he be left free and under no other ties than he was in before in the state of nature. For what appearance would there be of any compact? What new engagement if he were no further tied by any decrees of the society than he himself thought fit and did actually consent to? This would be still as great a liberty as he himself had before his compact, or any one else in the state of nature has who may submit himself and consent to any acts of it if he thinks fit.

For if the consent of the majority shall not in reason be received as the act of the whole and conclude every individual, nothing but the consent of every individual can make anything to be the act of the whole; but such a consent is next to impossible ever to be had if we consider the infirmities of health and avocations of business which in a number, though much less than that of a commonwealth, will necessarily keep many away from the public assembly. To which, if we add the variety of opinions and contrariety of interests which unavoidably happen in all collections of men, the coming into society upon such terms would be only like Cato's coming into the theatre only to go out again. Such a constitution as this would make the mighty leviathan of a shorter duration than the feeblest creatures, and not let it outlast the day it was born in; which cannot be supposed till we can think that rational creatures should desire and constitute societies only to be dissolved; for where the majority cannot conclude the rest, there they cannot act as one body, and consequently will be immediately dissolved again.

Whosoever, therefore, out of a state of nature unite into a community must be understood to give up all the power necessary to the ends for which they unite into society to the majority of the community, unless they expressly agreed in any number greater than the majority. And this is done by barely agreeing to unite into one political society, which is all the compact that is, or needs be, between the individuals that enter into or make up a commonwealth. And thus that which begins and actually constitutes any political society is nothing but the consent of any number of freemen capable of a majority to unite and incorporate into such a society. And this is that, and that only, which did or could give beginning to any lawful government in the world.

. . .

The Ends of Political Society and Government

Every man being, as has been shown, naturally free, and nothing being able to put him into subjection to any earthly power but only his own consent, it is to be considered what shall be understood to be a sufficient declaration of a man's consent to make him subject to the laws of any government. There is a common distinction of an express and a tacit consent which will concern our present case. Nobody doubts but an express consent of any man entering into any society makes him a perfect member of that society, a subject of that government. The difficulty is, what ought to be looked upon as a tacit consent, and how far it binds—i.e., how far any one shall be looked upon to have consented and thereby submitted to any government, where he has made no expressions of it at all. And to this I say that every man that has any possessions or enjoyment of any part of the dominions of any government does thereby give his tacit consent and is as far forth obliged to obedience to the laws of that government, during such enjoyment, as anyone under it; whether this his possession be of land to him and his heirs for ever, or a lodging only for a week, or whether it be barely traveling freely on the highway; and, in effect, it reaches as far as the very being of anyone within the territories of that government.

To understand this the better, it is fit to consider that every man, when he at first incorporates himself into any commonwealth, he, by his uniting himself thereunto, annexes also, and submits to the community, those possessions which he has or shall acquire that do not already belong to any other government; for it would be a direct contradiction for any one to enter into society with others for the securing and regulating of property, and yet to suppose his land, whose property is to be regulated by the laws of the society, should be exempt from the jurisdiction of that government to which he himself, the proprietor of the land, is a subject. By the same act, therefore, whereby any one unites his person, which was before free, to any commonwealth, by the same he unites his possessions which were before free to it also; and they become, both of them, person and possession, subject to the government and dominion of that commonwealth as long as it has a being. Whoever, therefore, from thenceforth by inheritance, purchase, permission, or otherwise, enjoys any part of the land so annexed to, and under the government of that commonwealth, must take it with the condition it is under—that is, of submitting to the government of the commonwealth under whose jurisdiction it is as far forth as any subject of it.

But since the government has a direct jurisdiction only over the land, and reaches the possessor of it—before he has actually incorporated himself in the society—only as he dwells upon and enjoys that, the obligation anyone is under by virtue of such enjoyment, to submit to the government, begins and ends with the enjoyment; so that whenever the owner, who has given nothing but such a tacit consent to the government, will, by donation, sale, or otherwise, quit the said possession, he is at liberty to go and incorporate himself into any other commonwealth, or to agree with others to begin a new one *in vacuis locis,* in any part of the world they can find free and unpossessed. Whereas he that has once, by actual agreement and any express declaration, given his consent to be of any commonwealth is perpetually and indispensably obliged to be and remain unalterably a subject to it, and can never be again in the liberty of the state of nature, unless by any calamity the government he was under comes to be dissolved, or else, by some public act, cuts him off from being any longer a member of it.

But submitting to the laws of any country, living quietly and enjoying privileges and protection under them, makes not a man a member of that society; this is only a local protection and homage due to and from all those who, not being in a state of war, come within the territories belonging to any government, to all parts whereof the force of its laws extends. But this no more makes a man a member of that society, a perpetual subject of that commonwealth, than it would make a man subject to another in whose family he found it convenient to abide for some time, though, while he continued in it, he were obliged to comply with the laws and submit to the government he found there. And thus we see that foreigners, by living all their lives under another government and enjoying the privileges and protection of it, though they are bound, even in conscience, to submit to its administration as far forth as any denizen, yet do not thereby come to be subjects or members of that commonwealth. Nothing can make any man so but his actually entering into it by positive engagement and express promise and compact. That is that which I think concerning the beginning of political societies and that consent which makes any one a member of any commonwealth.

If man in the state of nature be so free, as has been said, if he be absolute lord of his own person and possessions, equal to the greatest, and subject to nobody, why will he part with his freedom, why will he give up his empire and subject himself to the dominion and control of any other power? To which it is obvious to answer that though in the state of nature he has such a right, yet the enjoyment of it is very uncertain and constantly exposed to the invasion of others; for all being kings as much as he, every man his equal, and the greater part no strict observers of equity and justice, the enjoyment of the property he has in this state is very unsafe, very unsecure. This makes him willing to quit a condition which, however free, is full of fears and continual dangers; and it is not without reason that he seeks out and is willing to join in society with others who are already united, or have a mind to unite, for the mutual preservation of their lives, liberties, and estates, which I call by the general name 'property.'

The great and chief end, therefore, of men's uniting into commonwealths and putting themselves under government is the preservation of their property. To which in the state of nature there are many things wanting:

First, there wants an established, settled, known law, received and allowed by common consent to be the standard of right and wrong and the common measure to decide all controversies between them; for though the law of nature be plain and intelligible to all rational creatures, yet men, being biased by their interest as well as ignorant for want of studying it, are not apt to allow of it as a law binding to them in the application of it to their particular cases.

Secondly, in the state of nature there wants a known and indifferent judge with authority to determine all differences according to the established law; for every one in that state being both judge and executioner of the law of nature, men being partial to themselves, passion and revenge is very apt to carry them too far and with too much heat in their own cases, as well as negligence and unconcernedness to make them too remiss in other men's.

Thirdly, in the state of nature there often wants power to back and support the sentence when right, and to give it due execution. They who by any injustice offend will seldom fail, where they are able, by force, to make good their injustice; such resistance many times makes the punishment dangerous and frequently destructive to those who attempt it.

Thus mankind, notwithstanding all the privileges of the state of nature, being but in an ill condition while they remain in it, are quickly driven into society. Hence it comes to pass that we seldom find any number of men live any time together in this state. The inconveniences that they are therein exposed to by the irregular and uncertain exercise of the power every man has of punishing the transgressions of others make them take sanctuary under the established laws of government and therein seek the preservation of their property. It is this makes them so willingly give up every one his single power of punishing, to be exercised by such alone as shall be appointed to it amongst them; and by such rules as the community, or those authorized by them to that purpose, shall agree on. And in this we have the original right of both the legislative and executive power, as well as of the governments and societies themselves.

For in the state of nature, to omit the liberty he has of innocent delights, a man has two powers:

The first is to do whatsoever he thinks fit for the preservation of himself and others within the permission of the law of nature, by which law, common to them all, he and all the rest of mankind are one community, make up one society, distinct from all other creatures. And, were it not for the corruption and viciousness of degenerate men, there would be no need of any other, no necessity that men should separate from this great and natural community and by positive agreements combine into smaller and divided associations.

The other power a man has in the state of nature is the power to punish the crimes committed against the law. Both these he gives up when he joins in a private, if I may so call it, or particular politic society and incorporates into any commonwealth separate from the rest of mankind.

The first power, viz., of doing whatsoever he thought fit for the preservation of himself and the rest of mankind, he gives up to be regulated by laws made by the society, so far forth as the preservation of himself and the rest of that society shall require; which laws of the society in many things confine the liberty he had by the law of nature.

Secondly, the power of punishing he wholly gives up, and engages his natural force—which he might before employ in the execution of the law of nature by his own single authority, as he thought fit—to assist the executive power of the society, as the law thereof shall require; for being now in a new state, wherein he is to enjoy many conveniences from the labor, assistance, and society of others in the same community as well as protection from its whole strength, he is to part also with as much of his natural liberty, in providing for himself, as the good, prosperity, and safety of the society shall require, which is not only necessary, but just, since the other members of the society do the like.

But though men when they enter into society give up the equality, liberty, and executive power they had in the state of nature into the hands of the society, to be so far disposed of by the legislative as the good of the society shall require, yet it being only with an intention in every one the better to preserve himself, his liberty and property—for no rational creature can be supposed to change his condition with an intention to be worse—the power of the society, or legislative constituted by them, can never be supposed to extend farther than the common good, but is obliged to secure every one's property by providing against those three defects above-mentioned that made the state of nature so unsafe and uneasy. And so whoever has the legislative or supreme power of any commonwealth is bound to govern by established standing laws, promulgated and known to the people, and not by extemporary decrees; by indifferent and upright judges who are to decide controversies by those laws; and to employ the force of the community at home only in the execution of such laws, or abroad to prevent or redress foreign injuries, and secure the community from inroads and invasion. And all this to be directed to no other end by the peace, safety, and public good of the people.

. . .

Tyranny Wherever law ends, tyranny begins if the law be transgressed to another's harm. And whosoever in authority exceeds the power given him by the law, and makes use of the force he has under his command to compass that upon the subject which the law allows not, ceases in that to be a magistrate and, acting without authority, may be opposed as any other man who by force invades the right of another. This is acknowledged in subordinate magistrates. He that has authority to seize my person in the street may be opposed as a thief and a robber if he endeavors to break into my house to execute a writ, notwithstanding that I know he has such a warrant and such a legal authority as will empower him to arrest me abroad. And why this should not hold in the highest as well as in the most inferior magistrate, I would gladly be informed. Is it reasonable that the eldest brother, because he has the greatest part of his father's estate, should thereby have a right to take away any of his younger brother's portions? Or that a rich man who possessed a whole country should from thence have a right to seize, when he pleased, the cottage and garden of his poor neighbor? The being rightfully possessed of great power and riches, exceedingly beyond the greatest part of the sons of Adam, is so far from being an excuse, much less a reason, for rapine and oppression, which the endamaging another without authority is, that it is a great aggravation of it; for the exceeding the bounds of authority is no more a right in a great than in a petty officer, no more justifiable in a king than a constable; but is so much the worse in him in that he has more trust put in him, has already a much greater share than the rest of his brethren, and is supposed, from the advantages of his education, employment, and counselors, to be more knowing in the measures of right and wrong.

May the commands, then, of a prince be opposed? May he be resisted as often as any one shall find himself aggrieved, and but imagine he has not right done him? This will unhinge and overturn all politics, and, instead of government and order, leave nothing but anarchy and confusion.

To this I answer that force is to be opposed to nothing but to unjust and unlawful force; whoever makes any opposition in any other case draws on himself a just condemnation both from God and man.

. . .

Revolutions Revolutions happen not upon every little mismanagement in public affairs. Great mistakes in the ruling part, many wrong and inconvenient laws, and all the slips of human frailty will be born by the people without mutiny or murmur. But if a long train of abuses, prevarications, and artifices, all tending the same way, make the design visible to the people, and they cannot but feel what they lie under and see whither they are going, it is not to be wondered that they should then rouse themselves and endeavor to put the rule into such hands which may secure to them the ends for which government was at first erected, and without which ancient names and specious forms are so far from being better that they are much worse than the state of nature or pure anarchy—the inconveniences being all as great and as near, but the remedy farther off and more difficult.

The doctrine of a power in the people of providing for their safety anew by a new legislative, when their legislators have acted contrary to their trust by invading their property, is the best fence against rebellion, and the probablest means to hinder it; for rebellion being an opposition, not to persons, but authority which is founded only in the constitutions and laws of the government, those, whoever they be, who by force break through, and by force justify their violation of them, are truly and properly rebels; for when men, by entering into society and civil government, have excluded force and introduced laws for the preservation of property, peace, and unity amongst themselves, those who set up force again in opposition to the laws do *rebellare*—that is, bring back again the state of war—and are properly rebels; which they who are in power, by the pretense they have to authority, the temptation of force they have in their hands, and the flattery of those about them, being likeliest to do, the properest way to prevent the evil is to show them the danger and injustice of it who are under the greatest temptation to run into it. . . .

Who shall be judge whether the prince or legislative act contrary to their trust? This, perhaps, ill-affected and factious men may spread amongst the people, when the prince only makes use of his due prerogative. To this I reply: The people shall be judge; for who shall be judge whether his trustee or deputy acts well and according to the trust reposed in him but he who deputes him and must, by having deputed him, have still a power to discard him when he fails in his trust? If this be reasonable in particular cases of private men, why should it be otherwise in that of the greatest moment where the welfare of millions is concerned, and also where the evil, if not prevented, is greater and the redress very difficult, dear, and dangerous?

But further, this question, Who shall be judge? cannot mean that there is no judge at all; for where there is no judicature on earth to decide controversies amongst men, God in heaven is Judge. He alone, it is true, is Judge of the right. But every man is judge for himself, as in all other cases, so in this, whether another has put himself into a state of war with him, and whether he should appeal to the Supreme Judge, as Jephthah did.

If a controversy arise betwixt a prince and some of the people in a matter where the law is silent or doubtful, and the thing be of great consequence, I should think the proper umpire in such a case should be the body of the people; for in cases where the prince has a trust reposed in him and is dispensed from the common ordinary rules of the law, there, if any men find themselves aggrieved and think the prince acts contrary to or beyond that trust, who so proper to judge as the body of the people (who, at first, lodged that trust in him) how far they meant it should extend? But if the prince, or whoever they be in the administration, decline that way of determination, the appeal then lies nowhere but to heaven; force between either persons who have no known superior on earth, or which permits no appeal to a judge on earth, being properly a state of war wherein the appeal lies only to heaven; and in that state the injured party must judge for himself when he will think fit to make use of that appeal and put himself upon it.

To conclude, the power that every individual gave the society when he entered into it can never revert to the individuals again as long as the society lasts, but will always remain in the community, because without this there can be no community, no commonwealth, which is contrary to the original agreement; so also when the society has placed the legislative in any assembly of men, to continue in them and their successors with direction and authority for providing such successors, the legislative can never revert to the people while that government lasts, because having provided a legislative with power to continue for ever, they have given up their political power to the legislative and cannot resume it. But if they have set limits to the duration of their legislative and made this supreme power in any person or assembly only temporary, or else when by the miscarriages of those in authority it is forfeited, upon the forfeiture, or at the determination of the time set, it reverts to the society, and the people have a right to act as supreme and continue the legislative in themselves, or erect a new form, or under the old form place it in new hands, as they think good.

3

JEAN JACQUES ROUSSEAU

(1712–1778)

*The Social Contract**

Rousseau maintains that the state exists because of an explicit or implicit agreement among men to live together under certain conditions. The social contract theory takes the state to be an organic, rather homogeneous, whole in which government (sovereignty) is found in the will of the organism. The social contract is the tacit agreement of all citizens to abide by the General Will. In effect, the individual agrees that in all questions of government his will shall be such that the general consensus shall prevail. In return, Rousseau claims, "We receive every member as an indivisible part of the whole." It is perhaps important to note that Rousseau intended this theory to apply only to an ideal state of 20,000 inhabitants.

* Jean Jacques Rousseau, *The Social Contract* (1763), Chap. 1, with omissions.

MAN is born free, and everywhere he is in chains. Many a one believes himself the master of others, and yet he is a greater slave than they. How has this change come about? I do not know. What can render it legitimate? I believe that I can settle this question.

If I considered only force and the results that proceed from it, I should say that so long as a people is compelled to obey and does obey, it does well; but that, so soon as it can shake off the yoke and does shake it off, it does better; for, if men recover their freedom by virtue of the same right by which it was taken away, either they are justified in resuming it, or there was no justification for depriving them of it. But the social order is a sacred right which serves as a foundation for all others. This right, however, does not come from nature. It is therefore based on conventions. The question is to know what these conventions are. Before coming to that, I must establish what I have just laid down.

. . .

The Right of the Strongest

The strongest man is never strong enough to be always master, unless he transforms his power into right, and obedience into duty. Hence the right of the strongest—a right apparently assumed in irony, and really established in principle. But will this phrase never be explained to us? Force is a physical power; I do not see what morality can result from its effects. To yield to force is an act of necessity, not of will; it is at most an act of prudence. In what sense can it be a duty?

Let us assume for a moment this pretended right. I say that nothing results from it but inexplicable nonsense; for if force constitutes right, the effect changes with the cause, and any force which overcomes the first succeeds to its rights. As soon as men can disobey with impunity, they may do so legitimately; and since the strongest is always in the right, the only thing is to act in such a way that one may be the strongest. But what sort of a right is it that perishes when forces ceases? If it is necessary to obey by compulsion, there is no need to obey from duty; and if men are no longer forced to obey, obligation is at an end. We see, then, that this word *right* adds nothing to force; it here means nothing at all.

Obey the powers that be. If that means, Yield to force, the precept is good but superfluous; I reply that it will never be violated. All power comes from God, I admit; but every disease comes from him too; does it follow that we are prohibited from calling in a physician? If a brigand should surprise me in the recesses of a wood, am I bound not only to give up my purse when forced, but am I also morally bound to do so when I might conceal it? For, in effect, the pistol which he holds is a superior force.

Let us agree, then, that might does not make right, and that we are bound to obey none but lawful authorities. Thus my original question ever recurs.

Slavery

Since no man has any natural authority over his fellow-men, and since force is not the source of right, conventions remain as the basis of all lawful authority among men.

If an individual, says Grotius, can alienate his liberty and become the slave of a master, why should not a whole people be able to alienate theirs, and become subject to a king? In this there are many equivocal terms requiring explanation; but let us confine ourselves to the word *alienate*. To alienate is to give or sell. Now, a man who becomes another's slave does not give himself; he sells himself at the very least for his subsistence. But why does a nation sell itself? So far from a king supplying his subjects with their subsistence, he draws his from them; and, according to Rabelais, a king does not live on a little. Do subjects, then, give up their persons on condition that their property also shall be taken? I do not see what is left for them to keep.

It will be said that the despot secures to his subjects civil peace. Be it so; but what do they gain by that, if the wars which his ambition brings upon them, together with his insatiable greed and the vexations of his administration, harass them more than their own dissensions would? What do they gain by it if this tranquility is itself one of their miseries? Men live tranquilly also in dungeons; is that enough to make them contented there? The Greeks confined in the cave of the Cyclops lived peacefully until their turn came to be devoured.

To say that a man gives himself for nothing is to say what is absurd and inconceivable; such an act is illegitimate and invalid, for the simple reason that he who performs it is not in his right mind. To say the same thing of a whole nation is to suppose a nation of fools; and madness does not confer rights.

Even if each person could alienate himself, he could not alienate his children; they are born free men; their liberty belongs to them, and no one has a right to dispose of it except themselves. Before they have come to years of discretion, the father can, in their name, stipulate conditions for their preservation and welfare, but not surrender them irrevocably and unconditionally; for such a gift is contrary to the ends of nature, and exceeds the rights of paternity. In order, then, that an arbitrary government might be legitimate, it would be necessary that the people in each generation should have the option of accepting or rejecting it; but in that case such a government would no longer be arbitrary.

To renounce one's liberty is to renounce one's quality as a man, the rights and also the duties of humanity. For him who renounces everything there is no possible compensation. Such a renunciation is incompatible with man's nature, for to take away all freedom from his will is to take away all morality from his actions. In short, a convention which stipulates absolute authority on the one side and unlimited obedience on the other is vain and contradictory. Is it not clear that we are under no obligations whatsoever towards a man from whom we have a right to demand everything? And does not this single condition, without equivalent, without exchange, involve the nullity of the act? For what right would my slave have against me, since all that he has belongs to me? His rights being mine, this right of me against myself is a meaningless phrase.

. . .

The Social Pact

I assume that men have reached a point at which the obstacles that endanger their preservation in the state of nature overcome by their resistance the forces which each individual can exert with a view to maintaining himself in that state. Then this primitive condition can no longer subsist, and the human race would perish unless it changed its mode of existence.

Now, as men cannot create any new forces, but only combine and direct those that exist, they have no other means of self-preservation than to form by aggregation a sum of forces which may overcome the resistance, to put them in action by a single motive power, and to make them work in concert.

This sum of forces can be produced only by the combination of many; but the strength and freedom of each man being the chief instruments of his preservation, how can he pledge them without injuring himself, and without neglecting the cares which he owes to himself? This difficulty, applied to my subject, may be expressed in these terms:—

"To find a form of association which may defend and protect with the whole force of the community the person and property of every associate, and by means of which each, coalescing with all, may nevertheless obey only himself, and remain as free as before." Such is the fundamental problem of which the social contract furnishes the solution.

The clauses of this contract are so determined by the nature of the act that the slightest modification would render them vain and ineffectual; so that, although they have never perhaps been formally enunciated, they are everywhere the same, everywhere tacitly admitted and recognised, until, the social pact being violated, each man regains his original rights and recovers his natural liberty, whilst losing the conventional liberty for which he renounced it.

These clauses, rightly understood, are reducible to one only, viz. the total alienation to the whole community of each associate with all his rights; for, in the first place, since each gives himself up entirely, the conditions are equal for all; and, the conditions being equal for all, no one has any interest in making them burdensome to others.

Further, the alienation being made without reserve, the union is as perfect as it can be, and an individual associate can no longer claim anything; for, if any rights were left to individuals, since there would be no common superior who could judge between them and the public, each, being on some point his own judge, would soon claim to be so on all; the state of nature would still subsist, and the association would necessarily become tyrannical or useless.

In short, each giving himself to all, gives himself to nobody; and as there is not one associate over whom we do not acquire the same rights which we concede to him ourselves, we gain the equivalent of all that we lose, and more power to preserve what we have.

If, then, we set aside what is not of the essence of the social contract, we shall find that it is reducible to the following terms: "Each of us puts in common his person and his whole power under the supreme direction of the general will; and in return we receive every member as an indivisible part of the whole."

Forthwith, instead of the individual personalities of all the contracting parties, this act of association produces a moral and collective body, which is composed of as many members as the assembly has voices, and which receives from this same act its unity, its common self (*moi*), its life, and its will. This public person, which is thus formed by the union of all the individual members, formerly took the name of *city*, and now takes that of *republic* or *body politic*, which is called by its members *State* when it is passive, *sovereign* when it is active, *power* when it is compared to similar bodies. With regard to the associates, they take collectively the name of *people*, and are called individually *citizens*, as participating in the sovereign power, and *subjects*, as subjected to the laws of the State. But these terms are often confused and are mistaken one for another; it is sufficient to know how to distinguish them when they are used with complete precision.

The Sovereign

We see from this formula that the act of association contains a reciprocal engagement between the public and individuals, and that every individual, contracting so to speak with himself, is engaged in a double relation, viz. as a member of the sovereign towards individuals, and as a member of the State towards the sovereign. But we cannot apply here the maxim of civil law that no one is bound by engagements made with himself; for there is a great difference between being bound to oneself and to a whole of which one forms part.

We must further observe that the public resolution which can bind all subjects to the sovereign in consequence of the two different relations under which each of them is regarded cannot, for a contrary reason, bind the sovereign to itself; and that accordingly it is contrary to the nature of the body politic for the sovereign to impose on itself a law which it cannot transgress. As it can only be considered under one and the same relation, it is in the position of an individual contracting with himself; whence we see that there is not, nor can be, any kind of fundamental law binding upon the body of the people, not even the social contract. This does not imply that such a body cannot perfectly well enter into engagements with others in what does not derogate from this contract; for, with regard to foreigners, it becomes a simple being, an individual.

But the body politic or sovereign, deriving its existence only from the sanctity of the contract, can never bind itself, even to others, in anything that derogates from the original act, such as alienation of some portion of itself, or submission to another sovereign. To violate the act by which it exists would be to annihilate itself; and what is nothing produces nothing.

So soon as the multitude is thus united in one body, it is impossible to injure one of the members without attacking the body, still less to injure the body without the members feeling the effects. Thus duty and interest alike oblige the two contracting parties to give mutual assistance; and the men themselves should seek to combine in this twofold relationship all the advantages which are attendant on it.

Now, the sovereign, being formed only of the individuals that compose it, neither has nor can have any interest contrary to theirs; consequently the sovereign power needs no guarantee towards its subjects, because it is impossible that the body should wish to injure all its members; and we shall see hereafter that it can injure no one as an individual. The sovereign, for the simple reason that it is so, is always everything that it ought to be.

But this is not the case as regards the relation of subjects to the sovereign, which, notwithstanding the common interest, would have no security for the performance of their engagements, unless it found means to ensure their fidelity.

Indeed, every individual may, as a man, have a particular will contrary to, or divergent from, the general will which he has as a citizen; his private interest may prompt him quite differently from the common interest; his absolute and naturally independent existence may make him regard what he owes to the common cause as a gratuitous contribution, the loss of which will be less harmful to others than the payment of it will be burdensome to him; and, regarding the moral person that constitutes the State as an imaginary being because it is not a man, he would be willing to enjoy the rights of a citizen without being willing to fulfil the duties of a subject. The progress of such injustice would bring about the ruin of the body politic.

In order, then, that the social pact may not be a vain formulary, it tacitly includes this engagement, which can alone give force to the others,—that whoever refuses to obey the general will shall be constrained to do so by the whole body; which means nothing else than that he shall be forced to be free; for such is the condition which, uniting every citizen to his native land, guarantees him from all personal dependence, a condition that ensures the control and working of the political machine, and alone renders legitimate civil engagements, which, without it, would be absurd and tyrannical, and subject to the most enormous abuses.

The Civil State

The passage from the state of nature to the civil state produces in man a very remarkable change, by substituting in his conduct justice for instinct, and by giving his actions the moral quality that they previously lacked. It is only when the voice of duty succeeds physical impulse, and law succeeds appetite, that man, who till then had regarded only himself, sees that he is obliged to act on other principles, and to consult his reason before listening to his inclinations. Although, in this state, he is deprived of many advantages that he derives from nature, he acquires equally great ones in return; his faculties are exercised and developed; his ideas are expanded; his feelings are ennobled; his whole soul is exalted to such a degree that, if the abuses of this new condition did not often degrade him below that from which he has emerged, he ought to bless without ceasing the happy moment that released him from it for ever, and transformed him from a stupid and ignorant animal into an intelligent being and a man.

Let us reduce this whole balance to terms easy to compare. What man loses by the social contract is his natural liberty and an unlimited right to do anything which tempts him and which he is able to attain; what he gains is civil liberty and property in all that he possesses. In order that we may not be mistaken about these compensations, we must clearly distinguish natural liberty, which is limited only by the powers of the individual, from civil liberty, which is limited by the general will; and possession, which is nothing but the result of force or the right of first occupancy, from property, which can be based only on a positive title.

Besides the preceding, we might add to the acquisitions of the civil state moral freedom, which alone renders man truly master of himself; for the impulse of mere appetite is slavery, while obedience to a self-prescribed law is liberty. But I have already said too much on this head, and the philosophical meaning of the term *liberty* does not belong to my present subject.

. . .

The Law

By the social compact we have given existence and life to the body politic; the question now is to endow it with movement and will by legislation. For the original act by which this body is formed and consolidated determines nothing in addition as to what it must do for its own preservation.

What is right and comfortable to order is such by the nature of things, and independently of human conventions. All justice comes from God, He alone is the source of it; but could we receive it direct from so lofty a source, we should need neither government nor laws. Without doubt there is a universal justice emanating from reason alone; but this justice, in order to be admitted among us, should be reciprocal. Regarding things from a human standpoint, the laws of justice are inoperative among men for want of a natural sanction; they only bring good to the wicked and evil to the just when the latter observe them with every one, and no one observes them in return. Conventions and laws, then, are necessary to couple rights with duties and apply justice to its object. In the state of nature, where everything is in common, I owe nothing to those to whom I have promised nothing; I recognize as belonging to others what is useless to me. This is not the case in the civil state, in which all rights are determined by law.

But then, finally, what is a law? So long as men are content to attach to this word only metaphysical ideas, they will continue to argue without being understood; and when they have stated what a law of nature is, they will know no better what a law of the State is.

I have already said that there is no general will with reference to a particular object. In fact, this particular object is either in the State or outside of it. If it is outside the State, a will which is foreign to it is not general in relation to it; and if it is within the State, it forms part of it; then there is formed between the whole and its part a relation which makes of it two separate beings, of which the part is one, and the whole, less this same part, is the other. But the whole less one part is not the whole, and so long as the relation subsists, there is no longer any whole, but two unequal parts; whence it follows that the will of the one is no longer general in relation to the other.

But when the whole people decree concerning the whole people, they consider themselves alone; and if a relation is then constituted, it is between the whole object under one point of view and the whole object under another point of view, without any division at all. Then the matter respecting which they decree is general like the will that decrees. It is this act that I call a law.

When I say that the object of the laws is always general, I mean that the law considers subjects collectively, and actions as abstract, never a man as an individual nor a particular action. Thus the law may indeed decree that there shall be privileges, but cannot confer them on any person by name; the law can create several classes of citizens, and even assign the qualifications which shall entitle them to rank in these classes, but it cannot nominate such and such persons to be admitted to them; it can establish a royal government and a hereditary succession, but cannot elect a king or appoint a royal family; in a word, no function which had reference to an individual object appertains to the legislative power.

From this standpoint we see immediately that it is no longer necessary to ask whose office it is to make laws, since they are acts of the general will; nor whether the prince is above the laws, since he is a member of the State; nor whether the law can be unjust, since no one is unjust to himself; nor how we are free and yet subject to the laws, since the laws are only registers of our wills.

We see, further, that since the law combines the universality of the will with the universality of the object, whatever any man prescribes on his own authority is not a law; and whatever the sovereign itself prescribes respecting a particular object is not a law, but a decree, not an act of sovereignty, but of magistracy.

I therefore call any State a republic which is governed by laws, under whatever form of administration it may be; for then only does the public interest predominate and the commonwealth count for something. Every legitimate government is republican; I will explain hereafter what government is.

Laws are properly only the conditions of civil association. The people, being subjected to the laws, should be the authors of them; it concerns only the associates to determine the conditions of association. But how will they be determined? Will it be by a common agreement, by a sudden inspiration? Has the body politic an organ for expressing its will? Who will give it the foresight necessary to frame its acts and publish them at the outset? Or how shall it declare them in the hour of need? How would a blind multitude, which often knows not what it wishes because it rarely knows what is good for it, execute of itself an enterprise so great, so difficult, as a system of legislation? Of themselves, the people always desire what is good, but do not always discern it. The general will is always right, but the judgment which guides it is not always enlightened. It must be made to see objects as they are, sometimes as they ought to appear; it must be shown the good path that it is seeking, and guarded from the seduction of private interests; it must be made to observe closely times and places, and to balance the attraction of immediate and palpable advantages against the danger of remote and concealed evils. Individuals see the good which they reject; the public desire the good which they do not see. All alike have need of guides. The former must be compelled to conform their wills to their reason; the people must be taught to know what they require. Then from the public enlightenment results the union of the understanding and the will in the social body; and from that the close co-operation of the parts, and, lastly, the maximum power of the whole. Hence arises the need of a legislator.

4

SIR JOHN WOLFENDEN

(1906–)

*Evolution of British Attitudes Toward Homosexuality**

This article presents both a historical and a philosophic account of the discussions of the famous Wolfenden Committee appointed in England in 1956. The committee was established to consider the laws and practices related to homosexuality and prostitution in the United Kingdom. The purpose of the committee was to advise the government on what general principles might be applied to establish a consistent policy of law on these two specific types of behavior. The committee's recommendations were that homosexual behavior between consenting males in private should not be the concern of the criminal law, but that solicitation by prostitutes in public places ought to be illegal. The committee concluded that "the function of the criminal law in the area of moral behavior is to safeguard public order and decency and to protect those who for whatever reason are properly regarded as weak." The fact that an act is considered immoral ought not be involved in a decision of its criminality.

* From *The American Journal of Psychiatry,* 125 (1968), pp. 792–797.
Used by kind permission of the editor and Sir John Wolfenden.

IN order to dispel any exaggerated expectations, I want to make one thing clear from the start. I have no medical or legal qualifications of any kind. Rather more than 12 years ago I became involved, by accident and at the invitation of the then British Secretaries of State for Home Affairs and for Scotland, in the chairmanship of a departmental committee which they set up to inquire into homosexual offenses and offenses in connection with prostitution.

The General Approach of the Committee

Our precise terms of reference are perhaps worth quoting so that there will be no misunderstanding of what we were and what we were not to examine. We were instructed to consider: a) the law and practice relating to homosexual offenses and the treatment of persons convicted of such offenses by the courts; and b) the law and practice relating to offenses against the criminal law in connection with prostitution and solicitation for immoral purposes; and to report what changes, if any, were in our opinion desirable.

We were not, you will observe, concerned with homosexuality as such or with prostitution as such. This is a point which must be blindingly obvious to a gathering like this present one, but it is a point which we found the greatest difficulty in driving into the heads of the general public in Britain. We were concerned with offenses against the law in these two areas, and, in the case of homosexual offenses, with the treatment of offenders. We were also, for technical reasons which do not concern us here, a departmental committee, not a royal commission.

We were not a committee of experts. Rather, we were a jury listening to the technical evidence of experts, trying to weigh it, and trying to make up our minds on it. We had two distinguished lawyers and two distinguished doctors among our number, but their primary duty was less to behave as experts themselves than to interpret to the rest of us the technical evidence which others gave—and a highly important contribution they made.

At the first meeting I ventured to make three preliminary observations, along the following lines.

> We are assembled to try to advise the government on topics which are deeply controversial and to many people extremely distasteful. So let us be clear from the start that whatever we recommend, and I have no idea what that will be, it will almost certainly be passionately opposed by approximately one-half of the population. In short, we can't win. So our business is to listen to the evidence and make up our own minds, never looking over our shoulders to see what is likely to be the outside world's reception of our conclusions, whatever they may turn out to be.
>
> Secondly, I suggest that we should not be content with piecemeal recommendations about particular parts of our field. I hope we may be able to find some valid general principles and then apply them to our special concerns, so that we have a logical position which can be logically defended. Thirdly, although we are technically reporting to the Secretaries of State I hope we may produce a report which will be intelligible to the ordinary intelligent man and woman and may, whatever it turns out to say, be of some general educational value to the country as a whole.

That was our general line of approach, and for three years we worked fairly hard along that line.

It is perhaps worth pointing out that it is nearly 13 years ago that we started, and during that time things have changed quite a bit in many parts of the world. So perhaps a word about the background in Britain at that time is not out of place.

In the three or four years before our appointment there had been a number of rather sensational cases of prosecutions for homosexual offenses. There had been in consequence two quite different kinds of uneasiness expressed. On the one hand there was a widely-voiced fear that what was called "this kind of behavior" was becoming increasingly widespread, especially in certain intellectual and artistic circles, and was damaging the nation's moral fibre. On the other hand, there were increasingly open condemnations, by those who regarded themselves as liberal and progressive, not only of the law as it stood but of the arbitrary and almost capricious way in which it was being applied.

Simultaneously, on the other half of our remit, there was increasing alarm and indignation about the blatant and shameless behavior of prostitutes in public places in London and some of the provincial cities. There was a clamor that "something must be done." But nobody quite knew what. So, in accordance with the best governmental tradition, a departmental committee was set up to investigate.

I will not weary you with a blow-by-blow account of our deliberations or of the reception of our report,* when it was published by the press and the public. But there was one event which I hope you will forgive me for narrating in some detail, because it turned out to be cardinal to our whole thinking. We began, of course, by studying and trying to absorb preliminary memoranda from a wide variety of sources, official and unofficial; after we had done that we thought we were ready to hear oral evidence.

Our first oral witness was the then Lord Chief Justice of England, Lord Goddard. It is rather a disquieting experience for a layman like myself to have in the witness box, as it were, the Lord Chief Justice, open to interrogation and rigorous examination. Fortunately, I had known him personally for many years, so embarrassment was diluted by former acquaintance; but it was still a rather unusual and piquant situation. I explained, as he already knew, that I was not versed in the law. But, still seeking for underlying general principles, I asked him if he could help me, in our consideration of the law on these matters, by telling me what sort of actions he thought ought to be crimes.

After a long and impressive pause he said that that was a question which in that form he could not answer. I asked him if he would put it into a form in which he could answer it, and then answer it. There followed a fascinating hour of conversation on the nature of crime; and although you must not attribute to Lord Goddard anything of what follows it is only right to acknowledge that it was he who knowingly or unknowingly set our feet on the path we trod to the end.

A crime, and here I begin to dogmatize, is any action about which the competent legislative authority says "If you do that we shall punish you." The competent legislative authority may be, in Britain, Parliament in national affairs, or the headmaster of a school, or the relevant committee of a professional organization or a trade union. There is no form of behavior which of its own nature is criminal; an action is only criminal if somebody who is empowered to say so says that it is.

There are, on the other hand, ways of behaving which many people would regard as immoral or sinful. The word "sin" is not very popular nowadays (however prevalent the forms of behavior to which it applies) and the religious and theological presuppositions which underlie it are by no means universally accepted. But even if "sin" is out of fashion (the word, I mean, not the conduct) there still remain many people who would say that such and such an action is "wrong." Or if even that seems too direct and stark a monosyllable, they would agree that such and such an action was "not right."

* Report of the Committee on Homosexual Offences and Prostitution, 1957.

They may make this judgment for any one of a variety of reasons, depending on their ethical views—that it causes unhappiness, that it is contrary to man's nature, that it is dysgenic, or simply that they don't like it. Whatever their basic moral theory, there are some actions which they call good or right and others which they call bad or wrong or (at the very least) not right. All these adjectives imply moral judgment on some basis or other.

The question for the legislator, the question we could not avoid because we were required to report what changes, if any, in the law we thought ought to be made, was this: What actions, recognized as being wrong or sinful or not right, ought to be made into crimes? There is one circle, so to speak, of actions to which moral adjectives properly belong; they are good or bad, right or wrong. There is another to which adjectives of criminality belong; they are lawful or unlawful, legal or illegal. The question is how far these circles should be made to be identical.

In some societies there is no problem. Under the theocracy of Calvin's Geneva, it was clear that the laws must be such as to punish every action which that theocracy regards as sinful. If a headmaster makes the rules of a school for immature boys he can do so on the basis that if any boy obeys all the rules he will be living the moral life. But I myself happened to have had an experience which cured me of that particular point of view.

Many years ago I too was headmaster of a school. I was in fact in that context what I have earlier called "the competent legislative authority," and I had hauled before me one day, for the appropriate disciplinary action, a boy who had been apprehended in a normal schoolboy crime, copying the answers from the notebook of the boy next to him. Before proceeding with the processes of justice I asked him if he had anything to say. He said "Yes, sir." (He was a very nasty small boy, who is now, I expect, making a lot of money at the bar.) I asked him what. He said "Sir, there is no school rule against it."

You see. If you once begin to legislate in order to ensure that compliance with the law is synonymous with the moral life, you have to legislate for everything; and although that may be excusable in a society of immature persons (though I do not myself believe that it is) it seems to me to be quite inappropriate behavior in those who are legislating for adult mature citizens of a democracy.

The Disjunction of Crime and Immorality

Short of that complete identification of the criminal and the immoral, is there any position which makes more sense? We did not, of course, set the criminal and the morally wrong in opposition or antithesis to each other. But we did set them in disjunction from one another; and this is, I believe, a position which is confirmed by experience and common sense.

There are many daily infringements of the law which their perpetrators would not regard as immoral or repugnant to conscience. I do not know how it is with you, but I am prepared to believe that I break one law or another every day without knowing it—and if I do not know I am doing it my moral withers are unwrung. If I were slightly to exceed a speed limit (which I never do, because I do not drive a car) I should not, I suspect, regard myself as morally culpable in any very serious sense.

More important, the converse is true. There are a good many ways of behaving which most people would regard as morally reprehensible but which are not against the laws. Acts of meanness, selfishness, cowardice, cruelty are not criminal offenses except in those rare particular cases where laws have been made about them.

More important for our present concern, there are a good many forms of sexual behavior which most people would regard as deserving moral condemnation but which are not offenses against the criminal law. Adultery, in England at least (there is a fascinating doubt about the law in Scotland), is not a legal offense; nor, for that matter is fornication; nor, for some odd reason, is homosexual behavior between women. Yet all of these, in various degrees, might well be considered by many to be sinful, or wrong, or (at the very least) not right. So I think we were not being outrageous or provocative or mischievous when we suggested that it is legitimate to draw a distinction between what we may perhaps call, in time-saving monosyllables, crime and sin.

Granted that this is so, we go back to the question I asked of Lord Goddard: "What sort of actions ought to be crimes?" Or, to put it another way, at what level and in what instances or on what general principles ought the competent legislative authority to designate as crimes forms of behavior which are held to be sins?

Problems arise at once. I said "held to be sins." So held by whom? Whose pattern of moral judgments is to determine legislation? It is easy enough, as I hinted earlier, if one lives in Calvin's Geneva; and it may be that there were parallels in the early history of New England. But if you were to start with the competent legislative authority in Britain, our two Houses of Parliament, it would be mighty difficult to discover an agreed pattern or (as the lately fashionable word is) consensus of moral judgments that legislation could translate into a code of criminal law. Are we talking about sin as defined by Roman Catholic theology or by austere Puritanism? Are we talking about the current sexual standards of our mid-20th-century permissive society?

That is one problem. The second is this: if you once try to enshrine in the criminal law the accepted standards of any one age, how do you ever change the law if the accepted standards change? It is a commonplace that different standards of sexual behavior are the accepted standards in different places at the same time and in the same place at different times. Which standards at which place at which time should determine if a man is to be sent to prison?

The Proper Function of the Criminal Law

Our own conclusion—and it is time I came out with it instead of continuing to ask these tedious rhetorical questions—was this. We came to the view that the function of the criminal law in this area of behavior is to safeguard public order and decency and to protect those who for whatever reason are properly regarded as the weak and therefore deserving society's protection. We concluded that in this area the private behavior of an adult individual, male or female, is no concern of the criminal law. I stress "an adult individual" because we were as deeply concerned as any other collection of 15 citizens to protect children, the mentally weak, and the officially subordinate. But I suggest that if this guideline is followed a coherent and logical pattern emerges. Let me be more explicit.

It is no concern of the criminal law if two adult consenting males indulge in homosexual behavior in private. It may be a form of behavior of which you and I disapprove; we may be disgusted by it; we may, on all sorts of moral grounds, find it repugnant. But none of those subjective reactions of ours have anything to do with criminality. Every day I come across forms of behavior to which all these descriptions apply; but that fact does not entitle me to demand that those who behave in this way should be sent to prison.

I disapprove of adultery; and so do a good many other people. We do so because we think this sort of behavior is immoral, or wrong, or "not right." But I do not demand that adulterers and adulteresses should be subject to the criminal law. If men and women, or men and men, or women and women, indulge in sexual acts in public, I not only disapprove, I think the law ought to do something about it. And I think this because I think the law's business is to protect me and my wife and children from affronts against decency.

I do not think this because I think such behavior immoral. That seems to me not to be the point. I do not think the law has a right to enter, as it were, anybody's bedroom. Sexual behavior is nobody's business except that of those immediately concerned, unless their behavior offends against public order and decency.

This is the basis in logic for the two halves of our recommendations, that homosexual behavior between consenting males in private should be no concern of the criminal law and that solicitation by prostitutes in public places should render them liable to prosecution. We were not concerned with prostitution or fornication as such; we were concerned with the criminal law and its function as the protector of public order and decency.

It is easy to say that the Street Offences Act, which was introduced on the basis of our recommendations, did no more than sweep prostitutes off the streets and under the carpet—in fact into the striptease joints and cryptobrothels of notorious parts of London. Again, my withers are unwrung. We were not so starry-eyed as to imagine that prostitution can be abolished. Our objective was to make the streets of London tolerable for the ordinary citizen and safe for an attractive girl who is not a prostitute. And if prostitution continues, in London or elsewhere, I am not surprised.

Nor am I moved when I am told that I am a hypocrite or a self-deceiver if I think that because the streets of London are now less thickly populated by nightwalkers or loiterers the standard of sexual morals in London has improved. Quite simply, our objective was not social reform; it was something which was quite different and which was within our terms of reference as a committee. I may have all kinds of private and personal views about prostitution, but I am not so arrogant as to suppose that my personal views about sexual morality should be sanctified by the criminal law.

Legal Versus Moral Responsibility

May I give just one example of the difficulty which quite intelligent people seem to have in making this distinction? After our report was published I was in conversation with an extremely distinguished ecclesiastic in Britain, an old friend of mine. He took me sharply to task for what he called discrimination against the women. "Surely," he said, "you would agree that the man who goes with a prostitute is as guilty as the woman is." "My dear Archbishop," I said—because that is what he was—"Of course the man is as guilty as the woman is of what you and I would both call the sin of fornication. The man is not as guilty as the woman is of what I regard as the offense against public order and decency involved in cluttering up the streets of London and soliciting all the available male passersby."

I have tried to explain what our concerns were and what they were not. I am well aware that these are highly controversial matters, and I have heard much talk—perhaps more than most people—of national decadence, of unnatural behavior, or disgust and scorn. I believe, still, after 13 years, that we were right.

In all the debates in both Houses of Parliament, all the arguments, prejudices, convictions, apprehensions, indignations, sympathies have been marshalled, deployed, and recapitulated time after time. In the end what I regard as unsentimental logic prevailed. Gradually public opinion changed, not dramatically overnight but by what I regard as a dispassionate assessment of the nature of human beings and the nature of the criminal law. In the end, on the initiative of a Conservative peer, the Earl of Arran, in the House of Lords, and with the support of an eloquent advocate, Mr. Leo Abse, in the House of Commons, the law in Britain was changed, almost exactly ten years after the publication of our report.

It is not for me to say whether or not, from the legal or medical point of view, this is a good thing. Still less is it for me to say whether other countries, whose laws are what Britain's used to be, should change them. I never thought it my business, at home, to campaign for a change in the law. My colleagues and I took the responsibility of making certain recommendations for what we thought to be valid and defensible reasons. The legislators eventually accepted those recommendations and wrote them into the law. It is for them and for you to judge what public opinion is in these matters and to decide how far the law should lead public opinion or follow it. I am content to have our stated position judged in terms of rational thinking and human happiness.

5

JOHN STUART MILL
(1806–1873)

*Of the Limits to the Authority of Society over the Individual**

In his famous essay, On Liberty, *Mill discusses some of the same issues which confronted the Wolfenden Committee. He argues that the greatest possible latitude in personal freedom ought to be the aim of society. The government should use as its guideline what Mill calls the "self-protection principle," which maintains that society is justified in interfering with the conduct of individuals only in so far as it may harm others. The individual's own good is not sufficient reason for a law. Any act of what Mill calls private morality (self-regarding acts) is no concern of law. Society may only advise or caution on private matters. Mill argues that in no case ought the moral attitudes of the majority be the grounds for law. Certainly men have always judged others on the basis of their own standards of conduct and feelings, but this has led to religious and racial persecution in civil societies. If law were to use this tendency as a principle of public interference in the conduct of individuals which does not affect the public, then individual human liberty would be a meaningless idea.*

* *From* John Stuart Mill, *On Liberty* (London: John W. Parker & Son, 1859), Chap. IV.

WHAT, then, is the rightful limit to the sovereignty of the individual over himself? Where does the authority of society begin? How much of human life should be assigned to individuality, and how much to society?

Each will receive its proper share, if each has that which more particularly concerns it. To individuality should belong the part of life in which it is chiefly the individual that is interested; to society, the part which chiefly interests society.

Rules of Social Conduct

Though society is not founded on a contract, and though no good purpose is answered by inventing a contract in order to deduce social obligations from it, everyone who receives the protection of society owes a return for the benefit, and the fact of living in society renders it indispensable that each should be bound to observe a certain line of conduct towards the rest. This conduct consists, *first*, in not injuring the interests of one another; or rather certain interests, which, either by express legal provision or by tacit understanding, ought to be considered as rights; and *secondly*, in each person's bearing his share (to be fixed on some equitable principle) of the labors and sacrifices incurred for defending the society or its members from injury and molestation. These conditions society is justified in enforcing, at all costs to those who endeavor to withhold fulfillment. Nor is this all that society may do. The acts of an individual may be hurtful to others, or wanting in due consideration for their welfare, without going to the length of violating any of their constituted rights. The offender may then be justly punished by opinion, though not by law. As soon as any part of a person's conduct affects prejudicially the interests of others, society has jurisdiction over it, and the question whether the general welfare will or will not be promoted by interfering with it, becomes open to discussion. But there is no room for entertaining any such question when a person's conduct affects the interests of no persons besides himself, or need not affect them unless they like (all the persons concerned being of full age, and the ordinary amount of understanding). In all such cases, there should be perfect freedom, legal and social, to do the action and stand the consequences.

Compulsion versus Persuasion

It would be a great misunderstanding of this doctrine to suppose that it is one of selfish indifference, which pretends that human beings have no business with each other's conduct in life, and that they should not concern themselves about the well-doing or well-being of one another, unless their own interest is involved. Instead of any diminution, there is need of a great increase of disinterested exertion to promote the good of others. But disinterested benevolence can find other instruments to persuade people to their good than whips and scourges, either of the literal or the metaphorical sort. I am the last person to undervalue the self-regarding virtues: they are only second in importance, if even second, to the social. It is equally the business of education to cultivate both. But even education works by conviction and persuasion as well as by compulsion, and it is by the former only that, when the period of education is passed, the self-regarding virtues should be inculcated. Human beings owe to each other help to distinguish the better from the worse, and encouragement to choose the former and avoid the latter. They should be forever stimulating each other to increased exercise of their higher faculties, and increased direction of their feelings and aims towards wise instead of foolish, elevating instead of degrading, objects and contemplations. But neither one person, nor any number of persons, is warranted in saying to another human creature of ripe years, that he shall not do with his life for his own benefit what he chooses to do with it. He is the person most interested in his own well-being: the interest which any other person, except in cases of strong personal attachment, can have in it, is trifling, compared with that which he himself has; the interest which society has in him individually (except as to his conduct to others) is fractional, and altogether indirect; while with respect to his own feelings and circumstances, the most ordinary man or woman has means of knowledge immeasurably surpassing those that can be possessed by anyone else. The interference of society to overrule his judgment and purposes in what only regards himself must be grounded on general presumptions; which may be altogether wrong, and even if right, are as likely as not to be misapplied to individual cases, by persons no better acquainted with the circumstances of such cases than those are who look at them merely from without. In this department, therefore, of human affairs, individuality has its proper field of action. In the conduct of human beings towards one another it is necessary that general rules should for the most part be observed, in order that people may know what they have to expect; but in each person's own concerns his individual spontaneity is entitled to free exercise. Considerations to aid his judgment, exhortations to strengthen his will, may be offered to him, even obtruded on him, by others: but he himself is the final judge. All errors which he is likely to commit against advice and warning are far outweighed by the evil of allowing others to constrain him to what they deem his good.

Consequences of Actions Harmful Only to Self

I do not mean that the feelings with which a person is regarded by others ought not to be in any way affected by his self-regarding qualities or deficiencies. This is neither possible nor desirable. If he is eminent in any of the qualities which conduce to his own good, he is, so far, a proper object of admiration. He is so much the nearer to the ideal perfection of human nature. If he is grossly deficient in those qualities, a sentiment the opposite of admiration will follow. There is a degree of folly, and a degree of what may be called (though the phrase is not unobjectionable) lowness or depravation of taste, which, though it cannot justify doing harm to the person who manifests it, renders him necessarily and properly a subject of distaste, or, in extreme cases, even of contempt: a person could not have the opposite qualities in due strength without entertaining these feelings. Though doing no wrong to anyone, a person may so act as to compel us to judge him, and feel to him, as a fool, or as a being of an inferior order; and since this judgment and feeling are a fact which he would prefer to avoid, it is doing him a service to warn him of it beforehand, as of any other disagreeable consequence to which he exposes himself. It would be well, indeed, if this good office were much more freely rendered than the common notions of politeness at present permit, and if one person could honestly point out to another that he thinks him in fault, without being considered unmannerly or presuming. We have a right, also, in various ways, to act upon our unfavorable opinion of anyone, not to the oppression of his individuality, but in the exercise of ours. We are not bound, for example, to seek his society; we have a right to avoid it (though not to parade the avoidance), for we have a right to choose the society most acceptable to us. We have a right, and it may be our duty, to caution others against him, if we think his example or conversation likely to have a pernicious effect on those with whom he associates. We may give others a preference over him in optional good offices, except those which tend to his improvement. In these various modes a person may suffer very severe penalties at the hands of others for faults which directly concern only himself; but he suffers these penalties only in so far as they are the natural and, as it were, the spontaneous consequences of the faults themselves, not because they are purposely inflicted on him for the sake of punishment. A person who shows rashness, obstinacy, self-conceit—who cannot live within moderate means —who cannot restrain himself from hurtful indulgences—who pursues animal pleasures at the expense of those of feeling and intellect—must expect to be lowered in the opinion of others, and to have a less share of their favorable sentiments; but of this he has no right to complain, unless he has merited their favor by special excellence in his social relations, and has thus established a title to their good offices, which is not affected by his demerits towards himself.

Types of Actions Injurious to Others

What I contend for is, that the inconveniences which are strictly inseparable from the unfavorable judgment of others, are the only ones to which a person should ever be subjected for that portion of his conduct and character which concerns his own good, but which does not affect the interest of others in their relations with him. Acts injurious to others require a totally different treatment. Encroachment on their rights; infliction on them of any loss or damage not justified by his own rights; falsehood or duplicity in dealing with them; unfair or ungenerous use of advantages over them; even selfish abstinence from defending them against injury—these are fit objects of moral reprobation, and, in grave cases, of moral retribution and punishment. And not only these acts, but the dispositions which lead to them, are properly immoral, and fit subjects of disapprobation which may rise to abhorrence. Cruelty of disposition; malice and ill-nature; that most anti-social and odious of all passions, envy; dissimulation and insincerity, irascibility on insufficient cause, and resentment disproportioned to the provocation; the love of domineering over others; the desire to engross more than one's share of advantages (the *πλεονεξια* of the Greeks); the pride which derives gratification from the abasement of others; the egotism which thinks self and its concerns more important than everything else, and decides all doubtful questions in its own favor;—these are moral vices, and constitute a bad and odious moral character: unlike the self-regarding faults previously mentioned, which are not properly immoralities, and to whatever pitch they may be carried, do not constitute wickedness. They may be proofs of any amount of folly, or want of personal dignity and self-respect; but they are only a subject of moral reprobation when they involve a breach of duty to others, for whose sake the individual is bound to have care for himself. What are called duties to ourselves are not socially obligatory, unless circumstances render them at the same time duties to others. The term "duty to oneself," when it means anything more than prudence, means self-respect or self-development, and for none of these is anyone accountable to his fellow-creatures, because for none of them is it for the good of mankind that he be held accountable to them.

Distinction between Punishment for Offense against Self and Offense against Others

The distinction between the loss of consideration which a person may rightly incur by defect of prudence or of personal dignity, and the reprobation which is due to him for an offense against the rights of others, is not a merely nominal distinction. It makes a vast difference both in our feelings and in our conduct towards him whether he displeases us in things in which we think we have a right to control him, or in things in which we know that we have not. If he displeases us, we may express our distaste, and we may stand aloof from a person as well as from a thing that displeases us; but we shall not therefore feel called on to make his life uncomfortable. We shall reflect that he already bears, or will bear, the whole penalty of his error; if he spoils his life by mismanagement, we shall not, for that reason, desire to spoil it still further: instead of wishing to punish him, we shall rather endeavor to alleviate his punishment, by showing him how he may avoid or cure the evils his conduct tends to bring upon him. He may be to us an object of pity, perhaps of dislike, but not of anger or resentment; we shall not treat him like an enemy of society: the worst we shall think ourselves justified in doing is leaving him to himself, if we do not interfere benevolently by showing interest or concern for him. It is far otherwise if he has infringed the rules necessary for the protection of his fellow-creatures, individually or collectively. The evil consequences of his acts do not then fall on himself, but on others; and society, as the protector of all its members, must retaliate on him; must inflict pain on him for the express purpose of punishment, and must take care that it be sufficiently severe. In the one case, he is an offender at our bar, and we are called on not only to sit in judgment on him, but, in one shape or another, to execute our own sentence: in the other case, it is not our part to inflict any suffering on him, except what may incidentally follow from our using the same liberty in the regulation of our own affairs, which we allow to him in his.

Does a Person's Offense Ever Harm only Himself?

The distinction here pointed out between the part of a person's life which concerns only himself, and that which concerns others, many persons will refuse to admit. How (it may be asked) can any part of the conduct of a member of society be a matter of indifference to the other members? No person is an entirely isolated being; it is impossible for a person to do anything seriously or permanently hurtful to himself, without mischief reaching at least to his near connections, and often far beyond them. If he injures his property, he does harm to those who directly or indirectly derived support from it, and usually diminishes, by a greater or less amount, the general resources of the community. If he deteriorates his bodily or mental faculties, he not only brings evil upon all who depended on him for any portion of their happiness, but disqualifies himself for rendering the services which he owes to his fellow-creatures generally; perhaps becomes a burden on their affection or benevolence; and if such conduct were very frequent, hardly an offense that is committed would detract more from the general sum of good. Finally, if by his vices or follies a person does no direct harm to others, he is nevertheless (it may be said) injurious by his example; and ought to be compelled to control himself, for the sake of those whom the sight or knowledge of his conduct might corrupt or mislead.

And even (it will be added) if the consequences of misconduct could be confined to the vicious or thoughtless individual, ought society to abandon to their own guidance those who are manifestly unfit for it? If protection against themselves is confessedly due to children and persons under age, is not society equally bound to afford it to persons of mature years who are equally incapable of self-government? If gambling, or drunkenness, or incontinence, or idleness, or uncleanliness, are as injurious to happiness, and as great a hindrance to improvement, as many or most of the acts prohibited by law, why (it may be asked) should not law, so far as is consistent with practicability and social convenience, endeavor to repress these also? And as a supplement to the unavoidable imperfections of law, ought not opinion at least to organize a powerful police against these vices, and visit rigidly with social penalties those who are known to practice them? There is no question here (it may be said) about restricting individuality, or impeding the trial of new and original experiments in living. The only things it is sought to prevent are things which have been tried and condemned from the beginning of the world until now; things which experience has shown not to be useful or suitable to any person's individuality. There must be some length of time and amount of experience after which a moral or prudential truth may be regarded as established: and it is merely desired to prevent generation after generation from falling over the same precipice which has been fatal to their predecessors.

When an Offense against the Self Becomes an Offense against Others

I fully admit that the mischief which a person does to himself may seriously affect, both through their sympathies and their interests, those nearly connected with him and, in a minor degree, society at large. When, by conduct of this sort, a person is led to violate a distinct and assignable obligation to any other person or persons, the case is taken out of the self-regarding class, and becomes amenable to moral disapprobation in the proper sense of the term. If, for example, a man, through intemperance or extravagance, becomes unable to pay his debts, or, having undertaken the moral responsibility of a family, becomes from the same cause incapable of supporting or educating them, he is deservedly reprobated, and might be justly punished; but it is for the breach of duty to his family or creditors, not for the extravagance. If the resources which ought to have been devoted to them, had been diverted from them for the most prudent investment, the moral culpability would have been the same. George Barnwell murdered his uncle to get money for his mistress, but if he had done it to set himself up in business, he would equally have been hanged. Again, in the frequent case of a man who causes grief to his family by addiction to bad habits, he deserves reproach for his unkindness or ingratitude; but so he may for cultivating habits not in themselves vicious, if they are painful to those with whom he passes his life, or who from personal ties are dependent on him for their comfort. Whoever fails in the consideration generally due to the interests and feelings of others, not being compelled by some more imperative duty, or justified by allowable self-preference, is a subject of moral disapprobation for that failure, but not for the cause of it, nor for the errors, merely personal to himself, which may have remotely led to it. In like manner, when a person disables himself, by conduct purely self-regarding, from the performance of some definite duty incumbent on him to the public, he is guilty of a social offense. No person ought to be punished simply for being drunk; but a soldier or a policeman should be punished for being drunk on duty. Whenever, in short, there is a definite damage, or a definite risk of damage, either to an individual or to the public, the case is taken out of the province of liberty, and placed in that of morality or law.

But with regard to the merely contingent, or, as it may be called, constructive injury which a person causes to society, by conduct which neither violates any specific duty to the public, nor occasions perceptible hurt to any assignable individual except himself, the inconvenience is one which society can afford to bear, for the sake of the greater good of human freedom. If grown persons are to be punished for not taking proper care of themselves, I would rather it were for their own sake, than under pretense of preventing them from impairing their capacity of rendering to society benefits which society does not pretend it has a right to exact. But I cannot consent to argue the point as if society had no means of bringing its weaker members up to its ordinary standard of rational conduct, except waiting till they do something irrational, and then punishing them, legally or morally, for it. Society has had absolute power over them during all the early portion of their existence: it has had the whole period of childhood and nonage in which to try whether it could make them capable of rational conduct in life. The existing generation is master both of the training and the entire circumstances of the generation to come; it cannot indeed make them perfectly wise and good, because it is itself so lamentably deficient in goodness and wisdom; and its best efforts are not always, in individual cases, its most successful ones; but it is perfectly well able to make the rising generation, as a whole, as good as, and a little better than, itself. If society lets any considerable number of its members grow up mere children, incapable of being acted on by rational consideration of distant motives, society has itself to blame for the consequences. Armed not only with all the powers of education, but with the ascendency which the authority of a received opinion always exercises over the minds who are least fitted to judge for themselves; and aided by the *natural* penalties which cannot be prevented from falling on those who incur the distaste or the contempt of those who know them; let not society pretend that it needs, besides all this, the power to issue commands and enforce obedience in the personal concerns of individuals, in which, on all principles of justice and policy, the decision ought to rest with those who are to abide the consequences. Nor is there anything which tends more to discredit and frustrate the better means of influencing conduct than a resort to the worse. If there be among those whom it is attempted to coerce into prudence or temperance any of the material of which vigorous and independent characters are made, they will infallibly rebel against the yoke. No such person will ever feel that others have a right to control him in his concerns, such as they have to prevent him from injuring them in theirs; and it easily comes to be considered a mark of spirit and courage to fly in the face of such usurped authority, and do with ostentation the exact opposite of what it enjoins; as in the fashion of grossness which succeeded, in the time of Charles II, to the fanatical moral intolerance of the Puritans. With respect to what is said of the necessity of protecting society from the bad example set to others by the vicious or the self-indulgent, it is true that bad example may have a pernicious effect, especially the example of doing wrong to others with impunity to the wrong-doer. But we are now speaking of conduct which, while it does no wrong to others, is supposed to do great harm to the agent himself: and I do not see how those who believe this can think otherwise than that the example, on the whole, must be more salutary than hurtful; since, if it displays the misconduct, it displays also the painful or degrading consequences which, if the conduct is justly censured, must be supposed to be in all or most cases attendant on it.

Invalidity of Many of the Interferences by the Public

But the strongest of all the arguments against the interference of the public with purely personal conduct is that, when it does interfere, the odds are that it interferes wrongly, and in the wrong place. On questions of social morality, of duty to others, the opinion of the public, that is, of an overruling majority, though often wrong, is likely to be still oftener right; because on such questions they are only required to judge of their own interests; of the manner in which some mode of conduct, if allowed to be practiced, would affect themselves. But the opinion of a similar majority, imposed as a law on the minority, on questions of self-regarding conduct, is quite as likely to be wrong as right; for in these cases public opinion means, at the best, some people's opinion of what is good or bad for other people; while very often it does not even mean that; the public, with the most perfect indifference, passing over the pleasure or convenience of those whose conduct they censure, and considering only their own preference. There are many who consider as an injury to themselves any conduct which they have a distaste for, and resent it as an outrage to their feelings; as a religious bigot, when charged with disregarding the religious feelings of others, has been known to retort that they disregard his feelings, by persisting in their abominable worship or creed. But there is no parity between the feeling of a person for his own opinion, and the feeling of another who is offended at his holding it; no more than between the desire of a thief to take a purse, and the desire of the right owner to keep it. And a person's taste is as much his own peculiar concern as his opinion or his purse. It is easy for anyone to imagine an ideal public which leaves the freedom and choice of individuals in all uncertain matters undisturbed, and only requires them to abstain from modes of conduct which universal experience has condemned. But where has there been seen a public which set any such limit to its censorship? or when does the public trouble itself about universal experience? In its interferences with personal conduct it is seldom thinking of anything but the enormity of acting or feeling differently from itself; and this standard of judgment, thinly disguised, is held up to mankind as the dictate of religion and philosophy, by nine-tenths of all moralists and speculative writers. These teach that things are right because they are right; because we feel them to be so. They tell us to search in our own minds and hearts for laws of conduct binding on ourselves and on all others. What can the poor public do but apply these instructions, and make their own personal feelings of good and evil, if they are tolerably unanimous in them, obligatory on all the world?

6

LORD DEVLIN
(1905–)

*Law, Democracy and Morality**

Devlin has been a powerful and vocal opponent of the libertarian point of view as expressed by the Wolfenden Committee and John Stuart Mill. In his famous The Enforcement of Morals *lecture, Devlin defended the position that morality must be the basis of criminal law. His reasoning was that a society is nothing more than its basic cohesive moral beliefs. Society not only has the right to punish immorality, it is obligated to do so to preserve itself. Society cannot exist without morals. What then is the duty of the lawmaker in a democracy, Devlin asks. In this selection, Devlin attempts to wrestle with that issue. Criminal law should be properly used when the weight of public opinion on a public moral principle is outraged. The democratic legislator cannot pass laws which are too far removed from the common sense of the society or he does disservice to the democratic system. Yet that does not change the fact, as Devlin finds it, that a society's law must mirror morality, and that the majority's moral principles must be enforced on the erring minority.*

* Lord Devlin, "Law, Democracy, and Morality," *University of Pennsylvania Law Review,* 110:635 (1962), pp. 635–649. Copyright *University of Pennsylvania Law Review.* Used by kind permission of the *University of Pennsylvania Law Review.*

WHEN a state recognizes freedom of worship and of conscience, it sets a problem for jurists which they have not yet entirely succeeded in solving. Now, when the law divides right from wrong, it cannot appeal to any absolute authority outside itself as justifying the division. All the questions which before were settled by divine law as pronounced by the churches are thrown open to debate when the decision is taken to admit freedom of conscience.†

The nineteenth century English philosophers drew what appeared to be the logical conclusion from the change. While the political scien-

† This decision, and not the separation of church from state, is crucial. In England, the church has never been formally separated from the state, but by the beginning of the nineteenth century an Englishman was effectively set free to worship or not as he chose. It was freedom not to worship at all and to disbelieve in revelation that was important, for it deprived the law of spiritual sustenance. In the eyes of the law the only judgment upon right and wrong which a man could be expected to follow was that of his own conscience, and it did not matter whether he taught himself on matters of morals or was taught by others.

tists and constitution-makers of the age were engaged in separating church and state, the philosophers came near to separating law and morality. Austin taught that the only force behind the law was physical force, and Mill declared that the only purpose for which that force could rightfully be used against any member of the community was to prevent harm to others; his own good, physical or moral, was not sufficient warrant.

But this sort of thinking made no impact at all upon the development or administration of the English criminal law. This was doubtless because no practical problems arose. If there had been a deep division in the country on matters of morals—if there had been, for example, a large minority who wished to practice polygamy—the theoretical basis for legislation on morals would have had to have been scrutinized. But the Englishman's hundred religions about which Voltaire made his jibe gave rise to no differences on morals grave enough to affect the criminal law. Parliament added incest and homosexual offenses to the list of crimes without inquiring what harm they did to the community if they were committed in private; it was enough that they were morally wrong. The judges continued to administer the law on the footing that England was a Christian country. Reluctantly they recognized respectful criticism of Christian doctrine as permissible, and the crime of blasphemy virtually disappeared. But Christian morals remained embedded in the law.

Emergence of a Practical Problem

It is only recently that there has emerged a moral problem needing a practical solution. There have long been cases in which men have violated various precepts of moral law, but there has been no body of men who asserted that the law ought not to interfere with immoral behavior. But there is now in England, and I daresay in other countries, a body of men who see nothing wrong with the homosexual relationship. There are others, to be found mainly among the educated classes, who, while not themselves practicing homosexuality, are not repelled by it, think it a permissible way of life for those so constituted as to enjoy it, and deplore the misery the law inflicts on the comparatively few victims it detects. In September 1957 the Wolfenden Committee of thirteen distinguished men and women appointed by the Home Secretary recommended with only one dissenter that homosexual behaviour between consenting adults in private should no longer be a criminal offense; and they based their recommendation on the ground that such offenses were within "a realm of private morality and immorality which is, in brief and crude terms, not the law's business."* The Home Secretary did not accept this recommendation; nevertheless, the report, in addition to its sociological value, is an important statement on the relationship between the criminal and the moral law.

Another landmark was made in May of last year by the decision of the House of Lords in *Shaw v. Director of Public Prosecutions.*

* Homosexual Offenses and Prostitution Committee, *Report,* CMD. No. 247, at 24 (1957).

This case arose indirectly out of another recommendation by the Wolfenden Committee. They were asked to report also upon offenses in connection with prostitution; and as a result the Street Offences Act, 1959, which made it impossible for prostitutes to continue soliciting in the streets, was passed. Mr. Shaw naively considered that since Parliament had not prohibited the trade of prostitution, there could be nothing objectionable or illegal about his supplying for prostitutes some means of advertisement in place of that which Parliament had denied them. So he published a magazine, which he called "The Ladies' Directory," containing the names, addresses, and telephone numbers of prostitutes. If that were all that he had done and if he had been content to remunerate himself simply by the proceeds from the sale of the magazine, he would have committed no specific offense. But the magazine contained additional matter which made it an obscene libel; and by taking payment from the prostitutes themselves the defendant had committed the statutory offense of living "wholly or in part on the earnings of prostitution." The importance of the case comes from the first count in the indictment, which was independent of the two statutory offenses and alleged a conspiracy at common law to corrupt public morals, the particulars being that the defendant and the prostitutes who advertised themselves in his magazine conspired "to induce readers thereof to resort to the said advertisers for the purposes of fornication." The defense argued that there was no such general offense known to the law as a conspiracy to corrupt public morals, but the House of Lords held by a majority of four to one that there was and that the accused was rightly found guilty of it. Viscount Simonds said: "There remains in the courts of law a residual power to enforce the supreme and fundamental purpose of the law, to conserve not only the safety and order but also the moral welfare of the State";* and he approved the assertion of Lord Mansfield two centuries before that the Court of King's Bench was the *custos morum* of the people and had the superintendency of offenses *contra bonos mores.*

With this cardinal enunciation of principle the courts rejected the teaching of John Stuart Mill and proclaimed themselves keepers of the nation's morals. From what source do they draw that power and how do they ascertain the moral standards they enforce?

The Basis of Morals Legislation

The state may claim on two grounds to legislate on matters of morals. The Platonic ideal is that the state exists to promote virtue among its citizens. If that is its function, then whatever power is sovereign in the state—an autocrat, if there be one, or in a democracy the majority—must have the right and duty to declare what standards of morality are to be observed as virtuous and must ascertain them as it thinks best. This is not acceptable to Anglo-American thought. It invests the state with power of determination between good and evil, destroys freedom of conscience, and is the paved road to tyranny. It is against this concept of the state's power that Mill's words are chiefly directed.

The alternative ground is that society may legislate to preserve

* Shaw v. Director of Pub. Prosecutions, [1961] 2 Weekly L.R. 897, 917 (H.L.).

itself. This is the ground, I think, taken by Lord Simonds when he says that the purpose of the law is to conserve the moral welfare of the state; and all the speeches in the House show, especially when they are laying down the part to be played by the jury, that the work of the courts is to be the guarding of a heritage and not the creation of a system. "The ultimate foundation of a free society is the binding tie of cohesive sentiment."* What makes a society is a community of ideas, not political ideas alone but also ideas about the way its members should behave and govern their lives.

If men and women try to create a society in which there is no fundamental agreement about good and evil they will fail; if having based it on common agreement, the agreement goes, the society will disintegrate. For society is not something that is kept together physically; it is held by the invisible bonds of common thought. If the bonds were too far relaxed the members would drift apart. A common morality is part of the bondage. The bondage is part of the price of society; and mankind, which needs society, must pay its price.

A law that enforces moral standards must like any other law be enacted by the appropriate constitutional organ, the monarch or the legislative majority as the case may be. The essential difference between the two theories is that under the first the lawmaker must determine for himself what is good for his subjects. He may be expected to do so not arbitrarily but to the best of his understanding; but it is his decision, based on his judgment of what is best, from which alone the law derives authority. The democratic system of government goes some way—not all the way, for no representative can be the mirror of the voter's thoughts—to insure that the decision of the lawmaker will be acceptable to the majority, but the majority is not the whole. A written constitution may safeguard to a great extent and for a long time the conscience of a minority, but not entirely and forever; for a written constitution is only a fundamental enactment that is difficult to alter.

But under the second theory the lawmaker is not required to make any judgment about what is good and what is bad. The morals which he enforces are those ideas about right and wrong which are already accepted by the society for which he is legislating and which are necessary to preserve its integrity. He has not to argue with himself about the merits of monogamy and polygamy; he has merely to observe that monogamy is an essential part of the structure of the society to which he belongs. Naturally he will assume that the morals of his society are good and true; if he does not, he should not be playing an active part in government. But he has not to vouch for their goodness and truth. His mandate is to preserve the essentials of his society, not to reconstruct them according to his own ideas.

How does the lawmaker ascertain the moral principles that are accepted by the society to which he belongs? He is concerned only with the fundament that is surely accepted, for legal sanctions are inappropriate for the enforcement of moral standards that are in dispute. He does not therefore need the assistance of moral philosophers, nor

* Minersville School Dist. v. Gobitis, 310 U.S. 586, 596 (1940) (Frankfurter, J.).

does he have to study the arguments upon peripheral questions. He is concerned with what is acceptable to the ordinary man, the man in the jury box, who might also be called the reasonable man or the right-minded man. When I call him the man in the jury box, I do not mean to imply that the ordinary citizen when he enters the jury box is invested with some peculiar quality that enables him to pronounce *ex cathedra* on morals. I still think of him simply as the ordinary reasonable man, but by placing him in the jury box I call attention to three points. First, the verdict of a jury must be unanimous; so a moral principle, if it is to be given the force of law, should be one which twelve men and women drawn at random from the community can be expected not only to approve but to take so seriously that they regard a breach of it as fit for punishment. Second, the man in the jury box does not give a snap judgment but returns his verdict after argument, instruction, and deliberation. Third, the jury box is a place in which the ordinary man's views on morals become directly effective. The lawmaker who makes the mistake of thinking that what he has to preserve is not the health of society but a particular regimen, will find that particular laws wither away. An important part of the machinery for hastening obsolescence is the lay element in the administration of English justice, the man in the jury box and the lay magistrate. The magistrates can act by the imposition of nominal penalties; the juryman acts by acquittal. If he gravely dislikes a law or thinks its application too harsh, he has the power, which from time immemorial he has exercised, to return a verdict of acquittal that is unassailable. . . .

The View of the Philosophers

What I want to discuss immediately is the reaction that many philosophers and academic lawyers have to the doctrine I have just outlined. They dislike it very much. It reduces morality, they feel, to the level of a question of fact. What Professor H. L. A. Hart calls rationalist morality, which I take to be morality embodied in the rational judgment of men who have studied moral questions and pondered long on what the answers ought to be, will be blown aside by a gust of popular morality compounded of all the irrational prejudices and emotions of the man-in-the-street. Societies in the past have tolerated witch-hunting and burnt heretics: was that done in the name of morality? There are societies today whose moral standards permit them to discriminate against men because of their color: have we to accept that? Is reason to play no part in the separation of right from wrong?

The most significant thing about questions of this type is that none of the questioners would think them worth asking if the point at issue had nothing in it of the spiritual. It is a commonplace that in our sort of society questions of great moment are settled in accordance with the opinion of the ordinary citizen who acts no more and no less rationally in matters of policy than in matters of morals. Such is the consequence of democracy and universal suffrage. Those who have had the benefit of a higher education and feel themselves better equipped to solve the nation's problems than the average may find it distasteful to submit to herd opinion. History tells them that democracies are far from perfect and have in the past done many foolish and even wicked things. But they do not dispute that in the end the will of the people must prevail, nor do they seek to appeal from it to the throne of reason.

But when it comes to a pure point of morals—for example, is homosexuality immoral and sinful—the first reaction of most of us is different. That reaction illustrates vividly the vacuum that is created when a society no longer acknowledges a supreme spiritual authority. For most of the history of mankind this sort of question has been settled, for men in society as well as for men as individuals, by priests claiming to speak with the voice of God. Today a man's own conscience is for him the final arbiter: but what for society?

This question, it seems to me, has received less study than it ought to have. The lawyers have evaded it by means of the assumption, substantially justifiable in fact though not in theory, that Christian morality remains just as valid for the purposes of the law as it was in the days of a universal church. The philosophers seem to have assumed that because a man's conscience could do for him, if he so chose, all that in the age of faith the priest had done, it could likewise do for society all that the priest had done; it cannot, unless some way be found of making up a collective conscience.

It is said or implied that this can be done by accepting the sovereignty of reason which will direct the conscience of every man to the same conclusion. The humbler way of using the power of reason is to hold, as Aquinas did, that through it it is possible to ascertain the law as God ordered it, the natural law, the law as it ought to be; the prouder is to assert that the reason of man unaided can construct the law as it ought to be. If the latter view is right, then one must ask: As men of reason are all men equal? If they are, if every man has equivalent power of reasoning and strength of mind to subdue the baser faculties of feeling and emotion, there can be no objection to morality being a matter for the popular vote. The objection is sustainable only upon the view that the opinion of the trained and educated mind, reached as its owner believes by an unimpassioned rational process, is as a source of morals superior to the opinion of ordinary men.

To the whole of this thesis, however it be put and whether or not it is valid for the individual mind that is governed by philosophy or faith, the lawmaker in a democratic society must advance insuperable objections, both practical and theoretical. The practical objection is that after centuries of debate men of undoubted reasoning power and honesty of purpose have shown themselves unable to agree on what the moral law should be, differing sometimes upon the answer to the simplest moral problem. To say this is not to deny the value of discussion among moral philosophers or to overlook the possibility that sometime between now and the end of the world universal agreement may be reached, but it is to say that as a guide to the degree of definition required by the lawmaker the method is valueless. Theoretically the method is inadmissable. If what the reason has to discover is the law of God, it is inadmissable because it assumes, as of course Aquinas did, belief in God as a lawgiver. If it is the law of man and if a common opinion on any point is held by the educated elite, what is obtained except to substitute for the voice of God the voice of the Superior Person? A free society is as much offended by the dictates of an intellectual oligarchy as by those of an autocrat.

The Task of the Lawmaker

For myself I have found no satisfactory alternative to the thesis I have proposed. The opposition to it, I cannot help thinking, has not rid itself of the idea, natural to a philosopher, that a man who is seeking a moral law ought also to be in pursuit of absolute truth. If he were, they would think it surprising if he found truth at the bottom of the popular vote. I do not think it as far from this as some learned people suppose, and I have known them to search for it in what seem to me to be odder places. But that is a subject outside the scope of this paper, which is not concerned with absolute truth. I have said that a sense of right and wrong is necessary for the life of a community. It is not necessary that their appreciation of right and wrong, tested in the light of one set or another of those abstract propositions about which men forever dispute, should be correct. If it were, only one society at most could survive. What the lawmaker has to ascertain is not the true belief but the common belief.

When I talk of the lawmaker I mean a man whose business it is to make the law whether it takes the form of a legislative enactment or of a judicial decision, as contrasted with the lawyer whose business is to interpret and apply the law as it is. Of course the two functions often overlap; judges especially are thought of as performing both. No one now is shocked by the idea that the lawyer is concerned simply with the law as it is and not as he thinks it ought to be. No one need be shocked by the idea that the lawmaker is concerned with morality as it is. There are, have been, and will be bad laws, bad morals, and bad societies. Probably no lawmaker believes that the morality he is enacting is false, but that does not make it true. Unfortunately bad societies can live on bad morals just as well as good societies on good ones.

In a democracy educated men cannot be put into a separate category for the decision of moral questions. But that does not mean that in a free society they cannot enjoy and exploit the advantage of the superior mind. The lawmaker's task, even in a democracy, is not the drab one of counting heads or of synthesizing answers to moral questions set up in a Gallup poll. In theory a sharp line can be drawn between law and morality as they are—positive law and positive morality—and as they ought to be; but in practice no such line can be drawn, because positive morality, like every other basis for the law, is subject to change, and consequently the law has to be developed. A judge is tethered to the positive law but not tied to it. So long as he does not break away from the positive law, that is, from the precedents which are set for him or the clear language of the statute which he is applying, he can determine for himself the distance and direction of his advance. Naturally he will move towards the law as he thinks it ought to be. If he has moved in the right direction, along the way his society would wish to go, there will come a time when the tethering-point is uprooted and moved nearer to the position he has taken; if he has moved in the wrong direction, he or his successors will be pulled back.

The legislator as an enforcer of morals has far greater latitude than the modern judge. Legislation of that sort is not usually made an election issue but is left to the initiative of those who are returned to power. In deciding whether or not to take the initiative the relevant question nearly always is not what popular morality is but whether it should be enforced by the criminal law. If there is a reasonable doubt on the first point, that doubt of itself answers the whole question in the negative. The legislator must gauge the intensity with which a popular moral conviction is held, because it is only when the obverse is generally thought to be intolerable that the criminal law can safely and properly be used. But if he decides that point in favor of the proposed legislation, there are many other factors, some of principle and some of expediency, to be weighed, and these give the legislator a very wide discretion in determining how far he will go in the direction of the law as he thinks it ought to be. The restraint upon him is that if he moves too far from the common sense of his society, he will forfeit the popular goodwill and risk seeing his work undone by his successor.

The Place of the Educated Man

This is the method of lawmaking common to both our countries; the popular vote does not itself enact or veto; rather, the initiative is put into the hands of a very few men. Under this method the law reformer has a double opportunity. He may work upon the popular opinion which is the lawmaker's base, or he may influence the lawmaker directly. At each of these stages the educated man is at an advantage in a democratic society.

Let us consider the first stage. True it is that in the final count the word of the educated man goes for no more than that of any other sort of man. But in the making up of the tally he has or should have the advantage of powers of persuasion above the ordinary. I do not mean by that simply powers of reasoning. If he is to be effective he must be ready to persuade and not just to teach, and he must accept that reason is not the plain man's only guide. "The common morality of a society at any time," says Dean Rostow, "is a blend of custom and conviction, of reason and feeling, of experience and prejudice."* If an educated man is armed only with reason, if he is disdainful of custom and ignores strength of feeling, if he thinks of "prejudice" and "intolerance" as words with no connotations that are not disgraceful and is blind to religious conviction, he had better not venture outside his academy, for if he does he will have to deal with forces he cannot understand. Not all learned men are prepared like Bertrand Russell to sit on the pavement outside No. 10 Downing Street. Not all are

* Dean Rostow, *The Enforcement of Morals,* 1960 Camb. L. J. 197.

lucid as well as erudite. Many a man will find satisfaction in teaching others to do what he is not equipped to do himself; but it is naive for such a man to reproach judges and legislators for making what he deems to be irrational law, as if in a democratic society they were the agents only of reason and the controllers of a nation's thought.

The other advantage which the educated man possesses is that he has easier access to the ear of the lawmaker. I do not mean merely by lobbying. When—with such latitude as our democratic and judicial system allows—the lawmaker is determining the pace and direction of his advance from the law that is towards the law that ought to be, he does and should inform himself of the views of wise and experienced men and pay extra attention to them.

These are the ways by which well-informed and articulate men can play a part in the shaping of the law quite disproportionate to their numbers. Under a system in which no single question is submitted to the electorate for direct decision, an ardent minority for or against a particular measure may often count for more than an apathetic majority. Recently in England in the reform of the criminal law a minority has had some remarkable successes. In 1948 flogging was abolished as a judicial punishment; it is doubtful whether that would have been the result of a majority vote, and it is still uncertain whether the gain will be held. Some years later much the same body of opinion was very nearly successful in abolishing capital punishment; I do not believe that in the country as a whole there is a majority against capital punishment. In 1959 the common law on obscenity was altered by statute. Notwithstanding that the tendency of a book is to deprave and corrupt, it is a good defense if its publication is in the interests of some "object of general concern," such as literature or art; and the opinion of experts is made admissable on the merits of the work. Under this latter provision in the recent case of *Lady Chatterley's Lover,* thirty-five witnesses distinguished in the fields of literature and morals were permitted to discuss at large the merits of the book, and thus a specially qualified body of opinion was brought into direct communication with the jury. On the other hand there has so far been a failure to reform the law against homosexuality. The conclusion of the Wolfenden Committee is an indication—I believe a correct one—that a substantial majority of "educated opinion" is in favor of some modification; but I believe also that the Home Secretary was right in his conclusion that public opinion as a whole was too strongly against the proposed amendments to permit legislation.

I have been considering this subject on the assumption that the extent to which the moral law is translated into the law of the land is determined chiefly by the legislature. In England that has appeared to be so at any rate during the last hundred years. The law that is now consolidated in the Sexual Offences Act of 1956 is mainly the creation of statute. Incest, for example, all homosexual offenses, and carnal knowledge of girls under the age of sixteen were never crimes at common law. Parliament in a series of statutes felt its way cautiously towards the curbing of prostitution, approaching the situation obliquely and at several different angles. The second cardinal enunciation of principles in *Shaw*'s case, to which I must now return, is that in matters of morals the common law has abandoned none of its rights and duties; and the third relates to the function of the jury.

The Jury as the Decider of Moral Questions

What exactly is meant by a conspiracy to corrupt public morals? We all know what a conspiracy is in law. Since acts of immorality are rarely committed by one person only, it is not in this branch of the law an element of much importance; indeed, it is uncertain whether it is a necessary ingredient in the crime. What limits, if any, are implicit in the words "public" and "corrupt"? Is it corruption to offer an adult an opportunity of committing, not for the first time, an immoral act? If so, what element of publicity has there to be about it? In the course of a very strong dissenting speech Lord Reid reached the conclusion that the successful argument by the Crown made "unlawful every act which tends to lead a single individual morally astray."* Their lordships in the majority refrained—I think, deliberately—from defining their terms. They left the work to the jury. Lord Simonds said: "The uncertainty that necessarily arises from the vagueness of general words can only be resolved by the opinion of twelve chosen men and women."† On the question of what was meant by the words in the indictment Lord Tucker said: "It is for the jury to construe and apply these words to the facts proved in evidence and reach their own decision . . . ."‡ Lord Morris said: "Even if accepted public standards may to some extent vary from generation to generation, current standards are in the keeping of juries, who can be trusted to maintain the corporate good sense of the community and to discern attacks upon values that must be preserved."** Lord Hodson said that the function of *custos morum* would ultimately be performed by the jury: "[I]n the field of public morals it will thus be the morality of the man in the jury box that will determine the fate of the accused . . . ."***

The opinions in *Shaw*'s case will certainly give rise to much debate. Critics of the majority view complain that it removes from the criminal law on morals the element of reasonable certainty. The relationship between statute and common law surely needs further elucidation. In this respect the immediate impact of the case is sharp. The legislators in Whitehall, inching forward clause by clause towards their moral objectives, topped a rise only to find the flag of their ally, the common law, whom they erroneously believed to be comatose (the Crown cited only three reported cases of conspiracy to corrupt public morals since Lord Mansfield's dictum in 1763), flying over the whole territory, a small part of which they had laboriously occupied.

There is another important aspect of the case, and that is whether, in placing so heavy a burden on the jury, it has brought about a shift

* Shaw v. Director of Pub. Prosecutions, [1961] 2 Weekly L.R. 926 (H.L.) (Lord Reid).

† *Id.* at 919.

‡ *Id.* at 937.

** *Id.* at 938.

*** *Id.* at 940.

of responsibility for decisions in the moral field that affects the democratic process I have endeavoured to describe.

If the only question the jury had to decide was whether or not a moral belief was generally held in the community, the jury would, I think, be an excellent tribunal. It will be objected that the decision would not be that of a jury alone but of a jury assisted by a judge; and in the minds of many reformers, some of whom identify liberalism with relaxation, the views of a judge on what is immoral are suspect. It is true that on this question a judge usually takes the conservative view, but then, so does the British public.

This is, however, as I have now stressed several times, unlikely to be the issue. The argument will not usually be about the immorality of the act but about whether the arm of the law should be used to suppress it. Hitherto the role of the jury has been negative and never formally recognized. The jury resists the enforcement of laws which it thinks to be too harsh. The law has never conceded that it has the right to do that, but it has been accepted that in practice it will exercise its power in that way. The novelty in the dicta in *Shaw*'s case is that they formally confer on the jury a positive function in law enforcement. It cannot be intended that the jury's only duty is to draw the line between public morality and immorality. If, for example, a man and a woman were charged with conspiring to corrupt public morals by openly living in sin, a jury today might be expected to acquit. If homosexuality were to cease to be per se criminal and two men were to be similarly charged with flaunting their relationship in public, a jury today might be expected—I think that this is what Lord Simonds and Lord Tucker would contemplate—to convict. The distinction can be made only on the basis that one sort of immorality ought to be condemned and punished and the other not. That is a matter on which many people besides lawyers are qualified to speak and would desire to be heard before a decision is reached. When a minister submits the issue to Parliament, they can be heard; when a judge submits it to a jury, they cannot. The main burden of Lord Reid's trenchant criticism of the majority opinion is that it allows and requires the jury to perform the function of the legislator.

Of course the courts would never deny the supremacy of Parliament. If Parliament dislikes the fruits of the legal process, it can say so; frequently in the past it has altered the law declared by the courts. But in the legislative process the forces of inertia are considerable; and in matters of morals negative legislation is especially difficult, because relaxation is thought to imply approval. So whoever has the initiative has the advantage. For the moment it appears that the common law has regained the initiative.

Morality as a Question of Fact

Whether it retains it or not, *Shaw*'s case settles for the purposes of the law that morality in England means what twelve men and women think it means—in other words, it is to be ascertained as a question of fact. I am not repelled by that phrase, nor do I resent in such a matter submission to the mentality of the common man. Those who believe in God and that He made man in His image will believe also that He gave to each in equal measure the knowledge of good and evil, placing it not in the intellect wherein His grant to some was more bountiful than to others, but in the heart and understanding, building there in each man the temple of the Holy Ghost. Those who do not believe in God must ask themselves what they *mean* when they say that they believe in democracy. Not that all men are born with equal brains—we cannot believe that; but that they have at their command—and that in this they are all born in the same degree—the faculty of telling right from wrong: this is the whole meaning of democracy, for if in this endowment men were not equal, it would be pernicious that in the government of any society they should have equal rights.

To hold that morality is a question of fact is not to deify the *status quo* or to deny the perfectibility of man. The unending search for truth goes on and so does the struggle towards the perfect society. It is our common creed that no society can be perfect unless it is a free society; and a free society is one that is created not as an end in itself but as a means of securing and advancing the bounds of freedom for the individuals who live within it. This is not the creed of all mankind. In this world as it is no man can be free unless he lives within the protection of a free society; if a free man needed society for no other reason, he would need it for this, that if he stood alone his freedom would be in peril. In the free society there are men, fighters for freedom, who strain at the bonds of their society, having a vision of life as they feel it ought to be. They live gloriously, and many of them die gloriously, and in life and death they magnify freedom. What they gain and as they gain it becomes the property of their society and is to be kept: the law is its keeper. So there are others, defenders and not attackers, but also fighters for freedom, for those who defend a free society defend freedom. These others are those who serve the law. They do not look up too often to the heights of what ought to be lest they lose sight of the ground on which they stand and which it is their duty to defend—the law as it is, morality as it is, freedom as it is—none of them perfect but the things that their society has got and must not let go. It is the faith of the English lawyer, as it is of all those other lawyers who took and enriched the law that Englishmen first made, that most of what their societies have got is good. With that faith they serve the law, saying as Cicero said, "*Legum denique . . . omnes servi sumus ut liberi esse possimus.*" In the end we are all of us slaves to the law, for that is the condition of our freedom.

Further Reading

Cassier, Ernst. *The Myth of the State*. New Haven: Yale University Press, 1946.

d'Entrènes, A. P. *Natural Law*. London: Hutchinson, 1951.

Ebenstein, William. *Great Political Thinkers*. New York: Holt, Rinehart and Winston, 1951.

Gough, J. W. *John Locke's Political Philosophy*. Oxford: Clarendon Press, 1950.

Hart, H. L. A. *Law, Liberty and Morality*. Stanford: Stanford University Press, 1963.
———. *The Concept of Law*. Oxford: Clardon Press, 1961.
Hook, Sidney (ed.). *Law and Philosophy*. New York: New York University Press, 1964.
Kelsen, Hans. *What is Justice?* Berkeley: University of California Press, 1960.
Laslett, Peter. *Philosophy, Politics and Society*. Oxford: Basil Blackwell, 1967.
Olafson, Frederick A. *Society, Law and Morality*. Englewood Cliffs: Prentice-Hall, 1961.
Perelman, Charles. *The Idea of Justice and the Problem of Argument*. London: Routledge and Kegan Paul, 1963.
Stumpf, Samuel Enoch. *Morality and the Law*. Nashville: Vanderbilt University Press, 1966.

PART III

SOCIAL ACTION AND HUMAN NATURE

INTRODUCTORY READINGS

Martin Luther King, Jr.
Students for a Democratic Society

INQUIRY

SELECTED SOURCES

Marx

Marx and Engels

Mao

Thoreau

Gandhi

Camus

INTRODUCTORY READING

Martin Luther King, Jr.

I Have A Dream*

FIVE SCORE YEARS AGO, A GREAT AMERICAN, IN WHOSE SYMBOLIC shadow we stand, signed the Emancipation Proclamation. This momentous decree came as a great beacon light of hope to millions of Negro slaves who had been seared in the flames of withering injustice. It came as a joyous daybreak to end the long night of captivity.

But one hundred years later, we must face the tragic fact that the Negro is still not free. One hundred years later, the life of the Negro is still sadly crippled by the manacles of segregation and the chains of discrimination. One hundred years later, the Negro lives on a lonely island of poverty in the midst of a vast ocean of material prosperity. One hundred years later the Negro is still languishing in the corners of American society and finds himself an exile in his own land. So we have come here today to dramatize an appalling condition.

In a sense we have come to our nation's capital to cash a check. When the architects of our republic wrote the magnificent words of the Constitution and the Declaration of Independence, they were signing a promissory note to which every American was to fall heir. This note was a promise that all men would be guaranteed the inalienable rights of life, liberty, and the pursuit of happiness.

It is obvious today that America has defaulted on this promissory note insofar as her citizens of color are concerned. Instead of honoring this sacred obligation, America has given the Negro people a bad check, a check which has come back marked "insufficient funds." But we refuse to believe that the bank of justice is bankrupt. We refuse to believe that there are insufficient funds in

* Speech delivered in Washington D.C., August, 1963. Reprinted by permission of Joan Daves.

the great vaults of opportunity of this nation. So we have come to cash this check—a check that will give us upon demand the riches of freedom and the security of justice. We have also come to this hallowed spot to remind America of the fierce urgency of now. This is no time to engage in the luxury of cooling off or to take the tranquilizing drug of gradualism. *Now* is the time to rise from the dark and desolate valley of segregation to the sunlit path of racial justice. *Now* is the time to open the doors of opportunity to all of God's children. Now is the time to lift our nation from the quicksands of racial injustice to the solid rock of brotherhood.

It would be fatal for the nation to overlook the urgency of the moment and to underestimate the determination of the Negro. This sweltering summer of the Negro's legitimate discontent will not pass until there is an invigorating autumn of freedom and equality. Nineteen sixty-three is not an end, but a beginning. Those who hope that the Negro needed to blow off steam and will now be content will have a rude awakening if the nation returns to business as usual. There will be neither rest nor tranquility in America until the Negro is granted his citizenship rights. The whirlwinds of revolt will continue to shake the foundations of our nation until the bright day of justice emerges.

But there is something that I must say to my people who stand on the warm threshold which leads into the palace of justice. In the process of gaining our rightful place we must not be guilty of wrongful deeds. Let us not seek to satisfy our thirst for freedom by drinking from the cup of bitterness and hatred.

We must forever conduct our struggle on the high plane of dignity and discipline. We must not allow our creative protest to degenerate into physical violence. Again and again we must rise to the majestic heights of meeting physical force with soul force. The marvelous new militancy which has engulfed the Negro community must not lead us to distrust of all white people, for many of our white brothers, as evidenced by their presence here today, have come to realize that their destiny is tied up with our destiny and their freedom is inextricably bound to our freedom. We cannot walk alone.

And as we walk, we must make the pledge that we shall march ahead. We cannot turn back. There are those who are asking the devotees of civil rights, "When will you be satisfied?" We can never be satisfied as long as the Negro is the victim of unspeakable horrors of police brutality. We can never be satisfied as long as our bodies, heavy with the fatigue of travel, cannot gain lodging in the motels of the highways and the hotels of the cities. We cannot be satisfied as long as the Negro's basic mobility is from a smaller ghetto to a larger one. We can never be satisfied as long as a Negro in Mississippi cannot vote and a Negro in New York believes he has nothing for which to vote. No, no, we are not satisfied, and we will not be satisfied until justice rolls down like waters and righteousness like a mighty stream.

I am not unmindful that some of you have come here out of great trials and tribulations. Some of you have come from areas where your quest for freedom left you battered by the storms of persecution and staggered by the winds of police brutality. You have been the veterans of creative suffering. Continue to work with the faith that unearned suffering is redemptive.

Go back to Mississippi, go back to Alabama, go back to Georgia, go back to Louisiana, go back to the slums and ghettos of our northern cities, knowing that somehow this situation can and will be changed. Let us not wallow in the valley of despair.

I say to you today, my friends, that in spite of the difficulties and frustrations of the moment, I still have a dream. It is a dream deeply rooted in the American dream.

I have a dream that one day this nation will rise up and live out the true meaning of its creed: "We hold these truths to be self-evident: that all men are created equal."

I have a dream that one day on the red hills of Georgia the sons of former slaves and the sons of former slaveowners will be able to sit down together at the table of brotherhood.

I have a dream that one day even the state of Mississippi, a desert state, sweltering with the heat of injustice and oppression, will be transformed into an oasis of freedom and justice.

I have a dream that my four little children will one day live in a nation where they will not be judged by the color of their skin but by the content of their character.

I have a dream today.

I have a dream that one day the state of Alabama, whose governor's lips are presently dripping with the words of interposition and nullification, will be transformed into a situation where little black boys and black girls will be able to join hands with little white boys and white girls and walk together as sisters and brothers.

I have a dream today.

I have a dream that one day every valley shall be exalted, every hill and mountain shall be made low, the rough places will be made plain, and the crooked places will be made straight, and the glory of the Lord shall be revealed, and all flesh shall see it together.

This is our hope. This is the faith with which I return to the South. With this faith we will be able to hew out of the mountain of despair a stone of hope. With this faith we will be able to transform the jangling discords of our nation into a beautiful symphony of brotherhood. With this faith we will be able to work together, to pray together, to struggle together, to go to jail together, to stand up for freedom together, knowing that we will be free one day.

This will be the day when all of God's children will be able to sing with a new meaning, "My country 'tis of thee, sweet land of liberty, of thee I sing. Land where my fathers died, land of the pilgrim's pride, from every mountainside, let freedom ring."

And if America is to be a great nation this must become true. So let freedom ring from the prodigious hilltops of New Hampshire. Let freedom ring from the mighty mountains of New York. Let freedom ring from the heightening Alleghenies of Pennsylvania!

Let freedom ring from the snowcapped Rockies of Colorado!

Let freedom ring from the curvaceous peaks of California!

But not only that; let freedom ring from Stone Mountain of Georgia!

Let freedom ring from Lookout Mountain of Tennessee!

Let freedom ring from every hill and molehill of Mississippi. From every mountainside, let freedom ring.

When we let freedom ring, when we let it ring from every village and every hamlet, from every state and every city, we will be able to speed up that day when all of God's children, black men and white men, Jews and Gentiles, Protestants and Catholics, will be able to join hands and sing in the words of the old Negro spiritual, "Free at last! free at last! thank God Almighty, we are free at last!"

INTRODUCTORY READING

Students for a Democratic Society

Port Huron Statement*

WE ARE PEOPLE OF THIS GENERATION, BRED IN AT LEAST MODEST comfort, housed in universities, looking uncomfortably to the world we inherit.

. . .

Our work is guided by the sense that we may be the last generation in the experiment with living. But we are a minority—the vast majority of our people regard the temporary equilibriums of our society and the world as eternally-functional parts. In this is perhaps the outstanding paradox: We ourselves are imbued with urgency, yet the message of our society is that there is no viable alternative to the present. Beneath the reassuring tones of the politicians, beneath the common opinion that America will "muddle through," beneath the stagnation of those who have closed their minds to the future, is the pervading feeling that there simply are no alternatives, that our times have witnessed the exhaustion not only of Utopias, but of any new departures as well. Feeling the press of complexity upon the emptiness of life, people are fearful of the thought that at any moment things might thrust out of control. They fear change itself, since change might smash whatever invisible framework seems to hold back chaos for them now. For most Americans, all crusades are suspect, threatening. The fact that each individual sees apathy in his fellows perpetuates the common reluctance to organize for changes. The dominant institutions are complex enough to blunt the minds of their potential critics, and entrenched enough to swiftly dissipate or entirely repel the energies of protest and reform, thus limiting human expectancies. Then, too, we are a materially improved

* From mimeographed copy, distributed at the Convention of SDS in Port Huron, Michigan, June 11–15, 1962, with omissions.

society, and by our own improvements we seem to have weakened the case for change.

Some would have us believe that Americans feel contentment amidst prosperity—but might it not better be called a glaze above deeply-felt anxieties about their role in the new world? And if these anxieties produce a developed indifference to human affairs, do they not as well produce a yearning to believe there *is* an alternative to the present, that something *can* be done to change circumstances in the school, the workplaces, the bureaucracies, the government? It is to this latter yearning, at once the spark and engine of change, that we direct our present appeal. The search for truly democratic alternatives to the present, and a commitment to social experimentation with them, is a worthy and fulfilling human enterprise, one which moves us and, we hope, others today.

. . .

Making values explicit—an initial task in establishing alternatives—is an activity that has been devalued and corrupted. The conventional moral terms of the age, the politician moralities ("free world," "peoples democracies") reflect realities poorly, if at all, and seem to function more as ruling myths than as descriptive principles. But neither has our experience in the universities brought us moral enlightenment. Our professors and administrators sacrifice controversy to public relations; their curriculums change more slowly than the living events of the world; their skills and silence are purchased by investors in the arms race; passion is called unscholastic. The questions we might want raised—what is really important? can we live in a different and better way? if we wanted to change society, how would we do it? —are not thought to be questions of a "fruitful, empirical nature," and thus are brushed aside.

Unlike youth in other countries we are used to moral leadership being exercised and moral dimensions being clarified by our elders. But today, for us, not even the liberal and socialist preachments of the past seem adequate to the forms of the present. Consider the old slogans: Capitalism Cannot Reform Itself, United Front Against Fascism, General Strike, All Out on May Day. Or, more recently, No Cooperation with Commies and Fellow Travelers, Ideologies Are Exhausted, Bipartisanship, No Utopias. These are incomplete, and there are few new prophets. It has been said that our liberal and socialist predecessors were plagued by vision without program, while our own generation is plagued by program without vision. All around us there is astute grasp of method, technique—the committee, the *ad hoc* group, the lobbyist, the hard and soft sell, the make, the projected image—but, if pressed critically, such expertise is incompetent to explain its implicit ideals. It is highly fashionable to identify oneself by old categories, or by naming a respected political figure, or by explaining "how we would vote" on various issues.

Theoretic chaos has replaced the idealistic thinking of old—and, unable to reconstitute theoretic order, men have condemned idealism itself. Doubt has replaced hopefulness, and men act out a defeatism that is labelled realistic. The decline of utopia and hope is in fact one of the defining features of social life today. The reasons are various: The dreams of the older left were perverted by Stalinism and never recreated; the congressional stalemate makes men narrow their view of the possible; the specialization of human activity leaves little room for sweeping thought; the horrors of the twentieth century, symbolized in the gas ovens and concentration camps and atom bombs, have blasted hopefulness. To be idealistic is to be considered apocalyptic, deluded. To have no serious aspirations, on the contrary, is to be "tough-minded."

In suggesting social goals and values, therefore, we are aware of entering a sphere of some disrepute. Perhaps matured by the past, we have no sure formulas, no closed theories—but that does not mean values are beyond discussion and tentative determination. A first task of any social movement is to convince people that the search for orienting theories and the creation of human values is complex but worthwhile. We are aware that to avoid platitudes we must analyze the concrete conditions of social order. But to direct such an analysis we must use the guideposts of basic principles. Our own social values involve conceptions of human beings, human relationships, and social systems.

We regard *men* as infinitely precious and possessed of unfulfilled capacities for reason, freedom, and love. In affirming these principles we are aware of countering perhaps the dominant conceptions of man in the twentieth century: that he is a thing to be manipulated, and that he is inherently incapable of directing his own affairs. We oppose the depersonalization that reduces human beings to the status of things. If anything, the brutalities of the twentieth century teach that means and ends are intimately related, that vague appeals to "posterity" cannot justify the mutilations of the present. We oppose, too, the doctrine of human incompetence because it rests essentially on the modern fact that men have been "competently" manipulated into incompetence. We see little reason why men cannot meet with increasing skill the complexities and responsibilities of their situation, if society is organized not for minority participation but for majority participation in decision-making.

Men have unrealized potential for self-cultivation, self-direction, self-understanding, and creativity. It is this potential that we regard as crucial and to which we appeal—not to the human potentiality for violence, unreason, and submission to authority. The goal of man and society should be human independence: a concern not with image or popularity but with finding a meaning in life that is personally authentic; a quality of mind not compulsively driven by a sense of powerlessness, nor one which unthinkingly adopts status values, nor one which represses all threats to its habits, but one which has full, spontaneous access to present and past experiences, one which easily unites the fragmented parts of personal history, one which openly faces problems which are troubling and unresolved—one with an intuitive awareness of possibilities, an active sense of curiosity, an ability and willingness to learn.

This kind of independence does not mean egoistic individualism; the object is not to have one's way so much as it is to have a way that is one's own. Nor do we deify man—we merely have faith in his potential.

Human relationships should involve fraternity and honesty. Human interdependence is contemporary fact; human brotherhood must be willed, however, as a condition of future survival and as the most appropriate form of social relations. Personal links between man and man are needed, especially to go beyond the partial and fragmentary bonds of function that bind men only as worker to worker, employer to employee, teacher to student, American to Russian.

Loneliness, estrangement, isolation describe the vast distance between man and man today. These dominant tendencies cannot be overcome by better personnel management, nor by improved gadgets, but only when a love of man overcomes the idolatrous worship of things by man.

As the individualism we affirm is not egoism, the selflessness we affirm is not self-elimination. On the contrary, we believe in generosity of a kind that imprints one's unique individual qualities in the relation to other men, and to all human activity. Further, to dislike isolation is not to favor the abolition of privacy; the latter differs from isolation in that it occurs or is abolished according to individual will.

. . .

The very isolation of the individual—from power and community and ability to aspire—means the rise of a democracy without publics. With the great mass of people structurally remote and psychologically hesitant with respect to democratic institutions, those institutions themselves attenuate and become, in a fashion of the vicious circle, progressively less accessible to those few who aspire to serious participation in social affairs. The vital democratic connection between community and leadership, between the mass and the several elites, has been so wrenched and perverted that disastrous policies go unchallenged time and again. . . .

The first effort, then, should be to state a vision: What is the perimeter of human possibility in this epoch? . . . The second effort, if we are to be politically responsible, is to evaluate the prospects for obtaining at least a substantial part of that vision in our epoch: What are the social forces that exist, or that must exist, if we are to be successful? And what role have we ourselves to play as a social force?

"Students don't even give a damn about apathy," one has said. Apathy toward apathy begets a privately constructed universe, a place of systematic study schedules, two nights each week for beer, a girl or two, and early marriage—a framework infused with personality, warmth, and under control, no matter how unsatisfying otherwise.

Under these conditions university life loses all relevance to some. Four hundred thousand of our classmates leave college each year.

But apathy is not simply an attitude; it is a product of social institutions, and of the structure and organization of higher education itself. The extracurricular life is ordered according to *in loco parentis* theory, which ratifies the administration as the moral guardian of the young. The accompanying "let's pretend" theory of student extracurricular affairs validates student government as a training center for those who want to spend their lives in political pretense, and discourages initiative from more articulate, honest, and sensitive students. The bounds and style of controversy are delimited before controversy begins. The university "prepares" the student for "citizenship" through perpetual rehearsals and, usually, through emasculation of what creative spirit there is in the individual.

The academic life contains reinforcing counterparts to the way in which extracurricular life is organized. The academic world is founded in a teacher-student relation analogous to the parent-child relation which characterizes *in loco parentis*. Further, academia includes a radical separation of student from the material of study. That which is studied, the social reality, is "objectified" to sterility, dividing the student from life—just as he is restrained in active involvement by the deans controlling student government. The specialization of function and knowledge, admittedly necessary to our complex technological and social structure, has produced an exaggerated compartmentalization of study and understanding. This has contributed to: an overly parochial view, by faculty, of the role of its research and scholarship; a discontinuous and truncated understanding, by students, of the surrounding social order; a loss of personal attachment, by nearly all, to the worth of study as a humanistic enterprise.

There is, finally, the cumbersome academic bureaucracy extending throughout the academic as well as extracurricular structures, contributing to the sense of outer complexity and inner powerlessness that transforms so many students from honest searching to ratification of convention and, worse, to a numbness to present and future catastrophes. The size and financing systems of the university enhance the permanent trusteeship of the administrative bureaucracy, their power leading to a shift to the value standards of business and administrative mentality within the university. Huge foundations and other private financial interests shape the under-financed colleges and universities, making them not only more commercial but less disposed to diagnose society critically, less open to dissent. Many social and physical scientists, neglecting the liberating heritage of higher learning, develop "human relations" or "morale-producing" techniques for the corporate economy, while others exercise their intellectual skills to accelerate the arms race.

The university is located in a permanent position of social influence. Its educational function makes it indispensable and automatically makes it a crucial institution in the formation of social attitudes. In an unbelievably complicated world, it is the central institution for organizing, evaluating, and transmitting knowledge. . . . Social relevance, the accessibility to knowledge, and internal openness—these together make the university a potential base and agency in the movement of social change.

1. Any new left in America must be, in large measure, a left with real intellectual skills, committed to deliberativeness, honesty, and reflection as working tools. The university permits the political life to be an adjunct to the academic one, and action to be informed by reason.

2. A new left must be distributed in significant social roles throughout the country. The universities are distributed in such a manner.

3. A new left must consist of younger people who matured in the post-war world, and must be directed to the recruitment of younger people. The university is an obvious beginning point.

4. A new left must include liberals and socialists, the former for their relevance, the latter for their sense of thoroughgoing reforms in the system. The university is a more sensible place than a political party for these two traditions to begin to discuss their differences and look for political synthesis.

5. A new left must start controversy across the land, if national policies and national apathy are to be reversed. The ideal uni-

versity is a community of controversy, within itself and in its effects on communities beyond.

6. A new left must transform modern complexity into issues that can be understood and felt close-up by every human being. It must give form to the feelings of helplessness and indifference, so that people may see the political, social, and economic sources of their private troubles and organize to change society. In a time of supposed prosperity, moral complacency, and political manipulation, a new left cannot rely on only aching stomachs to be the engine force of social reform. The case for change, for alternatives that will involve uncomfortable personal efforts, must be argued as never before. The university is a relevant place for all of these activities.

But we need not indulge in illusions: The university system cannot complete a movement of ordinary people making demands for a better life. From its schools and colleges across the nation, a militant left might awaken its allies, and by beginning the process towards peace, civil rights, and labor struggles, reinsert theory and idealism where too often reign confusion and political barter. The power of students and faculty united is not only potential; it has shown its actuality in the South, and in the reform movements of the North.

To turn these possibilities into realities will involve national efforts at university reform by an alliance of students and faculty. They must wrest control of the educational process from the administrative bureaucracy. They must make fraternal and functional contact with allies in labor, civil rights, and other liberal forces outside the campus. They must import major public issues into the curriculum. . . . They must make debate and controversy, not dull pedantic cant, the common style for educational life. They must consciously build a base for their assault upon the loci of power.

As students for a democratic society, we are committed to stimulating this kind of social movement, this kind of vision and program in campus and community across the country. If we appear to seek the unattainable as it has been said, then let it be known that we do so to avoid the unimaginable.

INQUIRY

Inferiors revolt in order that they may be equal, and equals that they may be superior. Such is the state of mind which creates revolutions.

ARISTOTLE
Politics

Philosophers have only interpreted the world in various ways, but the real task is to change it.

KARL MARX
Eleven Theses on Feuerbach

AT the end of T. H. White's popular retelling of the legends of King Arthur, *The Once and Future King,* the king, old and defeated on the eve of his final battle, attempts to understand the failure of his dream. Arthur had had such high hopes for the perfectibility of man; his idea of the Round Table of Knights was based on those expectations. But, as Arthur puts it, "The whole structure depended on the first premise: that man was decent."*

Origins of Social Change

All major social action movements seem to be predicated upon some concept of human nature. Most, one would suspect, take an optimistic point of view. After all, if men were thought to be basically bestial or evil, there would be no reason for hope, and social revolution designed to improve the lot of mankind would be pointless. Stoic perseverance in the face of evil would be our greatest virtue. Or, if men were merely machines, with neither good nor bad natures, simply programmed series of stimulus-response mechanisms, no meaningful theory of social change would be sen-

* T. H. White, *The Once and Future King* (New York: G. P. Putnam's Sons, 1959), p. 666.

sible. A revolutionary, if one were ever to exist, would have to destroy the programmer or the builder.

What reasons do men provide for creating upheaval in social institutions? Why do the thoughts and actions of some men provide the catalyst for significant attacks on the status quo? Throughout the history of the United States, the social reformer, the radical, the revolutionary has played a dominant role. Today's revolutionaries on the campus and in the ghetto serve to remind us of the heritage of social action which we all share. The signers of the Declaration of Independence, the Samuel Adamses, Benjamin Franklins, of our tradition were not so-called respectable establishment people. They were the radicals whose ideas of reform, directed especially against the aristocracy, sparked the most violent social movement: armed revolution. We cannot allow ourselves the luxury of forgetting that most of our sacred social and political tradition was born in the violence of upheaval. Violence and disruption have been the method of most of the meaningful social change in our history.

In this chapter our concern lies with the attempt to understand the philosophic superstructure of social action. We are told that there are a number of psychological and sociological factors that produce revolutionaries, but is there also a philosophic element in the radical, an intellectual groundwork to his movement? Are there a series of interrelated ideas which underlie his compulsion to restructure his society? During a recent television interview, when asked to define a conservative, a young campus revolutionary responded, "someone who isn't hungry." Certainly there are few if any starving conservatives, but is the economic status of the individual always an index to his participation in social action movements? There seems to be more involved here than empty stomachs.

Sidney Lens, in his book *Radicalism in America,* makes the following claim:

> The radical has been a motor force of history. He has galvanized the "injured and oppressed" to remove roadblocks placed in the path of progress by the "rich and well-born." If he does not always get credit for this role, it is because current radicals are usually bitterly castigated by the organs of the status quo which they challenge while radicals of the past are made respectable by tradition.*

The history of the idea of revolution and social change is at least as old as Spartacus. We are now, however, particularly interested in two major expressions of Twentieth Century social action, the civil rights movement and the student-campus revolt. The roots of these movements might well be traced to our concern for human dignity and for equality in the human condition, but the great upheavals of socialism and communism of the last century provide philosophically fertile soil for beginning our inquiry. These movements followed what some have called the greatest of social and economic changes: the Industrial Revolution, which drastically altered the existing class structure and distribution of wealth, greatly polarizing

* Sidney Lens, *Radicalism in America* (New York: Thomas Y. Crowell Co., 1966), p. 1.

classes in the countries it affected. The new era of industry resulted in the oppression of large masses of unskilled workers. It was in response to this condition that the socialistic and communistic movements arose.

Socialism The basic design of socialism is to divide equally among the members of a community the basic means of production, distribution and exchange. All other social orders must be rejected in favor of the new order, which is only attainable by drastically altering existing institutions. Socialist philosophy has an undercurrent of optimism concerning the ability of men to reason and to progress toward a state of total equality. In the Erfurt Program the "social transformation" was to free not only the working man, but all humanity, even though only the uncorrupted laborer could institute the revolution of politico-economic power. In other words, despite his negative appraisals of contemporary situations, the socialist's demand for change was based on a notion of mankind as perfectible through his own efforts, worthy of respect not because of the property he commanded but because he is a man; and men can attain a greater degree of happiness in this world after the removal of the oppressive economic conditions which tend to establish class barriers.

The philosophical problems of revolution lead toward two major considerations, economic policy and human nature. Socialism and radicalism, with which we are concerned, understand the state to be the instrument of economic and humanistic reform. In contrast, anarchists, such as Thoreau, regard the state as the instrument of oppression and see no hope that it can avoid the control of the corrupt. Their aim therefore is society without government. Yet the anarchists do share with other revolutionaries certain principles of human value and the conviction that man can gain an equitable control over his social world.

Marxism Karl Marx, perhaps the world's most famous revolutionary, holds the position that an elite within society can take and hold power unless the great working masses are prepared to overthrow, violently if necessary, the rule of the status quo. He attacks the notion, prevalent in idealistic philosophy of the last century, that poverty and human misery are to be rationalized as parts of the plan for the universe of a greater or higher order of spirit. For Marx, the only time when misery among the working class is justified is when they are in the process of overthrowing the established capitalistic order.

Economics, the motivating force of mankind, serves to explain our present dilemma and class struggle. Marx tells us that the capitalist system alienates man from his very nature. The loss of identity with the product of one's labor is most common for the working class, but this is only symptomatic of the alienation which capitalism creates for all humanity.

No class, Marx argues, can afford to wait for the offer of suffrage from the ruling elite. Those without must unite to overthrow the oppression of those with, restoring a balance of economic power and, most importantly, re-identifying the worker with his life work. Yet no individual can produce the desired goal. Revolution, for Marx, is a social project, not a personal one. The world must be altered, and then men will change. Notice how this differs from the approach of many civil rights activists who express the feeling that nothing can change until individual men change their patterns of belief, their prejudices.

Practicality of Non-Violence

Let us consider Martin Luther King's famous "I Have a Dream" speech, given at the largest civil rights demonstration in our history, in Washington, D.C., in August, 1963. The particular language of the speech is worth noting, because it emphasizes the major tenets of King's movement: economic adjustment and social justice. These two ideas seem to be inseparable in his thinking. How are they to be accomplished? Nonviolently? His intention is to force the issue on the "high plane of dignity and discipline," involving "a meeting of physical force with soul force," similar to the teaching of M. K. Gandhi. But is this realistic? For Gandhi the act of *Satyagraha* is a lifelong endeavor which purifies the activist as he exacts reform. The *Satyagrahi* is not victory-centered. He attempts to bring his enemy into his understanding and thereby attain justice. King's concept of man is also basically optimistic; he believes passive resistance of the status quo will gradually eradicate its injustices. In the face of the history of intolerance and oppression against which King's revolution was mounted, is his view justified?

King had a dream; most other radicals have also had utopian ideas. Must a revolutionary have a vision, a new view of human character, which often ignores the historical facts? Is revolutionary thinking basically mythical? Is it a natural outgrowth of a commitment to a new or reborn subjective conception of human life and human nature? Is a kind of spiritual motivation involved?

Tactics of Successful Revolution

Social revolution produces conflicts within its philosophy between ideals and methods. What tactics are successful? Can a revolutionary realistically prescribe a tactical limit beyond which he will not go? Does the end always justify the means? Is it necessary at times to act with violence in order to shock a generally apathetic populace to recognition of the "cause"? Yet, seldom have revolutionaries appealed to these tactics to gain support. Must the revolution excite emotional and even philosophic interest before tactics can be discussed? Certainly the revolutionary's appeal can never solely be based on force; part of his attraction is derived from his underdog status.

Mao Tse-Tung, leader of China and tactician of revolutions, catalogues the procedures for a "people's war" and revolutionary government. In effect, the strategy of guerrilla combat is to turn the populace into a force hostile to the aims and means of the status quo's forces. Guerrillas on their own can hope to gain little. Revolutionary war, Mao tells us, "is a war of the masses; it can be waged only by mobilizing the masses and relying on them." What if the people fail to respond? Should the rebels terrorize the people on the theory that the people will join them for the promise of security (a tactic used at times by the Viet Cong in the villages of South Vietnam)?

Regis DeBray, French reporter on Latin American revolutions, makes the point in his famous little book, *Revolution dans la Revolution?,* that tactics cannot be exported, that the conditions of each new country determine the strategy of revolt: "The best teacher of Marxist-Leninism is the enemy, in face-to-face confrontation during the people's war."*

Most of the establishment's criticisms of student campus revolts have been aimed at the physical methods of such groups as the Students for a Democratic Society; few have been fired at their principles. Consider the following statements of Mario Biaggi, Congressman from New York, delivered in the House of Representatives, April 17, 1969:

> Surely it is not improper for young people to question the wisdom and policies that affect their very existence. When there is legal dissent—and I emphasize legal dissent—it is without a doubt, healthy and progressive because it is both an expression of interest and an act of faith in a democracy. . . . However, I am worried about the other side of the coin—the process of illegal dissent among a minority of students who have turned the campuses into an arena for oppression by revolutionaries, vandals and arsonists. . . . They must also understand completely that the pursuit of intellectual freedom is genuine and idealistic only when it is accomplished within the laws of our society.†

Is there a basic misunderstanding here of the theory and appeal of revolution? Ought one to take comfort in the thought that only a minority is involved? If the entire social structure has been judged corrupt, what restraints will the law exercise on the critics who would completely alter it?

Relation of Ideology to the Revolutionary Movement

There is a wide variety of tactics to which revolutionaries subscribe. Few revolutionaries promise to avoid violence at all cost. When is a riot an act of revolution? In regard to this, consider some of the major social action movements of our time and the massive disorders related to them: the civil rights movement—the Watts riot; the peace movement—the Chicago police riot at the Democratic convention of 1968; the student revolt—Columbia, 1967 and

* *Ramparts* (September, 1967), p. 55.
† *The Congressional Record,* Vol. 115, No. 61, P.E. 3065.

Harvard, 1969. Is there such a thing as a spontaneous revolution? Can a mob or a crowd initiate a social revolution? Or is the term "revolution" reserved for social upheavals based on principles? Are dreams necessary to revolutionary movements? Can you conceive of social change, gained through violence, and undirected by any dream? Would you call your conception a revolution? DeBray maintains that a guerrilla force must be both military, political, and ideological.

Representative Biaggi failed to grasp that societies, even democratic ones, by their very nature must outlaw and condemn the very drastic changes the militant students are seeking. In *New Left Notes** the SDS issued a minimum definition of a revolutionary organization. They maintain that the purpose of such an organization is to abolish the existing class structure in such a way as to prevent the re-division of society into classes. Furthermore they claim that a revolutionary organization "makes a unitary critique of the world, or is nothing . . . a total critique of all geographic areas where various forms of separate socio-economic powers exist, as well as a critique of all aspects of life." The SDS, however, then makes a rather remarkable statement of purpose:

> The organization dissolves any "revolutionary ideology" by revealing it to be the sign of failure of the revolutionary project, as the private property of new specialists of power, as the imposture of a new *representation* which erects itself above the real proletarianized life.

Is not the "real proletarianized life" a product of a revolutionary ideology? Perhaps this type of thinking is self-defeating. Is the ultimate state to be man without direction, or perhaps man with multitudinous directions? Will this insure an end to alienation? Certainly if men are to have similar goals and ideologies, myths have an important role to play. Without a commitment to the ideology of the "new man," does the revolution become what Rep. Biaggi called "vandalism and arson"?

The Relation of the Establishment to Its Ideals

Consider another related problem. In the name of preservation of the status quo, the establishment often discredits first the values it most wants to maintain, merely by its reaction to proposed change. Was the status quo preserved when the principles of justice valued so highly in the so-called American system were utterly neglected; when, one after another, white racists were freed in civil rights cases in the South despite the evidence against them? Does not such reaction by the establishment only stimulate the revolt and broaden its appeal? The conclusions drawn from Southern Justice were simple; revolutionary conclusions generally are. The privilege of a certain "elite" was apparently more important than the ideals that "elite" claimed to support. If such establishment reaction gen-

* Reprinted in *The Congressional Record* (April 28, 1969).

erally serves to strengthen the appeal of the cause of restructure, and violent social interaction usually follows, what position should the establishment take? Is the establishment always in the position of being unable to make significant moves? Must there always be revolutions? And is every revolution in its turn doomed to the fate it forced on the previous establishment? Is every revolutionary in a sense Sisyphus, Camus' absurd hero who rolls his rock eternally (Selected Source #6)?

We cannot forget that revolutions are internal social outgrowths. They are products of the values of the very structures they seek to destroy. They force us to re-consider our whole pattern of life. In a commencement address, William M. Thompson, 1969 Yale University Graduating Class Secretary, said: "Today as we leave Yale a sense of frustration and despair overwhelms us"; and at Harvard, the 1969 Student Speaker, Meldon Levine added:

> (Considering that we are) attempting to achieve the values you have taught us to cherish, your response has been astounding. . . . Tell them they have broken the best heads in the country. . . . You have convinced us that equality and justice were inviolable concepts and we have taken you seriously.

1

KARL MARX (1818–1883)

FRIEDRICH ENGELS (1820–1895)

*The Communist Manifesto**

The Communist Manifesto, *originally composed as a statement of objectives for the Communist League in England in 1848, serves as a basic formula for social change. Marx supported the theory that a small elite group could capture and hold social-political power if, and only if, the masses were prepared in advance for the revolution and could assist in overcoming the resistance forces of the status quo. For Marx, revolution must be fermented in the working class and can never be a co-operative effort with the bourgeoisie. These ideas are not new with Marx or Engels. They have a long history in the political and social philosophy of the Nineteenth Century. Marx himself asserted that he contributed only three new ideas to socialist thinking: (1) that classes are related to historic stages in the development of production, (2) that class struggle must end in the dictatorship of the working class, and (3) that the dictatorship of the working class is a positive step to the classless society.*

For Marxism, capitalistic society is inevitably immoral and unjust. The classless society will, according to Marx and Engels, provide self-regulatory controls and insure justice for all of its members. Capital, the Marxists argue, is not personal property but is a collective product and must therefore be used as a social power, not as a personal power. In the place of the capitalistic society of classes and class warfare, distrust and injustice, the Manifesto *promises: "an association in which the free development of each is the condition for the free development of all."*

* Karl Marx and Friedrich Engels, *Manifesto of the Communist Party*, S. Moore, trans. (New York: Socialist Labor Party, 1888), pp. 7–21.

A SPECTRE is haunting Europe—the spectre of Communism. All the powers of old Europe have entered into a holy alliance to exorcise this spectre; Pope and Czar, Metternich and Guizot, French Radicals and German police-spies.

Where is the party in opposition that has not been decried as communistic by its opponents in power? Where the Opposition that has not hurled back the branding reproach of Communism, against the more advanced opposition parties, as well as against its reactionary adversaries?

Two things result from this fact.

1. Communism is already acknowledged by all European Powers to be itself a Power.

2. It is high time that Communists should openly, in the face of the whole world, publish their views, their aims, their tendencies, and meet this nursery tale of the Spectre of Communism with a Manifesto of the party itself.

To this end, Communists of various nationalities have assembled in London, and sketched the following manifesto, to be published in the English, French, German, Italian, Flemish and Danish languages.

Bourgeois and Proletarians

The history of all hitherto existing society is the history of class struggles.

Freeman and slave, patrician and plebeian, lord and serf, guildmaster and journeyman, in a word, oppressor and oppressed, stood in constant opposition to one another, carried on an uninterrupted, now hidden, now open fight, a fight that each time ended, either in a revolutionary re-constitution of society at large, or in the common ruin of the contending classes.

In the earlier epochs of history, we find almost everywhere a complicated arrangement of society into various orders, a manifold graduation of social rank. In ancient Rome we have patricians, knights, plebeians, slaves; in the Middle Ages, feudal lords, vassals, guildmasters, journeymen, apprentices, serfs; in almost all of these classes, again, subordinate gradations.

The modern bourgeois society that has sprouted from the ruins of feudal society, has not done away with class antagonisms. It has but established new classes, new conditions of oppression, new forms of struggle in place of the old ones.

Our epoch, the epoch of the bourgeoisie, possesses, however, this distinctive feature: it has simplified the class antagonisms. Society as a whole is more and more splitting up into two great hostile camps, into two great classes directly facing each other: Bourgeoisie and Proletariat.

From the serfs of the Middle Ages sprang the chartered burghers of the earliest towns. From these burgesses the first elements of the bourgeoisie were developed.

The discovery of America, the rounding of the Cape, opened up fresh ground for the rising bourgeoisie. The East-Indian and Chinese markets, the colonization of America, trade with the colonies, the increase in the means of exchange and in commodities generally, gave to commerce, to navigation, to industry, an impulse never before known, and thereby, to the revolutionary element in the tottering feudal society, a rapid development.

The feudal system of industry, under which industrial production was monopolized by close guilds, now no longer sufficed for the growing wants of the new markets. The manufacturing system took its place. The guildmasters were pushed on one side by the manufacturing middle-class; division of labor between the different corporate guilds vanished in the face of division of labor in each single workshop.

Meantime the markets kept ever growing, the demand, ever rising. Even manufacture no longer sufficed. Thereupon, steam and machinery revolutionized industrial production. The place of manufacture was taken by the giant, Modern Industry, the place of the industrial middle-class, by industrial millionaires, the leaders of whole industrial armies, the modern bourgeois.

Modern industry has established the world-market, for which the discovery of America paved the way. This market has given an immense development to commerce, to navigation, to communication by land. This development has, in its turn, reacted on the extension of industry; and in proportion as industry, commerce, navigation, railways extended, in the same proportion the bourgeoisie developed, increased its capital, and pushed into the background every class handed down from the Middle Ages.

We see, therefore, how the modern bourgeoisie is itself the product of a long course of development, of a series of revolutions in the modes of production and of exchange.

Each step in the development of the bourgeoisie was accompanied by a corresponding political advance of that class. An oppressed class under the sway of the feudal nobility, an armed and self-governing association in the medieval commune, here independent urban republic (as in Italy and Germany), there taxable "third estate" of the monarchy (as in France), afterwards, in the period of manufacture proper, serving either the semi-feudal or the absolute monarchy as a counterpoise against the nobility, and, in fact, corner stone of the great monarchies in general, the bourgeoisie has at last, since the establishment of Modern Industry and of the world-market, conquered for itself, in the modern representative State, exclusive political sway. The executive of the modern State is but a committee for managing the common affairs of the whole bourgeoisie.

The bourgeoisie, historically, has played a most revolutionary part.

The bourgeoisie, wherever it has got the upper hand, has put an end to all feudal, patriarchal, idyllic relations. It has pitilessly torn asunder the motley feudal ties that bound man to his "natural superiors," and has left remaining no other nexus between man and man than naked self-interest, than callous "cash payment." It has drowned the most heavenly ecstasies of religious fervor, of chivalrous enthusiasm, of philistine sentimentalism, in the icy water of egotistical calculation. It has resolved personal worth into exchange value, and in place of the numberless indefeasible chartered freedoms, has set up that single, unconscionable freedom—Free Trade. In one word, for exploitation, veiled by religious and political illusions, it has substituted naked, shameless, direct, brutal exploitation.

The bourgeoisie has stripped of its halo every occupation hitherto honored and looked up to with reverent awe. It has converted the physician, the lawyer, the priest, the poet, the man of science, into its paid wage-laborers.

The bourgeoisie has torn away from the family its sentimental veil, and has reduced the family relation to a mere money relation.

The bourgeoisie has disclosed how it came to pass that the brutal display of vigor in the Middle Ages, which Reactionists so much admire, found its fitting complement in the most slothful indolence. It has been the first to show what man's activity can bring about. It has accomplished wonders far surpassing Egyptian pyramids, Roman aqueducts, and Gothic cathedrals; it has conducted expeditions that put in the shade all former Exoduses of nations and crusades.

The bourgeoisie cannot exist without constantly revolutionizing the instruments of production, and thereby the relations of production, and with them the whole relations of society. Conservation of the old modes of production in unaltered form, was, on the contrary, the first condition of existence for all earlier industrial classes. Constant revolutionizing of production, uninterrupted disturbance of all social conditions, everlasting uncertainty and agitation distinguish the bourgeois epoch from all earlier ones. All fixed, fast-frozen relations, with their train of ancient and venerable prejudices and opinions, are swept away, all new-formed ones become antiquated before they can ossify. All that is solid melts into air, all that is holy is profaned, and man is at last compelled to face with sober senses, his real conditions of life, and his relations with his kind.

Imperialism and the Bourgeoisie

The need of a constantly expanding market for its products chases the bourgeoisie over the whole surface of the globe. It must nestle everywhere, settle everywhere, establish connections everywhere.

The bourgeoisie has through its exploitation of the world-market given a cosmopolitan character to production and consumption in every country. To the great chagrin of Reactionists, it has drawn from under the feet of industry the national ground on which it stood. All old-established national industries have been destroyed or are daily being destroyed. They are dislodged by new industries, whose introduction becomes a life and death question for all civilized nations, by industries that no longer work up indigenous raw material, but raw material drawn from the remotest zones; industries whose products are consumed, not only at home, but in every quarter of the globe. In place of the old wants, satisfied by the productions of the country, we find new wants, requiring for their satisfaction the products of distant lands and climes. In place of the old local and national seclusion and self-sufficiency, we have intercourse in every direction, universal inter-dependence of nations. And as in material, so also in intellectual production. The intellectual creations of individual nations become common property. National one-sidedness and narrow-mindedness become more and more impossible, and from the numerous national and local literatures there arises a world-literature.

The bourgeoisie, by the rapid improvement of all instruments of production, by the immensely facilitated means of communication, draws all, even the most barbarian, nations into civilization. The cheap prices of its commodities are the heavy artillery with which it batters down all Chinese walls, with which it forces the barbarians' intensely obstinate hatred of foreigners to capitulate. It compels all nations, on pain of extinction, to adopt the bourgeois mode of production; it compels them to introduce what it calls civilization into their midst, i.e., to become bourgeois themselves. In a word, it creates a world after its own image.

The bourgeoisie has subjected the country to the rule of the towns. It has created enormous cities, has greatly increased the urban population as compared with the rural, and has thus rescued a considerable part of the population from the idiocy of rural life. Just as it has made the country dependent on the towns, so it has made barbarian and semi-barbarian countries dependent on the civilized ones, nations of peasants on nations of bourgeois, the East on the West.

The bourgeoisie keeps more and more doing away with the scattered state of the population, of the means of production, and of property. It has agglomerated population, centralized means of production, and has concentrated property in a few hands. The necessary consequence of this was political centralization. Independent, or but loosely connected provinces, with separate interests, laws, governments, and systems of taxation, became lumped together in one nation, with one government, one code of laws, one national class-interest, one frontier and one customs-tariff.

The bourgeoisie, during its rule of scarce one hundred years, has created more massive and more colossal productive forces than have all preceding generations together. Subjection of Nature's forces to man, machinery, application of chemistry to industry and agriculture, steam-navigation, railways, electric telegraphs, clearing of whole continents for cultivation, canalization of rivers, whole populations conjured out of the ground—what earlier century had even a presentiment that such productive forces slumbered in the lap of social labor?

The Revolutionary Potential of the Proletariat

We see then: the means of production and of exchange on whose foundation the bourgeoisie built itself up, were generated in feudal society. At a certain stage in the development of these means of production and of exchange, the conditions under which feudal society produced and exchanged, the feudal organization of agriculture and manufacturing industry, in one word, the feudal relations of property became no longer compatible with the already developed productive forces; they became so many fetters. They had to burst asunder; they were burst asunder.

Into their places stepped free competition, accompanied by a social and political constitution adapted to it, and by the economical and political sway of the bourgeois class.

A similar movement is going on before our own eyes. Modern bourgeois society with its relations of production, of exchange and of property, a society that has conjured up such gigantic means of production and of exchange, is like the sorcerer, who is no longer able to control the powers of the nether world whom he has called up by his spells. For many a decade past the history of industry and commerce is but the history of the revolt of modern productive forces against modern conditions of production, against the existence of the bourgeoisie and of its rule. It is enough to mention the commercial crises that by their periodical return put on its trial, each time more threateningly, the existence of the entire bourgeois society. In these crises a great part not only of the existing products, but also of the previously created productive forces, are periodically destroyed. In these crises there breaks out an epidemic that, in all earlier epochs, would have seemed an absurdity—the epidemic of over-production. Society suddenly finds itself put back into a state of momentary barbarism; it appears as if a famine, a universal war of devastation had cut off the supply of every means of subsistence; industry and commerce seem to be destroyed; and why? Because there is too much civilization, too much means of subsistence, too much industry, to much commerce. The productive forces at the disposal of society no longer tend to further the development of the conditions of bourgeois property; on the contrary, they have become too powerful for these conditions, by which they are fettered, and so soon as they overcome these fetters, they bring disorder into the whole of bourgeois society, endanger the existence of bourgeois property. The conditions of bourgeois society are too narrow to comprise the wealth created by them. And how does the bourgeoisie get over these crises? On the one hand by enforced destruction of a mass of productive forces; on the other, by the conquest of new markets, and by the more thorough exploitation of the old ones. That is to say, by paving the way for more extensive and more destructive crises, and by diminishing the means whereby crises are prevented.

The weapons with which the bourgeoisie felled feudalism to the ground are now turned against the bourgeoisie itself.

But not only has the bourgeoisie forged the weapons that bring death to itself; it has also called into existence the men who are to wield those weapons—the modern working-class—the proletarians.

In proportion as the bourgeoisie, i.e., capital, is developed, in the same proportion is the proletariat, the modern working-class, developed, a class of laborers, who live only so long as they find work, and who find work only so long as their labor increases capital. These laborers, who must sell themselves piecemeal, are a commodity, like every other article of commerce, and are consequently exposed to all the vicissitudes of competition, to all the fluctuations of the market.

Owing to the extensive use of machinery and to division of labor, the work of the proletarians has lost all individual character, and, consequently, all charm for the workman. He becomes an appendage of the machine, and it is only the most simple, most monotonous, and most easily acquired knack that is required of him. Hence, the cost of production of a workman is restricted, almost entirely, to the means of subsistence that he requires for his maintenance, and for the propagation of his race. But the price of a commodity, and also of labor, is equal to its cost of production. In proportion, therefore, as the repulsiveness of the work increases, the wage decreases. Nay more, in proportion as the use of machinery and division of labor increases, in the same proportion the burden of toil also increases, whether by prolongation of the working hours, by increase of the work enacted in a given time, or by increased speed of the machinery, etc.

Modern industry has converted the little workshop of the patriarchal master into the great factory of the industrial capitalist. Masses of laborers, crowded into the factory, are organized like soldiers. As privates of the industrial army they are placed under the command of a perfect hierarchy of officers and sergeants. Not only are they the slaves of the bourgeois class, and of the bourgeois State, they are daily and hourly enslaved by the machine, by the over-looker, and, above all, by the individual bourgeois manufacturer himself. The more openly this despotism proclaims gain to be its end and aim, the more petty, the more hateful and the more embittering it is.

The less the skill and exertion or strength implied in manual labor, in other words, the more modern industry becomes developed, the more is the labor of men superseded by that of women. Differences of age and sex have no longer any distinctive social validity for the working class. All are instruments of labor, more or less expensive to use, according to their age and sex.

No sooner is the exploitation of the laborer by the manufacturer, so far at an end, that he receives his wages in cash, then he is set upon by the other portions of the bourgeoisie, the landlord, the shopkeeper, the pawnbroker, etc.

The Growth of the Proletariat

The lower strata of the middle class—the small tradespeople, shopkeepers, and retired tradesmen generally, the handicraftsmen and peasants—all these sink gradually into the proletariat, partly because their diminutive capital does not suffice for the scale on which Modern Industry is carried on, and is swamped in the competition with the large capitalists, partly because their specialized skill is rendered worthless by new methods of production. Thus the proletariat is recruited from all classes of the population.

The proletariat goes through various stages of development. With its birth begins its struggle with the bourgeoisie. At first the contest is carried on by individual laborers, then by the workpeople of a factory, then by the operatives of one trade, in one locality, against the individual bourgeois who directly exploits them. They direct their attacks not against the bourgeois conditions of production, but against the instruments of production themselves; they destroy imported wares that compete with their labor, they smash to pieces machinery, they set factories ablaze, they seek to restore by force the vanished status of the workman of the Middle Ages.

At this stage the laborers still form an incoherent mass scattered over the whole country, and broken up by their mutual competition. If anywhere they unite to form more compact bodies, this is not yet the consequence of their own active union, but of the union of the bourgeoisie, which class, in order to attain its own political ends, is compelled to set the whole proletariat in motion, and is moreover yet, for a time, able to do so. At this stage, therefore, the proletarians do not fight their enemies, but the enemies of their enemies, the remnants of absolute monarchy, the landowners, the non-industrial bourgeois, the petty bourgeoisie. Thus the whole historical movement is concentrated in the hands of the bourgeoisie; every victory so obtained is a victory for the bourgeoisie.

But with the development of industry the proletariat not only increases in number, it becomes concentrated in greater masses, its strength grows, and it feels that strength more. The various interests and conditions of life within the ranks of the proletariat are more and more equalized, in proportion as machinery obliterates all distinctions of labor, and nearly everywhere reduces wages to the same low level. The growing competition among the bourgeois, and the resulting commercial crises, make the wages of the workers ever more fluctuating. The unceasing improvement of machinery, ever more rapidly developing, makes their livelihood more and more precarious; the collisions between individual workmen and individual bourgeois take more and more the character of collisions between two classes. Thereupon the workers begin to form combinations (Trades' Unions) against the bourgeois; they club together in order to keep up the rate of wages; they found permanent associations in order to make provision beforehand for these occasional revolts. Here and there the contest breaks out into riots.

Dimensions of the Class Struggle

Now and then the workers are victorious, but only for a time. The real fruit of their battles lies, not in the immediate result, but in the ever expanding union of the workers. This union is helped on by the improved means of communication that are created by modern industry, and that place the workers of different localities in contact with one another. It was just this contact that was needed to centralize the numerous local struggles, all of the same character, into one national struggle between classes. But every class struggle is a political struggle. And that union, to attain which the burghers of the Middle Ages, with their miserable highways, required centuries, the modern proletarians, thanks to railways, achieve in a few years.

This organization of the proletarians into a class, and consequently into a political party, is continually being upset again by the competition between the workers themselves. But it ever rises up again, stronger, firmer, mightier. It compels legislative recognition of particular interests of the workers, by taking advantage of the divisions among the bourgeoisie itself. Thus the ten-hour bill in England was carried.

Altogether collisions between the classes of the old society further, in many ways, the course of development of the proletariat. The bourgeoisie finds itself involved in a constant battle. At first with the aristocracy; later on, with those portions of the bourgeoisie itself, whose interests have become antagonistic to the progress of industry;

at all times, with the bourgeoisie of foreign countries. In all these battles it sees itself compelled to appeal to the proletariat, to ask for its help, and thus, to drag it into the political arena. The bourgeoisie itself, therefore, supplies the proletariat with its own elements of political and general education, in other words, it furnishes the proletariat with weapons for fighting the bourgeoisie.

Further, as we have already seen, entire sections of the ruling classes are, by the advance of industry, precipitated into the proletariat, or are at least threatened in their conditions of existence. These also supply the proletariat with fresh elements of enlightenment and progress.

Finally, in times when the class-struggle nears the decisive hour, the process of dissolution going on within the ruling class, in fact, within the whole range of old society, assumes such a violent, glaring character, that a small section of the ruling class cuts itself adrift, and joins the revolutionary class, the class that holds the future in its hands. Just as, therefore, at an earlier period, a section of the nobility went over to the bourgeoisie, so now a portion of the bourgeoisie goes over to the proletariat, and in particular, a portion of the bourgeois ideologists, who have raised themselves to the level of comprehending theoretically the historical movements as a whole.

Of all the classes that stand face to face with the bourgeoisie today, the proletariat alone is a really revolutionary class. The other classes decay and finally disappear in the face of modern industry; the proletariat is its special and essential product.

The lower middle class, the small manufacturer, the shopkeeper, the artisan, the peasant, all these fight against the bourgeoisie, to save from extinction their existence as fractions of the middle class. They are, therefore, not revolutionary, but conservative. Nay more, they are reactionary, for they try to roll back the wheel of history. If by chance they are revolutionary, they are so, only in view of their impending transfer into the proletariat, they thus defend not their present, but their future interests, they desert their own standpoint to place themselves at that of the proletariat.

The "dangerous class," the social scum, that passively rotting mass thrown off by the lowest layers of old society, may, here and there, be swept into the movement by a proletarian revolution; its conditions of life, however, prepare it far more for the part of a bribed tool of reactionary intrigue.

In the conditions of the proletariat, those of old society at large are already virtually swamped. The proletarian is without property; his relation to his wife and children has no longer anything in common with the bourgeois family-relations; modern industrial labor, modern subjection to capital, the same in England as in France, in America as in Germany, has stripped him of every trace of national character. Law, morality, religion, are to him so many bourgeois prejudices, behind which lurk in ambush just as many bourgeois interests.

All the preceding classes that got the upper hand, sought to fortify their already acquired status by subjecting society at large to their conditions of appropriation. The proletarians cannot become masters of the productive forces of society, except by abolishing their own previous mode of appropriation, and thereby also every other previous mode of appropriation. They have nothing of their own to secure and to fortify; their mission is to destroy all previous securities for, and insurances of, individual property.

All previous historical movements were movements of minorities, or in the interest of minorities. The proletarian movement is the self-conscious, independent movement of the immense majority, in the interest of the immense majority. The proletariat, the lowest stratum of our present society, cannot stir, cannot raise itself up, without the whole superincumbent strata of official society being sprung into the air.

Though not in substance, yet in form, the struggle of the proletariat with the bourgeoisie is at first a national struggle. The proletariat of each country must, of course, first of all settle matters with its own bourgeoisie.

In depicting the most general phases of the development of the proletariat, we traced the more or less veiled civil war, raging within existing society, up to the point where that war breaks out into open revolution, and where the violent overthrow of the bourgeoisie lays the foundation for the sway of the proletariat.

Hitherto, every form of society has been based, as we have already seen, on the antagonism of oppressing and oppressed classes. But in order to oppress a class, certain conditions must be assured to it under which it can, at least, continue its slavish existence. The serf, in the period of serfdom, raised himself to membership in the commune, just as the petty bourgeois, under the yoke of feudal absolutism, managed to develop into a bourgeois. The modern laborer, on the contrary, instead of rising with the progress of industry, sinks deeper and deeper below the conditions of existence of his own class. He becomes a pauper, and pauperism develops more rapidly than population and wealth. And here it becomes evident, that the bourgeoisie is unfit any longer to be the ruling class in society, and to impose its conditions of existence upon society as an over-riding law. It is unfit to rule, because it is incompetent to assure an existence to its slave within his slavery, because it cannot help letting him sink into such a state that it has to feed him, instead of being fed by him. Society can no longer live under this bourgeoisie, in other words, its existence is no longer compatible with society.

The essential condition for the existence, and for the sway of the bourgeois class, is the formation and augmentation of capital; the condition for capital is wage-labor. Wage-labor rests exclusively on competition between the laborers. The advance of industry, whose involuntary promoter is the bourgeoisie, replaces the isolation of the laborers, due to competition, by their revolutionary combination, due to association. The development of Modern Industry, therefore, cuts from under its feet the very foundation on which the bourgeoisie produces and appropriates products. What the bourgeoisie therefore produces, above all, are its own grave-diggers. Its fall and the victory of the proletariat are equally inevitable.

Proletarians and Communists

In what relation do the Communists stand to the proletarians as a whole?

The Communists do not form a separate party opposed to other working class parties.

They have no interests separate and apart from those of the proletariat as a whole.

They do not set up any sectarian principles of their own, by which to shape and mould the proletarian movement.

The Communists are distinguished from the other working class parties by this only: 1. In the national struggles of the proletarians of the different countries, they point out and bring to the front the common interests of the entire proletariat independently of all nationality. 2. In the various stages of development which the struggle of the working class against the bourgeoisie has to pass through, they always and everywhere represent the interests of the movement as a whole.

The Communists, therefore, are on the one hand, practically, the most advanced and resolute section of the working class parties of every country, that section which pushes forward all others; on the other hand, theoretically, they have over the great mass of the proletariat the advantage of clearly understanding the line of march, the conditions, and the ultimate general results of the proletarian movement.

The immediate aim of the Communists is the same as that of all the other proletarian parties: formation of the proletariat into a class, overthrow of the bourgeois supremacy, conquest of political power by the proletariat.

The theoretical conclusions of the Communists are in no way based on ideas or principles that have been invented, or discovered, by this or that would-be universal reformer.

The Abolition of Private Property

They merely express, in general terms, actual relations springing from an existing class struggle, from a historical movement going on under our very eyes. The abolition of existing property relations is not at all a distinctive feature of Communism.

All property relations in the past have continually been subject to historical change consequent upon the change in historical conditions.

The French Revolution, for example, abolished feudal property in favor of bourgeois property.

The distinguishing feature of Communism is not the abolition of property generally, but the abolition of bourgeois property. But modern bourgeois private property is the final and most complete expression of the system of producing and appropriating products, that is based on class antagonism, on the exploitation of the many by the few.

In this sense, the theory of the Communists may be summed up in the single sentence: Abolition of private property.

We Communists have been reproached with the desire of abolishing the right of personally acquiring property as the fruit of a man's own labor, which property is alleged to be the ground work of all personal freedom, activity and independence.

Hard-won, self-acquired, self-earned property! Do you mean the property of the petty artisan and of the small peasant, a form of property that preceded the bourgeois form? There is no need to abolish that; the development of industry has to a great extent already destroyed it, and is still destroying it daily.

Or do you mean modern bourgeois private property?

But does wage-labor create any property for the laborer? Not a bit. It creates capital, i.e., that kind of property which exploits wage-labor, and which cannot increase except upon condition of getting a new supply of wage-labor for fresh exploitation. Property, in its present form, is based on the antagonism of capital and wage-labor. Let us examine both sides of this antagonism.

To be a capitalist, is to have not only a purely personal, but a social status in production. Capital is a collective product, and only by the united action of many members, nay, in the last resort, only by the united action of all members of society, can it be set in motion.

Capital is therefore not a personal, it is a social power.

When, therefore, capital is converted into common property, into the property of all members of society, personal property is not thereby transformed into social property. It is only the social character of the property that is changed. It loses its class-character.

Let us now take wage-labor.

The average price of wage-labor is the minimum wage, i.e., that quantum of the means of subsistence, which is absolutely requisite to keep the laborer in bare existence as a laborer. What, therefore, the wage-laborer appropriates by means of his labor, merely suffices to prolong and reproduce a bare existence. We by no means intend to abolish this personal appropriation of the products of labor, an appropriation that is made for the maintenance and reproduction of human life, and that leaves no surplus wherewith to command the labor of others. All that we went to do away with is the miserable character of this appropriation, under which the laborer lives merely to increase capital, and is allowed to live only in so far as the interest of the ruling class requires it.

In bourgeois society, living labor is but a means to increase accumulated labor. In communist society, accumulated labor is but a means to widen, to enrich, to promote the existence of the laborer.

In bourgeois society, therefore, the past dominates the present; in communist society, the present dominates the past. In bourgeois society capital is independent and has individuality, while the living person is dependent and has no individuality.

And the abolition of this state of things is called by the bourgeois, abolition of individuality and freedom! And rightly so. The abolition of bourgeois individuality, bourgeois independence, and bourgeois freedom is undoubtedly aimed at.

By freedom is meant, under the present bourgeois conditions of production, free trade, free selling and buying.

But if selling and buying disappears, free selling and buying disappears also. This talk about free selling and buying, and all the other "brave words" of our bourgeoisie about freedom in general, have a meaning, if any, only in contrast with restricted selling and buying, with the fettered traders of the Middle Ages, but have no meaning when opposed to the Communistic abolition of buying and selling, of the bourgeois conditions of production, and of the bourgeoisie itself.

You are horrified at our intending to do away with private property. But in your existing society, private property is already done away with for nine-tenths of the population; its existence for the few is solely due to its non-existence in the hands of those nine-tenths. You reproach us, therefore, with intending to do away with a form of property, the necessary condition for whose existence is, the non-existence of any property for the immense majority of society.

In one word, you reproach us with intending to do away with your property. Precisely so; that is just what we intend.

From the moment when labor can no longer be converted into capital, money, or rent, into a social power capable of being monopolized, i.e., from the moment when individual property can no longer be transformed into bourgeois property, into capital, from that moment, you say, individuality vanishes.

You must, therefore, confess that by "individual" you mean no other person than the bourgeois, than the middle-class owner of property. This person must, indeed, be swept out of the way, and made impossible.

Communism deprives no man of the power to appropriate the products of society: all that it does is to deprive him of the power to subjugate the labor of others by means of such appropriation.

It has been objected, that upon the abolition of private property all work will cease, and universal laziness will overtake us.

According to this, bourgeois society ought long ago to have gone to the dogs through sheer idleness; for those of its members who work, acquire nothing, and those who acquire anything, do not work. The whole of this objection is but another expression of the tautology: that there can no longer be any wage-labor when there is no longer any capital.

All objections urged against the Communistic mode of producing and appropriating material products, have, in the same way, been urged against the Communistic modes of producing and appropriating intellectual products. Just as, to the bourgeois, the disappearance of class property is the disappearance of production itself, so the disappearance of class culture is to him identical with the disappearance of all culture.

That culture, the loss of which he laments, is, for the enormous majority, a mere training to act as a machine.

But don't wrangle with us so long as you apply, to our intended abolition of bourgeois property, the standard of your bourgeois notions of freedom, culture, law, etc. Your very ideas are but the outgrowth of the conditions of your bourgeois production and bourgeois property, just as your jurisprudence is but the will of your class made into a law for all, a will, whose essential character and direction are determined by the economic conditions of existence of your class.

The selfish misconception that induces you to transform into eternal laws of nature and of reason, the social forms springing from your present mode of production and form of property—historical relations that rise and disappear in the progress of production—this misconception you share with every ruling class that has preceded you. What you see clearly in the case of ancient property, what you admit in the case of feudal property, you are of course forbidden to admit in the case of your own bourgeois form of property.

Abolition of the Family

Abolition of the family! Even the most radical flare up at this infamous proposal of the Communists.

On what foundation is the present family, the bourgeois family, based? On capital, on private gain. In its completely developed form this family exists only among the bourgeoisie. But this state of things finds its complement in the practical absence of the family among the proletarians, and in public prostitution.

The bourgeois family will vanish as a matter of course when its complement vanishes, and both will vanish with the vanishing of capital.

Do you charge us with wanting to stop the exploitation of children by their parents? To this crime we plead guilty.

But, you will say, we destroy the most hallowed of relations, when we replace home education by social.

And your education! Is not that also social, and determined by the social conditions under which you educate, by the intervention, direct or indirect, of society by means of schools, etc.? The Communists have not invented the intervention of society in education; they do but seek to alter the character of that intervention, and to rescue education from the influence of the ruling class.

The bourgeois clap-trap about the family and education, about the hallowed co-relation of parent and child, becomes all the more disgusting, the more, by the action of Modern Industry, all family ties among the proletarians are torn asunder, and their children transformed into simple articles of commerce and instruments of labor.

But you Communists would introduce community of women, screams the whole bourgeoisie in chorus.

The bourgeois sees in his wife a mere instrument of production. He hears that the instruments of production are to be exploited in common, and, naturally, can come to no other conclusion, than that the lot of being common to all will likewise fall to the women.

He has not even a suspicion that the real point aimed at is to do away with the status of women as mere instruments of production.

For the rest, nothing is more ridiculous than the virtuous indignation of our bourgeois at the community of women which, they pretend, is to be openly and officially established by the Communists. The Communists have no need to introduce community of women; it has existed almost from time immemorial.

Our bourgeois, not content with having the wives and daughters of their proletarians at their disposal, not to speak of common prostitutes, take the greatest pleasure in seducing each other's wives.

Bourgeois marriage is in reality a system of wives in common and thus, at the most, what the Communists might possibly be reproached with, is that they desire to introduce, in substitution for a hypocritically concealed, an openly legalized community of women. For the rest, it is self-evident, that the abolition of the present system of production must bring with it the abolition of the community of women springing from that system, i.e., of prostitution both public and private.

Abolition of Nationality

The Communists are further reproached with desiring to abolish countries and nationalities.

The working men have no country. We cannot take from them what they have not got. Since the proletariat must first of all acquire political supremacy, must rise to be the leading class of the nation, must constitute itself the nation, it is, so far, itself national, though not in the bourgeois sense of the word.

National differences, and antagonisms between peoples, are daily more and more vanishing, owing to the development of the bourgeoisie, to freedom of commerce, to the world-market, to uniformity in the mode of production and in the conditions of life corresponding thereto.

The supremacy of the proletariat will cause them to vanish still faster. United action, of the leading civilized countries at least, is one of the first conditions for the emancipation of the proletariat.

In proportion as the exploitation of one individual by another is put an end to, the exploitation of one nation by another will also be put an end to. In proportion as the antagonism between classes within the nation vanishes, the hostility of one nation to another will come to an end.

Abolition of Religion

The charges against Communism made from a religious, a philosophical, and generally, from an ideological standpoint, are not deserving of serious examination.

Does it require deep intuition to comprehend that man's ideas, views, and conceptions, in one word, man's consciousness, changes with every change in the conditions of his material existence, in his social relations and in his social life?

What else does the history of ideas prove, than that intellectual production changes in character in proportion as material production is changed? The ruling ideas of each age have ever been the ideas of its ruling class.

When people speak of ideas that revolutionize society, they do but express the fact, that within the old society, the elements of a new one have been created, and that the dissolution of the old ideas keeps even pace with the dissolution of the old conditions of existence.

When the ancient world was in its last throes, the ancient religions were overcome by Christianity. When Christian ideas succumbed in the 18th century to rationalist ideas, feudal society fought its death-battle with the then revolutionary bourgeoisie. The ideas of religious liberty and freedom of conscience, merely gave expression to the sway of free competition within the domain of knowledge.

"Undoubtedly," it will be said, "religious, moral, philosophical and juridical ideas have been modified in the course of historical development. But religion, morality, philosophy, political science, and law, constantly survived this change.

"There are, besides, eternal truths, such as Freedom, Justice, etc., that are common to all states of society. But Communism abolishes eternal truths, it abolishes all religion, and all morality, instead of constituting them on a new basis; it therefore acts in contradiction to all past historical experience."

What does this accusation reduce itself to? The history of all past society has consisted in the development of class antagonisms, antagonisms that assume different forms at different epochs.

But whatever form they may have taken, one fact is common to all past ages, viz., the exploitation of one part of society by the other. No wonder, then, that the social consciousness of past ages, despite all the multiplicity and variety it displays, moves within certain common forms, or general ideas, which cannot completely vanish except with the total disappearance of class antagonisms.

The Communist revolution is the most radical rupture with traditional property-relations; no wonder that its development involves the most radical rupture with traditional ideas.

But let us have done with the bourgeois objections to Communism.

Victory of the Proletariat

We have seen above, that the first step in the revolution by the working class, is to raise the proletariat to the position of ruling class, to win the battle of democracy.

The proletariat will use its political supremacy, to wrest, by degrees, all capital from the bourgeoisie, to centralize all instruments of production in the hands of the State, i.e., of the proletariat organized as the ruling class; and to increase the total of productive forces as rapidly as possible.

Of course, in the beginning, this cannot be effected except by means of despotic inroads on the rights of property, and on the conditions of bourgeois production; by means of measures, therefore, which appear economically insufficient and untenable, but which, in the course of the movement, outstrip themselves, necessitate further inroads upon the old social order, and are unavoidable as a means of entirely revolutionizing the mode of production.

These measures will of course be different in different countries.

Nevertheless in the most advanced countries the following will be pretty generally applicable:

1. Abolition of property in land and application of all rents of land to public purposes.
2. A heavy progressive or graduated income tax.
3. Abolition of all right of inheritance.
4. Confiscation of the property of all emigrants and rebels.

5. Centralization of credit in the hands of the state, by means of a national bank with State capital and an exclusive monopoly.

6. Centralization of the means of communication and transport in the hands of the State.

7. Extension of factories and instruments of production owned by the State; the bringing into cultivation of waste lands, and the improvement of the soil generally in accordance with a common plan.

8. Equal liability of all to labor. Establishment of industrial armies, especially for agriculture.

9. Combination of agriculture with manufacturing industries; gradual abolition of the distinction between town and country, by a more equable distribution of population over the country.

10. Free education for all children in public schools. Abolition of children's factory labor in its present form. Combination of education with industrial production, etc., etc.

Withering Away of the State

When, in the course of development, class distinctions have disappeared, and all production has been concentrated in the hands of a vast association of the whole nation, the public power will lose its political character. Political power, properly so called, is merely the organized power of one class for oppressing another. If the proletariat during its contest with the bourgeoisie is compelled, by the force of circumstances, to organize itself as a class, if, by means of a revolution, it makes itself the ruling class, and, as such, sweeps away by force the old conditions of production, then it will, along with these conditions, have swept away the conditions for the existence of class antagonisms, and of classes generally, and will thereby have abolished its own supremacy as a class.

In place of the old bourgeois society, with its classes and class antagonisms, we shall have an association, in which the free development of each is the condition for the free development of all.

. . .

2

MAO TSE-TUNG

(1893–)

*On Practice**

Political and spiritual leader of China, Mao Tse-Tung served in Sun Yat-sen's revolutionary army (1911–12), studied Marx and Engels and Lenin's successful Russian Revolution of 1917, and then organized the Chinese Communist Party in the 1920's. In 1949 his armies drove the Chiang Kai-shek Nationalists from mainland China, and he became chairman of Central Government Council. Mao's works have become a major philosophical rally-point for contemporary radicals. He is totally opposed to compromise and peaceful co-existence with capitalism. His revolution is world-wide. His theories of guerrilla warfare, explaining the steps of a successful rebellion, were utilized in the strategies of the Viet Cong and in the Che Guevara's abortive Bolivian campaign.

The first of our selections of Mao's philosophy, "On Practice," was published in 1937. It is a criticism of the "dogmatists" and those with either leftist or rightist inclinations. In the broader sense it is an attempt to combine a theory of knowledge with practical application. The Marxist idea of man's nature plays a dominant role in Mao's thinking. Truth is to be attained through practice, knowledge through activity; subject and object are interdependent. Revolution produces not only external change but remolds the entire fabric of knowledge and the relationship of the knower to what is known, the subject to the world.

* Arthur P. Mendel, ed., *The Essential Works of Marxism* (New York: Bantam, 1961), pp. 499–513.

IN the study of the problem of knowledge pre-Marxist materialism leaves man's social nature and historical development out of account. Hence it cannot explain the dependence of cognition upon social practice—its dependence upon production and class struggle.

Productive Activity and Knowledge

First of all, a Marxist regards human productive activity as the most fundamental practice determining all other human activities. Cognitively man depends mainly upon his activity in material production for a gradual understanding of nature's phenomena, its characteristics, its laws, and its relation to himself; at the same time, through productive activity, man comes to understand gradually and in varying degrees certain human interrelations. None of such knowledge can be obtained apart from productive activity. In a classless society everyone in his capacity as one of its members works together with other members of society, comes into certain relations of production with them, and engages in production to solve the problem of man's material life. In various kinds of class societies, members of society from all classes come in different ways into certain relations of production with each other and engage in production to solve the same problem. This is the fundamental source of the development of human knowledge.

Productive activity is not the only form of man's social practice. There are various other forms—class struggle, political life, scientific and artistic activities. In short, man participates as a social being in every sphere of the actual life of society. Thus besides his cognition of things of material life, man comes to know in varying degrees the different kinds of human relations through his political and cultural life closely connected with his material life. Among these, class struggle in its various forms especially exerts a profound influence on the development of man's knowledge. In a class society everyone lives with a certain class status and all his thoughts are stamped with the seal of his class.

According to the Marxist, man's activity in social production develops step by step from a low stage to a high stage, and consequently man's knowledge, whether of nature or of society, also develops step by step from a low stage to a high stage, *viz.*, from the elementary to the advanced, and from the one-sided to the many-sided. For a very long period in human history, people were, as they could only be, limited to a phasic understanding of the history of society. This was due on the one hand to the constant distortion of it by the exploiting classes with their biased views, and on the other to the small scale of production which limited the breadth of view of the people. Not until the modern proletariat appeared along with greatly increased productive forces or big industry did man begin to have a comprehensive and historical understanding of the development of society and turn his knowledge of society into a science. This is none other than the science of Marxism.

According to the Marxist, man's social practice alone is the criterion of truth in his cognition of the external world, for in actuality human cognition becomes verified only when man arrives at the results predicted, through the process of social practice, *viz.*, through the processes of material production, of class struggle, and of scientific experiments. If anyone wants to be successful in his work or to achieve the anticipated results, he must make his ideas correspond to the laws of the external world; otherwise he will fail in practice. It is from failure that one derives lessons and corrects one's ideas so as to make them correspond to the laws of the external world. This is how one turns failure into success. This is exactly what is meant by failure being the mother of success, and by "a fall into the pit, a gain in your wit."

The epistemology of dialectical materialism raises practice to a position of primary importance. It regards human knowledge as being at no point separable from practice, refuting all the incorrect theories which deny the importance of practice or which separate knowledge from it.

Thus Lenin said, "Practice is more important than (theoretical) knowledge, because it not only has the virtue of universality but also the virtue of direct reality."

Marxist philosophy, dialectical materialism, has two most outstanding characteristics. One is its class nature: it openly declares itself to be in the service of the proletariat. The other is its practicality: it emphasizes the dependence of theory on practice, practice being the foundation of theory which in turn serves practice. One's theory or cognition is judged to be true or untrue not by how it is subjectively felt to be, but by what objectively the result is in social practice. The criterion of truth can only be social practice. The viewpoint which emphasizes practice is primary and basic in the epistemology of dialectical materialism.

Human Knowledge through Practice

But how after all does human knowledge arise from practice and serve practice in turn? This will be clear after an examination of the developing process of cognition.

At first man sees in the process of practice only the phenomena of things, their individual aspects, and their external relations to each other. For instance, a number of outside people came to Yenan on an observation tour. On the first day or two, they saw the topography, the streets, and the houses of Yenan; met people; went to feasts, evening parties, and mass meetings; heard what was talked about; read what was written: these are the phenomena of things, their individual aspects, and their external relations. This is called the perceptual stage of knowledge, namely, the stage of sensation and imagery. It is also the first stage of knowledge, the stage in which these different things in Yenan affected the sense organs of the gentlemen of the observation commission, gave rise to sensations, and left many images in their brain together with a crude outline of their external relations. In this stage one cannot as yet form profound concepts or draw logical conclusions.

With the continuation of man's social practice, the sensations and images of a thing are repeated innumerable times in his practice and then a sudden change in the cognitive process takes place in his brain resulting in the formation of concepts. Concepts as such represent no longer the phenomena of things, their individual aspects, or their external relations. Through concepts man comes to grasp a thing in its entirety, its essence, and its internal relations. Conception is not only quantitatively but also qualitatively different from perception. Proceeding from concepts, we can employ the method of judgment and inference and arrive at logical conclusions. What is known as "knit your brows, and the idea comes to your mind" in the *Tale of the Three Kingdoms* or "let me think" in our workaday language refers to the employment of concepts in our brain to form judgments and draw inferences. This is the second stage of knowledge.

The gentlemen of the observation commission after having gathered various kinds of data and in addition reflected on them may come to the judgment: The policy of the National Anti-Japanese United Front pursued by the Communist Party is thorough, sincere, and honest. If these gentlemen themselves were sincerely in favor of unity for national salvation, then after having made the above judgment they could go a step further and conclude that "the National Anti-Japanese United Front can succeed." In the complete process of knowing a thing this stage of conception, judgment, and inference is more important than the first stage. It is the stage of rational knowledge.

The real task of cognition is to arrive at thought through perception, at a gradual understanding of the internal contradictions of objective things, their laws, the internal relations between this and that process, that is, at rational knowledge. To repeat, the reason why rational knowledge is different from perceptual knowledge is that perceptual knowledge is knowledge of a thing in its individual aspects, its appearance, and its external relations, whereas rational knowledge, marking a great step in advance, is knowledge of a thing in its entirety, its essence, and its internal relations. When one arrives at rational knowledge, one is able to reveal the internal contradictions of the surrounding world and thus grasp the development of that world by considering it in its entirety—the internal relations of and between all its aspects.

Before the advent of Marxism none had proposed a theory of knowledge that takes account of the developing process of cognition that is based on practice, that proceeds from the elementary to the advanced, and that is dialectically materialistic. Marxist materialism for the first time correctly solved this problem, pointing out both materialistically and dialectically the ever-deepening process of cognition, a process that turns perceptual knowledge into rational knowledge through the complex and regularly recurring practices of man as a social being in his production and class struggle. Lenin said: "The abstract concept of matter, of a law of nature, of economic value or any other scientific (*i.e.*, correct and basic, not false or superficial) abstraction reflects nature more deeply, truly, and fully." What characterizes respectively the two stages of the process of cognition, according to Marxism-Leninism, is that in the lower stage knowledge appears in perceptual form and in the higher stage in rational form; each of these two stages, however, constitutes a stage in one united process of cognition. Perceptual knowledge and rational knowledge are different in nature, but not separate from each other, being united on the basis of practice.

It is our practice that proves that things perceived are not readily understood, and that only things understood are more profoundly perceived. It proves that perception only solves the problem of how things appear, and that understanding answers the question as to what their essence is. Thus these problems cannot be solved at all apart from practice. If anybody wants to know something, he cannot do otherwise than to come into contact with that thing, that is, to live (practice) in its setting.

In a feudal society one cannot know beforehand the laws of capitalist society, because, capitalist society not yet having appeared, there cannot be any practice appropriate to it. Marxism can only be the product of capitalist society. In the age of the capitalism of free competition, Marx could not know concretely beforehand some of the special laws of the age of imperialism, because this age, the last stage of capitalism, had not yet arrived and there was no practice appropriate to it. Only Lenin and Stalin could shoulder this task.

Aside from their genius, what enabled Marx, Engels, Lenin, and Stalin to formulate their theories was mainly their personal participation in the practice of the class struggle and scientific experiments of their time. Without the latter condition no genius could succeed in such a task. "A scholar knows all that is happening in the world without going out of his door" was only an empty phrase in the technologically undeveloped times of old. Although this dictum could be true in the present age of technological development, yet real knowledge through direct acquaintance is only for all those in the world who are engaged in actual practice. Through practice these people obtain knowledge which, when put into the hands of the scholar through the communication of language and technical devices, enables him indirectly to know about "all that is happening in the world."

If one wants to know directly some things or some kinds of things one can do so only through personal participation in the practical struggle to change existing conditions, to change those things or those kinds of things. Only thus can one come into contact with the phenomena of those things or those kinds of things; and only thus can the essence of those things or those kinds of things be revealed and understood. This is actually the path to knowledge along which everyone travels. Only some people deliberately argue to the contrary to confuse and confound.

The most ridiculous persons in the world are those "know-it-alls" who pick up crumbs of knowledge piecemeal and proclaim themselves, each of them, "the number one of the world." This serves merely to show that they have not taken proper measure of themselves.

Knowledge is a matter of science, and there is no room for the slightest insincerity or conceit. What is required is decidedly the opposite, sincerity and modesty. If one wants to have knowledge one has to participate in the practice of changing existing conditions. If one wants to know the taste of a pear one has to transform the pear by eating it oneself. If one wants to know the composition and properties of atoms one has to perform physical and chemical experiments to change their original state. If one wants to know the theory and method of revolution, one has to participate in revolution.

All knowledge originates from direct experience. But no one can directly experience everything. As a matter of fact, most of our knowledge is of things indirectly experienced. All our knowledge of ancient times and foreign lands belongs to this category, but for the ancients and foreigners it is knowledge of things directly experienced. If this kind of knowledge of the ancients and foreigners from their direct experience conforms to the requirements of "scientific abstraction" mentioned by Lenin and reflects objective things scientifically, then it is reliable knowledge, otherwise it is not. Hence one's knowledge consists of two parts: knowledge of things directly experienced and knowledge of things indirectly experienced. And what is indirectly experienced by one is nevertheless directly experienced by others. Hence taken as a whole, any kind of knowledge is inseparable from direct experience.

Origins of Knowledge

All knowledge originates in man's perception of the external world through his sense organs. If one denies perception, denies direct experience, and denies personal participation in the practice of changing existing conditions, one is not a materialist. This is exactly where the "know-it-alls" are ridiculous. The Chinese have an old saying: "If one doesn't enter the tiger's den, one cannot obtain tiger cubs." This statement is as true of epistemology as of man's practice. Knowledge is impossible if separated from practice.

In order to understand the dialectical materialist conception of the process of cognition based upon and issuing from the practice of changing existing conditions—the process of cognition in its gradually deepening movement—let us take a few examples.

The knowledge of capitalist society the proletariat had in the first period of its practice; the period of machine-smashing and spontaneous struggle, was only perceptual knowledge. It was only a knowledge of the individual aspects and the external relations of the various phenomena of capitalism. At that time the proletariat was what is called a *class in itself*. But when this class reached the second period of its practice, the period of conscious, organized economic and political struggle, there emerged the ideology of Marxism as a result of the practice of this class, its experience of constant and continuous struggle and the scientific summary and integration of all these experiences by Marx and Engels. When this ideology was used to educate the proletariat and enabled it to understand the essence of capitalist society, the relation of exploitation between classes, and its own historic task, it transformed itself into a *class for itself*.

The Chinese people came to know imperialism in the same way. The first stage was one of perceptual knowledge of the appearance of things. It was marked with the indiscriminately antiforeign struggle of the T'aip'ing (1850–1864) and the Boxer (1900) revolutionary movements. It was only in the second stage that the Chinese people arrived at rational knowledge. They saw the internal and external contradictions of imperialism. They also saw the essence of the exploitation of China's broad masses by imperialism in alliance with the comprador and feudal classes. This kind of knowledge came to light only about the time of the May Fourth Movement of 1919.

Let us look at war. If those who are to direct a war have no experience of it, they would not understand at first the deep underlying laws for conducting a particular war such as that of our Agrarian Revolution of the past ten years. In the beginning they merely go through the experience of much fighting and many defeats, but subsequently from such experience (of victories and especially of defeats) they are able to understand the inner thread that runs through the whole of the fighting, namely, the laws of that particular war. They thus understand strategy and tactics and are able to direct the fighting with confidence. At such a time if an inexperienced man is appointed to take over the command, he still will not be able to understand the correct laws of war until he has also suffered defeats and gathered experiences from them.

Comrades who are not brave enough to accept an assignment are often heard to say: "I have no confidence." Why have they no confidence? Because they have no systematic understanding of the nature of the work nor the conditions under which it will be undertaken. Probably they have had little or even no contact with this kind of work and hence cannot know the underlying laws. After a close analysis of the nature and conditions of the work, they feel more confident and are willing to undertake it. If those people have gained experiences in this work after a period of time, and if they are not given to approaching things subjectively, one-sidedly, or superficially, but endeavor to understand them with an open mind, they are able to draw their own conclusions as to how they should proceed and their courage to undertake the task will be greatly enhanced. Those are bound to stumble who approach problems only subjectively, one-sidedly, superficially, who, upon reaching any place, start to issue orders or directives self-assuredly without considering their environment, without viewing things in their totality (their history and their present state as a whole), without coming into contact with the essence of things (their qualities and the internal relations between one thing and another).

It is thus seen that the first step in the process of cognition is to come into contact with the things of the external world; this belongs to the stage of perception. The second step is to synthesize the data of perception, to rearrange and reconstruct them; this belongs to the stage of conception, judgment, and inference. It is only when the perceptual data are abundant, not fragmentary or incomplete, and are in correspondence with reality, instead of being illusory, that they can serve as the basis for valid concepts, judgments, and inferences.

Here, two important points are to be emphasized. To repeat what has already been mentioned before, the first one is the dependence of rational knowledge upon perceptual knowledge. If one thinks that rational knowledge need not be derived from perceptual knowledge, one is an idealist. In the history of philosophy there were the so-called rationalists who admitted only the reality of reason, but not the reality of experience, regarding reason alone as reliable and perceptual experience as unreliable. The mistake of this school consisted in turning things upside down. What is rational is reliable precisely because it originates from the senses, otherwise it would be like water without source or trees without roots and become something unreliable and self-engendered.

As to the sequence in the process of cognition, perceptual experience comes first. We point out with special emphasis the significance of social practice in the process of cognition precisely because it is only through social practice that human cognition comes to pass, that people begin to obtain perceptual experience from the external world. There could be no such thing as knowledge for a person who shuts his eyes, stops his ears, and totally cuts himself off from the external world. Knowledge starts from experience—this is epistemological materialism.

The second point is that knowledge depends upon a deepening process, upon developing from the perceptual into the rational. This is epistemological dialectics. If anyone thinks that knowledge may stop at the low stage of perception and that perceptual knowledge alone is reliable, but not rational knowledge, then one repeats the historical mistake of empiricism. The mistake of such a theory is that it fails to take into account the fact that although the data of perception are the reflection of certain realities of the external world—I am not speaking of the idealist empiricism which limits experience to the so-called introspection—yet these data concern merely the aspects and appearances of things. This kind of reflection is incomplete and it is not one of the essence of things. To reflect a thing in its entirety, its essence, and its underlying laws, it is necessary to ponder over the wealth of data, to remodel and to reconstruct them so as to form a system of concepts and theories by straining the refined from the crude, sifting the true from the false, deriving the yet unascertained from the ascertained, and probing into the deep-seated from the superficial. To do all these, it is necessary to leap from perceptual knowledge to rational knowledge.

Knowledge after this kind of reconstruction is not emptier or more unreliable, on the contrary, only what has been reconstructed scientifically on the basis of practice in the process of cognition can, as Lenin said, reflect nature or objective things more deeply, truly, fully. Vulgar plodders absorbed in daily trifles do not know this. They bow down before experience and despise theory, hence they cannot have a comprehensive grasp of the entire objective process, lack a clear direction and a long perspective, but are self-satisfied with one instance of success, one ray of light. Were these persons to lead a revolution, they would direct it to a dead end.

Rational knowledge depends upon perceptual knowledge and perceptual knowledge has to develop into rational knowledge. This is the epistemology of dialectical materialism. Both rationalism and empiricism in philosophy fail to account for the dialectical and historical nature of knowledge, and although each represents an aspect of truth (here it is materialist, not idealist, rationalism and empiricism that are in question), yet both are invalid so far as concerns their respective epistemology as a whole. The dialectical materialist process of cognition from the perceptual to the rational applies to a minor process of cognition such as knowing one thing or one undertaking, as well as to a major one such as knowing a society of a revolution.

But at this point the process of cognition is not yet concluded. If we stop the discussion of the dialectical materialist process of cognition merely at rational knowledge, we have touched upon only half of the problem. And from the point of view of Marxist philosophy we have only touched upon the half that is not quite so important. What Marxist philosophy considers most important is not understanding the laws of the external world and thereby explaining it, but actively changing the world by applying the knowledge of objective laws. Theory is important from the viewpoint of Marxism; its importance is sufficiently shown in the statement Lenin made: "Without a revolutionary theory there can be no revolutionary movement." But when Marxism emphasizes theory, it does so precisely and only because it can guide our actions. If we had a correct theory, but merely prated about it, pigeonholed it, and refused to act accordingly, then that theory, however good, would be totally devoid of significance.

Cognition starts with practice and through practice it reaches the theoretical plane, and then it has to go back to practice. The active effect of cognition not only manifests itself in the active leap from perceptual knowledge to rational knowledge, but also, what is more important, manifests itself in that leap from rational knowledge to revolutionary practice. After having grasped the laws of the world we must redirect this knowledge to the practice of changing the world, to the practice of production, of revolutionary class struggle and national struggle as well as of scientific experiments. This is the process of testing and developing theory, the continuation of the entire process of cognition.

Theory and Practice

The problem whether theories correspond to objective realities is not entirely solved in the process of cognition from the perceptual to the rational as mentioned before: there it cannot be entirely solved. The only way to solve this problem completely is to redirect rational knowledge to social practice and apply theory to practice to see whether it can achieve preconceived results. This is the reason why many theories of natural science are regarded as truths not only at the time of their discovery by natural scientists, but also subsequently when they are verified by scientific practice. The reason why Marxism-Leninism is regarded as truth lies in the fact that it was not only scientifically formulated by Marx, Engels, Lenin, and Stalin, but also subsequently verified in the revolutionary practice of class struggle and national struggle. Dialectical materialism is a universal truth because no one in his practice can escape from the sphere of its applicability.

The history of human knowledge tells us that the truth of many theories is incomplete but that this incompleteness is remedied when put to the test of practice. Many theories are incorrect, but their mistakes are corrected when put to the test of practice. That is why practice is the criterion of truth and why the standpoint of practice is "first and fundamental in the theory of knowledge." Stalin very well said: "Theory becomes aimless if it is not connected with revolutionary practice, just as practice gropes in the dark if its path is not illumined by revolutionary theory."

When we get to this point, is the process of cognition completed? Our answer is yes and no. By the reflection of the objective process and the effects of their own capacity for activity, men as social beings engaged in the practice of changing a certain objective process in a certain stage of its development (irrespective of whether the practice is one of changing a natural process or one of changing a social process) are enabled to advance their knowledge from the perceptual to the rational, bringing forth ideas, theories, plans, or programs which on the whole correspond to the laws of that objective process. These are then put into practice in the said process. If they enable us to realize the preconceived aim, *viz.*, when these ideas, theories, plans, or programs are changed or on the whole changed into facts through practice in that objective process, then so far as this concrete process is concerned, the process of cognition is regarded as completed. For example, in the process of changing nature, the realization of an engineering plan, the verification of a scientific hypothesis, the manufacturing of a utensil or instrument, and the reaping of agricultural produce; and in the process of changing society, the victory of a strike or of a war, the materialization of an educational plan—these can all be regarded as the realization of a preconceived aim.

But generally speaking, in the practice of changing either nature of society, people's original ideas, theories, plans, or programs are hardly ever realized without any change whatever. This is because those who are engaged in changing existing conditions are limited in many ways. They are limited not only by the scientific and technological conditions, but also by the objective process itself, both in its development and in the degree to which it reveals its aspects and its essence. In such a situation, on account of unforeseen circumstances discovered in practice, our ideas, theories, plans, or programs are often partially and sometimes even entirely changed. That is to say, the original ideas, theories, plans, or programs may not correspond partially or entirely to reality and are partially or entirely incorrect. It often happens that failures are repeated several times before our cognition is corrected of its errors and made into knowledge that corresponds to the laws of the objective process so that subjective things can be transformed into objective things, *viz.*, preconceived results can be achieved in practice. But in any case, at such a point, the process of one's knowing a certain objective process in a certain stage of its development is regarded as completed.

But as the objective process advances from stage to stage, one's process of cognition is by no means completed. As any objective process, whether natural or social, advances and develops in consequence of its internal contradictions and conflicts, one's cognitive process should also advance and develop accordingly. In terms of social movement, not only must a truly revolutionary leader be adept at correcting his ideas, theories, plans, or programs when they are mistaken, as mentioned above, but he must also be adept at making himself and his fellow participants in the revolution advance and change their subjective cognition accordingly when a certain objective process has already advanced from one stage of development to another. That is to say, he must propose the new revolutionary tasks and program in such a way as to correspond to the new changes in the circumstances. The situation in a revolutionary period changes quickly. If the cognition of revolutionaries does not change quickly with it they cannot lead the revolution towards victory. However, people's ideas often fall behind actual events because man's knowledge is limited by many social conditions.

Against "Rightists" and "Leftists"

We are opposed to the die-hards in the revolutionary ranks. Their ideas do not advance with the changing objective circumstances and have manifested themselves historically in the form of right opportunism. These people do not see that the conflict of the contradictions has already pushed the objective process forward and their cognition still remains at the old stage. All die-hards have shown this characteristic in their ideas. Their ideas having departed from social practice, they cannot advance at the head of the chariot of social progress as its guide. All they do is to trail behind and grumble that it runs rather too fast. They attempt to halt the chariot and drag it back.

We are also opposed to the idle talk of the "left." The ideas of these "leftists" are far ahead of a given stage of development of the objective process. Some of them regard their hallucinations as the truth; others strain themselves to realize at present an ideal which can only be realized in the future. They have separated themselves from the practice of the majority of the people and the realities of their time and their ideas, when translated into action, reveal themselves in the form of adventurism.

Idealism and mechanistic materialism, opportunism and adventurism are all characterized by the separation of the subjective from the objective, the divorce of knowledge from practice. The epistemology of Marxism-Leninism characterized by its scientific social practice cannot but be strongly opposed to these incorrect ideologies. A Marxist recognizes that the development of the total process of the universe is absolute, whereas the development of each particular process in this total process is relative. Hence in the great river of absolute truth man's knowledge of a particular process in each given stage of development is only relatively true. Absolute truth is compounded of a sum-total of relative truths.

The development of the objective process is full of contradictions and conflicts, and so is the development of the process of man's cognition. All the dialectical movements of the external world can sooner or later find their reflection in man's knowledge. The process of coming into being, development, and elimination in social practice as well as in human knowledge is infinite. As the practice of changing objective existing conditions based upon certain ideas, theories, plans, or programs moves forward step by step, man's knowledge of objective reality also deepens step by step. The movement or change of the world of objective realities is never finished, hence man's recognition of truth through practice is also never complete. Marxism-Leninism has in no way put an end to the discovery of truths, but continues to blaze the path towards the recognition of truths through practice. Our conclusion is that we stand for the concrete and historical unity of the subjective and the objective, of theory and practice, and of knowledge and action; we are against any incorrect ideology, whether right or "left," that departs from the realities of history.

At the present stage of the development of society the responsibility of correctly understanding the world and of changing it has already fallen with the whole weight of history upon the shoulders of the proletariat and its political party. This process of the practice of changing the world on the basis of a scientific knowledge of it has already reached a historic moment both in China and in the whole world, a moment of such importance as the world has never witnessed before. This change is none other than the complete overturn of the world of darkness both in China and elsewhere and the transformation of it into a world of light that never existed before.

The struggle of the proletariat and revolutionary people in changing the world consists in achieving the following tasks: to reconstruct the external world; to reconstruct their own subjective world, *i.e.*, to remold their faculty of knowing; and to change the relations between the subjective and external worlds. Such a change has already been effected in one part of the globe, namely, the Soviet Union. The people there are still expediting this process of change. The people of China and the rest of the world are either passing, or will pass, through this kind of change.

What is meant by the external world which is to be changed includes the persons who are opposed to that change. To be remolded they will have to go through a stage of compulsion before they enter into a stage of remolding of their own accord. When the whole of mankind of its own accord remolds itself and changes the world, that will be the age of World Communism.

The discovery of truths through practice, and through practice the verification and the development of them; the active development of perceptual knowledge into rational knowledge, and, by means of rational knowledge, the active direction of revolutionary practice and the reconstruction of the subjective and the external world; practice, knowledge, more practice, more knowledge, and the repetition *ad infinitum* of this cyclic pattern, and with each cycle, the elevation of the content of practice and knowledge to a higher level: such is the whole epistemology of dialectical materialism, such is its theory of the unity of knowledge and action.

3

MAO TSE-TUNG
(1893–   )

*People's War**

This selection from Mao comes out of the little red book Quotations of Chairman Mao, *which has become famous as the bible of Red Guards. These quotes form a call to arms and set forth Mao's theories of guerrilla warfare, the people's war, and of involving the people in the revolutionary effort.*

* Mao Tse-Tung, "People's War," *The Quotations of Chairman Mao,* pp. 88–98, with omissions.

1. The revolutionary war is a war of the masses; it can be waged only by mobilizing the masses and relying on them.

2. What is a true bastion of iron? It is the masses, the millions upon millions of people who genuinely and sincerely support the revolution. That is the real iron bastion which it is impossible, and absolutely impossible, for any force on earth to smash. . . .

Strategy and Goals

3. Unquestionably, victory or defeat in war is determined mainly by the military, political, economic and natural conditions on both sides. But not by these alone. It is also determined by each side's subjective ability in directing the war. In his endeavour to win a war, a military strategist cannot overstep the limitations imposed by the material conditions; within these limitations, however, he can and must strive for victory. The stage of action for a military strategist is built upon objective material conditions, but on that stage he can direct the performance of many a drama, full of sound and colour, power and grandeur.

4. The object of war is specifically "to preserve oneself and destroy the enemy" (to destroy the enemy means to disarm him or "deprive him of the power to resist", and does not mean to destroy every member of his forces physically). . . . It should be pointed out that destruction of

the enemy is the primary object of war and self-preservation the secondary, because only by destroying the enemy in large numbers can one effectively preserve oneself. Therefore attack, the chief means of destroying the enemy, is primary, while defence, a supplementary means of destroying the enemy and a means of self-preservation, is secondary. In actual warfare the chief role is played by defence much of the time and by attack for the rest of the time, but if war is taken as a whole, attack remains primary.

Means to the End

5. Our principles of operation are:

(1) Attack dispersed, isolated enemy forces first; attack concentrated, strong enemy forces later.

(2) Take small and medium cities and extensive rural areas first; take big cities later.

(3) Make wiping out the enemy's effective strength our main objective; do not make holding or seizing a city or place our main objective. Holding or seizing a city or place is the outcome of wiping out the enemy's effective strength, and often a city or place can be held or seized for good only after it has changed hands a number of times.

(4) In every battle, concentrate an absolutely superior force (two, three, four and sometimes even five or six times the enemy's strength), encircle the enemy forces completely, strive to wipe them out thoroughly and do not let any escape from the net. In special circumstances, use the method of dealing the enemy crushing blows, that is, concentrate all our strength to make a frontal attack and an attack on one or both of his flanks, with the aim of wiping out one part and routing another so that our army can swiftly move its troops to smash other enemy forces. Strive to avoid battles of attrition in which we lose more than we gain or only break even. In this way, although inferior as a whole (in terms of numbers), we shall be absolutely superior in every part and every specific campaign, and this ensures victory in the campaign. As time goes on, we shall become superior as a whole and eventually wipe out all the enemy.

(5) Fight no battle unprepared, fight no battle you are not sure of winning; make every effort to be well prepared for each battle, make every effort to ensure victory in the given set of conditions as between the enemy and ourselves.

(6) Give full play to our style of fighting—courage in battle, no fear of sacrifice, no fear of fatigue, and continuous fighting (that is, fighting successive battles in a short time without rest).

(7) Strive to wipe out the enemy when he is on the move. At the same time, pay attention to the tactics of positional attack and capture enemy fortified points and cities.

(8) With regard to attacking cities, resolutely seize all enemy fortified points and cities which are weakly defended. At opportune moments, seize all enemy fortified points and cities defended with moderate strength, provided circumstances permit. As for all strongly defended enemy fortified points and cities, wait till conditions are ripe and then take them.

(9) Replenish our strength with all the arms and most of the personnel captured from the enemy. Our army's main sources of manpower and *matériel* are at the front.

(10) Make good use of the intervals between campaigns to rest, train and consolidate our troops. Periods of rest, training and consolidation should not in general be very long, and the enemy should so far as possible be permitted no breathing space.

These are the main methods the People's Liberation Army has employed in defeating Chiang Kai-shek. They are the result of the tempering of the People's Liberation Army in long years of fighting against domestic and foreign enemies and are completely suited to our present situation. . . . our strategy and tactics are based on a people's war; no army opposed to the people can use our strategy and tactics.

6. Without preparedness superiority is not real superiority and there can be no initiative either. Having grasped this point, a force which is inferior but prepared can often defeat a superior enemy by suprise attack.

4

HENRY DAVID THOREAU

(1817–1862)

*Civil Disobedience**

Thoreau's ideas tend toward anarchy. "That government is best which governs not at all," he believes. Compare Thoreau's analysis of obedience to law with Plato's in the Crito. *Thoreau maintains that man's primary loyalty is to his own nature. He asserts that the majority of men are reduced to serving the state only with their bodies. Unjust laws, he counsels, ought not to be obeyed. But the problem is to find a criterion for distinguishing the just from the unjust law. Thoreau asks that conscience, not majority opinion, be the basis of law.*

* Henry David Thoreau, *Civil Disobedience* (Boston: 1849), with omissions.

I HEARTILY accept the motto,—"That government is best which governs least;" and I should like to see it acted up to more rapidly and systematically. Carried out, it finally amounts to this, which also I believe,—"That government is best which governs not at all;" and when men are prepared for it, that will be the kind of government which they will have. Government is at best but an expedient; but most governments are usually, and all governments are sometimes, inexpedient. The objections which have been brought against a standing army, and they are many and weighty, and deserve to prevail, may also at last be brought against a standing government. The standing army is only an arm of the standing government. The government itself, which is only the mode which the people have chosen to execute their will, is equally liable to be abused and perverted before the people can act through it. Witness the present Mexican war, the work of comparatively a few individuals using the standing government as their tool; for, in the outset, the people would not have consented to this measure.

The Impositions of Government upon its Citizens

This American government,—what is it but a tradition, though a recent one, endeavoring to transmit itself unimpared to posterity, but each instant losing some of its integrity? It has not the vitality and force of a single living man; for a single man can bend it to his will.

It is a sort of wooden gun to the people themselves. But it is not the less necessary for this; for the people must have some complicated machinery or other, and hear its din, to satisfy that idea of government which they have. Governments show thus how successfully men can be imposed on, even impose on themselves, for their own advantage. It is excellent, we must all allow. Yet this government never of itself furthered any enterprise, but by the alacrity with which it got out of its way. *It* does not keep the country free. *It* does not settle the West. *It* does not educate. The character inherent in the American people has done all that has been accomplished; and it would have done somewhat more, if the government had not sometimes got in its way. For government is an expedient by which men would fain succeed in letting one another alone; and, as has been said, when it is most expedient, the governed are most let alone by it. Trade and commerce, if they were not made of India-rubber, would never manage to bounce over the obstacles which legislators are continually putting in their way; and, if one were to judge these men wholly by the effects of their actions and not partly by their intentions, they would deserve to be classed and punished with those mischievous persons who put obstructions on the railroads.

But, to speak practically and as a citizen, unlike those who call themselves no-government men, I ask for, not at once no government, but *at once* a better government. Let every man make known what kind of government would command his respect, and that will be one step toward obtaining it.

After all, the practical reason why, when the power is once in the hands of the people, a majority are permitted, and for a long period continue, to rule is not because they are most likely to be in the right, nor because this seems fairest to the minority, but because they are physically the strongest. But a government in which the majority rule in all cases cannot be based on justice, even as far as men understand it. Can there not be a government in which majorities do not virtually decide right and wrong, but conscience?—in which majorities decide only those questions to which the rule of expediency is applicable?

Obedience to the State as Resignation of Conscience

Must the citizen ever for a moment, or in the very least degree, resign his conscience to the legislator? Why has every man a conscience, then? I think that we should be men first, and subjects afterward. It is not desirable to cultivate a respect for the law, so much as for the right. The only obligation which I have a right to assume is to do at any time what I think right. It is truly enough said, that a corporation has no conscience; but a corporation of conscientious men is a corporation *with* a conscience. Law never made men a whit more just; and, by means of their respect for it, even the well-disposed are daily made the agents of injustice. A common and natural result of an undue respect for law is, that you may see a file of soldiers, colonel, captain, corporal, privates, powder-monkeys, and all, marching in admirable order over hill and dale to the wars, against their wills, ay, against their common sense and consciences, which makes it very steep marching indeed, and produces a palpitation of the heart. They have no doubt that it is a damnable business in which they are concerned; they are all peaceably inclined. Now, what are they? Men at all? Or small movable forts and magazines, at the service of some unscrupulous man in power? Visit the Navy-yard, and behold a marine, such a man as an American government can make, or such as it can make a man with its black arts,—a mere shadow and reminiscence of humanity, a man laid out alive and standing, and already, as one may say, buried under arms with funeral accompaniments, though it may be,—

> "Not a drum was heard, not a funeral note,
> As his corse to the rampart we hurried;
> Not a soldier discharged his farewell shot
> O'er the grave where our hero we buried."

The mass of men serve the state thus, not as men mainly, but as machines, with their bodies. They are the standing army, and the militia, jailors, constables, posse comitatus, etc. In most cases there is no free exercise whatever of the judgment or of the moral sense; but they put themselves on a level with wood and earth and stones; and wooden men can perhaps be manufactured that will serve the purpose as well. Such command no more respect than men of straw or a lump of dirt. They have the same sort of worth only as horses and dogs. Yet such as these even are commonly esteemed good citizens. Others—as most legislators, politicians, lawyers, ministers, and office-holders—serve the state chiefly with their heads; and, as they rarely make any moral distinctions, they are as likely to serve the Devil, without *intending* it, as God. A very few, as heroes, patriots, martyrs, reformers in the great sense, and *men*, serve the state with their consciences also, and so necessarily resist it for the most part; and they are commonly treated as enemies by it. A wise man will only be useful as a man, and will not submit to be "clay," and "stop a hole to keep the wind away," but leave that office to his dust at least:—

> "I am too high-born to be propertied,
> To be a secondary at control,
> Or useful serving-man and instrument
> To any sovereign state throughout the world."

He who gives himself entirely to his fellow-men appears to them useless and selfish; but he who gives himself partially to them is pronounced a benefactor and philanthropist.

How does it become a man to behave toward this American government to-day? I cannot for an instant recognize that political organization as *my* government which is the *slave's* government also.

The Right of Revolution

All men recognize the right of revolution; that is, the right to refuse allegiance to, and to resist, the government, when its tyranny or its inefficiency are great and unendurable. But almost all say that such is not the case now. But such was the case, they think, in the Revolutions of '75. If one were to tell me that this was a bad government because it taxed certain foreign commodities brought to its ports, it is most probable that I should not make an ado about it, for I can do without them. All machines have their friction; and possibly this does enough good to counterbalance the evil. At any rate, it is a great evil to make a stir about it. But when the friction comes to have its machine, and oppression and robbery are organized, I say, let us not have such a machine any longer. In other words, when a sixth of the population of a nation which has undertaken to be the refuge of liberty are slaves, and a whole country is unjustly overrun and conquered by a foreign army, and subjected to military law, I think that it is not too soon for honest men to rebel and revolutionize. What makes this duty the more urgent is the fact that the country so overrun is not our own, but ours is the invading army. . . .

. . .

Unjust laws exist: shall we be content to obey them, or shall we endeavor to amend them, and obey them until we have succeeded, or shall we transgress them at once? Men generally, under such a government as this, think that they ought to wait until they have persuaded the majority to alter them. They think that, if they should resist, the remedy would be worse than the evil. But it is the fault of the government itself that the remedy *is* worse than the evil. *It* makes it worse. Why is it not more apt to anticipate and provide for reform? Why does it not cherish its wise minority? Why does it cry and resist before it is hurt? Why does it not encourage its citizens to be on the alert to point out its faults and *do* better than it would have them? Why does it always crucify Christ, and excommunicate Copernicus and Luther, and pronounce Washington and Franklin rebels?

One would think, that a deliberate and practical denial of its authority was the only offense never contemplated by government; else, why has it not assigned its definite, its suitable and proportionate penalty? If a man who has no property refuses but once to earn nine shillings for the state, he is put in prison for a period unlimited by any law that I know, and determined only by the discretion of those who placed him there; but if he should steal ninety times nine shillings from the state, he is soon permitted to go at large again.

If the injustice is part of the necessary friction of the machine of government, let it go, let it go; perchance it will wear smooth,—certainly the machine will wear out. If the injustice has a spring, or a pulley, or a rope, or a crank, exclusively for itself, then perhaps you may consider whether the remedy will not be worse than the evil; but if it is of such a nature that it requires you to be the agent of injustice to another, then, I say, break the law. Let your life be a counter friction to stop the machine. What I have to do is to see, at any rate, that I do not lend myself to the wrong which I condemn.

Reform

As for adopting the ways which the state has provided for remedying the evil, I know not of such ways. They take too much time, and a man's life will be gone. I have other affairs to attend to. I came into this world, not chiefly to make this a good place to live in, but to live in it, be it good or bad. A man has not everything to do, but something;

and because he cannot do *everything*, it is not necessary that he should do *something* wrong. It is not my business to be petitioning the Governor or the Legislature any more than it is theirs to petition me; and if they should not hear my petition, what should I do then? But in this case the state has provided no way: its very Constitution is the evil. This may seem to be harsh and stubborn and unconciliatory; but it is to treat with the utmost kindness and consideration the only spirit that can appreciate or deserves it. So is all change for the better, like birth and death, which convulse the body.

I do not hesitate to say, that those who call themselves Abolitionists should at once effectually withdraw their support, both in person and property, from the government of Massachusetts and not wait till they constitute a majority of one, before they suffer the right to prevail through them. I think that it is enough if they have God on their side, without waiting for that other one. Moreover, any man more right than his neighbors constitutes a majority of one already.

Refusal of Taxation

I meet this American government, or its representative, the state government, directly, and face to face, once a year—no more—in the person of its tax-gatherer; this is the only mode in which a man situated as I am necessarily meets it; and it then says distinctly, Recognize me; and the simplest, most effectual, and, in the present posture of affairs, the indispensablest mode of treating with it on this head, of expressing your little satisfaction with and love for it, is to deny it then. My civil neighbor, the tax-gatherer, is the very man I have to deal with,—for it is, after all, with men and not with parchment that I quarrel,—and he has voluntarily chosen to be an agent of the government. How shall he ever know well what he is and does as an officer of the government, or as a man, until he is obliged to consider whether he shall treat me, his neighbor, for whom he has respect, as a neighbor and well-disposed man, or as a maniac and disturber of the peace, and see if he can get over this obstruction to his neighborliness without a ruder and more impetuous thought or speech corresponding with his action. I know this well, that if one thousand, if one hundred, if ten men whom I could name,—if ten *honest* men only,—ay, if *one* HONEST man, in this State of Massachusetts, *ceasing* to *hold* slaves, were actually to withdraw from this copartnership, and be locked up in the county jail therefor, it would be the abolition of slavery in America. For it matters not how small the beginning may seem to be: what is once well done is done forever. But we love better to talk about it: that we say is our mission. Reform keeps many scores of newspapers in its service, but not one man. If my esteemed neighbor, the State's ambassador, who will devote his days to the settlement of the question of human rights in the Council Chamber, instead of being threatened with the prisons of Carolina, were to sit down the prisoner of Massachusetts, that State which is so anxious to foist the sin of slavery upon her sister,—though at present she can discover only an act of inhospitality to be the ground of a quarrel with her,—the Legislature would not wholly waive the subject the following winter.

Acceptance of Imprisonment

Under a government which imprisons any unjustly, the true place for a just man is also a prison. The proper place to-day, the only place which Massachusetts has provided for her freer and less desponding spirits, is in her prisons, to be put out and locked out of the State by her own act, as they have already put themselves out by their principles. It is there that the fugitive slave, and the Mexican prisoner on parole, and the Indian come to plead the wrongs of his race should find them; on that separate, but more free and honorable ground, where the State places those who are not *with* her, but *against* her,—the only house in a slave State in which a free man can abide with honor. If any think that their influence would be lost there, and their voices no longer afflict the ear of the State, that they would not be as an enemy within its walls, they do not know by how much truth is stronger than error, nor how much more eloquently and effectively he can combat injustice who has experienced a little in his own person. Cast your whole vote, not a strip of paper merely, but your whole influence. A minority is powerless while it conforms to the majority; it is not even a minority then; but it is irresistible when it clogs by its whole weight. If the alternative is to keep all just men in prison, or give up war and slavery, the State will not hesitate which to choose. If a thousand men were not to pay their tax-bills this year, that would not be a violent and bloody measure, as it would be to pay them, and enable the State to commit violence and shed innocent blood. This is, in fact, the definition of a peaceable revolution, if any such is possible. If the tax-gatherer, or any other public officer, asks me, as one has done, "But what shall I do?" my answer is, "If you really wish to do anything, resign your office." When the subject has refused allegiance, and the officer has resigned his office, then the revolution is accomplished. But even suppose blood should flow. Is there not a sort of blood shed when the conscience is wounded? Through this wound a man's real manhood and immortality flow out, and he bleeds to an everlasting death. I see this blood flowing now. . . .

Manhood through Self-reliance

When I converse with the freest of my neighbors, I perceive that, whatever they may say about the magnitude and seriousness of the question, and their regard for the public tranquillity, the long and the short of the matter is, that they cannot spare the protection of the existing government, and they dread the consequences to their property and families of disobedience to it. For my own part, I should not like to think that I ever rely on the protection of the State. But, if I deny the authority of the State when it presents its tax-bill, it will soon take and waste all my property, and so harass me and my children without end. This is hard. This makes it possible for a man to live honestly, and at the same time comfortably, in outward respects. It will not be worth the while to accumulate property; that would be sure to go again. You must hire or squat somewhere, and raise but a small crop, and eat that soon. You must live within yourself, and depend upon yourself always tucked up and ready for a start, and not have many affairs. A man may grow rich in Turkey even, if he will be in all respects a good subject of the Turkish government. Confucius said: "If a State is governed by the principles of reason, poverty and misery are subjects of shame; if a state is not governed by the principles of reason, riches and honors are the subjects of shame." . . . It costs me less in every sense to incur the penalty of disobedience to the State than it would to obey. I should feel as if I were worth less in that case. . . .

Thus, the State never intentionally confronts a man's sense, intellectual or moral, but only his body, his senses. It is not armed with superior wit or honesty, but with superior physical strength. I was not born to be forced. I will breathe after my own fashion. Let us see who is the strongest. What force has a multitude? They only can force me who obey a higher law than I. They force me to become like themselves. I do not hear of *men* being *forced* to live this way or that by masses of men. What sort of life were that to live? When I meet a government which says to me, "Your money or your life," why should I be in haste to give it my money? It may be in a great strait, and not know what to do: I cannot help that. It must help itself; do as I do. It is not worth the while to snivel about it. I am not responsible for the successful working of the machinery of society. I am not the son of the engineer. I perceive that, when an acorn and a chestnut fall side by side, the one does not remain inert to make way for the other, but both obey their own laws, and spring and grow and flourish as best they can, till one, perchance, overshadows and destroys the other. If a plant cannot live according to its nature, it dies; and so a man.

5

M. K. GANDHI

(1869–1948)

Satyagraha

Nationalist and spiritual leader of emerging India, Gandhi espoused a philosophy of passive resistance (Satyagraha: Truth-seeking) which has affected the revolutionary thinking of many black civil rights leaders, most notably Martin Luther King, Jr. Gandhi's is a philosophy of means, not necessarily ends. It is a way of life, not just a tactic. His organization and leadership of resistance movements in India eventually culminated in independence for his country. In 1947 Viscount Mountbatten, former viceroy of the Indian Empire, called Gandhi "The architect of India's freedom through non-violence." The Satyagraha method is not designed to humble one's opponents, but to lead them to find the truth.

In these selections, Gandhi recounts his thinking on the matter and method of passive resistance, an idea not original with Gandhi. Interestingly, it is a Western theory seen in the works of Thoreau and Tolstoy. On the question of means and ends Gandhi counters the tactical thinking of men like Mao with his theory of soul force, which elevates the resister instead of lowering him to the level of the brute force of his oppressor.

In defining his motives, Daniel Ellsberg, who exposed the "Pentagon Papers," said, "You know what Gandhi's term is for what is otherwise called nonviolent civil disobedience? He called it 'Satyagraha.' That means 'truth force.' The people always focus on the nonviolent aspect of this Gandhian approach, but, in fact, the theme of honesty and openness was at least as strong as the nonviolence. The courts, the press, the Congress—all together have been cooperating in a massive effort at truth telling."

Satyagraha, Civil Disobedience, Passive Resistance, Non-Co-operation*

Satyagraha is literally holding on to Truth and it means, therefore, Truth-force. Truth is soul or spirit. It is, therefore, known as soul-force. It excludes the use of violence because man is not capable of knowing the absolute truth and, therefore, not competent to punish. The word was coined in South Africa to distinguish the non-violent resistance of the Indians of South Africa from the contemporary "passive resistance" of the suffragettes and others. It is not conceived as a weapon of the weak.

Passive resistance is used in the orthodox English sense and covers the suffragette movement as well as the resistance of the Non-conformists. Passive resistance has been conceived and is regarded as a weapon of the weak. Whilst it avoids violence, being not open to the

* From *Young India* (1924), 23-3-1921. Used by permission of the Navajivan Trust.

weak, it does not exclude its use if, in the opinion of a passive resister, the occasion demands it. However, it has always been distinguished from armed resistance and its application was at one time confined to Christian martyrs.

Civil Disobedience is civil breach of unmoral statutory enactments. The expression was, so far as I am aware, coined by Thoreau to signify his own resistance to the laws of a slave State. He has left a masterly treatise on the duty of Civil Disobedience. But Thoreau was not perhaps an out and out champion of non-violence. Probably, also, Thoreau limited his breach of statutory laws to the revenue law, i.e. payment of taxes. Whereas the term Civil Disobedience as practised in 1919 covered a breach of any statutory and unmoral law. It signified the resister's outlawry in a civil, i.e., non-violent manner. He invoked the sanctions of the law and cheerfully suffered imprisonment. It is a branch of Satyagraha.

Non-co-operation predominantly implies withdrawing of co-operation from the State that in the non-co-operator's view has become corrupt and excludes Civil Disobedience of the fierce type described above. By its very nature, non-co-operation is even open to children of understanding and can be safely practised by the masses. Civil Disobedience presupposes the habit of willing obedience to laws without fear of their sanctions. It can, therefore, be practised only as a last resort and by a select few in the first instance at any rate. Non-co-operation, too, like Civil Disobedience is a branch of Satyagraha which includes all non-violent resistance for the vindication of Truth.

Means and Ends*

Reader: Why should we not obtain our goal, which is good, by any means whatsoever, even by using violence? Shall I think of the means when I have to deal with a thief in the house? My duty is to drive him out anyhow. You seem to admit that we have received nothing, and that we shall receive nothing by petitioning. Why, then, may we not do so by using brute force? And, to retain what we may receive we shall keep up the fear by using the same force to the extent that it may be necessary. You will not find fault with a continuance of force to prevent a child from thrusting its foot into fire? Somehow or other we have to gain our end.

Editor: Your reasoning is plausible. It has deluded many. I have used similar arguments before now. But I think I know better now, and I shall endeavour to undeceive you. Let us first take the argument that we are justified in gaining our end by using brute force because the English gained theirs by using similar means. It is perfectly true that they used brute force and that it is possible for us to do likewise, but by using similar means we can get only the same thing that they got. You will admit that we do not want that. Your belief that there is no connection between the means and the end is a great mistake. Through that mistake even men who have been considered religious have committed grievous crimes. Your reasoning is the same as saying that we can get a

* From *Indian Home Rule* (1922), Chap. XVI. Used by permission of the Navajivan Trust.

rose through planting a noxious weed. If I want to cross the ocean, I can do so only by means of a vessel; if I were to use a cart for that purpose, both the cart and I would soon find the bottom. "As is the God, so is the votary," is a maxim worth considering. Its meaning has been distorted and men have gone astray. The means may be likened to a seed, the end to a tree; and there is just the same inviolable connection between the means and the end as there is between the seed and the tree. I am not likely to obtain the result flowing from the worship of God by laying myself prostrate before Satan. If, therefore, any one were to say: "I want to worship God; it does not matter that I do so by means of Satan," it would be set down as ignorant folly. We reap exactly as we sow. The English in 1833 obtained greater voting power by violence. Did they by using brute force better appreciate their duty? They wanted the right of voting, which they obtained by using physical force. But real rights are a result of performance of duty; these rights they have not obtained. We, therefore, have before us in England the force of everybody wanting and insisting on his rights, nobody thinking of his duty. And, where everybody wants rights, who shall give them to whom? I do not wish to imply that they do no duties. They don't perform the duties corresponding to those rights; and as they do not perform that particular duty, namely, acquire fitness, their rights have proved a burden to them. In other words, what they have obtained is an exact result of the means they adopted. They used the means corresponding to the end. If I want to deprive you of your watch, I shall certainly have to fight for it; if I want to buy your watch, I shall have to pay for it; and if I want a gift, I shall have to plead for it; and, according to the means I employ, the watch is stolen property, my own property, or a donation. Thus we see three different results from three different means. Will you still say that means do not matter?

Now we shall take the example given by you of the thief to be driven out. I do not agree with you that the thief may be driven out by any means. If it is my father who has come to steal I shall use one kind of means. If it is an acquaintance I shall use another; and in the case of a perfect stranger I shall use a third. If it is a white man, you will perhaps say you will use means different from those you will adopt with an Indian thief. If it is a weakling, the means will be different from those to be adopted for dealing with an equal in physical strength; and if the thief is armed from top to toe, I shall simply remain quiet. Thus we have a variety of means between the father and the armed man. Again, I fancy that I should pretend to be sleeping whether the thief was my father or that strong armed man. The reason for this is that my father would also be armed and I should succumb to the strength possessed by either and allow my things to be stolen. The strength of my father would make me weep with pity; the strength of the armed man would rouse in me anger and we should become enemies. Such is the curious situation. From these examples we may not be able to agree as to the means to be adopted in each case. I myself seem clearly to see what should be done in all these cases, but the remedy may frighten you. I therefore hesitate to place it before you. For the time being I will leave you to guess it, and if you cannot, it is clear you will have to adopt different means in each case. You will also have seen that any means will not avail to drive away the thief. You will have to adopt means to fit each case. Hence it follows that your duty is not to drive away the thief by any means you like.

Let us proceed a little further. That well-armed man has stolen your property; you have harboured the thought of his act; you are filled with anger; you argue that you want to punish that rogue, not for your own sake, but for the good of your neighbours; you have collected a number of armed men, you want to take his house by assault; he is duly informed of it, he runs away; he too is incensed. He collects his brother robbers, and sends you a defiant message that he will commit robbery in broad daylight. You are strong, you do not fear him, you are prepared to receive him. Meanwhile, the robber pesters your neighbours. They complain before you. You reply that you are doing all for their sake, you do not mind that your own goods have been stolen. Your neighbours reply that the robber never pestered them before, and that he commenced his depredations only after you declared hostilities against him. You are between Scylla and Charybdis. You are full of pity for the poor men. What they say is true. What are you to do? You will be disgraced if you now leave the robber alone. You, therefore, tell the poor men: "Never mind. Come, my wealth is yours, I will give you arms, I will teach you how to use them; you should belabour the rogue; don't you leave him alone." And so the battle grows; the robbers increase in numbers; your neighbours have deliberately put themselves to inconvenience. Thus the result of wanting to take revenge upon the robber is that you have disturbed your own peace; you are in perpetual fear of being robbed and assaulted; your courage has given place to cowardice. If you will patiently examine the argument, you will see that I have not overdrawn the picture. This is one of the means. Now let us examine the other. You set this armed robber down as an ignorant brother; you intend to reason with him at a suitable opportunity; you argue that he is, after all, a fellow man; you do not know what prompted him to steal. You, therefore, decide that, when you can, you will destroy the man's motive for stealing. Whilst you are thus reasoning with yourself, the man comes again to steal. Instead of being angry with him you take pity on him. You think that this stealing habit must be a disease with him. Henceforth, you, therefore, keep your doors and windows open, you change your sleeping-place, and you keep your things in a manner most accessible to him. The robber comes again and is confused as all this is new to him; nevertheless, he takes away your things. But his mind is agitated. He inquires about you in the village, he comes to learn about your broad and loving heart, he repents, he begs your pardon, returns you your things, and leaves off the stealing habit. He becomes your servant, and you will find for him honourable employment. This is the second method. Thus, you see, different means have brought about totally different results. I do not wish to deduce from this that robbers will act in the above manner or that all will have the same pity and love like you, but I only wish to show that fair means alone can produce fair results, and that, at least in the majority of cases, if not indeed in all, the force of love and pity is infinitely greater than the force of arms. There is harm in the exercise of brute force, never in that of pity.

Now we will take the question of petitioning. It is a fact beyond dispute that a petition, without the backing of force, is useless. However, the late Justice Ranade used to say that petitions served a useful purpose because they were a means of educating people. They give the latter an idea of their condition and warn the rulers. From this point of view, they are not altogether useless. A petition of an equal is a sign of courtesy; a petition from a slave is a symbol of his slavery. A petition backed by force is a petition from an equal and, when he transmits his demand in the form of a petition, it testifies to his nobility. Two kinds of force can back petitions. "We shall hurt you if you do not give this," is one kind of force; it is the force of arms, whose evil results we have already examined. The second kind of force can thus be stated: "If you do not concede our demand, we shall be no longer your petitioners. You can govern us only so long as we remain the governed; we shall no longer have any dealings with you." The force implied in this may be described as love-force, soul-force, or, more popularly but less accurately, passive resistance. This force is indestructible. He who uses it perfectly understands his position. We have an ancient proverb which literally means: "One negative cures thirty-six diseases." The force of arms is powerless when matched against the force of love or the soul.

Now we shall take your last illustration, that of the child thrusting its foot into fire. It will not avail you. What do you really do to the child? Supposing that it can exert so much physical force that it renders you powerless and rushes into fire, then you cannot prevent it. There are only two remedies open to you—either you must kill it in order to prevent it from perishing in their flames, or you must give your own life because you do not wish to see it perish before your very eyes. You will not kill it. If your heart is not quite full of pity, it is possible that you will not surrender yourself by preceding the child and going into the fire yourself. You, therefore, helplessly allow it to go to the flames. Thus, at any rate, you are not using physical force. I hope you will not consider that it is still physical force, though of a low order, when you would forcibly prevent the child from rushing towards the fire if you could. That force is of a different order and we have to understand what it is.

Remember that, in thus preventing the child, you are minding entirely its own interest, you are exercising authority for its sole benefit. Your example does not apply to the English. In using brute force against the English you consult entirely your own, that is the national, interest. There is no question here either of pity or of love. If you say that the actions of the English, being evil, represent fire, and that they proceed to their actions through ignorance, and that therefore they occupy the position of a child and that you want to protect such a child, then you will have to overtake every evil action of that kind by whomsoever committed and, as in the case of the evil child, you will have to sacrifice yourself. If you are capable of such immeasurable pity, I wish you well in its exercise.

Satyagraha or Passive Resistance*

Reader: Is there any historical evidence as to the success of what you have called soul-force or truth-force? No instance seems to have happened of any nation having risen through soul-force. I still think that the evil-doers will not cease doing evil without physical punishment.

Editor: The poet Tulsidas has said: "Of religion, pity, or love, is the root, as egotism of the body. Therefore, we should not abandon pity so long as we are alive." This appears to me to be a scientific truth. I believe in it as much as I believe in two and two being four. The force of love is the same as the force of the soul or truth. We have evidence of its working at every step. The universe would disappear without the existence of that force. But you ask for historical evidence. It is, therefore, necessary to know what history means. The Gujarati equivalent means: "It so happened." If that is the meaning of history, it is possible to give copious evidence. But, if it means the doings of kings and emperors, there can be no evidence of soul-force or passive resistance in such history. You cannot expect silver ore in a tin mine. History, as we know it, is a record of the wars of the world, and so there is a proverb among Englishmen that a nation which has no history, that is, no wars, is a happy nation. How kings played, how they became enemies of one another, how they murdered one another, is found accurately recorded in history, and if this were all that had happened in the world, it would have been ended long ago. If the story of the universe had commenced with wars, not a man would have been found alive today. Those people who had been warred against have disappeared as, for instance, the natives of Australia of whom hardly a man was left alive by the intruders. Mark, please, that these natives did not use soul-force in self-defense, and it does not require much foresight to know that the Australians will share the same fate as their victims. "Those that take the sword shall perish by the Sword." With us the proverb is that professional swimmers will find a watery grave.

The fact that there are so many men still alive in the world shows that it is based not on the force of arms but on the force of truth or love. Therefore, the greatest and most unimpeachable evidence of the success of this force is to be found in the fact that, in spite of the wars of the world, it still lives on.

Thousands, indeed tens of thousands, depend for their existence on a very active working of this force. Little quarrels of millions of families in their daily lives disappear before the exercise of this force. Hundreds of nations live in peace. History does not and cannot take note of this fact. History is really a record of every interruption of the even working of the force of love or of the soul. Two brothers quarrel; one of them repents and re-awakens the love that was lying dormant in him; the two again begin to live in peace; nobody takes note of this. But if the two brothers, through the intervention of solicitors or some other reason, take up arms or go to law—which is another form of the exhibition of brute force—their doing would be immediately noticed in the press, they would be the talk of their neighbours and would

* From *Indian Home Rule,* Chap. XVII. Used by permission of the Navajivan Trust.

probably go down to history. And what is true of families and communities is true of nations. There is no reason to believe that there is one law for families and another for nations. History, then, is a record of an interruption of the course of nature. Soul-force, being natural, is not noted in history.

Reader: According to what you say, it is plain that instances of this kind of passive resistance are not to be found in history. It is necessary to understand this passive resistance more fully. It will be better, therefore, if you enlarge upon it.

Editor: Passive resistance is a method of securing rights by personal suffering; it is the reverse of resistance by arms. When I refuse to do a thing that is repugnant to my conscience, I use soul-force. For instance, the Government of the day has passed a law which is applicable to me. I do not like it. If by using violence I force the Government to repeal the law, I am employing what may be termed body-force. If I do not obey the law and accept the penalty for its breach, I use soul-force. It involves sacrifice of self.

Everybody admits that sacrifice of self is infinitely superior to sacrifice of others. Moreover, if this kind of force is used in a cause that is unjust, only the person using it suffers. He does not make others suffer for his mistakes. Men have before now done many things which were subsequently found to have been wrong. No man can claim that he is absolutely in the right or that a particular thing is wrong because he thinks so, but it is wrong for him so long as that is his deliberate judgment. It is therefore meet that he should not do that which he knows to be wrong, and suffer the consequence whatever it may be. This is the key to the use of soul-force.

Reader: You would then disregard laws—this is rank disloyalty. We have always been considered a law-abiding nation. You seem to be going even beyond the extremists. They say that we must obey the laws that have been passed, but that if the laws be bad, we must drive out the law-givers even by force.

Editor: Whether I go beyond them or whether I do not is a matter of no consequence to either of us. We simply want to find out what is right and to act accordingly. The real meaning of the statement that we are a law-abiding nation is that we are passive resisters. When we do not like certain laws, we do not break the heads of law-givers but we suffer and do not submit to the laws. That we should obey laws whether good or bad is a newfangled notion. There was no such thing in former days. The people disregarded those laws they did not like and suffered the penalties for their breach. It is contrary to our manhood if we obey laws repugnant to our conscience. Such teaching is opposed to religion and means slavery. If the Government were to ask us to go about without any clothing, should we do so? If I were a passive resister, I would say to them that I would have nothing to do with their law. But we have so forgotten ourselves and become so compliant that we do not mind any degrading law.

A man who has realized his manhood, who fears only God, will fear no one else. Man-made laws are not necessarily binding on him. Even the Government does not expect any such thing from us. They do not say: "You must do such and such a thing," but they say: "If you do not do it, we will punish you." We are sunk so low that we fancy that it is our duty and our religion to do what the law lays down. If man will only realize that it is unmanly to obey laws that are unjust, no man's tyranny will enslave him. This is the key to self-rule or home-rule.

It is a superstition and ungodly thing to believe that an act of a majority binds a minority. Many examples can be given in which acts of majorities will be found to have been wrong and those of minorities to have been right. All reforms owe their origin to the initiation of minorities in opposition to majorities. If among a band of robbers a knowledge of robbing is obligatory, is a pious man to accept the obligation? So long as the superstition that men should obey unjust laws exists, so long will their slavery exist. And a passive resister alone can remove such a superstition.

To use brute-force, to use gunpowder, is contrary to passive resistance, for it means that we want our opponent to do by force that which we desire but he does not. And, if such a use of force is justifiable, surely he is entitled to do likewise by us. And so we should never come to an agreement. We may simply fancy, like the blind horse moving in a circle round a mill, that we are making progress. Those who believe that they are not bound to obey laws which are repugnant to their conscience have only the remedy of passive resistance open to them. Any other must lead to disaster.

6

FRANTZ FANON

(1925–1961)

*Violence**

Fanon's works have become a blueprint for revolutionaries in the black world. He has become the new prophet of African as well as American black society. Many of the stratagems of the Black Left can be traced to Fanon's ideas. The call to violence as a cleansing agent, the emphasis on native culture and black identity, form an integral part of his message. Militant blacks in the United States, including leaders of the Black Panther Party, who consider their plight to be that of a colonized people, turn to Fanon for direction. Bobby Seale, in his book Seize the Time, *maintains that reading Fanon was the spark that ignited him and Huey Newton to start the Black Panther Party. It is not difficult to substitute the words "white establishment" for "settler" and the word "blacks" for "natives" and thereby understand Fanon's message to the black militant.*

Fanon maintains that violence is necessary to bring about liberation. Colonialism, he argues, creates a Manichean world of opposites, a world of compartments. By violence colonialism maintains itself, and only by greater violence can it be destroyed. Compare Fanon's thought to that of Gandhi. Such a comparison should point out the essential philosophical differences in the civil rights movement from its beginnings with Martin Luther King to its turn toward militancy.

* Frantz Fanon. *The Wretched of the Earth,* Copyright 1963 by *Presence Africaine.* Originally published by François Maspero, éditeur, Paris, France, under the title *Les Damnés de la terre,* copyright 1961 by François Maspero éditeur S. A. R. Evergreen Black Edition, Grove Press, Inc., 1965, pp. 40–41, 42–43, 46–48, 56–58, 71–75, 84–86, 88, 93–95. Used by permission of the publisher.

The Manichean World of Colonialism

EVERYTHING up to and including the very nature of pre-capitalist society, so well explained by Marx, must here be thought out again. The serf is in essence different from the knight, but a reference to divine right is necessary to legitimize this statutory difference. In the colonies, the foreigner coming from another country imposed his rule by means of guns and machines. In defiance of his successful transplantation, in spite of his appropriation, the settler still remains a foreigner. It is neither the act of owning factories, nor estates, nor a bank balance which distinguishes the governing classes. The governing race is first and foremost those who come from elsewhere, those who are unlike the original inhabitants, "the others."

The violence which has ruled over the ordering of the colonial world, which has ceaselessly drummed the rhythm for the destruction of native social forms and broken up without reserve the systems of reference of the economy, the customs of dress and external life, that same violence will be claimed and taken over by the native at the moment when, deciding to embody history in his own person, he surges into the forbidden quarters. To wreck the colonial world is henceforward a mental picture of action which is very clear, very easy to understand and which may be assumed by each one of the individuals which constitute the colonized people. To break up the colonial world does not mean that after the frontiers have been abolished lines of communication will be set up between the two zones. The destruction of the colonial world is no more and no less than the abolition of one zone, its burial in the depths of the earth or its expulsion from the country.

The natives' challenge to the colonial world is not a rational confrontation of points of view. It is not a treatise on the universal, but the untidy affirmation of an original idea propounded as an absolute. The colonial world is a Manichean world. It is not enough for the settler to delimit physically, that is to say with the help of the army and the police force, the place of the native. As if to show the totalitarian character of colonial exploitation the settler paints the native as a sort of quintessence of evil. Native society is not simply described as a society lacking in values. It is not enough for the colonist to affirm that those values have disappeared from, or still better never existed in, the colonial world. The native is declared insensible to ethics; he represents not only the absence of values, but also the negation of values. He is, let us dare to admit, the enemy of values, and in this sense he is the absolute evil. He is the corrosive element, destroying all that comes near him; he is the deforming element, disfiguring all that has to do with beauty or morality; he is the depository of maleficent powers, the unconscious and irretrievable instrument of blind forces. . . . All values, in fact, are irrevocably poisoned and diseased as soon as they are allowed in contact with the colonized race. The customs of the colonized people, their traditions, their myths—above all, their myths—are the very sign of that poverty of spirit and of their constitutional depravity. That is why we must put the DDT which destroys parasites, the bearers of disease, on the same level as the Christian religion which wages war on embryonic heresies and instincts, and on evil as yet unborn. The recession of yellow fever and the advance of evangelization form part of the same balance sheet. But the triumphant *communiqués* from the missions are in fact a source of information concerning the implantation of foreign influences in the core of the colonized people. I speak of the Christian religion, and no one need be astonished. The Church in the colonies is the white people's Church, the foreigner's Church. She does not call the native to God's ways but to the ways of the white man, of the master, of the oppressor. And as we know, in this matter many are called but few chosen.

At times this Manicheism goes to its logical conclusion and dehumanizes the native, or to speak plainly, it turns him into an animal. In fact, the terms the settler uses when he mentions the native are zoological terms. He speaks of the yellow man's reptilian motions, of the stink of the native quarter, of breeding swarms, of foulness, of spawn, of gesticulations. When the settler seeks to describe the native fully in exact terms he constantly refers to the bestiary. The European rarely hits on a picturesque style; but the native, who knows what is in the mind of the settler, guesses at once what he is thinking of. Those hordes of vital statistics, those hysterical masses, those faces bereft of all humanity, those distended bodies which are like nothing on earth, that mob without beginning or end, those children who seem to belong to nobody, that laziness stretched out in the sun, that vegetative rhythm of life—all this forms part of the colonial vocabulary . . . The native knows all this, and laughs to himself every time he spots an allusion to the animal world in the other's words. For he knows that he is not an animal; and it is precisely at the moment he realizes his humanity that he begins to sharpen the weapons with which he will secure its victory.

Western Values and Decolonization

As soon as the native begins to pull on his moorings, and to cause anxiety to the settler, he is handed over to well-meaning souls who in cultural congresses point out to him the specificity and wealth of Western values. But every time Western values are mentioned they produce in the native a sort of stiffening or muscular lockjaw. During the period of decolonization, the native's reason is appealed to. He is offered definite values, he is told frequently that decolonization need not mean regression, and that he must put his trust in qualities which are well-tried, solid, and highly esteemed. But it so happens that when the native hears a speech about Western culture he pulls out his knife—or at least he makes sure it is within reach. The violence with which the supremacy of white values is affirmed and the aggressiveness which has permeated the victory of these values over the ways of life and of thought of the native mean that, in revenge, the native laughs in mockery when Western values are mentioned in front of him. In the colonial context the settler only ends his work of breaking in the native when the latter admits loudly and intelligibly the supremacy of the white man's values. In the period of decolonization, the colonized masses mock at these very values, insult them, and vomit them up . . . During the struggle for liberation, at the moment that the native intellectual comes into touch again with his people, . . . all the Mediterranean values—the triumph of the human individual, of clarity, and of beauty—become lifeless, colorless knickknacks. All those speeches seem like collections of dead words; those values which seemed to uplift the soul are revealed as worthless, simply because they have nothing to do with the concrete conflict in which the people is engaged.

Individualism is the first to disappear. The native intellectual had learnt from his masters that the individual ought to express himself fully. The colonialist bourgeoisie had hammered into the native's mind the idea of a society of individuals where each person shuts himself up in his own subjectivity, and whose only wealth is individual thought. Now the native who has the opportunity to return to the people during the struggle for freedom will discover the falseness of this theory. The very forms of organization of the struggle will suggest to him a different vocabulary. Brother, sister, friend—these are words outlawed by the colonialist bourgeoisie, because for them my brother is my purse, my friend is part of my scheme for getting on. The native intellectual takes part, in a sort of auto-da-fé, in the destruction of all his idols: egoism, recrimination that springs from pride, and the childish stupidity of those who always want to have the last word. Such a colonized intellectual, dusted over by colonial culture, will in the same way discover the substance of village assemblies, the cohesion of people's committees, and the extraordinary fruitfulness of local meetings and groupments. Henceforward, the interests of one will be the interests of all, for in concrete fact *everyone* will be discovered by the troops, *everyone* will be massacred—or *everyone* will be saved. The motto "look out for yourself," the atheist's method of salvation, is in this context forbidden.

Self-criticism has been much talked about of late, but few people realize that it is an African institution. Whether in the *djemaas** of northern Africa or in the meetings of western Africa, tradition demands that the quarrels which occur in a village should be settled in public. It is communal self-criticism, of course, and with a note of humor, because everybody is relaxed, and because in the last resort we all want the same things. But the more the intellectual imbibes the atmosphere of the people, the more completely he abandons the habits of calculation, of unwonted silence, of mental reservations, and shakes off the spirit of concealment. And it is true that already at that level we can say that the community triumphs, and that it spreads its own light and its own reason.

The Native's Emotional Sensibilities and Ritual Practices

In the colonial world, the emotional sensitivity of the native is kept on the surface of his skin like an open sore which flinches from the caustic agent; and the psyche shrinks back, obliterates itself and finds outlet in muscular demonstrations which have caused certain very wise men to say that the native is a hysterical type. This sensitive emotionalism, watched by invisible keepers who are however in unbroken contact with the core of the personality, will find its fulfillment through eroticism in the driving forces behind the crisis' dissolution.

On another level we see the native's emotional sensibility exhausting itself in dances which are more or less ecstatic. This is why any study of the colonial world should take into consideration the phenomena of the dance and of possession. The native's relaxation takes precisely the form of a muscular orgy in which the most acute aggressivity and the most impelling violence are canalized, transformed, and conjured away. The circle of the dance is a permissive circle: it protects and permits. At certain times on certain days, men and women come together at a given place, and there, under the solemn eye of the tribe, fling themselves into a seemingly unorganized pantomime, which is in reality extremely systematic, in which by various means—shakes of the head, bending of

* Village assemblies.

the spinal column, throwing of the whole body backward—may be deciphered as in an open book the huge effort of a community to exorcise itself, to liberate itself, to explain itself. There are no limits—inside the circle. The hillock up which you have toiled as if to be nearer to the moon; the river bank down which you slip as if to show the connection between the dance and ablutions, cleansing and purification—these are sacred places. There are no limits—for in reality your purpose in coming together is to allow the accumulated libido, the hampered aggressivity, to dissolve as in a volcanic eruption. Symbolical killings, fantastic rides, imaginary mass murders—all must be brought out. The evil humors are undammed, and flow away with a din as of molten lava.

One step further and you are completely possessed. In fact, these are actually organized séances of possession and exorcism; they include vampirism, possession by djinns, by zombies, and by Legba, the famous god of the voodoo.

This disintegrating of the personality, this splitting and dissolution, all this fulfills a primordial function in the organism of the colonial world. When they set out, the men and women were impatient, stamping their feet in a state of nervous excitement; when they return, peace has been restored to the village; it is once more calm and unmoved.

During the struggle for freedom, a marked alienation from these practices is observed. The native's back is to the wall, the knife is at his throat (or, more precisely, the electrode at his genitals): he will have no more call for his fancies. After centuries of unreality, after having wallowed in the most outlandish phantoms, at long last the native, gun in hand, stands face to face with the only forces which contend for his life—the forces of colonialism. And the youth of a colonized country, growing up in an atmosphere of shot and fire, may well make a mock of, and does not hesitate to pour scorn upon the zombies of his ancestors, the horses with two heads, the dead who rise again, and the djinns who rush into your body while you yawn. The native discovers reality and transforms it into the pattern of his customs, into the practice of violence and into his plan for freedom.

We have seen that this same violence, though kept very much on the surface all through the colonial period, yet turns in the void. We have also seen that it is canalized by the emotional outlets of dance and possession by spirits; we have seen how it is exhausted in fratricidal combats. Now the problem is to lay hold of this violence which is changing direction. When formerly it was appeased by myths and exercised its talents in finding fresh ways of committing mass suicide, now new conditions will make possible a completely new line of action . . .

Violence in Action

Let us return to that atmosphere of violence, that violence which is just under the skin. We have seen that in its process toward maturity many leads are attached to it, to control it and show it the way out. Yet in spite of the metamorphoses which the colonial regime imposes upon it in the way of tribal or regional quarrels, that violence makes its way forward, and the native identifies his enemy and recognizes all his misfortunes, throwing all the exacerbated might of his hate and anger into this new channel. But how do we pass from the atmosphere of violence to violence in action? What makes the lid blow off? There is first of all the fact that this development does not leave the settler's blissful existence intact. The settler who "understands" the natives is made aware by several straws in the wind showing that something is afoot. "Good" natives become scarce; silence falls when the oppressor approaches; sometimes looks are black, and attitudes and remarks openly aggressive. The nationalist parties are astir, they hold a great many meetings, the police are increased and reinforcements of soldiers are brought in. The settlers, above all the farmers isolated on their land, are the first to become alarmed. They call for energetic measures.

The authorities do in fact take some spectacular measures. They arrest one or two leaders, they organize military parades and maneuvers, and air force displays. But the demonstrations and warlike exercises, the smell of gunpowder which now fills the atmosphere, these things do not make the people draw back. Those bayonets and cannonades only serve to reinforce their aggressiveness. The atmosphere becomes dramatic, and everyone wishes to show that he is ready for anything. And it is in these circumstances that the guns go off by themselves, for nerves are jangled, fear reigns and everyone is trigger-happy. A single commonplace incident is enough to start the machine-gunning . . .

The repressions, far from calling a halt to the forward rush of national consciousness, urge it on. Mass slaughter in the colonies at a certain stage of the embryonic development of consciousness increases that consciousness, for the hecatombs are an indication that between oppressors and oppressed everything can be solved by force. It must be remarked here that the political parties have not called for armed insurrection, and have made no preparations for such an insurrection. All these repressive measures, all those actions which are a result of fear are not within the leaders' intentions: they are overtaken by events. At this moment, then, colonialism may decide to arrest the nationalist leaders. But today the governments of colonized countries know very well that it is extremely dangerous to deprive the masses of their leaders; for then the people, unbridled, fling themselves into *jacqueries*, mutinies, and "brutish murders." The masses give free rein to their "bloodthirsty instincts" and force colonialism to free their leaders, to whom falls the difficult task of bringing them back to order. The colonized people, who have spontaneously brought their violence to the colossal task of destroying the colonial system, will very soon find themselves with the barren, inert slogan "Release X or Y." Then colonialism will release these men, and hold discussions with them. The time for dancing in the streets has come.

In certain circumstances, the party political machine may remain intact. But as a result of the colonialist repression and of the spontaneous reaction of the people the parties find themselves out-distanced by their militants . . .

What is the real nature of this violence? We have seen that it is the intuition of the colonized masses that their liberation must, and can only, be achieved by force. By what spiritual aberration do these men, without technique, starving and enfeebled, confronted with the military and economic might of the occupation, come to believe that violence alone will free them? How can they hope to triumph?

It is because violence (and this is the disgraceful thing) may constitute, in so far as it forms part of its system, the slogan of a political party. The leaders may call on the people to enter upon an armed struggle. This problematical question has to be thought over. When militarist Germany decides to settle its frontier disputes by force, we are not in the least surprised; but when the people of Angola, for example, decide to take up arms, when the Algerian people reject all means which are not violent, these are proofs that something has happened or is happening at this very moment. The colonized races, those slaves of modern times, are impatient. They know that this apparent folly alone can put them out of reach of colonial oppression. A new type of relations is established in the world. The underdeveloped peoples try to break their chains, and the extraordinary thing is that they succeed . . .

Freedom Through Violence

In the native's eagerness, the fact that he openly brandishes the threat of violence proves that he is conscious of the unusual character of the contemporary situation and that he means to profit by it. But, still on the level of immediate experience, the native, who has seen the modern world penetrate into the furthermost corners of the bush, is most acutely aware of all the things he does not possess. The masses by a sort of (if we may say so) child-like process of reasoning convince themselves that they have been robbed of all these things. That is why in certain underdeveloped countries the masses forge ahead very quickly, and realize two or three years after independence that they have been frustrated, that "it wasn't worth while" fighting, and that nothing could really change. In 1789, after the bourgeois revolution, the smallest French peasants benefited substantially from the upheaval. But it is a commonplace to observe and to say that in the majority of cases, for 95 per cent of the population of underdeveloped countries, independence brings no immediate change. The enlightened observer takes note of the existence of a kind of masked discontent, like the smoking ashes of a burnt-down house after the fire has been put out, which still threaten to burst into flames again.

So they say that the natives want to go too quickly. Now, let us never forget that only a very short time ago they complained of their slowness, their laziness, and their fatalism. Already we see that violence used in specific ways at the moment of the struggle for freedom does not magically disappear after the ceremony of trooping the national colors. It has all the less reason for disappearing since the reconstruction of the nation continues within the framework of cutthroat competition between capitalism and socialism . . .

This chain of reasoning which presumes very arithmetically the disappearance of the colonized people does not leave the native overcome with moral indignation. He has always known that his duel with the settler would take place in the arena. The native loses no time in lamentations, and he hardly ever seeks for justice in the colonial framework.

The fact is that if the settler's logic leaves the native unshaken, it is because the latter has practically stated the problem of his liberation in identical terms: "We must form ourselves into groups of two hundred or five hundred, and each group must deal with a settler." It is in this manner of thinking that each of the protagonists begins the struggle.

For the native, this violence represents the absolute line of action. The militant is also a man who works. The questions that the organization asks the militant bear the mark of this way of looking at things: "Where have you worked? With whom? What have you accomplished?" The group requires that each individual perform an irrevocable action . . . To work means to work for the death of the settler. This assumed responsibility for violence allows both strayed and outlawed members of the group to come back again and to find their place once more, to become integrated. Violence is thus seen as comparable to a royal pardon. The colonized man finds his freedom in and through violence. This rule of conduct enlightens the agent because it indicates to him the means and the end . . .

It is understandable that in this atmosphere, daily life becomes quite simply impossible. You can no longer be a fellah, a pimp, or an alcoholic as before. The violence of the colonial regime and the counter-violence of the native balance each other and respond to each other in an extraordinary reciprocal homogeneity. This reign of violence will be the more terrible in proportion to the size of the implantation from the mother country. The development of violence among the colonized people will be proportionate to the violence exercised by the threatened colonial regime . . .

Violence As a Positive and Creative Factor

The settler's work is to make even dreams of liberty impossible for the native. The native's work is to imagine all possible methods for destroying the settler. On the logical plane, the Manicheism of the settler produces a Manicheism of the native. To the theory of the "absolute evil of the native" the theory of the "absolute evil of the settler" replies.

The appearance of the settler has meant in the terms of syncretism the death of the aboriginal society, cultural lethargy, and the petrification of individuals. For the native, life can only spring up again out of the rotting corpse of the settler. This then is the correspondence, term by term, between the two trains of reasoning.

But it so happens that for the colonized people this violence, because it constitutes their only work, invests their characters with positive and creative qualities. The practice of violence binds them together as a whole, since each individual forms a violent link in the great chain, a part of the great organism of violence which has surged upward in reaction to the settler's violence in the beginning. The groups recognize each other and the future nation is already indivisible. The armed struggle mobilizes the people; that is to say, it throws them in one way and in one direction.

The mobilization of the masses, when it arises out of the war of liberation, introduces into each man's consciousness the ideas of a common cause, of a national destiny, and of a collective history. In the same way the second phase, that of the building-up of the nation, is helped on by the existence of this cement which has been mixed with blood and anger. Thus we come to a fuller appreciation of the originality of the words used in these underdeveloped countries. During the colonial period the people are called upon to fight against oppression; after national liberation, they are called upon to fight against poverty, illiteracy, and underdevelopment. The struggle, they say, goes on. The people realize that life is a unending contest.

We have said that the native's violence unifies the people . . . Violence is in action all-inclusive and national. It follows that it is closely involved in the liquidation of regionalism and of tribalism. Thus the national parties show no pity at all toward the caids and the customary chiefs. Their destruction is the preliminary to the unification of the people.

At the level of individuals, violence is a cleansing force. It frees the native from his inferiority complex and from his despair and inaction; it makes him fearless and restores his self-respect. Even if the armed struggle has been symbolic and the nation is demobilized through a rapid movement of decolonization, the people have the time to see that the liberation has been the business of each and all and that the leader has no special merit. From thence comes that type of aggressive reticence with regard to the machinery of protocol which young governments quickly show. When the people have taken violent part in the national liberation they will allow no one to set themselves up as "liberators." They show themselves to be jealous of the results of their action and take good care not to place their future, their destiny, or the fate of their country in the hands of a living god. Yesterday they were completely irresponsible; today they mean to understand everything and make all decisions. Illuminated by violence, the consciousness of the people rebels against any pacification. From now on the demagogues, the opportunists and the magicians have a difficult task. The action which has thrown them into a hand-to-hand struggle confers upon the masses a voracious taste for the concrete. The attempt at mystification becomes, in the long run, practically impossible.

7

ALBERT CAMUS
(1913–1960)

*The Myth of Sisyphus**

Camus was born in Algeria, the locale of his famous short novel The Stranger. *The heroes of his novels are what he calls "absurd men" fighting an unconcerned universe for a set of human values by which to organize their lives meaningfully. The goal is an elusive and difficult one. During the French occupation Camus was one of the leaders of the Resistance movement (the Underground). He served as chief editor of the Underground newspaper,* Combat. *At the time, he and Jean-Paul Sartre were friends and they have been linked philosophically to the same movement, existentialism. Camus, however, claimed he had refuted the basic tenets of existentialism by his works. On the whole, Camus' approach to the human situation is rather more hopeful than Sartre's. "Whoever puts his trust in the human condition is a madman, while whoever despairs because of events is a coward." Camus maintains that men are capable of human dignity and could live by higher values if they can come to understand the quality of human life, if they begin to respond humanly to other men.*

Consider what makes Sisyphus an absurd hero. Why must we imagine him happy? Is he symbolic of all revolutionaries, or are there really few revolutionaries his equal in character? Compare Camus' revolutionary to that of Marx and Engels.

* Albert Camus, *The Myth of Sisyphus and Other Essays* (New York: Alfred A. Knopf, 1955), pp. 88–91. Used by permission of the publishers, Random House, Inc. and Alfred A. Knopf, Inc.

THE gods had condemned Sisyphus to ceaselessly rolling a rock to the top of a mountain, whence the stone would fall back of its own weight. They had thought with some reason that there is no more dreadful punishment than futile and hopeless labor.

If one believes Homer, Sisyphus was the wisest and most prudent of mortals. According to another tradition, however, he was disposed to practice the profession of highwayman. I see no contradiction in this. Opinions differ as to the reasons why he became the futile laborer of the underworld. To begin with, he is accused of a certain levity in regard to the gods. He stole their secrets. Ægina, the daughter of Æsopus, was carried off by Jupiter. The father was shocked by that disappearance and complained to Sisyphus. He, who knew of the abduction, offered to tell about it on condition that Æsopus would give water to the citadel of Corinth. To the celestial thunderbolts he preferred the benediction of water. He was punished for this in the underworld. Homer tells us also that Sisyphus had put Death in chains. Pluto could not endure the sight of his deserted, silent empire. He dispatched the god of war, who liberated Death from the hands of her conqueror.

It is said also that Sisyphus, being near to death, rashly wanted to test his wife's love. He ordered her to cast his unburied body into the middle of the public square. Sisyphus woke up in the underworld. And there, annoyed by an obedience so contrary to human love, he obtained from Pluto permission to return to earth in order to chastise his wife. But when he had seen again the face of this world, enjoyed water and sun, warm stones and the sea, he no longer wanted to go back to the infernal darkness. Recalls, signs of anger, warnings were of no avail. Many years more he lived facing the curve of the gulf, the sparkling sea, and the smiles of earth. A decree of the gods was necessary. Mercury came and seized the impudent man by the collar and, snatching him from his joys, led him forcibly back to the underworld, where his rock was ready for him.

Sisyphus as the Absurd Hero

You have already grasped that Sisyphus is the absurd hero. He *is,* as much through his passions as through his torture. His scorn of the gods, his hatred of death, and his passion for life won him that unspeakable penalty in which the whole being is exerted toward accomplishing nothing. This is the price that must be paid for the passions of this earth. Nothing is told us about Sisyphus in the underworld. Myths are made for the imagination to breathe life into them. As for this myth, one sees merely the whole effort of a body straining to raise the huge stone, to roll it and push it up a slope a hundred times over; one sees the face screwed up, the cheek tight against the stone, the shoulder bracing the clay-covered mass, the foot wedging it, the fresh start with arms outstretched, the wholly human security of two earth-clotted hands. At the very end of his long effort measured by skyless space and time without depth, the purpose is achieved. Then Sisyphus watches the stone rush down in a few moments toward that lower world whence he will have to push it up again toward the summit. He goes back down to the plain.

Consciousness and the Absurd

It is during that return, that pause, that Sisyphus interests me. A face that toils so close to stones is already stone itself! I see that man going back down with a heavy yet measured step toward the torment of which he will never know the end. That hour like a breathing-space which returns as surely as his suffering, that is the hour of consciousness. At each of those moments when he leaves the heights and gradually sinks toward the lairs of the gods, he is superior to his fate. He is stronger than his rock.

If this myth is tragic, that is because its hero is conscious. Where would his torture be, indeed, if at every step the hope of succeeding upheld him? The workman of today works every day in his life at the same tasks, and this fate is no less absurd. But it is tragic only at the rare moments when it becomes conscious. Sisyphus, proletarian of the gods, powerless and rebellious, knows the whole extent of his wretched condition: it is what he thinks of during his descent. The lucidity that was to constitute his torture at the same time crowns his victory. There is no fate that cannot be surmounted by scorn.

Happiness and the Absurd

If the descent is thus sometimes performed in sorrow, it can also take place in joy. This word is not too much. Again I fancy Sisyphus returning toward his rock, and the sorrow was in the beginning. When the images of earth cling too tightly to memory, when the call of happiness becomes too insistent, it happens that melancholy rises in man's heart: this is the rock's victory, this is the rock itself. The boundless grief is too heavy to bear. These are our nights of Gethsemane. But crushing truths perish from being acknowledged. Thus, Œdipus at the outset obeys fate without knowing it. But from the moment he knows, his tragedy begins. Yet at the same moment, blind and desperate, he realizes that the only bond linking him to the world is the cool hand of a girl. Then a tremendous remark rings out: "Despite so many ordeals, my advanced age and the nobility of my soul make me conclude that all is well." Sophocles' Œdipus, like Dostoevsky's Kirilov, thus gives the recipe for the absurd victory. Ancient wisdom confirms modern heroism.

One does not discover the absurd without being tempted to write a manual of happiness. "What! by such narrow ways—?" There is but one world, however. Happiness and the absurd are two sons of the same earth. They are inseparable. It would be a mistake to say that happiness necessarily springs from the absurd discovery. It happens as well that the feeling of the absurd springs from happiness. "I conclude that all is well," says Œdipus, and that remark is sacred. It echoes in the wild and limited universe of man. It teaches that all is not, has not been, exhausted. It drives out of this world a god who had come into it with dissatisfaction and a preference for futile sufferings. It makes of fate a human matter, which must be settled among men.

All Sisyphus' silent joy is contained therein. His fate belongs to him. His rock is his thing. Likewise, the absurd man, when he contemplates his torment, silences all the idols. In the universe suddenly restored to its silence, the myriad wondering little voices of the earth rise up. Unconscious, secret calls, invitations from all the faces, they are the necessary reverse and price of victory. There is no sun without shadow, and it is essential to know the night. The absurd man says yes and his effort will henceforth be unceasing. If there is a personal fate, there is no higher destiny, or at least there is but one which he concludes is inevitable and despicable. For the rest, he knows himself to be the master of his days. At that subtle moment when man glances backward over his life, Sisyphus returning toward his rock, in that slight pivoting he contemplates that series of unrelated actions which becomes his fate, created by him, combined under his memory's eye and soon sealed by his death. Thus, convinced of the wholly human origin of all that is human, a blind man eager to see who knows that the night has no end, he is still on the go. The rock is still rolling.

I leave Sisyphus at the foot of the mountain! One always finds one's burden again. But Sisyphus teaches the higher fidelity that negates the gods and raises rocks. He too concludes that all is well. This universe henceforth without a master seems to him neither sterile nor futile. Each atom of that stone, each mineral flake of that night-filled mountain, in itself forms a world. The struggle itself toward the heights is enough to fill a man's heart. One must imagine Sisyphus happy.

Further Reading

Camus, Albert. *The Rebel.* New York: Alfred Knopf, 1956.

———. *Resistance, Rebellion and Death.* New York: Alfred Knopf, 1960.

Fanon, Frantz. *Black Skin, White Masks.* New York: Grove Press, 1967.

———. *Toward the African Revolution.* New York: Monthly Review Press, 1967.

Eagbert, Persons, Bassett. *Socialism and American Life.* Princeton: Princeton University Press, 1952.

Marcuse, Herbert. *Reason and Revolution.* New York: Humanities Press, 1954.

Marx, Karl. *Early Writings.* Trans. T. B. Bottomore. New York: McGraw-Hill, 1963.

Meisner, Maurice. *Li-Ta-Chao and the Origins of Chinese Marxism.* Cambridge: Harvard University Press, 1967.

Merton, Robert. *Social Theory and Social Structure.* New York: Free Press, 1957.

Popper, Karl. *The Open Society and Its Enemies.* Vols. 1 and 2. Princeton: Princeton University Press, 1962.

Schram, Stuart R. (Ed.) *Quotations from Chairman Mao Tse-Tung.* New York: Bantam Books, 1967.

PART IV

PERSONAL IDENTITY

INTRODUCTORY READINGS

Walt Kelly

Lewis Carroll

INQUIRY

SELECTED SOURCES

Locke

Hume

Ryle

Pears

Shoemaker

Walt Kelly

I Double (Bridge term)*

HERE IS A DISCUSSION OF PERSONAL SERPENTS AND WHICH IS THE right side of a mirror, head or tails.

* Walt Kelly, *The Pogo Papers* (New York; Simon and Schuster, 1952, 1953), pp. 60–1, 65–7, 69–73. Used by kind permission of Walt Kelly.

BEFORE YOU GO OFF TO VISIT YOUR BALD UNCLE, BALDWIN, MEBBE YOU'D BETTER FIND OUT WHO IS THIS PORKYPINE THAT LOOKS LIKE YOU.
WELL, I DUNNO.
BUT HE'S A STRANGER. DON'T YOU WANT TO KNOW HIM ?
ONE OF ME IS ABOUT ALL I KIN STOMACH.
BESIDES, I IS ANXIOUS TO GIT THIS PRESENT TO UNCLE BALDWIN SOMETHIN' TO KEEP HIS HAIR IN.... IT'S KIND OF A JOKE — ROUSES SOME FOLKS.
HE CAN KEEP IT IN A JAR... HA HA?
YEP! ONLY IN WATER... THEN, LIKE HORSE HAIRS, THEY CHANGE TO SNAKES... AN', SINCE THEY IS HIS PERSONAL SNAKES, HE CAN TRAIN 'EM TO NESTLE ON HIS HEAD LIKE A WIG... SHOULD BE MIGHTY COOL.
NATURAL WAVY, TOO.
I'D LIKE TO BORRY THE LOAN OF A CUP OF SUGAR....
HELP YOUR SELF... SON.
HOO BOY! IS THAT HOW YOU USES IT?
WHERE'D YOU GIT THE HAT?

LONG AS WE CAN'T DISCOVER WHO THAT STRANGE PORKYPINE IS, I GUESS YOU KIN GO HOME AN' READY UP FOR YO' VISIT TO UNCLE BALDWIN.
SOUN' LIKE SOMEBODY IS IN THERE, PORKY.
HUMPH!
POGO! IS YOU GOIN' ROUN' WITH THIS IMPOSTOR ?
DOES HE LOOK LIKE ME OR WORSE YET.. DO I LOOK LIKE HIM?
IT'S ACCORDIN' TO HOW THE MIRROR FALLS AN' DID YOU TOOK HEADS OR TAILS.

PORKY GETS A GRIP ON HIMSELF DESPITE CERTAIN PHYSICAL problems, holds himself at arm's length and hastily puts himself back.

I IS BEEN GOIN' OVER MY PAST, POGO, AN' UP TO NOW I IS NEVER DOUBTED I WAS ME.
THERE'S THE FELLER WHAT LOOKS LIKE YOU. SEEM'S IF HE'S A-PULLIN' OUT.
A-HOY!
SIR, THIS PLACE IS ONLY SWAMP ENOUGH TO HOLD ONE OF US....
WELL, THIS IS A MIGHTY DECENT GESTURE.
RIGHT! HERE'S A BAG PACKED FOR YOU....MY ADVICE IS FOR YOU TO HEAD OUT BRESH COUNTRY WAY... OFF TO DODD COUNTY OR SOME PLACE.
COME ON OVER WHEN YOU WANTS, POGO... I IS BAKED A CAKE.
THAT PORKYPINE WAS MIGHTY NICE, PACKIN' ME A BAG SO'S I COULD GO AWAY.
MEBBE HE IS YOU... HE GOT A GOOD HEART ON HIM.
FIGGER I MOUGHT OF PACKED A SANWICH OR TWO INSIDE?
OPEN HER UP AN' SEE IF THEY IS SOME LUNCH.

OW!
IF I COULD ONLY READ.....
HEY, ALBERT, WE IS A-GOIN' OVER TO PORKY'S HOUSE TO SEE IS PORKY.
SELECTED EPITHETS for the AMATEUR CARPENTER
SOME PORKYPINE IS AROUND... LOOKS JES' LIKE PORKY AN' US CAN'T TELL WHICH IS REALLY.
I'LL GO ALONG AN' FOO-LAVORATE THE IM-POSTORIN' SCAMP.
NATURAL, ACCORDIN' TO WHOM IS THE UNREAL McCOY!
DON'T LOOK AT ME..... I IS A PLAIN TOURIST.
Y'KNOW I GOT A HUNCH THIS OTHER FELLOW AIN'T ME 'CAUSE HE SAID HE BAKED A CAKE.
WHEREAS THE ONLY KIN I GOT WHAT CAN EVEN HALF BAKE IS MY BALD UNCLE, BALDWIN, OF WHOM I IS NEVER EVEN SEED HIM.....
THIS BOY CAN'T BE YO' UNCLE BALDWIN

THE PORKYPINE IN QUESTION GOT A HEAD OF HAIR ON HIM LIKE A THREE TOED ECHIDNA.
TRUE - TRUE
DING BING IT! WHAT A PLACE FOR A MAN OF MY STATION TO GIT BALDED OFF AT.... WISH NEPHEW PORKY HAD A MORE EFFICACIOUS STOCK OF TONIC.
UNCLE BALDWIN
I BEEN THINKIN'... THAT OTHER FELLA AIN'T UNCLE BALDWIN.
HE MEBBE IS RIGHT...THE SWAMP GOT ONLY ROOM ENOUGH FOR ONE SOUR PUSS.... I BETTER GO ON OFF ... I CAN'T TELL IF HE'S PORKY OR I IS.... BUT I DO KNOW IT DON'T PAY TO CROWD UP A PLACE WITH PORKYPINES.
EVENTUALLY EVER' MAN GOTTA FACE THE PROBLEM OF TRYIN' TO FIGGER IF IT'S WORTH-WHILE TO PROVE THAT HE IS HIMSELF.
G'BYE

HEREIN THE RAINS COME DOWN IN THE SOGGY ALONE AND WE FIND a firefly in every ointment.

DING BING IT! JES' WHEN A MIGRATORY MAN NEEDS A FISH, IT STARTS TO RAIN! THEM FISH AIN'T GONE BITE NOW-- GIT HAULED OUT AN' GIT ALL WET.
THEY'S DOWN BELOW SITTIN' ROUN' THE FIRE TELLIN' LIES 'BOUT THE BIG FISHERMANS WHO ALMOST CAUGHT 'EM--AN' I AINT GONE SIT OUTSIDE HERE....
--GITTIN' SOAKED TO THE SKIN OFFERIN' UNREQUITED LOVE TO A MESS OF INDOOR, UNSPORTIN', SUMMER SOLDIERIN', SEDENTARY, PISCATORY PUSSY FOOTERS! THEY KIN DIG THEIR OWN WORMS.
WHY DO IT GOTTA RAIN WHEN US IS LOOKIN' FOR SOME BODY?
IT'S PART OF THE PITY OF IT ALL.
THAT PORKYPINE COULDN'T GIT LOST IN SUNSHINE.
WOULDN'T BE IN CHARACTER

HE MIGHT NOT EVEN BE THE RIGHT PORKYPINE.
WELL, PERSON'LY...
ANY LOST CRITTUR WE FINDS IN THIS STORM WILL BE RIGHT ENOUGH FOR ME.
THIS PORKYPINE MAY BE SOME BOY WE DON'T MAYBE KNOW.
WE KNOWS HIM GOOD ENOUGH TO GIVE HIM A HAND.
BY JING! IF THIS IS OUR OL' BUDDY, WHY DON'T HE UP AN' SAY SO?
A MAN'S OWN FRIENDS OUGHT TO RECOGNIZE HIM.

Lewis Carroll

Who in the World am I?*

"CURIOUSER AND CURIOSIER!" CRIED ALICE (SHE WAS SO MUCH surprised, that for the moment she quite forgot how to speak good English). "Now I'm opening out like the largest telescope that ever was! Goodbye, feet!" (for when she looked down at her feet, they seemed to be almost out of sight, they were getting so far off). "Oh, my poor little feet, I wonder who will put on your shoes and stockings for you now, dears? I'm sure *I* shan't be able! I shall be a great deal too far off to trouble myself about you: you must manage the best way you can—but I must be kind to them," thought Alice, "or perhaps they won't walk the way I want to go! Let me see. I'll give them a new pair of boots every Christmas."

And she went on planning to herself how she would manage it. "They must go by the carrier," she thought; "and how funny it'll seem, sending presents to one's own feet! And how odd the directions will look!

Alice's Right Foot, Esq.,
Hearthrug,
near the Fender.
(with Alice's love).

Oh dear, what nonsense I'm talking!"

Just at this moment her head struck against the roof of the hall: in fact she was now rather more than nine feet high, and she at once took up the little golden key and hurried off to the garden door.

Poor Alice! It was as much as she could do, lying down on one side, to look through into the garden with one eye; but to get through was more hopeless than ever: she sat down and began to cry again.

*Lewis Carroll, *Alice's Adventures in Wonderland* (New York: Macmillan, 1865), Chap. II.

"You ought to be ashamed of yourself," said Alice, "a great girl like you," (she might well say this), "to go on crying in this way! Stop this moment, I tell you!" But she went on all the same, shedding gallons of tears, until there was a large pool all round her, about four inches deep and reaching half down the hall.

After a time she heard a little pattering of feet in the distance, and she hastily dried her eyes to see what was coming. It was the White Rabbit returning, splendidly dressed, with a pair of white kid gloves in one hand and a large fan in the other: he came trotting along in a great hurry, muttering to himself, as he came, "Oh! the Duchess, the Duchess! Oh! *won't* she be savage if I've kept her waiting!" Alice felt so desperate that she was ready to ask help of any one: so, when the Rabbit came near her, she began, in a low, timid voice, "If you please, sir—" The Rabbit started violently, dropped the white kid gloves and the fan, and scurried away into the darkness as hard as he could go.

Alice took up the fan and gloves, and, as the hall was very hot, she kept fanning herself all the time she went on talking. "Dear, dear! How queer everything is today! And yesterday things went on just as usual. I wonder if I've been changed in the night? Let me think: *was* I the same when I got up this morning? I almost think I can remember feeling a little different. But if I'm not the same, the next question is, 'Who in the world am I?' Ah, *that's* the great puzzle!" And she began thinking over all the children she knew that were of the same age as herself, to see if she could have been changed for any of them.

"I'm sure I'm not Ada," she said, "for her hair goes in such long ringlets, and mine doesn't go in ringlets at all; and I'm sure I can't be Mabel, for I know all sorts of things, and she, oh, she knows such a very little! Besides, *she's* she, and *I'm* I, and—oh dear, how puzzling it all is! I'll try if I know all the things I used to know. Let me see: four time five is twelve, and four times six is thirteen, and four times seven is—oh dear! I shall never get to twenty at that rate! However, the Multiplication Table doesn't signify: let's try Geography. London is the capital of Paris and Paris is the capital of Rome, and Rome—no, *that's* all wrong, I'm certain! I must have been changed for Mabel! I'll try and say '*How doth the little—*' " and she crossed her hands on her lap, as if she were saying lessons, and began to repeat it, but her voice sounded hoarse and strange, and the words did not come the same as they used to do:—

"How doth the little crocodile
  Improve his shining tail,
And pour the waters of the Nile
  On every golden scale!

"How cheerfully he seems to grin,
  How neatly spreads his claws,
And welcomes little fishes in,
  With gently smiling jaws!"

"I'm sure those are not the right words," said poor Alice, and her eyes filled with tears again as she went on, "I must be Mabel after all, and I shall have to go and live in that poky little house, and have next to no toys to play with, and oh, ever so many lessons to learn! No, I've made up my mind about it: if I'm Mabel, I'll stay down here! It'll be no use their putting their heads down and saying, 'Come up again, dear!' I shall only look up and say, 'Who am I, then? Tell me that first, and then, if I like being that person, I'll come up: if not, I'll stay down here till I'm somebody else'—but, oh dear!" cried Alice, with a sudden burst of tears, "I do wish they *would* put their heads down! I am so *very* tired of being all alone here!"

As she said this, she looked down at her hands, and was surprised to see that she had put on one of the Rabbit's little white kid gloves while she was talking. "How *can* I have done that?" she thought. "I must be growing small again." She got up and went to the table to measure herself by it, and found that, as nearly as she could guess, she was now about two feet high, and was going on shrinking rapidly: she soon found out that the cause of this was the fan she was holding, and she dropped it hastily, just in time to save herself from shrinking away altogether.

"That *was* a narrow escape!" said Alice, a good deal frightened at the sudden change, but very glad to find herself still in existence. "And now for the garden!"

INQUIRY

"God knows!" exclaimed he, at his wits' end. "I'm not myself—I'm somebody else—that's me yonder—no—that's somebody else got into my shoes. I was myself last night, but I fell asleep on the mountain, and they've changed my gun, and everything's changed, and I'm changed, and I can't tell what's my name, or who I am!"

WASHINGTON IRVING
Rip Van Winkle

IS having the same body that you had, say last week, a necessary condition of being the same person? That is one form of the classical philosophical problem of personal identity. In a broader sense, the problem is related to the kinds of criteria we apply when questions arise in our lives regarding whether or not someone is the same person as, for example, someone we used to know. In this chapter we will examine some proposals relative to determining personal identity (self-identity) and some of the problems which arise when these are applied. The Pogo Cartoon strip serves to illustrate for us some of the issues involved in personal identity.

Questions of Personal Identity

Porkypine is perplexed by the appearance in the swamp of his double, who has taken over Porkypine's daily activities and even his home. For all Porkypine knows (we, of course, know that it is an imposter) this other self may be a miraculous reconstruction of himself. That is, Porky could imagine that this other Porkypine might well be a real duplicate of himself. How does he convince his friends that he is not his look-alike?

One of our more popular science-fiction television shows employed an intriguing method of transporting a man between spaceship and planet. The body of a man was disintegrated in the spaceship and then reformulated at the desired location. We could suppose that the process is such that the machine which performs it makes a tape of the type and position of all the molecular structures of the body entering it. This taped information is then transported to the desired location and a kind of rebuilding process is begun. If a machine were to act as we have suggested, then could not the machine "re-create" (perhaps "assemble" is a better word) two or three duplicates, all having the same bodily structure as the disintegrated original? Suppose the operator of the machine were struck with the idea that three men like his captain would be better than only one; consequently he re-constitutes three bodies of the captain instead of the usual one on the next occasion when the captain must be transported.

We need not carry this conjecture further. Certain questions of identity, similar to those which arise for Porkypine and his swamp friends, naturally emerge. None of the three reconstructed captains would claim that he is the same person as any of the other two. All of them can see that they are not the same single person. (This distinction might not be possible if, for example, we were dealing with a schizophrenic or a "three faces of Eve" personality.) Yet they all claim to be the same person in another sense. They all claim to have been the captain who entered the transportation machine. Porkypine and Uncle Baldwin both claim to have been the same friend to the rest of the swamp creatures.

How might we settle the issue of who is who? Porkypine comments, "Eventually ever' man gotta face the problem of tryin' to figger if it's worthwhile to prove that he is himself." In the case of the three captains, we might have to conclude that none of them is the old captain. Certainly we could not learn which was the real captain by checking their memory statements or even by witnessing their behavior with the hope of recognizing certain familiar "captain" traits. Porkypine's case is not just that, however. No miraculous machine is involved. Two persons simply claim to be the same person, and they look alike. How do we draw distinctions here? What criteria are to be applied? As Pogo says, "A man's own friends ought to recognize him." What does "recognize" mean here? Consider the sentence, "Oh, it's you, I didn't recognize you." Imagine the circumstances in which you might say it.

In examining the issue more closely, we must remember that the philosophical problem of personal identity is not "What kind of a person am I?" but "What particular person am I?" Alice's predicament is of this latter type. She wants to be able to pin a particular label upon herself. Alice's case also suggests another interesting complication often related to the problem of personal identity: the concept of reincarnation (see also Part V). Yesterday things went as usual for Alice. She wonders if during the night she has somehow changed. "*Was* I the same when I got up this morning? I almost think I can remember feeling a little different."

We may have read accounts of persons who claim to have awakened some morning with a different set of memories than they had the night before. Perhaps such a person begins to recount events in which he could not possibly have participated. But his descriptions of these events are concise and correct. Let us say he claims to be a historical figure and that his memories, as far as it is possible to check, agree with the facts of the historical character's life. Of course, he still looks like the person he was before he began having these memories. Would we be inclined to say that he is now, strange as it may sound, the historical figure?

Notice that Alice as she ponders her identity touches on both bodily characteristics and mental abilities. But which is more important? Does what you can remember count more than the way you look? Alice doesn't even look as she used to.

"Same . . ."

The key to personal identity seems to lie in the way we use the word "same." "Same" implies a standard. It refers us to some criterion or rule. The fact that it is important at times in our daily lives to make claims about ourselves as "the same person that . . ." should give us a clue to the kinds of criteria we deem appropriate to the problem. We are told by scientists that within about seven years all the cells in the human body have been replaced by new cells. What makes us the same persons we were seven years ago? Is it more than the way we look? In many respects, of course, we are not the same persons. Perhaps our political views have changed or we have a different circle of friends or we have gotten false teeth or have just lost weight. What a difference comes over a formerly confirmed bachelor who marries and becomes an expectant father. Nonetheless, we do refer to our old acquaintances and even ourselves as the same persons despite the lapse of many years.

If you had purchased a car seven years ago, and in the course of time every part of that car had to be replaced by a new part, would you be inclined to call it the "same car" you bought seven years ago? If not, during which repair did the car cease to be the old car and become the new, different car? Certainly the car is not the original, but it is a seven-year-old car. A used car dealer would refer to it as such. What of a human being? What constitutes his identity and makes him recognizable even after seven years? Some people have difficulty recognizing themselves when reading their own old diaries.

Whenever questions of identity arise, we would like a clear-cut uncomplicated criterion to solve the problem. In normal circumstances these questions seldom do arise. Only when some extraordinary events interfere with daily life, or when it becomes necessary to establish identity to have an alibi, to recognize someone in a crowd, or to be recognized by someone, do we confront these issues; and, of course, the question of personal identity is also related to certain theories of after-life as discussed in Part V.

Imagine a legal case. The murder of a beachcomber is committed in a small seaside village. Three townsfolk are witnesses to the event. Seven years pass until a man is apprehended and charged with the murder, and the witnesses are called upon at the trial to identify him. Over the span of the years the accused, call him A, has changed his physical appearance drastically. He has married, become a father, a banker, a man of considerable standing in a large inland community. Only the tireless efforts of a police detective were able to trace a connection between the prominent banker and the murderer. But in a court of law one must be able to show beyond a reasonable doubt that A, the banker, is the *same* person, then known as B, the murderer of the beachcomber.

Locke's Analysis of Identity

John Locke distinguishes between the identity of men and the identity of persons. The "same man" for Locke refers to bodily continuity. If we were to know (in the sense that we recognize) a certain man in town, even if he should undergo a severe psychological maladjustment—perhaps even to the point of complete mental derangement—we would still call him the same man, assuming his bodily existence is continuous. But, as Locke points out, the personal identity of the man in question would not necessarily be the same. A "person" for Locke is a "thinking, intelligent being that has reason and reflection and can consider itself as itself in different times and places." If these mental capacities were not a vital part of our identities, then we would not differ in terms of distinguishing qualities from beasts or inanimate objects such as trees. Locke concludes that the identity of a person is a question of consciousness, memory, "as far as this consciousness can be extended backwards to any past action or thought, so far reaches the identity of that person." My personal identy, for Locke, might well be summarized as, "I am what I remember."

Is it possible for the same man not to be the same person? Consider the case of Charly, whose I.Q. changes from that of a moron to that of a genius in the story "Flowers for Algernon" and the movie *Charly*. Or, consider the plea of temporary insanity often used in murder trials. Sirhan Sirhan, the assassin of Robert F. Kennedy, claimed to have been in a trance with no memory of the murder incident and thus not the same person who pulled the trigger of the murder weapon and therefore not responsible for the crime.

There are problems with Locke's analysis of identity. Do we want to know, as in our murder case, that A and B are one in the same *man* (same body) or one in the same *person* (that A remembers or can be brought to remember having killed the beachcomber in the seaside village while he lived under the name B)? Suppose A claims no memory of B's life; he says he never heard of the beachcomber. We could make the case more complex here by introducing evidence that A suffered a tremendous mental shock, creating complete amnesia of his life as B, right after the alleged murder; but this complication is not necessary, for we have no way of checking on the contents of A's memory; we only know that he tells us he remembers nothing of the incident. Might we not be constructing a case of having the right man but the wrong person? We must be careful here not to let the discussion turn to the occult. (For those who consider reincarnation a possibility, Locke's view is of interest. We might want to say that a body that has been "informed" by the spirit of an historical figure is the same man, but not the same person, as before the reincarnation. But other problems related to his memory would be crucial: Is the subject only clairvoyant, a lucky guesser, etc.?)

Thomas Reid criticized Locke's theory of personal identity when he pointed out that the memory criterion has a tendency to people the world unnecessarily, thereby confusing the issue as to just who someone is. Reid cited the example of a general who remembers his valiant efforts on the battlefield (when a major, let us say), but has forgotten all of his activities as a schoolboy. Yet while he was a major performing the valiant deeds of battle he clearly remembered his school days. On Locke's account we would have to say that the general is the same person as the valiant major and that the major was the same person as the schoolboy, but that the schoolboy and the general are not the same person. If this seems complicated, that was part of Reid's point.

The Humian Idea of Self

A great deal of our Western tradition supports the theory that the identity of persons (personality?) is a non-physical matter and that there is something called "I," separate from the body, which need not exist within the particular body it now occupies.

David Hume attempts to uncover this thing "I." Hume concludes, however, that a man has no clear, constant idea of "self" as he carries on the various activities of living. You never catch your self when it is not doing something. In other words, your idea of yourself is constantly changing. You are happy, sad, relaxed, working on mathematical problems, doing philosophy; but there is no one invariable "I" or "self" which is ascertainable in this bundle of perceptions. For Hume, if there is no constant impression of "I," there can be no clear idea of "I" apart from the series of things "I" does. Identity is the imagined linking of a series of impressions. I am a bundle of the things I do, feel, think, etc. I am not a thing apart from my activities.

A Twentieth Century version of the Humian idea of self is expressed by Gilbert Ryle. Ryle refers to the problem as the "systematic" elusiveness of 'I'." Whenever I try to look into my own mind, to introspect my self in the many things I do, I discover that I always miss something: me in the present. I cannot introspect the act of my introspecting. Ryle suggests that what we call introspection is, in fact, retrospection. We can only consider the past events and activities we have performed and must always leave out the present act of so-called introspection. (Is this not Alice's predicament?) It is like attempting to jump on the shadow of one's outstretched hand. You never quite succeed.

Notice, however, that if we accept the Humian theory of the self we are left with acts, both mental and physical, but no actors. We have activities, but no agents performing them. Arthur Koestler, in his famous novel *Darkness at Noon,* has one of the major characters refer to the self, the pronoun "I," as a "grammatical fiction," something the language makes exist. Is the self nothing but a product of the imagination or language?

Consider again the trial of A for murder at the seaside village. An activity had occurred (the murder), but who did it? If there were no agents, no continuing "selves," just activities, who can be blamed? What happens to our theories of punishment? Learning? Common sense and our social, legal, and educational systems would lead us to believe that each of us is an Ego, a center or subject of experience. We attribute states of consciousness to ourselves and to others, and we act within our social framework as if each of us has a continuing identity. Is all of this a myth? Is it a product of our imagination and not of fact? If we have no perception of the self, why do we find it necessary to manufacture an entity to serve as a kind of ghostly actor in each of our experiences? What would the possessives "mine," "yours," etc. mean if this were the case?

Returning to the problems raised by the experiences of Alice and Porkypine, we see two major related issues. Alice wants to find out who she is, not unlike an amnesic; but Porkypine knows who he is, he wants to convince others. Certainly the methods by which they would proceed would differ. But are criteria of the body really of much help to either of them?

A Case of Exchange of Brains

Let us create one final situation for our consideration. Today's achievements in medical technology, especially in the area of organ transplants, suggest the possibility of a future experiment in which the brains of two individuals are exchanged.* A's body receives B's brain and B's body receives A's brain. In order to limit the realm of consideration somewhat, assume that A's body/B's brain dies during the operation, but that B's body/A's brain survives. Let us call our subject BA. BA awakens. Put yourself in his position. You see the familiar body, lifeless, being wheeled out of the room. You have A's brain and his memory traces, but, like Alice, this body does not quite feel right. You are released from the hospital (perhaps told to return weekly to a local philosopher for a progress report). To whose house do you go? Let us stipulate that A and B and their respective families had never met. You undoubtedly go to A's house; you remember none other. Mrs. A is at the door. What is to be your relationship with wife A and children A? How would you proceed to convince them that you are husband and father despite appearances? Think of the legal problems. Who is the widow? Who collects the life insurance?

Finally, imagine that BA is the banker arrested in the inland city and accused of killing the beachcomber at the seaside village. We

* This example was suggested by Sydney Shoemaker, *Self-Knowledge and Self-Identity* (Ithaca: Cornell University Press, 1963).

are inclined to identify people by their mental abilities and dispositions, but certainly it does matter that body B was seen to have committed a crime whether or not the brain in B's body has a personal memory of the event. Can we establish clear-cut identification criteria which will be applicable to all cases in which the problem arises?

1

JOHN LOCKE

(1632–1704)

*Same Man . . . Same Person**

Locke's interests lie mainly in practical and social matters. He is most famous for his contributions to government theory, which were influential in the thought of the founders of the American Republic. Locke's epistemological thinking is an attack on the theory that men are born with certain innate ideas that form the core of our human knowledge. Ideas, Locke claims, arise from sensations and reflections on those sensations. In other words, the source of knowledge is experience. Locke's philosophy is often cited as the first major exposition of English empiricism, the theory that knowledge arises not from deducible first principles, but from interactions with our environment. Locke, on the question of identity, draws a distinction between the recognition of material things and that of persons. We know that material things are the same on the basis of sense perception; they look the same. But ourselves? We know our identities through consciousness, intuition and memory.

* John Locke, *Essay Concerning Human Understanding* (1690), with omissions.

The Identity of Man

THIS also shows wherein the identity of the same *man* consists; viz. in nothing but a participation of the same continued life, by constantly fleeting particles of matter, in succession vitally united to the same organized body. He that shall place the identity of man in anything else, but, like that of other animals, in one fitly organized body, taken in any one instant, and from thence continued, under one organization of life, in several successively fleeting particles of matter united to it, will find it hard to make an embryo, one of years, mad and sober, the *same* man, by any supposition, that will not make it possible for Seth, Ismael, Socrates, Pilate, St. Austin, and Cæsar Borgia, to be the same man. For if the identity of *soul alone* makes the same *man;* and there be nothing in the nature of matter why the same individual spirit may not be united to different bodies, it will be possible that those men, living in distant ages, and of different tempers, may have been the same man: which way of speaking must be from a very strange use of the word man, applied to an idea out of which body and shape are excluded. And that way of speaking would agree yet worse with the notions of those philosophers who allow of transmigration, and are of opinion that the souls of men may, for their miscarriages, be detruded into the bodies of beasts, as fit habitations, with organs suited to the satisfaction of their brutal inclinations. But yet I think nobody, could he be sure that the *soul* of Heliogabalus were in one of his hogs, would yet say that hog were a *man* or *Heliogabalus.*

It is not therefore unity of substance that comprehends all sorts of identity, or will determine it in every case; but to conceive and judge of it aright, we must consider what idea the word it is applied to stands for: it being one thing to be the same *substance*, another the same *man*, and a third the same *person*, if *person*, *man*, and *substance*, are three names standing for three different ideas;—for such as is the idea belonging to that name, such must be the identity; which, if it had been a little more carefully attended to, would possibly have prevented a great deal of that confusion which often occurs about this matter, with no small seeming difficulties, especially concerning *personal* identity, which therefore we shall in the next place a little consider.

Same Man

An animal is a living organized body; and consequently the same animal, as we have observed, is the same continued *life* communicated to different particles of matter, as they happen successively to be united to that organized living body. And whatever is talked of other definitions, ingenious observation puts it past doubt, that the idea in our minds, of which the sound man in our mouths is the sign, is nothing else but of an animal of such a certain form. Since I think I may be confident, that, whoever should see a creature of his own shape or make, though it had no more reason all its life than a cat or a parrot, would call him still a *man;* or whoever should hear a cat or a parrot discourse, reason, and philosophize, would call or think it nothing but a *cat* or a *parrot;* and say, the one was a dull irrational man, and the other a very intelligent rational parrot. [A relation we have in an author of great note, is sufficient to countenance the supposition of a rational parrot. His words are:

A Rational Parrot

'I had a mind to know, from Prince Maurice's own mouth, the account of a common, but much credited story, that I had heard so often from many others, of an old parrot he had in Brazil, during his government there, that spoke, and asked, and answered common questions, like a reasonable creature: so that those of his train there generally concluded it to be witchery or possession; and one of his chaplains, who lived long afterwards in Holland, would never from that time endure a parrot, but said they all had a devil in them. I had heard many particulars of this story, and assevered by people hard to be discredited, which made me ask Prince Maurice what there was of it. He said, with his usual plainness and dryness in talk, there was something true, but a great deal false of what had been reported. I desired to know of him what there was of the first. He told me short and coldly, that he had heard of such an old parrot when he had been at Brazil; and though he believed nothing of it, and it was a good way off, yet he had so much curiosity as to send for it: that it was a very great and a very old one; and when it came first into the room where the prince was, with a great many Dutchmen about him, it said presently, *What a company of white men are here!* They asked it, what it thought that man was, pointing to the prince. It answered, *Some General or other.* When they brought it close to him, he asked it, *D'où venez-vous?* It answered, *De Marinnan.* The Prince, *À qui estes-vous?* The parrot, *À un Portugais.* The Prince, *Que fais-tu là?* Parrot, *Je garde les poulles.* The Prince laughed, and said, *Vous gardez les poulles?* The parrot answered, *Oui-moi; et je sçai bien faire;* and made the chuck four or five times that people use to make to chickens when they call them. I set down the words of this worthy dialogue in French, just as Prince Maurice said them to me. I asked him in what language the parrot spoke, and he said in Brazilian. I asked whether he understood Brazilian; he said No, but he had taken care to have two interpreters by him, the one a Dutchman that spoke Brazilian, and the other a Brazilian that spoke Dutch; that he asked them separately and privately, and both of them agreed in telling him just the same thing that the parrot had said. I could not but tell this odd story, because it is so much out of the way, and from the first hand, and what may pass for a good one; for I dare say this Prince at least believed himself in all he told me, having ever passed for a very honest and pious man: I leave it to naturalists to reason, and to other men to believe, as they please upon it; however, it is not, perhaps, amiss to relieve or enliven a busy scene sometimes with such digressions whether to the purpose or no.'

I have taken care that the reader should have the story at large in the author's own words, because he seems to me not to have thought it incredible; for it cannot be imagined that so able a man as he, who had sufficiency enough to warrant all the testimonies he gives of himself, should take so much pains, in a place where it had nothing to do, to pin so close, not only a man whom he mentions as his friend, but on a Prince in whom he acknowledges very great honesty and piety, a story which, if he himself thought incredible, he could not but also think ridiculous. The Prince, it is plain, who vouches this story, and our author, who relates it from him, both of them call this talker a parrot: and I ask any one else who thinks such a story fit to be told, whether, if this parrot, and all of its kind, had always talked, as we have a prince's word for it this one did,—whether, I say, they would not have passed for a race of *rational animals;* but yet, whether, for all that, they would have been allowed to be men, and not *parrots?*] For I presume it is not the idea of a thinking or rational being alone that makes the *idea of a man* in most people's sense: but of a body, so and so shaped, joined to it; and if that be the idea of a man, the same successive body not shifted all at once, must, as well as the same immaterial spirit, go to the making of the same man.

Personal Identity

This being premised, to find wherein personal identity consists, we must consider what *person* stands for;—which, I think, is a thinking intelligent being, that has reason and reflection, and can consider itself as itself, the same thinking thing, in different times and places; which it does only by that consciousness which is inseparable from thinking, and, as it seems to me, essential to it: it being impossible for any one to perceive without *perceiving* that he does perceive. When we see, hear, smell, taste, feel, meditate, or will anything, we know that we do so. Thus it is always as to our present sensations and perceptions: and by this every one is to himself that which he calls *self*:—it not being considered, in this case, whether the same self be continued in the same or divers substances. For, since consciousness always accompanies thinking, and it is that which makes every one to be what he calls self, and thereby distinguishes himself from all other thinking things, in this alone consists personal identity, i.e. the sameness of a rational being: and as far as this consciousness can be extended backwards to any past action or thought, so far reaches the identity of that person; it is the same self now it was then; and it is by the same self with this present one that now reflects on it, that that action was done.

Consciousness Makes Personal Identity

But it is further inquired, whether it be the same identical substance. This few would think they had reason to doubt of, if these perceptions, with their consciousness, always remained present in the mind, whereby the same thinking thing would be always consciously present, and, as would be thought, evidently the same to itself. But that which seems to make the difficulty is this, that this consciousness being interrupted always by forgetfulness, there being no moment of our lives wherein we have the whole train of all our past actions before our eyes in one view, but even the best memories losing the sight of one part whilst they are viewing another; and we sometimes, and that the greatest part of our lives, not reflecting on our past selves, being intent on our present thoughts, and in sound sleep having no thoughts at all, or at least none with that consciousness which remarks our waking thoughts,—I say, in all these cases, our consciousness being interrupted, and we losing the sight of our past selves, doubts are raised whether we are the same thinking thing, i.e. the same *substance* or no. Which, however reasonable or unreasonable, concerns not *personal* identity at all. The question being what makes the same person; and not whether it be the same identical substance, which always thinks in the same person, which, in this case, matters not at all: different substances, by the same consciousness (where they do partake in it) being united into one person, as well as different bodies by the same life are united into one animal, whose identity is preserved in that change of substances by the unity of one continued life. For, it being the same consciousness that makes a man be himself to himself, personal identity depends on that only, whether it be annexed solely to one individual substance, or can be continued in a succession of several substances. For as far as any intelligent being *can* repeat the idea of any past action with the same consciousness it had of it at first, and with the same consciousness it has of any present action; so far it is the same personal self. For it is by the consciousness it has of its present thoughts and actions, that it is *self to itself* now, and so will be the same self, as far as the same consciousness can extend to actions past or to come; and would be by distance of time, or change of substance, no more two persons, than a man be two men by wearing other clothes to-day than he did yesterday, with a long or a short sleep between: the same consciousness uniting those distant actions into the same person, whatever substances contributed to their production.

That this is so, we have some kind of evidence in our very bodies, all whose particles, whilst vitally united to this same thinking conscious self, so that *we feel* when they are touched, and are affected by, and conscious of good or harm that happens to them, are a part of ourselves; i.e. of our thinking conscious self. Thus, the limbs of his body are to every one a part of himself; he sympathizes and is concerned for them. Cut off a hand, and thereby separate it from that consciousness he had of its heat, cold, and other affections, and it is then no longer a part of that which is himself, any more than the remotest part of matter. Thus, we see the *substance* whereof personal self consisted at one time may be varied at another, without the change of personal identity; there being no question about the same person, though the limbs which but now were a part of it, be cut off.

Change of Substance and Personal Identity

But the question is, Whether if the same substance which thinks be changed, it can be the same person; or, remaining the same, it can be different persons?

And to this I answer: First, This can be no question at all to those who place thought in a purely material animal constitution, void of an immaterial substance. For, whether their supposition be true or no, it is plain they conceive personal identity preserved in something else than identity of substance; as animal identity is preserved in identity of life, and not of substance. And therefore those who place thinking in an immaterial substance only, before they can come to deal with these men, must show why personal identity cannot be preserved in the change of immaterial substances, or variety of particular immaterial substances, as well as animal identity is preserved in the change of material substances, or variety of particular bodies: unless they will say, it is one immaterial spirit that makes the same life in brutes, as it is one immaterial spirit that makes the same person in men. . . .

Consciousness (Memory) Alone Unites Activities into the Same Person

But though the same immaterial substance or soul does not alone, wherever it be, and in whatsoever state, make the same *man;* yet it is plain, consciousness, as far as ever it can be extended—should it be to ages past—unites existences and actions very remote in time into the same *person,* as well as it does the existences and actions of the immediately preceding moment: so that whatever has the consciousness of present and past actions, is the same person to whom they both belong. Had I the same consciousness that I saw the ark and Noah's flood, as that I saw an overflowing of the Thames last winter, or as that I write now, I could no more doubt that I who write this now, that saw the Thames overflowed last winter, and that viewed the flood at the general deluge, was the same *self*,—place that self in what *substance* you please—than that I who write this am the same *myself* now whilst I write (whether I consist of all the same substance, material or immaterial, or no) that I was yesterday. For as to this point of being the same self, it matters not whether this present self be made up of the same or other substances—I being as much concerned, and as justly accountable for any action that was done a thousand years since, appropriated to me now by this self-consciousness, as I am for what I did the last moment. . . .

Wherein Personal Identity Consists

This may show us wherein personal identity consists not in the identity of substance, but, as I have said, in the identity of consciousness, wherein if Socrates and the present mayor of Queinborough agree, they are the same person: if the same Socrates waking and sleeping do not partake of the same consciousness, Socrates waking and sleeping is not the same person. And to punish Socrates waking for what sleeping Socrates thought, and waking Socrates was never conscious of, would be no more of right, than to punish one twin for what his brother-twin did, whereof he knew nothing, because their outsides were so like, that they could not be distinguished; for such twins have been seen.

Clarification of Same Man and Same Person

But yet possibly it will still be objected,—Suppose I wholly lose the memory of some parts of my life, beyond a possibility of retrieving them, so that perhaps I shall never be conscious of them again; yet am I not the same person that did those actions, had those thoughts that I once was conscious of, though I have now forgot them? To which I answer, that we must here take notice what the word *I* is applied to; which, in this case, is the *man* only. And the same man being presumed to be the same person, I is easily here supposed to stand also for the same person. But if it be possible for the same man to have distinct incommunicable consciousness at different times, it is past doubt the same man would at different times make different persons; which, we see, is the sense of mankind in the solemnest declaration of their opinions, human laws not punishing the mad man for the sober man's actions, nor the sober man for what the mad man did,—thereby making them two persons: which is somewhat explained by our way of speaking in English when we say such an one is 'not himself,' or is 'beside himself'; in which phrases it is insinuated, as if those who now, or at least first used them, thought that self was changed; the self-same person was no longer in that man.

But yet it is hard to conceive that Socrates, the same individual man, should be two persons. To help us a little in this, we must consider what is meant by Socrates, or the same individual *man*.

First, it must be either the same individual, immaterial, thinking substance; in short, the same numerical soul, and nothing else.

Secondly, or the same animal, without any regard to an immaterial soul.

Thirdly, or the same immaterial spirit united to the same animal.

Now, take which of these suppositions you please, it is impossible to make personal identity to consist in anything but consciousness; or reach any further than that does.

For, by the first of them, it must be allowed possible that a man born of different women, and in distant times, may be the same man. A way of speaking which, whoever admits, must allow it possible for the same man to be two distinct persons, as any two that have lived in different ages without the knowledge of one another's thoughts.

By the second and third, Socrates, in this life and after it, cannot be the same man any way, but by the same consciousness; and so making human identity to consist in the same thing wherein we place personal identity, there will be no difficulty to allow the same man to be the same person. But then they who place human identity in consciousness only, and not in something else, must consider how they will make the infant Socrates the same man with Socrates after the resurrection. But whatsoever to some men makes a man, and consequently the same individual man, wherein perhaps few are agreed, personal identity can by us be placed in nothing but consciousness, (which is that alone which makes what we call *self,*) without involving us in great absurdities.

But is not a man drunk and sober the same person? why else is he punished for the fact he commits when drunk, though he be never afterwards conscious of it? Just as much the same person as a man that walks, and does other things in his sleep, is the same person, and is answerable for any mischief he shall do in it. Human laws punish both, with a justice suitable to *their* way of knowledge;—because, in these cases, they cannot distinguish certainly what is real, what counterfeit: and so the ignorance in drunkenness or sleep is not admitted as a plea. [For, though punishment be annexed to personality, and personality to consciousness, and the drunkard perhaps be not conscious of what he did, yet human judicatures justly punish him; because the fact is proved against him, but want of consciousness cannot be proved for him.] But in the Great Day, wherein the secrets of all hearts shall be laid open, it may be reasonable to think, no one shall be made to answer for what he knows nothing of; but shall receive his doom, his conscience accusing or excusing him.

Two Consciousnesses Acting in the Same Body?

Nothing but consciousness can unite remote existences into the same person: the identity of substance will not do it; for whatever substance there is, however framed, without consciousness there is no person: and a carcass may be a person, as well as any sort of substance be so, without consciousness.

Could we suppose two distinct incommunicable consciousnesses acting the same body, the one constantly by day, the other by night; and, on the other side, the same consciousness, acting by intervals, two distinct bodies: I ask, in the first case, whether the day and the night—man would not be two as distinct persons as Socrates and Plato? And whether, in the second case, there would not be one person in two distinct bodies, as much as one man is the same in two distinct clothings? Nor is it at all material to say, that this same, and this distinct consciousness, in the cases above mentioned, is owing to the same and distinct immaterial substances, bringing it with them to those bodies; which, whether true or no, alters not the case: since it is evident the personal identity would equally be determined by the consciousness, whether that consciousness were annexed to some individual immaterial substance or no. For, granting that the thinking substance in man must be necessarily supposed immaterial, it is evident that immaterial thinking thing may sometimes part with its past consciousness, and be restored to it again: as appears in the forgetfulness men often have of their past actions; and the mind many times recovers the memory of a past consciousness, which it had lost for twenty years together. Make these intervals of memory and forgetfulness to take their turns regularly by day and night, and you have two persons with the same immaterial spirit, as much as in the former instance two persons with the same body. So that self is not determined by identity or diversity of substance, which it cannot be sure of, but only by identity of consciousness. . . .

2

DAVID HUME

(1711–1776)

*On the Idea of the Self**

Hume is a thorough-going empiricist, skeptical of any arguments which could not be shown to be founded on perceptual knowledge. He reduces all thought to impressions of the senses and to ideas which are derived from those impressions. We have sense impressions of our bodies and the things we do. Our idea of self is the result of a collection of these various impressions. Self is a bundle of perceptions. It is an aggregation of physical and mental states, constantly changing as we are constantly doing different things. Any idea of stability or of a continuing entity called "self" must be a product of imagination, not of inspection. Thus, Hume discredits the idea that there is a constant entity called "I" which has my experiences, and claims that there is no self apart from the activities, mental and physical, which we perform.

* David Hume, *A Treatise of Human Nature* (1739), Section 6, Pt. IV, Bk. I.

THERE are some philosophers who imagine we are every moment intimately conscious of what we call our *self;* that we feel its existence and its continuance in existence; and are certain, beyond the evidence of a demonstration, both of its perfect identity and simplicity. The strongest sensation, the most violent passion, say they, instead of distracting us from this view, only fix it the more intensely, and make us consider their influence on *self* either by their pain or pleasure. To attempt a further proof of this were to weaken its evidence; since no proof can be derived from any fact of which we are so intimately conscious; nor is there anything of which we can be certain if we doubt of this.

Self is not any one Impression

Unluckily all these positive assertions are contrary to that very experience which is pleaded for them; nor have we any idea of *self,* after the manner it is here explained. For, from what impression could this idea be derived? This question it is impossible to answer without a manifest contradiction and absurdity; and yet it is a question which must necessarily be answered, if we would have the idea of self pass for clear and intelligible. It must be some one impression that gives rise to every real idea. But self or person is not any one impression, but that to which our several impressions and ideas are supposed to have a reference. If any impression gives rise to the idea of self, that impression must continue invariably the same, through the whole course of our lives; since self is supposed to exist after that manner. But there is no impression constant and invariable. Pain and pleasure, grief and joy, passions and sensations succeed each other, and never all exist at the same time. It cannot therefore be from any of these impressions, or from any other, that the idea of self is derived; and consequently there is no such idea.

But further, what must become of all our particular perceptions upon this hypothesis? All these are different, and distinguishable, and separable from each other, and may be separately considered, and may exist separately, and have no need of anything to support their existence. After what manner therefore do they belong to self, and how are they connected with it? For my part, when I enter most intimately into what I call *myself*, I always stumble on some particular perception or other, of heat or cold, light or shade, love or hatred, pain or pleasure. I never can catch *myself* at any time without a perception, and never can observe anything but the perception. When my perceptions are removed for any time, as by sound sleep, so long am I insensible of *myself*, and may truly be said not to exist. And were all my perceptions removed by death, and could I neither think, nor feel, nor see, nor love, nor hate, after the dissolution of my body, I should be entirely annihilated, nor do I conceive what is further requisite to make me a perfect nonentity. If any one, upon serious and unprejudiced reflection, thinks he has a different notion of *himself*, I must confess I can reason no longer with him. All I can allow him is, that he may be in the right as well as I, and that we are essentially different in this particular. He may, perhaps, perceive something simple and continued, which he calls *himself;* though I am certain there is no such principle in me.

Self as a Bundle of Perceptions

But setting aside some metaphysicians of this kind, I may venture to affirm of the rest of mankind, that they are nothing but a bundle or collection of different perceptions, which succeed each other with an inconceivable rapidity, and are in a perpetual flux and movement. Our eyes cannot turn in their sockets without varying our perceptions. Our thought is still more variable than our sight; and all our other senses and faculties contribute to this change; nor is there any single power of the soul, which remains unalterably the same, perhaps for one moment. The mind is a kind of theater, where several perceptions successively make their appearance; pass, repass, glide away, and mingle in an infinite variety of postures and situations. There is properly no *simplicity* in it at one time, nor *identity* in different, whatever natural propension we may have to imagine that simplicity and identity. The comparison of the theater must not mislead us. They are the successive perceptions only, that constitute the mind; nor have we the most distant notion of the place where these scenes are represented, or of the materials of which it is composed.

What then gives us so great a propension to ascribe an identity to these successive perceptions, and to suppose ourselves possessed of an invariable and uninterrupted existence through the whole course of our lives? In order to answer this question we must distinguish betwixt personal identity, as it regards our thought or imagination, and as it regards our passions or the concern we take in ourselves. The first is our present subject; and to explain it perfectly we must take the matter pretty deep, and account for that identity, which we attribute to plants and animals; there being a great analogy betwixt it and the identity of a self or person.

Identity and Diversity

We have a distinct idea of an object that remains invariable and uninterrupted through a supposed variation of time; and this idea we call that of *identity* or *sameness*. We have also a distinct idea of several different objects existing in succession, and connected together by a close relation; and this to an accurate view affords as perfect a notion of *diversity* as if there was no manner of relation among the objects. But though these two ideas of identity, and a succession of related objects, be in themselves perfectly distinct, and even contrary, yet it is certain that, in our common way of thinking, they are generally confounded with each other. That action of the imagination, by which we consider the uninterrupted and invariable object, and that by which we reflect on the succession of related objects, are almost the same to the feeling, nor is there much more effort of thought required in the latter case than in the former. The relation facilitates the transition of the mind from one object to another, and renders its passage as smooth as if it contemplated one continued object. This resemblance is the cause of the confusion and mistake, and makes us substitute the notion of identity, instead of that of related objects. However at one instant we may consider the related succession as variable or interrupted, we are sure the next to ascribe to it a perfect identity, and regard it as invariable and uninterrupted. Our propensity to this mistake is so great from the resemblance above mentioned, that we fall into it before we are aware; and though we incessantly correct ourselves by reflection, and return to a more accurate method of thinking, yet we cannot long sustain our philosophy, or take off this bias from the imagination. Our last resource is to yield to it, and boldly assert that these different related objects are in effect the same, however interrupted and variable. In order to justify to ourselves this absurdity, we often feign some new and unintelligible principle, that connects the objects together, and prevents their interruption or variation. Thus we feign the continued existence of the perceptions of our senses, to remove the interruption; and run into the notion of a *soul*, and *self*, and *substance*, to disguise the variation. But, we may further observe, that where we do not give rise to such a fiction, our propension to confound identity with relation is so great, that we are apt to imagine something unknown and mysterious, connecting the parts, beside their relation; and this I take to be the case with regard to the identity we ascribe to plants and vegetables. And even when this does not take place, we still feel a propensity to confound these ideas, though we are not able fully to satisfy ourselves in that particular, nor find anything invariable and uninterrupted to justify our notion of identity.

Thus the controversy concerning identity is not merely a dispute of words. For when we attribute identity, in an improper sense, to variable or interrupted objects, our mistake is not confined to the expression, but is commonly attended with a fiction, either of something invariable and uninterrupted, or of something mysterious and inexplicable, or at least with a propensity to such fictions. What will suffice to prove this hypothesis to the satisfaction of every fair inquirer, is to show, from daily experience and observation, that the objects which are variable or interrupted, and yet are supposed to continue the same, are such only as consist of a succession of parts, connected together by resemblance, contiguity, or causation. For as such a succession answers evidently to our notion of diversity, it can only be by mistake we ascribe to it an identity; and as the relation of parts, which leads us into this mistake, is really nothing but a quality, which produces an association of ideas, and an easy transition of the imagination from one to another, it can only be from the resemblance, which this act of the mind bears to that by which we contemplate one continued object, that the error arises. Our chief business, then, must be to prove, that all objects, to which we ascribe identity, without observing their invariableness and uninterruptedness, are such as consist of a succession of related objects.

The Same Object actually is a Succession of Related Objects

In order to this, suppose any mass of matter, of which the parts are contiguous and connected, to be placed before us; it is plain we must attribute a perfect identity to this mass, provided all the parts continue uninterruptedly and invariably the same, whatever motion or change of place we may observe either in the whole or in any of the parts. But supposing some very *small* or *inconsiderable* part to be added to the mass, or subtracted from it; though this absolutely destroys the identity of the whole, strictly speaking, yet as we seldom think so accurately, we scruple not to pronounce a mass of matter the same, where we find so trivial an alteration. The passage of the thought from the object before the change to the object after it, is so smooth and easy, that we scarce perceive the transition, and are apt to imagine, that it is nothing but a continued survey of the same object.

There is a very remarkable circumstance that attends this experiment; which is, that though the change of any considerable part in a mass of matter destroys the identity of the whole, yet we must measure the greatness of the part, not absolutely, but by its *proportion* to the whole. The addition or diminution of a mountain would not be sufficient to produce a diversity in a planet; though the change of a very few inches would be able to destroy the identity of some bodies. It will be impossible to account for this, but by reflecting that objects operate upon the mind, and break or interrupt the continuity of its actions, not according to their real greatness, but according to their proportion to each other; and therefore, since this interruption makes an object cease to appear the same, it must be the uninterrupted progress of the thought which constitutes the imperfect identity.

Change and Identity

This may be confirmed by another phenomenon. A change in any considerable part of a body destroys its identity; but it is remarkable, that where the change is produced *gradually* and *insensibly*, we are less apt to ascribe to it the same effect. The reason can plainly be no other, than that the mind, in following the successive changes of the body, feels an easy passage from the surveying its condition in one moment, to the viewing of it in another, and in no particular time perceives any interruption in its actions. From which continued perception, it ascribes a continued existence and identity to the object.

But whatever precaution we may use in introducing the changes gradually, and making them proportionable to the whole, it is certain, that where the changes are at last observed to become considerable, we make a scruple of ascribing identity to such different objects. There is, however, another artifice, by which we may induce the imagination to advance a step further; and that is, by producing a reference of the parts to each other, and a combination to some *common end* or purpose. A ship, of which a considerable part has been changed by frequent reparations, is still considered as the same; nor does the difference of the materials hinder us from ascribing an identity to it. The common end, in which the parts conspire, is the same under all their variations, and affords an easy transition of the imagination from one situation of the body to another.

But this is still more remarkable, when we add a *sympathy* of parts to their *common end*, and suppose that they bear to each other the reciprocal relation of cause and effect in all their actions and operations. This is the case with all animals and vegetables; where not only the several parts have a reference to some general purpose, but also a mutual dependence on, and connection with, each other. The effect of so strong a relation is, that though every one must allow, that in a very few years both vegetables and animals endure a *total* change, yet we still attribute identity to them, while their form, size, and substance, are entirely altered. An oak that grows from a small plant to a large tree is still the same oak, though there be not one particle of matter or figure of its parts the same. An infant becomes a man, and is sometimes fat, sometimes lean, without any change in his identity.

We may also consider the two following phenomena, which are remarkable in their kind. The first is, that though we commonly be able to distinguish pretty exactly betwixt numerical and specific identity, yet it sometimes happens that we confound them, and in our thinking and reasoning employ the one for the other. Thus, a man who hears a noise that is frequently interrupted and renewed, says it is still the same noise, though it is evident the sounds have only a specific identity or resemblance, and there is nothing numerically the same but the cause which produced them. In like manner it may be said, without breach of the propriety of language, that such a church, which was formerly of brick, fell to ruin, and that the parish rebuilt the same church of freestone, and according to modern architecture. Here neither the form nor materials are the same, nor is there anything common to the two objects but their relation to the inhabitants of the parish; and yet this alone is sufficient to make us denominate them the same. But we must observe, that in these cases the first object is in a manner annihilated before the second comes into existence; by which means, we are never presented, in any one point of time, with the idea of difference and multiplicity; and for that reason are less scrupulous in calling them the same.

Secondly, we may remark, that though, in a succession of related objects, it be in a manner requisite that the change of parts be not sudden nor entire, in order to preserve the identity, yet where the objects are in their nature changeable and inconstant, we admit of a more sudden transition than would otherwise be consistent with that relation. Thus, as the nature of a river consists in the motion and change of parts, though in less than four-and-twenty hours these be totally altered, this hinders not the river from continuing the same during several ages. What is natural and essential to anything is, in a manner, expected; and what is expected makes less impression, and appears of less moment than what is unusual and extraordinary. A considerable change of the former kind seems really less to the imagination than the most trivial alteration of the latter; and by breaking less the continuity of the thought, has less influence in destroying the identity.

Personal Identity is a Fictitious Idea

We now proceed to explain the nature of *personal identity,* which has become so great a question in philosophy, especially of late years, in England, where all the abstruser sciences are studied with a peculiar ardor and application. And here it is evident the same method of reasoning must be continued which has so successfully explained the identity of plants, and animals, and ships, and houses, and of all compounded and changeable productions either of art or nature. The identity which we ascribe to the mind of man is only a fictitious one, and of a like kind with that which we ascribe to vegetable and animal bodies. It cannot therefore have a different origin, but must proceed from a like operation of the imagination upon like objects.

But lest this argument should not convince the reader, though in my opinion perfectly decisive, let him weigh the following reasoning, which is still closer and more immediate. It is evident that the identity which we attribute to the human mind, however perfect we may imagine it to be, is not able to run the several different perceptions into one, and make them lose their characters of distinction and difference, which are essential to them. It is still true that every distinct perception which enters into the composition of the mind, is a distinct existence, and is different, and distinguishable, and separable from every other perception, either contemporary or successive. But as, notwithstanding this distinction and separability, we suppose the whole train of perceptions to be united by identity, a question naturally arises concerning this relation of identity, whether it be something that really binds our several perceptions together, or only associates their ideas in the imagination; that is, in other words, whether, in pronouncing concerning the identity of a person, we observe some real bond among his perception, or only feel one among the ideas we form of them. This question we might easily decide, if we would recollect what has been already proved at large, that the understanding never observes any real connection among objects, and that even the union of cause and effect, when strictly examined, resolves itself into a customary association of ideas. For from thence it evidently follows, that identity is nothing really belonging to these different perceptions, and uniting them altogether, but is merely a quality which we attribute to them, because of the union of their ideas in the imagination when we reflect upon them. Now, the only qualities which can give ideas a union in the imagination, are these three relations above mentioned. These are the uniting principles in the ideal world, and without them every distinct object is separable by the mind, and may be separately considered, and appears not to have any more connection with any other object than if disjoined by the greatest difference and remoteness. It is therefore on some of these three relations of resemblance, contiguity, and causation, that identity depends; and as the very essence of these relations consists in their producing an easy transition of ideas, it follows that our notions of personal identity proceed entirely from the smooth and uninterrupted progress of the thought along a train of connected ideas, according to the principles above explained.

Identity is a Product of the Relations between Resemblance and Causation

The only question, therefore, which remains is, by what relations this uninterrupted progress of our thought is produced, when we consider existence of a mind or thinking person. And here it is evident we must confine ourselves to resemblance and causation, and must drop contiguity, which has little or no influence in the present case.

To begin with *resemblance;* suppose we could see clearly into the breast of another, and observe that succession of perceptions which constitutes his mind or thinking principle, and suppose that he always preserves the memory of a considerable part of past perceptions, it is evident that nothing could more contribute to the bestowing a relation on this succession amidst all its variations. For what is the memory but a faculty, by which we raise up the images of past perceptions? And as an image necessarily resembles its object, must not the frequent placing of these resembling perceptions in the chain of thought, convey the imagination more easily from one link to another, and make the whole seem like the continuance of one object? In this particular, then, the memory not only discovers the identity, but also contributes to its production, by producing the relation of resemblance among the perceptions. The case is the same, whether we consider ourselves or others.

As to *causation;* we may observe that the true idea of the human mind, is to consider it as a system of different perceptions or different existences, which are linked together by the relation of cause and effect, and mutually produce, destroy, influence, and modify each other. Our impressions give rise to their correspondent ideas; and these ideas, in their turn, produce other impressions. One thought chases another, and draws after it a third, by which it is expelled in its turn. In this respect, I cannot compare the soul more properly to anything than to a republic or commonwealth, in which the several members are united by the reciprocal ties of government and subordination, and give rise to other persons who propagate the same republic in the incessant changes of its parts. And as the same individual republic may not only change its members, but also its laws and constitutions; in like manner the same person may vary his character and disposition, as well as his impressions and ideas, without losing his identity. Whatever changes he endures, his several parts are still connected by the relation of causation. And in this view our identity with regard to the passions serves to corroborate that with regard to the imagination, by the making our distant perceptions influence each other, and by giving us a present concern for our past or future pains or pleasures.

As memory alone acquaints us with the continuance and extent of this succession of perceptions, it is to be considered, upon that account chiefly, as the source of personal identity. Had we no memory, we never should have any notion of causation, nor consequently of that chain of causes and effects, which constitute our self or person. But having once acquired this notion of causation from the memory, we can extend the same chain of causes, and consequently the identity of our persons beyond our memory, and can comprehend times, and circumstances, and actions, which we have entirely forgot, but suppose in general to have existed. For how few of our past actions are there, of which we have any memory? Who can tell me, for instance, what his thoughts and actions on the first of January 1715, the eleventh of March 1719, and the third of August 1733? Or will he affirm, because he has entirely forgot the incidents of these days, that the present self is not the same person with the self of that time; and by that means overturn all the most established notions of personal identity? In this view, therefore, memory does not so much *produce* as *discover* personal identity, by showing us the relation of cause and effect among our different perceptions. It will be incumbent on those who affirm that memory produces entirely our personal identity, to give a reason why we can thus extend our identity beyond our memory.

The whole of this doctrine leads us to a conclusion, which is of great importance in the present affair, viz. that all the nice and subtile questions concerning personal identity can never possibly be decided, and are to be regarded rather as grammatical than as philosophical difficulties. Identity depends on the relations of ideas; and these relations produce identity, by means of that easy transition they occasion. But as the relations, and the easiness of the transition may diminish by insensible degrees, we have no just standard by which we can decide any dispute concerning the time when they acquire or lose a title to the name of identity. All the disputes concerning the identity of connected objects are merely verbal, except so far as the relation of parts gives rise to some fiction or imaginary principle of union, as we have already observed.

3

GILBERT RYLE

(1900–)

*The Systematic Elusiveness of "I"**

Ryle is interested in the way in which the word "I" is used and to what it is meant to refer. He claims that it is an index word, a word that serves to keep the subject of a sentence clear by referring back to someone. When anyone tries to pin down the "I," to introspect "I," he is bound to fail. "I" is always systematically in the past while the present "I" is looking for it. Something essential to such an introspection is always left out, namely the "I" that is attempting to find itself. You may find influences of Hume in Ryle's analysis. Ryle does not deny that there is a self. His claim is that a self can never be discovered in the activities of men.

* Gilbert Ryle, *The Concept of Mind* (New York: Barnes & Noble, 1949), pp. 195–198. Reprinted by kind permission of the publishers, Barnes & Noble, Inc.

WE are now in a position to account for the systematic elusiveness of the notion of 'I,' and the partial non-parallelism between it and the notion of 'you' or 'he'. To concern oneself about oneself in any way, theoretical or practical, is to perform a higher order act, just as it is to concern oneself about anybody else. To try, for example, to describe what one has just done, or is now doing, is to comment upon a step which is not itself, save *per accidens,* one of commenting. But the operation which is the commenting is not, and cannot be, the step on which that commentary is being made. Nor can an act of ridiculing be its own butt. A higher order action cannot be the action upon which it is performed. So my commentary on my performances must always be silent about one performance, namely itself, and this performance can be the target only of another commentary. Self-commentary, self-ridicule and self-admonition are logically condemned to eternal penultimacy. Yet nothing that is left out of any particular commentary or admonition is privileged thereby to escape comment or admonition for ever. On the contrary it may be the target of the very next comment or rebuke.

The point may be illustrated in this way. A singing-master might criticise the accents or notes of a pupil by mimicking with exaggerations each word that the pupil sang; and if the pupil sang slowly enough, the master could parody each word sung by the pupil before the next came to be uttered. But then, in a mood of humility, the singing-master tries to criticise his own singing in the same way, and more than that to mimic with exaggerations each word that he utters, including those that he utters in self-parody. It is at once clear, first, that he can never get beyond the very earliest word of his song and, second, that at any given moment he has uttered one noise which has yet to be mimicked—and it makes no difference how rapidly he chases his notes with mimicries of them. He can, in principle, never catch more than the coat-tails of the object of his pursuit, since a word cannot be a parody of itself. None the less, there is no word that he sings which remains unparodied; he is always a day late for the fair, but every day he reaches the place of yesterday's fair. He never succeeds in jumping on to the shadow of his own head, yet he is never more than one jump behind.

An ordinary reviewer may review a book, while a second order reviewer criticises reviews of the book. But the second order review is not a criticism of itself. It can only be criticised in a further third order review. Given complete editorial patience, any review of any order could be published, though at no stage would all the reviews have received critical notices. Nor can every act of a diarist be the topic of a record in his diary; for the last entry made in his diary still demands that the making of it should in its turn be chronicled.

This, I think, explains the feeling that my last year's self, or my yesterday's self, could in principle be exhaustively described and accounted for, and that your past or present self could be exhaustively described and accounted for by me, but that my today's self perpetually slips out of any hold of it that I try to take. It also explains the apparent non-parallelism between the notion of 'I' and that of 'you', without construing the elusive residuum as any kind of ultimate mystery.

There is another thing which it explains. When people consider the problems of the Freedom of the Will and try to imagine their own careers as analogous to those of clocks or water-courses, they tend to boggle at the idea that their own immediate future is already unalterably fixed and predictable. It seems absurd to suppose that what I am just about to think, feel or do is already preappointed, though people are apt to find no such absurdity in the supposition that the futures of other people are so preappointed. The so-called 'feeling of spontaneity' is closely connected with this inability to imagine that what I am going to think or do can already be anticipated. On the other hand, when I consider what I thought and did yesterday, there seems to be no absurdity in supposing that that could have been forecast, before I did it. It is only while I am actually trying to predict my own next move that the task feels like that of a swimmer trying to overtake the waves that he sends ahead of himself.

The solution is as before. A prediction of a deed or a thought is a higher order operation, the performance of which cannot be among the things considered in making the prediction. Yet as the state of mind in which I am just before I do something may make some difference to what I do, it follows that I must overlook at least one of the data relevant to my prediction. Similarly, I can give you the fullest possible advice what to do, but I must omit one piece of counsel, since I cannot in the same breath advise you how to take that advice. There is therefore no paradox in saying that while normally I am not at all surprised to find myself doing or thinking what I do, yet when I try most carefully to anticipate what I shall do or think, then the outcome is likely to falsify my expectation. My process of pre-envisaging may divert the course of my ensuing behaviour in a direction and degree of which my prognosis cannot take account. One thing that I cannot prepare myself for is the next thought that I am going to think.

The fact that my immediate future is in this way systematically elusive to me has, of course, no tendency to prove that my career is in principle unpredictable to prophets other than myself, or even that it is inexplicable to myself after the heat of the action. I can point to any other thing with my index-finger, and other people can point at this finger. But it cannot be the object at which it itself is pointing. Nor can a missile be its own target, though anything else may be thrown at it.

This general conclusion that any performance can be the concern of a higher order performance, but cannot be the concern of itself, is connected with what was said earlier about the special functioning of index words, such as 'now', 'you' and 'I'. An 'I' sentence indicates whom in particular it is about by being itself uttered or written by someone in particular. 'I' indicates the person who utters it. So, when a person utters an 'I' sentence, his utterance of it may be part of a higher order performance, namely one, perhaps of self-reporting, self-exhortation or self-commiseration, and this performance itself is not dealt with in the operation which it itself is. Even if the person is, for special speculative purposes, momentarily concentrating on the Problem of the Self, he has failed and knows that he has failed to catch more than the flying coattails of that which he was pursuing. His quarry was the hunter.

To conclude, there is nothing mysterious or occult about the range of higher order acts and attitudes, which are apt to be inadequately covered by the umbrella-title 'self-consciousness'. They are the same in kind as the higher order acts and attitudes exhibited in the dealings of people with one other. Indeed the former are only a special application of the latter and are learned first from them. If I perform the third order operation of commenting on a second order act of laughing at myself for a piece of manual awkwardness, I shall indeed use the first personal pronoun in two different ways. I say to myself, or to the company, 'I was laughing at myself for being butter-fingered'. But so far from this showing that there are two 'Mes' in my skin, not to speak, yet, of the third one which is still commenting on them, it shows only that I am applying the public two-pronoun idiom in which we talk of her laughing at him; and I am applying this linguistic idiom, because I am applying the method of inter-personal transaction which the idiom is ordinarily employed to describe.

Before concluding, it is worth mentioning that there is one influential difference between the first personal pronoun and all the rest. 'I', in my use of it, always indicates me and only indicates me. 'You', 'she' and 'they' indicate different people at different times. 'I' is like my own shadow; I can never get away from it, as I can get away from your shadow. There is no mystery about this constancy, but I mention it because it seems to endow 'I' with a mystifying uniqueness and adhesiveness. 'Now' has something of the same besetting feeling.

4

D. F. PEARS
(1921–   )

*Hume on Personal Identity**

Pears attacks Hume's view of personal identity on the ground that Hume fails to include in his account what Pears takes to be absolutely essential to identity questions: bodily reference and the existence of others. As Pears puts it, "questions of particular identity presuppose the existence of other people. If other people did not exist, there would be nobody for me not to be." The awareness of other people involves bodily identification, and as Pears points out, Hume totally avoids that element of identification. Pears claims that Hume tends toward solipsism, the idea that the individual self is the whole of reality, that other people have no existence independent from oneself. Solipsistic thinking is unrealistic. We live among others in space and time. Pears concludes that Hume tried to formulate a theory of personal identity in egocentric terms and that this failed; the fact that Hume's theory was very carefully constructed probably demonstrates that other attempts to formulate a theory of personal identity in these terms can never be successful either.

* D. F. Pears, ed., *David Hume, A Symposium* (New York: St. Martin's Press, 1963), pp. 43–54. Used by permission of the publishers, St. Martin's Press, Inc.

A PERSON is sometimes said to have no strong sense of his own identity. What that usually means is that he lacks some of the things that give inner stability and continuity to a human life: for instance, he may be uncertain about his beliefs, feelings and desires; he may not know the sort of person that he is, or the sort of person that he wants to be. But there is also another way in which a person may lose the sense of his own identity: he may be afflicted with amnesia and simply forget who he is. Someone in this situation would probably need the help of the police in order to re-establish his own identity, and, of course, he would want them to tell him not only the sort of person that he was, but also the particular person that he was. These two pieces of information are connected with one another, and in Nigel Dennis's novel *Cards of Identity* the victims are deprived of both at once. But it is easy to see that they are different things, and the philosophical problem of personal identity is in fact concerned with only one of them—particular identity.

Most people know their own particular identities. I know who I am, and I can produce enough facts to establish who I am. Anyone who wonders what these facts would be in his own case has only to imagine himself being questioned by the police. But what about other people? Every day I see a great number of other people whose particular identities are unknown to me. So there is a striking contrast between one's knowledge of one's own particular identity and one's knowledge of the particular identities of other people. But it is not such a complete contrast as it seems to be at first sight. For though I know enough facts to establish my own particular identity, there are also a great many facts of this kind that I do not know. For example, I know my name, address and telephone number, but I do not know whether I am the person who walked through the gate of this college exactly twenty-nine minutes ago.

Personal Identity is Particular Identity

The philosophical problem of personal identity is concerned with particular identities. It begins when one asks how such statements of personal identity are established. But that is only the beginning. For suppose that some philosopher gave a completely satisfactory account of the criteria that we use in order to establish that these statements are true. Then it would still be possible for someone to argue, in a sceptical way, that those criteria were inadequate, because they did not really add up to anything that could properly be called identity. This is how Hume's treatment of the problem develops. And other developments are possible: for instance, it might be argued that the real person is the soul, and that the real criteria of personal identity have nothing to do with the body. But whatever happens in the end, we can at least insist that any philosophical treatment of this subject should begin with a realistic account of the ways in which we ask and answer questions about the particular identities of people. After all, that is what it is all about.

Hume's treatment of the subject is surprisingly unrealistic. His account of the way in which questions of personal identity are asked and answered is out of touch with the familiar facts which ought to have been its starting-point. In everyday life one asks questions not only about one's own identity but also about the identities of other people. But Hume only considers questions about his own identity. It is true that he intends that what he says about himself should be applied by his readers to themselves. But this does not alter the situation. For each of his readers will consider the problem only in its application to his own case, as Hume himself does. So though Hume's use of the pronoun 'I' is, in a way, impersonal, it always excludes consideration of other people. That is very unrealistic. So too is his account of the way in which questions of personal identity are answered. For he never mentions the fact that we use physical criteria in answering them, but always confines himself to facts about the inner life of the person concerned. We might take the example that I gave just now and use it again in order to show how crippling these two limitations are. Suppose that I wish to establish that I am not the person who walked through the gate of this college exactly twenty-nine minutes ago. Then Hume would perhaps allow that I might do it by recalling what time it was when I entered this college. But this is not the only way of establishing that I am not that person. For I might get someone else to testify that my body has been in this room for more than twenty-nine minutes, and thus establish an alibi. And this alibi would bring in both the things that are missing in Hume's account—the use of physical criteria in answering identity-questions, and the posing of identity-questions about other people (since my witness poses an identity-question about me).

When Hume looked in his own mind for the criteria of his identity as a person, he found only a succession of impressions and ideas, related to one another in various ways. He failed to find any impression of the self that is supposed to have these impressions and ideas. He took this failure to be of the utmost importance. For he assumed that, if his adversaries were correct in thinking that the self is a mental substance, perhaps a soul, in which impressions and ideas inhered, then there would have to be a separate impression of the self. But there is no such impression, and therefore the continued identity of a person could only consist in certain relations between the impressions and ideas that were the contents of his mind.

These relations between impressions and ideas were, according to him, similarity and causation. It sounds very odd to our ears when we hear Hume saying that the continued identity of a person consists in the fact that his impressions and ideas form a series in which many of the elements are related by similarity and causation. But we have to remember that he is speaking from the eighteenth century in antique psychological terms. If we express his thesis in a different terminology, it sounds less odd. For it is quite natural to say that the continued identity of a person consists in the fact that his mental life contains many repetitions, and that its development is governed by causal laws.

How would these facts be used by someone who was trying to answer a question about the particular identity of a person? Perhaps it is not immediately clear how he would use them. If he were asking the other question that I mentioned at the beginning of this essay, the question whether a person's life had inner stability and continuity, it is very obvious how he would use them. For stability and continuity depend, to a large extent, on recurrent patterns and consistent developments of thought and feeling. But suppose that I were wondering about a question of particular identity; for example, whether a man talking to me on a railway journey was the man who talked to me several weeks ago in the station buffet. How would I use Hume's two factors? I think that they would make some contribution towards the solution of my problem. For example, the man might say things that fitted the character revealed in the earlier conversation. If he did, that would not *prove* that he was the same man, since two different people can have similar characters and views. In fact, the possibility of very extensive similarities, both psychological and psychical, between two different people creates a difficulty which can be completely overcome only by appealing to space, time and motion, as is done by people who produce alibis. Nevertheless consistency of character is some help in answering questions of particular identity.

Hume's Rejection of His Own Theory

Hume was dissatisfied with his two factors, but the reason for his dissatisfaction was not the difficulty that is presented by the possibility of extensive similarities, and so he was not led to recognise the importance of space, time, and motion which are, of course, involved in the physical criteria of personal identity. His reason for feeling dissatisfied was not that a statement of particular identity might turn out to be false in spite of the fact that his two crieria had been fulfilled—for example, that the travelling companion might not be the same man again after all—but rather that, whoever the man was, there would be something inadequate about his psychological history. For he thought that, though what he had said about the psychological history of a person was the very most that a careful empiricist could say, nevertheless it was inadequate, since it did not add up to anything that could properly be called identity. All that he had found was a series of impressions and ideas. Although the series itself lasted as long as the life of the person, it contained no permanent element; indeed, all its elements were so brief as to be almost momentary. It is true that the series as a whole exhibited various kinds of pattern and structure, but it had no background and no observer, rather like a piece of music in empty space. And Hume did not think that this was enough to deserve the name 'personal identity.' It might, indeed, be *called* personal identity, but only by courtesy and as a kind of fiction.

Now it might be thought that Hume was not entirely sincere when he expressed himself dissatisfied with his own theory of personal identity. For it is characteristic of his philosophy to take a generally accepted idea and to demonstrate that its foundation in human experience is inadequate. Of course, if it had no foundation at all, he would reject it completely. But what usually happens is that he finds adequate support only for a very reduced version of the original idea. And when he expresses dismay at the difference between the reduced idea, which is well founded, and the original idea, which is ill founded, he is usually being ironical, and he is implying that the original idea is largely pretentious nonsense. This kind of irony is very noticeable in his account of perception, and in his treatment of causal necessity. And it might be thought that there is a good deal of the same irony in his expression of dissatisfaction with his theory of personal identity, particularly since the theory was in conflict with an accepted religious doctrine. But this would be a complete misinterpretation. In the appendix to the *Treatise* he makes it absolutely clear that he regards his account of personal identity as totally unsatisfactory; and yet he confesses that he has nothing better to put in its place.

His total withdrawal of his theory of personal identity is neglected by some commentators, who talk as if he had made up his mind on the subject once and for all. But the withdrawal is a fact, and an important one. For if we look at his philosophy as a whole, we see that it has a serious consequence. His philosophy is, for the most part, neither abstract nor remote from human interests. It ranges very widely over morality, politics, aesthetics and religion. In all this he constantly appeals to the idea of the self. But the idea of the self was precisely the idea that he was unable to place on an adequate foundation. So there is an important weakness, a weakness which he himself admits, in the theoretical basis of his science of human nature.

What exactly was the weakness? Hume gave his account of it in the appendix to the *Treatise*. But it is arguable that his diagnosis was wrong, and that the weakness was really something other than what he took it to be. So in the remainder of this essay I shall be occupied with two things. First, I shall try to explain Hume's version of what was wrong with his theory of personal identity: and then I shall argue that what is really wrong with it is something else, which he himself did not recognise.

First let us look at his own diagnosis of his failure. Now it is an important fact about him that he wished to achieve in the science of human nature what Newton had achieved in astronomy. Where Newton used mechanics, he would use what we now call psychology, and he compares his law of the association of ideas with Newton's law of gravitation. I think that the fact that he regarded his work in this way really explains why he was willing to reduce the accepted idea of causal necessity and the accepted idea of a material object, and yet could not bring himself to reduce the accepted idea of personal identity. For he was prepared, or at least half prepared, to reduce the external world to phenomena in the human mind. But this meant that his theory of the self had to bear a great weight, and so it was essential that it should remain strong and unreduced. But when he reviewed it in the appendix to the *Treatise,* it seemed to him to be too thin and weak. He said that, if the self were a substance in which impressions and ideas inhered, or if there were a real connexion between impressions and ideas, he would be satisfied. But since neither of these two things was the case, he remained dissatisfied.

But would he really have been in a better position if he had been able to say that the self is a substance, or that there is a real connexion between impressions and ideas? Certainly he might have claimed to have justified the sense that we have of the stability and continuity of our lives. On the other hand, perhaps he would not have felt the need for some unattainable kind of connexion between the elements in our psychological histories if he had realised the importance of intentional connexions, instead of being so preoccupied with mechanical ones. However, suppose that he had succeeded in establishing one of the two things which, according to him, could not be established. Would that have helped him to solve the philosophical problem of the particular identity of persons? As I pointed out earlier, some of the factors that give stability and continuity to a human life can be used by a person who asks himself a question of particular identity. So this might be true of the two factors that Hume wished that he could find, but admitted that he could not find. Whether it would in fact be true is a difficult question, which I shall not attempt to answer here.

Personal Identity and Bodily Criteria

In any case, there is another deficiency in Hume's theory. He not only does not find adequate criteria for answering questions of particular identity, but also fails to provide a setting in which such questions can even be asked. This came about in the following way. When he asked himself a question about his own particular identity, he always confined himself to earlier impressions and ideas, and did not consider earlier speech, behaviour and actions. Perhaps he could have avoided this restriction, but it was at least very natural for a philosopher who admitted that he could give no rational account of our belief in the physical world. Anyway, the consequence was that he would ask himself whether, for example, he was the person who had a certain idea, which was not expressed in words, on New Year's Day 1735. But the trouble with this kind of question was that, if he had any reason to believe that the idea occurred at all, he could not fail to believe that it occurred in the series that was himself, David Hume. For only his own unaided memory vouched for the occurrence of the idea. Consequently he could never be in a position in which he could ask himself whether he was the person who . . . : if he had any doubt about the answer, he would equally doubt whether the question was properly framed.

This situation can be avoided only if questions of particular identity are framed in such a way that they make some reference to speech, behaviour and actions, or, more generally, to the body and its history. It is exceedingly important that this is so even when the identity-question is one that a person asks about himself. For example, when I ask myself whether I am the person who walked through the gate of this college at a particular moment today, I must have some way of knowing that there was such a person even if he was not myself. And that means that I must be able to use something other than my memory of my own psychological history. Otherwise there will be no possibility of my knowing that there was such a person unless he was myself. Questions of particular personal identity presuppose the existence of other people. If other people did not exist, there would be nobody for me not to be. And I must have some way of knowing that other people exist.

Now we are aware of other people only through their bodies. Whether this is a contingent fact or a necessary fact, it is the human predicament. And since we are in this predicament, any philosophical theory of personal identity must be based on our physical existence in space and time. That is absolutely essential. But what Hume tried to do was to work out a theory of personal identity that did not rely on our knowledge of the external world or on our awareness of other people. In this he necessarily failed, not only because he could not explain completely how questions of personal identity are answered, but because he could not explain at all how they are asked.

Hume was not a solipsist, but he suffered from a tendency to solipsism. As always happens in such a case, the attempt to describe the internal world without the external world led to a curious distortion. For Hume's impressions and ideas gradually began to take over the characteristics of material objects. In his discussion of personal identity he talked as if they could exist in isolation, floating in a kind of impersonal medium. And his version of the theory that the self is a substance, which he is reluctantly forced to reject, is based on obvious analogies with the body. When the external world is neglected, it usually makes itself felt in this way.

Earlier in this essay I said that Hume's theory of personal identity is unrealistic. That is true. It is unrealistic because it fails to take account of the fact that we live together in space and time, and communicate through our bodies. But though this is a true judgement about Hume's theory, it is an inadequate one. For it is not as if he simply overlooked these obvious facts through carelessness. If that were so, his theory would be of little interest. What makes it interesting is that it is a careful attempt to work out a theory of personal identity within an egocentric framework. The attempt failed, conspicuously and avowedly, because Hume was more consistent and clear-sighted than others who tried to do the same thing. That kind of failure is important. What it probably shows is that the thing cannot be done.

5

SYDNEY S. SHOEMAKER

(1931–   )

*Personal Identity and Memory**

Shoemaker examines the claims of philosophers, such as Locke, who stress the importance of memory to personal identity. He asks if memory is really a criterion of identity and, if so, is it the sole criterion. Also, what is the relationship between remembering an event and being the same person as the one who participated in the remembered event? The key lies in how we use the word "remember." How do we know if someone is using the phrase, "I remember . . . " correctly? Can we distinguish clearly bodily criteria and memory in this case? Shoemaker argues that we do not use any criteria of identity when making claims on the basis of memory. The criteria of personal identity arise in third person cases, and memory in such cases is only part of the picture. Unless accompanied by bodily criteria, memory statements of others would fail to provide sufficient grounds for identification. In other words, if memory claims are to be significant in establishing identity, there must be some way of checking those claims. We must know what the person making a memory claim means, and to know that is to involve some form of bodily identity. A criterion of "same person" is prior to establishing memory claims.

* From *Journal of Philosophy,* Vol. LVI, No. 22 (October 22, 1959), pp. 868–882. Used by kind permission of *The Journal of Philosophy* and Professor Shoemaker.

PERSONS, unlike other things, make statements about their own pasts, and can be said to know these statements to be true. This fact would be of little importance, as far as the problem of personal identity is concerned, if these statements were always grounded in the ways in which people's statements about the past history of things other than themselves are grounded. But while our statements about our own pasts are sometimes based on diaries, photographs, fingerprints, and the like, normally they are not. Normally they are based on our own memories, and the way in which one's memory provides one with knowledge concerning one's own past is quite unlike the way in which it provides one with knowledge concerning the past history of another person or thing. It is largely for this reason, I believe, that in addition to whatever problems there are about the notion of identity in general there has always been felt to be a special problem about *personal* identity. It is, for example, the way in which one knows one's own past that has led some philosophers to hold that personal identity is the only *real* identity that we have any knowledge of, the identity we ascribe to ships and stones being only, as Thomas Reid expressed it, "something which, for convenience of speech, we call identity."* What I wish to do in this paper is to consider how the concept of memory and the concept of personal identity are related. In particular, I want to consider the view that memory provides a criterion of personal identity, or, as H. P. Grice expressed it some years ago, that "the self is a logical construction and is to be defined in terms of memory."†

Personal Identity as Bodily Identity

1. Clearly the concepts of memory and personal identity are not logically independent. As has often been pointed out, it is a logical truth that, if a person remembers a past event, then he, the very person who remembers, must have been a witness to that event. It is partly this logical truth that has led some philosophers to hold that personal identity can be wholly or partially defined in terms of memory. And this view may seem to be supported by the fact that we sometimes use, as grounds for saying that a person was present when an event occurred, the fact that he apparently remembers the event, i.e., is able to give a correct and detailed account of it and does not appear to have anything accept this view. For it might be held that while there is a logical relaother than his own memory on the basis of which he could know of it.

But it does not seem, off-hand, that these considerations force us to tionship between the concepts of memory and personal identity, this is because the former is definable or analyzable in terms of the latter, and not *vice versa*. The assertion that a person A remembers an event X can plausibly be analyzed as meaning (1) that A now has knowledge of X, (2) that A's knowledge is not grounded inductively or based on the testimony of other persons, and (3) that A witnessed X when it occurred. To know with certainty that A remembers X, it might be held, we would have to know all three of these conditions were satisfied, and we could know that (3) is satisfied only if we had a criterion of personal identity by which we could judge that A, the person who now has knowledge of X, is identical with one of the persons who witnessed X. Obviously our criterion of identity here could not be the fact that A remembers X, for we know this fact only if we had already established that such an identity holds.

The view just described, I think, must be the view of any philosopher who thinks that the identity of a human body is the sole criterion of personal identity. And this view seems compatible with the fact that sometimes, when we do not have independent grounds for saying that a person witnessed an event, we accept his being able to describe the event as evidence that we was a witness to it. For it might be held that in such cases we are reasoning inductively. We have, it might be said,

* Thomas Reid, *Essays on the Intellectual Powers of Man*, A. D. Woozley, ed. (London: Macmillan, 1941), p. 206.

† H. P. Grice, "Personal Identity," *Mind*, Vol. L (October, 1941), p. 340.

found out empirically (using bodily identity as our criterion of personal identity) that when someone claims to remember a past event it is generally the case that such an event did occur and that he was a witness to it. On this view it is an inductively established correlation, and not any logical relationship between memory and personal identity, that justifies us in using the memory claims of persons as evidence for identity judgments about them.

Cases of Bodily Transfer

2. On the view just described the criteria of personal identity are simply the criteria of bodily identity (i.e., I suppose, spatio-temporal continuity). But it is often argued that bodily identity is not even a necessary condition of personal identity, let alone a sufficient condition, and the same arguments have been alleged to show that memory is a criterion of personal identity. We must now consider some of these arguments.

Considerable attention has been paid, in discussions of personal identity, to so-called "puzzle cases," ostensible cases of what I will call "bodily transfer." It has been argued that if certain imaginable events were to occur we would be obliged to say, or at least would have good grounds for saying, that someone had changed bodies, i.e., had come to have a body that is numerically different from the body that had been his in the past. Locke, it may be recalled, thought it conceivable that the soul of a prince might "enter and inform" the body of a cobbler, "carrying with it the consciousness of the prince's past life," and said that if this happened the cobbler would become "the same person with the prince, accountable only for the prince's actions."* And it is certainly imaginable that a cobbler, living somewhere in the Bronx, might awake some morning and show great surprise at the appearance of his body, that he might claim to find his surroundings, and the persons who claim to know him, totally unfamiliar, that he might exhibit a detailed knowledge of the past life of Prince Philip, reporting the Prince's actions as his own, and that he might, in his subsequent behavior, exhibit all of the mannerisms, interests, and personality and character traits that Prince Philip had displayed in the past. Let us imagine this happening immediately after the death of the man now known as Prince Philip.

What we say about such cases is clearly relevant to the question whether memory is a criterion of personal identity. If the above case inclines us to say that bodily transfer is possible, this is largely because the cobbler is imagined to be able to describe in detail, thereby giving evidence of being able to remember, the past life of Prince Philip. That this so much inclines us to admit the possibility of bodily transfer, whether or not we do admit it, seems to be grounds for saying that bodily identity is not our sole criterion of personal identity, and that memory, and perhaps also sameness of personality, has a place among our criteria.

* John Locke, *An Essay Concerning Human Understanding*, Vol. I, Fraser, ed. (Oxford: The Clarendon Press, 1894), p. 457.

Many philosophers have held that personal identity and bodily identity are logically quite distinct. This view is implied by the Cartesian conception of the mind (or soul) as a substance distinct from the body, and it also seems to be implied by the view of Locke, that it is "same consciousness" that "makes" the same person, and by the views of those philosophers, such as Hume and (at one time) Russell, who have held that the persistence of a person through time consists simply in the occurrence of a series of mental events ("perceptions," "experiences") that are bound together by a non-physical relationship of "co-personality" (perhaps the relation "being the memory of"). In short, it is implied by any view according to which the identity of a person is essentially the identity of a mind, and according to which a mind (whether regarded as a Cartesian "spiritual substance" or a Humeian "bundle" of mental events) is something logically distinct from a human body. To hold such a view is to admit the possibility of bodily transfer, and it is partly the prevalence of such views that accounts for the attention that philosophers have paid to "puzzle cases" such as the one I have described. But it is hardly plausible to suppose that those who have held such views have come to hold them because they have been persuaded by such cases that bodily transfer is possible. For even if it is admitted that such cases would be cases of bodily transfer, it by no means follows that personal identity and bodily identity are logically independent. It does not follow that bodily transfer could become the rule rather than the exception, and it certainly does not follow that a person could exist without having a body at all. Indeed, the view that bodily transfer is possible is quite compatible with a completely behavioristic view concerning the nature of mind and a completely materialistic conception of the nature of a person. After all, in the case I have imagined it is bodily and behavioral facts (the behavior of the cobbler and the past behavior of Prince Philip) that incline one to say that a bodily transfer has occurred.

So while such cases provide some grounds for thinking that memory is among the criteria of personal identity, we must look further if we wish to account for the plausibility of the view that the criteria of personal identity are "mental" or "psychological," one version of which being the view that memory is, to the exclusion of bodily identity, the sole criterion of personal identity. But we need not look much further; all that we have to do, in fact, is to describe such cases in the first person rather than in the third person. For it is when one considers the way in which one knows, or seems to know, one's *own* identity that it becomes plausible to regard personal identity as something logically independent of bodily identity. One does not have to observe, or (it seems) know anything about, the present state of one's body in order to make past tense statements about oneself on the basis of memory. But such statements imply the persistence of a person through time, and it is natural to regard them as expressing knowledge of one's own identity, knowledge that a "present self" (that to which the word "I" refers) is identical with a "past self" (the person who did such and such in the past). One is inclined to suppose that the real criteria of personal identity must be criteria that one uses in making statements about one's own identity. And since it appears that one can make such statements, and know them to be true, without first knowing the facts that would justify an assertion about the identity of one's body, the conclusion would seem to be that bodily identity cannot be a criterion of personal identity. The real criteria of personal identity, it seems, cannot be bodily or behavioral criteria of any sort, but must be criteria that one can know to be satisfied in one's own case without knowing anything about one's body. For similar reasons one is inclined to reject the view that the notion of memory is definable or analyzable in terms of the notion of personal identity. For when one says that one remembers a past event it is surely not the case that one has first established that one is the same as someone who witnessed the event, and then concluded, on the basis of this fact and others, that one remembers the event. That one remembers an event seems, from one's own point of view, a brute, unanalyzable fact. But if there is a logical relationship between the concepts of memory and personal identity, and if the former is not definable or analyzable in terms of the latter, what seems to follow is that the latter is somehow definable in terms of the former, and that memory provides the criterion of personal identity.

Memory as a Criterion of Personal Identity

3. Whether or not memory is *a* criterion of personal identity, it is not *the* criterion. As I will argue later, it cannot be the sole criterion that we use in making identity statements about other persons. And while it is true that one does not use bodily identity as a criterion of personal identity when one says on the basis of memory that one did something in the past, this is not because one uses something else as a criterion, but is rather because one uses no criterion at all.

Suppose that I make the statement "I broke the front window yesterday." If this statement is based on a criterion of personal identity it must be the case that I know that someone broke the front window yesterday, and that I have found out, by use of my criterion, that that person was myself. And my statement must be based, at least in part, on what I know about that person as he was at the time at which he broke the window. Let us suppose that my own memory is my only source of knowledge concerning the past event in question, for that is the sort of case that we are interested in. Then my statement must be a conclusion from what I remember about the person who broke the window yesterday, and perhaps from other facts as well (facts about my "present self"), and my criterion of identity must be what justifies me in drawing this conclusion from these facts. Presumably, if I had remembered different facts about that person I would have drawn a different conclusion, namely that he was not myself. It should be noted that, if all of this were so, then, strictly speaking, it would be incorrect for me to say "*I remember* that I broke the front window yesterday." For if my statement "I broke the front window yesterday" expresses a conclusion *from* what I remember it is not itself a memory statement, i.e., is not simply a description or report of what I actually remember. We must distinguish statements that are "based" on memory simply in the sense of being memory statements from those that are "based" on memory in the sense of being conclusions drawn from remembered facts.* If one thinks that one cannot make a first person past tense statement except on the basis of a criterion of identity, one must accept the consequence that no such statement can be a memory statement. In the case at hand, if my statement is grounded on a criterion of identity then what I actually remember cannot be that *I* broke the window yesterday, but must be that someone of such and such a description broke the window, the assertion that it was myself being a conclusion from what I remember about the person.

Now it is a logical truth, as I have already said, that if a person remembers a past event then he, that same person, must have been a witness to the event, i.e., must have been present when it occurred and in a position to know of its occurrence. So if I remember someone breaking the front window yesterday it follows that I was present at the time. And since, if I remember this, I am entitled to say "I remember someone breaking the front window yesterday," I am also entitled to say "I was present yesterday when the front window was broken." But this last statement is a first person past tense statement, so let us see whether it can be grounded on any criterion of personal identity. Clearly it cannot be. It is not, as it would have to be if based on a criterion of identity, a conclusion from what I know about someone who existed in the past. What I know about the past, in the case we are considering, is what I remember, but this statement is not a conclusion from *what* I remember at all; it is a conclusion from the fact *that I remember something,* not from any of the facts that I remember.

But if I can know that I was present when an action was done without using a criterion of identity, why can't I know in this way that I did the action? Is it that I must employ a criterion in order to know *which* of the persons present was myself? In that case, presumably, I would not need to employ my criterion if I remembered that only one person was present, for that person would obviously have to be myself. But the trouble is that he would have to be myself *no matter what* I remembered about him. i.e., even if the remembered facts were such that I would have to conclude, in accordance with my criterion, that he was *not* myself. If I had a criterion of identity that I could use in such cases, it seems to me, it would be possible for me to remember someone doing a certain action, discover by the use of my criterion that he was not myself, and then find, by consulting my memory of the event, that he was the only person present when the action was done. And clearly this is not possible.

It is sometimes suggested that one is able to identify a remembered "past self" as one's own self by the fact that one is able to remember the private thoughts, feelings, sensations, etc., of that self. There does seem to be a sense in which my own thoughts and feelings are the only ones that I can remember. Certainly they are the only ones that I can

*Roughly speaking, a statement is a memory statement if (supposing it to be an honest assertion) it cannot be false unless the speaker has misremembered. A conclusion from what is remembered, on the other hand, can be false without there being a mistaken memory. E.g., I mistakenly identify the man I saw as John when in fact it was his identical twin.

ramember *having*. But it is a mistake to conclude from this that memory is used as a first person criterion of personal identity. The sentence "I remember having a headache yesterday" does not differ in meaning from the sentence "I remember my having a headache yesterday." But if what I remember when I remember a past headache is *my having* a headache, or that *I* had a headache, my statement "I had a headache" is a memory statement, not a conclusion from what I remember, and cannot be grounded on any criterion of identity. If, however, what I remember is that someone had a headache, or that a headache occurred, it is clear that the remembered facts provide no grounds for the conclusion that *I* had a headache. Nor can we say, as some have said, that the relation "being the memory of" is the relation of "co-personality" between mental events, and that I know that a past sensation was mine because I have established that one of my present mental states is a memory of it and therefore co-personal with it. For, contrary to what Hume and others seem to have supposed, in the sort of case we are considering it makes no sense to speak of comparing one's present memory with a past sensation and finding that the one is the memory of (on Hume's theory, that it resembles) the other. One could make such a comparison only if one knew of the past sensation on some grounds other than one's memory of it, and our concern here is with cases in which one's memory is one's only source of knowledge concerning the past events in question. In such a case, comparing a past sensation with one's memory of it could only be comparing one's memory with itself—and comparing something with itself (if that means anything) is certainly not a way of discovering whether two events are related in a certain way. One can raise the question whether two events are related in a particular way (in *any* given way) only if one knows of the occurrence of both events. And if one knows of one of the events on the basis of memory, one must, in inquiring whether it is related in some way to the other event, be relying on one's memory of it, and clearly cannot be raising any question as to whether one does remember it (or whether one of one's present mental states is a memory of it). Indeed, if one's knowledge of a past sensation is memory knowledge it is misleading to say that one knows that one remembers a particular past sensation. It makes sense to speak of knowing that one remembers a particular event (knowing of an event that one remembers it) only where it would also make sense to speak of knowing of that event that one does not remember it (as is the case if one's knowledge of an event is based on something other than, or in addition to, one's memory). When I say that I have a headache I am not mentioning some particular headache and reporting, as a fact that I know about it, that it is experienced by me; likewise, when I say that I remember a headache I am not, in most cases, saying of some particular headache that I remember it. Normally I can identify a past sensation only as one that I remember (or, as I should prefer to say, one that I remember having). And when this is so there cannot arise any question concerning the ownership of the sensation, and there is no room for the employment of criteria of ownership or criteria of personal identity.

4. If, as I have argued, one does not use criteria of identity in making statements about one's own past on the basis of memory, the criteria of personal identity must be third person criteria. And if memory were the sole criterion of personal identity it would have to be the sole criterion that we use in making identity statements about persons other than ourselves. It is easily shown, however, that if we did not have some criterion other than memory that we could use in making statements of personal identity we could not use what others remember, or claim to remember, as evidence of any sort (criteriological or otherwise) for identity statements about them.

To begin with, if the word "remember" is to have any meaning it must be possible to establish whether someone is using it correctly. If some of the utterances that persons make are to count as memory claims, and therefore as evidence of what they remember or seem to remember, it must be possible to establish what a person means by the words he utters. But establishing what a person means by a term, or whether he is using it correctly, involves observing his use of it in various circumstances and over a period of time. This, of course, involves being able to know that it was one and the same person who uttered a given word on two different occasions, and to be able to know this one must have a criterion of identity. What could this criterion be if not bodily identity? It could not be any "psychological" criterion (such as memory or sameness of personality), for the use of such criteria (if criteria they are) involves accepting what a person says as indicating what his psychological state is (e.g., that he seems to remember doing a certain thing), and one could not do this if one were trying to establish what he means by, or whether he understands, the expressions he is using. In *some* circumstances, at least, bodily identity must be a criterion of personal identity.

Moreover, memory claims can be mistaken, and there must, accordingly, be such a thing as checking on the truth of a memory claim, i.e., establishing whether a person remembers something without taking his word for it that he does. And this, if he claims to have done a certain thing in the past, would involve establishing whether he, the person who claims this, is the same as someone who did do such an action in the past. In establishing this we could not use memory as our criterion of personal identity, and it is difficult to see what we could use if not bodily identity. And if, in such cases, we could not use bodily identity (or something other than memory) as a criterion of identity, it would not be possible to establish whether someone understands the use of the term "remember," and that term could not so much as have a meaning. It is, I believe, a logical or conceptual truth, not a contingent truth, that memory beliefs, and therefore honest memory claims, are generally true. If someone frequently prefaced past tense statements with the words "I remember that," and these statements generally turned out to be false, this would be grounds for saying that he did not understand the use of these words. We would not think that we had succeeded in teaching a child the use of the word "remember" if he commonly said "I remember doing such and such" when he had not done the thing in question. Again, suppose that we had discovered a new people whose language we did not know, and that someone had proposed a way of translating their language that involved regarding a certain class of statements (or utterances) as memory statements. Clearly, if all or most of those statements turned out to be false if translated as proposed, there could be no reason for accepting that way of translating them as correct, and there would be every reason for rejecting it as mistaken. But if it is a conceptual truth that memory claims are generally true, establishing that someone understands the use of the term "remember" must surely involve establishing whether his memory claims (or what appear to be his memory claims) are true or false. And to be able to do this we must have something other than memory that we can use as a criterion of personal identity.

If Bodily Identity were the Sole Criterion . . .

5. The arguments of the last section may seem to give support to the view that bodily identity is, to the exclusion of memory, the sole criterion of personal identity. But this view seems to me to be mistaken. Bodily identity is certainly *a* criterion of personal identity, and if it were not, I have argued, nothing else could be so much as evidence of personal identity. But I do not think that it can be the sole criterion, and I think that there is an important sense in which memory, though certainly not the sole criterion, is one of the criteria.

Let us consider one consequence of the view that bodily identity is the sole criterion of personal identity. As I said in section 1, if this view were correct it would have to be the case that we are reasoning inductively when we use the fact that someone claims to remember something as grounds for a statement about his past. It would be a contingent fact, one that we have discovered empirically, that most memory claims are true, or that people generally remember what they claim to remember. This would, indeed, be nothing other than the fact that the memory claims that issue from the mouth of a certain body generally correspond to events in the past history of that same body. But I have argued that it is a logical fact, not a contingent fact, that memory claims are generally true. If this is so, inferences of the form "He claims to remember doing X, so he probably did X" are not simply inductive inferences, for they are warranted by a generalization that is logically rather than empirically true.

Now let us return briefly to the case of the cobbler and the prince. If one is inclined to use the memory claims of the cobbler as grounds that he is (has become) the prince, the inference one is inclined to make is not of the form "He claims to remember doing X, so he probably did do X," but is of a more complex sort. Roughly, it is of the form "He claims to remember doing X, Y, and Z under such and such circumstances and at such and such times and places, and X, Y, and Z were done by someone under precisely those circumstances and at those times and places, so there is reason to believe that he is the person who did those actions." But it seems to me that if inferences of the first sort are not inductive, neither are inferences of the second sort. And I think that to say that inferences of the second sort are legitimate (as they certainly are, at least under certain circumstances), and that they are non-inductive, is tantamount to saying that memory is a criterion of personal identity.

It should be noted that if such inferences were merely inductive, and if bodily identity were the sole criterion of personal identity, it would be patently absurd to make such an inference in a case in which the body of the person making a memory claim is known not to be identical with the body of the person who did the action that he claims to remember. The absurdity would be that of asserting something to be true, or probably true, on the basis of indirect evidence, when one has direct and conclusive evidence that it is false. But in the imaginary case I have described, the claim that the cobbler is (has become) the prince does not, I think, strike us as having *this* sort of absurdity. I have not attempted to say whether, if the events I have described were to occur, it would be correct to say that the cobbler had become the prince, and I do not know how this question could be settled. But this in itself seems to me significant. The fact that such cases so much as incline us to admit the possibility of bodily transfer, or leave us in doubt as to what to say, seems to me *prima facie* evidence that memory is a criterion of personal identity. It is not as if our doubts were due to ignorance of empirical facts that, if known, would settle the issue. Doubts of that sort are easily removed, for we need only add further details to the description of the case. But if, knowing all of the relevant facts, we are in doubt as to how we should answer a question of identity, this is surely an indication that the case is such that the question is not unambiguously decidable by our criterion of identity. This, in turn, suggests that there is a conflict of criteria. In the case at hand, our doubts are evidence that one criterion of personal identity, namely bodily identity, is in conflict with another, namely memory.

Memory Claims and Personal History

But now I must try to meet an objection. It might be argued that while the inference "He claims to remember doing X, so he probably did X" is not inductive, we are nevertheless reasoning inductively when we take what a person says as evidence for a statement about his past history. For what justifies us in taking the sounds that a person utters as expressing a memory claim? As was argued earlier, if a question arises as to whether a person understands the use of the word "remember," or is using it to mean what we mean by it, the question can be settled only by establishing, independently of what he says, whether the things that he claims (or apparently claims) to remember are things he actually did, endured, or witnessed in the past. If in a number of cases it turns out that the actions that he apparently claims to remember having done are actions that he actually did, this is evidence that he does understand the use of such words as "remember," and that his apparent memory claims are really memory claims and can generally be relied upon. Must it not be much the same sort of considerations, i.e., our having observed certain correlations between the sounds that people utter and what they have done in the past, that justifies our general reliance on people's memory claims, or rather our acceptance of people's utterances as memory claims? If so, it would seem that our use of people's memory claims as evidence for statements about their own pasts, including identity statements about them, is, in the end, inductively based. Though it is a logical fact that memory claims are generally true, what does this come to except the fact that if there did not exist correlations of the sort mentioned none of the utterances of persons would be memory claims? But the existence of such correlations is a contingent fact, and it is on this contingent fact, it might be argued, that inferences of the sort "He claims to remember doing X, so he probably did X" are ultimately based. As for the case of the cobbler and the prince, it might be argued that if what I said in section 4 is correct then the fact that I have imagined would be evidence, not that the cobbler had become the prince, but rather that his utterances were not memory claims at all, and that he did not understand the use of the term "remember."

To take the last point first, suppose that we were in doubt as to whether the cobbler really understood the words that he was using. Could we not satisfy ourselves that he did by observing his subsequent behavior, and by establishing (using bodily identity as our criterion of personal identity) that when he claims to have done an action that occurred *after* the alleged bodily transfer it is generally the case that he did do that action? When we are trying to establish whether a person understands the words he utters we must, I have argued, use bodily identity as a criterion of identity, but it does not follow from this that there cannot, in exceptional cases, be personal identity in the absence of bodily identity.

As for the rest of the objection, it is certainly true that unless there existed certain correlations between the sounds people utter and events in the past histories of those who utter them it would be impossible to have knowledge of the past that is based on the memory claims of other persons. These correlations are those that must exist if any of the utterances that people make are to be memory claims. But it cannot be the case, I believe, that we regard certain of the utterances of other persons as memory claims *because* we have established, inductively, that such correlations hold. To be sure, from the fact that a person utters the sounds that I would utter if making a certain memory claim it does not necessarily follow that he speaks the language that I speak and means by those sounds what I would mean by them. Under exceptional circumstances I might raise a question as to whether what sounds to me like a memory claim is really one, and such a question could be settled empirically, by observing the behavior of the person who made the claim. But except when we have definite grounds for supposing the contrary, we must, I believe, regard other persons as speaking a language, our own if the words sound familiar, without having any general empirical justification for doing so. Let us consider whether it would be possible for me to question whether there is anyone at all (other than myself) who speaks the language that I speak, and then to discover empirically, by observing correlations between the sounds people utter and their present and past behavior, that those around me do speak the language that I speak and that certain of their utterances are memory claims and can generally be relied upon. In carrying on such an investigation I would, of course, have to rely on my own memory. But one's memory can be mistaken. It is essential to the very notion of memory that there be a distinction between remembering something and merely seeming to remember something. And for there to be such a distinction there must be such a thing as checking up on one's own memory and finding that one does, or does not, remember what one seems to remember. As Wittgenstein pointed out,* there are and must be circumstances in which we would accept other sorts of evidence concerning the past as more authoritative than our own memories. But an important—I think essential—check on one's own memory is the testimony of other persons. And this sort of check would not be available to me if I could not even regard the utterances of other persons as testimony until I had completed my investigation and established the required set of correlations. Unless there were some persons whose utterances I would be willing to accept as memory claims without having conducted such an investigation I would in effect be admitting no distinction between remembering and merely seeming to remember, and I could therefore make no distinction between finding the correlations and merely seeming to have found them.

It is, I should like to say, part of the concept of a person that persons are capable of making memory statements about their own pasts. Since it is a conceptual truth that memory statements are generally true, it is a conceptual truth that persons are capable of knowing their own pasts in a special way, a way that does not involve the use of criteria of personal identity, and it is a conceptual truth (or a logical fact) that the memory claims that a person makes can be used by others as grounds for statements about the past history of that person. This, I think, is the kernel of truth that is embodied in the view that personal identity can be defined in terms of memory.

Further Reading

Ayer, A. J. *The Concept of A Person.* London: Macmillan, 1963.

Campbell, C. A. *On Selfhood and Godhood.* London: George Allen & Unwin, Ltd., 1957.

Chappell, V. C. (Ed.) *The Philosophy of David Hume.* New York: Modern Library, 1963.

Gustafson, Donald (Ed.) *Essays in Philosophical Psychology.* Garden City: Doubleday, 1964.

Laird, John. *Problems of the Self.* London: Macmillan, 1917.

MacMurray, John. *The Self as Agent.* London: Faber and Faber, 1953.

Shoemaker, Sydney. *Self-Knowledge and Self-Identity.* Ithaca: Cornell University Press, 1963.

Wittgenstein, Ludwig. *The Blue and Brown Books.* Oxford: Blackwell, 1958.

* Ludwig Wittgenstein, *Philosophical Investigations* (Oxford: Basil Blackwell, 1953), Pt. I, paras. 56 and 265.

PART V

DUALISM AND SURVIVAL

INTRODUCTORY READING

The Will of James Kidd

INQUIRY

SELECTED SOURCES

Plato

Saint Paul

Samuel

Ayer

Ryle

Passmore

Broad

Price

Flew

Ramsey

Taylor

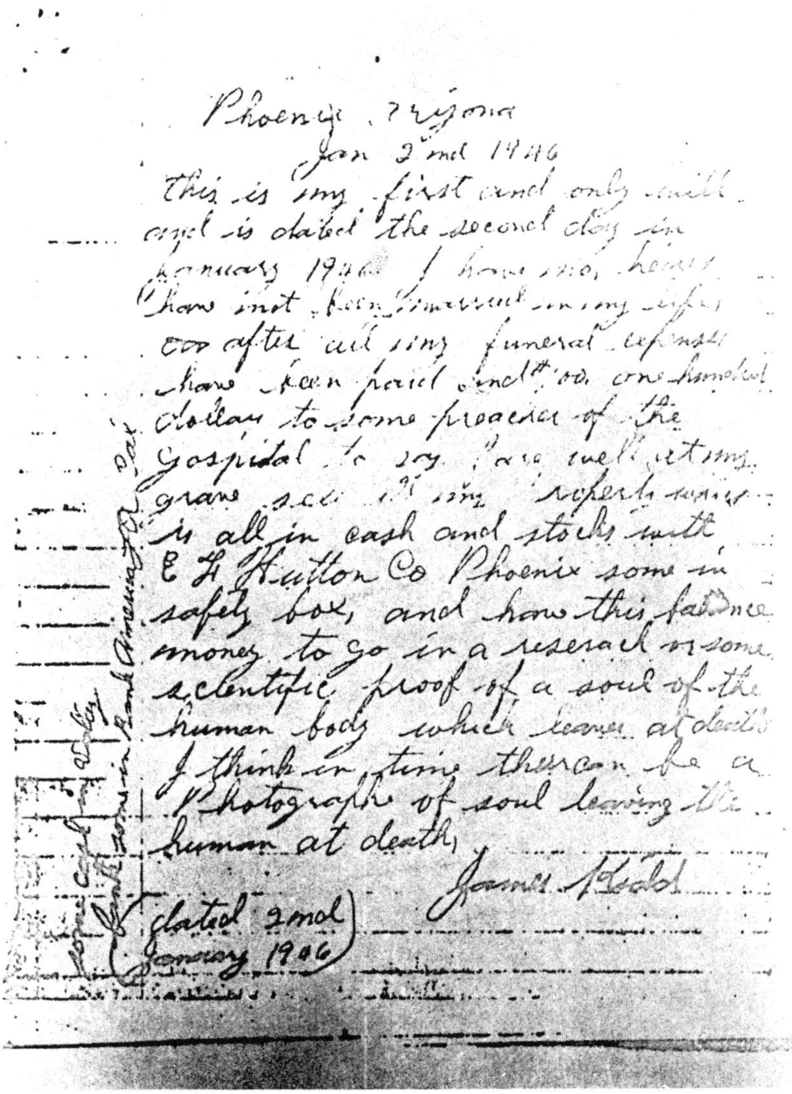

Phoenix Arizona
Jan 2nd 1946

this is my first and only will and is dated the second day in January 1946. I have no heires (have not been married in my life) after all my funeral expenses have been paid and $100, one hundred dollars, to some preacher of the gospital to say farewell at my grave sell all property which is in cash and stocks with E F Hutton Co Phoenix some in safety box, and have this balance money to go in a research or some scientific proof of a soul of the human body which leaves at death I think in time their can be a Photograph of soul leaving the human at death,

James Kidd

dated 2nd
January 1946
[on side margin]: some cash in Valley bank some in Bank America LA Cal

INQUIRY

nobody nowhere
except yourself
not even a mirror
to make you two
not a soul
except your own
maybe
and even that
not there
maybe
or not yours
maybe
because you're what's called
dead
you've reached your station

Descend

LAWRENCE FERLINGHETTI
"The Long Street"*

THE Will of James Kidd has been taken seriously. During the spring and summer of 1967 it was probated in the Superior Court of the State of Arizona. Among the many claimants to the estate, which was valued at $200,000, were philosophers, psychologists, neurologists, religious and academic institutions and certain individuals who said that they had special powers of communication with the dead or unique theories on "soul-searching."

Suppose we want to prove that the soul of a human being leaves his body at death. Where do we begin? What, in fact, are we looking for? The belief that individuals do "live" after their deaths is certainly widespread. But is it really possible to imagine yourself disembodied? Does the phrase, "the funeral of my body" sound strange? If you are dead, then you did not survive. "The dead" and "the survivors" are exclusive categories. Furthermore, consider what might be meant by "disembodied person." A person has a point of view; but what would be the point of view of the disembodied?

Antony Flew tells us that "persons are what we meet." We learn about being a person and identifying persons through our physical experiences. We point out persons, we shake hands, pat persons on the back. How could we identify something disembodied as a person (note Part IV)? If we are to deal with the Kidd Will, we must wrestle with problems related to those above.

A good deal of Western religious tradition and much of our literature incorporates the idea that man is a combination of physical processes and mental processes, outer and inner existences. The physical is public and the mental is private. Note the following description of man from the famous American novel *Moby Dick,* by Herman Melville:

> To be sure, in cold weather you may carry your house aloft with you, in the shape of a watch-coat; but properly speaking the thickest watch-coat is no more of a house than the unclad body; for as the soul is glued inside of its fleshy tabernacle, and cannot freely move about in it, nor even move out of it, without running great risk of perishing (like an ignorant pilgrim crossing the snowy Alps in winter); so a watch-coat is not so much of a house as it is a mere envelope, or additional skin encasing you.*

Asking children about death shows us, as Maria H. Nagy demonstrates in her studies on the "Child's View of Death," how early in life we distinguish between these "parts" of ourselves. A child of nine years and four months says:

> What is death? Well I think it is a part of a person's life. . . . Only one part of it is earthly. As in school, we go on to a different class. To die means to begin a new life. Everyone has to die once, but the soul lives on.†

This type of thinking is called *dualistic* because it emphasizes the belief that there are two essentially different parts of man. (This conception is opposed to monism—the view that there is only one fundamental reality—and to pluralism—the doctrine that there are many fundamental realities.) The two "parts" of man are taken by dualist philosophers to be irreducible to each other; that is, minds and mental activity can never be explained totally by reference to the physical, nor can bodies and physical activities be explained completely by reference to the mental. Dualists might consider it probable that a man (a mind or soul) could survive his physical death.

* Herman Melville, *Moby Dick,* Chap. 28.

† Maria H. Nagy, "The Child's View of Death," *Journal of Genetic Psychology,* 73 (1948), pp. 3–27.

Dualism and the idea of personal immortality have been linked in the history of Western thinking, though they need not necessarily be so related. St. Paul, for example, expressed the notion that man is a physical thing, but that by a miraculous act of God he will be re-created in another kind of body after his physical death. If this were to happen, the major philosophical problem of survival would revolve around establishing a criterion for "same person" (again see Part IV). We would want to know that the re-created person was, in some way, the same as the original person. Those who would agree with Paul would find the Kidd Will puzzling. For them there is nothing to leave the body at physical death, and thus nothing to prove scientifically.

For the great Greek philosopher, Plato, distinguishing between body and soul is of major importance. This contrast is essential to his theory of knowledge (how men come to have knowledge) and also to his definition of true happiness. In the *Phaedo* he develops the idea that a philosopher ought to welcome death because death forces complete separation of the body and soul; and the pure soul is able to contemplate the Eternal Forms of knowledge (true ideas) unfettered by the desires of the body.

The theory of forms and recollected knowledge is based on the idea that there are many universal concepts, such as Beauty, Justice, and Equality, which are essential to the way we think, but which we do not derive from sense experiences. Where do we get this knowledge? From the mind's recalling that which is already implanted in it, Plato answers. It is as if in a pre-natal state our souls lived in the "heaven of ideas." The post-natal world in which we live is a mirror image, an imperfect set of copies, of the real world of ideas. Now encased in bodies, our souls have forgotten the knowledge of the real and must by thought recollect what they once knew. But simply establishing the soul's pre-birth existence is not sufficient to say that it lives beyond physical death.

Plato argues that the soul is not a compound thing. It is not composed of parts. If something has no parts, that is, if it is basically simple, then it cannot be divided or broken up. Decay, as we know it in the physical world, is a slow breaking apart of complex structures. The singular cannot decay; it is indestructible. (Nothing short of an act of God would annihilate it). The soul for Plato, then, is immortal because it is a complete entity, simple and irreducible.

Plato further contends that the way the soul has conducted itself while in the body will determine the type of its after-life existence. If a soul has been concerned only with satisfying the cravings of the body it is ignorant and evil and will be punished. If a soul gains wisdom it is virtuous and can expect a rewarding after-life of true happiness. It is no wonder that the philosopher welcomes death. Certainly many of our dualistic ideas have developed through Platonic thinking.

The Renaissance philosopher Rene Descartes, called by many the father of modern philosophy, gives a concise statement of the "official doctrine" of dualism:

Because I know certainly that I exist, and that meanwhile I do not remark that any other thing necessarily pertains to my nature or essence, excepting that I am a thinking thing, I rightly conclude that my essence consists solely in the fact that I am a thinking thing (or a substance whose whole essence or nature is to think.) And although possibly (or rather certainly, as I shall say in a moment) I possess a body with which I am very intimately conjoined, yet because, on the one side, I have a clear and distinct idea of myself inasmuch as I am only a thinking and unextended thing, and as, on the other, I possess a distinct idea of body, inasmuch as it is only an extended and unthinking thing, it is certain that this I (that is to say, my soul by which I am what I am), is entirely and absolutely distinct from my body, and can exist without it.*

"I have my Body, I am my Mind."

Notice that not only does Descartes think of himself as a combination of two different entities, a mind and a body, but the essence, the real Descartes, is identified with his mind or soul. H. D. Lewis put this idea in the phrase, "I have my body, I am my mind." The identification of the person with the soul or mind is quite crucial to our problem. Even if we could show that souls do not die with bodies, unless the individual is, in some essential way, his soul, we could not say that he had survived physical death. But why are we prone to think of ourselves as souls? If we were to ask any ordinary man what distinguishes men from animals, he would likely tell us that only men have souls or minds. Would he, however, express the belief, as Mr. Kidd did, that it will one day be *proved* that we (our souls) leave our bodies at death?

Does the existence of a separate soul or mind explain anything that cannot already be accounted for by reference to physical activities? Dualists tell us that there is a major difference between something physical and something mental. I come to know of physical things through my senses, in a somewhat indirect way. On the other hand, I know that certain mental processes, such as thinking, intending, willing, deciding, are going on in me regardless of data received from my senses. I have knowledge of this "mental me" in an immediate way, in a direct way. My mental world is private. You never know what I'm thinking (intending, hoping, etc.) unless I tell you. The dualist would say that we know we have these private sides of ourselves and also that a great deal of our activity is explainable only if we assume that we intend mentally to do something physical. He might say, for example, I intend to open the door; therefore I raise my arm, take the knob and open the door. My opening the door is no accident, nor simply a series of mechanical gestures.

This type of thinking, however has been challenged. If mental states are private, some philosophers have argued, then we cannot account for the fact that we explain many of the activities of others by reference to their mental states: "John is depressed." "John is in pain." How could we understand what another person means by

* Rene Descartes, *Meditations*, (1641).

"I am in pain" if his pain were a totally private thing? I could not discover whether he means by "pain" what I mean by "pain." As long as our so-called mental or internal states are private, the statement "He is in pain" cannot really be a comment about him, but it is a round-about statement about what it is like when I use "pain" in reference to myself.

Twentieth Century philosopher Ludwig Wittgenstein (see Part VII) offers an interesting analogy to this problem.* He tells us to suppose that everyone has a box with something in it which is called a "beetle." No one can look into anyone else's box, and each of us knows what a "beetle" is only by looking at our own "beetle." Might not everyone have something different in his box? Perhaps someone has an empty box. The concept of beetle then could not even be "something in the box." The word "beetle" would have to be used in such a way as not to be the name of anything. "Beetle" is useless; it could mean anything or nothing. If we knew our mental state only by looking within ourselves, then referring to mental states in others would be as meaningless as talking about the "beetles."

Mind and Body Affect Each Other

Certain philosophers also have attacked the notion of most dualists that the mind and the body affect each other; that is, many dualists claim that the mind interacts with the body, communicating its intentions and will to the body, and causing the body to act. However, if the mind is purely mental and the body purely physical, they have nothing in common. There are no grounds for transactions between them. Can you imagine a purely physical thing being moved to act by the "force" of reason? If there is no body in mind (minds apparently can be influenced only by thoughts) and if there is no mind in body (bodies are influenced only by physical forces), then minds can never influence bodies and bodies can never influence minds. The separation of the two terms must be blurred if we are to talk of interactions between them. The value of dualism, some philosophers argue, must decrease if the process of separating man into two distinct entities confuses the explanation of most of our common human activities: walking, hating, eating, deciding, loving, etc. Might we not conclude that minds (souls) are nothing but imagined ghosts in the machines of our bodies?

It is possible that Mr. Kidd (perhaps other dualists as well) mistakenly applied concepts of physical matters to matters concerning the soul. This is not uncommon. We say, "The man has sold his house," and "The man has sold his soul;" "The airplane leaves the terminal at midnight," "The soul leaves the body at death." It seems quite natural to talk this way. If it is possible for one to sell his house, why not his soul? If it is possible for someone to take a picture of an airplane as it leaves the terminal, why not a picture of the soul as it leaves the body at death? However, we might remind ourselves that

* Ludwig Wittgenstein, *Philosophical Investigations,* G. E. M. Anscombe, trans. (New York: Macmillan, 1953), #293.

there are many things we can say about houses and airplanes which we cannot say about souls. For example, one might inquire at the ticket counter as to how late a certain plane was in leaving the terminal. But such a question would not be appropriate concerning a certain soul leaving the body at death. Continue the comparison. "Where is your house?" but not "Where is your soul?" "I see my arm," but not "I see my soul." Have we uncovered a trap of language into which many of us have fallen at times? Should we give up on the Kidd Will as the product of such a confusion? Have we grounds to conclude that souls do not leave bodies at death?

The Survival Hypotheses

Mr. Kidd's Will demands physical evidence of survival, but what would count as such evidence? Can we even conceive of what is involved in the so-called "survival hypothesis"? During the court hearings on the Will, various mediums claimed that their abilities to contact the "dead" constituted the scientific proof Kidd sought or that they at least established a high probability that survival is a fact. Do we have any way of evaluating such "evidence"? Perhaps this again is a question of personal identity. We would want proof that the subject with whom we are communicating through a medium is the same person we once knew. Further, can we have any idea what it is like to be "alive" in some other world—the world of the dead?

H. H. Price claims that our experience of dreaming is a key to an intelligible account of "Another World." When we dream, he tells us, we enter a world of mental images; we are not stimulated sensually in the normal ways, and the laws of behavior in dreams are not those of physics. Yet, so long as the dream lasts we are not aware that it is a dream (excepting during so-called "lucid dreams"). We take the dream to be reality. Price suggests that the "Next World" might be like our dream world. It might be a world of images. The process of "imaging" would replace normal sense perceiving. Instead of receiving stimuli through the senses, we would be stimulated by our mental images, thoughts, emotions and wishes. Price argues that we would certainly "feel as much alive" in our image world as we do in the present physical world. The word "survival" then would be appropriate to what happened to us.

But where is this "Next World?" Where is the world of your dreams? This is a particularly perplexing problem. Suppose you dreamed last night that you got on the boat to heaven and by some chance you had brought your dice along. In your dream the boat takes up space and the dice have spatial co-ordinates in relation to the other objects in the boat. But the question, "Where is the boat and where are the dice?" beyond giving the dream spatial co-ordinates, is meaningless. You, the dreamer, are in bed, but the boat is nowhere in the bedroom. You might want to say that the objects of your dreams are in your head, but this would be intelligible only in a metaphorical way. Certainly the boat is not in your head. It is not a miniature boat because you are in it. How could you be in your head (in the boat to heaven) and also in your bedroom? Might you not begin to wonder which is the real you?

The phrase "in my dream" is the problem. We might think that it is like "in my house," a place with physical space co-ordinates. But dreams are not places, like Denver, Colorado, locatable in the physical world. You would never say, "I've been to Los Angeles, Rome, and Dreamland." The boat to heaven is not to be found in the physical world because it is nowhere in the physical world. It takes up space only in your dream world. But what does "space" mean in the dream context? Is there more than one space?

Price suggests, based on the model of the dream, that the "Next World" can be thought of as a space not locatable in the physical world. Nonetheless, it would be a place of spatial co-ordinates for those who image there. As each of us has his own dream worlds, Price allows that there will be many "Next Worlds," and, perhaps by telepathy, intercommunication between these other-worldly heavens and hells would be possible.

If we accept Price's account of the survival hypothesis and "Another World," are we in a better position to meet the requirements of the Kidd Will? Can we imagine a photograph of a soul leaving the body at death? Notice that we do not use movement words to describe the process of beginning to dream. We do not say of the sleeper: Now he is halfway to his dream, now three-quarters of the way; he has reached his dream world. He simply starts to dream. On this analogy, might not a dualist such as Price argue that one could not photograph the soul leaving the human body at death because its leaving the body and arriving in "Another World" are simultaneous events? There is nowhere to put the camera, nowhere to aim it. Might not even the dualist maintain that Kidd was confused in his understanding of either what a camera does or of what a soul is?

If the soul is totally non-physical, then all movement words would be inappropriate in regard to it. We would be hard-pressed to explain how a non-physical thing could be localized in a physical thing in the first place, and then how it could perform a physical act, leaving one place for another. But if we say that "leaving" makes no sense when we are talking of a non-physical entity, then must not such phrases as "in my body," etc., also be meaningless in reference to the soul? Where then is the soul? Why must we have souls at all?

1

PLATO
(427–347 B.C.)

*The Immortality of the Soul and Afterlife**

A student of Socrates and apparently greatly influenced by the latter's searching inquiries into questions about man, Plato was one of the first philosophers to develop a dualistic theory of man. Much of Plato's philosophy is written in the form of dialogues, discussions among men. These are generally led by Plato's representation of his teacher Socrates. Plato uses Socrates to present his own theories, while the rest of the participants set forth other popular ideas. Many of the dialogues have almost a dramatic effect.

None of the dialogues is more moving than the Phaedo, *which recounts the last day of Socrates' life. The court of Athens convicted him of two crimes, corrupting the youth and impiety, and sentenced him to death. His friends, among whom was Phaedo, join their teacher in his cell. The discussion turns to questions of death and after-life and is centered on Socrates' claim that the philosopher ought to welcome death. Socrates presents a series of arguments to prove that the souls of men are immortal and that the "personality" of a man is lodged in his soul. The myth at the end of the dialogue gives moral significance to the concept of immortality because, according to Plato, the after-life of the soul is either comfortable or torturous depending upon the good or evil in the soul.*

* Plato, *Phaedo*, B. Jowett, trans. (1898), with omissions.

The Doctrine of Recollection

YOUR favourite, doctrine, Socrates, that knowledge is simply recollection, if true, also necessarily implies a previous time in which we have learned that which we now recollect. But this would be impossible unless our soul had been in some place before existing in the form of man; here then is another proof of the soul's immortality.

But tell me, Cebes, said Simmias, interposing, what arguments are urged in favour of this doctrine of recollection. I am not very sure at the moment that I remember them.

One excellent proof, said Cebes, is afforded by questions. If you put a question to a person in a right way, he will give a true answer of himself, but how could he do this unless there were knowledge and right reason already in him? And this is most clearly shown when he is taken to a diagram or to anything of that sort.

But if, said Socrates, you are still incredulous, Simmias, I would ask you whether you may not agree with me when you look at the matter in another way;—I mean, if you are still incredulous as to whether knowledge is recollection?

Incredulous I am not, said Simmias; but I want to have this doctrine of recollection brought to my own recollection, and, from what Cebes has said, I am beginning to recollect and be convinced: but I should still like to hear what you were going to say.

This is what I would say, he replied:—We should agree, if I am not mistaken, that what a man recollects he must have known at some previous time.

Very true.

And what is the nature of this knowledge or recollection? I mean to ask, Whether a person who, having seen or heard or in any way perceived anything, knows not only that, but has a conception of something else which is the subject, not of the same but of some other kind of knowledge, may not be fairly said to recollect that of which he has the conception? . . .

And shall we proceed a step further, and affirm that there is such a thing as equality, not of one piece of wood or stone with another, but that, over and above this, there is absolute equality? Shall we say so?

Say so, yes, replied Simmias, and swear to it, with all the confidence in life.

And do we know the nature of this absolute essence?

To be sure, he said.

And whence did we obtain our knowledge? Did we not see equalities of material things, such as pieces of wood and stones, and gather from them the idea of an equality which is different from them? For you will acknowledge that there is a difference. Or look at the matter in another way:—Do not the same pieces of wood or stone appear at one time equal, and at another time unequal?

That is certain.

But are real equals ever unequal? or is the idea of equality the same as of inequality?

Impossible, Socrates.

Then these (so-called) equals are not the same with the idea of equality?

I should say, clearly not, Socrates.

And yet from these equals, although differing from the idea of equality, you conceived and attained that idea?

Very true, he said.

Which might be like, or might be unlike them?

Yes.

But that makes no difference: whenever from seeing one thing you conceived another, whether like or unlike, there must surely have been an act of recollection?

Very true.

But what would you say of equal portions of wood and stone, or other material equals? and what is the impression produced by them?

Are they equals in the same sense in which absolute equality is equal? or do they fall short of this perfect equality in a measure?

Yes, he said, in a very great measure too.

And must we not allow, that when I or any one, looking at any object, observes that the thing which he sees aims at being some other thing, but falls short of, and cannot be, that other thing, but is inferior, he who makes this observation must have had a previous knowledge of that to which the other, although similar, was inferior?

Certainly.

And has not this been our own case in the matter of equals and of absolute equality?

Precisely.

Then we must have known equality previously to the time when we first saw the material equals, and reflected that all these apparent equals strive to attain absolute equality, but fall short of it?

Very true.

And we recognize also that this absolute equality has only been known, and can only be known, through the medium of sight or touch, or of some other of the senses, which are all alike in this respect?

Yes, Socrates, as far as the argument is concerned, one of them is the same as the other.

From the senses then is derived the knowledge that all sensible things aim at an absolute equality of which they fall short?

Yes.

Then before we began to see or hear or perceive in any way, we must have had a knowledge of absolute equality, or we could not have referred to that standard the equals which are derived from the senses? —for to that they all aspire, and of that they fall short.

No other inference can be drawn from the previous statements.

And did we not see and hear and have the use of our other senses as soon as we were born?

Certainly.

Then we must have acquired the knowledge of equality at some previous time?

Yes.

That is to say, before we were born, I suppose?

True.

And if we acquired this knowledge before we were born, and were born having the use of it, then we also knew before we were born and at the instant of birth not only the equal or the greater or the less, but all other ideas; for we are not speaking only of equality, but of beauty, goodness, justice, holiness, and of all which we stamp with the name of essence in the dialectical process, both when we ask and when we answer questions. Of all this we may certainly affirm that we acquired the knowledge before birth?

We may.

But if, after having acquired, we have not forgotten what in each case we acquired, then we must always have come into life having knowledge, and shall always continue to know as long as life lasts—for knowing is the acquiring and retaining knowledge and not forgetting. Is not forgetting, Simmias, just the losing of knowledge?

Quite true, Socrates.

But if the knowledge which we acquired before birth was lost by us at birth, and if afterwards by the use of the senses we recovered what we previously knew, will not the process which we call learning be a recovering of the knowledge which is natural to us, and may not this be rightly termed recollection? . . .

The Soul as Life and Immortal

Do you think that every man is able to give an account of these very matters about which we are speaking?

Would that they could, Socrates, but I rather fear that to-morrow, at this time, there will no longer be any one alive who is able to give an account of them such as ought to be given.

Then you are not of opinion, Simmias, that all men know these things?

Certainly not.

They are in process of recollecting that which they learned before?

Certainly.

But when did our souls acquire this knowledge?—not since we were born as men?

Certainly not.

And therefore, previously?

Yes.

Then, Simmias, our souls must also have existed without bodies before they were in the form of man, and must have had intelligence.

Here lies the point:—You want to have it proven to you that the soul is imperishable and immortal, and the philosopher who is confident in death appears to you to have but a vain and foolish confidence, if he believes that he will fare better in the world below than one who has led another sort of life, unless he can prove this: and you say that the demonstration of the strength and divinity of the soul, and of her existence prior to our becoming men, does not necessarily imply her immortality. Admitting the soul to be longlived, and to have known and done much in a former state, still she is not on that account immortal; and her entrance into the human form may be a sort of disease which is the beginning of dissolution, and may at last, after the toils of life are over, end in that which is called death. And whether the soul enters into the body once only or many times, does not, as you say, make any difference in the fears of individuals. For any man, who is not devoid of sense, must fear, if he has no knowledge and can give no account of the soul's immortality. This, or something like this, I suspect to be your notion, Cebes; and I designedly recur to it in order that nothing may escape us, and that you may, if you wish, add or subtract anything.

But, said Cebes, as far as I see at present, I have nothing to add or subtract: I mean what you say that I mean.

Tell me, then, what is that of which the inherence will render the body alive?

The soul, he replied.

And is this always the case?

Yes, he said, of course.

Then whatever the soul possesses, to that she comes bearing life?

Yes, certainly.

And is there any opposite to life?

There is, he said.

And what is that?

Death.

Then the soul, as has been acknowledged, will never receive the opposite of what she brings.

Impossible, replied Cebes.

And now, he said, what did we just now call that principle which repels the even?

The odd.

And that principle which repels the musical or the just?

The unmusical, he said, and the unjust.

And what do we call that principle which does not admit of death?

The immortal, he said.

And does the soul admit of death?

No.

Then the soul is immortal?

Yes, he said.

And may we say that this has been proven?

Yes, abundantly proven, Socrates, he replied.

Supposing that the odd were imperishable, must not three be imperishable?

Of course.

And if that which is cold were imperishable, when the warm principle came attacking the snow, must not the snow have retired whole and unmelted—for it could never have perished, nor could it have remained and admitted the heat?

True, he said.

Again, if the uncooling or warm principle were imperishable, the fire when assailed by cold would not have perished or have been extinguished, but would have gone away unaffected?

Certainly, he said.

And the same may be said of the immortal: if the immortal is also imperishable, the soul when attacked by death cannot perish; for the preceding argument shows that the soul will not admit of death, or ever be dead, any more than three or the odd number will admit of the even, or fire, or the heat in the fire, of the cold. Yet a person may say: 'But although the odd will not become even at the approach of the even, why may not the odd perish and the even take the place of the odd?' Now to him who makes this objection, we cannot answer that the odd principle is imperishable; for this has not been acknowledged, but if this had been acknowledged, there would have been no difficulty in contending that at the approach of the even the odd principle and the number three took their departure; and the same argument would have held good of fire and heat and any other thing.

Very true.

And the same may be said of the immortal: if the immortal is also imperishable, then the soul will be imperishable as well as immortal; but if not, some other proof of her imperishableness will have to be given.

No other proof is needed, he said; for if the immortal, being eternal, is liable to perish, then nothing is imperishable.

Yes, replied Socrates, and yet all men will agree that God, and the essential form of life, and the immortal in general, will never perish.

Yes, all men, he said—that is true; and what is more, gods, if I am not mistaken, as well as men.

Seeing then that the immortal is indestructible, must not the soul, if she is immortal, be also imperishable?

Most certainly.

Then when death attacks a man, the mortal portion of him may be supposed to die, but the immortal retires at the approach of death and is preserved safe and sound?

True.

Then, Cebes, beyond question, the soul is immortal and imperishable, and our souls will truly exist in another world!

I am convinced, Socrates, said Cebes, and have nothing more to object; but if my friend Simmias, or any one else, has any further objection to make, he had better speak out, and not keep silence, since I do not know to what other season he can defer the discussion, if there is anything which he wants to say or to have said.

But I have nothing more to say, replied Simmias; nor can I see any reason for doubt after what has been said. But I still feel and cannot help feeling uncertain in my own mind, when I think of the greatness of the subject and the feebleness of man.

Yes, Simmias, replied Socrates, that is well said: and I may add that first principles, even if they appear certain, should be carefully considered; and when they are satisfactorily ascertained, then, with a sort of hesitating confidence in human reason, you may, I think, follow the course of the argument; and if that be plain and clear, there will be no need for any further enquiry.

Very true.

Afterlife of the Soul

But then, O my friends, he said, if the soul is really immortal, what care should be taken of her, not only in respect of the portion of time which is called life, but of eternity! And the danger of neglecting her from this point of view does indeed appear to be awful. If death had only been the end of all, the wicked would have had a good bargain in dying, for they would have been happily quit not only of their body, but of their own evil together with their souls. But now, inasmuch as the soul is manifestly immortal, there is no release or salvation from evil except the attainment of the highest virtue and wisdom. For the soul when on her progress to the world below takes nothing with her but nurture and education; and these are said greatly to benefit or greatly to injure the departed, at the very beginning of his journey thither.

For after death, as they say, the genius of each individual, to whom he belonged in life, leads him to a certain place in which the dead are gathered together, whence after judgment has been given they pass into the world below, following the guide, who is appointed to conduct them from this world to the other: and when they have there received their due and remained their time, another guide brings them back again after many revolutions of ages. Now this way to the other world is not, as Aeschylus says in the Telephus, a single and straight path—if that were so no guide would be needed, for no one could miss it; but there are many partings of the road, and windings, as I infer from the rites and sacrifices which are offered to the gods below in places where three ways meet on earth. The wise and orderly soul follows in the straight path and is conscious of her surroundings; but the soul which desires the body, and which, as I was relating before, has long been fluttering about the lifeless frame and the world of sight, is after many struggles and many sufferings hardly and with violence carried away by her attendant genius: and when she arrives at the place where the other souls are gathered, if she be impure and have done impure deeds, whether foul murders or other crimes which are the brothers of these, and the works of brothers in crime—from that soul every one flees and turns away; no one will be her companion, no one her guide, but alone she wanders in extremity of evil until certain times are fulfilled, and when they are fulfilled, she is borne irresistibly to her own fitting habitation; as every pure and just soul which has passed through life in the company and under the guidance of the gods has also her own proper home. I can tell you a charming tale, Simmias, which is well worth hearing.

And we, Socrates, replied Simmias, shall be charmed to listen to you.

The Myth of the Phaedo: A Description of the "Other World"

There are diverse regions in the hollows on the face of the globe everywhere, some of them deeper and more extended than that which we inhabit, others deeper but with a narrower opening than ours, and some are shallower and also wider. All have numerous perforations, and there are passages broad and narrow in the interior of the earth, connecting them with one another; and there flows out of and into them, as into basins, a vast tide of water, and huge subterranean streams of perennial rivers, and springs hot and cold, and a great fire, and great rivers of fire, and streams of liquid mud, thin or thick (like the rivers of mud in Sicily, and the lava streams which follow them), and the regions about which they happen to flow are filled up with them. And there is a swinging or see-saw in the interior of the earth which moves all this up and down, and is due to the following cause:—There is a chasm which is the vastest of them all, and pierces right through the whole earth; this is that chasm which Homer describes in the words,—

> 'Far off, where is the inmost depth beneath the earth;'

and which he in other places, and many other poets, have called Tartarus. And the see-saw is caused by the streams flowing into and out of this chasm, and they each have the nature of the soil through which they flow. And the reason why the streams are always flowing in and out, is that the watery element has no bed or bottom, but is swinging and surging up and down, and the surrounding wind and air do the same; they follow the water up and down, hither and thither, over the earth—just as in the act of respiration the air is always in process of inhalation and exhalation;—and the wind swinging with the water in and out produces fearful and irresistible blasts: when the waters retire with a rush into the lower parts of the earth, as they are called, they flow through the earth in those regions, and fill them up like water raised by a pump, and then when they leave those regions and rush back hither, they again fill the hollows here, and when these are filled, flow through subterranean channels and find their way to their several places, forming seas, and lakes, and rivers, and springs. Thence they again enter the earth, some of them making a long circuit into many lands, others going to a few places and not so distant; and again fall into Tartarus, some at a point a good deal lower than that at which they rose, and others not much lower, but all in some degree lower than the point from which they came. And some burst forth again on the opposite side, and some on the same side, and some wind round the earth with one or many folds like the coils of a serpent, and descend as far as they can, but always return and fall into the chasm. The rivers flowing in either direction can descend only to the centre and no further, for opposite to the rivers is a precipice.

Now these rivers are many, and mighty, and diverse, and there are four principal ones, of which the greatest and outermost is that called Oceanus, which flows round the earth in a circle; and in the opposite direction flows Acheron, which passes under the earth through desert places into the Acherusian lake: this is the lake to the shores of which the souls of the many go when they are dead, and after waiting an appointed time, which is to some a longer and to some a shorter time, they are sent back to be born again as animals. The third river passes out between the two, and near the place of outlet pours into a vast region of fire, and forms a lake larger than the Mediterranean Sea, boiling with water and mud; and proceeding muddy and turbid, and winding about the earth, comes, among other places, to the extremities of the Acherusian lake, but mingles not with the waters of the lake, and after making many coils about the earth plunges into Tartarus at a deeper level. This is that Pyriphlegethon, as the stream is called, which throws up jets of fire in different parts of the earth. The fourth river goes out on the opposite side, and falls first of all into a wild and savage region, which is all of a dark blue colour, like lapis lazuli; and this is that river which is called the Stygian river, and falls into and forms the Lake Styx, and after falling into the lake and receiving strange powers in the waters, passes under the earth, winding round in the opposite direction, and comes near the Acherusian lake from the opposite side to Pyriphlegethon. And the water of this river too mingles with no other, but flows round in a circle and falls into Tartarus over against Pyriphlegethon; and the name of the river, as the poets say, is Cocytus.

The Myth: Treatment of Souls

Such is the nature of the other world; and when the dead arrive at the place to which the genius of each severally guides them, first of all, they have sentence passed upon them, as they have lived well and piously or not. And those who appear to have lived neither well nor ill, go to the river Acheron, and embarking in any vessels which they may find, are carried in them to the lake, and there they dwell and are purified of their evil deeds, and having suffered the penalty of the wrongs which they have done to others, they are absolved, and receive the rewards of their good deeds, each of them according to his deserts. But those who appear to be incurable by reason of the greatness of their crimes—who have committed many and terrible deeds of sacrilege, murders foul and violent, or the like—such are hurled into Tartarus which is their suitable destiny, and they never come out. Those again who have committed crimes, which, although great, are not irremediable—who in a moment of anger, for example, have done some violence to a father or a mother, and have repented for the remainder of their lives, or, who have taken the life of another under the like extenuating circumstances—these are plunged into Tartarus, the pains of which they are compelled to undergo for a year, but at the end of the year the wave casts them forth—mere homicides by way of Cocytus, parricides and matricides by Pyriphlegethon—and they are borne to the Acherusian lake, and there they lift up their voices and call upon the victims whom they have slain or wronged, to have pity on them, and to be kind to them, and let them come out into the lake. And if they prevail, then they come forth and cease from their troubles; but if not, they are carried back again into Tartarus and from thence into the rivers unceasingly, until they obtain mercy from those whom they have wronged: for that is the sentence inflicted upon them by their judges. Those too who have been pre-eminent for holiness of life are released from this earthly prison, and go to their pure home which is above, and dwell in the purer earth; and of these, such as have duly purified themselves with philosophy live henceforth altogether without the body, in mansions fairer still which may not be described, and of which the time would fail me to tell.

The Hope of the Philosopher

Wherefore, Simmias, seeing all these things, what ought not we to do that we may obtain virtue and wisdom in this life? Fair is the prize, and the hope great!

A man of sense ought not to say, nor will I be very confident, that the description which I have given of the soul and her mansions is exactly true. But I do say that, inasmuch as the soul is shown to be immortal, he may venture to think, not improperly or unworthily, that something of the kind is true. The venture is a glorious one, and he ought to comfort himself with words like these, which is the reason why I lengthen out the tale. Wherefore, I say, let a man be of good cheer about his soul, who having cast away the pleasures and ornaments of the body as alien to him and working harm rather than good, has sought after the pleasures of knowledge; and has arrayed the soul, not in some foreign attire, but in her own proper jewels, temperance, and justice, and courage, and nobility, and truth—in these adorned she is ready to go on her journey to the world below, when her hour comes. You, Simmias and Cebes, and all other men, will depart at some time or other. Me already, as a tragic poet would say, the voice of fate calls. Soon I must drink the poison; and I think that I had better repair to the bath first, in order that the women may not have the trouble of washing my body after I am dead.

2

SAINT PAUL

(?–64)

*Death and the Spiritual Body**

Paul was the most ardent leader and most influential writer/theologian of the early Christian Church. Basic to Paul's thinking is the concept of belief in salvation by faith as opposed to the traditional Jewish concept of salvation by obedience to the law. In I Corinthians he addresses himself to the question of resurrection of bodies, a major tenet of Christian doctrine. Paul seems to imply that a new body, a spiritual body (soma pneumatikon) *will replace the earthly body. God, by his will, recreates the human being, embodying his old dispositions and memory in a new mold in a resurrection world. Paul does not imply the clear-cut dualism of Plato. In fact, he seems to suggest that some kind of body is a necessary element of man. When a man dies, he is no more, he is annihilated; but God has the power of reconstituting him in a new body.*

* I Cor. 15, Revised Standard Version of *The Holy Bible.*

NOW I would remind you, brethren, in what terms I preached to you the gospel, which you received, in which you stand, by which you are saved, if you hold it fast—unless you believed in vain.

For I delivered to you as of first importance what I also received, that Christ died for our sins in accordance with the scriptures, that he was buried, that he was raised on the third day in accordance with the scriptures, and that he appeared to Cephas, then to the twelve. Then he appeared to more than five hundred brethren at one time, most of whom are still alive, though some have fallen asleep. Then he appeared to James, then to all the apostles. Last of all, as to one untimely born, he appeared also to me. For I am the least of the apostles, unfit to be called an apostle, because I persecuted the church of God. But by the grace of God I am what I am, and his grace toward me was not in vain. On the contrary, I worked harder than any of them, though it was not I, but the grace of God which is with me. Whether then it was I or they, so we preach and so you believed.

The Doctrine of Resurrection of the Dead

Now if Christ is preached as raised from the dead, how can some of you say that there is no resurrection of the dead? But if there is no resurrection of the dead, then Christ has not been raised; if Christ has not been raised, then our preaching is in vain and your faith is in vain.

We are even found to be misrepresenting God, because we testified of God that he raised Christ, whom he did not raise if it is true that the dead are not raised. For if the dead are not raised, then Christ has not been raised. If Christ has not been raised, your faith is futile and you are still in your sins. Then those also who have fallen asleep in Christ have perished. If in this life we who are in Christ have only hope, we are of all men most to be pitied.

But in fact Christ has been raised from the dead, the first fruits of those who have fallen asleep. For as by a man came death, by a man has come also the resurrection of the dead. For as in Adam all die, so also in Christ shall all be made alive. But each in his own order: Christ the first fruits, then at his coming those who belong to Christ. Then comes the end, when he delivers the kingdom to God the Father after destroying every rule and every authority and power. For he must reign until he has put all his enemies under his feet. The last enemy to be destroyed is death. "For God has put all things in subjection under his feet." But when it says, "All things are put in subjection under him," it is plain that he is excepted who put all things under him. When all things are subjected to him, then the Son himself will also be subjected to him who put all things under him, that God may be everything to every one.

Otherwise, what do people mean by being baptized on behalf of the dead? If the dead are not raised at all, why are people baptized in their behalf? Why am I in peril every hour? I protest, brethren, by my pride in you which I have in Christ Jesus our Lord, I die every day! What do I gain if, humanly speaking, I fought with beasts at Ephesus? If the dead are not raised, "Let us eat and drink, for tomorrow we die." Do not be deceived: "Bad company ruins good morals." Come to your right mind, and sin no more. For some have no knowledge of God. I say this to your shame.

"Resurrection Bodies"

But some one will ask, "How are the dead raised? With what kind of body do they come?" You foolish man! What you sow does not come to life unless it dies. And what you sow is not the body which is to be, but a bare kernel, perhaps of wheat or of some other grain. But God gives it a body as he has chosen, and to each kind of seed its own body. For not all flesh is alike, but there is one kind for men, another for animals, another for birds, and another for fish. There are celestial bodies and there are terrestrial bodies; but the glory of the celestial is one, and the glory of the terrestrial is another. There is one glory of the sun, and another glory of the stars; for star differs from star in glory.

So is it with the resurrection of the dead. What is sown is perishable, what is raised is imperishable. It is sown in dishonor, it is raised in glory. It is sown in weakness, it is raised in power. It is sown a physical body, there is also a spiritual body. Thus it is written, "The first man Adam became a living being"; the last Adam became a life-giving spirit. But it is not the spiritual which is first but the physical, and then the spiritual. The first man was from the earth, a man of dust; the second man is from heaven. As was the man of dust, so are those who are of the dust; and as is the man of heaven, so are those who are of heaven. Just as we have borne the image of the man of dust, we shall also bear the image of the man of heaven. I tell you this, brethren: flesh and blood cannot inherit the kingdom of God, nor does the perishable inherit the imperishable.

Lo! I tell you a mystery. We shall not all sleep, but we shall all be changed, in a moment, in the twinkling of an eye, at the last trumpet. For the trumpet will sound, and the dead will be raised imperishable, and we shall be changed. For this perishable nature must put on the imperishable, and this mortal nature must put on immortality. When the perishable puts on the imperishable, and the mortal puts on immortality, then shall come to pass the saying that is written:

"Death is swallowed up in victory."
"O death, where is thy victory?
O death, where is thy sting?"

The sting of death is sin, and the power of sin is the law. But thanks be to God, who gives us the victory through our Lord Jesus Christ.

Therefore, my beloved brethren, be steadfast, immovable, always abounding in the work of the Lord, knowing that in the Lord your labor is not in vain.

3

LORD SAMUEL
(1870–1963)

A. J. AYER
(1910–)

GILBERT RYLE
(1900–)

*Philosophers' Symposium on the Physical Basis of Mind**

This discussion is taken from the British Broadcasting Corporation's Third Programme. It was part of a series of talks on the topic, "The Physical Basis of Mind." Seven scientists spoke first, and then the three philosophers contributed the concluding symposium. Each philosopher speaks uninterrupted. Lord Samuel takes the position that the real philosophic problem lies in finding a basis for mind-body unity and that science has taken us nowhere toward this aim. A. J. Ayer, on the other hand, argues that a physicalist bias is doomed to failure because the very nature of our idea of the mental is that it is not and cannot be physical or discoverable in any physical object. Ayer claims that we are misled by our conceptual patterns of thinking, and he concludes that "talking about minds and talking about bodies are different ways of classifying and interpreting experience." Gilbert Ryle attacks the whole idea of dualism and of mind language as the invention of a kind of ghost in the mechanism of the body. His story of the peasants and the steam-engine is most enlightening in helping to understand his attack. Notice that Ryle is not claiming that men are only mechanisms, but that the dualistic theory necessitates a machine/ghost conception of man. He then points out some of the consequences of that type of thinking.

* From B.B.C. Journal, *The Listener* (1950). Reprinted in P. Laslett, ed., *The Physical Basis of Mind* (Oxford: B. H. Blackwell, 1950). Reprinted by kind permission of the British Broadcasting Co. and Professors Ayer and Ryle.

Lord Samuel

We have made no progress towards explaining how the mind is attached to the body.

In so short a broadcast, I can only offer baldly my own conclusions on the question debated in this most interesting, and indeed exciting, discussion, without attempting any survey of the previous contributions.

The discussion has been an approach, from the side of physiology, to one of the oldest and most fundamental of the problems of philosophy—the relation between mind and matter. For centuries, philosophers of different schools have made strenuous efforts to resolve one into the other. Some have sought to show that mind is nothing more than an emanation, in the course of evolution, from matter; others that matter is nothing more than a concept of mind, which alone is real. Those efforts have been unsuccessful: neither view has won general assent.

The materialists appear to ignore the obvious lessons of daily experience. We see, every moment, events which cannot be accounted for by derivations, however subtle, from physical or chemical processes. Watch a chess-player deliberating for a quarter of an hour whether to move his queen here or a pawn there. At last he stretches out his hand and does the one or the other: or he may do neither; using his vocal organs, he may say, "I resign this game." The physiologist may reveal the nervous and muscular mechanism which operates the hand or the tongue, but not the process which has decided the player's action. Or consider a novelist making up a story, a musician writing a symphony, a scientist engaged in a mathematical calculation; or, indeed, something much simpler, a bird building its nest, and choosing the right materials for each stage; or a cat waiting for a pause in the traffic before crossing the street. All these, and all such, are engaged in some process that is different in kind from electrical attractions and repulsions, or from the processes that unite particles into atoms, atoms into molecules, molecules into objects, and move them about relatively to one another.

The idealists do not account for the fact, which we are bound to accept from astronomy, geology, and anthropology—if we think at all, and if we accept anything at all—that the stars and the planets and this earth existed aeons before man existed; that the universe carried on its activities then—and may properly be assumed to carry them on now—independently of man's perceiving and observing, timing and measuring. The material universe cannot, therefore, be a product of human thought. If it is said that matter may still be an emanation of mind—the mind of God—that is merely an evasion, removing the problem outside the scope of the argument.

The whole effort—to resolve mind into matter or else matter into mind—is the outcome of what T. H. Green called "the philosophic craving for unity." But a craving is something irrational, and we had better beware of becoming addicts. What ground is there for requiring any such unification, either of the one kind or of the other? An essential duality in nature is the alternative that is left.

For those who have proceeded on that assumption, it has been natural and usual to regard the living conscious body as the province of mind and the outside material universe as the province of matter. This series of addresses, which is now concluding, has been most valuable in showing that that is an error; it has put the boundary between the two in the wrong place. The eminent scientists who have taken part in it have clearly established that the acceptance of sense stimuli, the transmission of their effects along the nerve fibres, and their activation of different parts of the brain, are mechanical. Whether the approach is from bio-physics or bio-chemistry, anatomy or pathology, the conclusion is the same—these are material activities, obeying mechanical laws. Dr. Russell Brain who spoke on "Speech and Thought" tells us that "all stimuli reach the brain as electrical patterns"; Professor Le Gros Clark and others describe with great clarity the mechanism of the nervous system as a whole. We must conclude that these processes, although inside the body, are not essentially different from the physical processes that are going on outside; rather they are a continuation. When we feel an electric shock, the nerve fibres that carry the current are performing a function similar in kind to that of the copper wire between the battery and the hand. When we hear a sound, the mechanism of the auditory organs, including the relevant part of the brain, is specialized, no doubt, but is not fundamentally of a different order from the air-waves which had carried the sound. It follows that the meeting-place between mind and matter in our own experience is not where we had supposed it to be; it is not at the boundary between body and not-body, but is internal.

The Meeting-place of Brain and Mind

That, however, does not solve the problem: it merely shifts it. Some meeting-place there must be to account for the brain-mind relation. And we are bound to assume that, although the two are of different orders, they must have something in common, because there is a meeting-place; because the two interconnect and interact; because body (including brain) does in fact condition and influence mind, and mind does in fact condition and influence body.

The painter or sculptor is conditioned and influenced by his materials; the composer by the musical instruments that exist in his time; the architect by the available building materials; the craftsman by his tools; the captain and crew by their ship. But also the artist, composer, architect, craftsman, or navigator chooses the things that he will use and decides the purposes that they shall serve. So with mind and body.

This discussion has helped to clarify the whole problem by establishing the fact that the meeting-place is not at the points where external stimuli impinge upon the nervous system; it is at the points where mind accepts and utilizes the sense-data offered by the brain. But the discussion has not been able to answer the question what it is that takes over at those points; and therefore it could not even begin to consider how the connection may be made.

Here again our scientists are substantially agreed. Professor Le Gros Clark said at the end of his broadcast: "No more than the physiologist is the anatomist able even to suggest how the physico-chemical phenomena associated with the passage of nervous impulses from one part of the brain to another can be translated into a mental experience." Dr. Penfield compares the mechanism of nerve-cell connections to a telephone switchboard. He asks: "What is the real relationship of this mechanism to the mind?" He says that "there is a difference between automatic action and voluntary action: . . . that something else finds its dwelling-place between the sensory complex and the motor mechanism, that there is a switchboard operator as well as a switchboard." Sir Charles Sherrington has written elsewhere, "That our being should consist of *two* fundamental elements offers, I suppose, no greater inherent improbability than that it should rest on one only." Again, "We have to regard the relation of mind to brain as still not merely unsolved, but still devoid of a basis for its very beginning." And he had ended his stimulating contribution to the present discussion by saying, "Aristotle, 2,000 years ago, was asking how is the mind attached to the body? We are asking that question still."

That, it seems, is where we are now at a standstill. Until science and philosophy can help us to move on from that position we cannot hope that the universe will, for us, be rationalized.

A. J. Ayer

But this is to misconceive the problem

I wonder if Lord Samuel has made it completely clear exactly what the problem is that the philosophers are here called upon to solve? The scientists who have spoken in this series have shown very fully and convincingly how various mental processes—thinking, feeling, perceiving, remembering—are causally dependent upon processes in the brain, but to some of them at least the character of this connection still appears mysterious. Thus, Sir Charles Sherrington remarks that "it is a far cry from an electrical reaction in the brain to suddenly seeing the world around one, with all its distances, colours, and chiaro-curo": and Professor Adrian confesses to the same "misgivings" when he says that "the part of the picture of the brain which may always be missing is of course the part which deals with the mind, the part which ought to explain how a particular pattern of nerve impulses can produce an idea; or the other way round, how a thought can decide which nerve cells are to come into action."

If this is a genuine problem, it is hard to see why further information about the brain should be expected to solve it. For however much we amplify our picture of the brain, it remains still a picture of something physical, and it is just the question how anything physical can interact with something that is not that is supposed to constitute our difficulty. If what we are seeking is a bridge across a seemingly impassable river it will not help us merely to elevate one of the banks. It looks, indeed, as if some of the previous speakers were hoping to discover in the brain something describable as the locus of the mind; as if mind and brain could be conceived as meeting at a point in space or as somehow shading into one another: but to me this is not even an intelligible hypothesis. What would it be like to come upon this junction? By what signs would you recognize it if you found it? Descartes had the same problem, and he met it by suggesting that mind and body came together in the pineal gland; but how this conjecture could conceivably be tested he did not explain. The reason he had the problem—the reason why we have it still—is that matter and mind were conceived by him from the outset as distinct orders of being; it is as if there were two separate worlds, such that every event had to belong to one or other of them, but no event could belong to both. But from these premises it follows necessarily that there can be no bridge or junction; for what would the bridge consist of? Any event that you discovered would have to fall on one or other side of it. So, if there is a difficulty here, it is not because our factual information is scanty, but because our logic is defective. Perhaps this whole manner of conceiving the distinction between mind and matter is at fault. In short, our problem is not scientific but philosophical.

Let us consider, then, what can be meant by saying that a particular pattern of nerve impulses "produces an idea," or that "a thought decides" which nerve cells are to come into action. What are the facts on which such assertions are based? The facts are that the physiologist makes certain observations, and that these observations fall into different categories. On the one hand there are the observations which lead him to tell his story about nerve cells and electrical impulses. That is to say, the story is an interpretation of the observations in question. On the other hand there are the observations which he interprets by saying that the subject of his experiment is in such and such a "mental" state, that he is thinking, or resolving to perform some action, or feeling some sensation, or whatever it may be. It is then found to be the case that these two sorts of observations can be correlated with one another; that whenever an observation of the first type can be made, there is good reason to suppose that an observation of the second type can be made also. For example, when the scientists make observations which they interpret by saying that such and such nerve cells are undergoing such and such electrical disturbances, they can also make observations which are interpreted by saying that the subject is having sensations of a certain type. Again, when they are able to make such observations as are interpreted by saying that the subject is resolving to perform some action, they can also make further observations which are interpreted by saying that certain impulses are passing through certain of his nerve fibres. It seems to me that when it is asserted that the two events in question—the mental and the physical—are causally connected, that the pattern of nerve impulses "produces" the sensation, or that the thought "decides" which nerve cells are to operate, all that is meant, or at least all that can properly be meant, is that these two sets of observations are correlated in the way that I have described. But if this is so, where is the difficulty? There is nothing especially mysterious about the fact that two different sets of observations are correlated; that, given the appropriate conditions, they habitually accompany one another. You may say that this fact requires an explanation; but such an explanation could only be some theory from which the fact of this correlation could be deduced. And in so far as the theory was not a mere redescription of the facts which it was intended to explain, it would serve only to fit them into a wider context. We should learn from it that not only were these observations correlated, but certain further types of observation were correlated with them. To ask *why* something occurs, if it is not simply equivalent to asking *how* it occurs, is to ask what other things are associated with it. Once the facts are fully described, there is no mystery left.

If there seems to be a mystery in this case, it is because we are misled by our conceptual systems; not by the facts themselves but by the pictures which we use to interpret the facts. The physiologist's story is complete in itself. The characters that figure in it are nerve cells, electrical impulses, and so forth. It has no place for an entirely different cast, of sensations, thoughts, feelings, and the other *personae* of the mental play. And just because it has no place for them they do not intervene in it. The muddle arises from trying to make them intervene, as I am afraid Lord Samuel does. We then get a confused, indeed an unintelligible, story of electrical impulses being transmuted into sensations, or of mental processes interleaved with disturbances of the nervous cells. The picture we are given is that of messengers travelling through the brain, reaching a mysterious entity called the mind, receiving orders from it, and then travelling on. But since the mind has no position in space—it is by definition not the sort of thing that can have a position in space—it does not literally make sense to talk of physical signals reaching it; nor are there such temporal gaps in the procession of nervous impulses as would leave room for the mental characters to intervene. In short, the two stories will not mix. It is like trying to play *Hamlet*, not without the Prince of Denmark, but with Pericles, the Prince of Tyre. But to say that the two stories will not mix is not to say that either of them is superfluous. Each is an interpretation of certain phenomena and they are connected by the fact that, in certain conditions, when one of them is true, the other is true also.

My conclusion is, then, that mind and body are not to be conceived as two disparate entities between which we have to make, or find, some sort of amphibious bridge, but that talking about minds and talking about bodies are different ways of classifying and interpreting our experiences. I do not say that this procedure does not give rise to serious philosophical problems; how, for example, to analyse statements about the thoughts and feelings of others; or how far statements about people's so-called mental processes are equivalent to statements about their observable behaviour. But once we are freed from the Cartesian fallacy of regarding minds as immaterial substances, I do not think that the discovery of causal connections between what we choose to describe respectively as mental and physical occurrences implies anything by which we need to be perplexed.

Gilbert Ryle

Which should not be set in general terms

The story is told of some peasants who were terrified at the sight of their first railway-train. Their pastor therefore gave them a lecture explaining how a steam-engine works. One of the peasants then said, "Yes, pastor, we quite understand what you say about the steam-engine. But there is really a horse inside, isn't there?" So used were they to horse-drawn carts that they could not take in the idea that some vehicles propel themselves.

We might invent a sequel. The peasants examined the engine and peeped into every crevice of it. They then said, "Certainly we cannot see, feel, or hear a horse there. We are foiled. But we know there is a horse there, so it must be a ghost-horse which, like the fairies, hides from mortal eyes."

The pastor objected, "But, after all, horses themselves are made of moving parts, just as the steam-engine is made of moving parts. You know what their muscles, joints, and bloodvessels do. So why is there a mystery in the self-propulsion of a steam-engine, if there is none in that of a horse? What do you think makes the horse's hooves go to and fro?" After a pause a peasant replied, "What makes the horse's hooves go is four extra little ghost-horses inside."

Poor simple-minded peasants! Yet just such a story has been the official theory of the mind for the last three very scientific centuries. Several, though not all, of the scientists in this series have automatically posed their problem in this very way. I think that Lord Samuel still accepts the whole story, and that Professor Ayer would like to reject it, but does not see how to do so. For the general terms in which the scientists have set their problem of mind and body, we philosophers have been chiefly to blame, though we have been obsessed, not by the rustic idea of horses, but by the newer idea of mechanical contrivances. The legend that we have told and sold runs like this. A person consists of two theatres, one bodily and one non-bodily. In his Theatre A go on the incidents which we can explore by eye and instrument. But a person also incorporates a second theatre, Theatre B. Here there go on incidents which are totally unlike, though synchronized with those that go on in Theatre A. These Theatre B episodes are changes in the states, not of bits of flesh, but of something called "consciousness," which occupies no space. Only the proprietor of Theatre B has first-hand knowledge of what goes on in it. It is a secret theatre. The experimentalist tries to open its doors, but it has no doors. He tries to peep through its windows, but it has no windows. He is foiled.

We tend nowadays to treat it as obvious that a person, unlike a newt, lives the two lives, life A and life B, each completely unlike, though mysteriously geared to the other. Ingrained hypotheses do feel obvious, however redundant they may be. The peasants in my story correctly thought that a steam-engine was hugely different from a cart and automatically but incorrectly explained the difference by postulating a ghost-horse inside. So most of us, correctly thinking that there are huge differences between a clock and a person, automatically but incorrectly explain these differences by postulating an extra set of ghost-works inside. We correctly say that people are not like clocks, since people mediate, calculate, and invent things; they make plans, dream dreams, and shirk their obligations; they get angry, feel depressed, scan the heavens, and have likes and dislikes; they work, play, and idle; they are sane, crazy, or imbecile; they are skilful at some things and bunglers at others. Where we go wrong is in explaining these familiar actions and conditions as the operations of a secondary set of secret works.

Everybody knows quite well when to describe someone as acting absent-mindedly or with heed, as babbling deliriously or reasoning coherently, as feeling angry but not showing it, as wanting one thing but pretending to want another, as being ambitious, patriotic, or miserly. We often get our accounts and estimates of other people and of ourselves wrong; but we more often get them right. We did not need to learn the legend of the two theatres before we were able to talk sense about people and to deal effectively with them. Nor has this fairly newfangled legend helped us to do it better.

When we read novels, biographies, and reminiscences, we do not find the chapters partitioned into Section A, covering the hero's "bodily" doings, and Section B, covering his "mental" doings. We find unpartitioned accounts of what he did and thought and felt, of what he said to others and to himself, of the mountains he tried to climb and the problems he tried to solve. Should an examiner mark the paper written by the candidate's hand but refuse to assess the candidate's wits? Theorists themselves, when actually describing people, sensibly forget Theatre A and Theatre B. Sir Charles Sherrington paid a well-deserved compliment to Professor Adrian, but he did not pay one cool compliment to Professor Adrian A and another warmer compliment to Professor Adrian B.

In saying that a person is not to be described as a mind coupled with a body I am not saying, with some truculent thinkers, that people are just machines. Nor are engines just wagons or live bodies just corpses. What is wrong with the story of the two theatres is not that it reports differences which are not there but that it misrepresents differences which are there. It is a story with the right characters but the wrong plot. It is an attempt to explain a genuine difference—or rather a galaxy of differences—but its effect, like that of the peasants' theory, is merely to reduplicate the thing to be explained. It says, "The difference between a machine like a human body on the one hand and a human being on the other, is that in a human being, besides the organs which we do see, there is a counterpart set of organs which we do not see; besides the causes and effects which we can witness, there is a counterpart series of causes and effects which we cannot witness." So now we ask, "But what explains the differences between what goes on in the Theatre B of a sane man and what goes on in that of a lunatic? A third theatre, Theatre C?"

No, what prevents us from examining Theatre B is not that it has no doors or windows, but that there is no such theatre. What prevented the peasants from finding the horse, was not that it was a ghost-horse, but that there was no horse. None the less, the engine *was* different from a wagon and ordinary people *are* different not only from machines, but also from animals, imbeciles, infants, and corpses. They also differ in countless important ways from one another. I have not begun to show how we should grade these differences. I have only shown how we should not grade them.

One last word. In ordinary life (save when we want to sound knowing) we seldom use the noun "mind" or the adjective "mental" at all. What we do is to talk of people, of people calculating, conjuring, hoping, resolving, tasting, bluffing, fretting, and so on. Nor, in ordinary life, do we talk of "matter" or of things being "material." What we do is to talk of steel, granite, and water; of wood, moss, and grain; of flesh, bone, and sinew. The umbrella-titles "mind" and "matter" obliterate the very differences that ought to interest us. Theorists should drop both these words. "Mind" and "matter" are echoes from the hustings of philosophy, and prejudice the solutions of all problems posed in terms of them.

4

JOHN PASSMORE

(1914–   )

*The Humpty-Dumpty Argument**

Passmore, taking a cue from Ryle, also attacks the whole fabric of dualistic thinking. Passmore claims, perhaps a bit too hastily, that no creative contemporary philosophers are dualists: that philosophers have found unanswerable what Passmore terms the Humpty-Dumpty Argument. This major criticism rests on the problem of interaction between mind and body, which a dualist must assume to explain much of human behavior. Minds and bodies are supposed to work together in most of our activities, but, Passmore argues, where are they related so as to affect each other? Body, according to the dualists, is all physical and mind is all mental. There seems to be no common meeting ground. To the dualists, the kinds of things—persuasive argument, reason, emotion—which might affect mind are not physical, and the things which affect bodies—force, weight, etc.—are certainly not mental. Man has been taken apart, and all the king's horses and men cannot seem to put him back together again without erasing the original clear-cut distinctions of the dualism.

* John Passmore, *Philosophical Reasoning* (New York: Basic Books, 1961), pp. 38–40, 53–57. Excerpts from Chapter 3, "The Two-Worlds Argument," of *Philosophical Reasoning* by John Passmore, Basic Books, Inc., Publishers, New York, 1969. Used by permission of the publisher.

THE general tendency of philosophy is towards monism, in one or the other of its two very different varieties. There have, of course, been distinguished dualists—Plato and Descartes, for example—but they have been the exception. Few philosophers have been satisfied with a doctrine which preserves that sort of absolute separation between the mind and the body, the eternal and the temporal, the supernatural and the natural, which is to be found in the orthodox Christian theologies. This is an important fact about philosophers; the rejection of dualism is indeed one of the few points on which almost all the creative philosophers of modern times have agreed. Why this unwonted unanimity?

Two Types of Monism

I have suggested that there are two different sorts of monism; let us call them 'existence-monism' and 'entity-monism.' Entity-monism is the doctrine that 'ultimately' there is only one real entity. What we normally regard as distinct things—whether they be chairs, or musical compositions, or human beings—are, all of them, appearances of this one entity. Some philosophers describe themselves as materialistic monists, others as spiritualistic monists. But obviously this will not do. For if all differences are unreal, the one real entity cannot properly be described as material rather than as spiritual, or as spiritual rather than material. The most that can be said (if even this can be said) is that there is 'the One' or 'the Absolute.' For anybody to say: 'My monism is corporeal in type' is a contradiction in terms—if, that is, his monism is an entity-monism.

Entity-monism has had relatively few, although some distinguished, exponents. The case is quite different with what, for want of a better name, I have called 'existence-monism.' Existence-monism is difficult to define in general terms. But we might put it thus: when we say that something exists, or that things of a certain kind exist, this *exist* or *exists* has an invariant meaning whatever the 'something' or the 'kind' may be, i.e. there are not sorts, or levels, or orders of existence. More accurately, what is asserted by 'X exists' can always be asserted by a proposition which contains an 'is' which has, in this sense, an invariant meaning. Existence-monism, unlike entity-monism, does admit of varieties. Philosophers might say, and have said, that to exist is to be perceived, or to be in process, or to be spatio-temporal, or to be a possible subject for physical investigation, or to be a thing with properties, and so on.

The possible variations are, one might even think, limitless; any predicate might serve. But most of them we should at once rule out. Nobody could now win credence who asserted that to be is to be a quantity of water, however plausible that doctrine might have looked to Thales. This would not be only for empirical reasons. We should not bring it against Thales' view, simply, that scientists had looked at some substance in a laboratory and found that it was not watery. The objection would run deeper: that 'to be' cannot involve the possession of some specific descriptive property (whatever qualms we might suffer if we were asked to define that phrase more exactly). Such a property as wateriness cannot have the sort of priority which Thales' theory would ascribe to it. So it is not only wateriness in particular but any similar predicate which is now being ruled out. Water is the sort of thing to which we *ascribe* existence; and 'water exists here' is not the mere tautology 'the water here is watery'.

Contrast the view that 'to be is to have a place in Space-Time'; this sort of difficulty does not arise, or not so obviously, for Space-Time is not the sort of thing to which existence is ascribed or which is used to distinguish one thing from another. 'Spatio-temporality exists here', if it means anything at all, does assert the mere identity 'this spatio-temporal region is spatio-temporal'. Of course, specific spatio-temporal predicates are used as modes of distinction—something, that is, may be distinguished from its fellows in virtue of its position, or duration, or size, or shape; but the more general property of being 'spatio-temporal' is not ordinarily a distinguishing predicate—although metaphysicians sometimes try to turn it into one by alleging that there is a non-spatio-temporal kind of existence. As for those who say that 'to be is to be an object of thought', they always pay a certain homage to the force of what I am arguing by setting out to show, in Berkeley's manner, that it would be self-contradictory to attempt to use 'object of thought' as if it were a descriptive predicate.

It is not my present object, although by now it might appear to be, to define monism and to distinguish its types. What I want to do, simply, is to consider why most creative philosophers have been attracted by some sort of existence-monism, whether it has taken the form of an explicitly argued phenomenalism, idealism, physicalism, naturalism, or has merely been the implicit assumption, certainly widespread, that the traditional dichotomies of Mind and Body, God and Nature, are obviously untenable.

The Two-World Argument

The convergence on existence-monism arises, I want to suggest, because philosophers have come to accept as unanswerable a particular philosophical argument, which I have called the 'two-worlds argument', but might, more frivolously, have described as the Humpty Dumpty argument. Its basic point is that once we break up any system in a certain kind of way, it becomes quite impossible to put the pieces together again in a single situation: and yet, unless they can be so put together, the whole point of the breaking-up is lost. . . .

Ryle in *The Concept of Mind* puts the two-world argument in a more fundamental way, which links it with our previous discussion. 'The problem,' he writes, 'how a person's mind and body influence one another is notoriously charged with theoretical difficulties. What the mind wills, the legs, arms and the tongue execute; what affects the ear and the eye has something to do with what the mind perceives; grimaces and smiles betray the mind's moods and bodily castigations lead, it is hoped, to moral improvement. But the actual transactions between the episodes of the private history and those of the public history remain mysterious, since by definition they can belong to neither series. They could not be reported among the happenings described in a person's autobiography of his inner life, but nor could they be reported among those described in someone else's biography of that person's overt career. They can be inspected neither by introspection nor by laboratory experiment. They are theoretical shuttlecocks which are forever being bandied from the physiologist back to the psychologist and from the psychologist back to the physiologist.' He continues thus: 'Underlying this partly metaphorical representation of the bifurcation of a person's two lives, there is a seemingly more profound and philosophical assumption. It is assumed that there are two kinds of existence or status. What exists or happens may have the status of physical existence, or it may have the status of mental existence' (pp. 12–13).

Transactions Between Mind and Body

Ryle suggests in this passage that *by definition* the transaction between mind and body can belong to neither the mental nor the physical series. If the mental series is defined as containing only such transactions as are mental this is, of course, true. The two-world argument then becomes a very simple one indeed. It consists in saying: 'According to you, everything is either a part of the mental series or a part of the bodily series, and no transaction can belong to the mental series unless it is between members of the mental series, or to the bodily series unless it is between members of the bodily series. But then you have left no room whatever for transactions between the mental and the bodily series.' More commonly, however, the dualist presumes that the mental series can include any transaction in which one ingredient is mental, and the physical series any transaction in which one ingredient is physical; so that mental-physical transactions belong to *both* series. Describing my mental life I can say, 'At this moment I influenced my body' and describing my physical life I can say: 'At this moment I was influenced by my mind.' Then argument is needed to show that there is something about the conditions laid down for series-membership that would rule out this sort of double membership. But Ryle makes two points on which I have been insisting; first, that if we suppose that the mental life is known in one way and the physical in another, it will be impossible to give any account of our knowledge of the transaction between the two lives; and, secondly, that the crucial questions in the end, all the same, are not epistemological but ontological.

Mind and body are supposed to differ not only in properties, as an explosion differs from a lighted match, but in ontological status; the conditions which have to be fulfilled by a mind in order to exist, on the traditional theory, are entirely different from those which have to be fulfilled by a physical object. To assert that a physical body exists is to say that something is going on at a particular time in a particular place, something which is describable in principle by physical laws. To say that a mind exists is to say that at a particular time, but not in a particular place, something is happening which is describable only by spiritual laws, e.g. by teleological as distinct from efficient causality. Then the difficulty can be put thus; it has to be granted that in some sense the mind influences the body and vice versa. But the only force the mind has at its disposal is spiritual force, the power of rational persuasion; and the only thing that can move it is a purpose. On the other side, a body has no force at its disposal except material force and nothing can influence it except mechanical pressure. This means that bodies cannot appeal to minds to act; they can only push; and minds cannot influence bodies by putting purposes before them, because bodies are not susceptible to this sort of influence. So there is no possible way in which one could influence the other. We cannot nominate any particular place—whether it be the pineal gland or the synapse—where mind interacts with body, because mind is no more in that place, nor next to it, than anywhere else. Yet if once we say that mind itself is spatial, subject to physical force, capable of exercising physical force, and so on, the supposed ontological contrast breaks down.

The "Ontological Gap" Between the Mental and the Non-mental

This type of argument is sometimes described as 'the argument against interactionism'. But if interactionism is simply the view that the mental can affect the non-mental—that, for example, if I am worried about something, this can affect my digestion—then it is obviously true. What the two-world argument is concerned to show is that interactionism cannot be true *if there is an ontological gap between the mental and the non-mental;* it is directed against the gap, not against the interaction.

Parallelism

Once again, evasive action may be taken. 'Psycho-physical parallelism' is the best known form of evasion. Notwithstanding appearances, the parallelist argues, there is in fact no interaction between the mental and the non-mental, for such an interaction is ontologically impossible. Mental events and non-mental events belong to two distinct series, even although the series run parallel to one another. But what does 'parallel' mean here? Not that certain events in the one series are *like* events in the other; this has been ruled out in advance. Nor that they occur in the same place, for the same reason. The only possible parallelism is a temporal one; certain events in the mental series occur at the same time as, or prior to, or subsequent to, certain events in the non-mental series. But this relation is not close enough to do justice to the admitted facts. Events in my mind are related temporally to all sorts of events, inside and outside my body; what 'parallelism' fails to explain is the *special* relation between what goes on in my brain and what goes on in my mind.

Even at the level of temporal relationships, parallelism jams into the single notion of 'being parallel' the fact that my mental operations are regularly preceded and regularly followed by such and such physical operations and the fact that they regularly occur at the same time as certain such operations. (Is my nervousness 'parallel' to the changes it produces in my stomach or to the changes in the brain which coincide with it?) But in any case parallelism does not even *look* plausible once the 'parallelism' between mental and non-mental has been spelled out into 'some temporal relationship or other'; for such a relationship holds between any two things we care to mention. Yet to make the relation more intimate—as it very clearly is—at once threatens the ontological gap.

The Failure of Dualism to Maintain its Own Distinctions

The difficulties in the two-world thesis cannot be solved, either, by setting up a third entity in Descartes' manner—very, very subtle animal spirits. For, no matter how subtle, the problem persists of relating such spirits to mind if they are describable in terms of physical science; and if they are not, the problem of relating them to body. Or, if they exhibit the properties both of the spiritual and the physical, then again all ground has gone for supposing that the mental and the physical must belong to sharply sundered realms of existence.

It will now be apparent why so many philosophers have held some form of existence-monism, rejecting the view that universals and particulars, minds and bodies, God and Nature, belong to different orders of existence. For even to state such a theory, its exponents are obliged to destroy the ontological contrast which the theory is supposed to be setting up; and this becomes even more obvious as soon as they try to use the theory as a matter of explanation, a use which is the *raison d'être* of the theory. From this point on philosophers have said very different things: some that everything is changing and complex; others that nothing is; some that everything is describable in terms of physical laws; others that nothing is; some that existence-monism, properly understood, leads to entity-monism, others that it does not. These various paths I cannot now follow; but if philosophy can really show, by its own peculiar arguments, not by experimental inference or by mathematical deduction (and surely I have used neither of these), that dualism is untenable, it has made a contribution of the first importance, sufficient by itself to dispel the view that philosophy is either no more than personal vision or no more than analysis.

5

C. D. BROAD

(1887–)

*Mind / Body: Two-Sided Interaction**

Broad has written extensively in many areas of philosophy, but he is perhaps best known for his works in the area of philosophical psychology. He is a dualist and in this essay he attempts to defend the theory of interactionism, the idea that the mind and the body act upon each other though they are irreducible entities. The two major sources of attack on the idea of interaction have been philosophical and scientific. Broad meets the objections of both types by showing how the philosophical arguments against interaction are inconclusive, while the scientific theories are not really incompatible with the dualist position. Compare Broad's arguments with those of Passmore and Taylor.

THERE is a question which has been argued about for some centuries now under the name of "Interaction"; this is the question whether minds really do act on the organisms which they animate, and whether organisms really do act on the minds which animate them. (I must point out at once that I imply no particular theory of mind or body by the word "to animate". I use it as a perfectly neutral name to express the fact that a certain mind is connected in some peculiarly intimate way with a certain body and under normal conditions with no other body. This is a fact even on a purely behaviouristic theory of mind; on such a view to say that the mind M animates the body B would mean that the body B, in so far as it behaves in certain ways, *is* the mind M. A body which did not act in these ways would be said not to be animated by a mind. And a different Body B′, which acted in the same general way as B, would be said to be animated by a different mind M′.)

The problem of Interaction is generally discussed at the level of enlightened common-sense; where it is assumed that we know pretty well what we mean by "mind", by "matter" and by "causation". Obviously no solution which is reached at that level can claim to be ultimate. If what we call "matter" should turn out to be a collection of spirits of low intelligence, as Leibniz thought, the argument that mind and body are so unlike that their interaction is impossible would be-

* C. D. Broad, *The Mind and Its Place in Nature* (London: 1925), Chap. III, pp. 95–113. Reprinted by permission of Routledge & Kegan Paul Ltd.

come irrelevant. Again, if causation be nothing but regular sequence and concomitance, as some philosophers have held, it is ridiculous to regard psychoneural parallelism and interaction as mutually exclusive alternatives. For interaction will mean no more than parallelism, and parallelism will mean no less than interaction. Nevertheless I am going to discuss the arguments here at the common-sense level, because they are so incredibly bad and yet have imposed upon so many learned men.

We start then by assuming a developed mind and a developed organism as two distinct things, and by admitting that the two are now intimately connected in some way or other which I express by saying that "this mind *animates* this organism". We assume that bodies are very much as enlightened common-sense believes them to be; and that, even if we cannot define "causation", we have some means of recognising when it is present and when it is absent. The question then is: "Does a mind ever act on the body which it animates, and does a body ever act on the mind which animates it?" The answer which common-sense would give to both questions is: "Yes, certainly." On the face of it my body acts on my mind whenever a pin is stuck into the former and a painful sensation thereupon arises in the latter. And, on the face of it, my mind acts on my body whenever a desire to move my arm arises in the former and is followed by this movement in the latter. Let us call this common-sense view "Two-sided Interaction". Although it seems so obvious it has been denied by probably a majority of philosophers and a majority of physiologists. So the question is: "Why should so many distinguished men, who have studied the subject, have denied the apparently obvious fact of Two-sided Interaction?"

The arguments against Two-sided Interaction fall into two sets:—Philosophical and Scientific. We will take the philosophical arguments first; for we shall find that the professedly scientific arguments come back in the end to the principles or prejudices which are made explicit in the philosophical arguments.

Philosophical Arguments Against Two-sided Interaction

No one can deny that there is a close correlation between certain bodily events and certain mental events, and conversely. Therefore anyone who denies that there is action of mind on body and of body on mind must presumbaly hold (*a*) that concomitant variation is not an adequate criterion of causal connexion, and (*b*) that the other feature which is essential for causal connexion is absent in the case of body and mind. Now the common philosophical argument is that minds and mental events are so extremely unlike bodies and bodily states that it is inconceivable that the two should be causally connected. It is certainly true that, if minds and mental events are just what they seem to be to introspection and nothing more, and if bodies and bodily events are just what enlightened common-sense thinks them to be and nothing more, the two *are* extremely unlike. And this fact is supposed to show that, however closely correlated certain pairs of events in mind and body respectively may be, they cannot be causally connected.

Evidently the assumption at the back of this argument is that concomitant variation, together with a high enough degree of likeness, is an adequate test for causation; but that no amount of concomitant variation can establish causation in the absence of a high enough degree of likeness. Now I am inclined to admit part of this assumption. I think it is practically certain that causation does not simply *mean* concomitant variation. (And, if it did, *cadit quœstio.*) Hence the existence of the latter is not *ipso facto* a proof of the presence of the former. Again, I think it is almost certain that concomitant variation between A and B is not in fact a sufficient sign of the presence of a *direct* causal relation between the two. (I think it may perhaps be a sufficient sign of *either* a direct causal relation between A and B *or* of several causal relations which indirectly unite A and B through the medium of other terms C, D, etc.) So far I agree with the assumptions of the argument. But I cannot see the least reason to think that the other characteristic, which must be added to concomitant variation before we can be sure that A and B are causally connected, is a high degree of likeness between the two. One would like to know just how unlike two events may be before it becomes impossible to admit the existence of a causal relation between them. No one hesitates to hold that draughts and colds in the head are causally connected, although the two are extremely unlike each other. If the unlikeness of draughts and colds in the head does not prevent one from admitting a causal connexion between the two, why should the unlikeness of volitions and voluntary movements prevent one from holding that they are causally connected? To sum up. I am willing to admit that an adequate criterion of causal connexion needs some other relation between a pair of events beside concomitant variation; but I do not believe for a moment that this other relation is that of qualitative likeness.

This brings us to a rather more refined form of the argument against Interaction. It is said that, whenever we admit the existence of a causal relation between two events, these two events (to put it crudely) must also form parts of a single substantial whole. *E.g.*, all physical events are spatially related and form one great extended whole. And the mental events which would commonly be admitted to be causally connected are always events in a single mind. A mind is a substantial whole of a peculiar kind too. Now it is said that between bodily events and mental events there are no relations such as those which unite physical events in different parts of the same Space or mental events in the history of the same mind. In the absence of such relations, binding mind and body into a single substantial whole, we cannot admit that bodily and mental events can be causally connected with each other, no matter how closely correlated their variations may be.

This is a much better argument than the argument about qualitative likeness and unlikeness. If we accept the premise that causal relations can subsist only between terms which form parts of a single substantial whole must we deny that mental and bodily events can be causally connected? I do not think that we need. (i) It is of course perfectly true that an organism and the mind which animates it do not form a physical whole, and that they do not form a mental whole; and these, no doubt, are the two kinds of substantial whole with which we are most familiar. But it does not follow that a mind and its organism do not form a substantial whole of *some* kind. There, plainly, is the extraordinarily intimate union between the two which I have called "animation" of one by the other. Even if the mind be just what it seems to introspection, and the body be just what it seems to perception aided by the more precise methods of science, this seems to me to be enough to make a mind and its body a substantial whole. Even so extreme a dualist about Mind and Matter as Descartes occasionally suggests that a mind and its body together form a quasi-substance; and, although we may quarrel with the language of the very numerous philosophers who have said that the mind is "the form" of its body, we must admit that such langauge would never have seemed plausible unless a mind and its body together had formed something very much like a single substantial whole.

(ii) We must, moreover, admit the possibility that minds and mental events have properties and relations which do not reveal themselves to introspection, and that bodies and bodily events may have properties and relations which do not reveal themselves to perception or to physical and chemical experiment. In virtue of these properties and relations the two together may well form a single substantial whole of the kind which is alleged to be needed for causal interaction. Thus, if we accept the premise of the argument, we have no right to assert that mind and body *cannot* interact; but only the much more modest proposition that introspection and perception do not suffice to assure us that mind and body are so interrelated that they *can* interact.

(iii) We must further remember that the Two-sided Interactionist is under no obligation to hold that the *complete* conditions of any mental event are bodily or that the complete conditions of any bodily event are mental. He needs only to assert that some mental events include certain bodily events among their necessary conditions, and that some bodily events include certain mental events among their necessary conditions. If I am paralysed my volition may not move my arm; and, if I am hypnotised or intensely interested or frightened, a wound may not produce a painful sensation. Now, if the complete cause and the complete effect in all interaction include both a bodily and a mental factor, the two wholes will be related by the fact that the mental constituents belong to a single mind, that the bodily constituents belong to a single body, and that this mind animates this body. This amount of connexion should surely be enough to allow of causal interaction.

This will be the most appropriate place to deal with the contention that, in voluntary action, and there only, we are immediately acquainted with an instance of causal connexion. If this be true the controversy is of course settled at once in favour of the Interactionist. It is generally supposed that this view was refuted once and for all by Mr. Hume in his *Enquiry concerning Human Understanding* (Sect. VII, Part I). I should not care to assert that the doctrine in question is true; but I do think that it is plausible, and I am quite sure that

Mr. Hume's arguments do not refute it. Mr. Hume uses three closely connected arguments. (1) The connexion between a successful volition and the resulting bodily movement is as mysterious and as little self-evident as the connexion between any other event and its effect. (2) We have to learn from experience which of our volitions will be effective and which will not. *E.g.*, we do not know, until we have tried, that we can voluntarily move our arms and cannot voluntarily move our livers. And again, if a man were suddenly paralysed, he would still expect to be able to move his arm voluntarily, and would be surprised when he found it kept still in spite of his volition. (3) We have discovered that the immediate consequence of a volition is a change in our nerves and muscles, which most people know nothing about; and it is not the movement of a limb, which most people believe to be its immediate and necessary consequence.

The second and third arguments are valid only against the contention that we know immediately that a volition to make a certain movement is the *sufficient* condition for the happening of that movement. They are quite irrelevant to the contention that we know immediately that the volition is a *necessary* condition for the happening of just that movement at just that time. No doubt many other conditions are also necessary, *e.g.*, that our nerves and muscles shall be in the right state; and these other necessary conditions can be discovered only by special investigation. Since our volitions to move our limbs are in fact followed in the vast majority of cases by the willed movement, and since the other necessary conditions are not very obvious, it is natural enough that we should think that we know immediately that our volition is the *sufficient* condition of the movement of our limbs. If we think so, we are certainly wrong; and Mr. Hume's arguments prove that we are. But they prove nothing else. It does not follow that we are wrong in thinking that we know, without having to wait for the result, that the volition is a *necessary* condition of the movement.

It remains to consider the first argument. Is the connexion between cause and effect as mysterious and as little self-evident in the case of the voluntary production of bodily movement as in all other cases? If so, we must hold that the first time a baby wills to move its hand it is just as much surprised to find its hand moving as it would be to find its leg moving or its nurse bursting into flames. I do not profess to know anything about the infant mind; but it seems to me that this is a wildly paradoxical consequence, for which there is no evidence or likelihood. But there is no need to leave the matter there. It is perfectly plain that, in the case of volition and voluntary movement, there *is* a connexion between the cause and the effect which is not present in other cases of causation, and which does make it plausible to hold that in this one case the nature of the effect can be foreseen by merely reflecting on the nature of the cause. The peculiarity of a volition as a cause-factor is that it involves as an essential part of it the idea of the effect. To say that a person has a volition to move his arm involves saying that he has an idea of his arm (and not of his leg or his liver) and an idea of the position in which he wants his arm to be. It is simply silly in view of this fact to say that there is no closer connexion between the desire to move my arm and the movement of my arm than there is between this desire and the movement of my leg or my liver. We cannot detect any analogous connexion between cause and effect in causal transactions which we view wholly from outside, such as the movement of a billiard-ball by a cue. It is therefore by no means unreasonable to suggest that, in the one case of our own voluntary movements, we can see without waiting for the result that such and such a volition is a necessary condition of such and such a bodily movement.

It seems to me then that Mr. Hume's arguments on this point are absolutely irrelevant, and that it may very well be true that in volition we positively know that our desire for such and such a bodily movement is a necessary (though not a sufficient) condition of the happening of just that movement at just that time. On the whole then I conclude that the philosophical arguments certainly do not disprove Two-sided Interaction, and that they do not even raise any strong presumption against it. And, while I am not prepared definitely to commit myself to the view that, in voluntary movement, we positively *know* that the mind acts on the body, I do think that this opinion is quite plausible when properly stated and that the arguments which have been brought against it are worthless. I pass therefore to the scientific arguments.

Scientific Arguments Against Two-sided Interaction

There are, so far as I know, two of these. One is supposed to be based on the physical principle of the Conservation of Energy, and on certain experiments which have been made on human bodies. The other is based on the close analogy which is said to exist between the structures of the physiological mechanism of reflex action and that of vountary action. I will take them in turn.

(1) The Argument from Energy

It will first be needful to state clearly what is asserted by the principle of the Conservation of Energy. It is found that, if we take certain material systems, *e.g.*, a gun, a cartridge, and a bullet, there is a certain magnitude which keeps approximately constant throughout all their changes. This is called "Energy". When the gun has not been fired it and the bullet have no motion, but the explosive in the cartridge has great chemical energy. When it has been fired the bullet is moving very fast and has great energy of movement. The gun, though not moving fast in its recoil, has also great energy of movement because it is very massive. The gases produced by the explosion have some energy of movement and some heat-energy, but much less chemical energy than the unexploded charge had. These various kinds of energy can be measured in common units according to certain conventions. To an innocent mind there seems to be a good deal of "cooking" at this stage, *i.e.*, the conventions seem to be chosen and various kinds and amounts of concealed energy seem to be postulated in order to make the principle come out right at the end. I do not propose to go into this in detail, for two reasons. In the first place, I think that the conventions adopted and the postulates made, though somewhat suggestive of the fraudulent company-promoter, can be justified by their coherence with certain experimental facts, and that they are not simply made *ad hoc.* Secondly, I shall show that the Conservation of Energy is absolutely irrelevant to the question at issue, so that it would be a waste of time to treat it too seriously in the present connexion. Now it is found that the total energy of all kinds in this system, when measured according to these conventions, is approximately the same in amount though very differently distributed after the explosion and before it. If we had confined our attention to a part of this system and *its* energy this would not have been true. The bullet, *e.g.*, had no energy at all before the explosion and a great deal afterwards. A system like the bullet, the gun, and the charge is called a "Conservative System"; the bullet alone, or the gun and the charge, would be called "Non-conservative Systems". A conservative system might therefore be defined as one whose total energy is redistributed, but not altered in amount, by changes that happen within it. Of course a given system might be conservative for some kinds of change and not for others.

So far we have merely defined a "Conservative System", and admitted that there are systems which, for some kinds of change at any rate, answer approximately to our defiinition. We can now state the Principle of the Conservation of Energy in terms of the conceptions just defined. The principle asserts that every material system is either itself conservative, or, if not, is part of a larger material system which is conservative. We may take it that there is good inductive evidence for this proposition.

The next thing to consider is the experiments on the human body. These tend to prove that a living body, with the air that it breathes and the food that it eats, forms a conservative system to a high degree of approximation. We can measure the chemical energy of the food given to a man, and that which enters his body in the form of Oxygen breathed in. We can also, with suitable apparatus, collect, measure and analyse the air breathed out, and thus find its chemical energy. Similarly, we can find the energy given out in bodily movement, in heat, and in exertion. It is alleged that, on the average, whatever the man may do, the energy of his bodily movements is exactly accounted for by the energy given to him in the form of food and of Oxygen. If you take the energy put in food and Oxygen, and subtract the energy given out in waste-products, the balance is almost exactly equal to the energy put out in bodily movements. Such slight differences as are found are as often on one side as on the other, and are therefore probably due to unavoidable experimental errors. I do not propose to criticise the interpretation of these experiments in detail, because, as I shall show soon, they are completely irrelevant to the problem of whether mind and body interact. But there is just one point that I will make before passing on. It is perfectly clear that such experiments can tell us only what happens on the average over a long time. To know whether the balance was accurately kept at every moment we should have to kill the patient at each moment and analyse his body so as to find out the energy present then in the form of stored-up products. Obviously we cannot keep on killing the patient in order to analyse him, and then reviving him in order to go on with the experiment. Thus it would seem that the results of the experiment are perfectly compatible with the presence of quite large excesses or defects in the total bodily energy at certain moments, provided that these average out over longer periods. However, I do not want to press this criticism; I am quite ready to accept for our present purpose the traditional interpretation which has been put on the experiments.

We now understand the physical principle and the experimental facts. The two together are generally supposed to prove that mind and body cannot interact. What precisely is the argument, and is it valid? I imagine that the argument, when fully stated, would run somewhat as follows: "I will to move my arm, and it moves. If the volition has anything to do with causing the movement we might expect energy to flow from my mind to my body. Thus the energy of my body ought to receive a measurable increase, not accounted for by the food that I eat and the Oxygen that I breathe. But no such physically unaccountable increases of bodily energy are found. Again, I tread on a tin-tack, and a painful sensation arises in my mind. If treading on the tack has anything to do with causing the sensation we might expect energy to flow from my body to my mind. Such energy would cease to be measurable. Thus there ought to be a noticeable decrease in my bodily energy, not balanced by increases anywhere in the physical system. But such unbalanced decreases of bodily energy are not found." So it is concluded that the volition has nothing to do with causing my arm to move, and that treading on the tack has nothing to do with causing the painful sensation.

Is this argument valid? In the first place it is important to notice that the conclusion does not follow from the Conservation of Energy and the experimental facts alone. The real premise is a tacitly assumed proposition about causation; viz., that, if a change in A has anything to do with causing a change in B, energy must leave A and flow into B. This is neither asserted nor entailed by the Conservation of Energy. What *it* says is that, *if* energy leaves A, it must appear in something else, say B; so that A and B together form a conservative system. Since the Conservation of Energy is not itself the premise for the argument against Interaction, and since it does not entail that premise, the evidence for the Conservation of Energy is not evidence against Interaction. Is there any independent evidence for the premise? We may admit that it *is* true of many, though not of all, transactions within the physical realm. But there are cases where it is not true even of purely physical transactions; and, even if it were always true in the physical realm, it would not follow that it must also be true of trans-physical causation. Take the case of a weight swinging at the end of a string hung from a fixed point. The total energy of the weight is the same at all positions in its course. It is thus a conservative system. But at every moment the direction and velocity of the weight's motion are different, and the proportion between its kinetic and its potential energy is constantly changing. These changes are caused by the pull of the string, which acts in a different direction at each different moment. The string makes no difference to the total energy of the weight; but it makes all the difference in the world to the particular way in which the energy is distributed between the potential and the kinetic forms. This is evident when we remember that the weight would begin to move in an utterly different course if at any moment the string were cut.

Here, then, we have a clear case even in the physical realm where a system is conservative but is continually acted on by something which affects its movement and the distribution of its total energy. Why should not the mind act on the body in this way? If you say that you can see how a string can affect the movement of a weight, but cannot see how a volition could affect the movement of a material particle, you have deserted the scientific argument and have gone back to one of the philosophical arguments. Your real difficulty is either that volitions are so very unlike movements, or that the volition is in your mind whilst the movement belongs to the physical realm. And we have seen how little weight can be attached to these objections.

The fact is that, even in purely physical systems, the Conservation of Energy does not explain what changes will happen or when they will happen. It merely imposes a very general limiting condition on the changes that are possible. The fact that the system composed of bullet, charge, and gun, in our earlier example, is conservative does not tell us that the gun ever will be fired, or when it will be fired if at all, or what will cause it to go off, or what forms of energy will appear if and when it does go off. The change in this case is determined by pulling the trigger. Likewise the mere fact that the human body and its neighbourhood form a conservative system does not explain any particular bodily movement; it does not explain why I ever move at all, or why I sometimes write, sometimes walk, and sometimes swim. To explain the happening of these particular movements at certain times it seems to be essential to take into account the volitions which happen from time to time in my mind; just as it is essential to take the string into account to explain the particular behaviour of the weight, and to take the trigger into account to explain the going off of the gun at a certain moment. The difference between the gun-system and the body-system is that a little energy does flow into the former when the trigger is pulled, whilst it is alleged that none does so when a volition starts a bodily movement. But there is not even this amount of difference between the body-system and the swinging weight.

Thus the argument from energy has no tendency to disprove Two-sided Interaction. It has gained a spurious authority from the august name of the Conservation of Energy. But this impressive principle proves to have nothing to do with the case. And the real premise of the argument is not self-evident, and is not universally true even in purely intra-physical transactions. In the end this scientific argument has to lean on the old philosophic arguments; and we have seen that these are but bruised reeds. Nevertheless, the facts brought forward by the argument from energy do throw some light on the *nature* of the interaction between mind and body, assuming this to happen. They do suggest that all the energy of our bodily actions comes out of and goes back into the physical world, and that minds neither add energy to nor abstract it from the latter. What they do, if they do anything, is to determine that at a given moment so much energy shall change from the chemical form to the form of bodily movement; and they determine this, so far as we can see, without altering the total amount of energy in the physical world.

(2) The Argument from the Structure of the Nervous System

There are purely reflex actions, like sneezing and blinking, in which there is no reason to suppose that the mind plays any essential part. Now we know the nervous structure which is used in such acts as these. A stimulus is given to the outer end of an efferent nerve; some change or other runs up this nerve, crosses a synapsis between this and an afferent nerve, travels down the latter to a muscle, causes the muscle to contract, and so produces a bodily movement. There seems no reason to believe that the mind plays any essential part in this process. The process may be irreducibly vital, and not merely physico-chemical; but there seems no need to assume anything more than this. Now it is said that the whole nervous system is simply an immense complication of interconnected nervous arcs. The result is that a change which travels inwards has an immense number of alternative paths by which it may travel outwards. Thus the reaction to a given stimulus is no longer one definite movement, as in the simple reflex. Almost any movement may follow any stimulus according to the path which the afferent disturbance happens to take. This path will depend on the relative resistance of the various synapses at the time. Now a variable response to the same stimulus is characteristic of deliberate as opposed to reflex action.

These are the facts. The argument based on them runs as follows. It is admitted that the mind has nothing to do with the causation of purely reflex actions. But the nervous structure and the nervous processes involved in deliberate action do not differ in kind from those involved in reflex action; they differ only in degree of complexity. The variability which characterizes deliberate action is fully explained by the variety of alternative paths and the variable resistances of the synapses. So it is unreasonable to suppose that the mind has any more to do with causing deliberate actions than it has to do with causing reflex actions.

I think that this argument is invalid. In the first place I am pretty sure that the persons who use it have before their imagination a kind of picture of how mind and body must interact if they interact at all. They find that the facts do not answer to this picture, and so they conclude that there is no interaction. The picture is of the following kind.

They think of the mind as sitting somewhere in a hole in the brain, surrounded by telephones. And they think of the efferent disturbance as coming to an end at one of these telephones and there affecting the mind. The mind is then supposed to respond by sending an afferent impulse down another of these telephones. As no such hole, with efferent nerves stopping at its walls and afferent nerves starting from them, can be found, they conclude that the mind can play no part in the transaction. But another alternative is that this picture of how the mind must act if it acts at all is wrong. To put it shortly, the mistake is to confuse a gap in an explanation with a spatio-temporal gap, and to argue from the absence of the latter to the absence of the former.

The Interactionist's contention is simply that there is a gap in any purely physiological explanation of deliberate action; *i.e.*, that all such explanations fail to account completely for the facts because they leave out one necessary condition. It does not follow in the least that there must be a spatio-temporal breach of continuity in the physiological conditions, and that the missing condition must fill this gap in the way in which the movement of a wire fills the spatio-temporal interval between the pulling of a bell-handle and the ringing of a distant bell. To assume this is to make the mind a kind of physical object, and to make its action a kind of mechanical action. Really, the mind and its actions are not literally in Space at all, and the time which is occupied by the mental event is no doubt *also* occupied by some part of the physiological process. Thus I am inclined to think that much of the force which this argument actually exercises on many people is simply due to the presupposition about the *modus operandi* of interaction, and that it is greatly weakened when this presupposition is shown to be a mere prejudice due to our limited power of envisaging unfamiliar alternative possibilities.

We can, however, make more detailed objections to the argument than this. There is a clear introspective difference between the mental accompaniment of voluntary action and that of reflex action. What goes on in our minds when we decide with difficulty to get out of a hot bath on a cold morning is obviously extremely different from what goes on in our minds when we sniff pepper and sneeze. And the difference is qualitative; it is not a mere difference of complexity. This difference has to be explained somehow; and the theory under discussion gives no plausible explanation of it. The ordinary view that, in the latter case, the mind is not acting on the body at all; whilst, in the former, it is acting on the body in a specific way, does at least make the introspective difference between the two intelligible.

Again, whilst it is true that deliberate action differs from reflex action in its greater variability of response to the same stimulus, this is certainly not the whole or the most important part of the difference between them. The really important difference is that, in deliberate action, the response is varied *appropriately* to meet the special circumstances which are supposed to exist at the time or are expected to arise later; whilst reflex action is not varied in this way, but is blind and almost mechanical. The complexity of the nervous system explains the *possibility* of variation; it does not in the least explain why the alternative which actually takes place should as a rule be appropriate and not merely haphazard. And so again it seems as if some factor were in operation in deliberate action which is not present in reflex action; and it is reasonable to suppose that this factor is the volition in the mind.

It seems to me that this second scientific argument has no tendency to disprove interaction; but that the facts which it brings forward do tend to suggest the particular form which interaction probably takes if it happens at all. They suggest that what the mind does to the body in voluntary action, if it does anything, is to lower the resistance of certain synapses and to raise that of others. The result is that the nervous current follows such a course as to produce the particular movement which the mind judges to be appropriate at the time. On such a view the difference between reflex, habitual, and deliberate actions for the present purpose becomes fairly plain. In pure reflexes the mind cannot voluntarily affect the resistance of the synapses concerned, and so the action takes place in spite of it. In habitual action it deliberately refrains from interfering with the resistance of the synapses, and so the action goes on like a complicated reflex. But it *can* affect these resistances if it wishes, though often only with difficulty; and it is ready to do so if it judges this to be expedient. Finally, it may lose the power altogether. This would be what happens when a person becomes a slave to some habit, such as drug-taking.

I conclude that, at the level of enlightened common-sense at which the ordinary discussion of Interaction moves, no good reason has been produced for doubting that the mind acts on the body in volition, and that the body acts on the mind in sensation. The philosophic arguments are quite inconclusive; and the scientific arguments, when properly understood, are quite compatible with Two-sided Interaction. At most they suggest certain conclusions as to the form which interaction probably takes if it happens at all.

6

H. H. PRICE

(1899–)

*Survival and the Idea of "Another World"**

Professor Price of Oxford University has been influential in contemporary philosophy in the area of epistemology (theory of knowledge). In this article, he deals with the Survival Hypothesis: the theory that man can survive death. Price is not involved in establishing empirical criteria to decide the issue. He is seeking to understand what is involved in the concept of personal survival of death and whether or not such an idea is intelligible to us. In other words, Price is trying to make sense of the concepts involved; he is trying to find relationships between what we know to be the case and what we believe about survival of death. Price's analysis starts with the common experience of dreams from which he thinks an analogy to survival can be drawn. Survival would have to take place in some world or other. Price sees the intelligibility of the hypothesis as resting on our ability to give some reasonable account of "Another World." He tries to establish that the dream world provides the model for our thinking about other worlds.

Upon learning of the Kidd Will, Professor Price commented that Mr. Kidd might have wanted a photograph of a so-called "extra body" said to exist by those who have claimed "out-of-body experiences." Price wrote: "The idea is, I think that each of us has this 'extra body' all the time and that normally it is coincident with, or interpenetrates, the physical organism. It is also alleged to be quite different from the 'astral body' which is supposed to be the permanent 'vehicle of the soul' in its post mortum *existence. Apparently it is supposed to leave the physical organism at death. But after a while it disintegrates, whereas the 'astral body' continues. So even if it were photographed this would hardly give Mr. Kidd what he wanted: and even the 'astral body' (if there is such a thing) couldn't be identified with the soul. Nor could it be photographed, for it would surely be in another space."*

* From *Proceedings of the Society for Psychical Research,* Vol. L, Pt. 182 (January, 1953) pp. 1–25. Reprinted by kind permission of the editor and the author.

THIS year is the seventieth anniversary of the foundation of the Society for Psychical Research. From the very beginning, the problem of survival has been one of the main interests of the Society; and that is my excuse, if any excuse is needed, for discussing some aspects of the problem this evening. I shall not, however, talk about the evidence for survival. In this lecture I am concerned only with the conception of survival; with the *meaning* of the Survival Hypothesis, and not with its truth or falsity. When we consider the Survival Hypothesis, whether we believe it or disbelieve it, what is it that we have in mind? Can we form any idea, even a rough and provisional one, of what a disembodied human life might be like? Supposing we cannot, it will follow that what is called the Survival Hypothesis is a mere set of words and not a hypothesis at all. The evidence adduced in favour of it might still be evidence for something, and perhaps for something important, but we should no longer have the right to claim that it is evidence for survival. There cannot be evidence for something which is completely unintelligible to us.

Evidence for Survival

Now let us consider the situation in which we find ourselves after seventy years of psychical research. A very great deal of work has been done on the problem of survival, and much of the best work by members of our Society. Yet there are the widest differences of opinion about the results. A number of intelligent persons would maintain that we now have a very large mass of evidence in favour of survival; that some of it is of very good quality indeed, and cannot be explained away unless we suppose that the super-normal cognitive powers of some embodied human minds are vastly more extensive and more accurate than we can easily believe them to be; in short, that on the evidence available the Survival Hypothesis is more probable than not. Some people—and not all of them are silly or credulous—would even maintain that the Survival Hypothesis is proved, or as near to being so as any empirical hypothesis can be. On the other hand, there are also many intelligent persons who entirely reject these conclusions. Some of them, no doubt, have not taken the trouble to examine the evidence. But others of them have; they may even have given years of study to it. They would agree that the evidence is evidence of *something*, and very likely of something important. But, they would say, it cannot be evidence of survival; there *must* be some alternative explanation of it, however difficult it may be to find out. Why do they take this line? I think it is because they find the very conception of survival unintelligible. The very idea of a "discarnate human personality" seems to them a muddled or absurd one; indeed not an idea at all, but just a phrase—an emotionally exciting one, no doubt—to which no clear meaning can be given.

Moreover, we cannot just ignore the people who have not examined the evidence. Some of our most intelligent and most highly educated contemporaries are among them. These men are well aware, by this time, that the evidence does exist, even if their predecessors fifty years ago were not. If you asked them why they do not trouble to examine it in detail, they would be able to offer reasons for their attitude. And one of their reasons, and not the least weighty in their eyes, is the contention I mentioned just now, that the very idea of survival is a muddled or absurd one. To borrow an example from Whately Carington, we know pretty well what we mean by asking whether Jones has survived a shipwreck. We are asking whether he continues to live after the shipwreck has occurred. Similarly it makes sense to ask whether he survived a railway accident, or the bombing of London. But if we substitute "his own death" for "a shipwreck," and ask whether he has survived it, our question (it will be urged) becomes unintelligible. Indeed, it *looks* self-contradictory, as if we were asking whether Jones is still alive at a time when he is no longer alive—whether Jones is both alive and not alive at the same time. We may try to escape from this logical absurdity by using phrases like "discarnate existence," "alive, but disembodied." But such phrases, it will be said, have no clear meaning. No amount of facts, however well established, can have the slightest tendency to support a meaningless hypothesis, or to answer an unintelligible question. It would therefore be a waste of time to examine such facts in detail. There are other and more important things to do.

If I am right so far, questions about the meaning of the word "survival" or of the phrase "life after death" are not quite so arid and academic as they may appear. Anyone who wants to maintain that there is empirical evidence for survival ought to consider these questions, whether he thinks the evidence strong or weak. Indeed, anyone who thinks there is a *problem* of survival at all should ask himself what his conception of survival is.

The Importance of an Idea of "Another World"

Now why should it be thought that the very idea of life after death is unintelligible? Surely it is easy enough to conceive (whether or not it is true) that experiences might occur after Jones's death which are linked with experiences which he had before his death, in such a way that his personal identity is preserved? But, it will be said, the idea of after-death *experiences* is just the difficulty. What kind of experiences could they conceivably be? In a disembodied state, the supply of sensory stimuli is perforce cut off, because the supposed experient has no sense organs and no nervous system. There can therefore be no sense-perception. One has no means of being aware of material objects any longer; and if one has not, it is hard to see how one could have any emotions or wishes either. For all the emotions and wishes we have in this present life are concerned directly or indirectly with material objects, including of course our own organisms and other organisms, especially other human ones. In short, one could only be said to have experiences at all, if one is aware of some sort of a *world*. In this way, the idea of survival is bound up with the idea of "another world" or a "next world." Anyone who maintains that the idea of survival is after all intelligible must also be claiming that we can form some conception, however rough and provisional, of what "the next world" or "the other world" might be like. The skeptics I have in mind would say that we can form no such conception at all; and this, I think, is one of the main reasons why they hold that the conception of survival itself is unintelligible. I wish to suggest, on the contrary, that we *can* form some conception, in outline at any rate, of what a "next world" or "another world" might be like, and consequently of the kind of experiences which disembodied minds, if indeed there are such, might be supposed to have.

The thoughts which I wish to put before you on this subject are not at all original. Something very like them is to be found in the chapter on survival in Whately Carington's book *Telepathy*,* and in the concluding chapter of Professor C. J. Ducasse's book *Nature, Mind and Death*.† Moreover, if I am not mistaken, the Hindu conception of *Kama Loka* (literally, "the world of desire") is essentially the same as the one I wish to discuss; and something very similar is to be found in Mahayana Buddhism. In these two religions, of course, there is not just one "other world" but several different "other worlds," which we are supposed to experience in succession; not merely the next world, but the next but one, and another after that. But I think it will be quite enough for us to consider just the next world, without troubling ourselves about any additional other worlds which there might be. It is a sufficiently difficult task, for us Western people, to convince ourselves that it makes sense to speak of any sort of after-death world at all. Accordingly, with your permission, I shall use the expressions "next world" and "other world" interchangeably. If anyone thinks this is an oversimplification, it will be easy for him to make the necessary corrections.

The Next World as Analogous to the Dream-world

The next world, I think, might be conceived as a kind of dream-world. When we are asleep, sensory stimuli are cut off, or at any rate are prevented from having their normal effects upon our brain-centres. But we still manage to have experiences. It is true that sense-perception no longer occurs, but something sufficiently like it does. In sleep, our image-producing powers, which are more or less inhibited in waking life by a continuous bombardment of sensory stimuli, are released from this inhibition. And then we are provided with a multitude of objects of awareness, about which we employ our thoughts and towards which we have desires and emotions. These objects which we are aware of behave in a way which seems very queer to us when we wake up. The laws of their behaviour are not the laws of physics. But however queer their behaviour is, it does not at all disconcert us at the time and our personal identity is not broken.

A World of Mental Images

In other words, my suggestion is that the next world, if there is one, might be a world of mental images. Nor need such a world be so "thin and insubstantial" as you might think. Paradoxical as it may sound, there is nothing imaginary about a mental image. It is an actual entity, as real as anything can be. The seeming paradox arises from the ambiguity of the verb "to imagine." It does sometimes mean "to have mental images." But more usually it means "to entertain propositions without believing them"; and very often they are false propositions, and moreover we *dis*believe them in the act of entertaining them. This is what happens, for example, when we read Shakespeare's play *The Tempest*, and that is why we say that Prospero and Ariel are "imaginary characters." Mental images are not in this sense imaginary at all. We do actually experience them, and they are no more imaginary than sensa-

* Whately Carington, *Telepathy* (London: Methuen & Co., Ltd., 1945).

† C. J. Ducasse, *Nature, Mind and Death* (La Salle, Ill.: Open Court Publishing Co., 1951).

tions. To avoid the paradox, though at the cost of some pedantry, it would be well to distinguish between *imagining* and *imaging,* and to have two different adjectives "imaginary" and "imagy." In this terminology, it is imaging, and not imagining, that I wish to talk about; and the next world, as I am trying to conceive of it, is an *imagy* world, but not on that account an imaginary one.

Indeed, to those who experienced it an image-world would be just as "real" as this present world is; perhaps so like it, that they would have considerable difficulty in realizing that they were dead. We are, of course, sometimes told in mediumistic communications that quite a lot of people do find it difficult to realize that they are dead; and this is just what we should expect if the next world is an image-world. Lord Russell and other philosophers have maintained that a material object in this present physical world is nothing more nor less than a complicated system of *appearances.* So far as I can see, there might be a set of visual images related to each other perspectivally, with front views and side views and back views all fitting neatly together in the way that ordinary visual appearances do now. Such a group of images might contain tactual images too. Similarly it might contain auditory images and smell images. Such a family of interrelated images would make a pretty good object. It would be quite a satisfactory substitute for the material objects which we perceive in this present life. And a whole world composed of such families of mental images would make a perfectly good world.

It is possible, however, and indeed likely, that some of those images would be what Francis Galton called *generic* images. An image representing a dog or a tree need not necessarily be an exact replica of some individual dog or tree one has perceived. It might rather be a representation of a *typical* dog or tree. Our memories are more specific on some subjects than on others. How specific they are depends probably on the degree of interest we had in the individual objects or events at the time when we perceived them. An event which moved us deeply is likely to be remembered specifically and in detail; and so is an individual object to which we were much attached (for example, the home of our childhood). But with other objects which interested us less and were less attended to, we retain only a "general impression" of a whole class of objects collectively. Left to our own resources, as we should be in the other world, with nothing but our memories to depend on, we should probably be able to form only generic images of such objects. In this respect, an image-world would not be an exact replica of this one, not even of those parts of this one which we have actually perceived. To some extent it would be, so to speak, a generalized picture, rather than a detailed reproduction.

Imaging

Let us now put our question in another way, and ask what kind of experience a disembodied human mind might be supposed to have. We can then answer that it might be an experience in which *imaging* replaces sense-perception: "replaces" it, in the sense that imaging would perform much the same function as sense-perception performs now, by providing us with objects about which we could have thoughts, emotions and wishes. There is no reason why we should not be "as much alive," or at any rate *feel* as much alive, in an image-world as we do now in this present material world, which we perceive by means of our sense-organs and nervous systems. And so the use of the word "survival" ("life after death") would be perfectly justifiable.

Being or Feeling Alive in an Image-world

It will be objected, perhaps, that one cannot be said to be alive unless one has a body. But what is meant here by "alive"? It is surely conceivable (whether or not it is true) that *experiences* should occur which are not causally connected with a physical organism. If they did, should we or should we not say that "life" was occurring. I do not think it matters much whether we answer Yes or No. It is purely a question of definition. If you define "life" in terms of certain very complicated physico-chemical processes, as some people would, then of course life after death is by definition impossible, because there is no longer anything to be alive. In that case, the problem of survival (*life* after bodily death) is misnamed. Instead, it ought to be called the problem of after-death *experiences*. And this is in fact the problem with which all investigators of the subject have been concerned. After all, what people want to know, when they ask whether we survive death, is simply whether experiences occur after death, or what likelihood, if any, there is that they do; and whether such experiences, if they do occur, are linked with each other and with *ante mortem* ones in such a way that personal identity is preserved. It is not physico-chemical processes which interest us, when we ask such questions. But there is another sense of the words "life" and "alive" which may be called the psychological sense; and in this sense "being alive" just *means* "having experiences of certain sorts." In this psychological sense of the word "life," it is perfectly intelligible to ask whether there is life after death, even though life in the physiological sense does *ex hypothesi* come to an end when someone dies. Or, if you like, the question is whether one could *feel* alive after bodily death, even though (by hypothesis) one would not *be* alive at the time. It will be just enough to satisfy most of us if the *feeling* of being alive continues after death. It will not make a halfpennyworth of difference that one will not then *be* alive in the physiological or biochemical sense of the word.

It may be said, however, that "feeling alive" (life in the psychological sense) cannot just be equated with having experiences in general. Feeling alive, surely, consists in having experiences of a special sort, namely *organic sensations*—bodily feelings of various sorts. In our present experience, these bodily feelings are not as a rule separately attended to unless they are unusually intense or unusually painful. They are a kind of undifferentiated mass in the background of consciousness. All the same, it would be said, they constitute our feeling of being alive; and if they were absent (as surely they must be when the body is dead) the feeling of being alive could not be there.

I am not at all sure that this argument is as strong as it looks. I think we should still feel alive—or alive enough—provided we experienced emotions and wishes, even if no organic sensations accompanied these experiences, as they do now. But in case I am wrong here, I would suggest that *images* of organic sensations could perfectly well provide what is needed. We can quite well image to ourselves what it feels like to be in a warm bath, even when we are not actually in one; and a person who has been crippled can image what it felt like to climb a mountain. Moreover, I would ask whether we do not feel alive when we are dreaming. It seems to me that we obviously do—or at any rate quite alive enough to go on with.

Psychical Bodies

This is not all. In an image-world, a dream-like world such as I am trying to describe, there is no reason at all why there should not be *visual* images resembling the body which one had in this present world. In this present life (for all who are not blind) visual percepts of one's own body form as it were the constant centre of one's perceptual world. It is perfectly possible that visual images of one's own body might perform the same function in the next. They might form the continuing centre or nucleus of one's image world, remaining more or less constant while other images altered. If this were so, we should have an additional reason for expecting that recently dead people would find it difficult to realize that they were dead, that is, disembodied. To all appearances they *would* have bodies just as they had before, and pretty much the same ones. But, of course, they might discover in time that these image-bodies were subject to rather peculiar causal laws. For example, it might be found that in an image-world our wishes tend *ipso facto* to fulfil themselves in a way they do not now. A wish to go to Oxford might be immediately followed by the occurrence of a vivid and detailed set of Oxford-like images; even though, at the moment before, one's images had resembled Piccadilly Circus or the palace of the Dalai Lama in Tibet. In that case, one would realize that "going somewhere"—transferring one's body from one place to another—was a rather different process from what it had been in the physical world. Reflecting on such experiences, one might come to the conclusion that one's body was not after all the same as the physical body one had before death. One might conclude perhaps that it must be a "spiritual" or "psychical" body, closely resembling the old body in appearance, but possessed of rather different causal properties. It has been said, of course, that phrases like "spiritual body" or "psychical body" are utterly unintelligible, and that no conceivable empirical meaning could be given to such expressions. But I would rather suggest that they might be a way (rather a misleading way perhaps) of referring to a set of body-like images. If our supposed dead empiricist continued his investigations, he might discover that his whole world—not only his own body, but everything else he was aware of—had different causal properties from the physical world, even though everything in it had shape, size, colour, and other qualities which material objects have now. And so eventually, by the exercise of ordinary inductive good sense, he could draw the conclusion that he was in "the next world" or "the other world" and no longer in this one. If, however, he were a very dogmatic philosopher, who distrusted inductive good sense and preferred a priori reasoning, I do not know what condition he would be in. Probably he would never discover that he was dead at all. Being persuaded, on a priori grounds, that life after death was impossible, he might insist on thinking that he must still be in this world, and refuse to pay any attention to the new and strange causal laws which more empirical thinkers would notice.

I think, then, that there is no difficulty in conceiving that the experience of feeling alive could occur in the absence of a physical organism; or, if you prefer to put it so, a disembodied personality could *be* alive in the psychological sense, even though by definition it would not be alive in the physiological or biochemical sense.

Personal Identity and Disembodiment

Moreover, I do not see why disembodiment need involve the destruction of personal identity. It is, of course, sometimes supposed that personal identity depends on the continuance of a background of organic sensation—the "mass of bodily feeling" mentioned before. (This may be called the somato-centric analysis of personal identity.) We must notice, however, that this background of organic sensation is not literally the same from one period of time to another. The very most that can happen is that the organic sensations which form the background of my experience now should be *exactly similar* to those which were the background of my experience a minute ago. And as a matter of fact, the present ones need not *all* be exactly similar to the previous ones. I might have a twinge of toothache now which I did not have then. I may even have an over-all feeling of lassitude now which I did not have a minute ago, so that the whole mass of bodily feeling, and not merely part of it, is rather different; and this would not interrupt my personal identity at all. The most that is required is only that the majority (not all) of my organic sensations should be closely (not exactly) similar to those I previously had. And even this is only needed if the two occasions are close together in my private time series; the organic sensations I have now might well be very unlike those I used to have when I was one year old. I say "in my private times series." For when I wake up after eight hours of dreamless sleep my personal identity is not broken, though in the physical or public time series there has been a long interval between the last organic sensations I experienced before falling asleep, and the first ones I experience when I wake up. But if similarity, and not literal sameness, is all that is required of this "continuing organic background," it seems to me that the continuity of it could be perfectly well preserved if there were organic *images* after death very like the organic *sensations* which occurred before death.

As a matter of fact, this whole "somato-centric" analysis of personal identity appears to me highly disputable. I should have thought that Locke was much nearer the truth when he said that personal identity depends on memory. But I have tried to show that even if the "somato-centric" theory of personal identity is right, there is no reason why personal identity need be broken by bodily death, provided there are images after death which sufficiently resemble the organic sensations one had before; and this is very like what happens when one falls asleep and begins dreaming.

"People are What You Meet"

There is, however, another argument against the conceivability of a disembodied person, to which some present-day linguistic philosophers would attach great weight. It is neatly expressed by Mr. A. G. N. Flew when he says, "people are what you meet."* By "a person" we are supposed to mean a human organism which behaves in certain ways, and especially one which speaks and can be spoken to. And when we say, "this is the same person whom I saw yesterday," we are supposed to mean just that it is the same human organism which I saw yesterday, and also that it behaves in a recognizably similar way.

"People are what you meet." With all respect to Mr. Flew, I would suggest that he does not in this sense "meet" *himself*. He might indeed have had one of those curious out-of-body experiences which are occasionally mentioned in our records, and he might have seen his body from outside (if he has, I heartily congratulate him); but I do not think we should call this "meeting." And surely the important question is, what constitutes my personal identity *for myself*. It certainly does not consist in the fact that other people can "meet" me. It might be that I was for myself the same person as before, even at a time when it was quite impossible for others to meet me. No one can "meet" me when I am dreaming. They can, of course, come and look at my body lying in bed; but this is not "meeting," because no sort of social relations are possible between them and me. Yet, although temporarily "unmeetable," during my dreams I am still, for myself, the same person that I was. And if I went on dreaming *in perpetuum*, and could never be "met" again, this need not prevent me from continuing to be, for myself, the same person.

As a matter of fact, however, we can quite easily conceive that "meeting" of a kind might still be possible between discarnate experients. And therefore, even if we do make it part of the definition of "a person," that he is capable of being met by others, it will still make sense to speak of "discarnate persons," provided we allow that telepathy is possible between them. It is true that a special sort of telepathy would be needed; the sort which in life produces *telepathic apparitions*. It would not be sufficient that *A*'s thoughts or emotions should be telepathically affected by *B*'s. If such telepathy were sufficiently prolonged and continuous, and especially if it were reciprocal, it would indeed have some of the characteristics of social intercourse; but I do not think we should call it "meeting," at any rate in Mr. Flew's sense of the word. It would be necessary, in addition, that *A* should be aware of something which could be called "*B*'s body," or should have an experience not too

* *University*, Vol. II, No. 2, 38, in a symposium on "Death" with Professor D. M. Mackinnon. Mr. Flew obviously uses "people" as the plural of "person"; but if we are to be linguistic, I am inclined to think that the nuances of "people" are not quite the same as those of "person." When we used the word "person," in the singular or the plural, the notion of consciousness is more prominently before our minds than it is when we use the word "people."

unlike the experience of *seeing* another person in this life. This additional condition would be satisfied if *A* experienced a telepathic apparition of *B*. It would be necessary, further, that the telepathic apparition by means of which *B* "announces himself" (if one may put it so) should be recognizably similar on different occasions. And if it were a case of meeting some person *again* whom one had previously known in this world, the telepathic apparition would have to be recognizably similar to the physical body which that person had when he was still alive.

There is no reason why an image-world should not contain a number of images which are telepathic apparitions, and if it did, one could quite intelligently speak of "meeting other persons" in such a world. All the experiences I have when I meet another person in this present life could still occur, with only this difference, that percepts would be replaced by images. It would also be possible for another person to "meet" me in the same manner, if I, as a telepathic agent could cause him to experience a suitable telepathic apparition, sufficiently resembling the body I used to have when he formerly "met" me in this life.

The Space of the Next World

I now turn to another problem which may have troubled some of you. If there be a next world, *where* is it? Surely it must be somewhere. But there does not seem to be any room for it. We can hardly suppose that it is up in the sky (i.e., outside the earth's atmosphere) or under the surface of the earth, as Homer and Vergil seemed to think. Such suggestions may have contented our ancestors, and the Ptolemaic astronomy may have made them acceptable, for some ages, even to the learned; but they will hardly content us. Surely the next world, if it exists, must be somewhere; and yet, it seems, there is nowhere for it to be.

The answer to this difficulty is easy if we conceive of the next world in the way I have suggested, as a dream-like world of mental images. Mental images, including dream images, are in a space of their own. They do have spatial properties. Visual images, for instance, have extension and shape, and they have spatial relations to one another. But they have no spatial relation to objects in the physical world. If I dream of a tiger, my tiger-image has extension and shape. The dark stripes have spatial relation to the yellow parts, and to each other; the nose has a spatial relation to the tail. Again, the tiger image as a whole may have spatial relations to another image in my dream, for example to an image resembling a palm tree. But suppose we have to ask how far it is from the foot of my bed, whether it is three inches long, or longer or shorter; is it not obvious that these questions are absurd ones? We cannot answer them, not because we lack the necessary information or find it impracticable to make the necessary measurements, but because the questions themselves have no meaning. In the space of the physical world these images are nowhere at all. But in relation to other images of mine, each of them is somewhere. Each of them is extended, and its parts are in spatial relations to one another. There is no a priori reason why all extended entities must be in physical space.

If we now apply these considerations to the next world, as I am conceiving of it, we see that the question "where is it?" simply does not arise. An image-world would have a space of its own. We could not find it anywhere in the space of the physical world, but this would not in the least prevent it from being a spatial world all the same. If you like, it would be its own "where."

I am tempted to illustrate this point by referring to the fairy-tale of Jack and the Beanstalk. I am not of course suggesting that we should take the story seriously. But if we were asked to try to make sense of it, how should we set about it? Obviously the queer world which Jack found was not at the top of the beanstalk in the literal, spatial sense of the words "at the top of." Perhaps he found some very large pole rather like a beanstalk, and climbed up it. But (we shall say) when he got to the top he suffered an abrupt change of consciousness, and began to have a dream or waking vision of a strange country with a giant in it. To choose another and more respectable illustration: In Book VI of Vergil's *Aeneid,* we are told how Aeneas descended into the Cave of Avernus with the Sibyl and walked from there into the other world. If we wished to make the narrative of the illustrious poet intelligible, how should we set about it? We should suppose that Aeneas did go down into the cave, but that once he was there he suffered a change of consciousness, and all the strange experiences which happened afterwards—seeing the River Styx, the Elysian Fields and the rest—were part of a dream or vision which he had. The space he passed through in his journey was an image-space, and the River Styx was not three Roman miles, or any other number of miles, from the cave in which his body was.

"Passing" (Leaving) from This World to the Next: a Change of Consciousness

It follows that when we speak of "passing" from this world to the next, this passage is not to be thought of as any sort of movement in space. It should rather be thought of as a change of consciousness, analogous to the change which occurs when we "pass" from waking experience to dreaming. It would be a change from the perceptual type of consciousness to another type of consciousness in which perception ceases and imaging replaces it, but unlike the change from waking consciousness to dreaming in being irreversible. I suppose that nearly everyone nowadays who talks of "passing" from this world to the other does think of the transition in this way, as some kind of irreversible change of consciousness, and not as a literal spatial transition in which one goes from one place to another place.

The Image-world is a Real World

So much for the question "where the next world is," if there be one. I have tried to show that if the next world is conceived of as a world of mental images, the question simply does not arise. I now turn to another difficulty. It may be felt that an image-world is somehow a deception and a sham, not a *real* world at all. I have said that it would be a kind of dream-world. Now when one has a dream in this life, surely the things one is aware of in the dream are not *real* things. No doubt the dreamer really does have various mental images. These images do actually occur. But this is not all that happens. As a result of having these images, the dreamer believes, or takes for granted, that various material objects exist and various physical events occur; and these beliefs are mistaken. For example, he believes that there is a wall in front of him and that by a mere effort of will he succeeds in flying over the top of it. But the wall did not really exist, and he did not really fly over the top of it. He was in a state of delusion. Because of the images which he really did have, there *seemed* to him to be various objects and events which did not really exist at all. Similarly, you may argue, it may *seem* to discarnate minds (if indeed there are such) that there is a world in which they live, and a world not unlike this one. If they have mental images of the appropriate sort, it may even *seem* to them that they have bodies not unlike the ones they had in this life. But surely they will be mistaken. It is all very well to say, with the poet, that "dreams are real while they last"—that dream-objects are only called "unreal" when one wakes up, and normal sense-perceptions begin to occur with which the dream experiences can be contrasted. And it is all very well to conclude from this that if one did *not* wake up, if the change from sense-perception to imaging were irreversible, one would not call one's dream objects unreal, because there would then be nothing with which to contrast them. But would they not still *be* unreal for all that? Surely discarnate minds, according to my account of them, would be in a state of permanent delusion; whereas a dreamer in this life (fortunately for him) is only in a temporary one. And the fact that a delusion goes on for a long time, even forever and ever, does not make it any less delusive. Delusions do not turn themselves into realities just by going on and on. Nor are they turned into realities by the fact that their victim is deprived of the power of detecting their delusiveness.

Now, of course, if it were true that the next life (supposing there is one) is a condition of permanent delusion, we should just have to put up with it. We might not like it: we might think that a state of permanent delusion is a bad state to be in. But our likes and dislikes are irrelevant to the question. I would suggest, however, that this argument about the "delusiveness" or "unreality" of an image-world is based on confusion.

One may doubt whether there is any clear meaning in using the words "real" and "unreal" *tout court,* in this perfectly general and unspecified way. One may properly say, "this is real silver, and that is not," "this is a real pearl and that is not," or again "this is a real pool of water, and that is only a mirage." The point here is that something *X* is mistakenly believed to be something else *Y*, because it does resemble *Y* in some respects. It makes perfectly good sense, then, to say that *X* is not really *Y*. This piece of plated brass is not real silver, true enough. It only looks like silver. But for all that, it cannot be called "unreal" in the unqualified sense, in the sense of not existing at all. Even the mirage is something, though it is not the pool of water you took it to be. It is a perfectly good set of visual appearances, though it is not related to other appearances in the way you thought it was; for example, it does not have the relations to tactual appearances, or to visual appearances from other places, which you expected it to have. You may properly say that the mirage is not a real pool of water, or even that it is not a real physical object, and that anyone who thinks it is must be in a state of delusion. But there is no clear meaning in saying that it is just "unreal" *tout court,* without any further specification or explanation. In short, when the word "unreal" is applied to something, one means that it is different from something else, with which it might be mistakenly identified; what that something else is may not be explicitly stated, but it can be gathered from the context.

What, then, could people mean by saying that a next world such as I have described would be "unreal"? If they are saying anything intelligible, they must mean that it is different from something else, something else which it does resemble in some respects, and might therefore be confused with. And what is that something else? It is the present physical world in which we now live. An image-world, then, is only "unreal" in the sense that it is not really physical, though it might be mistakenly thought to be physical by some of those who experience it. But this only amounts to saying that the world I am describing would be an *other* world, other than this present physical world, which is just what it ought to be; other than this present physical world, and yet sufficiently like it to be possibly confused with it, because images do resemble percepts. And what would this otherness consist in? First, in the fact that it is in a *space* which is other than physical space; secondly, and still more important, in the fact that the *causal laws* of an image-world would be different from the laws of physics. And this is also our ground for saying that the events we experience in dreams are "unreal," that is, not really physical, though mistakenly believed by the dreamer to be so. They do in some ways closely resemble physical events, and that is why the mistake is possible. But the causal laws of their occurrence are quite different, as we recognize when we wake up; and just occasionally we recognize it even while we are still asleep.

Now let us consider the argument that the inhabitants of the other world, as I have described it, would be in a state of delusion. I admit that some of them might be. That would be the condition of the people described in the mediumistic communications already referred to—the people who "do not realize that they are dead." Because their images are so like the normal percepts they were accustomed to in this life, they believe mistakenly that they are still living in the physical world. But, as I have already tried to explain, their state of delusion need not be permanent and irremediable. By attending to the relations between one image and another, and applying the ordinary inductive methods by which we ourselves have discovered the causal laws of this present world in which *we* live, they too could discover in time what the causal laws of *their* world are. These laws, we may suppose, would be more like the laws of Freudian psychology than the laws of physics. And once the discovery was made, they would be cured of their delusion. They would find out, perhaps with surprise, that the world they were experiencing was *other* than the physical world which they experienced before, even though like it in some respects.

Would the Next World be Subjective?

Let us now try to explore the conception of a world of mental images a little more fully. Would it not be a "*subjective*" world? And surely there would be many *different* next worlds, not just one; and each of them would be private. Indeed, would there not be as many next worlds as there are discarnate minds, and each of them wholly private to the mind which experiences it? In short, it may seem that each of us, when dead, would have his own dream-world, and there would be no common or public next world at all.

"Subjective," perhaps, is a rather slippery word. Certainly, an image-world would have to be subjective in the sense of being mind-dependent, dependent for its existence upon mental processes of one sort or another; images, after all, are mental entities. But I do not think that such a world need be completely private, if telepathy occurs in the next life. I have already mentioned the part which telepathic apparitions might play in it in connection with Mr. Flew's contention that "people are what you meet." But there is more to be said. It is reasonable to suppose that in a disembodied state telepathy would occur more frequently than it does now. It seems likely that in this present life our telepathic powers are constantly being inhibited by our need to adjust ourselves to our physical environment. It even seems likely that many telepathic "impressions" which we receive at the unconscious level are shut out from consciousness by a kind of biologically motivated censorship. Once the pressure of biological needs is removed, we might expect that telepathy would occur continually, and manifest itself in consciousness by modifying and adding to the images which one experiences. (Even in this life, after all, some dreams are telepathic.)

If this is right, an image-world such as I am describing would not be the product of one single mind only, nor would it be purely private. It would be the joint product of a group of telepathically interacting minds and public to all of them. Nevertheless, one would not expect it to have unrestricted publicity. It is likely that there would still be *many* next worlds, a different one for each group of like-minded personalities. I admit I am not quite sure what might be meant by "like-minded" and "unlike-minded" in this connection. Perhaps we could say that two personalities are like-minded if their memories or their characters are sufficiently similar. It might be that Nero and Marcus Aurelius do not have a world in common, but Socrates and Marcus Aurelius do.

So far, we have a picture of many "semi-public" next worlds, if one may put it so; each of them composed of mental images, and yet not wholly private for all that, but public to a limited group of telepathically interacting minds. Or, if you like, after death everyone does have his own dream, but there is still some overlap between one person's dream and another's, because of telepathy.

7

ANTONY FLEW

(1923–   )

*Can a Man Witness His Own Funeral?**

Flew, though perhaps better known as the editor of Logic and Language *and the author of various works on the British Empiricists as well as religious and epistemological problems, has been actively involved in the issues arising out of parapsychological research. He and H. H. Price carried on a series of debates on Price's "Survival and the Idea of 'Another World'" and on issues related to the question of survival. This selection, though not directed specifically at Price, is an attack on the position of Price and of any dualist that seriously maintains the possibility and/or intelligibility of survival of death. When Flew asks whether a man can witness his own funeral he refers to the situation in which a person would be watching the funeral of his own body from some other point of view. The key words are "survivor," "dead," "person," and "body." Flew argues that it would take a radical change in the meanings of these words for us to make sense of the idea of witnessing one's own funeral. The dualist conception of man is inconsistent with the ways we generally use language. What is needed, Flew maintains, is a clearer idea of a person. He tells us that persons are what we meet. What would it be like to meet a disembodied person?*

* From *Hibbert Journal* (1956), pp. 242–250. Used by permission of the Hibbert Trust.

"Whether we are to live in a future state, as it is the most important question which can possibly be asked, so it is the most intelligible one which can be expressed in language" (Bishop Butler in the dissertation *Of Personal Identity*).

I The purposes of this paper are, *first*, to try to begin to raise what Butler called "strange perplexities"* about the meaningfulness of this question and, *second*, to attempt to dispose of the counter-thesis, maintained by Schlick, that it must be significant because the possibility being discussed is not merely conceivable but also imaginable. These

* *Op. cit.*

are very strictly limited objectives. We shall not, and shall not pretend to, do more than attack these two of the vast complex of problems, both logical and empirical, compendiously described as the questions of Survival and Immortality.

II Survival of Death is Self-Contradictory

Now suppose someone offers the gambit "We all of us survive death" or "We all of us live forever." Might we not reply "Whatever in the world do you mean? For, in the ordinary senses of the words you use, the former sentence is self-contradictory and the latter denies one of the most securely established of all empirical generalisations; for it is the contrary of that traditional darling of the logicians 'All men are mortal'." As the objections to the two sentences are different, let us deal with each of them separately.

"We all of us survive death" is self-contradictory because we use the words "death" and "survival" and their derivatives in such a way that the classification of the crew of a torpedoed ship into "Dead" and "Survivors" is both exclusive and exhaustive. Every member of the crew must (logical "must") have either died or survived: and no member of the crew could (logical "could") have both died and survived. It is easy to overlook that "We all of us survive death" is self-contradictory because we all habitually and wisely give all utterances the benefit of the doubt. Generously assuming that other people usually have something intelligible to express even when they speak or write in unusual or incorrect ways, we attempt to attach sense even to expressions which are strictly self-contradictory. This tendency is frequently exploited by advertisers. Posters advertising the film *Bachelor Husband* catch the eye precisely because the expression "bachelor husband" is self-contradictory, and therefore paradoxical. We tend to puzzle over the title, to ponder—doubtless to the advertiser's eventual profit—over the non-linguistic improprieties suggested by this linguistically improper expression. If we see the headline "We survived death!" we do not just exclaim (in the tone of voice of rigid logical schoolmasters) "Nonsense: you either survive or you die!", but, curiosity aroused, we read on to learn how the death was only 'death' (in inverted commas), that the people in question had only pretended, been reported, appeared, to die; but had not of course in fact died. Sometimes, for instance, people show all the usual 'symptoms' of death, all the usually reliable signs that they will not walk, or talk, or joke again, but then, surprisingly, recover and do walk and talk and joke once more. This happened quite often in World War II: Russian doctors in particular reported many cases of patients who showed the usual indications of death—the heart not beating and so forth—but were brought back to life by shock treatments, blood transfusions, and suchlike. These patients thus survived 'death' (in inverted commas). The doctors then adapted their language—or at least the language of *Soviet War News* (London) was adapted—to meet the new situation: "We cannot survive death" was retained as the expression of a necessary truth; and the expression "clinical death" was introduced as a more precise and less awkward substitute for "death" (in inverted commas) to refer to the condition of the patients who showed all the usual 'symptoms' but who nevertheless might or might not survive to tell the tale. "We survive death" thus was, and remains, self-contradictory. The paradox use of "survives death" in advertising and headlines, and the inverted-comma use of 'death' in which people can be said to return from the "dead" (in inverted commas), do not in the least weigh against this contention. They positively reinforce it: it is precisely because "He survived death" is self-contradictory that it is a good headline; it is precisely because "to survive death" is self-contradictory that the doctors put the word "death" between warning inverted commas when first they had to report that a patient survived 'death,' and later introduced the new expression "clinical death" to replace the makeshift 'death' (in inverted commas) when similar cases occurred repeatedly.

"We Live Forever" is False as a Matter of Fact

"We all of us live forever" is, on the other hand, not self-contradictory but just as a matter of fact false, being as it is the flat contrary of the massively confirmed generalisation "All men are mortal." (Though if you choose to use the latter expression to express not a factual generalisation but an artificial truth of logic, making it true by definition that all *men* are mortal, thus incurring the probably unwelcome consequence that on this definition neither the prophet Elijah nor—on the Roman view—the Virgin Mary can count as human beings; then, of course, "we all of us [men] live forever" will on your definition become self-contradictory, and not merely false as a matter of manifest empirical fact.) But, like "We all of us survive death," "We all of us live forever" has what we might call 'headline value.' Both are 'shockers' and thus catch the eye and arouse curiosity. They make us wonder what the writer is up to, what is the story which he is going to tell under these arresting headlines. For surely he cannot really be intending to say something so obviously nonsensical or so notoriously false as what at first glance he seems to be saying.

Now many stories have been and still more could be told under these headlines. People have claimed that "We all of us live for ever, *because* the evil (and sometimes even the good) that men do lives after them." People have argued that "We survive death, *because* our descendants will live on after we are dead." And in the variety and irrelevance of their supporting reasons they have revealed the variety and irrelevance of the theses which they have been concerned to maintain when they used these and similar paradoxical expressions. The only use with which we are concerned here—and certainly the only use which would justify Butler's claim that here was "the most important question which can possibly be asked"—is that in which they are intended to support or express what Wisdom has called "the logically unique expectation,"* the expectation that we shall see and feel, or at any rate and more noncommittally, that we shall 'have experiences' after we are dead. Therefore we shall take it that the person who has said "We all of us survive

* In 'Gods' *PAS* 44/5, reprinted in *Logic and Language* I, A. G. N. Flew, ed. (Blackwell, 1951).

death" or "We all of us live forever" was making a move intended to justify such expectations.

And against this move the simple-minded counter-move is to attempt a sort of philosophical fools' mate. Clearly this expectation cannot (logical "cannot") be well grounded unless we are going to exist after our deaths. But we have been insisting that it is not merely false but actually self-contradictory to say that we survive death. So we cannot (logical "cannot") exist after our deaths. Therefore these logically unique expectations cannot be well founded. Indeed the suggestion on which they are based, the assumption which they presuppose (*viz.* that "We survive death") is self-contradictory and therefore senseless.

III Presuppositions of the Dualist Concept of Man

Well, of course there are several possible defences against this sort of attack; and the possible variations on these defences are innumerable. The traditional one depends on the distinction between body and mind, or body and soul (what Professor Ryle, unaccountably ignoring Plato, insists on calling the *Cartesian* Myth; a notion which—far from being a philosopher's fancy—is incapsulated in the idiom of innumerable languages and is a widespread, though not universal, element in folklore and religion). The first stage is to maintain that people consist of two elements, one, the body, visible, tangible and corporeal, the other, the mind or soul, invisible, intangible and incorporeal. The second stage is to maintain that we are our souls or minds. This stage is indispensable: unless we are our souls the survival of our souls will not be our survival; and the news that our souls were to be preserved after we died would be of no more importance or concern to us than the news that any other parts of us—our appendices, say—were to be preserved. Granted these two presuppositions (and "presuppositions" is surely the *mot juste*: for they are rarely either distinguished from one another or argued for) it is then significant and even plausible to say that we (our incorporeal souls, that is) survive death (which is "the mere death of the body"). The desire to allow doctrines of personal immortality to be significant and plausible is one of the main drives behind dualist conceptions, and one perhaps insufficiently stressed by Professor Ryle in *The Concept of Mind.* But this is a vast and another subject; here we propose to concentrate exclusively on one more modern defence, that which claims that "I shall survive my death" cannot be self-contradictory and therefore senseless, because it refers to a possibility which is not merely conceivable but imaginable.

The Argument that Survival of Death is Imaginable

This argument was used by Moritz Schlick* "I take it for granted that . . . we are concerned with the question of survival after 'death'."—[His inverted commas. These surely tacitly concede the claim that "to survive death" is a self-contradictory expression: compare the similar tacit admission made in the tombstone insistence "Not dead but sleep-

* *Philosophical Review* (July, 1936), p. 356. Reprinted in Feigl and Sellars' *Readings in Philosophical Analysis,* pp. 159–60.

ing". A.F.] I think we may agree with Professor Lewis when he says about this hypothesis: "Our understanding of what would verify it has no lack of clarity. In fact I can easily imagine, e.g. witnessing the funeral of my own body and continuing to exist without a body, for nothing is easier than to describe a world which differs from our ordinary world only in the complete absence of all data which I would call parts of my own body. We must conclude that immortality, in the sense defined, should not be regarded as a metaphysical 'problem', but is an empirical hypothesis, because it possesses logical verifiability. It could be verified by following the prescription 'Wait until you die!'." A briefer and more puckish version of the same argument can be found in John Wisdom's unending saga *Other Minds*. "I know indeed what it would be like to witness my own funeral—the men in tall silk hats, the flowers, and the face beneath the glass-topped coffin"* and it is also deployed by Dr. Casimir Lewy in his 'Is the Notion of Disembodied Existence Self-contradictory?'

So far as I know this argument has never been challenged: presumably partly because we can most of us imagine (image) a scene such as Wisdom describes; and partly because no one wants to arrogate to himself the right to decide what Wisdom or Schlick or anyone other than he himself can or cannot imagine (image). But the argument can and should be challenged: and it can be done without arbitrarily prescribing any limit to Wisdom's obviously very considerable imaginative powers. For there is all the difference in the world between: imagining what it would be like to witness my own funeral (which requires only a minor effort); and imagining what it would be like to witness me witnessing *my own* funeral (which is logically impossible. Or at least, less dogmatically, is very far from being a logically straightforward matter). If it really is I who witness it then it is not my funeral but only 'my funeral' (in inverted commas): and if it really is my funeral then I cannot be a witness, for I shall be dead and in the coffin.

Imagining My Own Funeral

Of course I can imagine many situations which might be described as my watching 'my own funeral' (in inverted commas): I can remember Harry Lime in the film *The Third Man* watching 'his own funeral,' and of course I can imagine being in the same situation as Harry Lime; but it was not really Harry Lime's own funeral, and what I can imagine would not really be mine. Again I can imagine my own funeral—I shall not try to better Wisdom's whimsical description of such a scene—but now what I am imagining is not *my* witnessing *my own* funeral but merely my own funeral. (Parenthetically, it should be pointed out that Wisdom is far too good a writer to have committed himself to the former—and improper—description of his imaginings (imagings). What he wrote was "I know indeed what it would be like to witness my own funeral." Unfortunately, this will not, under examination, support his thesis: which requires that he should be able to imagine his surviving his own death and his witnessing his own funeral: which seems

* *Mind* (1942), p. 2 and *Other Minds* (Blackwell, 1952), p. 36.

to be impossible, since the latter supposition, like the former, is apparently self-contradictory).

But surely this is merely slick? Surely I can perfectly well imagine my own funeral, really my own funeral with my body in the coffin and not a substitute corpse or a weight of bricks; with me there watching it all, but invisible, intangible, a disembodied spirit? Well, yes, this seems all right: until someone asks the awkward question "Just how does all this differ from your imagining your own funeral without your being there at all (except as the corpse in the coffin)?"

Certainly Schlick could imagine, as he claimed, "the funeral of his own body": though it is perhaps a pity that he should describe what he imagined in this way and not, more naturally, as "his own funeral." But then he goes on to talk of imagining his "continuing to exist without a body": which he tries to justify by claiming that "nothing is easier than to describe a world which differs from our ordinary world only in the complete absence of all data which I would call parts of my own body." But the fact that we can all of us describe, or even imagine, a world which would differ from our ordinary world only in the complete absence of all data describable as parts of our respective bodies has not, by itself, the slightest tendency to show that anyone could imagine or describe a world in which, after his funeral, he continued to exist without a body. By itself it merely shows that we can each imagine what the world would be like if he were obliterated from it entirely, and no trace of his corpse remained. Schlick has misdescribed what he could imagine. Misled by the fact that a man can easily imagine what his funeral will be like, and hence what it would be like to watch it, it is tempting to insist that he can imagine what it would be like *for him* to watch *his own* funeral. Schlick is thus able to "conclude that immortality, in the sense defined . . . is an empirical hypothesis. . . . It could be verified by following the prescription 'Wait until you die!'." But he has not defined a sense of "immortality" at all: apparently he has merely misdescribed some rather humdrum exercises of his imagination in an extremely exciting and misleading way. He has failed to say anything to prevent his opponent from objecting to his conclusion: "But, on the contrary, nothing whatever could be verified (by me) by (my) following the prescription 'Wait until you die!': (for me my) death is so final that it is logically impossible (for me) to survive it to verify any hypotheses at all."

IV We have now fulfilled the two strictly limited purposes of this paper. But perhaps it is worth while to add comments on three other possible objections to the attempted philosophical fools' mate; emphasising that nothing we have said or shall say must be interpreted to mean that we ourselves consider it to be decisive. *First* it may be said that this is all too cut and dried, the logic of our ordinary language is not as sharp, clear, and uncomplicated as has been made out. This is true and important. To take only one example: any adequate treatment of the logic of survival and immortality (the enquiry initiated by Plato's *Phaedo*) would demand the use of the distinction between death and dissolution; just as any full discussion of the logic of metempsychosis and pre-existence (the enquiry initiated by Plato's *Meno*) would have to take account of the parallel distinction between birth and conception. But for our first purpose, the raising of "strange perplexities," soft shading and rich detail is confusing, while for the second, dealing with one counter-move crudely made, it is unnecessary.

The Sense of "Disembodied Person"

Second, it may be suggested that, although Schlick and Wisdom as a matter of fact only succeeded in imagining their own funerals and the world going on without them (and then misdescribed and/or mistook the significance of what they did imagine), it would nevertheless be quite possible to imagine all sorts of bizarre phenomena which we should feel inclined to describe as "the activities of disembodied people" or even as "evidence of survival." This again is true and important. Anyone who has read at all widely in the literature of psychical research must often have felt inclined to apply such expressions to phenomena, or putative phenomena, recorded in this literature. But it is all too easy to misinterpret what we shall be doing if we do allow ourselves to describe such *outré* phenomena in these paradoxical ways. In fact we shall be attaching sense to an expression—"disembodied person"—for which previously no sense had been provided: either directly as an idiomatic expression; or indirectly through the uses given to its constituent words. We are thereby introducing a new sense of the word "person." Yet it may appear to us and to others as if we have discovered a new sort of person, or a new state in which a person can be. Whereas a disembodied person is no more a special sort of person than is an imaginary person: and (except in the Services—which have their peculiar sense of the word "disembodied") disembodiment is no more a possible state of a person than is non-existence.

Now it is perfectly possible to specify a sense for the expression "disembodied person": just as it is possible to attach sense to any expression, even one which on present usage would be self-contradictory. The difficulty is to attach a sense to it so that some expression incorporating it will, if true, provide a ground for the logically unique expectation. In their present use person words have logical liaisons of the very greatest importance: personal identity is the necessary condition of both accountability and expectation; which is only to say that it is unjust to reward or punish someone for something unless (as a minimum condition) he is the same person who did the deed; and also that it is absurd to expect experiences for Flew in 1984 unless (as a minimum condition) there is going to be a person in existence in 1984 who will be the same person as I. The difficulty, not necessarily insuperable, is to change the use of person words so radically that it becomes significant to talk of people surviving dissolution, without changing it to such an extent that these vital logical liaisons are lost.

The *third* obvious criticism returns us to the traditional foundation for what we might call a "logic of immortality." The objection might be made that it has been assumed throughout that people are merely bodies, that people are bodies and nothing more. Even though we have excluded discussion of the traditional dualisms from this paper, this criticism has to be met. It is met by pointing out that no one has either argued or assumed anything of the sort. What has been done is merely to take for granted the ordinary meaning and use of person words, and to use them—we hope—in the conventional and proper way: a very different matter. People are what you meet. Person words refer to men and women like you and me and the other fellow. They are taught by pointing at people: indeed how else could they or should they be taught? They do not refer to anything invisible and elusive, to any mysterious incorporeal substances. Even children can be taught them, can and do know what is meant by "Father," "I," "man," "person," or "butcher." But that is not to say that they refer merely or at all to bodies. "Person" is no synonym for "body": though "body" is used peculiarly in the Services as a slightly pejorative substitute for "person," the degrading point of the substitution would be lost if the words were really synonymous; there is a difference, a difference of life and death, between "We brought a person down from the foot of the Z'mutt ridge" and "We brought a body down from the foot of the Z'mutt ridge." Person words do not mean either bodies or souls nor yet any combination of the two: "I" is no synonym for "my body" nor yet for "my mind" or "my soul" nor yet for any combination of these (as anyone who tries a few substitutions must soon discover). If we are indeed compound of two such disparate elements, that is a contingent fact about people and not part of what is meant by "person" and other person words. To suggest that it has been assumed that people are merely bodies is surely to reveal that you yourself assume that everyone must be a dualist—or at least a dualist with one component missing—a sort of one-legged dualist. And this is a mistake. But though this third criticism is mistaken, it does go straight to the heart of the matter. For the whole position does depend on the fact that people are what you meet: we do not just meet the sinewy containers in which other people are kept; they do not just encounter the fleshy houses which we ourselves inhabit. The whole position depends on the obvious, crucial, but constantly neglected fact that person words mean what they do mean. This paper has consisted in insistent and obstinate underlining of this fact; and in pointing out two implications of it, important but limited in scope: that Butler was wrong to deny that there were logical difficulties about the notion of a future life; and that Schlick's short way with these difficulties will not do. Perhaps attention to it can transform discussion of the problems of Survival and Immortality in a way very similar to that in which Moore's insistence that we do know that some material things exist has transformed discussions of Idealism and of the problems of Epistemology. As Berkeley, with his usual insight, remarked, "the grand mistake is that we know not what we mean by 'we', 'selves' or 'mind', etc."

8

IAN RAMSEY

(1915–)

*Persons and Funerals**

Ramsey attempts to provide an alternative to Flew's analysis of witnessing one's own funeral. He surveys some of the classic attempts to deal with identity and death. Ramsey agrees with Joseph Butler's theory that persons are more than observable behaviors or bodies. People are, as Butler puts it, "those who act conscientiously." Men are more than merely objects. And meeting people, Ramsey argues against Flew, is not merely bumping into objects. Ramsey does not disagree with Flew's belief in the logical impossibility of witnessing one's own funeral, but argues that Flew tries to put in logical terms what is only felt. That which is "more than the body" cannot be eliminated on logical grounds. We have only intimations of it. Ramsey maintains that we can only "tell tales" in regard to this problem. Notice that this is similar to the role myth plays for Plato in the Phaedo.

* From *Hibbert Journal* (1956), pp. 330–338. Used by permission of the Hibbert Trust.

I In this article I would like to outline the possibility of an alternative treatment of some of the points Professor Flew makes in his article on our inability to witness our own funerals.

Summary of Flew's Position

For our purpose we may summarize Flew's article as follows:

(a) "Person words refer to men and women like you and me and the other fellow"—people who walk and talk and joke with us. There is thus no significant difference between "father," "I," "person" and "butcher." Nor does this imply that all these words are synonymous with "body." On the contrary, the difference between "father," "I," "person" or "butcher" and the appropriate body is the difference (says Flew) between life and death. The butcher's body is what is there alone when the butcher is dead; the butcher is more than this, precisely because he is alive.

(b) Thus there are (contrary to Butler's view, Flew would say) logical difficulties about a "future life": for all that we mean by "life" is brought to an end by death. After death *we* no longer walk, talk, joke, climb mountains or become buried under snow. All that remains is a body. *We* are no longer "alive." Therefore, as we use language, we cannot talk about being "alive" after "death."

(c) Then again (contrary to Schlick's view, he would say) we cannot imagine witnessing our own funeral; whatever we can imagine *ourselves witnessing* belongs to a situation in which we are alive—i.e. before our death. Certainly I can imagine thereafter the funeral of my body, but not the funeral of myself. "Ramsey imagining Ramsey's funeral"="Ramsey imagining the funeral of Ramsey's body," but this does not represent "Ramsey then witnessing Ramsey's funeral," for Ramsey is not "there" to witness it. We may be more than bodies, but what we are *more* perishes at death. For Flew death is so final to empirical existence that it is logically impossible to survive it. Death obliterates "I" and replaces it by "body." As for any talk of "an invisible intangible disembodied spirit," this is devoid of empirical relevance. My imagining my "invisible intangible disembodied spirit" watching my own funeral does not differ at all, says Flew, from merely imagining my funeral without being there at all, except as the body in the coffin. We have no sense in which to talk of the invisible spirit "being there."

The fact that I cannot witness my own funeral is thus used by Flew to illustrate his major point that, while "I" is more than "my body," nevertheless after death all that is left of me is my body. There is no "I" and nothing "mine." We cannot talk significantly about persons "living" after death, therefore *a fortiori* we cannot talk of anything post-death being "mine" such as "my funeral." And all this is because (we are told) person words mean what they do.

II But what in fact do person words mean? How do we use person words? Flew's answer would no doubt be to give examples of "live butchers," "live fathers" and so on, and what is distinctive about a "person" would then be distinctive about their observable behaviour, the kind of observable behaviour which ceases when they die. A butcher is "alive" —he then weighs the sausages, talks with us, and (if we are lucky) jokes as well. Once there is the dead body, no such behaviour occurs; "person" and "living" are both inapplicable to the butcher's body.

But is "life" and "personal behaviour" no more than walking, talking, joking, weighing sausages and the like? Is there nothing perceptually elusive about characteristically personal situations? Is personal behaviour no more than behaviour which is observable or in principle observable, including in the last phrase all that psychosomatic medicine, deep analysis and the like might reveal? Is a person what we can point at without needing to do more to know what "person" means? Are there no situations which already give an empirical anchorage to the phrase "invisible intangible disembodied spirit" and thus give us a sense for its "being there"? These are the crucial questions which Flew's paper raises for us, and to answer them let us take further two of the classical references which Flew gives, and add a third which he does not, before concluding with some generalisations of our own.

Butler's Theory of People as Those Who Act Conscientiously

(1) First, then, Butler. He quotes from Butler: "It is as easy to conceive—that we may exist out of bodies as in them, that we might have animated bodies of any other organs and senses wholly different from those now given us, and that we may hereafter animate these same new bodies variously modified and organised—as to conceive how we can animate such bodies as our present." (*Analogy*, Ch. 1). Butler does *not* of course say that it is *easy* to conceive that we may exist out of bodies or in them, nor that it is easy to know what we mean by "animate." For Butler (*pace* Flew) nothing—certainly not a doctrine of a future life—was easy; all philosophical theology had its logical difficulties. Hence, written over the *Analogy* is Butler's peculiar doctrine of probability which was his endeavour to show, by analogy with morality, or conscientious behaviour, that the logical difficulties of theology in general and the doctrine of a future life in particular could nevertheless be reasonably associated with a "full" or "real" assent. But this is a broader point which in this article we must set aside. Suffice it for now to recognize that Butler's point is that there is something puzzling and mysterious about human existence; that we know mighty little about it; and that those who have attacked the possibility of a future life have been taking too cut-and-dried a view of human existence. Despite what Flew says, Butler's whole attitude in this *Analogy* was: Nothing is without its logical difficulties, least of all theology.

However, what was Butler's positive claim? We certainly do not do justice to it, nor represent it fairly, by associating him with those who think of people as "elusive entities" which are kept in "sinewy containers" or which inhabit "fleshy houses." Let us always remember that his desire to meet his opponents by talking their language means that we must take great care to read his assertions in their wider context, and I think we must be specially careful before we associate him with what seem to be the implications of his argument, or of particular phrases in them.

Now reading Chapter 1 of the *Analogy* in its widest context, and taking it along with the Dissertation *Of Personal Identity* we can see better what Butler's positive point was. He may not take us very far, but he does go some way in a positive direction.

(i) He was, like Flew, convinced that we "ourselves" are not "gross bodies"; that "systems of matter" are not "ourselves." But about the more he would have claimed that there is something mysterious, and this is his major difference from Flew, who does not, I think, do justice to Butler's position when he implies that the mystery for Butler can be expressed in the puzzle: How could the "elusive entity" "animate" a human body?

The "elusive entity" is not for Butler properly pictured as a soul which does some animating, though many theologians and philosophers—and many of those Butler was arguing against—would have taken that view. Butler is too much the empiricist for that. What is elusive is "we", and the mystery and puzzle is about "ourselves."

(ii) "We" are "living beings," and part of ourselves is a body. "We" are "the same living agents" though the body changes, and this identity we know by a "natural sense." No person "in his wits" can act on the assumption that he may not be the same person tomorrow. The claim is that here in self-awareness—in the awareness of oneself as a living being—is something peculiarly incorrigible and authentic (nor do I necessarily stretch that word as far as some existentialists) and in such a situation we are *inter alia* aware of that which is more than spatio-temporal.

Now of course such a *claim* by itself *proves* nothing, but let us notice that Butler is appealing to a certain "fact." He is claiming that in our awareness of ourselves—whatever situation it is, for example, which justifies us in saying that we are the "same person"—is a situation which cannot be reduced to observable behaviour, let alone to bodies. Other illuminating situations are for Butler those of morality, or "conscientious" behaviour. People, for Butler, are those who act "conscientiously," not just what we meet—like brick walls in the dark—and if we profess not to recognize such "conscientious" behaviour (whose degree of spatio-temporal transcendence is so often misleadingly expressed by a denial of utilitarianism) all we can say in the end is that persons are people like ourselves. But even this is not proof against misunderstanding. For we must now insist that "we ourselves" (no matter how plausible such an account might be of other people)* are not "objects," even when that word is used in neither its Army sense nor any other pejorative sense. The fact that there are "objects" at all implies at least one (logically different) "subject," and that as a matter of logical necessity, as a condition of our talking significantly about "objects" at all. If there is no logically peculiar "subject" I do not see what is meant by talking about "objects." Persons, then, are people like ourselves; but it might be said: are not we "objects"? Don't we talk, walk, joke, cut up meat? I hope so, but my point is that this does *not* exhaust our behaviour, which is characteristically more than anything which can be cashed in terms of such "objects" though plainly it includes reference to them.

Berkeley's Theory

(2) Berkeley would make the same point. We are each aware of distinctive situations (he would say) which cannot satisfactorily be exhausted in observational terms, i.e. in "objects." Such peculiarly elusive situations are (for Berkeley) given in our experience of activity. "An agent, an active mind or spirit, cannot be an idea, or like an idea. Whence it should seem to follow that those words which denote an active principle, soul or spirit do not in a strict and proper sense stand for ideas. And yet they are not insignificant neither, since I understand what is signified by the term *I* or *myself*, and know what it means, although it be no idea, nor like an idea . . . but that which . . . operates about them. Certainly it must be allowed that we have some notion that we understand or know what is meant by, the terms *myself, will* . . . *love, hate,* and so forth; although, to speak exactly, these words do not suggest so many distinct ideas." (*Alciphron*, Seventh Dialogue).

* It is the logical egalitarianism which has been the traditional undoing of the empiricist.

Here is that experience of "self-activity" which, when they have wished to emphasise its perceptual elusiveness, men have spoken of in terms of "free-will"—a contorted phrase expressing the best of intentions with the worst of logic. For the phrase tries to claim that here in "will" is a situation which escapes, is "free" from the net of "object" language. To talk of "free will" has been to claim that here was something not reducible to predictability stories, causal stories, or any other of the technical tales which would all profess to reduce it, and more importantly a "person," to "objects"—spatio-temporal events. Flew's quotation from *Philosophical Commentaries* is very significant. Since quoting it in an earlier article he has wisely added a footnote to the effect that Berkeley uses it "albeit with a different intent." But it might have been even better to say what the different intent was. The full sentence in the *Philosophical Commentaries* runs as follows:*

> But the Great Mistake is that we know
> not wt we mean by we or selves or mind etc.
> tis most sure & certain that our Ideas are distinct from
> the Mind i.e. the Will, and the Spirit.

We know what we mean by ideas; but all such "objects" can be distinguished from "we," "selves" and so on which are thus left logically problematical. They cannot be talked of in straightforward idea language; in *that* language we know not what we mean by "we," "selves," etc. Here is the point of view I have already exemplified from *Alciphron;* and we may remember that, as developed in Berkeley's doctrine of Notions, it provided in *Alciphron* the basis of a philosophical theology, empirical at that.

I am aware that this does not prove Flew wrong and Berkeley right, but we come to see better where the difference between them lies. Berkeley is claiming that there are certain situations which are not only more than "bodies," but are more than any "ideas," i.e. more than any empirical "objects" whatever, more than anything which ordinary empirical language used straightforwardly can exhaust. This, Flew would deny.

Hume's Feeling of Personal Identity

(3) Which brings us conveniently to Hume. If anyone ever tried to exhaust personality and self-identity in terms of ideas, if anyone ever tried to deal with personality in straightforward observational language, it was Hume. I have no need to go here over ground I have covered elsewhere. But for convenience I may summarise my view as follows. In the Appendix to Volume 2 of *A Treatise on Human Nature,* Hume is puzzled because he has a "feeling" of "personal identity" when reflecting on "the train of past perceptions that compose a mind." "The ideas . . . are felt to be connected together," but "connection" is something which we never "perceive." Here then seems to be something we cannot perceive, something which is not an idea nor an impression and yet which is needed to account for the facts, and Hume is puzzled by the problem.

* *Phil. Comm.,* A. A. Luce, ed., No. 847, p. 301.

But is not the clear inference that "feeling" is something perceptually odd, something which cannot be adequately talked of in terms of words for ideas and impressions? The situation in which Hume confesses that he has a "feeling of personal identity" is one of those odd situations which Butler describes in terms of "natural sense," and in relation to which Berkeley talked of "notions" besides ideas, those odd situations which enable us to claim that people are what we meet, *and more.*

Those who objected to Flew that he assumed that "people are bodies and nothing more," were expressing a good point misleadingly. The good point was that he was assuming "person" words referred to something that could be empirically cashed in terms of what's seen, heard, smelt, talked about by psychosomatic medicine, psychiatrists and so on. The contrary claim is that persons are *in part* "invisible and elusive," in part "mysterious," but those who assert it need *not* talk of them as "incorporeal substances." There is no need for Flew to foist the traditional jargon onto everyone who wishes to do justice to facts which they believe him to have overlooked; such jargon can only too easily be misread to make its sponsors look silly fools.

III Meeting and Personal Situations

So we come back to our main contention. Persons may be what you meet; but what is meeting? There is a jostling in the crowd, when people are scarcely more than bodies. There is the exchange of noises, as in a discussion, when, as Flew would agree, "people" are much more than their bodies. We meet "people" in warfare and on hunger marches, and there is again more in this meeting than before. But what of the "people" we meet in the intimacies of our own family, or in the confidences that we share with no more than one or two friends? Is this just another member of the series we have been elaborating—the crowd, the discussion, the hunger march, or is something here disclosed which is characteristically different from anything the other situations normally show? Is it not significant that while we "meet" "people," we generally use the word "person" in relation to "love" (or "hate") which Berkeley was wise enough to see are logical kinsmen of "I" and "myself"? If people are what we meet; might it not be said that persons are what we love? At least it might be agreed that we do not generally use "persons" and "people" interchangeably, and this itself might suggest that there is some characteristic difference between "people" and "person" situations.

Here at any rate is the crucial difference between Flew and myself. *I am claiming that there are certain characteristically personal situations to be evoked in certain ways which are not wholly tractable in terms of (public) behaviour stories, even if these are complex enough to cover part, i.e. the public part, of what is meant by attitudes, emotions and the like.* This he would deny. Plainly one important question to settle the difference between us is: "Can such situations be evoked or not?" But let us see how the difference between us is somewhat more subtle than the question suggests. I am claiming that there are certain stories which, when told, might evoke the kind of situation I have in mind. Now this may seem a very odd way in which to conduct an argument, but we have to realise that, if I am right, it is *logically impossible* to describe in straightforward perceptual language the kind of situation to which I wish to call attention;—it is logically impossible to play a straightforward kind of explanation game and to have the result we need. For the kind of situation which I am claiming occurs, if it does occur, is more than perceptual language will straightforwardly deal with. To settle the difference between Flew and myself, we must begin therefore by telling such odd stories as we may hope to evoke a characteristic situation. If, when such situations are evoked, a person feels disinclined to accept their religious valuation, the second move must be to ask him to state his alternative account, in the confident hope that before he has gone very far we shall find him encountering the same kind of difficulties as beset Berkeley and Hume. Further, in looking for possible stories to effect the disclosure, let us remember that the traditional phrases of the past can all be regarded as quarries for producing this philosopher's stone, e.g. "timeless self," and even "invisible intangible disembodied spirit." These and countless other phrases, if rubbed and developed in the right direction, have a chance of evoking the kind of situation we want. At the same time let us realise that such phrases as we have quoted have for very many people lost their complex logical placings, and viewed as straightforward phrases they hinder rather than help, conceal rather than reveal, the tale that we mean to tell.

IV Death and Witnessing My Own Funeral

But to come to Flew's paper again. It is interesting to reflect that among the various stories by which suitable situations may be evoked, are stories about death and funerals. For instance, take the case of "death." Plainly the word can mean many things. Biological "death" talks of biochemical reactions, decomposition, a breakdown of organic processes, and all such stories as are commonplace in the laboratories of physiology, anatomy, bio-chemistry and the rest. Socially, "death" is that occasion after which a man no longer throws his darts or dinner parties. "Death" for the psychologist is that point beyond which we have no longer the appropriate behaviour response. "Death" for the statistician is something which involves the pay-out of insurance premiums. Now suppose we begin to reflect . . . yes, the day will come when in my case there is this breakdown of organic processes . . . this cessation of the social round . . . this failure of appropriate behaviour responses . . . this pay-out of premiums . . . suppose, in other words, we begin to pare off from our existence all the features that the word "death" can cover, whereupon our lives become less and less . . . and less. . . . What is the outcome? As is well known, some become mad, terror-stricken, and are said to be "beside themselves," or "out of their mind", and not surprisingly, because for them "I" has disappeared, since they were never more than could have been known by the competent pathologist, psychologist, social worker, economist, and so on. Yet others talk of "peace," "immortality," "Heaven," "eternal life in Christ Jesus," and so on, and these, whatever their differences, are they for whom there is evoked at some point or other in the story what we have called a characteristically personal situation, and the *differences* between these various situations do not now concern us. All that matters at the moment is that the contemplation of death (and funerals) can often reveal to us what we are more than the biological man, the social man, the economic man, the psychological man. By contemplating enough translations of "X is dead" (where X does not=I, but the man whose funeral I am witnessing) what is peculiar about the proposition "I am dead" (which we can never, for obvious reasons, significantly assert) becomes apparent.

We would agree with all that Flew says about the difficulty of witnessing our own funerals. Indeed the difficulty concerns more than funerals. "I am witnessing X's funeral," is neither more nor less problematical than "I am witnessing X's running," when X does not=I. But both cases are altogether different when X=I, and from this difference arises the claim that self-awareness, whether evoked by funeral stories or running stories or any other way, is logically odd.

Can a man witness his own funeral? We can give no answer one way or the other, and that for logical reasons; for while, if I am right, we have reason to know what "I" will refer to at the time of my funeral, we cannot significantly link it with the word "witnessing." Flew would say that "my funeral"=an event involving all that is then left of me, and therefore I cannot witness it. We would say that, while "my funeral" is an event which certainly involves my body, nevertheless our *present* self-awareness yields a situation *not* wholly reducible either to my body or to any public objects, or to anything spatio-temporal. So "Ramsey's funeral" then, no more than "Ramsey's present public behaviour, dispositional and all that," covers all that of which Ramsey is aware when he is aware of himself. That situation covers all such public behaviour *and more*. And it is this "*more*" for which, on the day of my funeral, philosophical friends, if they feel so inclined, can spend their time choosing logically appropriate phrases: I for my part will be content to enjoy "it" untroubled then (I hope) by the need to give it a logical mapping. Meanwhile, let alone at my funeral, there is a part of what is given in my *present* awareness of which we cannot use temporal words such as "change" or "cease," or even a spatial word like "there," still less a word like "witness", *unless* we are prepared to give a very complex logical account of what we are saying, the kind of complex account which such logical conundrums as "witnessing with the eye of faith," or "being there in spirit" summarise and sponsor. It is such a complex structure that we need to give to talk about "invisible disembodied spirits being there"; and it is not surprising that such a phrase appears to be absurd rubbish if its logical grammar is assimilated to an ordinary assertion, instead of being anchored in that kind of situation for whose evoking its complex logical structure is suitable currency. None so blind as those who insist that the language of the open-eyed must be logically indistinguishable from that which they know already.

Does death obliterate everything (except the body) that is now covered by the assertion "I am alive"? No! For though death leaves a body and brings all talking, walking and cutting meat to an end, it does not bring to an end what we know now, in certain situations, as something which is "more than" the body and any and all spatio-temporal elements that those situations contain. But let me repeat that this point will never be fully *argued;* all we can do is to tell tales until the penny drops and the vision comes, when we see what some people might mean, and have meant, by "person" words. Here is the cure, a therapeutic recipe, for empirical myopia. We have already an intimation of immortality, and though I cannot talk straightforwardly about witnessing my funeral (let alone be right or wrong in so doing) none can assert that my body is all that is left of me at death, if already they have known me (or at any rate themselves) as more than a walker, a talker, or a weigher of sausages.

9

RICHARD TAYLOR
(1919–   )

*How to Bury the Mind-Body Problem**

Taylor denies that there are such things as minds. His philosophy is that of a materialist: only matter is real, so-called mental activity does not exist. But Taylor realizes that he must show that the dualistic analysis of certain forms of human behavior is inferior to a materialistic analysis. For Taylor, reference to the capacities of matter can explain all the dualist's mental activities. Taylor explores our notions of "living" and "not living" as we apply them to different things. The Greek tradition suggests that a living thing has something which a non-living thing does not. Plato called it "soul." Aristotle and his followers simply identified it with "life." If life or soul is a possession, then we can see how Mr. Kidd might have been led to think of losing life as the leaving of a possession from the body. Taylor argues, however, that the difference between a living and a non-living being is to be found in abilities and capacities, things one is able to do, the other not. You are living not because you have something, but because you can do something. Man is a highly organized material system. But can matter think?

* From *American Philosophical Quarterly*, Vol. 6, No. 2 (April, 1969), pp. 136–143. Reprinted by permission of the editor and Professor Taylor.

THE mind-body problem, in all its variants, is a philosophical fabrication resting on no genuine data at all. It has arisen from certain presuppositions about matter and human nature familiar to philosophy from the time of the Pythagoreans, presuppositions which have persisted just to the extent that they have been left unexamined. And they have not been questioned very much simply because they are so familiar.

There are vexing, unsolved problems of psychology and problems of mental health, but there are no mind-body problems. And there are problems of "philosophical psychology," as they are sometimes called today—problems of perception, sensation, the analysis of deliberation, of purposeful behavior, and so on—but there are no mind-body problems.

The reason why there are no mind-body problems is the most straightforward imaginable: It is because there are no such things as *minds* in the first place. There being no minds, there are in strictness no mental states or events; there are only certain familiar states, capacities, and abilities which are conventionally but misleadingly called "mental." They are so-called, partly in deference to certain philosophical presuppositions, and partly as a reflection of our lack of understanding of them, that is of our ignorance.

Men and women are not minds, nor do they "have" minds. It is not merely that they do not "have" minds the way they have arms and legs; they do not have minds in any proper sense at all. And just as no man or woman has or ever has had any mind, so also are cats, dogs, frogs, vegetables, and the rest of living creation without minds—though philosophers of the highest rank, such as Aristotle, have felt driven to say that all living things, vegetables included, must have souls (else how could they be *living* things?) just as others of similar eminence, like Descartes, have thought that men must have minds, else how could they be *thinking* things? Today, when philosophers talk about mind-body problems, and advance various claims concerning the possible relationships between "mental" and "physical" states and events, they are, of course, talking about men. But they might as well be talking about frogs, because the presuppositions that give rise to these theories apply to other animals as well as to men.

Philosophical Arguments for the Existence or Nonexistence of Things

There cannot be any philosophical argument proving that something does or does not exist, so long as the description or definition of it is self-consistent. Thus there cannot be a philosophical argument proving that men do or do not, as some medieval thinkers believed, have an indestructible bone in their bodies. One can only say that such a bone has never been found (which is not a philosophical argument) and then exhibit the groundlessness or falsity of the presuppositions that gave rise to the belief in the first place. (In this case it was certain presuppositions concerning the requirements of the resurrection of the body.) Similarly, there can be no philosophical argument proving that men do or do not have souls, spirits, or minds, or that there are not *sui generis* mental states or events, assuming that these can be described in a self-consistent way. One can only note that such things have never been found in any man, living or dead, and then exhibit the arbitrariness and apparent falsity of the presuppositions that give rise to these opinions in the first place. Now of course, as far as *finding* them goes, many philosophers claim to find them all the time, *within themselves*. They are alleged to be *private* things, deeply hidden, discernible only by their possessors. All they really "find," however, are the most commonplace facts about themselves that are perfectly well known to anyone who knows anything at all—but of this, more later.

The Grand Presupposition of the Mind-Body Problem

What I must do now, then, is consider the presupposition that has given birth to the so-called "mind-body" problem, and show that there is nothing in it at all that anyone needs to believe; that, on the contrary, we have good evidence that it is false.

The presupposition can be tersely expressed by saying: *Matter cannot think.* That is the way a Cartesian would put it, but philosophers now spell it out a little better. Thus, we are apt to be told that thinking, choosing, deliberating, reasoning, perceiving, and even feeling, are not concepts of physics and chemistry, so that these terms have no application to bodies. Since, however, men do think, choose, deliberate, reason, perceive and feel, it follows that men are not "mere bodies." They are instead minds or souls or, as it is more common to say today "selves" or "persons," and such terms as "is thinking," 'is choosing," 'is perceiving," etc., are not physical or bodily but *personal* predications. A man may be in one clear sense a physical object, having arms and legs and so on, but a person is not just that visible and palpable object; there is more to a self or person than this. For it is the self or person that thinks, chooses, deliberates, feels, and so on, and not his body or some part of it.

Again—and this is really only another way of expressing the same presupposition—we are apt to be told that thoughts, choices, reasons, feelings, etc., are not physical things. It makes no sense to ask how large a thought is, whether it is soluble in alcohol, and so on. Yet these things do exist—any man can be aware of them, "within himself." Hence, that "self" within which such things occur must be something more than or other than the body. It might be just the totality of all those nonphysical ("mental") things, but in any case it is mental in nature, so a self or person is not the same thing as his body.

Or again, in case one boggles at calling thoughts, feelings, and the like, "things," at least (it is said) no one can deny that they are events or states. But they are not events or states that occur or obtain in the laboratories of physicists and chemists—except in the sense that they sometimes occur in physicists and chemists themselves, who sometimes happen to be in laboratories. No one could ever truly represent whatever might be happening in a test tube or vacuum tube as the transpiring of a thought or feeling. These things just do not—indeed, obviously could not—happen in test tubes or vacuum tubes, because they are not the *kind* of event involving changes of matter. They are a kind of "mental" event. And since these things do, obviously, happen in men, then things happen in men which are nonphysical, "mental," in nature. And so on.

"Selves" or "Persons" as Minds and Bodies

The word "self" and the plural "selves" are fairly common items of contemporary philosophical vocabulary. These words never occur outside of philosophy, except as suffixes to personal pronouns, but in philosophical contexts they are sometimes taken to denote rather extraordinary things. Selves are, indeed, about the strangest inhabitants of nature that one can imagine—except that, as sometimes described in philosophy, they are not even imaginable in the first place, being quite nonphysical. You cannot poke a self with a stick; the nearest you can come to that is to poke his body. The self that has that body is not supposed to be quite the same thing as his body—that is a (mere) physical object, a possible subject matter for physics and chemistry.

That is not what thinks, reasons, deliberates, and so on; it is the self that does things like this.

At the same time, selves are never doubted to be the same things as *persons,* and persons are thought to be the same things as people, as men. And there is no doubt at all that men are visible, palpable objects, having arms and legs and so on: That they are, in short, physical objects. So the thing becomes highly ambiguous. We do not, in contexts in which it would seem silly or embarrassing to do so, have to say that selves (men) are spirit beings (minds) which in some sense or other happen to "have" bodies. Clearly men are visible and palpable things, that is, are bodies. We can say that all right. But at the same time we need not say—indeed, *must* not say—that men are just (mere) bodies. There is, after all, a difference between a man's body, and that which thinks, perceives, feels, deliberates, and so on; and those are things that men (selves) do, not things that bodies do. Or again, there is, after all, a difference between bodily predicates (weighs 160 pounds, falls, is warm, etc.) and personal predicates (chooses, believes, loves his country, etc.). The former can be predicated of a man's body, just like any other body, but it would "make no sense" to predicate the latter of any (mere) body, and hence of any man's body. They are only predicated of persons. So even though selves are persons and persons are men and men are visible, palpable beings, we must not think that they are just nothing but physical beings. They are physical bodies with minds, or, as some would prefer, minds with physical bodies or, as most writers on this subject want to say, they are somehow *both.*

So the "mental" is discriminated from the (merely) "physical," and the mind-body problem emerges at once: What is the *connection* between them? What is the relationship between men's minds and their bodies? Or between mental and physical events? Or between personal and physical predicates? Anyone who raises this question—for these all amount to one and the same question—can see at once that it is going to be extremely difficult to answer. And this means that it is capable of nourishing a vast amount of philosophy. It has, in fact, kept philosophers on scattered continents busy for hundreds of years, and even today claims much of the time of philosophical faculties and their proteges. It seems a conceit to undertake to put an end to all this, but that is what I propose now to do.

Mentalism and Materialism

Consider the following two theses:

(I) A person is not something that has, possesses, utilizes, or contains a mind. That is, a person is not one thing and his mind another thing. A person or self and his mind are one and the same thing.

(II) A person is not something that has, possesses, utilizes, or occupies a body. That is, a person is not one thing and his body another thing. A person or self and his body are one and the same thing.

We can call these two theses "mentalism" and "materialism" respectively, since the first asserts that men are minds and not bodies, and the second that they are bodies and not minds.

Now the first thing to note about these two rather crudely stated theses is that both of them cannot be true, since each asserts what the other denies. They could, of course, both be false, since a person might be identical neither with his body nor with his mind (though it is hard to think of any other candidate for the title of "person"), or a person might somehow be identical with the two of them at once. These two simple theses are, nevertheless, a good starting point for discussion, and I am going to maintain that (II), the materialist thesis, is absolutely true.

Philosophers have tended to regard (I), or some more sophisticated version of it, as correct, and to dismiss (II) as unworthy of consideration. In fact, however—and it is hard to see how this could have been so generally overlooked—*any* philosophical argument in favor of (I) against (II) is just as good an argument for (II) against (I). This I shall illustrate shortly.

In the meantime, let us give what is due to the humble fact that there are considerations drawn from common sense, indeed from the common knowledge of mankind, which favor, without proving (II). It is common knowledge that there are such things as human bodies, that there are men and women in the world. There is also one such body which everyone customarily, and without the least suggestion of absurdity, refers to as himself; he sees himself in the mirror, dresses himself, scratches himself, and so on. This is known, absolutely as well as anything can be known, and if any man were to profess doubt about it—if he doubted, for example, that there are such physical objects in the world as men and women, and therefore doubted the reality of his own body—then that man would have to be considered *totally* ignorant. For there is nothing more obvious than this. A man would be ignorant indeed if he did not know that there are such things as the sun, moon, earth, rivers, and lakes. I have never met anyone so ignorant as that. But a man who did not even know that there are men and women in the world, and that he—his body—was one of them, would be totally ignorant.

Now there is no such common knowledge of the existence of minds or souls. No one has ever found such a thing anywhere. Belief in such things rests either on religious persuasion or on philosophical arguments, sometimes on nothing but the connotations of familiar words. Such beliefs are opinions, easily doubted, and nothing that anyone knows. If a man denies that such things exist, as many have, then he exhibits no ignorance; he expresses only scepticism or doubt concerning certain religious or philosophical presuppositions or arguments.

If, accordingly, we are seeking some sort of thing with which to identify persons, then this is a *prima facie* consideration in favor of identifying them with their bodies, with things we know to be real, rather than with things postulated to suit the requirements of philosophical arguments or religious faith. This does not prove that men are nothing but bodies, of course, but it is enough to show that, since we know there are such things as persons, and we know there are such things as men (living human bodies), we had better regard these as the very same things *unless* there are some facts which would prohibit our doing so. And I shall maintain that there are no such facts. There are only philosophical arguments, not one of which proves anything.

The arguments for mentalism. I shall now consider the arguments I know, already adumbrated, in favor of what I have called mentalism. Of course not all philosophers who take seriously the mind-body problem subscribe to this simple thesis as I have formulated it, but the more sophisticated versions can be considered as we go along, and it will be seen that the arguments for these are equally inconclusive.

The first argument. There are certain predicates that undoubtedly apply to persons, but not to their bodies. Persons and their bodies cannot, therefore, be the same. One can sometimes truly say of a person, for example, that he is intelligent, sentimental, that he loves his country, believes in God, holds strange theories on the doctrine of universals, and so on. But it would sound very odd—indeed, not even make sense—to assert any such things of any physical object whatever and hence of any man's body. It would at best be a confusion of categories to say that a certain man's *body* loves its country, for example.

Reply. If the foregoing is considered a good argument for the non-identity of persons and bodies, then the following is obviously just as good an argument for not identifying them with their minds: There are certain predicates that undoubtedly apply to persons, but not to their minds. A person and his mind cannot, therefore, be the same. One can sometimes truly say of a person, for example, that he is walking, ran into a post, is feverish, or that he fell down. But it would sound very odd—indeed not even make sense—to assert such things of any mind whatever. It would at best be a confusion of categories to say, for instance, that a certain man's *mind* ran into a post.

Considerations such as these have led many philosophers to affirm that a person or the "true self" is neither a mind, nor a body. Hence, a person must be (a) something else altogether or, as some would prefer to say, the term "person" must express a "primitive" concept or (b) both mind and body; i.e., a person must be something having both mental and physical properties.

The former of these alternatives is simply evasive. Persons are real beings, so there must be existing things which are persons. If when we bump into a man we are not bumping into a person, and if at the same time we are not referring to a person when we say of someone that he is thinking, then it is quite impossible to see what is left to fill the role of a person. The word "person" may indeed be a primitive one, but this, I think, only means that such arguments as the two just cited are equally good and equally bad.

The second alternative that persons are beings having both mental and physical properties, is obviously only as good as the claim that there are such things as "mental properties" to begin with. Indeed, it is not even that good, for just as a physical property can be nothing but a property of a physical thing, i.e., a body, so also a mental property can be nothing but the property of a mental thing, i.e., a mind. For something to count as a physical property of something it is sufficient, and necessary, that the thing in question is a physical object. By the same token, for something to count as a mental property it is sufficient, and necessary, that it be the property that some mind possesses. Any property whatsoever that can be truly claimed to be the property of some body, animate or inanimate, is a physical property; the assertion that some body possesses a nonphysical property is simply a contradiction. This second alternative, that persons are beings possessing both physical and mental properties, therefore amount to saying that a person is at one and the same time *two* utterly different things—a body with its physical properties and a mind with its mental properties. These are not supposed to be two things in the same sense that a family, for instance, is a plurality of beings consisting of husband, wife, and perhaps one or more children, but two wholly disparate kinds of beings having, as Descartes put it, nothing in common. Now this is no resolution of the antithesis between what I have called mentalism and materialism. It is only a reformulation of that issue. For now we can surely ask: Which of these two is the person, the true self? The body which has a mind, or the mind which has a body? And we are then back where we started.

The second argument. This argument consists of pointing out the rather remarkable things that a person can do but which, it is alleged, no physical object, of whatever complexity, can do, from which it of course follows that a person is not a physical object and hence not identical with his own body. A person, for example, can reason, deliberate about ends and means, plan for the future, draw inferences from evidence, speculate, and so on. No physical objects do such things, and even complicated machines can at best only simulate these activities. Indeed, it would not even make sense to say that a man's body was, for example, speculating on the outcome of an election, though this would not be an absurd description of some person. A person, therefore, is not the same thing as his body, and can only be described in terms of certain concepts of mind.

Reply. This argument is not very different from the first; it only substitutes activities for properties which are baptized "mental." And one reply to it is the same as to the first argument; namely, that since persons often do things that no mind could do—for instance, they run races, go fishing, raise families, and so on—then it follows that persons are not minds.

A far better reply, however, and one that is not so question-begging as it looks, is to note that since men do reason, deliberate, plan, speculate, draw inferences, run races, go fishing, raise families, and so on, and since the men that do all such things are the visible, palpable beings that we see around us all the time, then it follows that *some* physical objects—namely, men—do all these things. All are, accordingly, the activities of physical objects; they are not activities divided between a physical object, the visible man, on the one hand, and some invisible thing, his mind, on the other.

Consider the statement: "I saw George yesterday; he was trying to get from Albany to Montpelier." Now this statement obviously refers, in a normal context, to a person, and it is perfectly clear that the name "George" and the pronoun "he" refer to *one and the same* being, that person. And what they both refer to is something that was seen, a certain man's body; they do not refer to some unseen thing, of which that body is some sort of visible manifestation. If that were so, then the statement would not really be true. And in any case, it would be embarrassingly silly to suppose that a more accurate rendition of the thought expressed in this statement might be: "I saw George's body yesterday. His mind was trying to figure out how to get (how to get what?) from Albany to Montpelier." It is, accordingly, one and the same thing which (a) is seen, and (b) figures and plans, and that thing is undoubtedly the physical object George. Now if conventions incline us to describe figuring out something as a "mental" activity, then we shall have to say that some purely physical objects—namely, living men—engage in mental activities. But this is simply misleading, if not contradictory, for it suggests that we are ascribing to a physical object an activity of something that is not physical, but mental. It would, therefore, be far better to say that some physical objects, namely, men or persons, sometimes perform physical activities such as figuring and planning which are quite unlike those we are accustomed to finding in certain other physical objects such as machines and the like.

The third argument. This argument, the commonest of all, is to the effect that while there may or may not be such things as "minds" (whatever that might mean), there are indisputably certain nonphysical things which are quite properly called "mental," as anyone can verify within himself. Indeed, it is sometimes claimed that nothing, not even the reality of our own bodies, is as certain as the existence of these mental things, which are perceived "directly."

Reply. What are here referred to as mental entities are, of course, such things as thoughts, mental images, after-images, sensations, feelings, and so on. Pains are frequently mentioned in this context, being, presumably, things whose existence no one would question. Having got to this point then the next step, of course, is to speculate on the connection between these mental things and certain "physical" states of the body. They evidently are not the same, and yet it is hard to see what the connection could be. Speculation also extends to such questions as whether two or more men might have "the same" pain, or why it is impossible that they should in view of the fact that they can hold common possession of ordinary "physical" things like clocks and books. Again, curiosity is aroused by the fact that a mental image, for instance, seems to have color, and yet it somehow can be perceived only by one person, its owner. Again, images sometimes seem to have shape—enough so that a perceiver can distinguish one from another, for instance—and yet no assignable size. Here, really, is a gold mine for philosophical speculation, and such speculations have filled, as they still fill, volumes.

Now surely there is a *better* way to express all that is known to be true in all this, and it is a way that does not even permit these odd theories to get started. What we know is true, and all we know is true, is that men think, sense, imagine, feel, etc. It is sheer redundancy to say that men think things called "thoughts," sense things called "sensations," imagine "images," and feel "feelings." There are no such things.

And to say there are no such things is *not* to deny that men think, sense, imagine, and feel.

What, for instance, does it mean to say a man feels a pain in his foot? Absolutely nothing, except that his foot hurts. But this hurting, what sort of thing is it? It is not a thing at all; not a thing felt, and certainly not a mental thing that is felt *in his foot*. It is a state, and in no sense a state of his mind, but a straightforward state of his foot. But can that be a *physical* state? Well, it is assuredly a state of his foot, and that is a physical object; there is nothing else—no spirit foot, no spirit being, no spirit mind—that it can be a state of. Why, then, cannot other people have that same state? Why cannot other people feel the same pain I feel in my foot? And if it is a physical state, why cannot we open the foot and *see* it there? Or make some straightforward test of its presence in another man's foot?

To ask questions like these is just not to understand what is meant by describing an object as being in a certain state. Consider a piece of molten lead. Now this molten state, what sort of thing is it? The answer is that it is not a thing at all; it is a state or condition of a thing. Is it a physical state? Well, it is a state of the lead, and that is a physical object; there is nothing else for it to be a state of. Why, then, cannot another piece of lead have that same state? Why cannot something else have the molten state of this piece of lead? Of course something else can, in the only meaningful sense that can be attached to such a question; that is, another piece of lead, or some things which are not lead can melt the same way this piece of lead melted. To ask why another piece of lead cannot have the molten state of this piece of lead is, of course, unintelligible, unless it is interpreted the way just suggested, in which case the answer is that it can. But similarly, to ask why another man cannot have the pain that this man is feeling is also unintelligible, unless construed as the question why other men cannot suffer pain, in which case its presupposition is wrong—they can. And if the piece of lead's being melted is a "physical" state, why can we not separate the lead into drops and see that state? Simply because it is a state of the lead, and not some other thing contained in the lead. Indeed, to separate it into drops *is* to see, not its meltedness (there is no such thing), but that it is melted—that is just the test. We do no have to *ask* the lead whether it is melted, and rely upon its testimony; we can tell by its behavior. And in the same way we can sometimes—admittedly not always—see that a man is suffering, without having to ask him. That we sometimes go wrong here does not result from the fact that his suffering is something quite hidden within him, which he alone can find and then report; there is nothing hidden, and nothing for him to find. Still, there is a straightforward way of testing whether a piece of lead is melted, and there is no similarly straightforward way of testing whether a man's foot hurts—he may only be pretending it does. Does this indicate that there might be a pain, which he has found in his foot but might conceal, as he might conceal the contents of his wallet? Surely not; it shows only that men, unlike pieces of lead, are capable of dissimulating. No philosophy was needed to unearth that commonplace fact. It is easier to test for the presence of some states of properties than others, and this is true not only of the states of men's bodies, but of everything under the sun. But things that are hard to establish do not, just by virtue of that, warrant the title of "mental."

Similar remarks can be made about images, which are frequent candidates for the role of mental entities. When queried about their mental imagery, people often will describe it in colorful detail and even with pride, not unlike the regard one might have for a precious gem accessible only to himself. It turns out, though, that all one thereby describes is his power of imagination, which is, of course, sometimes quite great. To say that one has a lively imagination, even great powers of imagination, does not mean that he can create within his mind, *ex nihilo,* things called "images" and composed of some mental, nonphysical, spiritual material. There is no material that is non-material, and there are no images composed of this or anything else—except, of course, those physical objects (pictures, etc.) visible to anyone who can see, which are rightly called images of things. When someone *sees* something, there is (i) the man who sees, and (ii) the thing seen; for instance, some building or scene. There is not, between these, a third thing called the appearance of what is seen; philosophers are pretty much agreed on this. But similarly, when someone *imagines* something or, as it is misleadingly put, "forms an image" of it, there is (i) the man who imagines, and (ii) sometimes, but not always, something that he imagines; for instance, some building or scene, which might or might not be real. There is not, between these, a third thing called the image of what is imagined. There is just the imagining of the thing in question. And to say that a man is imagining something is to say what he is doing, or perhaps to refer to some state he is in; it is not to refer to some inner thing that he creates and, while it lasts, exclusively possesses.

It is enough, it seems to me, to point this out; that is, to point out that we can say all we want to say about men's powers of imagination without ever introducing the substantive "an image." Philosophy is robbed of nothing by the disposal of these, and there is absolutely no fact about human nature which requires us to affirm their existence. But if one does insist upon the reality of mental images, and professes, for instance, to find them right in his own mind by introspecting—and it is astonishing how eager students of philosophy seem to be to make this claim—then we can ask some very embarrassing questions. Suppose, for instance, one professes to be able to form a very clear image of, say, the campus library—he can bring it before his mind, hold it there, perhaps even turn it bottom side up, and banish it at will. We ask him, then, to hold it before his mind and count the number of steps in the image, the number of windows, the number and disposition of pigeons on the roof, and so on. He could do these things if he had a photograph of the thing before him. But he cannot do them with the image, in spite of the fact that it is supposed to be right there "before his mind," easily and "directly" inspectable. He can tell how many steps there are only if he has sometime counted the steps on the building itself (or in a photograph of it) and now *remembers*—but that is not counting the steps in the image. Or he can *imagine* that it has, say, 30 steps, and then *say* "30"—but that is not counting anything either;

it is only a performance. The image he professes to "have" there, so clearly and with such detail, does not even exist. He claims to have produced in his mind an image of the library; but all he has actually done is imagine the library.

What, then, is imagining something? Is it an activity, a state, or what? It does not really matter here how we answer that; it is only *not* the producing of an entity called a "mental image." Let us suppose for this context, then, that to be imagining something is to be in a certain *state*. Is it, then, a *physical* state? Well, it is a state of a man, just as drunkenness, sleep, perspiration, obesity, etc., are sometimes states of this man or that. What is meant by asking whether these are "physical" states, other than asking whether they are states of a physical object? What shall we say of being in a state of sleep, for instance? It is the state of a man, and a man is a physical—that is, a visible and palpable —being. You cannot poke a man's state of imagining something with a stick; all you can do is poke him. That is true. But you cannot poke his somnolence with a stick either. There is nothing to poke; there is only the man sleeping, or the man imagining, or the man becoming drunk, or whatever.

How then can a man, if he is nothing but a (mere) physical object, be in such a state as this, that is, of imagining something? If he is only a body and can do this, why cannot sticks and stones be in such a state, for are they not bodies too? The answer is: For just the same reason that sticks and stones cannot be drunken, asleep, perspiring, obese, or hungry; namely, that they are sticks and stones and not men. The reason is not that they lack minds. Even if they had them, they still could not be drunken, asleep, perspiring, obese or hungry, for they would still be sticks and stones and not men.

The fourth (and last) argument. It is fairly common for people, including philosophers, to say that they can perfectly well imagine surviving the death of their bodies, which would be quite impossible for anyone who supposed that he and his body were one and the same thing. Admittedly no one knows whether there is any survival of death, but it is at least not necessarily false. The doctrine of metempsychosis, for example, though there may be no reason for believing it, cannot be shown to be impossible just on philosophical grounds. It would be impossible, however, if a person and his body were identical, and so would any other form of survival. We know the fate of the body: dust. If I am the same as my body, then it is logically impossible that I should not share that fate.

Reply. All this argument shows is that not everyone, perhaps even no one, *knows* that he and his body are one and the same thing. It does not in the least show that, in fact, they are not. Some things, like the Evening Star and the Morning Star, which some are accustomed to thinking of and describing as different things, nevertheless do turn out to be the same.

Suppose a god were to promise me a life after death—promising, perhaps, to have me (the very person that I am) reborn elsewhere with a different body. Now such a promise might quicken a real hope in me, provided I am capable (as everyone is) of thinking of myself as being something different from my body. But the fact that I can think such a distinction does not show that there is one, and in case there is not—in case I happen to be identical with my body—then of course no god could fulfill such a promise. Consider this analogy: If an enemy of our country did not know that Albany is (the same thing as) the capital of New York, then he might be very interested in a proposal to bomb the one but to spare the other. It would nevertheless be a proposal that no one could carry out. The fact that someone who is ignorant of this identity can entertain the possibility of its being carried out does not show that it is possible; it shows only that he does not know that it is not.

The Soul as Life and the Soul as Thought

It is useful in concluding, I think, to compare the philosophical conception of the mind with what was once the philosophical conception of life. It was once pretty much taken for granted that men and other animals *possess* something which inanimate things lack, namely, life, and that it is *because* they possess this that they can do all sorts of things that inanimate things cannot do, such as move themselves, assimulate nourishment, reproduce their kind, and so on. Aristotle classified the souls of living things according to the abilities they imparted to their owners, and thought that even vegetables had souls. Indeed, an animal's *life* and *soul* were generally thought to be one and the same thing. The very word "animal" had its origin in this belief. Socrates, according to Plato, was even able to convince himself of his own immortality on the basis of this notion for, he thought, if it is only because he *has* a life or soul to begin with that he is a living man, then it is idle to fear the death of that very soul. Life seemed to him identical with his soul, but accidental to his body, indeed even foreign to such a thing of clay. A similar model was at work in Descartes' philosophy when he declared that the soul could never stop thinking. Thought seemed to him identical with his soul, but positively foreign to his body.

Now of course we still talk of life that way, but we no longer take such common modes of speech as descriptive of any reality. We speak of a man "losing" his life, of a man "taking" another's life, of the "gift" of life, and even of the 'breath" of life which God is supposed to infuse into an otherwise *lifeless* body. But these are plainly metaphors. No one supposes that a man or animal moves, assimilates nourishment, reproduces, and so on *because* it is possessed of life. We no longer think of life as something added to an animal body, some separable thing that quickens matter. To distinguish something as a living animal is only to call attention to the very complicated way the matter of its body is organized and to a large class of capacities which result from such organization. A living body is simply one in which certain processes, some of them frightfully complex and ill understood, take place. A living body, in short, differs from a non-living one, not in what it possesses, but in what it does, and these are facts about it that can be verified in a straightforward way.

I have been urging a similar way of speaking of the mind; not as something mysteriously *embodied* here and there, and something that is supposed to *account* for the more or less intelligent behavior of certain beings. A being capable of more or less intelligent thought and action differs from one lacking such capacities, not in something it possesses, but precisely in what it does. And this, incidentally, explains why a man tends to regard it as a deep insult to be told that he had no mind. It is not because he is thus divested in our eyes of some possession dearly prized, but rather, because such a remark is quite rightly taken to mean that he lacks certain important and distinctively human abilities and capacities. If a man is assured that his possession of certain more or less intellectual abilities is in no way in question, he feels divested of nothing upon learning that among his parts or possessions there is none that is properly denoted "a mind."

Does Matter Think?

Probably every philosopher has felt more or less acutely at one time or another a profound puzzlement in the idea of (mere) matter doing those various things rightly ascribable only to persons. How, it is wondered, can a body think, deliberate, imagine things, figure and plan, and so on?

This is really no proper source of bafflement, however. No one can say, *a priori,* what the highly organized material systems of one's body are or are not capable of. It was once thought incredible that matter, unquickened by any soul, could be alive, for matter seemed to inquirers to be inert or lifeless by its very nature. Yet we see around us all the time specimens of living matter—in the merest insects, for instance—so philosophical prejudice has had to yield to the fact. Similarly, I submit, we see around us all the time specimens of thinking matter; that is, material beings which deliberate, imagine, plan, and so on. For men do in fact do these things, and when we see a man, we are seeing a material being—a dreadfully complex and highly organized one, to be sure, but no less a visible and palpable object for that. In any case, the seeming mystery or incredibility that may attach to the idea of matter exercising intellectual capacities is hardly dissolved by postulating something *else* to exercise those capacities. If there is a difficulty in comprehending how a body can do such things, there is surely no less difficulty in seeing how something which is not a body can do them any better.

Further Reading

Broad, C. D. *Mind and Its Place in Nature.* London: Routledge & Kegan Paul, 1925.

Ducasse, C. J. *The Belief in Life After Death.* Springfield: Charles C. Thomas, 1961.

Flew, Antony. *Body, Mind, and Death.* New York: Macmillan, 1964.

Haldane and Ross. *Descartes' Philosophical Works,* Vol. I and II. Cambridge: Cambridge University Press, 1911.

Hook, Sidney (Ed.) *Dimensions of Mind.* New York: New York University Press, 1960.

Lovejoy, A. O. *The Revolt Against Dualism*. Lasalle: Open Court, 1955.

Murphy, Gardner. *Challenge of Psychical Research*. New York: Harper & Brothers, 1961.

Ryle, Gilbert. *The Concept of Mind*. London: Hutchinson, 1949.

Smythies, J. R. (Ed.) *Brain and Mind*. London: Routledge & Kegan Paul, 1965.

Wisdom, John. *Problems of Mind and Matter*. Cambridge: Cambridge University Press, 1934.

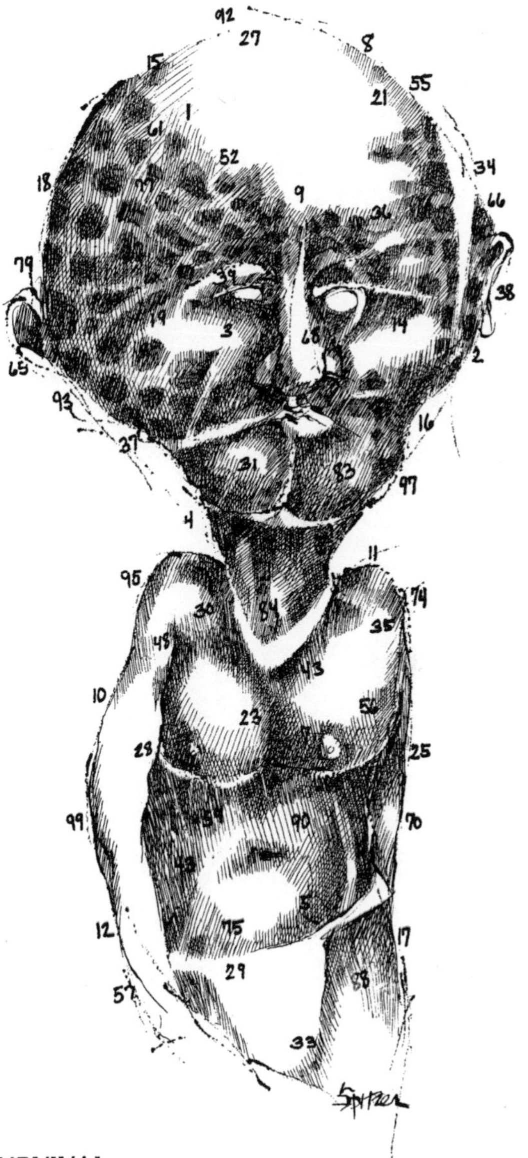

PART VI

FAITH AND GOD

INTRODUCTORY READINGS

Genesis 22:1–14

Tennessee Williams

INQUIRY

SELECTED SOURCES

Kierkegaard

Blanshard

Tillich

Bhagavad-Gita

Asvaghosha

Aquinas

Nietzsche

Russell

Copleston

Genesis 22: 1-14*

AND IT CAME TO PASS AFTER THESE THINGS, THAT GOD DID TEMPT Abraham, and said unto him, Abraham: and he said, Behold, *here I am.*

And he said, Take now thy son, thine only *son* Isaac, whom thou lovest, and get thee into the land of Moriah; and offer him there for a burnt offering upon one of the mountains which I will tell thee of.

And Abraham rose up early in the morning, and saddled his ass, and took two of his young men with him, and Isaac his son, and clave the wood for the burnt offering, and rose up, and went unto the place of which God had told him.

Then on the third day Abraham lifted up his eyes, and saw the place afar off.

And Abraham said unto his young men, Abide ye here with the ass; and I and the lad will go yonder and worship, and come again to you.

And Abraham took the wood of the burnt offering, and laid *it* upon Isaac his son; and he took the fire in his hand, and a knife; and they went both of them together.

And Isaac spake unto Abraham his father, and said, My father: and he said, Here *am* I, my son. And he said, Behold the fire and the wood: but where *is* the lamb for a burnt offering?

And Abraham said, My son, God will provide himself a lamb for a burnt offering: so they went both of them together.

And they came to the place which God had told him of; and Abraham built an altar there, and laid the wood in order, and bound Isaac his son, and laid him on the altar upon the wood.

And Abraham stretched forth his hand, and took the knife to slay his son.

* From *The Holy Bible,* King James Version.

And the Angel of the LORD called unto him out of heaven, and said, Abraham, Abraham: and he said, Here *am* I.

And he said, Lay not thine hand upon the lad, neither do thou any thing unto him: for now I know that thou fearest God, seeing thou hast not withheld thy son, thine only *son*, from me.

And Abraham lifted up his eyes, and looked, and behold behind him a ram caught in a thicket by his horns: and Abraham went and took the ram, and offered him up for a burnt offering in the stead of his son.

Tennessee Williams

Sebastian in the Encantadas*

MRS. VENABLE:

. . .

One long-ago summer—now, why am I thinking of this?—my son, Sebastian, said, "Mother?—Listen to this!"—He read me Herman Melville's description of the Encantadas, the Galápagos Islands. Quote—take five and twenty heaps of cinders dumped here and there in an outside city lot. Imagine some of them magnified into mountains, and the vacant lot, the sea. And you'll have a fit idea of the general aspect of the Encantadas, the Enchanted Isles—extinct volcanos, looking much as the world at large might look—after a last conflagration—end quote. He read me that description and said that we had to go there. And so we did go there that summer on a chartered boat, a four-masted schooner, as close as possible to the sort of boat that Melville must have sailed on. . . . We saw the Encantadas, but on the Encantadas we saw something Melville *hadn't* written about. We saw great sea-turtles crawl up out of the sea for their annual egg-laying. . . . Once a year the female of the sea-turtle crawls up out of the equatorial sea onto the blazing sand-beach of a volcanic island to dig a pit in the sand and deposit her eggs there. It's a long and dreadful thing, the depositing of the eggs in the sand-pits, and when it's finished the exhausted female turtle crawls back to the sea half-dead. She never sees her offspring, but we did. Sebastian knew exactly when the sea-turtle eggs would be hatched out and we returned in time for it. . . .

DOCTOR:

You went back to the—?

* Tennessee Williams, *Suddenly Last Summer* (New York: New Directions, 1958), pp. 18–21.

MRS. VENABLE:

Terrible Encantadas, those heaps of extinct volcanos, in time to witness the hatching of the sea-turtles and their desperate flight to the sea!

(*There is a sound of harsh bird-cries in the air. She looks up.*)

—The narrow beach, the color of caviar, was all in motion! But the sky was in motion, too. . . .

DOCTOR:

The sky was in motion, too?

MRS. VENABLE:

—Full of flesh-eating birds and the noise of the birds, the horrible savage cries of the—

DOCTOR:

Carnivorous birds?

MRS. VENABLE:

Over the narrow black beach of the Encantadas as the just hatched sea-turtles scrambled out of the sand-pits and started their race to the sea. . . .

DOCTOR:

Race to the sea?

MRS. VENABLE:

To escape the flesh-eating birds that made the sky almost as black as the beach!

(*She gazes up again: we hear the wild, ravenous, harsh cries of the birds. The sound comes in rhythmic waves like a savage chant.*)

And the sand all alive, all alive, as the hatched sea-turtles made their dash for the sea, while the birds hovered and swooped to attack and hovered and—swooped to attack! They were diving down on the hatched sea-turtles, turning them over to expose their soft undersides, tearing the undersides open and rending and eating their flesh. Sebastian guessed that possibly only a hundredth of one per cent of their number would escape to the sea. . . .

DOCTOR:

What was it about this spectacle on the beach that fascinated your son?

MRS. VENABLE:

My son was looking for—

(*Stops short: continues evasively—*)

Let's just say he was interested in sea-turtles.

DOCTOR:

You started to say that your son was looking for something.

MRS. VENABLE:

(*defiantly*)

All right, I started to say that my son was looking for God and I stopped myself because I was afraid that if I said he was looking for God, you'd say to yourself, 'Oh, a pretentious young crack-pot!'—which Sebastian was not. All poets look for God, all good poets do, and they have to look harder for Him than priests do since they don't have the help of such famous guide-books and well-organized expeditions as priests have with their scriptures and churches. All right! Well, now I've said it, my son was looking for God. I mean for a clear image of Him. He spent that whole blazing equatorial day in the crow's nest of the schooner watching that thing on the beach of the Encantadas till it was too dark to see it, and when he came back down the rigging, he said, Well, now I've see Him!—and he meant God . . .

INQUIRY

Man has never been the same since God died,
He has taken it very hard.
Why, you'd think it was only yesterday
The way he takes it.

EDNA ST. VINCENT MILLAY
Conversation at Midnight

WHY was Abraham going to kill his son? No doubt you have heard of persons who, for whatever reasons, took their children from their homes and killed them; but such accounts usually are found in sensational tabloids, not in holy writ. Imagine your reaction if Abraham were your neighbor and you were reading of this event in the daily newspaper. He was willing to perform and all but completed an act which almost all societies would deem criminal and most moral codes would call evil. Would the fact that he claimed that God had directed him to do this thing sway your opinion of him? In a recent bizarre murder trial in Florida the fact that the accused claimed to talk with God was taken by friends and a psychiatrist as evidence for their conclusion that he was "psychotic, schizophrenic, a paranoid type." Even though your neighbor Abraham did not complete the act this time, would it not be wise to lock him up for society's protection? Assuredly you would no longer want him for a neighbor. How could you trust him?

The traditional interpretation of the story of Abraham aims to lead us into taking comfort in a God who rewards Abraham for obedience. Abraham was being tested by God; he had faith in God, and God is good, so everything turned out fine. We may go on and tell it to others without ever seeing the events from Abraham's point of view. Abraham had great faith in God; we may even add that all of us ought to follow his lead. But what do we mean by "great faith in God"? What is it that Abraham had or did which sets him apart and makes this a significant story?

In this chapter we shall examine the idea of faith and the concept of God. The statement "He had faith" is the key. Consider Abraham. Does he know something many of us do not know? Perhaps faith is a kind of knowledge, a certain sort of knowing, which is different from the kind of knowing we have in science and other human activities. Think of situations in which we normally use the word "faith." Mothers talk of having faith in baby aspirin. We might ask one of them on what evidence does she base this faith. She would most likely respond by recounting experiences: her own, her mother's, a neighbor's, or a report in *Parent's Magazine*. These experiences are offered as proof of the reliability of the object of her faith; and we might imagine that her "faith," used in this sense, could be strengthened or weakened by the addition of supporting or refuting evidence. Faith, used in this way, is either reasonable or unreasonable, given the evidence. If faith is not knowledge, at least it is not incompatible with our usual methods of obtaining knowledge. But is this what the religious man means when he talks of having faith? What would we think of our mother if she shook her head and said, "I have no evidence; I just give him the pills. I have faith they'll work." How much evidence is necessary to support a religious faith, and how much to destroy it?

We often talk as if faith were one of a number of ways of gaining truth; there is scientific truth, common sense truth, religious truth, etc. We frequently distinguish between what we call religious knowledge and scientific knowledge and imply that both will lead in the long run to "truth." Consider Job's claim, "I know that my redeemer liveth."* Is the word "know" used here in the same way as in the statement, "I know it's raining out"? Or, "I know that water is composed of hydrogen and oxygen"? Paul Tillich calls faith an act of ultimate concern which can only be expressed symbolically. It is not a matter of knowledge. It is a state of being something, not of knowing something.

Faith is Acceptance of Certain Statements as Truths

Some major religions take the position that faith is the acceptance of certain statements as truths, statements revealed through prophecy, scripture, or ecclesiastical authority. The Bible, for instance, is accepted not only as inspiration from the divinity but as the written word of God. Thus faith amounts to believing certain propositions about the way things are upon scientifically insufficient evidence. The phrase "taking it on faith" comes to mean the opposite of knowing for certain: believing without or despite evidence. A good deal of criticism of religion arises because of this view of faith.

What evidence has Abraham to support his willingness to sacrifice his son? What could he expect to result from his actions? The man who knows something can predict certain things on the basis of his knowledge, but Abraham knows nothing of the events he is to perform except that he thinks he is called upon to perform them. How

* Job, 19:25

can he be sure this is really the command of God? Abraham's position is not comparable to that of Agamemnon, who sacrificed his daughter with the assurance of the Greek gods that if he did so the winds would blow, carrying his ships to Troy and victory. If this is truly a test of Abraham's faith, then Abraham cannot expect anything. Or at least we might imagine that he expects the worst as he walks with his son to the mountain. Abraham cannot know this is only a test.

If we think of faith (Abraham's faith) as unrelated to knowledge, then we can understand why no amount of contradictory evidence affects the determination of the faithful. Consider how you might convince a man of faith that he is misguided, wasting his time, foolish. What kind of evidence can you bring to bear against him? Construct an argument which might convince Abraham to return home before this sacrifice thing goes too far. But Abraham tells you that all of your arguments have occurred to him. He is not a fool. He knows what he is doing and what the circumstances are liable to be when he returns home. If he did not recognize the gravity of his deed, his act of faith would be of little significance. Why then does he proceed?

To Have Faith is to Have a Particular Point of View

To have faith, according to both Kierkegaard and Tillich, is to have a particular point of view. You and the man of faith might agree on all of the physical facts of a situation (an event in daily life or even the structure of the universe), but your interpretation of those facts might differ sharply from his. How would you then convince him that he is wrong? Bringing more facts to the argument in support of your position is not likely to help, for he does not disagree with you on the facts.

Here is an example suggested by Walt Kelly's "Pogo" cartoon strip. Albert, the alligator, announces to the other residents of the swamp that he has just discovered that they are living in the land of the Invisible Indians. Pogo asks what evidence Albert has to support his claim. Albert's answer is, "Look around," to which Pogo responds, "I don't see anything." And Albert retorts, "You see!" What is the difference between there being Invisible Indians and there being no Indians at all? What evidence for the existence of the Invisible Indians could be offered? Suppose you asked Albert if an Invisible Indian would leave a trail (broken twigs, bent brush, tracks), and he responded that these Indians are also intangible. You wonder why anyone would be interested in such Indians, to which Albert responds that of course we may not *know* whether the Indians are there, but certainly they might be there. And that, to him, is a very important "might."

Having faith is one thing, of course; the object of faith is quite another. Faith in a home remedy for chest colds and faith in the existence of a divine being are not on the same plane. Do we learn anything about the latter from examining the former?

One of the major philosophical problems related to religion is to determine a meaning for the statement "God exists" and how, if at all, it is to be used. Returning to your conversation with the man of faith, you discover that despite your argument on the facts, the man of faith finds it necessary to include the statement "God exists" as an explanation of those facts. You are not prepared to accept that without proof. Physical data as proof has been ruled out because you both agree on the physical facts. The man of faith could appeal to the powers of reflection and logic. Many "proofs" of the existence of God have been devised solely on the basis of definition and logic. St. Anselm's famous argument (used in a revised form by Descartes) rests on the kind of being we say that God is (called the "ontological argument" because "ontology" refers to the science of being). When Moses asked God at the burning bush to identify himself, God answered, "I am who I am."* If God is a perfect being, the ontological argument goes, and to be perfect is to lack nothing; then the perfect being must exist, for lacking existence would be an imperfection. Therefore, God exists. There are major problems with this type of thinking, as you may well imagine; not the least important of these is the claim of some philosophers that existence destroys perfection. A perfect circle, for example, cannot exist. All existing circles are less than perfect. It is suggested that the perfect God can only be perfect if he does not exist.

St. Thomas Aquinas' series of five logical proofs of God's existence begin with appeals to our common experience and then proceed logically to the necessity of a first or prime being. He seems to think that all processes must have begun somewhere. But is this necessarily the case, or is it only a psychological necessity in our patterns of thinking about our environment? Perhaps it is not even a psychological necessity but merely a handy device for seeming to prove something we assume. In order to be convinced by St. Thomas' proofs you must think that the question "Why do things happen as they do?" or the question "Where did the universe come from?" is sensible.

But just because we can ask a question does not make it meaningful or assure that it can be given a meaningful answer. Some questions should not be asked because any answer to them will be inadequate. There are inappropriate questions. "Have you stopped lying yet?" To say "Yes" may be another lie. It also admits that you have been lying right along, but this is incriminating. To say "No" is to say you are still lying, which is, of course, another lie, for you are not. Who could answer a question about the origin of the universe without being in the position of our liar? Even if we were to accept the existence of a first cause or prime being demonstrated through logical means, why would we call it God? Men don't want just any kind of a God, and Aquinas' proofs do not demonstrate that the First Cause of the universe is loving, merciful, just, or char-

* Exodus, 3:14.

acterized by any of the other attributes generally associated with God. We know that God has these attributes, Aquinas tells us, because we have faith.

The attributes of God are very important to the religious man. We are told by religious people, as well as by Scripture, that God is (among other things) a loving being; we are also told that he is an all-powerful being, that no task is too difficult for his mastery. Yet, as many philosophers (John Stuart Mill in particular) have pointed out, the world is filled with evil and suffering. If God were both loving and all powerful, he ought to want to destroy the suffering and evil, and he ought to have the power to do so. Yet God doesn't seem to do anything to alter the evil state of affairs. Therefore we have no grounds for believing that God is loving; or, if he is loving, that he is powerful enough to overcome the evil of our situation.

How can a man of faith counter such an argument? Must he simply deny that there is evil or suffering in the world? He could claim that evil is an illusion, the result of our imperfect ability to understand the universe and God's plan; but, as in the Book of Job, such appeals to the imperfections of men do little to comfort the sufferer (and, in fact, reflect back upon God). If God is good and also the creator of the universe, he must be in some way responsible for the evil and suffering of his creatures.

Nietzsche argues (see Selected Sources) that there is no real human freedom (despite our illusion that we are free to act as we choose) if we accept the traditional notions of God as creator. Ultimately God must take the blame and punishment for our evil doings.

> How he raged at us, this wrath-snorter, because we understood him badly! But why did he not speak more clearly? And if the fault lay in our ears, why did he give us ears that heard him badly? If there was dirt in our ears, well! Who put it in them?

God is Dead

Nietzsche's prophet, Zarathustra, announces to man that God is dead. This concept has played a major role in contemporary theology. The statement is meant by Nietzsche to be taken as an historical pronouncement. Modern man no longer can have any relationship with God. Nietzsche does not mean that men no longer believe in God or that God is actually dead. His claim is that man has lost his own image as a responsible and dignified being in the centuries of feeling subservient to his image of God. Without an idea of meaningful human existence, the concept of God is valueless. Nietzsche is saying that the personality of man was incorporated in the idea of a personal god, and that because men have lost sight of themselves, they can find no way of identifying with God. Ugly man cannot stand the perfection and mercy of God. It demeans man, and so God must be killed for man to save face. Nietzsche says:

> Away with such a God! Better to have no God, better to set up destiny on one's own account, better to be a fool, better to be God oneself!

A non-personal God, a pantheistic God or nature-God, might be more appealing. Such a concept of God would serve both as an explanation of nature and would not be distinguishable from nature or the events in nature. But join Sebastian in the crow's-nest watching that "thing" on the beach of the Encantadas. What you see is not a pleasant sight. Very little of nature is as blissful as a Walt Disney movie. Why call it God? What difference does it make to call a particular set of natural circumstances, no matter how awe-inspiring, God? Imagine what a religious relationship with such a God would involve. Is Sebastian having a religious experience?

In the Hindu scriptures and philosophy, attaining oneness with all of nature, with Brahman, the impersonal world-soul, is the highest goal of man. Loss of self-identity in the Whole is the supreme aim of life. The salvation of man from his daily predicaments is said to consist in identification with and insight into the essential singularity of the world-soul and in freedom from the point of view of seeing things in nature as "particularizations." For the Hindu, true religion is coming to see All without being confused by the diversity of parts. Sankara tells us that outside of God, who appears in many ways, there is nothing to be conceived. The *Bhagavad-Gita* demonstrates the applicability of this way of thinking. As long as oneness with God is reached, the requirements of living can be met without concern. One kills in war, but it should lead no one to grieve because in Brahman nothing is really changed. In life one does what is unavoidable.

We do not suggest that Sebastian was influenced by Hindu thinking. Nonetheless, these ideas provide a way of understanding Sebastian's apparently mystical experience. Certainly Sebastian has no reason to act on his experience; nothing is called for from him. Abraham felt compelled to act. For Abraham there was something to do, and only he could do it. Abraham's faith demanded action. What would be the meaning of "faith" in Sebastian's case? We are told that he was looking for God. How did he know he had found God on that gory beach of the Encantadas?

1

SØREN KIERKEGAARD
(1813–1855)

*Faith and Abraham**

Kierkegaard is a dominant influence in theology today. His philosophy is existential, and his major concern is finding "authentic existence," salvation from the corruption of the social life of external convention. For Kierkegaard philosophy and truth are a subjective, individual matter. He attacks institutionalized Christianity as superficial and hypocritical and calls for understanding of the total commitment of a "knight of faith" in a subjectively oriented life. Kierkegaard's favorite example of a man called to act on faith is the Abraham-Isaac story in Genesis. *Abraham acts without hope; he "leaps" to faith when his despair cannot be explained by reason or morality. Objectivity, Kierkegaard argues, is meaningless to faith. Abraham acts because he believes, and he does what cannot be rationally defended because he has restructured his life. He does nothing glorious. He does the absurd. We cannot understand his faith, Kierkegaard tells us; one must live it existentially. Seen from the point of view of faith, Abraham's actions have great significance in his life; his world can never be the same.*

* Søren Kierkegaard, *Fear and Trembling and The Sickness unto Death,* transl. with Introduction and Notes by Walter Lowrie (Copyright 1941, 1954 by Princeton University Press; Princeton Paperback, 1968), "Problemata-Preliminary Expectoration." Reprinted by permission of Princeton University Press.

NO, not one shall be forgotten who was great in the world. But each was great in his own way, and each in proportion to the greatness of that which he *loved.* For he who loved himself became great by himself, and he who loved other men became great by his selfless devotion, but he who loved God became greater than all. Everyone shall be remembered, but each became great in proportion to his *expectation.* One became great by expecting the possible, another by expecting the eternal, but he who expected the impossible became greater than all. Everyone shall be remembered, but each was great in proportion to the greatness of that with which he *strove.* For he who strove with the world became great by overcoming the world, and he who strove with himself became great by overcoming himself, but he who strove with God became greater than all. So there was strife in the world, man against man, one against a thousand, but he who strove with God was greater than all. So there was strife upon earth: there was one who overcame all by his power, and there was one who overcame God by his impotence. There was one who relied upon himself and gained all, there was one who secure in his strength sacrificed all, but he who believed God was greater than all. There was one who was great by reason of his power, and one who was great by reason of his wisdom, and one who was great by reason of his hope, and one who was great by reason of his love; but Abraham was greater than all, great by reason of his power whose strength is impotence, great by reason of his wisdom whose secret is foolishness, great by reason of his hope whose form is madness, great by reason of the love which is hatred of oneself.

By faith Abraham went out from the land of his fathers and became a sojourner in the land of promise. He left one thing behind, took one thing with him: he left his earthly understanding behind and took faith with him—otherwise he would not have wandered forth but would have thought this unreasonable. By faith he was a stranger in the land of promise, and there was nothing to recall what was dear to him, but by its novelty everything tempted his soul to melancholy yearning—and yet he was God's elect, in whom the Lord was well pleased! Yea, if he had been disowned, cast off from God's grace, he could have comprehended it better; but now it was like a mockery of him and of his faith. There was in the world one too who lived in banishment from the fatherland he loved. He is not forgotten, nor his Lamentations when he sorrowfully sought and found what he had lost. There is no song of Lamentations by Abraham. It is human to lament, human to weep with them that weep, but it is greater to believe, more blessed to contemplate the believer.

By faith Abraham received the promise that in his seed all races of the world would be blessed. Time passed, the possibility was there, Abraham believed; time passed, it became unreasonable, Abraham believed. There was in the world one who had an expectation, time passed, the evening drew nigh, he was not paltry enough to have forgotten his expectation, therefore he too shall not be forgotten. Then he sorrowed, and sorrow did not deceive him as life had done, it did for him all it could, in the sweetness of sorrow he possessed his delusive expectation. It is human to sorrow, human to sorrow with them that sorrow, but it is greater to believe, more blessed to contemplate the believer. There is no song of Lamentations by Abraham. He did not mournfully count the days while time passed, he did not look at Sarah with a suspicious glance, wondering whether she were growing old, he did not arrest the course of the sun, that Sarah might not grow old, and his expectation with her. He did not sing lullingly before Sarah his mournful lay. Abraham became old, Sarah became a laughingstock in the land, and yet he was God's elect and inheritor of the promise that in his seed all the races of the world would be blessed. So were it not better if he had not been God's elect? What is it to be God's elect? It is to be denied in youth the wishes of youth, so as with great pains to get them fulfilled in old age. But Abraham believed and held fast the expectation. If Abraham had wavered, he would have given it up. If he had said to God, "Then perhaps it is not after all Thy will that it should come to pass, so I will give up the wish. It was my only wish, it was my bliss. My soul is sincere, I hide no secret malice because Thou didst deny it to me"—he would not have been forgotten, he would have saved many by his example, yet he would not be the father of faith. For it is great to give up one's wish, but it is greater to hold it fast after having given it up, it is great to grasp the eternal, but it is greater to hold fast to the temporal after having given it up.

Then came the fulness of time. If Abraham had not believed, Sarah surely would have been dead of sorrow, and Abraham, dulled by grief, would not have understood the fulfilment but would have smiled at it as at a dream of youth. But Abraham believed, therefore he was young; for he who always hopes for the best becomes old, and he who is always prepared for the worst grows old early, but he who believes preserves an eternal youth. Praise therefore to that story! For Sarah, though stricken in years, was young enough to desire the pleasure of motherhood, and Abraham, though gray-haired, was young enough to wish to be a father. In an outward respect the marvel consists in the fact that it came to pass according to their expectation, in a deeper sense the miracle of faith consists in the fact that Abraham and Sarah were young enough to wish, and that faith had preserved their wish and therewith their youth. He accepted the fulfilment of the promise, he accepted it by faith, and it came to pass according to the promise and according to his faith—for Moses smote the rock with his rod, but he did not believe.

Then there was joy in Abraham's house, when Sarah became a bride on the day of their golden wedding.

But it was not to remain thus. Still once more Abraham was to be tried. He had fought with that cunning power which invents everything, with that alert enemy which never slumbers, with that old man who outlives all things—he had fought with Time and preserved his faith. Now all the terror of the strife was concentrated in one instant. "And God tempted Abraham and said unto him, Take Isaac, thine only son, whom thou lovest, and get thee into the land of Moriah, and offer him there for a burnt offering upon the mountain which I will show thee."

So all was lost—more dreadfully than if it had never come to pass! So the Lord was only making sport of Abraham! He made miraculously the preposterous actual, and now in turn He would annihilate it. It was indeed foolishness, but Abraham did not laugh at it like Sarah when the promise was announced. All was lost! Seventy years of faithful expectation, the brief joy at the fulfilment of faith. Who then is he that plucks away the old man's staff, who is it that requires that he himself shall break it? Who is he that would make a man's gray hairs comfortless, who is it that requires that he himself shall do it? Is there no compassion for the venerable oldling, none for the innocent child? And yet Abraham was God's elect, and it was the Lord who imposed the trial. All would now be lost. The glorious memory to be preserved by the human race, the promise in Abraham's seed—this was only a whim, a fleeting thought which the Lord had had, which Abraham should now obliterate. That glorious treasure which was just as old as faith in Abraham's heart, many, many years older than Isaac, the fruit of Abraham's life, sanctified by prayers, matured in conflict—the blessing upon Abraham's lips, this fruit was now to be plucked prematurely and remain without significance. For what significance had it when Isaac was to be sacrificed? That sad and yet blissful hour when Abraham was to take leave of all that was dear to him, when yet once more he was to lift up his head, when his countenance would shine like that of the Lord, when he would concentrate his whole soul in a blessing which was potent to make Isaac blessed all his days—this time would not come! For he would indeed take leave of Isaac, but in such a way that he himself would remain behind; death would separate them, but in such a way that Isaac remained its prey. The old man would not be joyful in death as he laid his hands in blessing upon Isaac, but he would be weary of life as he laid violent hands upon Isaac. And it was God who tried him. Yea, woe, woe unto the messenger who had come before Abraham with such tidings! Who would have ventured to be the emissary of this sorrow? But it was God who tried Abraham.

Yet Abraham believed, and believed for this life. Yea, if his faith had been only for a future life, he surely would have cast everything away in order to hasten out of this world to which he did not belong. But Abraham's faith was not of this sort, if there be such a faith; for really this is not faith but the furthest possibility of faith which has a presentiment of its object at the extremest limit of the horizon, yet is separated from it by a yawning abyss within which despair carries on its game. But Abraham believed precisely for this life, that he was to grow old in the land, honored by the people, blessed in his generation, remembered forever in Isaac, his dearest thing in life, whom he embraced with a love for which it would be a poor expression to say that he loyally fulfilled the father's duty of loving the son, as indeed is evinced in the words of the summons, "the son whom thou lovest." Jacob had twelve sons, and one of them he loved; Abraham had only one, the son whom he loved.

Yet Abraham believed and did not doubt, he believed the preposterous. If Abraham had doubted—then he would have done something else, something glorious; for how could Abraham do anything but what is great and glorious! He would have marched up to Mount Moriah, he would have cleft the fire-wood, lit the pyre, drawn the knife—he would have cried out to God, "Despise not this sacrifice, it is not the best thing I possess, that I know well, for what is an old man in comparison with the child of promise; but it is the best I am able to give Thee. Let Isaac never come to know this, that he may console himself with his youth." He would have plunged the knife into his own breast. He would have been admired in the world, and his name would not have been forgotten; but it is one thing to be admired, and another to be the guiding star which saves the anguished.

But Abraham believed. He did not pray for himself, with the hope of moving the Lord—it was only when the righteous punishment was decreed upon Sodom and Gomorrha that Abraham came forward with his prayers.

We read in those holy books: "And God tempted Abraham, and said unto him, Abraham, Abraham, where art thou? And he said, Here am I." Thou to whom my speech is addressed, was such the case with thee? When afar off thou didst see the heavy dispensation of providence approaching thee, didst thou not say to the mountains, Fall on me, and to the hills, Cover me? Or if thou wast stronger, did not thy foot move slowly along the way, longing as it were for the old path? When a call was issued to thee, didst thou answer, or didst thou not answer perhaps in a low voice, whisperingly? Not so Abraham: joyfully, buoyantly, confidently, with a loud voice, he answered, "Here am I." We read further: "And Abraham rose early in the morning"—as though it were to a festival, so he hastened, and early in the morning he had come to the place spoken of, to Mount Moriah. He said nothing to Sarah, nothing to Eleazar. Indeed who could understand him? Had not the temptation by its very nature exacted of him an oath of silence? He cleft the wood, he bound Isaac, he lit the pyre, he drew the knife. My hearer, there was many a father who believed that with his son he lost everything that was dearest to him in the world, that he was deprived of every hope for the future, but yet there was none that was the child of promise in the sense that Isaac was for Abraham. There was many a father who lost his child; but then it was God, it was the unalterable, the unsearchable will of the Almighty, it was His hand took the child. Not so with Abraham. For him was reserved a harder trial, and Isaac's fate was laid along with the knife in Abraham's hand. And there he stood, the old man, with his only hope! But he did not doubt, he did not look anxiously to the right or to the left, he did not challenge heaven with his prayers. He knew that it was God the Almighty who was trying him, he knew that it was the hardest sacrifice that could be required of him; but he knew also that no sacrifice was too hard when God required it—and he drew the knife.

Who gave strength to Abraham's arm? Who held his right hand up so that it did not fall limp at his side? He who gazes at this becomes paralyzed. Who gave strength to Abraham's soul, so that his eyes did not grow dim, so that he saw neither Isaac nor the ram? He who gazes at this becomes blind.—And yet rare enough perhaps is the man who becomes paralyzed and blind, still more rare one who worthily recounts what happened. We all know it—it was only a trial.

If Abraham when he stood upon Mount Moriah had doubted, if he had gazed about him irresolutely, if before he drew the knife he had by chance discovered the ram, if God had permitted him to offer it instead of Isaac—then he would have betaken himself home, everything would have been the same, he has Sarah, he retained Isaac, and yet how changed! For his retreat would have been a flight, his salvation an accident, his reward dishonor, his future perhaps perdition. Then he would have borne witness neither to his faith nor to God's grace, but would have testified only how dreadful it is to march out to Mount Moriah. Then Abraham would not have been forgotten, nor would Mount Moriah, this mountain would then be mentioned, not like

Ararat where the Ark landed, but would be spoken of as a consternation, because it was here that Abraham doubted.

Venerable Father Abraham! In marching home from Mount Moriah thou hadst no need of a panegyric which might console thee for thy loss; for thou didst gain all and didst retain Isaac. Was it not so? Never again did the Lord take him from thee, but thou didst sit at table joyfully with him in thy tent, as thou dost in the beyond to all eternity. Venerable Father Abraham! Thousands of years have run their course since those days, but thou hast need of no tardy lover to snatch the memorial of thee from the power of oblivion, for every language calls thee to remembrance—and yet thou dost reward thy lover more gloriously than does any other; hereafter thou dost make him blessed in thy bosom; here thou dost enthral his eyes and his heart by the marvel of thy deed. Venerable Father Abraham! Second Father of the human race! Thou who first wast sensible of and didst first bear witness to that prodigious passion which disdains the dreadful conflict with the rage of the elements and with the powers of creation in order to strive with God; thou who first didst know that highest passion, the holy, pure and humble expression of the divine madness which the pagans admired—forgive him who would speak in praise of thee, if he does not do it fittingly. He spoke humbly, as if it were the desire of his own heart, he spoke briefly, as it becomes him to do, but he will never forget that thou hadst need of a hundred years to obtain a son of old age against expectation, that thou didst have to draw the knife before retaining Isaac; he will never forget that in a hundred and thirty years thou didst not get further than to faith.

2

BRAND BLANSHARD

(1892–)

*Kierkegaard on Faith**

Blanshard attacks Kierkegaard's concept of faith as non-rational. Blanshard points out that Kierkegaard's faith is beyond reasonable understanding. Kierkegaard claims that we find what is absolutely true when we commit ourselves to the unintelligible and self-contradictory. Blanshard responds that such a definition of truth only creates meaningless assertions and a complete lack of common truths in religion. Blanshard's claim is that Kierkegaard can never succeed in establishing a basis for faith in the total subjectivity that is left after he has destroyed all uses of reason. Why must religion be reasonable? Does Kierkegaard have an insight that Blanshard ignores? Is Blanshard's concern with Kierkegaard's life relevant to his case against Kierkegaard's theory of faith and truth?

* From *The Personalist,* Vol. XLIX, No. 1 (Winter, 1968). Used by kind permission of Professor Blanshard and *The Personalist.*

AT the center of Kierkegaard's thought is the idea of human life as lived on various plateaus, each with its special characteristics. The idea probably came from Hegel. Just as Hegel recognized three main stages on the way to the Absolute—being, essence, and the notion—so Kierkegaard distinguished three "stages on life's way," the aesthetic, the ethical, and the religious. The first two were preparatory stages, rungs on the ladder that led to the third, where the clearest and surest insights of which men are capable were to be reached. This highest stage was again divided into two, A and B, each with its special features. Of these it is 3B, the last stage of all, that is of most interest to the philosopher, since it carries us to the highest summit that man's knowledge can attain.

But Kierkegaard insists that this summit is not attained through any process of reflective thought. The final step is a passionate, non-rational "leap of faith," a commitment of feeling and will. What is the commitment *to*? Not to a way of life merely, as some readers have supposed, but also to Christian belief. And the central Christian belief, he holds, is the belief in the incarnation. "The object of faith is thus God's reality in existence as a particular individual, the fact that God has existed as an individual human being." This is the distinctive fact of Christianity, which marks it out from all other religions. And according to Kierkegaard it is a fact incapable of establishment by any process of objective thought. You can never *prove* the existence of any past fact. It might seem, then, that the proper attitude is one of doubt and suspended judgment, just as it would be if we were asked to accept the existence of King Arthur. The two facts, however, are not comparable. For the unique Christian fact, if a fact at all, is one of overwhelming moment, upon whose acceptance our eternal happiness depends, and if there is any chance of its reality, an attitude of reserve and detachment would be flippancy. So, "while objective knowledge rambles comfortably on by way of the long road of approximation without being impelled by the urge of passion, subjective knowledge counts every delay a deadly peril, and the decision so infinitely important and so instantly pressing that it is as if the opportunity had already passed." The decision is what James called a "forced option"; we cannot evade it, since with so high a prize at stake, to evade decision is in effect to reject the offer as illusory.

Faith as Non-Rational

The man who attempts to make this decision on the ground of evidence is in an even worse position than we have suggested. For the incarnation is not a fact of more or less probability; to our reason it is an impossibility. Kierkegaard admits it to be a "contradiction that God has existed in human form." It is not knowable or even thinkable. "To speculate upon it is a misunderstanding, and the farther one goes in this direction the greater is the misunderstanding. When one finally reaches the stage of not only speculating about it, but of understanding it speculatively, one has reached the highest pitch of misunderstanding." The attempt to know religious truth by the intellect is thus fundamentally misguided because destined to defeat by the nature of its object. "For the absurd is the object of faith, and the only object that can be believed."

Fortunately this defeat of intelligence does not leave us without recourse. Faith remains. But there must be no looking back, no longing for the unprofitable old fleshpots of rational understanding and certainty. One must recognize the sophisticated intellect for the dangerous thing it is, and be content to become a child again. "When faith requires of a man to give up his reason, it becomes equally difficult for the cleverest and the most stupid person to believe, or it becomes in a sense more difficult for the clever." The difficulty must be overcome, not by thinking more critically, which is futile, but by a resolute act of will. The leap of faith is a daring, passionate non-rational commitment to the paradoxical and the unintelligible. "Faith begins where thought leaves off." "Without risk there is no faith." "The truth is precisely the venture which chooses an objective uncertainty with the passion of the infinite . . . the above definition of truth is an equivalent expression for faith. . . . Faith is precisely the contradiction between the infinite passion of the individual's inwardness and the objective uncertainty." "Faith is what the Greeks termed divine madness."

We shall say more in a moment about such faith as a means of insight in theology. But Kierkegaard's best known illustration of the meaning of faith is drawn not from theology, but from morals. The ultimate source of right and wrong is the will of God, and "the knight of faith," like the knights of the Round Table, will at every moment of life be in the service of his royal master. Not that he needs to renew the appeal to this will at every moment consciously; for the lower-level guidance of his own ethical faculties will normally suffice. The ethical level, says Kierkegaard, is the level of "the universal." By this cryptic pronouncement he seems to mean one or other of two things; either that the moral man will, in Kantian fashion, ask what conduct could in principle be consistently adopted by everybody, or, in Hegelian fashion, ask what the community would generally approve. Most modern moralists would regard either of these appeals as hopelessly inadequate, but Kierkegaard had little grasp of ethical theory. His chief contribution to it is to say that at times it breaks down, and that when it does, our resort must to be to a "teleological suspension of the ethical" at Divine behest. The nature of this behest can be ascertained only by faith.

The Crucial Case of Abraham and Isaac

How is he to show that our natural faculties do break down in morals? The most effective way would be to show that our clearest moral judgment may stand in radical conflict with the divine will. Can any case of such conflict be cited? Yes; we find it in scripture itself. The most revolting act of which a human being is capable is to destroy his own flesh and blood. In the book of Genesis we find Abraham commanded by God to do just this, to take his only son, the son of his old age on whom the joy and hope of his life were concentrated, to the summit of Mount Moriah, to bind him, cut his throat, and use his body as a burnt offering. Anthropologists who have studied this legend have considered that it is probably a relic of the custom of human sacrifice which once held in many parts of the world, and apparently even in the prehistoric past of the Hebrew people. However that may be, Kierkegaard takes it in all historic and symbolic seriousness. Is it not the point of this story, which is clearly inspired, that it was Abraham's duty, and may at any moment be ours, to trample down the affections of the natural man and all his nicely calculated goods and evils? Kierkegaard's answer is an emphatic Yes.

In his essay *Fear and Trembling* he goes into the matter with gusto and in detail. After a "Preliminary Expectoration," as he calls it, in which he spews philosophy, ethics and even reflective theology out of his mouth as incompetent to deal with the case, he goes on to consider what is implied in the command to Abraham. There have been cases in history and literature in which a father's killing of a child may in some degree be reconciled with our moral sense. Brutus ordered the execution of his sons, but they were, after all, guilty of treason, and does not a general's duty to the state take precedence of his own affections? Jephthah made a grateful vow to Heaven to offer as a sacrifice the first person he met on his return from victory, and if this happened to be his daughter, he would nonetheless be breaking a sacred oath by sparing her. If Agamemnon kills Iphigenia, it is to appease the wrath of Artemis, who holds the power of destruction over his fleet and army. These are not, therefore, pure cases of "the teleological suspension of the ethical"; in all of them the killing of the child is dreadful, but it is not entirely pointless. The great thing about the act demanded of Abraham was that it was pointless absolutely. Isaac was wholly innocent; Abraham loved him beyond anyone else in the world; no conceivable good to anyone could be anticipated from killing him. It was an act in which every human consideration was lined up on one side and on the other nothing at all but the command from on high to kill. Abraham bowed to it and drew his knife. The fact that at the last moment he was relieved of the need to strike is irrelevant in appraising him. Whether he actually killed or not, he showed that he possessed the one thing needful, namely the readiness to kill.

For Kierkegaard this makes him the perfect knight of faith. "Venerable father Abraham! Second father of the human race! Thou who first didst know that highest passion, the holy, pure, and humble expression of the divine madness . . ." Abraham is "great by reason of his wisdom whose secret is foolishness, great by reason of his hope whose form is madness, great by reason of love which is hatred of oneself." He surrendered himself to the "paradox which is capable of transforming a murder into a holy act well pleasing to God." "Abraham believed and did not doubt, he believed the preposterous." "He believed by virtue of the absurd; for all human reckoning had long since ceased to function." He was called upon to renounce the moral for the religious, the finite for the infinite. "This is . . . clear to the knight of faith, so the only thing that can save him is the absurd, and this he grasps by faith." Here is the meaning of that most deceptive phrase, "the teleological suspension of the ethical." "Teleological" means "for an end," but what Kierkegaard is praising here is the abandonment of all thought of ends and the doing of something that in every human point of view is productive of nothing but evil. "As soon as the will begins to look right and left for results, the individual begins to become immoral."

Kierkegaard as a Moral Nihilist

What are we to say of a rhapsody (in forty thousand words) in praise of pure and holy murder, of a defense of the humanly immoral on the ground that it is religious duty? Kierkegaard, in choosing such ground, believes that he has cut off the possibility of rational criticism. And clearly if an appeal is taken to the unintelligible and the irrational, it is begging the question to protest against it on any grounds of sense or reason. Sense and reason have been deliberately left behind. But we can at least point out that the irrationalist defense is double-edged. If it undercuts its opponents, it also undercuts itself, in the sense that it has forgone all right to the rational criticism of others. If opponents claim a divine warrant for the opposite of what Kierkegaard proclaims, all he can do is denounce them as impostors.

Of course there have been countless claims of this sort. There were Jewish leaders who claimed a divine imperative to destroy the Amalekites, man, woman, and child. There were Christians—St. Louis described himself as one—who thought the proper Christian reply to an argumentative Jew was to bury one's sword in him to the hilt. John Woolman felt a divine interdict against his preparing papers as a magistrate for the sale of a slave. John Newton, the hymn-writer, reported that some of his sweetest hours of communion with the divine were spent while he was the captain of a slave-ship, separated by a few planks from a weltering mass of human misery. Joseph Smith claimed to know that the divine will approved of plural wives; Mohammed made a like claim, but limited the divine approval to four; the Christian fathers limited it still further to one; and St. Paul construed it as favoring those who did not marry at all. St. Basil, St. Gregory of Nyssa and St. Ambrose thought it a divine imperative that one should not accept interest on loans. St. Abraham the hermit appears to have thought it the divine will that, beginning with the day of his conversion and continuing for fifty years, he should wash neither his face nor his feet. There are few practices too trivial or too eccentric to have been included among actions enjoined or prohibited by divine will. If claims to such guidance are to be above rational criticism, what we have is a chaos of voices, each announcing itself as authoritative, each denouncing its opponents as deceivers, and none of them able to defend themselves against the others.

Abraham was enabled by faith to see what ordinary men were unable to see. What exactly was this? It was that an act which, so far as the human mind could judge, was productive only of evil was nevertheless right—a duty because the will of God. For the person who possesses the insight, the principles and consequences involved in the act are held to be irrelevant; its character as seen by faith is its true character, which takes precedence of any judgment of our merely human faculties. Faith thus revealed to Abraham in the most dramatic and decisive way that it may be duty to reduce rather than to increase, to destroy rather than to create, the values recognized by reason and conscience.

Now when "the knight of faith" claims that he has had this kind of insight, can we credit what he says? It is hard to take the claim seriously. A person may *say* that it is really better that the powers of youth should be frustrated than fulfilled, that excruciating pain is better than pleasure, that sorrow and anguish are better than happiness, but can we believe that he has in fact seen these things to be true? The question is not, of course, whether pain, misery, and the destruction of life may be *means* leading to later goods; this is true enough, but is irrelevant here; for we are expressly forbidden to try to justify the divine command by any such considerations. What was presented as Abraham's duty, what he was honored for accepting, was the production of these evils without any thought of compensating goods. When the question is thus clearly put, one must take leave to doubt not only whether such insight occurs in fact, but whether it could possibly occur. For what the insight amounts to is that there is no such thing as good or evil, right or wrong, better or worse. If the killing of innocent youth without regard to consequences may be right, then anything may be right, since our moral sense has proved delusive at the very point of its greatest confidence. If pleasure is intrinsically evil and pain intrinsically good, if misery is in truth more desirable than happiness, then the clearest and surest judgments about values are worthless, and it is no longer possible to hold that anything is really better than anything else. The entire realm of values, including moral values, becomes a mirage. Now one may talk as if it were, but one cannot live or think accordingly. Daily and hourly we make choices implying judgments that it is better to be happy or enlightened or at peace than it is to be the opposite; indeed the person who chooses to affirm that nothing is better than anything else presumably assumes that it is better so to affirm than not to do so. The Kierkegaardian "knight of faith," in electing the "absurd," is divesting himself of the shackles of all insights. But to do that is to be not a saint, but a moral nihilist.

Rational Morals Repudiated

Those who accept Kierkegaard's knight of faith as the true saint may well pause over this conclusion. The popularity of his religious ethics in our schools of theology is a genuine anomaly. The Christian saint, we must admit, has at times been a strange character whose asceticism and other-worldliness have set him apart from the run of men and caused him to be regarded with uncomprehending wonder. Still, in the main he has accepted and exemplified the values most prized by his fellows and has been honored by them accordingly; he has believed in the superiority of love to hate, in the relief of human misery, in refusing to count his own good as more important than that of others. These are virtues that we can see to be virtues with our unaided human faculties. But for Kierkegaard as for Luther, these faculties are corrupt; all the principles laid down by them are open to a "teleological suspension of the ethical" imposed from above; they are subject at any moment to cancellation by "the absurd"; and if, in the face of such a suspension we retain our old adherence to love or loyalty or even conscience in its natural sense, the charge of immorality is compounded with a charge of impiety. Furthermore, the saint or knight of faith, according to Kierkegaard, is a man whose leading concern is not the welfare of others, but his own "eternal happiness," a description, incidentally that applied to himself. "If ever a person was self-centered it was Kierkegaard; he hardly ever thinks of anyone but himself."* What we have in this strange version of Christianity is thus an insistence on the selfish character of the religious motive, combined with an insistence that the values of the Christian life, so far as these can be understood, are provisional only, and may at any time be overridden. Kierkegaard revelled in paradox; "if anyone has ever used

* H. J. Paton, *The Modern Predicament,* 120.

the slogan *credo quia absurdum*," says Emil Brunner, "it was Kierkegaard."* Those who love daylight, even in religion, will greet the absurd with less acclaim. To them it will still seem odd that one should have to become immoral in order to be religious. They may recall Halevy's remark that "virtue is more dangerous than vice, because its excesses are not subject to the restraints of conscience."

Rational Theology Repudiated

We have been dealing with the absurdity apprehended by faith in the field of morals. But it will be remembered that the central dogmas of the creed are also apprehended by faith, and are regarded as equally absurd. Sometimes the absurd is presented as the merely improbable. "Faith has in fact two tasks: to take care in every moment to discover the improbable, the paradox; and then to hold it fast with the passion of inwardness." Sometimes, as we have seen, the paradox that must be held fast is more than improbable; it is impossible. The central fact of Christianity, Kierkegaard holds, is the incarnation. "The object of faith is . . . the fact that God has existed as an individual human being." But he admits that by rational standards, this fact is inconceivable and inconsistent with itself. A being who is eternal or out of time cannot have measured out his life in human years. A being who is omnipresent could not be confined in his movements to a small area in the eastern Mediterranean. A being who is omniscient cannot grow in knowledge, or a being who is perfect grow in grace. A son who is a separate person from his father cannot also be one with the father; still less can three persons be one. So speaks logic. But faith requires us to put logic aside and accept what Kierkegaard admits to be a "contradiction." "In my God-relationship I have to learn precisely to give up my finite understanding, and therewith the custom of discrimination which is natural to me . . ." A man must somehow learn "to relinquish his understanding and his thinking, and to keep his soul fixed upon the absurd . . ." He must achieve "a crucifixion of the understanding," and by a leap of faith embrace the improbable and even impossible as nevertheless certain.

The difficulty with this claim is to attach definite meaning to it. If we were told that though a certain belief were improbable, we should try to make ourselves believe it, that would be intelligible, whether ethical or not. If we were told that a belief, though beyond our present understanding was vouched for by others who did understand it, and that through provisionally accepting this assurance we might come to understand it ourselves, that too would make sense. But if we are told that although a belief is both unintelligible and self-contradictory, we shall see that it is absolutely true and certain if we commit ourselves to it passionately enough, we can only question whether the proposer knows what he is asking of us. The law of contradiction is not a principle that is valid in some cases and not in others; if it is invalid in any case, it is invalid *as such* and therefore in every case. But if it is thus universally invalid, then in no case does the

* *Revelation and Reason*, 310.

assertion of something as true exclude the truth of its denial, and *nothing* is true rather than untrue. And that makes assertion meaningless, for *what* could one be asserting? Just as Kierkegaard's ethics implies the denial of a realm of value, so his trans-logical truth undermines truth as we know it. Not that he saw this implication or held to it. If he had, he would not have argued at all. He was in fact proud of his prowess as a dialectician, and took pleasure in pitting himself against Hegel. But his philosophy terminates in a rejection of those very principles of logic on which he proceeded as a philosopher. He can hardly have it both ways. If the logic he assumes in his philosophy is valid, then the faith which stands at the summit of "the stages on life's way" is meaningless. If that irrational faith is accepted, the principles on which reflection conducts itself are everywhere impugned. In that case, Kierkegaard should merely smile like Buddha and remain silent.

What would he reply to all this? Probably that he was not concerned with the truth of doctrines at all; "Christianity is not a doctrine but an existential communication expressing an existential contradiction." He would fall back on his notion of subjectivity; ". . . the passion of the infinite is the truth. But the passion of the infinite is precisely subjectivity, and thus subjectivity becomes the truth." (This is of course an illicit minor, if logic still has any importance.) He would renew his attack on the attempt to understand, insisting that "the objective acceptance of Christianity is paganism or thoughtlessness." He would remind us that religion is a commitment of the will, that "Christianity wishes to intensify passion to its highest pitch," not to induce in us belief or comprehension. But we have seen that this will not do. Christianity does include beliefs, and it insists rightly or wrongly that these beliefs are true in the common and ancient sense. To adopt Kierkegaard's new sense, peculiar to himself and inconsistently held, which reduces truth to a passionate commitment of feeling and will, would not save Christianity; on the contrary, it would largely destroy it. For it implies that there are no common truths for Christians to accept, no common principles by which their lives may be guided, indeed no common Deity for them to contemplate and worship. The Kierkegaardian subjectivity would dissolve these things away into a set of processes in individual minds where there would be as many Christianities as there were persons to exercise their "inwardness" and their passion.

The Thinker and His Thought

In this review of Kierkegaard on faith and reason, we have been examining the thought, not the man. *Ad hominem* reasoning, besides being distasteful, is never conclusive and is often self-defeating. But I do not wish to conceal my own belief that psychological causes as distinct from logical reasons had much to do with his conclusions. I cannot think that a psychopathologist would have much trouble in connecting the irrationalism of his thought with the irrationality of his temper. He said himself that his thought must be understood through his personality, and his personality was profoundly abnormal

—so abnormal as to have cut him off from his fellows, his friends, and his own family. His alternations of exaltation and depression, his temptations to suicide, the feverish activity of an over-pressed brain in darkened rooms, the hysterical-sounding claims to being "a genius in a market town" and his comparison of himself to Christ, the frantic excoriations of church and clergy in his later years, his own report that he had stood on the verge of insanity—it would be a mistake to pass over these things as if they were wholly irrelevant. They suggest, though with a force difficult to assess, that Kierkegaard's singularities of thought were less the product of judicial reflection than the by-product of a sick spirit.

I will take two examples that may serve to make clear what I mean. First, his overwhelming, persistent, and surely morbid sense of guilt. This was partly an infection from his father, who lived in terror of having committed the unpardonable sin, partly the reaction to youthful irregularities on the part of an excessively introspective mind brought up in a theological hothouse. Georg Brandes reminds us that "he lived his life through in an atmosphere saturated with theology and theological discussion; at least three fourths of his near acquaintances appear to have been theologians, chaplains, ministers, bishops, clerics of every rank." This atmosphere kept alive and flourishing in Kierkegaard's anxious mind a conviction which, if exposed to the air and light of free secular discussion, would probably have been dissipated, the inherited Lutheran conviction that we were born in sin, utterly corrupted by it, and doomed by it to condemnation unless faith could somehow be won. Kierkegaard, like his father, lived in fear. "The whole of existence frightens me; from the smallest fly to the mystery of the incarnation everything is unintelligible to me, most of all myself; the whole of existence is poisoned in my sight, particularly myself." The cure for this fear was faith, and Kierkegaard was terrified that, by losing his faith, he might also lose his "eternal happiness"; he must therefore keep it at all costs.

He saw clearly the tendency of "objective thinking" to undermine and disintegrate this faith. Is there any wonder that an imaginative mind, living in a "sickness unto death" of fear, despair, and dread, should come to conceive of philosophy as the enemy? If one wished to preserve one's faith, it was safer not to play the philosophical game at all. "The ungodly calmness with which the irresolute man would begin in the case of God (for he would begin with doubt), precisely this is insubordination; for thereby God is deposed from the throne, from being the Lord. And when one has done this, one really has chosen another master, wilfulness . . ." To argue the case with the philosopher is to risk defeat on an issue too important by far to be dealt with by a match of wits. It is better to ignore him, to insist that faith is one thing and reason another, and to settle the issue decisively by a leap of faith. That is the only escape from despair.

For the other example of how Kierkegaard's thought is rooted in his life, we may refer to his too celebrated love affair. Much in his philosophy seems to have been a rationalization, in the Freudian sense, of his conduct in this affair. He had long contemplated with growing passion a neighbor's daughter, a girl in her teens named Regina Olsen. He at last declared himself, led her on to a whole-hearted reciprocating passion, then threw her abruptly over and went off to Berlin where he wrote up his experience in *The Diary of a Seducer* and other edifying discourses. By merely secular standards, his behavior was that of a cad, and he seems to have realized this, for running through much of his work from this time on, there is a veiled attempt to justify himself. To his credit, he has occasional doubts. "If I had had faith, I would have remained with Regina," he once confided to his diary.

But the line he more commonly took was that he threw her over because he did have faith, or at least because renouncing her would give exaltation to his spiritual life. He prefers to write about it in parables, but the reference is unmistakeable. "Love for that princess became for him the expression for an eternal love, assumed a religious character, was transfigured into a love for the Eternal Being, which did to be sure deny him the fulfilment of his love, yet reconciled him again by the eternal consciousness of its validity in the form of eternity, which no reality can take from him." In this treatment of her, the simple Regina was unable to share "the eternal consciousness of its validity in the form of eternity," and was broken-hearted. Kierkegaard probably realized that, as mentally and sexually abnormal, he was no fit person to marry at all, and if he had rested his desertion on such ground, one could understand it, though wondering why the discovery came so late. But such an explanation was not satisfactory to a mind in which a messianic egotism was mixed in unwholesome fashion with eroticism and piety. He had done wrong; he knew it; and if he was to retain his picture of himself as genius and saint, he must explain his action by lofty motives. He chose the loftiest. As Buber suggested, God was Regina's successful rival. The desertion was in obedience to a secret imperative from on high, which, like the hero of *Fear and Trembling*, he was ready to obey, whatever the cost in renunciation. Regarding this book, Professor Paton has passed judgment in terms with which, severe as they are, it is hard to disagree.

> . . . What makes it nauseating as a professedly religious work is that, as he himself said, it is a "mystification" which reproduces his own life. In other words, it is an account of his unhappy love affair with Regina Olsen, an account in which his own deplorable behaviour is supposed to be similar to that of Abraham. We may pity his unhappy and diseased temperament, but neurosis is a poor qualification for setting up as a religious guide . . . Self-centeredness is the very antithesis of religion; and if the paradox of faith is—as he says—a willingness "to do the terrible and to do it for its own sake" (as well as for God's sake), then the less of this kind of faith we have the better.*

Concluding Disillusioned Postscript

This is a grim note on which to end a study of Kierkegaard. He is a figure who of late years has received almost lyrical praise for the profundity of his thought and the penetration of his psychological

* *The Modern Predicament,* 120.

insight. We have been assured that he "belongs to all time and to all humanity, just as surely as do Plato and Aristotle, Spinoza and Hume and Kant and Hegel."* We have been assured over and over of how profound he is. "Kierkegaard's explanation of the dialectical relation of freedom and fate in sin is one of the profoundest in Christian thought," and again, "Kierkegaard's analysis of the relation of anxiety to sin is the profoundest in Christian thought."† "Harnack's once celebrated essay on *The Essence of Christianity* seems incredibly trivial when one has read S. K."‡ I recall that, stimulated by such fair words, I approached his books with high expectation. My experience was like that of John Laird, who wrote, after a determined attempt on *Either/Or:* "By the time I had finished the first enormous volume I was sadly disconsolate. Even in a wide literary interpretation of 'philosophy'—and no other could be appropriate—I found very little that seemed to be worth stating in a formal way." One reads a few puzzling pages with the feeling that the writer must be catching his breath and getting slowly under way; some definite point will soon emerge. It does not. One reads on with gathering disillusionment, coming in the end to realize that Kierkegaard, if a philosopher at all, is a distinct species of philosopher, and that it is useless to look for clearly stated theses, still less for ordered arguments in support of them. He combined an undisciplined intellect with a remorseless, facile, unchecked, limitless, compulsive loquacity; he was, as Disraeli said of Gladstone, "inebriated with the exuberance of his own verbosity." He is alleged to have written twenty-two books by the time he was thirty-five; and since they have no firm construction, no obvious beginning or end, or any internal reason why they should ever end, one can read them only by allowing one's critical sense to be lulled into drowsiness and one's mind to be floated along on the tide of words.

Unfortunately, no sooner has one made one's peace with the indiscipline of thought and style than one must begin the battle over again with the man himself. The self-absorption, the strange blend of piety and contempt (his two dominant emotions, Georg Brandes said), the dogmatism, the proclamations of unappreciated genius, the imprecations on church and clergy, the gospel of universal guilt and despair, the homilies on love from a mind that was simmering with hatreds, the scorn for those who, in religion, try to understand—these things have an effect that the reader must manage to suppress if he is to go on. He must remind himself that though this is a sick and twisted mind, such minds have, on occasion, shown a sharp eye for truth.

What was the truth that Kierkegaard saw? The great insight claimed for him is that in religion objective thinking breaks down and that the insight it seeks is obtainable by faith. As for the inadequacy of thought, a case can certainly be made for it, and such a case was actually presented with a force of statement and argument far beyond Kierkegaard's range by an English contemporary, Dean Mansel.

* D. F. Swenson in E. Geismar, *Søren Kierkegaard,* xvii.

† R. Niebuhr, *The Nature and Destiny of Man,* I, 263; I, 182, note.

‡ W. Lowrie, *Kierkegaard,* 5.

Kierkegaard's own case is unimpressive. His contention that thought cannot deal with existence is put so obscurely that there is difficulty in extracting from it a meaning clear enough to refute. Furthermore, he seems never to have worked out what was involved for the normal exercise of reason by its breakdown at crucial points—for ethics by the suspension of its clearest rules, and for logic by the admission of contradictions to the status of higher truths. As a philosopher he employed with scornful confidence the reason which, as a theologian, he dismissed with equal scorn. He was too impatient to get on with his writing to declare a moratorium on it while he achieved coherence in this theory of knowledge.

What of the second half of the great insight attributed to him—that where reason fails faith succeeds? Unfortunately this is more obscure than the first. Perhaps it is inevitably so. When one has bid good-bye to reason and made the prodigious non-rational leap into the rarefied air of paradox, one should presumably say nothing, since anything one did say would have to be said in the distorting accents of the reason one has left behind. The silence, nevertheless, is a pity. Men struggle onward and upward along the stages on life's way; a hardy few reach the summit; and when they descend, the many waiting below ask a report on the splendid vision from the top. Kierkegaard, so voluble elsewhere, here finds his tongue at last tied. The stage that was supposed to cast illumination downward on all the others turns out to be strangely dark and empty. Practically, indeed, it is rather worse than empty. Kierkegaard insists that the love felt by the knight of faith is not mere human love, and if one can make any inference from his own practice, he was right, since the love displayed in that practice permitted a selfishness and harshness toward others—toward Hans Andersen and Regina and his mother and his brother and Bishop Mynster and the unfortunate "Christians" about him—which the lower love would not have allowed. Nor is the insight of faith into truth comparable with a merely human knowledge. Just as it gave Luther the power to see through and around Aristotle, so it gave Kierkegaard the power to see how superficial were all the systems of philosophy, and to see of science, without the need to study it, that if it differed from faith at any point, it was wrong.

In the end Kierkegaard stands, in his thought as in his life, a defeated figure. He was like a business man who builds up a commercial empire by condemning and buying up the businesses of all his competitors on the strength of promissory notes which he cannot redeem. He indicts reason; he indicts rational ethics; he indicts love and justice of the merely human variety; he indicts with eloquent contempt the Christianity practiced around him. He invites them all to accept subordination to one directing head in return for grandiose, even infinite, promises. But when they present their claims, they find the bank empty. The large promises of a new directorate are never fulfilled. Just how reason is to be rectified or ethics reformed, just what the new golden affections are that are to replace the old leaden ones, just what we are to believe or do or feel—these all-important directions never transpire. Faith has leaped so high that it has shot up beyond the earth's atmosphere to where thought and conscience can no longer breathe. These may be poor things, but we know them, and know that they have served us not badly. We shall do well to keep them, even when notes are flourished before us that are stamped in infinite denominations, unless we can be sure that the issuing bank is solvent. That assurance Kierkegaard never supplies.

3

PAUL TILLICH (1886–1967)

*Faith and Religious Symbols**

Tillich is a major Protestant theologian of the Twentieth Century. He insists that the existence of God cannot be demonstrated because the object of such a proof would have nothing to do with the faith upon which religious men act. (Compare Tillich's idea of God as "ultimate concern" with the proofs of God in Aquinas.) Tillich's conception is of a God "beyond the God of Theism," a personal God that is not an object in the demonstrable world. Tillich, influenced by existentialistic thinking, sees man as concerned with his own being. Man is a being of concerns, and some concerns are more basic than others. Religion is the expression of the system of ultimate concerns. It is a system of symbols representing the inexpressible concerns at the root of our way of life. Perhaps this whole idea is best summarized in Tillich's rather paradoxical phrase, "God is the symbol of God." The word serves to express the ultimate immediacy of one's concern and gives us a concrete object on which to focus. This, Tillich argues, is not dissimilar from the worship of a sacred tree or the statue of Apollo. Faith is not, however, in symbols, but in ultimate concerns expressed through symbols.

* Paul Tillich, *Dynamics of Faith* (New York: Harper and Row, 1957), pp. 1–2, 8–12, 44. Copyright © 1957 by Paul Tillich. Reprinted by permission of Harper & Row, Publishers.

Faith as Ultimate Concern

FAITH is the state of being ultimately concerned: the dynamics of faith are the dynamics of man's ultimate concern. Man, like every living being, is concerned about many things, above all about those which condition his very existence, such as food and shelter. But man, in contrast to other living beings, has spiritual concerns—cognitive, aesthetic, social, political. Some of them are urgent, often extremely urgent, and each of them as well as the vital concerns can claim ultimacy for a human life or the life of a social group. If it claims ultimacy it demands the total surrender of him who accepts this claim, and it promises total fulfillment even if all other claims have to be subjected to it or rejected in its name. If a national group makes the life and growth of the nation its ultimate concern, it demands that all other concerns, economic well-being, health and life, family, aesthetic and cognitive truth, justice and humanity, be sacrificed. The extreme nationalisms of our century are laboratories for the study of what ultimate concern means in all aspects of human existence, including the smallest concern of one's daily life. Everything is centered in the only god, the nation—a god who certainly proves to be a demon, but who shows clearly the unconditional character of an ultimate concern.

But it is not only the unconditional demand made by that which is one's ultimate concern, it is also the promise of ultimate fulfillment which is accepted in the act of faith. The content of this promise is not necessarily defined. It can be expressed in indefinite symbols or in concrete symbols which cannot be taken literally, like the "greatness" of one's nation in which one participates even if one has died for it, or the conquest of mankind by the "saving race," etc. In each of these cases it is "ultimate fulfillment" that is promised, and it is exclusion from such fulfillment which is threatened if the unconditional demand is not obeyed.

An example—and more than an example—is the faith manifest in the religion of the Old Testament. It also has the character of ultimate concern in demand, threat and promise. The content of this concern is not the nation—although Jewish nationalism has sometimes tried to distort it into that—but the content is the God of justice, who, because he represents justice for everybody and every nation, is called the universal God, the God of the universe. He is the ultimate concern of every pious Jew, and therefore in his name the great commandment is given: "You shall love the Lord your God with all your heart, and with all your soul, and with all your might" (Deut. 6:5). This is what ultimate concern means and from these words the term "ultimate concern" is derived. They state unambiguously the character of genuine faith, the demand of total surrender to the subject of ultimate concern. The Old Testament is full of commands which make the nature of this surrender concrete, and it is full of promises and threats in relation to it. Here also are the promises of symbolic indefiniteness, although they center around fulfillment of the national and individual life, and the threat is the exclusion from such fulfillment through national extinction and individual catastrophe. Faith, for the men of the Old Testament, is the state of being ultimately and unconditionally concerned about Jahweh and about what he represents in demand, threat and promise.

Another example—almost a counter-example, yet nevertheless equally revealing—is the ultimate concern with "success" and with social standing and economic power. It is the god of many people in the highly competitive Western culture and it does what every ultimate concern must do: it demands unconditional surrender to its laws even if the price is the sacrifice of genuine human relations, personal conviction, and creative *eros*. Its threat is social and economic defeat, and its promise—indefinite as all such promises—the fulfillment of one's being. It is the breakdown of this kind of faith which characterizes and makes religiously important most contemporary literature. Not false calculations but a misplaced faith is revealed in novels like *Point of No Return*. When fulfilled, the promise of this faith proves to be empty.

Faith is the state of being ultimately concerned. The content matters infinitely for the life of the believer, but it does not matter for the formal definition of faith. And this is the first step we have to make in order to understand the dynamics of faith.

Faith as ultimate concern is an act of the total personality. It happens in the center of the personal life and includes all its elements. Faith is the most centered act of the human mind. It is not a movement of a special section or a special function of man's total being. They all are united in the act of faith. But faith is not the sum total of their impacts. It transcends every special impact as well as the totality of them and it has itself a decisive impact on each of them.

. . .

The Source of Faith

We have described the act of faith and its relation to the dynamics of personality. Faith is a total and centered act of the personal self, the act of unconditional, infinite and ultimate concern. The question now arises: what is the source of this all-embracing and all-transcending concern? The word "concern" points to two sides of a relationship, the relation between the one who is concerned and his concern. In both respects we have to imagine man's situation in itself and in his world. The reality of man's ultimate concern reveals something about his being, namely, that he is able to transcend the flux of relative and transitory experiences of his ordinary life. Man's experiences, feelings, thoughts are conditioned and finite. They not only come and go, but their content is of finite and conditional concern—unless they are elevated to unconditional validity. But this presupposes the general possibility of doing so; it presupposes the element of infinity in man. Man is able to understand in an immediate personal and central act the meaning of the ultimate, the unconditional, the absolute, the infinite. This alone makes faith a human potentiality.

Human potentialities are powers that drive toward actualization. Man is driven toward faith by his awareness of the infinite to which he belongs, but which he does not own like a possession. This is in abstract terms what concretely appears as the "restlessness of the heart" within the flux of life.

The unconditional concern which is faith is the concern about the unconditional. The infinite passion, as faith has been described, is the passion for the infinite. Or, to use our first term, the ultimate concern is concern about what is experienced as ultimate. In this way, we have turned from the subjective meaning of faith as a centered act of the personality to its objective meaning, to what is meant in the act of faith. It would not help at this point of our analysis to call that which is meant in the act of faith "God" or "a god." For at this step we ask: What in the idea of God constitutes divinity? The answer is: It is the element of the unconditional and of ultimacy. This carries the quality of divinity. If this is seen, one can understand why almost every thing "in heaven and on earth" has received ultimacy in the history of human religion. But we also can understand that a critical principle was and is at work in man's religious consciousness, namely, that which is really ultimate over against what claims to be ultimate but is only preliminary, transitory, finite.

The term "ultimate concern" unites the subjective and the objective side of the act of faith—the *fides qua creditur* (the Faith through which one believes) and the *fides quae creditur* (the faith which is believed). The first is the classical term for the centered act of the personality, the ultimate concern. The second is the classical term for that toward which this act is directed, the ultimate itself, expressed in symbols of the divine. This distinction is very important, but not ultimately so, for the one side cannot be without the other. There is no faith without a content toward which it is directed. There is always something meant in the act of faith. And there is no way of having the content of faith except in the act of faith. All speaking about divine matters which is not done in the state of ultimate concern is meaningless. Because that which is meant in the act of faith cannot be approached in any other way than through an act of faith.

In terms like ultimate, unconditional, infinite, absolute, the difference between subjectivity and objectivity is overcome. The ultimate of the act of faith and the ultimate that is meant in the act of faith are one and the same. This is symbolically expressed by the mystics when they say that their knowledge of God is the knowledge God has of himself; and it is expressed by Paul when he says (I Cor. 13) that he will know as he is known, namely, by God. God never can be object without being at the same time subject. Even a successful prayer is, according to Paul (Rom. 8), not possible without God as Spirit praying within us. The same experience expressed in abstract language is the disappearance of the ordinary subject-object scheme in the experience of the ultimate, the unconditional. In the act of faith that which is the source of this act is present beyond the cleavage of subject and object. It is present as both and beyond both.

This character of faith gives an additional criterion for distinguishing true and false ultimacy. The finite which claims infinity without having it (as, e.g., a nation or success) is not able to transcend the subject-object scheme. It remains an object which the believer looks at as a subject. He can approach it with ordinary knowledge and subject it to ordinary handling. There are, of course, many degrees in the endless realm of false ultimacies. The nation is nearer to true ultimacy than is success. Nationalistic ecstasy can produce a state in which the subject is almost swallowed by the object. But after a period the subject emerges again, disappointed radically and totally, and by looking at the nation in a skeptical and calculating way does injustice even to its justified claims. The more idolatrous a faith the less it is able to overcome the cleavage between subject and object. For that is the difference between true and idolatrous faith. In true faith the ultimate concern is a concern about the truly ultimate; while in idolatrous faith preliminary, finite realities are elevated to the rank of ultimacy. The inescapable consequence of idolatrous faith is "existential disappointment," a disappointment which penetrates into the very existence of man! This is the dynamics of idolatrous faith; that it is faith, and as such, the centered act of a personality; that the centering point is something which is more or less on to the periphery; and that, therefore, the act of faith leads to the loss of the center and to a disruption of the personality. The ecstatic character of even an idolatrous faith can hide this consequence only for a certain time. But finally it breaks into the open.

. . .

The Meaning of Symbol

Man's ultimate concern must be expressed symbolically, because symbolic language alone is able to express the ultimate. This statement demands explanation in several respects. In spite of the manifold research about the meaning and function of symbols which is going on in contemporary philosophy, every writer who uses the term "symbol" must explain his understanding of it.

Symbols have one characteristic in common with signs; they point beyond themselves to something else. The red sign at the street corner points to the order to stop the movements of cars at certain intervals. A red light and the stopping of cars have essentially no relation to each other, but conventionally they are united as long as the convention lasts. The same is true of letters and numbers and partly even words. They point beyond themselves to sounds and meanings. They are given this special function by convention within a nation or by international conventions, as the mathematical signs. Sometimes such signs are called symbols; but this is unfortunate because it makes the distinction between signs and symbols more difficult. Decisive is the fact that signs do not participate in the reality of that to which they point, while symbols do. Therefore, signs can be replaced for reasons of expediency or convention, while symbols cannot.

This leads to the second characteristic of the symbol: It participates in that to which it points: the flag participates in the power and dignity of the nation for which it stands. Therefore, it cannot be replaced except after an historic catastrophe that changes the reality of the nation which it symbolizes. An attack on the flag is felt as an attack on the majesty of the group in which it is acknowledged. Such an attack is considered blasphemy.

The third characteristic of a symbol is that it opens up levels of reality which otherwise are closed for us. All arts create symbols for a level of reality which cannot be reached in any other way. A picture and a poem reveal elements of reality which cannot be approached scientifically. In the creative work of art we encounter reality in a dimension which is closed for us without such works. The symbol's fourth characteristic not only opens up dimensions and elements of reality which otherwise would remain unapproachable but also unlocks dimensions and elements of our soul which correspond to the dimensions and elements of reality. A great play gives us not only a new vision of the human scene, but it opens up hidden depths of our own being. Thus we are able to receive what the play reveals to us in reality. There are within us dimensions of which we cannot become aware except through symbols, as melodies and rhythms in music.

Symbols cannot be produced intentionally—this is the fifth characteristic. They grow out of the individual or collective unconscious and cannot function without being accepted by the unconscious dimension of our being. Symbols which have an especially social function, as political and religious symbols, are created or at least accepted by the collective unconscious of the group in which they appear.

The sixth and last characteristic of the symbol is a consequence of the fact that symbols cannot be invented. Like living beings, they grow and they die. They grow when the situation is ripe for them, and they die when the situation changes. The symbol of the "king" grew in a special period of history, and it died in most parts of the world in our period. Symbols do not grow because people are longing for them, and they do not die because of scientific or practical criticism. They die because they can no longer produce response in the group where they originally found expression.

These are the main characteristics of every symbol. Genuine symbols are created in several spheres of man's cultural creativity. We have mentioned already the political and the artistic realm. We could add history and, above all, religion, whose symbols will be our particular concern.

Religious Symbols

We have discussed the meaning of symbols generally because, as we said, man's ultimate concern must be expressed symbolically! One may ask: Why can it not be expressed directly and properly? If money, success or the nation is someone's ultimate concern, can this not be said in a direct way without symbolic language? Is it not only in those cases in which the content of the ultimate concern is called "God" that we are in the realm of symbols? The answer is that everything which is a matter of unconditional concern is made into a god. If the nation is someone's ultimate concern, the name of the nation becomes a sacred name and the nation receives divine qualities which far surpass the reality of the being and functioning of the nation. The nation then stands for and symbolizes the true ultimate, but in an idolatrous way. Success as ultimate concern is not the national desire of actualizing potentialities, but is readiness to sacrifice all other values of life for the sake of a position of power and social predominance. The anxiety about not being a success is an idolatrous form of the anxiety about divine condemnation. Success is grace; lack of success, ultimate judgment. In this way concepts designating ordinary realities become idolatrous symbols of ultimate concern.

The reason for this transformation of concepts into symbols is the character of ultimacy and the nature of faith. That which is the true ultimate transcends the realm of finite reality infinitely. Therefore, no finite reality can express it directly and properly. Religiously speaking, God transcends his own name. This is why the use of his name easily becomes an abuse or a blasphemy. Whatever we say about that which concerns us ultimately, whether or not we call it God, has a symbolic meaning. It points beyond itself while participating in that to which it points. In no other way can faith express itself adequately. The language of faith is the language of symbols. If faith were what we have shown that it is not, such an assertion could not be made. But faith, understood as the state of being ultimately concerned, has no language other than symbols. When saying this I always expect the question: Only a symbol? He who asks this question shows that he has not understood the difference between signs and symbols nor the power of symbolic language, which surpasses in quality and strength the power of any nonsymbolic language. One should never say "only a symbol," but one should say "not less than a symbol." With this in mind we can now describe the different kinds of symbols of faith.

God is the Fundamental Symbol of Faith

The fundamental symbol of our ultimate concern is God. It is always present in any act of faith, even if the act of faith includes the denial of God. Where there is ultimate concern, God can be denied only in the name of God. One God can deny the other one. Ultimate concern cannot deny its own character as ultimate. Therefore, it affirms what is meant by the word "God." Atheism, consequently, can only mean the attempt to remove any ultimate concern—to remain unconcerned about the meaning of one's existence. Indifference toward the ultimate question is the only imaginable form of atheism. Whether it is possible is a problem which must remain unsolved at this point. In any case, he who denies God as a matter of ultimate concern affirms God, because he affirms ultimacy in his concern. God is the fundamental symbol for what concerns us ultimately. Again it would be completely wrong to ask: So God is nothing but a symbol? Because the next question has to be: A symbol for what? And then the answer would be: For God! God is symbol for God. This means that in the notion of God we must distinguish two elements: the element of ultimacy, which is a matter of immediate experience and not symbolic in itself, and the element of concreteness, which is taken from our ordinary experience and symbolically applied to God. The man whose ultimate concern is a sacred tree has both the ultimacy of concern and the concreteness of the tree which symbolizes his relation to the ultimate. The man who adores Apollo is ultimately concerned, but not in an abstract way. His ultimate concern is symbolized in the divine figure of Apollo. The man who glorifies Jahweh, the God of the Old Testament, has both an ultimate concern and a concrete image of what concerns him ultimately. This is the meaning of the seemingly cryptic statement that God is the symbol of God. In this qualified sense God is the fundamental and universal content of faith.

It is obvious that such an understanding of the meaning of God makes the discussions about the existence or non-existence of God meaningless. It is meaningless to question the ultimacy of an ultimate concern. This element in the idea of God is in itself certain. The symbolic expression of this element varies endlessly through the whole history of mankind. Here again it would be meaningless to ask whether one or another of the figures in which an ultimate concern is symbolized does "exist." If "existence" refers to something which can be found within the whole of reality, no divine being exists. The question is not this, but: which of the innumerable symbols of faith is most adequate to the meaning of faith? In other words, which symbol of ultimacy expresses the ultimate without idolatrous elements? This is the problem, and not the so-called "existence of God"—which is in itself an impossible combination of words. God as the ultimate in man's ultimate concern is more certain than any other certainty, even that of oneself. God as symbolized in a divine figure is a matter of daring faith, of courage and risk.

God is the basic symbol of faith, but not the only one. All the qualities we attribute to him, power, love, justice, are taken from finite experiences and applied symbolically to that which is beyond finitude and infinity. If faith calls God "almighty," it uses the human experience of power in order to symbolize the content of its infinite concern, but it does not describe a highest being who can do as he pleases. So it is with all the other qualities and with all the actions, past, present and future, which men attribute to God. They are symbols taken from our daily experience, and not information about what God did once upon a time or will do sometime in the future. Faith is not the belief in such stories, but it is the acceptance of symbols that express our ultimate concern in terms of divine actions.

Another group of symbols of faith are manifestations of the divine in things and events, in persons and communities, in words and documents. This whole realm of sacred objects is a treasure of symbols. Holy things are not holy in themselves, but they point beyond themselves to the source of all holiness, that which is of ultimate concern.

4

*Bhagavad-Gita**

These are selections from the Hindu epic the Bhagavad-Gita. *The Krishna in the form of a charioteer meets King Arjuna on the battlefield. The King is not willing to fight his relatives. Krishna assures the King that he ought not to worry about killing, that it is his duty as King to do so, and that in Brahman there is no real slaying, for all is eternal. Life should be the achievement of oneness with God, and there are various ways of attaining peace of soul. The goal is that self-identity be lost in exchange for identification with Brahman.*

* *Bhagavad-Gita* Swami Paramananda, trans. (Boston: The Ramakrishna Vedanta Society, 1903), Chaps. 1, 2, 4, 5, 6, 9, 12, 18.

Arjuna's Grief

Arjuna said:

O Krishna, seeing these my kinsmen, gather here desirous to fight, my limbs fail me, my mouth is parched; my body shivers, my hair stands on end, my Gandiva (bow) slips from my hand, my skin is burning. O Keshava (Krishna, the slayer of Keshi), I am not able to stand upright, my mind is in a whirl and I see adverse omens. O Krishna, neither do I see any good in slaying my own people in this strife. I desire neither victory, nor kingdom, nor pleasures. Teachers, uncles, sons and grandsons, grandfathers, fathers-in-law, brothers-in-law, besides other kinsmen, for whose sake empire, enjoyment and pleasures are desired, they themselves stand here in battle, forsaking life and wealth. What avail, then, is kingdom, enjoyment, or even life, O Govinda (Krishna)? These warriors I do not wish to kill, even though I am killed by them, not even for the dominion over the three worlds, how much less for the sake of this earth, O slayer of Madhu. . . .

With my nature overpowered by pity and depression and mind confused about duty, I implore Thee (O Krishna) tell me with certainty what is good for me. I am Thy disciple, instruct me, who have taken refuge in Thee. For I see not what can remove this grief which withers my senses, even if I should obtain unrivalled and flourishing dominion over the earth and rulership over the gods.

Sanjaya said:

Gudakesha (Arjuna), the conqueror of his foes, having thus spoken to the Lord of the senses (Krishna), said: "I shall not fight, O Govinda!" and became silent. O descendant of King Bharata, Hrishikesha (Krishna), as if smilingly, spoke these words to him (Arjuna), who was thus grief-stricken in the midst of the two armies.

The Yoga of Knowledge Frees One from Karma

The Blessed Lord said:

Thou hast been mourning for those who should not be mourned for and yet thou speakest (apparent) words of wisdom; but the truly wise mourn not either for the dead or for the living. It is not that I have never existed before, nor thou, nor all these kings. Nor is it that all of us shall cease to exist hereafter. As in this body the embodied soul passes through childhood, youth and old age, in the same manner it goes from one body to another; therefore the wise are never deluded regarding it (the soul). O son of Kunti, the feelings of heat, cold, pleasure, pain, are produced from the contact of the senses with sense-objects; they are with beginning and end, transitory. Therefore, O Bharata, endure them (bravely). O mighty among men, he is fit to attain immortality who is serene and not afflicted by these sensations, but is the same in pleasure and pain. There is no existence for the unreal and the real can never be non-existent. The Seers of Truth know the nature and final ends of both. Know That to be indestructible by which all this is pervaded. No one is ever able to destroy that Immutable. These bodies are perishable; but the dwellers in these bodies are eternal, indestructible and impenetrable. Therefore fight, O descendant of Bharata!

He who considers this (Self) as a slayer or he who thinks that this (Self) is slain, neither of these knows the Truth. For It does not slay, nor is It slain. This (Self) is never born, nor does It die, nor after once having been, does It go into non-being. This (Self) is unborn, eternal, changeless, ancient. It is never destroyed even when the body is destroyed. O son of Pritha, how can he slay or cause the slaying of another who knows this (Self) to be indestructible, eternal, unborn and immutable? As man casts off worn-out garments and puts on others which are new, similarly the embodied soul, casting off worn-out bodies, enters into others which are new. Sword cannot pierce It (Self), fire cannot burn It, water cannot wet It, and air cannot dry It. It cannot be pierced, nor burned, nor wet, nor dried. It is eternal, all-pervading, unchangeable, immovable, everlasting. This (Self) is said to be unmanifested, unthinkable, unchangeable; therefore knowing this to be so, thou shouldst not grieve. But even if thou thinkest that this (Self) is subject to constant birth and death, even then, O mighty-armed, thou shouldst not grieve. For that which is born death is certain, and for the dead birth is certain. Therefore grieve not over that which is unavoidable.

Thus I have declared unto thee the wisdom of Self-realization. Listen now, O son of Pritha, regarding Yoga, by knowing which thou shalt be freed from the bonds of Karma (cause and effect). In this (Yoga) there is neither waste of effort nor possibility of evil results. Even a little practice of this (Yoga) delivers one from great fear. O son of Kuru, in this (Yoga), the well-resolved mind is single and one-pointed; but the purposes of the irresolute mind are many-branched and endless. O son of Pritha, those who delight in the flowery speech of the unwise and are satisfied with the mere letter of the Vedas (Scriptures) saying: "There is naught else"; and those who are full of desires for self-gratification regarding heaven as their highest goal, and are engaged in many intricate Scriptural rites just to secure pleasure and power as the result of their deeds for their future incarnations; whose discrimination is stolen away by the love of power and pleasure and who are thus deeply attached therein, (for such people) it is impossible to obtain either firm conviction (in purpose) or God-consciousness.

The Vedas deal with the three *Gunas.* O Arjuna, be thou free from these three Gunas; free from the pairs of opposites (cold and heat, pleasure and pain); ever steadfast, be thou free from (thoughts of) acquiring or keeping and self-possessing. To the Brahmana, the knower of Truth, all the Vedas are of as little use as a small water-tank is during the time of a flood, when water is everywhere. To work alone thou hast the right, but never to the fruits thereof. Be thou neither actuated by the fruits of action, nor be thou attached to inaction. O Dhananjaya, abandoning attachment and regarding success and failure alike, be steadfast in Yoga and perform thy duties. Evenmindedness is called Yoga. O Dhananjaya, work (with desire for results) is far inferior to work with understanding. Therefore seek refuge in the Yoga of understanding. Wretched indeed are those who work for results.

Oneness with Brahman

Arjuna said:

O Keshava, what are the signs of the man of steady wisdom, one who has attained God-consciousness? How does the man of steady wisdom speak? How does he sit? How does he walk?

The Blessed Lord said:

O Partha, when a man is satisfied in the Self by Self alone and has completely cast out all desires from the mind, then he is said to be of steady wisdom. He whose mind is not agitated in calamities and who has no longing for pleasure, free from attachment, fear and anger, he indeed is said to be a saint of steady wisdom. He who is free from all attachment and neither rejoices on receiving good nor is vexed on receiving evil, his wisdom is well-established. When he completely withdraws his senses from sense-objects as the tortoise withdraws its limbs, then his wisdom becomes well-established. The embodied, through the practice of abstinence (i.e. not giving food to the senses), can deaden the feelings of the senses, but longing still lingers in the heart; all longings drop off when he has seen the Supreme. O son of Kunti, dangerous are the senses, they even carry away forcibly the mind of a discriminative man who is striving for perfection. The man of steady wisdom, having subdued them all (senses), becomes fixed in Me, the Supreme. His wisdom is well-established whose senses are under control. Thinking of sense-objects, man becomes attached thereto. From attachment arises longing and from longing anger is born. From anger arises delusion; from delusion, loss of memory is caused. From loss of memory, the discriminative faculty is ruined and from the ruin of discrimination, he perishes.

But the self-subjugated attains peace and moves among objects with the senses under control, free from any longing or aversion. In peace there is an end to all misery and the peaceful mind soon becomes well-established in wisdom. There is no wisdom for the unsteady and there is no meditation for the unsteady and for the unmeditative there is no peace. How can there be any happiness for the peaceless? For the mind that yields to the uncontrolled and wandering senses, carries away his wisdom just as a boat on water is carried away by wind. Therefore, O mighty-armed, his wisdom is established whose senses are well-restrained from all objects of sense. That which is night to all beings, therein the self-subjugated remains awake; and in that where all beings are awake, that is night for the knower of Self: As the ocean remains calm and unaltered though the waters flow into it, similarly a self-controlled saint remains unmoved when desires enter into him; such a saint alone attains peace, but not he who craves the objects of desire.

That man attains peace who, abandoning all desires, moves about without attachment and longing, without the sense of "I" and "mine." O son of Pritha, this is the state of dwelling in Brahman (absolute Truth); having attained this, no one is ever deluded. Being established in this knowledge even at the end of life, one attains oneness with Brahman (The Supreme). . . .

Sacrifices O sinless one, in this world twofold is the path described by me. The path of wisdom is for the meditative and the path of work is for the active. A man does not attain to freedom from action by non-performance of action, nor does he attain to perfection merely by giving up action. No one can ever rest even for an instant without performing action, for all are impelled by the Gunas (qualities), born of Prakriti (Nature), to act incessantly. He who, restraining the organs of action, sits holding thoughts of sense-objects in mind, that self-deluded one is called a hypocrite. But, O Arjuna, he who, controlling the senses by the mind, follows without attachment the path of action with his organs of action, he is esteemed. . . .

Him the sages call wise whose undertakings are devoid of desire for results and of plans, whose actions are burned by the fire of wisdom. Having abandoned attachment for the fruits of action, ever content and dependent on none, though engaged in action, yet he does nothing. Being freed from longing, with self under control, and giving up all sense of possession (ownership), he is not tainted by sin merely by performing bodily action. Content with whatever comes without effort, undisturbed by the pairs of opposites (pleasure and pain, heat and cold), free from envy, even-minded in success and failure, though acting (he) is not bound. One whose attachment is gone, who is liberated, whose mind is well-established in wisdom, who works for sacrifice alone, his whole Karma melts away. Brahman (absolute Truth) is the offering, Brahman is the oblation, the sacrificial fire is (another form of) Brahman and by Brahman is the sacrifice performed. Thus, by performing actions with the consciousness of Brahman, he reaches Brahman alone.

Some Yogis offer sacrifices to the Devas, while other perform sacrifice in the fire of Brahman by offering self by the self alone. Some offer the sense of hearing and other senses as oblation in the fire of control; still others offer sound and other sense-objects as oblation in the fire of the senses. Others offer all the actions of the senses and the functions of the vital forces as oblation in the fire of self-control, lighted by wisdom. Some offer wealth as sacrifice; some, austerity and Yoga as sacrifice; still others, of rigid vow and self-control, offer study of the Scriptures and wisdom as sacrifice. Yet others offer as sacrifice the outgoing breath in the incoming and the incoming breath in the outgoing, stopping the courses of the outgoing and incoming breaths; thus they constantly practice Pranayama. Whereas others, regulating their food, offer the functions of the vital forces in the Prana itself as sacrifice. All the knowers of sacrifice, burning off their sins (impurities) by the performance of sacrifice and drinking the nectar of the remnant of sacrifice, go to the eternal Brahman (absolute Truth). O best of the Kurus (Arjuna), not even this world is for the non-performer of sacrifice, how much less is the other (world). All these various sacrifices are given in the Vedas (the revelation of Brahman or absolute Truth). Know them all to be born of action; knowing thus thou shalt be freed. O Parantapa (Arjuna), wisdom-sacrifice is far superior to the sacrifice performed with material objects. The entire realm of action, O Partha, ends in wisdom. . . .

Yoga of Renunciation

Arjuna said:

O Krishna, renunciation of action thou praisest and then again Yoga (performance of action); tell me with certainty which of the two is better?

The Blessed Lord said:

Renunciation (of action) and performance of action both lead to liberation. But of the two, performance of action is superior to renunciation of action.

He who performs actions, surrendering them to Brahman and abandoning all attachment, is not polluted by sin, as a lotus-leaf by water. Karma Yogins, for self-purification alone, perform actions with body, with mind, with intellect, even with the senses, abandoning all attachment. The steady-minded, by giving up all (attachment for) the fruits of action, obtains peace, born of steadfastness. The unsteady (fickle), being attached to fruits through desire, is ever bound (by action).

He who has conquered himself by the Self, he is the friend of himself; but he whose self is unconquered, his self acts as his own enemy like an external foe. The Supreme Self of the self-subjugated and serene-minded, is ever undisturbed in heat and cold, pleasure and pain, as well as in honor and dishonor. He who is satisfied with wisdom and direct vision of Truth, who has conquered the senses and is ever undisturbed, to whom a lump of earth, a stone and gold are the same, that

Yogi is said to be a Yukta (a saint of established wisdom). He is esteemed who looks with equal regard upon well-wishers, friends, enemies, neutrals, a mediator, the hateful, relatives, upon the righteous and the unrighteous.

A Yogi should constantly practice concentration of the heart, remaining in seclusion alone, subduing his body and mind and being free from longing and possession (sense of ownership). In a cleanly spot having established his seat firmly, neither too high nor too low, with a cloth, skin and Kusha grass, placed one on the other; being seated there, making the mind one-pointed and subduing the activities of mind and senses, let him practice Yoga for self-purification. Let him hold his body, head and neck erect and motionless, fixing the gaze on the tip of his nose, not looking around. Being serene-hearted and fearless ever steadfast in the vow of Brahmacharya and controlling the mind, let him sit steadfastly absorbed in thoughts of Me, regarding Me as his supreme goal. Thus ever keeping himself steadfast, the Yogi of subdued mind attains eternal peace and freedom, which abide in Me. But, O Arjuna, (the practice of) Yoga is not for him who eats too much or who does not eat at all, nor for him who sleeps too much or keeps awake (in excess). He who is moderate in eating and recreation, moderate in his efforts in work, moderate in sleep and wakefulness (his practice of) Yoga becomes the destroyer of all misery.

When the mind, completely subdued, rests in Self alone, free from longing for all objects of desire, then he is said to be a Yukta (steadfast in Self-knowledge). As a lamp placed in a windless spot does not flicker, the same simile is used to define a Yogi of subdued mind, practicing union with the Self. . . .

Meditation

He whose passions are quieted and mind perfectly tranquil, who has become one with Brahman, being freed from all impurities, to such a Yogi comes supreme bliss. Thus constantly holding the mind steadfast, the Yogi, whose sins are shaken off, easily attains the infinite bliss, born of contact with Brahman. He whose heart is steadfastly engaged in Yoga, looks everywhere with the eyes of equality, seeing the Self in all beings in the Self. He who sees Me in all and all in Me, from him I vanish not, nor does he vanish from Me.

[Now] I shall declare to thee, who art without evil thought, this great secret, wisdom together with realization, knowing which thou shalt be freed from evil. This is the king of sciences, king of secrets, the supreme purifier; it is realized by direct perception and is endowed with righteousness, easily performed and imperishable. O Parantapa (Arjuna), the men who have no faith in this Dharma (science of Self-knowledge), without attaining Me, return to the path of death and re-birth. By My unmanifested Form all this world is pervaded; all beings dwell in Me, but I do not dwell in them. Behold My Divine Yoga! Beings do not dwell in Me; (although) the Creator and Supporter of all beings, (yet) My Self dwells not in them. As the air, vast and always moving everywhere, exists in Akasha (space and ether), even so, know thou, all beings exist in Me. O son of Kunti, all beings, at the end of a cycle, go back to my Prakriti (Nature); again, at the beginning of a cycle, I send them forth. Ruling over My Prakriti, I send forth again and again this vast multitude of beings, who are helplessly impelled by Nature.

O conqueror of wealth (Arjuna), these acts (of creation and dissolution) do not bind Me, sitting as one unconcerned and unattached to these acts. O son of Kunti, with Me as the presiding Deity, Prakriti (Nature) sends forth the moving and the unmoving. For this reason the world wheels round and round. Fools, unaware of My Supreme state, as the great Lord of beings, disregard Me dwelling in human form. They are of vain hopes, of vain deeds, of vain knowledge, and senseless, possessed with the deluding nature of Rakshasas (unclean, passionate and godless creatures) and Asuras (creatures of darkness and of ignorance). But, O son of Kunti, the great-souled ones, possessing the Divine Nature, knowing Me as Immutable and as the Source of being, worship Me with single-minded devotion. . . .

He who, with devotion offereth to Me a leaf, a flower, a fruit and water, that love-offering I accept, made by the pure-hearted. Whatever thou doest, whatever thou eatest, whatever thou offerest as oblation, whatever thou givest and the austerities thou performest, O son of Kunti, do that as an offering to Me. Thus thou shalt be freed from the bonds of action that bears good and evil fruit; and thy soul, being steadfastly engaged in this devotion of renunciation, liberated thou shalt come unto me.

Alike am I to all beings; hated or beloved there is none to Me. But those who worship Me with devotion, they are in Me and I am in them. Even if the most wicked worships Me with undivided devotion, he should be regarded as good, for he is rightly resolved. Very soon he becomes a righteous soul and attains to eternal peace. Know thou, O son of Kunti, that my devotee never perishes. O Partha, even those who are of inferior birth,—women, Vaishyas (merchant class) and Sudras (servant class),—even they, by taking refuge in Me, attain to the Supreme Goal.

What need is there, then, to speak of the holy Brahmanas and the royal Sages! Having come into this transitory and joyless world, do thou worship Me. Fill thy mind with Me, be thou My devotee, worship Me and bow down to Me; thus, steadfastly uniting thy heart with Me alone and regarding Me as thy Supreme Goal, thou shalt come unto Me. . . .

Devotion

But those who contemplate the Imperishable, the Undefinable, Unmanifested, Omnipresent, Unthinkable, Unchangeable, Immovable and Eternal, having subdued all the senses, even-minded everywhere, and engaged in doing good to all beings, verily they attain unto Me. Greater is their difficulty whose minds are set on the Unmanifested, for the goal of the Unmanifested is very arduous for the embodied to attain. But those who, surrendering all actions to Me and regarding Me as the Supreme Goal, worship Me with single-hearted devotion, for them whose hearts are thus fixed on Me, O son of Pritha, I become ere long the Saviour from the ocean of mortal Samsara (world of birth and death). Fix thy mind on Me alone and rest thine understanding in Me, thus thou shalt doubtlessly live in Me hereafter. O Dhananjaya, if thou art unable to fix thy mind steadfastly on Me, then, by faithful practice of devotion, do thou seek to reach Me. If thou art also unable to practice devotion, then be thou intent on working for Me. Even by performing actions for My sake, thou shalt attain perfection. If thou art not able to do even this, then, taking refuge in Me alone, and self-controlled, do thou surrender the fruits of all actions.

Knowledge is indeed better than blind practice; meditation excels knowledge; surrender of the fruits of action is more esteemed than meditation. Peace immediately follows surrender. He who hates no creature and is friendly and compassionate to all, who is free from attachment and egotism, equal-minded in pleasure and pain, and forgiving, who is ever content and meditative, self-subjugated and possessed with firm conviction, with mind and intellect dedicated to Me, he who is thus devoted to Me is dear to Me. He by whom the world is not afflicted and who is not afflicted by the world, who is free from elation, envy, fear and anxiety, he is dear to Me. He who is free from all external dependence, pure, efficient, unattached, undisturbed, and has given up all (selfish) undertakings, he who is thus devoted to Me is dear to Me. He who neither rejoices, nor hates, nor sorrows, nor desires and who has renounced good and evil, he who is thus full of devotion is dear to Me. He who is the same to friend and foe and also in honor and dishonor, the same in heat and cold, pleasure and pain, free from all attachment, he who is alike in praise and blame, is silent, content with everything, homeless, steadyminded, such a devoted soul is dear to Me.

Those who follow this immortal Dharma (teaching) as declared (by Me) and who are possessed with faith, regarding Me as the Supreme Goal, such devotees are exceedingly dear to Me. . . .

Thus wisdom, most profound of all secrets, has been declared unto thee by Me; pondering over it fully, do as thou likest. Hear again My Supreme Word, most profound of all; for thou art My dearly beloved, therefore I shall speak for thy good.

Fill thy heart with Me, be thou devoted to Me, do thou worship Me and bow down to Me. Thus thou shalt attain unto Me. Truly I promise thee, for thou art dear to Me. Giving up all Dharmas (righteous and unrighteous actions), come unto Me alone for refuge. I shall free thee from all sins; grieve not. This should never be spoken by thee to one who is devoid of austerity or without devotion, nor to one who does not render service, nor to one who speaks ill of Me. He who, with supreme devotion to Me, will declare this deeply profound secret to My devotees, doubtless he shall come unto Me. There is none among men who does dearer service to Me than he, nor shall there be any other on earth dearer to Me than he. And he who shall study this Sacred Dialogue between us, by him I shall be worshipped with sacrifice of wisdom. Such is My conviction. And even that man who shall hear this, full of faith and without malice, he too, being freed from evil, shall attain to the sacred region of those of righteous deeds.

ASVAGHOSHA

(c.f.100 A.D.)

*The Soul as All Things**

In Brahman, according to Hinduism, all identity is lost, including a distinction between Brahman and the worshiper. Asvaghosha interprets Brahman as pantheistic. The emphasis on the whole is apparent. All things are in one soul; we only think that there is diversity and change in the world because we are impure, ignorant. The simile of the water and the waves is of particular interest. Can this paradox—of two being one and not one, two and not two, and neither one or two—be explained short of an appeal to mysticism?

* *Asvaghosha's Discourse on the Awakening of Faith in the Mahayana,* T. Suzuki, trans. (Chicago: Open Court Publishing Co., 1900), pp. 55–57, 60–62, 65–68, 79.

IN the one soul we may distinguish two aspects. The one is the soul as suchness, the other is the soul as birth-and-death. Each in itself constitutes all things, and both are so closely interrelated that one cannot be separated from the other.

The Soul as Suchness

What is meant by the soul as suchness, is the oneness of the totality of things, the great all-including whole, the quintessence of the Doctrine. For the essential nature of the soul is uncreate and eternal.

All things, simply on account of our confused subjectivity, appear under the forms of individuation. If we could overcome our confused subjectivity, the signs of individuation would disappear, and there would be no trace of a world of (individual and isolated) objects.

Therefore all things in their fundamental nature are not namable or explicable. They cannot be adequately expressed in any form of language. They are without the range of apperception. They (things in their fundamental nature) have no signs of distinction. They possess absolute sameness. They are subject neither to transformation, nor to destruction. They are nothing but the one soul, for which suchness is another designation. Therefore they cannot be (fully) explained by words or exhausted by reasoning. . . .

The Soul as Birth-and-Death

The soul as birth-and-death comes forth (as the law of causation) from the Tathâgata's womb. But the immortal (i.e., suchness) and the mortal (i.e., birth-and-death) coincide with each other. Though they are not identical, they are not a duality. (Thus when the absolute soul assumes a relative aspect by its self-affirmation) it is called the all-conserving mind.

The same mind has a twofold significance as the organiser and the producer of all things.

Again it embraces two principles: (1) Enlightenment; (2) Nonenlightenment.

Enlightenment is the highest quality of the mind; it is free from all (the limiting) attributes of subjectivity. As it is free from all (limiting) attributes of subjectivity, it is like unto space, penetrating everywhere, as the unity of all. . . .

The multitude of people are said to be lacking in enlightenment, because ignorance prevails there from all eternity, because there is a constant succession of confused subjective states from which they have never been emancipated.

But when they transcend their subjectivity, they can then recognise that all states of mentation, viz., their appearance, presence, change, and disappearance (in the field of consciousness) have no (genuine) reality. They are neither in a temporal nor in a spatial relation with the one soul, for they are not self-existent. . . .

Though all modes of consciousness and mentation are mere products of ignorance, ignorance in its ultimate nature is identical and not-identical with enlightenment *a priori;* and therefore ignorance in one sense is destructible, while in the other sense it is indestructible.

This may be illustrated by (the simile of) the water and the waves which are stirred up in the ocean. Here the water can be said to be identical (in one sense) and not-identical (in the other sense) with the waves. The waves are stirred up by the wind, but the water remains the same. When the wind ceases, the motion of the waves subsides; but the water remains the same.

Likewise, when the mind of all creatures which in its own nature is pure and clean, is stirred up by the wind of ignorance, the waves of mentality make their appearance. These three (i.e., the mind, ignorance, and mentality), however, have no (absolute) existence, and they are neither unity nor plurality.

But the mind though pure in its essence is the source of the awakened (or disturbed) mentality. When ignorance is annihilated, the awakened mentality is tranquilised, whilst the essence of the wisdom remains unmolested. . . .

While the essence of the mind is eternally clean and pure, the influence of ignorance makes possible the existence of a defiled mind. But in spite of the defiled mind, the mind (itself) is eternal, clear, pure, and not subject to transformation.

Further as its original nature is free from particularisation, it knows in itself no change whatever, though it produces everywhere the various modes of existence.

When the oneness of the totality of things is not recognised, then ignorance as well as particularisation arises, and all phases of the defiled mind are thus developed.

5

THOMAS AQUINAS

(1225–1274)

*Five Ways of Proving the Existence of God**

Of all Roman Catholic theologians St. Thomas Aquinas is perhaps the best known. The span of his influence upon the church and its basic views is immense. For Thomas there are two levels of knowledge: reason and faith. When reason reaches its limit, faith must take over to reveal the truths of religion. But the proof of the existence of God falls in the realm of reason. God's existence is not simply self-evident to man. It is a matter of logic and rational demonstration. Thomas argues inductively from data to generalization. He tells us that because we see the world in certain ways (there seems to be order, pattern to the world), we must admit to the existence of a being responsible for that which we see or we could not understand the very concepts we use in talking about our world. The universe, Aquinas claims, was created out of nothing by a God who is its First Mover, First Cause, Necessary Being and Highest Perfection.

* *Basic Writings of St. Thomas Aquinas*, A. C. Pegis, ed. (New York: Random House, 1945), Question 2, Articles 2 and 3. Used by permission of the publishers.

Objection 1 It seems that the existence of God cannot be demonstrated. For it is an article of faith that God exists. But what is of faith cannot be demonstrated, because a demonstration produces scientific knowledge, whereas faith is of the unseen, as is clear from the Apostle (*Heb.* xi. 1). Therefore it cannot be demonstrated that God exists.

Objection 2 Further, essence is the middle term of demonstration. But we cannot know in what God's essence consists, but solely in what it does not consist, as Damascene says. Therefore we cannot demonstrate that God exists.

Objection 3 Further, if the existence of God were demonstrated, this could only be from His effects. But His effects are not proportioned to Him, since He is infinite and His effects are finite, and between the finite and infinite there is no proportion. Therefore, since a cause cannot be demonstrated by an effect not proportioned to it, it seems that the existence of God cannot be demonstrated.

On the contrary, the Apostle says: *The invisible things of Him are clearly seen, being understood by the things that are made* (*Rom.* i. 20). But this would not be unless the existence of God could be demonstrated through the things that are made; for the first thing we must know of anything is, whether it exists.

I answer that, Demonstration can be made in two ways: One is through the cause, and is called *propter quid,* and this is to argue from what is prior absolutely. The other is through the effect, and is called a demonstration *quia;* this is to argue from what is prior relatively only to us. When an effect is better known to us than its cause, from the effect we proceed to the knowledge of the cause. And from every effect the existence of its proper cause can be demonstrated, so long as its effects are better known to us; because, since every effect depends upon its cause, if the effect exists, the cause must pre-exist. Hence the existence of God, in so far as it is not self-evident to us, can be demonstrated from those of His effects which are known to us.

Reply Objection 1 The existence of God and other like truths about God, which can be known by natural reason, are not articles of faith, but are preambles to the articles, for faith presupposes natural knowledge, even as grace presupposes nature and perfection the perfectible. Nevertheless, there is nothing to prevent a man, who cannot grasp a proof, from accepting, as a matter of faith, something which in itself is capable of being scientifically known and demonstrated.

Reply Objection 2 When the existence of a cause is demonstrated from an effect, this effect takes the place of the definition of the cause in proving the cause's existence. This is especially the case in regard to God, because, in order to prove the existence of anything, it is necessary to accept as a middle term the meaning of the name, and not its essence, for the question of its essence follows on the question of its existence. Now the names given to God are derived from His effects, as will be later shown. Consequently, in demonstrating the existence of God from His effects, we may take for the middle term the meaning of the name *God.*

Reply Objection 3 From effects not proportioned to the cause no perfect knowledge of that cause can be obtained. Yet from every effect the existence of the cause can be clearly demonstrated, and so we can demonstrate the existence of God from His effects; though from them we cannot know God perfectly as He is in His essence.

On the contrary, It is said in the person of God: *I am Who am* (*Exod. iii.* 14).

I answer that, The existence of God can be proved in five ways.

The first and more manifest way is the argument from motion. It is certain, and evident to our senses, that in the world some things are in motion. Now whatever is moved is moved by another, for nothing can be moved except it is in potentiality to that towards which it is moved whereas a thing moves inasmuch as it is in act. For motion is nothing else than the reduction of something from potentiality to actuality. But nothing can be reduced from potentiality to actuality, except by something in a state of actuality. Thus that which is actually hot, as fire, makes wood, which is potentially hot, to be actually hot, and thereby moves and changes it. Now it is not possible that the same thing should be at once in actuality and potentiality in the same respect, but only in different respects. For what is actually hot cannot simultaneously be potentially hot; but it is simultaneously potentially cold. It is therefore impossible that in the same respect and in the same way a thing should be both mover and moved, i. e., that it should move itself. Therefore, whatever is moved must be moved by another. If that by which it is moved be itself moved, then this also must needs be moved by another, and that by another again. But this cannot go on to infinity, because then there would be no first mover, and, consequently, no other mover, seeing that subsequent movers move only inasmuch as they are moved by the first mover, as the staff moves only because it is moved by the hand. Therefore, it is necessary to arrive at a first mover, moved by no other; and this everyone understands to be God.

The second way is from the nature of efficient cause. In the world of sensible things we find there is an order of efficient causes. There is no case known (neither is it, indeed, possible) in which a thing is found to be the efficient cause of itself; for so it would be prior to itself, which is impossible. Now in efficient causes it is not possible to go on to infinity, because in all efficient causes following in order, the first is the cause of the intermediate cause, and the intermediate is the cause of the ultimate cause, whether the intermediate cause be several, or one only. Now to take away the cause is to take away the effect. Therefore, if there be no first cause among efficient causes, there will be no ultimate, nor any intermediate, cause. But if in efficient causes it is possible to go on to infinity, there will be no first efficient cause, neither will there be an ultimate effect, nor any intermediate efficient causes; all of which is plainly false. Therefore it is necessary to admit a first efficient cause, to which everyone gives the name of God.

The third way is taken from possibility and necessity, and runs thus. We find in nature things that are possible to be and not to be, since they are found to be generated, and to be corrupted, and consequently, it is possible for them to be and not to be. But it is impossible for these always to exist, for that which can not be at some time is not. Therefore, if everything can not be, then at one time there was nothing in existence. Now if this were true, even now there would be nothing in existence, because that which does not exist begins to exist only through something already existing. Therefore, if at one time nothing was in existence, it would have been impossible for anything to have begun to exist; and thus even now nothing would be in existence—

which is absurd. Therefore, not all beings are merely possible, but there must exist something the existence of which is necessary. But every necessary thing either has its necessity caused by another, or not. Now it is impossible to go on to infinity in necessary things which have their necessity caused by another, as has been already proved in regard to efficient causes. Therefore we cannot but admit the existence of some being having of itself its own necessity, and not receiving it from another, but rather causing in others their necessity. This all men speak of as God.

The fourth way is taken from the gradation to be found in things. Among beings there are some more and some less good, true, noble, and the like. But *more* and *less* are predicated of different things according as they resemble in their different ways something which is the maximum, as a thing is said to be hotter according as it more nearly resembles that which is hottest; so that there is something which is truest, something best, something noblest, and, consequently, something which is most being, for those things that are greatest in truth are greatest in being, as it is written in *Metaph.* II (*Metaph.* Ia, 1 993b30). Now the maximum in any genus is the cause of all in that genus, as fire, which is the maximum of heat, is the cause of all hot things, as is said in the same book (993b25). Therefore there must also be something which is to all beings the cause of their being, goodness, and every other perfection; and this we call God.

The fifth way is taken from the governance of the world. We see that things which lack knowledge, such as natural bodies, act for an end, and this is evident from their acting always, or nearly always in the same way, so as to obtain the best result. Hence it is plain that they achieve their end, not fortuitously, but designedly. Now whatever lacks knowledge cannot move towards an end, unless it be directed by some being endowed with knowledge and intelligence; as the arrow is directed by the archer. Therefore some intelligent being exists by whom all natural things are directed to their end; and this being we call God.

6

FRIEDRICH NIETZSCHE

(1844–1900)

*The Deaths of God**

Nietzche's analysis of the deaths of God emphasizes the ways in which man's conception of divinity degrades his conception of himself. He is foretelling the collapse of the value system to which contemporary man is committed. The prophet Zarathustra meets the retired pope, the last pope to serve the dying god. Later he meets the ugliest man in the world who has murdered God in self-defense. Nietzsche tells us that when Gods die they do so in many ways. The Christian God choked on sympathy; he raged at his own failure to create a perfect man; he had to be killed because his pity knew no modesty. Why does Nietzsche choose such bizarre and inglorious ways to describe God's death? Perhaps this is a mirror of the way men are forced to see themselves in relation to their traditional God-concept. One could, no doubt, draw totally bleak pictures from Nietzsche's pronouncement, but Nietzsche sees the death of God as the birth of a new world.

* Friedrich Nietzsche, *Thus Spake Zarathustra*, T. Common, trans. (London: George Allen & Unwin, Ltd., 1909), Sections 66 and 67.

The Retired Pope

NOT long, however, after Zarathustra had freed himself from the magician, he again saw a person sitting beside the path which he followed, namely a tall, black man, with a haggard, pale countenance: *this man* grieved him exceedingly. "Alas," said he to his heart, "there sitteth disguised affliction; methinketh he is of the type of the priests: what do *they* want in my domain?

What! Hardly have I escaped from that magician, and must another necromancer again run across my path,—

—Some sorcerer with laying-on-of-hands, some sombre wonder-worker by the grace of God, some anointed world-maligner, whom, may the devil take!

But the devil is never at the place which would be his right place: he always cometh too late, that cursed dwarf and clubfoot!"—

Thus cursed Zarathustra impatiently in his heart, and considered how with averted look he might slip past the black man. But behold, it came about otherwise. For at the same moment had the sitting one already perceived him; and not unlike one whom an unexpected happiness overtaketh, he sprang to his feet, and went straight towards Zarathustra.

"Whoever thou art, thou traveller," said he, "help a strayed one, a seeker, an old man, who may here easily come to grief!

The world here is strange to me, and remote; wild beasts also did I hear howling; and he who could have given me protection—he is himself no more.

I was seeking the last pious man, a saint and an anchorite, who, alone in his forest, had not yet heard of what all the world knoweth at present."

"*What* doth all the world know at present?" asked Zarathustra. "Perhaps that the old God no longer liveth, in whom all the world once believed?"

"Thou sayest it," answered the old man sorrowfully. "And I served that old God until his last hour.

Now, however, am I out of service, without master, and yet not free; likewise am I no longer merry even for an hour, except it be in recollections.

Therefore did I ascend into these mountains, that I might finally have a festival for myself once more, as becometh an old pope and church-father: for know it, that I am the last pope!—a festival of pious recollections and divine services.

Now, however, is he himself dead, the most pious of men, the saint in the forest, who praised his God constantly with singing and mumbling.

He himself found I no longer when I found his cot—but two wolves found I therein, which howled on account of his death,—for all animals loved him. Then did I haste away.

Had I thus come in vain into these forests and mountains? Then did my heart determine that I should seek another, the most pious of all those who believe not in God—, my heart determined that I should seek Zarathustra!"

Thus spake the hoary man, and gazed with keen eyes at him who stood before him. Zarathustra however seized the hand of the old pope and regarded it a long while with admiration.

"Lo! thou venerable one," said he then, "what a fine and long hand! That is the hand of one who hath ever dispensed blessings. Now, however, doth it hold fast him whom thou seekest, me, Zarathustra.

It is I, the ungodly Zarathustra, who saith: 'Who is ungodlier than I, that I may enjoy his teaching?' "—

Thus spake Zarathustra, and penetrated with his glances the thoughts and arrear-thoughts of the old pope. At last the latter began:

"He who most loved and possessed him hath now also lost him most—:

—Lo, I myself am surely the most godless of us at present? But who could rejoice at that!"—

God Choked to Death on Sympathy

—"Thou servedst him to the last?" asked Zarathustra thoughtfully, after a deep silence, "thou knowest *how* he died? Is it true what they say, that sympathy choked him;

—That he saw how *man* hung on the cross, and could not endure it;—that his love to man became his hell, and at last his death?"— —

The old pope however did not answer, but looked aside timidly, with a painful and gloomy expression.

"Let him go," said Zarathustra, after prolonged meditation, still looking the old man straight in the eye.

"Let him go, he is gone. And though it honoureth thee that thou speakest only in praise of this dead one, yet thou knowest as well as I *who* he was, and that he went curious ways."

"To speak before three eyes," said the old pope cheerfully (he was blind of one eye), "in divine matters I am more enlightened than Zarathustra himself—and may well be so.

My love served him long years, my will followed all his will. A good servant, however, knoweth everything, and many a thing even which a master hideth from himself.

He was a hidden God, full of secrecy. Verily, he did not come by his son otherwise than by secret ways. At the door of his faith standeth adultery.

Whoever extolleth him as a God of love, doth not think highly enough of love itself. Did not that God want also to be judge? But the loving one loveth irrespective of reward and requital.

When he was young, that God out of the Orient, then was he harsh and revengeful, and built himself a hell for the delight of his favourites.

At last, however, he became old and soft and mellow and pitiful, more like a grandfather than a father, but most like a tottering old grandmother.

There did he sit shrivelled in his chimney-corner, fretting on account of his weak legs, world-weary, will-weary, and one day he suffocated of his all-too-great pity."— —

"Thou old pope," said here Zarathustra interposing, "hast thou seen *that* with thine eyes? It could well have happened in that way: in that way, *and* also otherwise. When gods die they always die many kinds of death.

The Problem of Evil

Well! At all events, one way or other—he is gone! He was counter to the taste of mine ears and eyes; worse than that I should not like to say against him.

I love everything that looketh bright and speaketh honestly. But he—thou knowest it, forsooth, thou old priest, there was something of thy type in him, the priest-type—he was equivocal.

He was also indistinct. How he raged at us, this wrath-snorter, because we understood him badly! But why did he not speak more clearly?

And if the fault lay in our ears, why did he give us ears that heard him badly? If there was dirt in our ears, well! who put it in them?

Too much miscarried with him, this potter who had not learned thoroughly! That he took revenge on his pots and creations, however, because they turned out badly—that was a sin against *good taste*.

There is also good taste in piety: *this* at last said: 'Away with *such* a God! Better to have no God, better to set up destiny on one's own account, better to be a fool, better to be God oneself!' "

—"What do I hear!" said then the old pope, with intent ears; "O Zarathustra, thou art more pious than thou believest, with such an unbelief! Some god in thee hath converted thee to thine ungodliness.

Is it not thy piety itself which no longer letteth thee believe in a God? And thine over-great honesty will yet lead thee even beyond good and evil!

Behold, what hath been reserved for thee? Thou hast eyes and hands and mouth, which have been predestined for blessing from eternity. One doth not bless with the hand alone.

Nigh unto thee, though thou professest to be the ungodliest one, I feel a hale and holy odour of long benedictions: I feel glad and grieved thereby.

Let me be thy guest, O Zarathustra, for a single night! Nowhere on earth shall I now feel better than with thee!"—

"Amen! So shall it be!" said Zarathustra, with great astonishment; "up thither leadeth the way, there lieth the cave of Zarathustra.

Gladly, forsooth, would I conduct thee thither myself, thou venerable one; for I love all pious men. But now a cry of distress calleth me hastily away from thee.

In my domain shall no one come to grief; my cave is a good haven. And best of all would I like to put every sorrowful one again on firm land and firm legs.

Who, however, could take *thy* melancholy off thy shoulders? For that I am too weak. Long, verily, should we have to wait until some one re-awoke thy God for thee.

For that old God liveth no more: he is indeed dead."—

Thus spake Zarathustra.

The Ugliest Man

—And again did Zarathustra's feet run through mountains and forests, and his eyes sought and sought, but nowhere was he to be seen whom they wanted to see—the sorely distressed sufferer and crier. On the whole way, however, he rejoiced in his heart and was full of gratitude. "What good things," said he, "hath this day given me, as amends for its bad beginning! What strange interlocutors have I found!

At their words will I now chew a long while as at good corn; small shall my teeth grind and crush them, until they flow like milk into my soul!"—

When, however, the path again curved round a rock, all at once the landscape changed, and Zarathustra entered into a realm of death. Here bristled aloft black and red cliffs, without any grass, tree, or bird's voice. For it was a valley which all animals avoided, even the beasts of prey, except that a species of ugly, thick, green serpent came here to die when they became old. Therefore the shepherds called this valley: "Serpent-death."

Zarathustra, however, became absorbed in dark recollections, for it seemed to him as if he had once before stood in this valley. And much heaviness settled on his mind, so that he walked slowly and always more slowly, and at last stood still. Then, however, when he opened his eyes, he saw something sitting by the wayside shaped like a man, and hardly like a man, something nondescript. And all at once there came over Zarathustra a great shame, because he had gazed on such a thing. Blushing up to the very roots of his white hair, he turned aside his glance, and raised his foot that he might leave this ill-starred place. Then, however, became the dead wilderness vocal: for from the ground a noise welled up, gurgling and rattling, as water gurgleth and rattleth at night through stopped-up water-pipes; and at last it turned into human voice and human speech:—it sounded thus:

"Zarathustra! Zarathustra! Read my riddle! Say, say! *What is the revenge on the witness?*

I entice thee back; here is smooth ice! See to it, see to it, that thy pride does not here break its legs!

Thou thinkest thyself wise, thou proud Zarathustra! Read then the riddle, thou hard nut-cracker,—the riddle that I am! Say then: who am *I!*"

—When however Zarathustra had heard these words,—what think ye then took place in his soul? *Pity overcame him;* and he sank down all at once, like an oak that hath long withstood many tree-fellers,—heavily, suddenly, to the terror even of those who meant to fell it. But immediately he got up again from the ground, and his countenance became stern.

"I know thee well," said he, with a brazen voice, *"thou art the murderer of God!* Let me go.

Thou couldst not *endure* him who beheld *thee,*—who ever beheld thee through and through, thou ugliest man. Thou tookest revenge on this witness!"

Thus spake Zarathustra and was about to go; but the nondescript grasped at a corner of his garment and began anew to gurgle and seek for words. "Stay," said he at last—

—"Stay! Do not pass by! I have divined what axe it was that struck thee to the ground: hail to thee, O Zarathustra, that thou art again upon thy feet!

Thou hast divined, I know it well, how the man feeleth who killed him,—the murderer of God. Stay! Sit down here beside me; it is not to no purpose.

Pity and Dignity

To whom would I go but unto thee? Stay, sit down! Do not however look at me! Honour thus—mine ugliness!

They persecute me: now art *thou* my last refuge. *Not* with their hatred, *not* with their bailiffs;—Oh, such persecution would I mock at, and be proud and cheerful!

Hath not all success hitherto been with the well-persecuted ones? And he who persecuteth well learneth readily to be *obsequent*—when once he is—put behind! But it is their *pity*—

—Their pity is it from which I flee away and flee to thee. O Zarathustra, protect me, thou, my last refuge, thou sole one who divinedst me:

—Thou hast divined how the man feeleth who killed *him*. Stay! And if thou wilt go, thou impatient one, go not the way that I came. *That* way is bad.

Art thou angry with me because I have already racked language too long? Because I have already counselled thee? But know that it is I, the ugliest man,

—Who have also the largest, heaviest feet. Where *I* have gone, the way is bad. I tread all paths to death and destruction.

But that thou passedst me by in silence, that thou blushedst—I saw it well: thereby did I know thee as Zarathustra.

Every one else would have thrown to me his alms, his pity, in look and speech. But for that—I am not beggar enough: that didst thou divine.

For that I am too *rich*, rich in what is great, frightful, ugliest, most unutterable! Thy shame, O Zarathustra, *honoured* me!

With difficulty did I get out of the crowd of the pitiful,—that I might find the only one who at present teacheth that 'pity is obtrusive' —thyself, O Zarathustra!

—Whether it be the pity of a God, or whether it be human pity, it is offensive to modesty. And unwillingness to help may be nobler than the virtue that rusheth to do so.

That however—namely, pity—is called virtue itself at present by all petty people:—they have no reverence for great misfortune, great ugliness, great failure.

Beyond all these do I look, as a dog looketh over the backs of thronging flocks of sheep. They are petty, good-wooled, good-willed, grey people.

As the heron looketh contemptuously at shallow pools, with backward-bent head, so do I look at the throng of grey little waves and wills and souls.

Too long have we acknowledged them to be right, those petty people: *so* we have at last given them power as well;—and now do they teach that 'good is only what petty people call good.'

And 'truth' is at present what the preacher spake who himself sprang from them, that singular saint and advocate of the petty people, who testified of himself: 'I—am the truth.'

That immodest one hath long made the petty people greatly puffed up,—he who taught no small error when he taught: 'I—am the truth.'

Hath an immodest one ever been answered more courteously?—Thou, however, O Zarathustra, passedst him by, and saidst: 'Nay! Nay! Three times Nay!'

Thou warnedst against his error; thou warnedst—the first to do so—against pity:—not every one, not none, but thyself and thy type.

Thou art ashamed of the shame of the great sufferer; and verily when thou sayest: 'From pity there cometh a heavy cloud; take heed, ye men!'

The Murder of God in Self-defense

—When thou teachest: 'All creators are hard, all great love is beyond their pity:' O Zarathustra, how well versed dost thou seem to me in weather-signs!

Thou thyself, however,—warn thyself also against *thy* pity! For many are on their way to thee, many suffering, doubting, despairing, drowning, freezing ones—

I warn thee also against myself. Thou hast read my best, my worst riddle, myself, and what I have done. I know the axe that felleth thee.

But he—*had to* die: he looked with eyes which beheld *everything*,—he beheld men's depths and dregs, all his hidden ignominy and ugliness.

His pity knew no modesty: he crept into my dirtiest corners. This most prying, over-intrusive, over-pitiful one had to die.

He ever beheld *me:* on such a witness I would have revenge—or not live myself.

The God who beheld everything, *and also man:* that God had to die! Man cannot *endure* it that such a witness should live."

Thus spake the ugliest man. Zarathustra however got up, and prepared to go on: for he felt frozen to the very bowels.

"Thou nondescript," said he, "thou warnedst me against thy path. As thanks for it I praise mine to thee. Behold, up thither is the cave of Zarathustra.

My cave is large and deep and hath many corners; there findeth he that is most hidden his hiding-place. And close beside it, there are a hundred lurking-places and by-places for creeping, fluttering, and hopping creatures.

Thou outcast, who hast cast thyself out, thou wilt not live amongst men and men's pity? Well then, do like me! Thus wilt thou learn also from me; only the doer learneth.

And talk first and foremost to mine animals! The proudest animal and the wisest animal—they might well be the right counsellors for us both!"— —

Thus spake Zarathustra and went his way, more thoughtfully and slowly even than before: for he asked himself many things, and hardly knew what to answer.

"How poor indeed is man," thought he in his heart, "how ugly, how wheezy, how full of hidden shame!

They tell me that man loveth himself. Ah, how great must that self-love be! How much contempt is opposed to it!

Even this man hath loved himself, as he hath despised himself,—a great lover methinketh he is, and a great despiser.

No one have I yet found who more thoroughly despised himself: even *that* is elevation. Alas, was *this* perhaps the higher man whose cry I heard?

I love the great despisers. Man is something that hath to be surpassed."— —

7

BERTRAND RUSSELL

(1872–1970)

AND

FATHER F. C. COPLESTON

(1907–)

*The Existence of God—A Debate**

This debate between Russell and Copleston was originally broadcast on the B.B.C.'s Third Programme series. Russell is widely known as both a philosopher and a political activist. In matters of religion he has taken an agnostic point of view. Copleston, on the other hand, is a leading Catholic philosopher and historian of philosophy. The debate ranges over many of the issues related to the existence of God, particularly those arguments for God's existence based on moral issues and on religious experiences. Copleston argues that the existence of God is the only thing that will "make sense of man's moral experience and of religious experience." Russell, however, argues that there are many ways of accounting for the feeling of moral obligation and for so-called "religious experiences" which do not necessitate the existence of a God.

* This debate was broadcast in 1948. It is used by permission of the British Broadcasting Corporation and Earl Russell and Father Copleston.

COPLESTON: As we are going to discuss the existence of God, it might perhaps be as well to come to some provisional agreement as to what we understand by the term "God." I presume that we mean a supreme personal being—distinct from the world and creator of the world. Would you agree—provisionally at least—to accept this statement as the meaning of the term "God"?

RUSSELL: Yes, I accept this definition.

COPLESTON: Well, my position is the affirmative position that such a being actually exists, and that His existence can be proved philosophically. Perhaps you would tell me if your position is that of agnosticism or of atheism. I mean, would you say that the non-existence of God can be proved?

RUSSELL: No, I should not say that: my position is agnostic.

COPLESTON: Would you agree with me that the problem of God is a problem of great importance? For example, would you agree that if God does not exist, human beings and human history can have no other purpose than the purpose they choose to give themselves, which—in practice—is likely to mean the purpose which those impose who have the power to impose it?

RUSSELL: Roughly speaking, yes, though I should have to place some limitation on your last clause.

COPLESTON: Would you agree that if there is no God—no absolute Being—there can be no absolute values? I mean, would you agree that if there is no absolute good that the relativity of values results?

RUSSELL: No, I think these questions are logically distinct. Take, for instance, G. E. Moore's *Principia Ethica,* where he maintains that there is a distinction of good and evil, that both of these are definite concepts. But he does not bring in the idea of God to support that contention.

COPLESTON: Well, suppose we leave the question of good till later, till we come to the moral argument, and I give first a metaphysical argument. I'd like to put the main weight on the metaphysical argument based on Leibniz's argument from "Contingency" and then later we might discuss the moral argument. Suppose I give a brief statement on the metaphysical argument and that then we go on to discuss it?

RUSSELL: That seems to me to be a very good plan.

The Argument from Contingency

COPLESTON: Well, for clarity's sake, I'll divide the argument into distinct stages. First of all, I should say, we know that there are at least some beings in the world which do not contain in themselves the reason for their existence. For example, I depend on my parents, and now on the air, and on food, and so on. Now, secondly, the world is simply the real or imagined totality or aggregate of individual objects, none of which contain in themselves alone the reason for their existence. There isn't any world distinct from the objects which form it, any more than the human race is something apart from the members. Therefore, I should say, since objects or events exist, and since no object of experience contains within itself the reason of its existence, this reason, the totality of objects, must have a reason external to itself. That reason must be an existent being. Well, this being is either itself the reason for its own existence, or it is not. If it is, well and good. If it is not, then we must proceed farther. But if we proceed to infinity in that sense, then there's no explanation of existence at all. So, I should say, in order to explain existence, we must come to a being which contains within itself the reason for its own existence, that is to say, which cannot not exist.

RUSSELL: This raises a great many points and it is not altogether easy to know where to begin, but I think that, perhaps, in answering your argument, the best point at which to begin is the question of necessary being. The word "necessary," I should maintain, can only be applied significantly to propositions. And, in fact, only to such as are analytic—

that is to say—such as it is self-contradictory to deny. I could only admit a necessary being if there were a being whose existence it is self-contradictory to deny. I should like to know whether you would accept Leibniz's division of propositions into truths of reason and truths of fact. The former—the truths of reason—being necessary.

COPLESTON: Well, I certainly should not subscribe to what seems to be Leibniz's idea of truths of reason and truths of fact, since it would appear that, for him, there are in the long run only analytic propositions. It would seem that for Leibniz truths of fact are ultimately reducible to truths of reason. That is to say, to analytic propositions, at least for an omniscient mind. Well, I couldn't agree with that. For one thing, it would fail to meet the requirements of the experience of freedom. I don't want to uphold the whole philosophy of Leibniz. I have made use of his argument from contingent to necessary being, basing the argument on the principle of sufficient reason, simply because it seems to me a brief and clear formulation of what is, in my opinion, the fundamental metaphysical argument for God's existence.

RUSSELL: But, to my mind, "a necessary proposition" has got to be analytic. I don't see what else it can mean. And analytic propositions are always complex and logically somewhat late. "Irrational animals are animals" is an analytic proposition; but a proposition such as "This is an animal" can never be analytic. In fact, all the propositions that can be analytic are somewhat late in the build-up of propositions.

COPLESTON: Take the proposition "If there is a contingent being then there is a necessary being." I consider that that proposition hypothetically expressed is a necessary proposition. If you are going to call every necessary proposition an analytic proposition, then—in order to avoid a dispute in terminology—I would agree to call it analytic, though I don't consider it a tautological proposition. But the proposition is a necessary proposition only on the supposition that there is a contingent being. That there is a contingent being actually existing has to be discovered by experience, and the proposition that there is a contingent being is certainly not an analytic proposition, though once you know, I should maintain, that there is a contingent being, it follows of necessity that there is a necessary being.

RUSSELL: The difficulty of this argument is that I don't admit the idea of a necessary being and I don't admit that there is any particular meaning in calling other beings "contingent." These phrases don't for me have a significance except within a logic that I reject.

COPLESTON: Do you mean that you reject these terms because they won't fit in with what is called "modern logic"?

RUSSELL: Well, I can't find anything that they could mean. The word "necessary," it seems to me, is a useless word, except as applied to analytic propositions, not to things.

COPLESTON: In the first place, what do you mean by "modern logic"? As far as I know, there are somewhat differing systems. In the second place, not all modern logicians surely would admit the meaninglessness of metaphysics. We both know, at any rate, one very eminent modern thinker whose knowledge of modern logic was profound, but who certainly did not think that metaphysics are meaningless or, in particular, that the problem of God is meaningless. Again, even if all modern logicians held that metaphysical terms are meaningless, it would not follow that they were right. The proposition that metaphysical terms are meaningless seems to me to be a proposition based on an assumed philosophy. The dogmatic position behind it seems to be this: What will not go into my machine is non-existent, or it is meaningless; it is the expression of emotion. I am simply trying to point out that anybody who says that a particular system of modern logic is the sole criterion of meaning is saying something that is over-dogmatic; he is dogmatically insisting that a part of philosophy is the whole of philosophy. After all, a "contingent" being is a being which has not in itself the complete reason for its existence, that's what I mean by a contingent being. You know, as well as I do, that the existence of neither of us can be explained without reference to something or somebody outside us, our parents, for example. A "necessary" being, on the other hand, means a being that must and cannot not exist. You may say that there is no such being, but you will find it hard to convince me that you do not understand the terms I am using. If you do not understand them, then how can you be entitled to say that such a being does not exist, if that is what you do say?

RUSSELL: Well, there are points here that I don't propose to go into at length. I don't maintain the meaninglessness of metaphysics in general at all. I maintain the meaninglessness of certain particular terms—not on any general ground, but simply because I've not been able to see an interpretation of those particular terms. It's not a general dogma—it's a particular thing. But those points I will leave out for the moment. And I will say that what you have been saying brings us back, it seems to me, to the ontological argument that there is a being whose essence involves existence, so that his existence is analytic. That seems to me to be impossible, and it raises, of course, the question what one means by existence, and as to this, I think a subject named can never be significantly said to exist but only a subject described. And that existence, in fact, quite definitely is not a predicate.

COPLESTON: Well, you say, I believe, that it is bad grammar, or rather bad syntax to say for example "T. S. Eliot exists"; one ought to say, for example, "He, the author of *Murder in the Cathedral,* exists." Are you going to say that the proposition, "The cause of the world exists," is without meaning? You may say that the world has no cause; but I fail to see how you can say that the proposition that "the cause of the world exists" is meaningless. Put it in the form of a question: "Has the world a cause?" or "Does a cause of the world exist?" Most people surely would understand the question, even if they don't agree about the answer.

RUSSELL: Well, certainly the question "Does the cause of the world exist?" is a question that has meaning. But if you say "Yes, God is the cause of the world" you're using God as a proper name; then "God exists" will not be a statement that has meaning; that is the position that I'm maintaining. Because, therefore, it will follow that it cannot be an analytic proposition ever to say that this or that exists. For example, suppose you take as your subject "the existent round-square," it would look like an analytic proposition that "the existent round-square exists," but it doesn't exist.

COPLESTON: No, it doesn't, then surely you can't say it doesn't exist unless you have a conception of what existence is. As to the phrase "existent round-square," I should say that it has no meaning at all.

RUSSELL: I quite agree. Then I should say the same thing in another context in reference to a "necessary being."

COPLESTON: Well, we seem to have arrived at an impasse. To say that a necessary being is a being that must exist and cannot not exist has for me a definite meaning. For you it has no meaning.

RUSSELL: Well, we can press the point a little, I think. A being that must exist and cannot not exist, would surely, according to you, be a being whose essence involves existence.

COPLESTON: Yes, a being the essence of which is to exist. But I should not be willing to argue the existence of God simply from the idea of His essence because I don't think we have any clear intuition of God's essence as yet. I think we have to argue from the world of experience to God.

RUSSELL: Yes, I quite see the distinction. But, at the same time, for a being with sufficient knowledge it would be true to say "Here is this being whose essence involves existence!"

COPLESTON: Yes, certainly if anybody saw God, he would see that God must exist.

RUSSELL: So that I mean there is a being whose essence involves existence although we don't know that essence. We only know there is such a being.

COPLESTON: Yes, I should add we don't know the essence *a priori*. It is only *a posteriori* through our experience of the world that we come to a knowledge of the existence of that being. And then one argues, the essence and existence must be identical. Because if God's essence and God's existence was not identical, then some sufficient reason for this existence would have to be found beyond God.

RUSSELL: So it all turns on this question of sufficient reason, and I must say you haven't defined "sufficient reason" in a way that I can understand—what do you mean by sufficient reason? You don't mean cause?

COPLESTON: Not necessarily. Cause is a kind of sufficient reason. Only contingent being can have a cause. God is His own sufficient reason; and He is not cause of Himself. By sufficient reason in the full sense I mean an explanation adequate for the existence of some particular being.

RUSSELL: But when is an explanation adequate? Suppose I am about to make a flame with a match. You may say that the adequate explanation of that is that I rub it on the box.

COPLESTON: Well, for practical purposes—but theoretically, that is only a partial explanation. An adequate explanation must ultimately be a total explanation, to which nothing further can be added.

RUSSELL: Then I can only say that you're looking for something which can't be got, and which one ought not to expect to get.

COPLESTON: To say that one has not found it is one thing; to say that one should not look for it seems to me rather dogmatic.

RUSSELL: Well, I don't know. I mean, the explanation of one thing is another thing which makes the other thing dependent on yet another, and you have to grasp this sorry scheme of things entire to do what you want, and that we can't do.

COPLESTON: But are you going to say that we can't, or we shouldn't even raise the question of the existence of the whole of this sorry scheme of things—of the whole universe?

RUSSELL: Yes. I don't think there's any meaning in it at all. I think the word "universe" is a handy word in some connections, but I don't think it stands for anything that has a meaning.

COPLESTON: If the word is meaningless, it can't be so very handy. In any case, I don't say that the universe is something different from the objects which compose it (I indicated that in my brief summary of the proof), what I'm doing is to look for the reason, in this case the cause of the objects—the real or imagined totality of which constitute what we call the universe. You say, I think that the universe—or my existence if you prefer, or any other existence—is unintelligible?

RUSSELL: First may I take up the point that if a word is meaningless it can't be handy. That sounds well but isn't in fact correct. Take, say, such a word as "the" or "than." You can't point to any object that those words mean, but they are very useful words; I should say the same of "universe." But leaving that point, you ask whether I consider that the universe is unintelligible. I shouldn't say unintelligible—I think it is without explanation. Intelligible, to my mind, is a different thing. Intelligible has to do with the thing itself intrinsically and not with its relations.

COPLESTON: Well, my point is that what we call the world is intrinsically unintelligible, apart from the existence of God. You see, I don't believe that the infinity of the series of events—I mean a horizontal series, so to speak—if such an infinity could be proved, would be in the slightest degree relevant to the situation. If you add up chocolates you get chocolates after all and not a sheep. If you add up chocolates to infinity, you presumably get an infinite number of chocolates. So if you add up contingent beings to infinity, you still get contingent beings, not a necessary being. An infinite series of contingent beings will be, to my way of thinking, as unable to cause itself as one contingent being. However, you say, I think, that it is illegitimate to raise the question of what will explain the existence of any particular object?

RUSSELL: It's quite all right if you mean by explaining it, simply finding a cause for it.

COPLESTON: Well, why stop at one particular object? Why shouldn't one raise the question of the cause of the existence of all particular objects?

RUSSELL: Because I see no reason to think there is any. The whole concept of cause is one we derive from our observation of particular things; I see no reason whatsoever to suppose that the total has any cause whatsoever.

COPLESTON: Well, to say that there isn't any cause is not the same thing as saying that we shouldn't look for a cause. The statement that there isn't any cause should come, if it comes at all, at the end of the inquiry, not the beginning. In any case, if the total has no cause, then to my way of thinking it must be its own cause, which seems to me impossible. Moreover, the statement that the world is simply there if in answer to a question, presupposes that the question has meaning.

RUSSELL: No, it doesn't need to be its own cause, what I'm saying is that the concept of cause is not applicable to the total.

COPLESTON: Then you would agree with Sartre that the universe is what he calls "gratuitous"?

RUSSELL: Well, the word "gratuitous" suggests that it might be something else; I should say that the universe is just there, and that's all.

COPLESTON: Well, I can't see how you can rule out the legitimacy of asking the question how the total, or anything at all comes to be there. Why something rather than nothing, that is the question? The fact that we gain our knowledge of causality empirically, from particular causes, does not rule out the possibility of asking what the cause of the series is. If the word "cause" were meaningless or if it could be shown that Kant's view of the matter were correct, the question would be illegitimate I agree; but you don't seem to hold that the word "cause" is meaningless, and I do not suppose you are a Kantian.

RUSSELL: I can illustrate what seems to me your fallacy. Every man who exists has a mother, and it seems to me your argument is that therefore the human race must have a mother, but obviously the human race hasn't a mother—that's a different logical sphere.

COPLESTON: Well, I can't really see any parity. If I were saying "every object has a phenomenal cause, therefore, the whole series has a phenomenal cause," there would be a parity; but I'm not saying that; I'm saying, every object has a phenomenal cause if you insist on the infinity of the series—but the series of phenomenal causes is an insufficient explanation of the series. Therefore, the series has not a phenomenal cause but a transcendent cause.

RUSSELL: That's always assuming that not only every particular thing in the world, but the world as a whole must have a cause. For that assumption I see no ground whatever. If you'll give me a ground I'll listen to it.

COPLESTON: Well, the series of events is either caused or it's not caused. If it is caused, there must obviously be a cause outside the series. If it's not caused then it's sufficient to itself, and if it's sufficient to itself it is what I call necessary. But it can't be necessary since each member is contingent, and we've agreed that the total has no reality apart from its members, therefore, it can't be necessary. Therefore, it can't be (caused)—uncaused—therefore it must have a cause. And I should like to observe in passing that the statement "the world is simply there and is inexplicable" can't be got out of logical analysis.

RUSSELL: I don't want to seem arrogant, but it does seem to me that I can conceive things that you say the human mind can't conceive. As for things not having a cause, the physicists assure us that individual quantum transitions in atoms have no cause.

COPLESTON: Well, I wonder now whether that isn't simply a temporary inference.

RUSSELL: It may be, but it does show that physicists' minds can conceive it.

COPLESTON: Yes, I agree, some scientists—physicists—are willing to allow for indetermination within a restricted field. But very many scientists are not so willing. I think that Professor Dingle, of London University, maintains that the Heisenberg uncertainty principle tells us something about the success (or the lack of it) of the present atomic theory in correlating observations, but not about nature in itself, and many physicists would accept this view. In any case, I don't see how physicists can fail to accept the theory in practice, even if they don't do so in theory. I cannot see how science could be conducted on any other assumption than that of order and intelligibility in nature. The physicist presupposes, at least tacitly, that there is some sense in investigating nature and looking for the causes of events, just as the detective presupposes that there is some sense in looking for the cause of a murder. The metaphysician assumes that there is sense in looking for the reason or cause of phenomena, and, not being a Kantian, I consider that the metaphysician is as justified in his assumption as the physicist. When Sartre, for example, says that the world is gratuitous, I think that he has not sufficiently considered what is implied by "gratuitous."

RUSSELL: I think—there seems to me a certain unwarrantable extension here; a physicist looks for causes; that does not necessarily imply that there are causes everywhere. A man may look for gold without assuming that there is gold everywhere; if he finds gold, well and good, if he doesn't he's had bad luck. The same is true when the physicists look for causes. As for Sartre, I don't profess to know what he means, and I shouldn't like to be thought to interpret him, but for my part, I do think the notion of the world having an explanation is a mistake. I don't see why one should expect it to have, and I think what you say about what the scientist assumes is an over-statement.

COPLESTON: Well, it seems to me that the scientist does make some such assumption. When he experiments to find out some particular truth, behind that experiment lies the assumption that the universe is not simply discontinuous. There is the possibility of finding out a truth by experiment. The experiment may be a bad one, it may lead to no result, or not to the result that he wants, but that at any rate there is the possibility, through experiment, of finding out the truth that he assumes. And that seems to me to assume an ordered and intelligible universe.

RUSSELL: I think you're generalizing more than is necessary. Undoubtedly the scientist assumes that this sort of thing is likely to be found and will often be found. He does not assume that it will be found, and that's a very important matter in modern physics.

COPLESTON: Well, I think he does assume or is bound to assume it tacitly in practice. It may be that, to quote Professor Haldane, "when I light the gas under the kettle, some of the water molecules will fly off as vapor, and there is no way of finding out which will do so," but it doesn't follow necessarily that the idea of chance must be introduced except in relation to our knowledge.

RUSSELL: No it doesn't—at least if I may believe what he says. He's finding out quite a lot of things—the scientist is finding out quite a lot of things that are happening in the world, which are, at first, beginnings of causal chains—first causes which haven't in themselves got causes. He does not assume that everything has a cause.

COPLESTON: Surely that's a first cause within a certain selected field. It's a relatively first cause.

RUSSELL: I don't think he'd say so. If there's a world in which most events, but not all, have causes, he will then be able to depict the probabilities and uncertainties by assuming that this particular event you're interested in probably has a cause. And since in any case you won't get more than probability that's good enough.

COPLESTON: It may be that the scientist doesn't hope to obtain more than probability, but in raising the question he assumes that the question of explanation has a meaning. But your general point then, Lord Russell, is that it's illegitimate even to ask the question of the cause of the world?

RUSSELL: Yes, that's my position.

COPLESTON: If it's a question that for you has no meaning, it's of course very difficult to discuss it, isn't it?

RUSSELL: Yes, it is very difficult. What do you say—shall we pass on to some other issue?

Religious Experience

COPLESTON: Let's. Well, perhaps I might say a word about religious experience, and then we can go on to moral experience. I don't regard religious experience as a strict proof of the existence of God, so the character of the discussion changes somewhat, but I think it's true to say that the best explanation of it is the existence of God. By religious experience I don't mean simply feeling good. I mean a loving, but unclear, awareness of some object which irresistibly seems to the experiencer as something transcending the self, something transcending all the normal objects of experience, something which cannot be pictured or conceptualized, but of the reality of which doubt is impossible—at least during the experience. I should claim that cannot be explained adequately and without residue, simply subjectively. The actual basic experience at any rate is most easily explained on the hypothesis that there is actually some objective cause of that experience.

RUSSELL: I should reply to that line of argument that the whole argument from our own mental states to something outside us, is a very tricky affair. Even where we all admit its validity, we only feel justified in doing so, I think, because of the consensus of mankind. If there's a crowd in a room and there's a clock in a room, they can all see the clock. The fact that they can all see it tends to make them think that it's not an hallucination: whereas these religious experiences do tend to be very private.

COPLESTON: Yes, they do. I'm speaking strictly of mystical experience proper, and I certainly don't include, by the way, what are called visions. I mean simply the experience, and I quite admit it's indefinable, of the transcendent object or of what seems to be a transcendent object. I remember Julian Huxley in some lecture saying that religious experience, or mystical experience, is as much a real experience as falling in love or appreciating poetry and art. Well, I believe that when we appreciate poetry and art we appreciate definite poems or a definite work of art. If we fall in love, well, we fall in love with somebody and not with nobody.

RUSSELL: May I interrupt for a moment here. That is by no means always the case. Japanese novelists never consider that they have achieved a success unless large numbers of real people commit suicide for love of the imaginary heroine.

COPLESTON: Well, I must take your word for these goings on in Japan. I haven't committed suicide, I'm glad to say, but I have been strongly influenced in the taking of two important steps in my life by two biographies. However, I must say I see little resemblance between the real influence of those books on me and the mystic experience proper, so far, that is, as an outsider can obtain an idea of that experience.

RUSSELL: Well, I mean we wouldn't regard God as being on the same level as the characters in a work of fiction. You'll admit there's a distinction here?

COPLESTON: I certainly should. But what I'd say is that the best explanation seems to be the not purely subjectivist explanation. Of course, a subjectivist explanation is possible in the case of certain people in whom there is little relation between the experience and life, in the case of deluded people and hallucinated people, and so on. But when you get what one might call the pure type, say St. Francis of Assisi, when you get an experience that results in an overflow of dynamic and creative love, the best explanation of that it seems to me is the actual existence of an objective cause of the experience.

RUSSELL: Well, I'm not contending in a dogmatic way that there is not a God. What I'm contending is that we don't know that there is. I can only take what is recorded as I should take other records and I do find that a very great many things are reported, and I am sure you would not accept things about demons and devils and what not—and they're reported in exactly the same tone of voice and with exactly the same conviction. And the mystic, if his vision is veridical, may be said to know that there are devils. But I don't know that there are.

COPLESTON: But surely in the case of the devils there have been people speaking mainly of visions, appearances, angels or demons and so on. I should rule out the visual appearances, because I think they can be explained apart from the existence of the object which is supposed to be seen.

RUSSELL: But don't you think there are abundant recorded cases of people who believe that they've heard Satan speaking to them in their hearts, in just the same way as the mystics assert God—and I'm not talking of an external vision, I'm talking of a purely mental experience. That seems to be an experience of the same sort as mystics' experience of God, and I don't see that from what mystics tell us you can get any argument for God which is not equally an argument for Satan.

COPLESTON: I quite agree, of course, that people have imagined or thought they have heard or seen Satan. And I have no wish in passing to deny the existence of Satan. But I do not think that people have claimed to have experienced Satan in the precise way in which mystics claim to have experienced God. Take the case of a non-Christian, Plotinus. He admits the experience is something inexpressible, the object is an object of love, and therefore, not an object that causes horror and disgust. And the effect of that experience is, I should say, borne out, or I mean the validity of the experience is borne out in the records of the life of Plotinus. At any rate it is more reasonable to suppose that he had that experience if we're willing to accept Porphyry's account of Plotinus's general kindness and benevolence.

RUSSELL: The fact that a belief has a good moral effect upon a man is no evidence whatsoever in favor of its truth.

COPLESTON: No, but if it could actually be proved that the belief was actually responsible for a good effect on a man's life, I should consider it a presumption in favor of some truth, at any rate of the positive part of the belief if not of its entire validity. But in any case I am using the character of the life as evidence in favor of the mystic's veracity and sanity rather than as a proof of the truth of his beliefs.

RUSSELL: But even that I don't think is any evidence. I've had experiences myself that have altered my character profoundly. And I thought at the time at any rate that it was altered for the good. Those experiences were important, but they did not involve the existence of something outside me, and I don't think that if I'd thought they did, the fact that they had a wholesome effect would have been any evidence that I was right.

COPLESTON: No, but I think that the good effect would attest your veracity in describing your experience. Please remember that I'm not saying that a mystic's mediation or interpretation of his experience should be immune from discussion or criticism.

RUSSELL: Obviously the character of a young man may be—and often is—immensely affected for good by reading about some great man in history, and it may happen that the great man is a myth and doesn't exist, but the boy is just as much affected for good as if he did. There have been such people. Plutarch's *Lives* take Lycurgus as an example, who certainly did not exist, but you might be very much influenced by reading Lycurgus under the impression that he had previously existed. You would then be influenced by an object that you'd loved, but it wouldn't be an existing object.

COPELSTON: I agree with you on that, of course, that a man may be influenced by a character in fiction. Without going into the question of what it is precisely that influences him (I should say a real value) I think that the situation of that man and of the mystic are different. After all the man who is influenced by Lycurgus hasn't got the irresistible impression that he's experienced in some way the ultimate reality.

RUSSELL: I don't think you've quite got my point about these historical characters—these unhistorical characters in history. I'm not assuming what you call an effect on the reason. I'm assuming that the young man reading about this person and believing him to be real loves him—which is quite easy to happen, and yet he's loving a phantom.

COPLESTON: In one sense he's loving a phantom, that's perfectly true, in the sense, I mean, that he's loving X or Y who doesn't exist. But at the same time, it is not, I think, the phantom as such that the young man loves; he perceives a real value, an idea which he recognizes as objectively valid, and that's what excites his love.

RUSSELL: Well, in the same sense we had before about the characters in fiction.

COPLESTON: Yes, in one sense the man's loving a phantom—perfectly true. But in another sense he's loving what he perceives to be a value.

The Moral Argument

RUSSELL: But aren't you now saying in effect, I mean by God whatever is good or the sum total of what is good—the system of what is good, and, therefore, when a young man loves anything that is good he is loving God. Is that what you're saying, because if so, it wants a bit of arguing.

COPLESTON: I don't say, of course, that God is the sum total or system of what is good in the pantheistic sense; I'm not a pantheist, but I do think that all goodness reflects God in some way and proceeds from Him, so that in a sense the man who loves what is truly good, loves God even if he doesn't advert to God. But still I agree that the validity of such an interpretation of a man's conduct depends on the recognition of God's existence, obviously.

RUSSELL: Yes, but that's a point to be proved.

COPLESTON: Quite so, but I regard the metaphysical argument as probative, but there we differ.

RUSSELL: You see, I feel that some things are good and that other things are bad. I love the things that are good, that I think are good, and I hate the things that I think are bad. I don't say that these things are good because they participate in the Divine goodness.

COPLESTON: Yes, but what's your justification for distinguishing between good and bad or how do you view the distinction between them?

RUSSELL: I don't have any justification any more than I have when I distinguish between blue and yellow. What is my justification for distinguishing between blue and yellow? I can see they are different.

COPLESTON: Well, that is an excellent justification, I agree, You distinguish blue and yellow by seeing them, so you distinguish good and bad by what faculty?

RUSSELL: By my feelings.

COPLESTON: By your feelings. Well, that's what I was asking. You think that good and evil have reference simply to feeling?

RUSSELL: Well, why does one type of object look yellow and another look blue? I can more or less give an answer to that thanks to the physicists, and as to why I think one sort of thing good and another evil, probably there is an answer of the same sort, but it hasn't been gone into in the same way and I couldn't give it you.

COPLESTON: Well, let's take the behavior of the Commandant of Belsen. That appears to you as undesirable and evil and to me too. To Adolf Hitler we suppose it appeared as something good and desirable. I suppose you'd have to admit that for Hitler it was good and for you it is evil.

RUSSELL: No, I shouldn't quite go so far as that. I mean, I think people can make mistakes in that as they can in other things. If you have jaundice you see things yellow that are not yellow. You're making a mistake.

COPLESTON: Yes, one can make mistakes, but can you make a mistake if it's simply a question of reference to a feeling or emotion? Surely Hitler would be the only possible judge of what appealed to his emotions.

RUSSELL: It would be quite right to say that it appealed to his emotions, but you can say various things about that; among others, that if that sort of thing makes that sort of appeal to Hitler's emotions, then Hitler makes quite a different appeal to my emotions.

COPLESTON: Granted. But there's no objective criterion outside feeling then for condemning the conduct of the Commandant of Belsen, in your view?

RUSSELL: No more than there is for the color-blind person who's in exactly the same state. Why do we intellectually condemn the color-blind man? Isn't it because he's in the minority?

COPLESTON: I would say because he is lacking in a thing which normally belongs to human nature.

RUSSELL: Yes, but if he were in the majority, we shouldn't say that.

COPLESTON: Then you'd say that there's no criterion outside feeling that will enable one to distinguish between the behavior of the Commandant of Belsen and the behavior, say, of Sir Stafford Cripps or the Archbishop of Canterbury.

RUSSELL: The feeling is a little too simplified. You've got to take account of the effects of actions and your feelings towards those effects. You see, you can have an argument about it if you say that certain sorts of occurrences are the sort you like and certain others the sort you don't like. Then you have to take account of the effects of actions. You can very well say that the effects of the actions of the Commandant of Belsen were painful and unpleasant.

COPLESTON: They certainly were, I agree, very painful and unpleasant to all the people in the camp.

RUSSELL: Yes, but not only to the people in the camp, but to outsiders contemplating them also.

COPLESTON: Yes, quite true in imagination. But that's my point. I don't approve of them, and I know you don't approve of them, but I don't see what grounds you have for not approving of them, because after all, to the Commandant of Belsen himself, they're pleasant, those actions.

RUSSELL: Yes, but you see I don't need any more ground in that case than I do in the case of color perception. There are some people who think everything is yellow, there are people suffering from jaundice, and I don't agree with these people. I can't prove that the things are not yellow, there isn't any proof, but most people agree with me that they're not yellow, and most people agree with me that the Commandant of Belsen was making mistakes.

COPLESTON: Well, do you accept any moral obligation?

RUSSELL: Well, I should have to answer at considerable length to answer that. Practically speaking—yes. Theoretically speaking I should have to define moral obligation rather carefully.

COPLESTON: Well, do you think that the word "ought" simply has an emotional connotation?

RUSSELL: No, I don't think that, because you see, as I was saying a moment ago, one has to take account of the effects, and I think right conduct is that which would probably produce the greatest possible balance in intrinsic value of all the acts possible in the circumstances, and you've got to take account of the probable effects of your action in considering what is right.

COPLESTON: Well, I brought in moral obligation because I think that one can approach the question of God's existence in that way. The vast majority of the human race will make, and always have made, some distinction between right and wrong. The vast majority I think has some consciousness of an obligation in the moral sphere. It's my opinion that the perception of values and the consciousness of moral law and obligation are best explained through the hypothesis of a transcendent ground of value and of an author of the moral law. I do mean by "author of the moral law" an arbitrary author of the moral law. I think, in fact, that those modern atheists who have argued in the converse way "there is no God; therefore, there are no absolute values and no absolute law," are quite logical.

RUSSELL: I don't like the word "absolute." I don't think there is anything absolute whatever. The moral law, for example, is always changing. At one period in the development of the human race, almost everybody thought cannibalism was a duty.

COPLESTON: Well, I don't see that differences in particular moral judgments are any conclusive argument against the universality of the moral law. Let's assume for the moment that there are absolute moral values, even on that hypothesis it's only to be expected that different individuals and different groups should enjoy varying degrees of insight into those values.

RUSSELL: I'm inclined to think that "ought," the feeling that one has about "ought," is an echo of what has been told one by one's parents or one's nurses.

COPLESTON: Well, I wonder if you can explain away the idea of the "ought" merely in terms of nurses and parents. I really don't see how it can be conveyed to anybody in other terms than itself. It seems to me that if there is a moral order bearing upon the human conscience, that that moral order is unintelligible apart from the existence of God.

RUSSELL: Then you have to say one or other of two things. Either God only speaks to a very small percentage of mankind—which happens to include yourself—or He deliberately says things that are not true in talking to the consciences of savages.

Copleston: Well, you see, I'm not suggesting that God actually dictates moral precepts to the conscience. The human being's idea of the content of the moral law depends certainly to a large extent on education and environment, and a man has to use his reason in assessing the validity of the actual moral ideas of his social group. But the possibility of criticizing the accepted moral code presupposes that there is an objective standard, that there is an ideal moral order, which imposes itself (I mean the obligatory character of which can be recognized). I think that the recognition of this ideal moral order is part of the recognition of contingency. It implies the existence of a real foundation of God.

Russell: But the law-giver has always been, it seems to me, one's parents or someone like. There are plenty of terrestrial law-givers to account for it, and that would explain why people's consciences are so amazingly different in different times and places.

Copleston: It helps to explain differences in the perception of particular moral values, which otherwise are inexplicable. It will help to explain changes in the matter of the moral law in the content of the precepts as accepted by this or that nation, or this or that individual. But the form of it, what Kant calls the categorical imperative, the "ought," I really don't see how that can possibly be conveyed to anybody by nurse or parent because there aren't any possible terms, so far as I can see, with which it can be explained. It can't be defined in other terms than itself, because once you've defined it in other terms than itself you've explained it away. It's no longer a moral "ought." It's something else.

Russell: Well, I think the sense of "ought" is the effect of somebody's imagined disapproval, it may be God's imagined disapproval, but it's somebody's imagined disapproval. And I think that is what is meant by "ought."

Copleston: It seems to me to be external customs and taboos and things of that sort which can most easily be explained simply through environment and education, but all that seems to me to belong to what I call the matter of the law, the content. The idea of the "ought" as such can never be conveyed to a man by the tribal chief or by anybody else, because there are no other terms in which it could be conveyed. It seems to me entirely——[Russell breaks in].

Russell: But I don't see any reason to say that—I mean we all know about conditioned reflexes. We know that an animal, if punished habitually for a certain sort of act, after a time will refrain. I don't think the animal refrains from arguing within himself, "Master will be angry if I do this." He has a feeling that that's not the thing to do. That's what we can do with ourselves and nothing more.

Copleston: I see no reason to suppose that an animal has a consciousness of moral obligation; and we certainly don't regard an animal as morally responsible for his acts of disobedience. But a man has a consciousness of obligation and of moral values. I see no reason to suppose that one could condition all men as one can "condition" an animal, and I don't suppose you'd really want to do so even if one could. If "behaviorism" were true, there would be no objective moral distinction between the emperor Nero and St. Francis of Assisi. I can't help feeling, Lord Russell, you know, that you regard the conduct of the Commandant at Belsen as morally reprehensible, and that you yourself would never under any circumstances act in that way, even if you thought, or had reason to think, that possibly the balance of the happiness of the human race might be increased through some people being treated in that abominable manner.

RUSSELL: No. I wouldn't imitate the conduct of a mad dog. The fact that I wouldn't do it doesn't really bear on this question we're discussing.

COPLESTON: No, but if you were making a utilitarian explanation of right and wrong in terms of consequences, it might be held, and I suppose some of the Nazis of the better type would have held that although it's lamentable to have to act in this way, yet the balance in the long run leads to greater happiness. I don't think you'd say that, would you? I think you'd say that that sort of action is wrong—and in itself, quite apart from whether the general balance of happiness is increased or not. Then, if you're prepared to say that, then I think you must have some criterion of right and wrong, that is outside the criterion of feeling, at any rate. To me, that admission would ultimately result in the admission of an ultimate ground of value in God.

RUSSELL: I think we are perhaps getting into confusion. It is not direct feeling about the act by which I should judge, but rather a feeling as to the effects. And I can't admit any circumstances in which certain kinds of behavior, such as you have been discussing, would do good. I can't imagine circumstances in which they would have a beneficial effect. I think the persons who think they do are deceiving themselves. But if there were circumstances in which they would have a beneficial effect, then I might be obliged, however reluctantly, to say—"Well, I don't like these things, but I will acquiesce in them," just as I acquiesce in the Criminal Law, although I profoundly dislike punishment.

COPLESTON: Well, perhaps it's time I summed up my position. I've argued two things. First, that the existence of God can be philosophically proved by a metaphysical argument; secondly, that it is only the existence of God that will make sense of man's moral experience and of religious experience. Personally, I think that your way of accounting for man's moral judgments leads inevitably to a contradiction between what your theory demands and your own spontaneous judgments. Moreover, your theory explains moral obligation away, and explaining away is not explanation. As regards the metaphysical argument, we are apparently in agreement that what we call the world consists simply of contingent beings. That is, of beings no one of which can account for its own existence. You say that the series of events needs no explanation: I say that if there were no necessary being, no being which must exist and cannot not exist, nothing would exist. The infinity of the series of contingent beings, even if proved, would be irrelevant. Something does exist; therefore, there must be something which accounts for this fact, a being which is outside the series of contingent beings. If you had admitted this, we could then have discussed whether that being is personal, good, and so on. On the actual point discussed, whether there is or is not a necessary being, I find myself, I think, in agreement with the great majority of classical philosophers.

You maintain, I think, that existing beings are simply there, and that I have no justification for raising the question of the explanation of their existence. But I would like to point out that this position cannot be substantiated by logical analysis; it expresses a philosophy which itself stands in need of proof. I think we have reached an impasse because our ideas of philosophy are radically different; it seems to me that what I call a part of philosophy, that you call the whole, insofar at least as philosophy is rational. It seems to me, if you will pardon my saying so, that besides your own logical system—which you call "modern" in opposition to antiquated logic (a tendentious adjective)—you maintain a philosophy which cannot be substantiated by logical analysis. After all, the problem of God's existence is an existential problem whereas logical analysis does not deal directly with problems of existence. So it seems to me, to declare that the terms involved in one set of problems are meaningless because they are not required in dealing with another set of problems, is to settle from the beginning the nature and extent of philosophy, and that is itself a philosophical act which stands in need of justification.

RUSSELL: Well, I should like to say just a few words by way of summary on my side. First, as to the metaphysical argument: I don't admit the connotations of such a term as "contingent" or the possibility of explanation in Father Copleston's sense. I think the word "contingent" inevitably suggests the possibility of something that wouldn't have this what you might call accidental character of just being there, and I don't think this is true except in the purely causal sense. You can sometimes give a causal explanation of one thing as being the effect of something else, but that is merely referring one thing to another thing and there's no—to my mind—explanation in Father Copleston's sense of anything at all, nor is there any meaning in calling things "contingent" because there isn't anything else they could be. That's what I should say about that, but I should like to say a few words about Father Copleston's accusation that I regard logic as all philosophy—that is by no means the case. I don't by any means regard logic as all philosophy. I think logic is an essential part of philosophy and logic has to be used in philosophy, and in that I think he and I are at one. When the logic that he uses was new—namely, in the time of Aristotle, there had to be a great deal of fuss made about it; Aristotle made a lot of fuss about that logic. Nowadays it's become old and respectable, and you don't have to make so much fuss about it. The logic that I believe in is comparatively new, and therefore I have to imitate Aristotle in making a fuss about it; but it's not that I think it's all philosophy by any means—I don't think so. I think it's an important part of philosophy, and when I say that, I don't find a meaning for this or that word, that is a position of detail based upon what I've found out about that particular word, from thinking about it. It's not a general position that all words that are used in metaphysics are nonsense, or anything like that which I don't really hold.

As regards the moral argument, I do find that when one studies anthropology or history, there are people who think it their duty to perform acts which I think abominable, and I certainly can't, therefore, attribute Divine origin to the matter of moral obligation, which Father Copleston doesn't ask me to; but I think even the form of moral obligation, when it takes the form of enjoining you to eat your father or what not, doesn't seem to me to be such a very beautiful and noble thing; and, therefore, I cannot attribute a Divine origin to this sense of moral obligation, which I think is quite easily accounted for in quite other ways.

Further Reading

Baillie, John. *The Interpretation of Religion.* Nashville: Abingdon Press, 1928.

Flew, Antony. *God and Philosophy.* New York: Harcourt, Brace and World, 1966.

Freud, Sigmund. *The Future of an Illusion.* New York: Liveright Publishing, 1955.

Hick, John. *Faith and Knowledge.* Ithaca: Cornell University Press, 1957.

Kaufmann, Walter. *Religion from Tolstoy to Camus.* New York: Harper Brothers, 1961.

Kierkegaard, Søren. *Christian Discourses.* London: Oxford Press, 1940.

Lewis, H. D. *Our Experience of God.* London: George Allen & Unwin Ltd., 1959.

Plantinga, Alvin. *God and Other Minds.* Ithaca: Cornell University Press, 1967.

Russell, Bertrand. *Mysticism and Logic.* London: George Allen & Unwin, Ltd., 1917.

Tillich, Paul. *My Search for Absolutes.* New York: Simon & Shuster, 1967.

PART VII

TRAGEDY AND AESTHETIC CRITICISM

INTRODUCTORY READINGS

Herman Melville

Arthur Miller

INQUIRY

SELECTED SOURCES

Plato

Aristotle

Auden

Roberts

Wittgenstein

Herman Melville

The Chase—Third Day*

THE MORNING OF THE THIRD DAY DAWNED FAIR AND FRESH, AND once more the solitary night-man at the fore-mast-head was relieved by crowds of the daylight look-outs, who dotted every mast and almost every spar.

"D'ye see him?" cried Ahab; but the whale was not yet in sight.

"In his infallible wake, though; but follow that wake, that's all. Helm there; steady, as thou goest, and hast been going. What a lovely day again! were it a new-made world, and made for a summerhouse to the angels, and this morning the first of its throwing open to them, a fairer day could not dawn upon that world. Here's food for thought, had Ahab time to think; but Ahab never thinks; he only feels, feels, feels; *that's* tingling enough for mortal man! to think's audacity. God only has that right and privilege. Thinking is, or ought to be, a coolness and a calmness; and our poor hearts throb, and our poor brains beat too much for that. And yet, I've sometimes thought my brain was very calm—frozen calm, this old skull cracks so, like a glass in which the contents turned to ice, and shiver it. And still this hair is growing now; this moment growing, and heat must breed it; but no, it's like that sort of common grass that will grow anywhere, between the earthy clefts of Greenland ice or in Vesuvius lava. How the wild winds blow it; they whip it about me as the torn shreds of split sails lash the tossed ship they cling to. A vile wind that has no doubt blown ere this through prison corridors and cells, and wards of hospitals, and ventilated them, and now comes blowing hither as innocent as fleeces. Out upon it!—it's tainted. Were I the wind, I'd blow no more on such a wicked, miserable world. I'd crawl somewhere to a cave, and slink there. And yet, 'tis a noble and heroic thing, the

* Herman Melville, *Moby Dick* (1851), Chap. 99, and the Epilogue.

wind! who ever conquered it? In every fight it has the last and bitterest blow. Run tilting at it, and you but run through it. Ha! a coward wind that strikes stark naked men, but will not stand to receive a single blow. Even Ahab is a braver thing—a nobler thing than *that*. Would now the wind but had a body; but all the things that most exasperate and outrage mortal man, all these things are bodiless, but only bodiless as objects, not as agents. There's a most special, a most cunning, oh, a most malicious difference! And yet, I say again, and swear it now, that there's something all glorious and gracious in the wind. These warm Trade Winds, at least, that in the clear heavens blow straight on, in strong and steadfast, vigorous mildness; and veer not from their mark, however the baser currents of the sea may turn and tack, and mightiest Mississippies of the land swift and swerve about, uncertain where to go at last. And by the eternal Poles! these same Trades that so directly blow my good ship on; these Trades, or something like them—something so unchangeable, and full as strong, blow my keeled soul along! To it! Aloft there! What d'ye see?"

"Nothing, sir."

"Nothing! and noon at hand! The doubloon goes a-begging! See the sun! Aye, aye, it must be so. I've oversailed him. How, got the start? Aye, he's chasing *me* now; not I, *him*—that's bad; I might have known it, too. Fool! the lines—the harpoons he's towing. Aye, aye, I have run him by last night. About! about! Come down, all of ye, but the regular look-outs! Man the braces!"

Steering as she had done, the wind had been somewhat on the *Pequod's* quarter, so that now being pointed in the reverse direction, the braced ship sailed hard upon the breeze as she rechurned the cream in her own white wake.

"Against the wind he now steers for the open jaw," murmured Starbuck to himself, as he coiled the new-hauled main-brace upon the rail. "God keep us, but already my bones feel damp within me, and from the inside wet my flesh. I misdoubt me that I disobey my God in obeying him!"

"Stand by to sway me up!" cried Ahab, advancing to the hempen basket. "We should meet him soon."

"Aye, aye, sir," and straightway Starbuck did Ahab's bidding, and once more Ahab swung on high.

A whole hour now passed; gold-beaten out to ages. Time itself now held long breaths with keen suspense. But at last, some three points off the weather bow, Ahab descried the spout again, and instantly from the three mast-heads three shrieks went up as if the tongues of fire had voiced it.

"Forehead to forehead I meet thee, this third time, Moby Dick! On deck there!—brace sharper up; crowd her into the wind's eye.

He's too far off to lower yet, Mr. Starbuck. The sails shake! Stand over that helmsman with a top-maul! So, so; he travels fast, and I must down. But let me have one more good round look aloft here at the sea; there's time for that. An old, old sight, and yet somehow so young; aye, and not changed a wink since I first saw it, a boy, from the sand-hills of Nantucket! The same!—the same!—the same to Noah as to me. There's a soft shower to leeward. Such lovely leewardings! They must lead somewhere—to something else than common land, more palmy than the palms. Leeward! the White Whale goes that way; look to windward, then; the better if the bitterer quarter. But good-by, good-by, old mast-head! What's this?—green? aye, tiny mosses in these warped cracks. No such green weather stains on Ahab's head! There's the difference now between man's old age and matter's. But aye, old mast, we both grow old together; sound in our hulls, though, are we not, my ship? Aye, minus a leg, that's all. By heaven, this dead wood has the better of my live flesh every way. I can't compare with it; and I've known some ships made of dead trees outlast the lives of men made of the most vital stuff of vital fathers. What's that he said? he should still go before me, my pilot; and yet to be seen again? But where? Will I have eyes at the bottom of the sea, supposing I descend those endless stairs? and all night I've been sailing from him, wherever he did sink to. Aye, aye, like many more thou told'st direful truth as touching thyself, O Parsee; but, Ahab, there thy shot fell short. Good-by, mast-head—keep a good eye upon the whale, the while I'm gone. We'll talk tomorrow, nay, tonight, when the White Whale lies down there, tied by head and tail."

He gave the word; and still gazing round him, was steadily lowered through the cloven blue air to the deck.

In due time the boats were lowered; but as standing in his shallop's stern, Ahab just hovered upon the point of the descent, he waved to the mate, who held one of the tackle-ropes on deck—and bade him pause.

"Starbuck!"

"Sir?"

"For the third time my soul's ship starts upon this voyage, Starbuck."

"Aye, sir, thou wilt have it so."

"Some ships sail from their ports, and ever afterwards are missing, Starbuck!"

"Truth, sir: saddest truth."

"Some men die at ebb tide; some at low water; some at the full of the flood; and I feel now like a billow that's all one crested comb, Starbuck. I am old; shake hands with me, man."

Their hands met; their eyes fastened; Starbuck's tears the glue.

"Oh, my Captain, my Captain!—noble heart—go not—go not! —see, it's a brave man that weeps; how great the agony of the persuasion then!"

"Lower away!" cried Ahab, tossing the mate's arm from him. "Stand by the crew!"

In an instant the boat was pulling round close under the stern.

"The sharks! the sharks!" cried a voice from the low cabin-window there; "O master, my master, come back!"

But Ahab heard nothing; for his own voice was high-lifted then; and the boat leaped on.

Yet the voice spake true; for scarce had he pushed from the ship, when numbers of sharks, seemingly rising from out the dark waters beneath the hull, maliciously snapped at the blades of the oars, every time they dipped in the water; and in this way accompanied the boat with their bites. It is a thing not uncommonly happening to the whale-boats in those swarming seas; the sharks at times apparently following them in the same prescient way that vultures hover over the banner of marching regiments in the east. But these were the first sharks that had been observed by the *Pequod* since the White Whale had been first descried; and whether it was that Ahab's crew were all such tiger-yellow barbarians, and therefore their flesh more musky to the senses of the sharks—a matter sometimes well known to affect them, however it was, they seemed to follow that one boat without molesting the others.

"Heart of wrought steel!" murmured Starbuck gazing over the side, and following with his eyes the receding boat—"canst thou yet ring boldly to that sight?—lowering thy keel among ravening sharks, and followed by them, open-mouthed to the chase; and this the critical third day?—For when three days flow together in one continuous intense pursuit; be sure the first is the morning, the second the noon, and the third the evening and the end of that thing—be that end what it may. Oh! my God! what is this that shoots through me, and leaves me so deadly calm, yet expectant—fixed at the top of a shudder! Future things swim before me, as in empty outlines and skeletons; all the past is somehow grown dim. Mary, girl; thou fadest in pale glories behind me; boy! I seem to see but thy eyes grown wondrous blue. Strangest problems of life seem clearing; but clouds sweep between—Is my journey's end coming? My legs feel faint; like his who has footed it all day. Feel thy heart—beats it yet? Stir thyself, Starbuck!—stave it off—move, move! speak aloud!—Mast-head there! See ye my boy's hand on the hill?—Crazed;—aloft there!—keep thy keenest eye upon the boats:—mark well the whale!—Ho! again!—drive off that hawk! see! he pecks—he tears the vane"—pointing to the red flag flying at the main-truck—"Ha, he soars away with it!—Where's the old man now? see'st thou that sight, oh, Ahab!—shudder, shudder!"

The boats had not gone very far, when by a signal from the mast-heads—a downward-pointed arm, Ahab knew that the whale had sounded; but intending to be near him at the next rising, he held on his way a little sideways from the vessel; the becharmed crew maintaining the profoundest silence, as the head-beat waves hammered and hammered against the opposing bow.

"Drive, drive in your nails, oh, ye waves! to their uttermost heads drive them in! ye but strike a thing without a lid; and no coffin and no hearse can be mine:—and hemp only can kill me! Ha! ha!"

Suddenly the waters around them slowly swelled in broad circles; then quickly upheaved, as if sideways sliding from a submerged berg of ice, swiftly rising to the surface. A low rumbling sound was heard; a subterraneous hum; and then all held their breaths; as bedraggled with trailing ropes, and harpoons, and lances, a vast form shot lengthwise, but obliquely from the sea. Shrouded in a thin drooping veil of mist, it hovered for a moment in the rainbowed air; and then fell swamping back into the deep. Crushed thirty feet upward, the waters flashed for an instant like heaps of fountains, then brokenly sank in a shower of flakes, leaving the circling surface creamed like new milk round the marble trunk of the whale.

"Give way!" cried Ahab to the oarsmen, and the boats darted forward to the attack; but maddened by yesterday's fresh irons that corroded in him, Moby Dick seemed combinedly possessed by all the angels that fell from heaven. The wide tiers of welded tendons overspreading his broad white forehead, beneath the transparent skin, looked knitted together; as head on, he came churning his tail among the boats; and once more flailed them apart; spilling out the irons and lances from the two mates' boats, and dashing in one side of the upper part of their bows, but leaving Ahab's almost without a scar.

While Daggoo and Queequeg were stopping the strained planks; and as the whale swimming out from them, turned, and showed one entire flank as he shot by them again; at that moment a quick cry went up. Lashed round and round to the fish's back; pinioned in the turns upon turns in which, during the past night, the whale had reeled the involutions of the lines around him, the half-torn body of the Parsee was seen; his sable raiment frayed to shreds; his distended eyes turned full upon old Ahab.

The harpoon dropped from his hand.

"Befooled, befooled!"—drawing in a long lean breath—"Aye, Parsee! I see thee again.—Aye, and thou goest before; and this, *this* then is the hearse that thou didst promise. But I hold thee to the last letter of thy word. Where is the second hearse? Away, mates, to the ship! those boats are useless now; repair them if ye can in time, and return to me; if not, Ahab is enough to die—Down, men; the first thing that but offers to jump from this boat I stand in, that thing I harpoon. Ye are not other men, but my arms and my legs; and so obey me.—Where's the whale? gone down again?"

But he looked too nigh the boat; for as if bent upon escaping with the corpse he bore, and as if the particular place of the last encounter had been but a stage in his leeward voyage, Moby Dick was now again steadily swimming forward; and had almost passed the ship, which thus far had been sailing in the contrary direction to him, though for the present her headway had been stopped. He seemed swimming with his utmost velocity, and now only intent upon pursuing his own straight path in the sea.

"Oh! Ahab," cried Starbuck, "not too late is it, even now, the third day, to desist. See! Moby Dick seeks thee not. It is thou, thou, that madly seekest him!"

Setting sail to the rising wind, the lonely boat was swiftly impelled to leeward, by both oars and canvas. And at last when Ahab was sliding by the vessel, so near as plainly to distinguish Starbuck's face as he leaned over the rail, he hailed him to turn the vessel about, and follow him, not too swiftly, at a judicious interval. Glancing upward he saw Tashtego, Queequeg, and Daggoo, eagerly mounting to the three mast-heads; while the oarsmen were rocking in the two staved boats which had just been hoisted to the side, and were busily at work in repairing them. One after the other, through the port-holes, as he sped, he also caught flying glimpses of Stubb and Flask, busying themselves on deck among bundles of new irons and lances. As he saw all this; as he heard the hammers in the broken boats; far other hammers seemed driving a nail into his heart. But he rallied. And now marking that the vane or flag was gone from the mainmast-head, he shouted to Tashtego, who had just gained that perch, to descend again for another flag, a hammer and nails, and so nail it to the mast.

Whether fagged by the three days' running chase, and the resistance to his swimming in the knotted hamper he bore; or whether it was some latent deceitfulness and malice in him: whichever was true, the White Whale's way now began to abate, as it seemed, from the boat so rapidly nearing him once more; though indeed the whale's last start had not been so long a one as before. And still as Ahab glided over the waves the unpitying sharks accompanied him; and so pertinaciously stuck to the boat; and so continually bit at the plying oars, that the blades became jagged and crunched, and left small splinters in the sea, at almost every dip.

"Heed them not! those teeth but give new rowlocks to your

oars. Pull on! 'tis the better rest, the sharks' jaw than the yielding water."

"But at every bite, sir, the thin blades grow smaller and smaller!"

"They will last long enough! pull on!—But who can tell"—he muttered—"whether these sharks swim to feast on the whale or on Ahab?—But pull on! Aye, all alive, now—we near him. The helm! take the helm! let me pass"—and so saying, two of the oarsmen helped him forward to the bows of the still flying boat.

At length as the craft was cast to one side, and ran ranging along with the White Whale's flank, he seemed strangely oblivious of its advance—as the whale sometimes will—and Ahab was fairly within the smoky mountain mist, which, thrown off from the whale's spout, curled round his great Monadnock hump; he was even thus close to him; when, with body arched back, and both arms lengthwise high-lifted to the poise, he darted his fierce iron, and his far fiercer curse into the hated whale. As both steel and curse sank to the socket, as if sucked into a morass, Moby Dick sidewise writhed; spasmodically rolled his nigh flank against the bow, and, without staving a hole in it, so suddenly canted the boat over, that had it not been for the elevated part of the gunwale to which he then clung, Ahab would once more have been tossed into the sea. As it was, three of the oarsmen—who foreknew not the precise instant of the dart, and were therefore unprepared for its effects—these were flung out; but so fell, that, in an instant two of them clutched the gunwale again, and rising to its level on a combing wave, hurled themselves bodily inboard again; the third man helplessly dropping astern, but still afloat and swimming.

Almost simultaneously, with a mighty volition of ungraduated, instantaneous swiftness, the White Whale darted through the weltering sea. But when Ahab cried out to the steersman to take new turns with the line, and hold it so; and commanded the crew to turn round on their seats, and tow the boat up to the mark; the moment the treacherous line felt that double strain and tug, it snapped in the empty air!

"What breaks in me? Some sinew cracks!—'tis whole again; oars! oars! Burst in upon him!"

Hearing the tremendous rush of the sea-crashing boat, the whale wheeled round to present his blank forehead at bay; but in that evolution, catching sight of the nearing black hull of the ship; seemingly seeing in it the source of all his persecutions; bethinking it—it may be—a larger and nobler foe; of a sudden, he bore down upon its advancing prow, smiting his jaws amid fiery showers of foam.

Ahab staggered; his hand smote his forehead. "I grow blind; hands! stretch out before me that I may yet grope my way. Is't night?"

"The whale! The ship!" cried the cringing oarsmen.

"Oars! oars! Slope downward to thy depths. Oh, sea, that ere it be forever too late, Ahab may slide this last, last time upon his mark! I see: the ship! the ship! Dash on, my men! will ye not save my ship?"

But as the oarsmen violently forced their boats through the sledge-hammering seas, the before whale-smitten bow-ends of two planks burst through, and in an instant almost, the temporarily disabled boat lay nearly level with the waves; its half-wading, splashing crew, trying hard to stop the gap and bale out the pouring water.

Meantime, for that one beholding instant, Tashtego's mast-head hammer remained suspended in his hand; and the red flag, half-wrapping him as with a plaid, then streamed itself straight out from him, as his own forward-flowing heart; while Starbuck and Stubb, standing upon the bowsprit beneath, caught sight of the down-coming monster just as soon as he.

"The whale, the whale! Up helm, up helm! Oh, all ye sweet powers of air, now hug me close! Let not Starbuck die, if die he must, in a woman's fainting fit. Up helm, I say—ye fools, the jaw! the jaw! Is this the end of all my bursting prayers? all my life-long fidelities? Oh, Ahab, Ahab, lo, thy work. Steady! helmsman, steady. Nay, nay! Up helm again! He turns to meet us! Oh, his unappeasable brow drives on toward one, whose duty tells him he cannot depart. My God, stand by me now!"

"Stand not by me, but stand under me, whoever you are that will now help Stubb; for Stubb, too, sticks here. I grin at thee, thou grinning whale! Whoever helped Stubb, or kept Stubb awake, but Stubb's own unwinking eye? And now poor Stubb goes to bed upon a mattress that is all too soft; would it were stuffed with brushwood! I grin at thee, thou grinning whale! Look ye, sun, moon, and stars! I call ye assassins of as good a fellow as ever spouted up his ghost. For all that, I would yet ring glasses with thee, would ye but hand the cup! Oh, oh! oh, oh! thou grinning whale, but there'll be plenty of gulping soon! Why fly ye not, O Ahab! For me, off shoes and jacket to it; let Stubb die in his drawers! A most moldy and over-salted death, though;—cherries! cherries! cherries! Oh, Flask, for one red cherry ere we die!"

"Cherries? I only wish that we were where they grow. Oh, Stubb, I hope my poor mother's drawn my part-pay ere this; if not, few coppers will now come to her, for the voyage is up."

From the ship's bows, nearly all the seamen now hung inactive; hammers, bits of planks, lances, and harpoons, mechanically retained in their hands, just as they had darted from their various employments; all their enchanted eyes intent upon the whale, which from side to side strangely vibrating his predestinating head, sent a broad band of overspreading semicircular foam before him as he rushed. Retribution, swift vengeance, eternal malice were in his whole aspect, and spite of all that mortal man could do, the solid white buttress of his forehead smote the ship's starboard bow, till men and timbers reeled. Some fell flat upon their faces. Like dislodged trucks, the heads of the harpooneers aloft shook on their bull-like necks. Through the breach, they heard the waters pour, as mountain torrent down a flume.

"The ship! The hearse!—the second hearse!" cried Ahab from the boat; "its wood could only be American!"

Diving beneath the settling ship, the whale ran quivering along its keel; but turning under water, swiftly shot to the surface again, far off the other bow, but within a few yards of Ahab's boat, where, for a time, he lay quiescent.

"I turn my body from the sun. What ho, Tashtego! let me hear thy hammer. Oh! ye three unsurrendered spires of mine; thou uncracked keel; and only god-bullied hull; thou firm deck, and haughty helm, and Pole-pointed prow—death-glorious ship! must ye then perish, and without me? Am I cut off from the last fond pride of meanest shipwrecked captains? Oh, lonely death on lonely life! Oh, now I feel my topmost greatness lies in my topmost grief. Ho, ho! from all your furthest bounds, pour ye now in, ye bold billows of my whole foregone life, and top this one piled comber of my death! Toward thee I roll, thou all-destroying but unconquering whale; to the last I grapple with thee; from hell's heart I stab at thee; for hate's sake I spit my last breath at thee. Sink all coffins and all hearses to one common pool! and since neither can be mine, let me then tow to pieces, while still chasing thee, though tied to thee, thou damned whale! *Thus,* I give up the spear!"

The harpoon was darted; the stricken whale flew forward; with igniting velocity the line ran through the groove;—ran foul. Ahab stooped to clear it; he did clear it; but the flying turn caught him round the neck, and voicelessly as Turkish mutes bowstring their victim, he was shot out of the boat, ere the crew knew he was gone. Next instant, the heavy eye-splice in the rope's final end flew out of the stark-empty tub, knocked down an oarsman, and smiting the sea, disappeared in its depths.

For an instant, the tranced boats crew stood still; then turned. "The ship? Great God, where is the ship?" Soon they through dim, bewildering mediums saw her sidelong fading phantom, as in the gaseous Fata Morgana; only the uppermost masts out of water; while fixed by infatuation, or fidelity, or fate, to their once lofty perches, the pagan harpooneers still maintained their sinking lookouts on the sea. And now, concentric circles seized the lone boat itself, and all its crew, and each floating oar, and every lance-pole, and spinning, animate and inanimate, all round and round in one vortex, carried the smallest chip of the *Pequod* out of sight.

But as the last whelmings intermixingly poured themselves over the sunken head of the Indian at the mainmast, leaving a few inches of the erect spar yet visible, together with long streaming yards of the flag, which calmly undulated, with ironical coincidings, over the destroying billows they almost touched—at that instant, a red arm and a hammer hovered backwardly uplifted in the open air, in the act of nailing the flag faster and yet faster to the subsiding spar. A sky-hawk that tauntingly had followed the main-truck downward from its natural home among the stars, pecking at the flag, and incommoding Tashtego there; this bird now chanced to intercept its broad fluttering wing between the hammer and the wood; and simultaneously feeling that ethereal thrill, the submerged savage beneath, in his death-gasp, kept his hammer frozen there; and so the bird of heaven, with archangelic shrieks, and his imperial beak thrust upward, and his whole captive form folded in the flag of Ahab, went down with his ship, which, like Satan, would not sink to hell till she had dragged a living part of heaven along with her, and helmeted herself with it.

Now small fowls flew screaming over the yet yawning gulf; a sullen white surf beat against its steep sides; then all collapsed, and the great shroud of the sea rolled on as it rolled five thousand years ago.

Epilogue "AND I ONLY AM ESCAPED TO TELL THEE"—JOB.

The drama's done. Why then here does any one step forth?—Because one did survive the wreck.

It so chanced, that after the Parsee's disappearance, I was he whom the Fates ordained to take the place of Ahab's bowsman, when that bowsman assumed the vacant post; the same, who, when on the last day the three men were tossed from out of the rocking boat, was dropped astern. So, floating on the margin of the ensuing scene, and in full sight of it, when the half-spent suction of the sunken ship reached me, I was then, but slowly, drawn toward the closing vortex. When I reached it, it had subsided to a creamy pool. Round and round, then, and ever contracting toward the buttonlike black bubble at the axis of that slowly wheeling circle, like another Ixion I did revolve. Till, gaining that vital center, the black bubble upward burst; and now, liberated by reason of its cunning spring, and, owing to its great buoyancy, rising with great force, the coffin life-buoy shot lengthwise from the sea, fell over, and floated by my side. Buoyed up by that coffin, for almost one whole day and night, I floated on a soft and dirge-like main. The unharming sharks, they glided by as if with pad-locks on their mouths; the savage sea-hawks sailed with sheathed beaks. On the second day, a sail drew near, nearer, and picked me up at last. It was the devious-cruising *Rachel,* that in her retracing search after her missing children, only found another orphan.

Arthur Miller

Requiem*

CHARLEY:

It's getting dark, Linda.

Linda doesn't react. She stares at the grave.

BIFF:

How about it, Mom? Better get some rest, heh? They'll be closing the gate soon.

Linda makes no move. Pause.

HAPPY, *deeply angered:*

He had no right to do that. There was no necessity for it. We would've helped him.

CHARLEY, *grunting:*

Hmmm.

BIFF:

Come along, Mom.

LINDA:

Why didn't anybody come?

CHARLEY:

It was a very nice funeral.

LINDA:

But where are all the people he knew? Maybe they blame him.

CHARLEY:

Naa. It's a rough world, Linda. They wouldn't blame him.

LINDA:

I can't understand it. At this time especially. First time in thirty-five years we were just about free and clear. He only needed a little salary. He was even finished with the dentist.

CHARLEY:

No man only needs a little salary.

* Arthur Miller, *Death of A Salesman* (New York: Viking Press, 1949), pp. 137–139. Copyright 1949 by Arthur Miller. Used by permission of the publisher.

LINDA:

I can't understand it.

BIFF:

There were a lot of nice days. When he'd come home from a trip; or on Sundays, making the stoop; finishing the cellar; putting on the new porch; when he built the extra bathroom; and put up the garage. You know something, Charley, there's more of him in that front stoop than in all the sales he ever made.

CHARLEY:

Yeah. He was a happy man with a batch of cement.

LINDA:

He was so wonderful with his hands.

BIFF:

He had the wrong dreams. All, all, wrong.

HAPPY, *almost ready to fight Biff:*

Don't say that!

BIFF:

He never knew who he was.

CHARLEY, *stopping Happy's movement and reply. To Biff:*

Nobody dast blame this man. You don't understand: Willy was a salesman. And for a salesman, there is no rock bottom to the life. He don't put a bolt to a nut, he don't tell you the law or give you medicine. He's a man way out there in the blue, riding on a smile and a shoeshine. And when they start not smiling back—that's an earthquake. And then you get yourself a couple of spots on your hat, and you're finished. Nobody dast blame this man. A salesman is got to dream, boy. It comes with the territory.

BIFF:

Charley, the man didn't know who he was.

HAPPY, *infuriated:*

Don't say that!

BIFF:

Why don't you come with me, Happy?

HAPPY:

I'm not licked that easily. I'm staying right in this city, and I'm gonna beat this racket! *He looks at Biff, his chin set.* The Loman Brothers!

BIFF:

I know who I am, kid.

HAPPY:

All right, boy. I'm gonna show you and everybody else that Willy Loman did not die in vain. He had a good dream. It's the only dream you can have—to come out number-one man. He fought it out here, and this is where I'm gonna win it for him.

BIFF, *with a hopeless glance at Happy, bends toward his mother:*

Let's go, Mom.

LINDA:

I'll be with you in a minute. Go on, Charley. *He hesitates.* I want to, just for a minute. I never had a chance to say good-by.

Charley moves away, followed by Happy. Biff remains a slight distance up and left of Linda. She sits there, summoning herself. The flute begins, not far away, playing behind her speech.

LINDA:

Forgive me, dear. I can't cry. I don't know what it is, but I can't cry. I don't understand it. Why did you ever do that? Help me, Willy, I can't cry. It seems to me that you're just on another trip. I keep expecting you. Willy, dear, I can't cry. Why did you do it? I search and search and I search, and I can't understand it, Willy. I made the last payment on the house today. Today, dear. And there'll be nobody home. *A sob rises in her throat.* We're free and clear. *Sobbing more fully, released:* We're free. *Biff comes slowly toward her.* We're free . . . We're free . . .

Biff lifts her to her feet and moves out up right with her in his arms. Linda sobs quietly. Bernard and Charley come together and follow them, followed by Happy. Only the music of the flute is left on the darkening stage as over the house the hard towers of the apartment buildings rise into sharp focus, and

The Curtain Falls

INQUIRY

They say they can't believe it, it's a sacrilegious shame
Now who would want to hurt such a hero of the game
But you know I predicted it I knew he had to fall
How did it happen, I hope his suffering was small
Tell me every detail I've got to know it all
And do you have a picture of the pain.

PHIL OCHS
Crucifixion *

WHY do we like to go to the theater to watch imaginary heroes facing imaginary trials and suffering imaginary pains and committing imaginary murders and suicides? What is there about the characters of tragic literature which attracts us? Newspapers are filled with daily tragic events, family misfortunes, the assassination of our leaders. Have we not had enough? There is something both frightening and exhilarating about Captain Ahab and Macbeth; there is something both pitiful and inspiring in Willy Loman of *Death of a Salesman* and Blanche DuBois of *Streetcar Named Desire*. Certainly we do not suggest to our children that these characters are worthy of emulation. What do these tragic heroes of literature share in common with us? What if anything is to be learned from a philosophic consideration of them?

Art as an Imitation of Appearances

Tragedy, as a literary genre, is rooted in the same Greek soil as philosophy. The traditional Greek concept considered all art as imitative. Plato described art, painting in particular, as imitations of appearances, copies of copies. He felt art to be unworthy of much consideration, because knowledge of reality for Plato was to be found only in the contemplation of ideas and never in the vagueness and vulgarity of earthly appearances. For these reasons he tells us that dramatic poetry ought to be excluded from his perfect state,

* Used by kind permission of Phil Ochs and Barricade Music.

the Republic. It is "ruinous to the understanding of the hearers, and . . . the knowledge of true nature is the only antidote to them (those who watch the drama.)"*

Aristotle, who did not share Plato's theory of knowledge, did, however, agree that art is an imitation. It seems natural to question the value of art, if it is felt to be purely imitative. After all, why settle for an imitation if you can get the real thing? Is art of value only for its decorative appeal? What other reason for keeping a copy? Paintings, no matter how realistic in appearance, always seem to fail to capture completely what they represent. Few of us are fooled by paintings, taking them to be the real things. But not all art attempts realism.

Tragedy as an Expression of the Universal Values of Human Life

Aristotle alleviates some of these problems when he says that artists "imitate things as they ought to be." He further clarifies what ought to be the subject of artistic imitations: men in action. Art, and especially tragedy, should be an expression of the universal values of human life, according to Aristotle. In this regard, tragedy is of superior worth to history. In the tragic drama, Aristotle maintains, the interplay of human values in life as we think it ought to be lived provides guidelines and examples for understanding value conflicts in actual situations. This type of imitative theater becomes a laboratory for the examination of a whole spectrum of value commitments.

The making of value judgments, the placing of degrees of worth on things, people, events, and ideas is one of the most fundamental of human activities. Nietzsche and the other existentialists have called man a valuing animal. Nietzsche writes in *Thus Spoke Zarathustra,* "Values did man only assign to things in order to maintain himself—he created only the significance of things, a human significance! Therefore, calleth he himself 'man', that is, the valuator."†

The Theory of Catharsis

Aristotle established certain principles of tragedy which have been used in criticism even today. One of the most significant of Aristotle's theories is catharsis, the purging of the emotions of pity and fear, which has been called both a psychotherapeutic and a moral technique. John Milton remarks in the preface to *Samson Agonistes* that tragedy as understood by Aristotle is the "moralest" of poems because it has the power of raising pity and fear and of purging the mind, leaving the audience "with a kind of delight." Milton closes his play with these lines: "From this great event/ With peace and consolation hath dismissed/ And calm of mind, all passion spent."‡

The value of tragedy, understood in the Aristotelian sense, lies in its ability to involve and then purify an audience's emotions. We enjoy tragedy because it focuses upon our basic emotions as men.

* See Selected Sources.

† Friedrich Nietzsche, *Thus Spoke Zarathustra,* Thomas Common, trans. (London: George Allen & Unwin Ltd., 1909), p. 60.

‡ John Milton, *Samson Agonistes* (1671).

We see an essentially good man suffer as the result of some fault in his character; we pity him and we fear for his outcome as well as our own. Aristotle tells us that the best character for a tragic hero is neither a saintly nor a devilish man. Instead the hero ought to be a man who befalls evil not due to vice on his part, but because of a flaw in his very personality or an error in his judgment. The emotions of pity and fear are generated in the audience because the hero suffers out of proportion with his faults.

It is true that we pity men who suffer unjustly. But if the suffering or punishment of a man's error is justified, we do not feel pity for him. Few of us have pity for the murderer as he faces the electric chair. It would appear that if we are to feel pity for the tragic hero, his misfortune cannot result simply from his character. But if the suffering in the Greek tragedy is a product of the punishment of the guilty by a moral universe, must we not conclude that one of the requirements of Aristotle's theory is that the universe display a tendency to irrationality, causing men to suffer far in excess of what their crime warrants?

What events produce in you a feeling of pity for an individual? Notice how questions of justice, good, bad, right, and wrong begin to enter your thinking about pity. Can you imagine a situation in which you would grant the justice of the punishment and still pity the sufferer? What values take on the most importance in such thinking?

Tragedy and the Understanding of Values

Why does tragedy, perhaps art in general, better satisfy our need to examine and understand values and value conflicts than history does? History attempts to recount the actions of men as they were, to narrate the story of the way in which the goods and bads of human existence motivated human action. Why then turn to tragedy? Does history tell too much of the truth?

Does the style of tragedy change with the evolution of cultural values over the years? Does tragedy still serve the purposes outlined for it by Aristotle? Consider Captain Ahab, in Melville's *Moby Dick*. W. H. Auden calls him a Christian tragic hero. Ahab embodies both the best and worst of man as seen from the Christian point of view. He is possessed with an irrational hatred of a particular white whale. We might at first think there is nothing unusual about a whaleboat captain venting all of his energies against a whale that has so horribly dismembered him. Perhaps Ahab's plight leads us to pity him. But Herman Melville shows us that other whalemen also dismembered by whales hold no such single-minded grudges as Captain Ahab bears. Ahab sees himself as wronged. He interprets the acts of the whale as maliciously intended, as purposely directed toward him. He attributes to a whale the power to do evil willfully.

The Tragedy of Possibility

Moby Dick, like many of the plays of William Shakespeare, involves us with a set of values different from those of classical tragedy. Auden calls this type of tragedy "the tragedy of possibility." In

Ahab's case, his future—possibly a good and prosperous life—and his error—his prideful attempt to seek vengeance on a whale—are both within his power of choice. He is not an evil man. He is a respected member of the religious community, a husband and father, a successful captain in his trade. There are no secrets of his life of which he is ignorant. His fate is not directed by the blind unfolding of patterns of necessity. Ahab is burned to the soul with a hatred of Moby Dick and of the universe which allows such an "evil" to exist. Ahab does not serenely accept his destiny, because he has no destiny until he chooses what it shall be. He challenges the great seas, the heavens, the universe. Of course Ahab must lose, but why?

Central to most Christian thinking is the idea that men are free to choose the lives they lead. When men sin, choose evil over good, the responsibility and the consequences of their actions rest not with God. God always remains purely good, while men are faced with the alternatives of good and evil and can by improper choices create their own adverse destinies. This is tragic, of course, because it might have been otherwise.

Augustine and some later philosophers such as Leibniz see the inclusion of free will in the world as an element of God's goodness. A man with free choice is thought by these philosophers to be a far greater accomplishment of a good God than a totally determined creature who could act only in certain prescribed ways. With free choice may come wrong choices and the consequence of punishment. Augustine summarizes the position as follows:

> Though sinful souls are censured, do not let that provoke you to say in your heart that it would have been better if they did not exist. They are censured because they are compared with what they might have been if they had not willed to sin. God, their Maker, is to be gloriously praised for the human faculties with which he has endowed them not only because he justly subjects them to his order when they sin, but also because he made them such that, even when soiled with sin, they are not surpassed in dignity by corporeal light, for which God is rightly praised.*

Melville realizes the potentials of a hero within a Christian framework of values and the control over destiny which men can exert. He writes:

> Would to God these blessed calms would last. But the mingled, mingling threads of life are woven by warp and woof: calms crossed by storms, a storm for every calm. There is no steady unretracing progress in this life; we do not advance through fixed gradations, and at the last one pause: through infancy's unconscious spell, boyhood's thoughtless faith, adolescence's doubt, then scepticism, then disbelief, resting in manhood's pondering repose of If. But once gone through, we trace round again, and are infants, boys, and men, and Ifs eternally.†

* Augustine, "On Free Will," *Augustine's Earlier Writings*. J. H. S. Burleigh, trans. (London: The Westminster Press, 1953).
† Herman Melville, *Moby Dick*, Chap. 78.

"Ifs eternally"—if only Hamlet had killed the king in the chapel, if only Ahab had gone to the aid of the Rachel. The sense of the tragic in Christian thinking lies in the recognition of these alternatives by the audience. Is this also our criterion for everyday tragedy? "If only he had listened to his mother . . . "; "If he had not taken the old country road—we told him to take the new super highway. . . ."

In this regard consider the tragic assassination of Senator Robert F. Kennedy. The tragedy there does not lie completely in "Ifs," at least not in "Ifs" related to particular events: "If he had not run for the presidential nomination . . . "; "If he had not entered the California primary . . . "; "If he had not been at the Ambassador Hotel. . . ." All seem inadequate in understanding the tragedy. It lies instead in the fact that Robert Kennedy was who he was. We could, no doubt, say that if Robert Kennedy had not been Robert Kennedy there would have been no tragedy; and this sounds strangely like the Greek idea of fate, does it not?

Ahab goes to his death cursing, spitting hate at the white whale. He does not die with the uplifted spirit of a Greek hero, but he does realize a sense of victory: "Oh how I feel my topmost greatness lies in my topmost grief." Ahab is not reunited with nature, as was the Greek, Oedipus, at Colonus. Ahab reaches peace with himself. But do the other tenets of Christian thinking preclude this type of literature from being truly tragic?

The basic doctrines of Christianity cannot be called tragic in any sense. Faith in rebirth, resurrection, and the grace of God would seem to take some of the sting out of suffering. Saint Paul claims to rejoice in his "thorn in the flesh," and we are told that the early Christians sought out martyrdom. The narrative of the life of Christ in the Gospels does not provide a basis for tragedy. We could imagine the account being turned into tragedy, but that could be accomplished only at the cost of ending it with the crucifixion and the words of Christ, "My God, my God, Why hast Thou forsaken me?" But this would destroy the story's central purpose and its religious significance. It is not a tragedy, and it provides no basis for the tragic ideal, at least in the Greek sense.

The Twentieth Century

It is argued by Preston Roberts that Twentieth Century authors are concerned with the pathetic side of life. He claims that writers such as Tennessee Williams and Arthur Miller dwell on the "underground aspects of existence,"* compulsive forces which drive men to their doom despite the human spirit. Roberts maintains that the tragic characters in the literature of this century usually are defeated by their own emotional insecurity and their inability to adapt to changing circumstances. This is neither the classical fault of ignorance nor the Christian sin of pride.

Why do we pity Willy Loman in *Death of a Salesman?* Roberts

* See Selected Sources.

tells us that we do so because the hero suffers in excess of what he morally and religiously deserves, and that, furthermore, we realize that there is no way out of the predicament for the hero who is not even responsible for his plight. Willy Loman commits suicide, but he is not totally an aimless brute led by powerful forces to his destruction. Willy has broken a law of our society, the law that one must be successful, and in so doing he fails to achieve the life goal that he has valued for so long. Willy Loman is a failure where success is all that counts. But is his fate really tragic, or just stupid?

Perhaps tragedy is an antique. Contemporary man looks at it, collects it, but he cannot sit in it. It crumbles under the weight of his problems. Do the plays of the Theater of the Absurd, the Happening Theater, the Shock Theater assume the role in our culture formerly played by tragedy? Martin Esslin says of the theater of the Absurd that it attempts to make man "face up to the human condition as it really is, to free him from illusions that are bound to cause constant maladjustment and disappointment."* Is this goal more successfully achieved if men turn into rhinoceroses, if two bums pratfall aimlessly around the stage, if parents live in ash-cans, than if a foolish old salesman torments himself for his failures?

If we assume that tragedy is dead, that our society can no longer find great significance in its struggles, how do we account for the immense popularity of the motion picture versions of traditional tragedies such as Shakespeare's *Romeo and Juliet?* Who does not know that story? The fact that the context and significance of certain values has changed seems to be a matter of history. Can we really appreciate the art of another time?

* Martin Esslin, *The Theater of the Absurd* (Garden City, N.Y.: Doubleday, 1961), p. 316

1

PLATO
(427–347 B.C.)

*Art in the Republic**

In this selection, taken from The Republic, *Plato presents Socrates discussing the value of art—painting, poetry, and drama in particular—in the perfect state. Through Socrates, Plato attacks the value of artistic endeavor. Poetry must be banned from the state. His reason is not simply that poetry excites emotional activity and thereby disrupts the rational community. He attacks the arts as imitations of copies of that which is real. Again the "Theory of Ideas," Plato's epistemology, is central to his analysis. The ideas are real and the things in this world are copies of the ideas. Art produces copies of the things in this world; therefore art is thrice removed from reality and can be of little value to rational man.*

Plato gives what may be one of his best accounts of the "Theory of Ideas" in this selection. He argues that each form must be singular. There can be only one of each because each is ideal. Notice how names play an important role. God can make only one ideal bed, Plato tells us, because if there were two ideal beds there would have to be a third, more ideal bed which would serve as the criterion of "bed" for the other two. The carpenter in this world is the creator of beds which are copies based on the ideal bed. But the artist, Plato maintains, does nothing but imitate and does not create. The imitator has no knowledge of the real and of truth, for he is too far removed from it. If art does not have truth, it cannot appeal to reason, and thus it must seek to satisfy emotions and other lesser parts of man, Plato argues. Men who are excited emotionally cannot be governed rationally; therefore, art has no place in the perfect state.

* Plato, *The Republic,* B. Jowett, trans. (Oxford: The Clarendon Press, 1892), Book X, with omissions.

OF the many excellences which I perceive in the order of our State, there is none which upon reflection pleases me better than the rule about poetry.

To what do you refer?

To the rejection of imitative poetry, which certainly ought not to be received; as I see far more clearly now that the parts of the soul have been distinguished.

What do you mean?

Poetry Distorts Understanding

Speaking in confidence, for I should not like to have my words repeated to the tragedians and the rest of the imitative tribe—but I do not mind saying to you, that all poetical imitations are ruinous to the understanding of the hearers, and that the knowledge of their true nature is the only antidote to them.

Explain the purpose of your remark.

Well, I will tell you, although I have always from my earliest youth had an awe and love of Homer, which even now makes the words falter on my lips, for he is the great captain and teacher of the whole of that charming tragic company; but a man is not to be reverenced more than the truth, and therefore I will speak out.

Very good, he said.

Listen to me then, or rather, answer me.

Put your question.

Can you tell me what imitation is? for I really do not know.

A likely thing, then, that I should know.

Why not? for the duller eye may often see a thing sooner than the keener.

Very true, he said; but in your presence, even if I had any faint notion, I could not muster courage to utter it. Will you inquire yourself?

Well then, shall we begin the inquiry in our usual manner: Whenever a number of individuals have a common name, we assume them to have also a corresponding idea or form:—do you understand me?

I do.

Let us take any common instance; there are beds and tables in the world—plenty of them, are there not?

Yes.

But there are only two ideas or forms of them—one the idea of a bed, the other of a table.

True.

And the maker of either of them makes a bed or he makes a table for our use, in accordance with the idea—that is our way of speaking in this and similar instances—but no artificer makes the ideas themselves: how could he?

Impossible.

And there is another artist,—I should like to know what you would say of him.

Who is he?

One who is the maker of all the works of all other workmen.

What an extraordinary man!

Wait a little, and there will be more reason for your saying so. For this is he who is able to make not only vessels of every kind, but plants and animals, himself and all other things—the earth and heaven, and the things which are in heaven or under the earth; he makes the gods also.

He must be a wizard and no mistake.

Oh! you are incredulous, are you? Do you mean that there is no such maker or creator, or that in one sense there might be a maker of all these things but in another not? Do you see that there is a way in which you could make them all yourself?

What way?

An easy way enough; or rather, there are many ways in which the feat might be quickly and easily accomplished, none quicker than that of turning a mirror round and round—you would soon enough make the sun and the heavens, and the earth and yourself, and other animals and plants, and all the other things of which we were just now speaking, in the mirror.

Yes, he said; but they would be appearances only.

Very good, I said, you are coming to the point now. And the painter too is, as I conceive, just such another—a creator of appearances, is he not?

Of course.

But then I suppose you will say that what he creates is untrue. And yet there is a sense in which the painter also creates a bed?

Yes, he said, but not a real bed.

And what of the maker of the bed? were you not saying that he too makes, not the idea which, according to our view, is the essence of the bed, but only a particular bed?

Yes, I did.

Then if he does not make that which exists he cannot make true existence, but only some semblance of existence; and if any one were to say that the work of the maker of the bed, or of any other workman, has real existence, he could hardly be supposed to be speaking the truth.

At any rate, he replied, philosophers would say that he was not speaking the truth.

No wonder, then, that his work too is an indistinct expression of truth.

No wonder.

Suppose now that by the light of the examples just offered we inquire who this imitator is?

If you please.

The Imitator as Thrice Removed from Truth

Well then, here are three beds: one existing in nature, which is made by God, as I think that we may say—for no one else can be the maker?

No.

There is another which is the work of the carpenter?

Yes.

And the work of the painter is a third?

Yes.

Beds, then, are of three kinds, and there are three artists who superintend them: God, the maker of the bed, and the painter?

Yes, there are three of them.

God, whether from choice or from necessity, made one bed in nature and one only; two or more such ideal beds neither ever have been nor ever will be made by God.

Why is that?

Because even if He had made but two, a third would still appear behind them which both of them would have for their idea, and that would be the ideal bed and not the two others.

Very true, he said.

God knew this, and He desired to be the real maker of a real bed, not a particular maker of a particular bed, and therefore He created a bed which is essentially and by nature one only.

So we believe.

Shall we, then, speak of Him as the natural author or maker of the bed?

Yes, he replied; inasmuch as by the natural process of creation He is the author of this and of all other things.

And what shall we say of the carpenter—is not he also the maker of the bed?

Yes.

But would you call the painter a creator and maker?

Certainly not.

Yet if he is not the maker, what is he in relation to the bed?

I think, he said, that we may fairly designate him as the imitator of that which the others make.

Good, I said; then you call him who is third in the descent from nature an imitator?

Certainly, he said.

And the tragic poet is an imitator, and therefore, like all other imitators, he is thrice removed from the king and from the truth?

That appears to be so. . . .

That there are three arts which are concerned with all things, one which uses, another which makes, a third which imitates them?

Yes.

And the excellence or beauty or truth of every structure, animate or inanimate, and of every action of man, is relative to the use for which nature or the artist has intended them.

True.

Then the user of them must have the greatest experience of them, and he must indicate to the maker the good or bad qualities which develop themselves in use; for example, the flute-player will tell the flute-maker which of his flutes is satisfactory to the performer; he will tell him how he ought to make them, and the other will attend to his instructions?

Of course.

The one knows and therefore speaks with authority about the goodness and badness of flutes, while the other, confiding in him, will do that what he is told by him?

True.

The instrument is the same, but about the excellence or badness of it the maker will only attain to a correct belief; and this he will gain from him who knows, by talking to him and being compelled to hear what he has to say, whereas the user will have knowledge?

True.

But will the imitator have either? Will he know from use whether or no his drawing is correct or beautiful? or will he have right opinion from being compelled to associate with another who knows and gives him instructions about what he should draw?

Neither.

Then he will no more have true opinion than he will have knowledge about the goodness or badness of his imitations?

I suppose not.

The imitative artist will be in a brilliant state of intelligence about his own creations?

Nay, very much the reverse.

And still he will go on imitating without knowing what makes a thing good or bad, and may be expected therefore to imitate only that which appears to be good to the ignorant multitude?

Just so.

Thus far then we are pretty well agreed that the imitator has no knowledge worth mentioning of what he imitates. Imitation is only a kind of play or sport, and the tragic poets, whether they write in Iambic or in Heroic verse, are imitators in the highest degree?

Very true.

Art Appeals to the Irrational Faculties of Man

And now tell me, I conjure you, has not imitation been shown by us to be concerned with that which is thrice removed from the truth?

Certainly.

And what is the faculty in man to which imitation is addressed?

What do you mean?

I will explain: The body which is large when seen near, appears small when seen at a distance?

True.

And the same objects appear straight when looked at out of the water, and crooked when in the water; and the concave becomes convex, owing to the illusion about colours to which the sight is liable. Thus every sort of confusion is revealed within us; and this is that weakness of the human mind on which the art of conjuring and of deceiving by light and shadow and other ingenious devices imposes, having an effect upon us like magic.

True.

And the arts of measuring and numbering and weighing come to the rescue of the human understanding—there is the beauty of them—and the apparent greater or less, or more or heavier, no longer have the mastery over us, but give way before calculation and measure and weight?

Most true.

And this, surely, must be the work of the calculating and rational principle in the soul?

To be sure.

And when this principle measures and certifies that some things are equal, or that some are greater or less than others, there occurs an apparent contradiction?

True.

But were we not saying that such a contradiction is impossible—the same faculty cannot have contrary opinions at the same time about the same thing?

Very true.

Then that part of the soul which has an opinion contrary to measure is not the same with that which has an opinion in accordance with measure?

True.

And the better part of the soul is likely to be that which trusts to measure and calculation?

Certainly.

And that which is opposed to them is one of the inferior principles of the soul?

No doubt.

This was the conclusion at which I was seeking to arrive when I said that painting or drawing, and imitation in general, when doing their own proper work, are far removed from truth, and the companions and friends and associates of a principle within us which is equally removed from reason, and that they have no true or healthy aim.

Exactly.

The imitative art is an inferior who marries an inferior, and has inferior offspring.

Very true.

And is this confined to the sight only, or does it extend to the hearing also, relating in fact to what we term poetry?

Probably the same would be true of poetry.

Do not rely, I said, on a probability derived from the analogy of painting; but let us examine further and see whether the faculty with which poetical imitation is concerned is good or bad.

By all means.

We may state the question thus:—Imitation imitates the actions of men, whether voluntary or involuntary, on which, as they imagine, a good or bad result has ensued, and they rejoice or sorrow accordingly. Is there anything more?

No, there is nothing else.

But in all this variety of circumstances is the man at unity with himself—or rather, as in the instance of sight there was confusion and opposition in his opinions about the same things, so here also is there not strife and inconsistency in his life? Though I need hardly raise the question again, for I remember that all this has been already admitted; and the soul has been acknowledged by us to be full of these and ten thousand similar oppositions occurring at the same moment?

And we were right, he said.

Yes, I said, thus far we were right; but there was an omission which must now be supplied.

What was the omission?

Were we not saying that a good man, who has the misfortune to lose his son or anything else which is most dear to him, will bear the loss with more equanimity than another?

Yes.

But will he have no sorrow, or shall we say that although he cannot help sorrowing, he will moderate his sorrow?

The latter, he said, is the truer statement.

Tell me: will he be more likely to struggle and hold out against his sorrow when he is seen by his equals, or when he is alone?

It will make a great difference whether he is seen or not.

When he is by himself he will not mind saying or doing many things which he would be ashamed of any one hearing or seeing him do?

True.

There is a principle of law and reason in him which bids him resist, as well as a feeling of his misfortune which is forcing him to indulge his sorrow?

True.

But when a man is drawn in two opposite directions, to and from the same object, this, as we affirm, necessarily implies two distinct principles in him?

Certainly.

One of them is ready to follow the guidance of the law?

How do you mean?

The law would say that to be patient under suffering is best, and that we should not give way to impatience, as there is no knowing whether such things are good or evil; and nothing is gained by impatience; also, because no human thing is of serious importance, and grief stands in the way of that which at the moment is most required.

What is most required? he asked.

That we should take counsel about what has happened, and when the dice have been thrown order our affairs in the way which reason deems best; not, like children who have had a fall, keeping hold of the part struck and wasting time in setting up a howl, but always accustoming the soul forthwith to apply a remedy, raising up that which is sickly and fallen, banishing the cry of sorrow by the healing art.

Yes, he said, that is the true way of meeting the attacks of fortune.

Yes, I said; and the higher principle is ready to follow this suggestion of reason?

Clearly.

And the other principle, which inclines us to recollection of our troubles and to lamentation, and can never have enough of them, we may call irrational, useless, and cowardly?

Indeed, we may.

And does not the latter—I mean the rebellious principle—furnish a great variety of materials for imitation? Whereas the wise and calm temperament, being always nearly equable, is not easy to imitate or to appreciate when imitated, especially at a public festival when a promiscuous crowd is assembled in a theatre. For the feeling represented is one to which they are strangers.

Certainly.

Then the imitative poet who aims at being popular is not by nature made, nor is his art intended, to please or to affect the rational principle in the soul; but he will prefer the passionate and fitful temper, which is easily imitated?

Clearly.

And now we may fairly take him and place him by the side of the painter, for he is like him in two ways: first, inasmuch as his creations have an inferior degree of truth—in this, I say, he is like him; and he is also like him in being concerned with an inferior part of the soul; and therefore we shall be right in refusing to admit him into a well-ordered State, because he awakens and nourishes and strengthens the feelings and impairs the reason. As in a city when the evil are permitted to have authority and the good are put out of the way, so in the soul of man, we maintain, the imitative poet implants an evil constitution, for he indulges the irrational nature which has no discernment of greater and less, but thinks the same thing at one time great and at another small—he is a manufacturer of images and is very far removed from the truth.

Exactly.

Poetry Has the Power of Harming the Good

But we have not yet brought forward the heaviest count in our accusation:—the power which poetry has of harming even the good (and there are very few who are not harmed), is surely an awful thing?

Yes, certainly, if the effect is what you say.

Hear and judge: The best of us, as I conceive, when we listen to a passage of Homer, or one of the tragedians, in which he represents some pitiful hero who is drawling out his sorrows in a long oration, or weeping, and smiting his breast—the best of us, you know, delight in giving way to sympathy, and are in raptures at the excellence of the poet who stirs our feelings most.

Yes, of course I know.

But when any sorrow of our own happens to us, then you may observe that we pride ourselves on the opposite quality—we would fain be quiet and patient; this is the manly part, and the other which delighted us in the recitation is now deemed to be the part of a woman.

Very true, he said.

Now can we be right in praising and admiring another who is doing that which any one of us would abominate and be ashamed of in his own person?

No, he said, that is certainly not reasonable.

Nay, I said, quite reasonable from one point of view.

What point of view?

If you consider, I said, that when in misfortune we feel a natural hunger and desire to relieve our sorrow by weeping and lamentation, and that this feeling which is kept under control in our own calamities is satisfied and delighted by the poets;—the better nature in each of us, not having been sufficiently trained by reason or habit, allows the sympathetic element to break loose because the sorrow is another's; and the spectator fancies that there can be no disgrace to himself in praising and pitying any one who comes telling him what a good man he is, and making a fuss about his troubles; he thinks that the pleasure is a gain, and why should he be supercilious and lose this and the poem too? Few persons ever reflect, as I should imagine, that from the evil of other men something of evil is communicated to themselves. And so the feeling of sorrow which has gathered strength at the sight of the misfortunes of others is with difficulty repressed in our own.

How very true!

And does not the same hold also of the ridiculous? There are jests which you would be ashamed to make yourself, and yet on the comic stage, or indeed in private, when you hear them, you are greatly amused by them, and are not at all disgusted at their unseemliness;—the case of pity is repeated;—there is a principle in human nature which is disposed to raise a laugh, and this which you once restrained by reason, because you were afraid of being thought a buffoon, is now let out again; and having stimulated the risible faculty at the theatre, you are betrayed unconsciously to yourself into playing the comic poet at home.

Quite true, he said.

And the same may be said of lust and anger and all the other affections, of desire and pain and pleasure, which are held to be inseparable from every action—in all of them poetry feeds and waters the passions instead of drying them up; she lets them rule, although they ought to be controlled, if mankind are ever to increase in happiness and virtue.

I cannot deny it.

Therefore, Glaucon, I said, whenever you meet with any of the eulogists of Homer declaring that he has been the educator of Hellas, and that he is profitable for education and the ordering of human things, and that you should take him up again and again and get to know him and regulate your whole life according to him, we may love and honour those who say these things—they are excellent people, as far as their lights extend; and we are ready to acknowledge that Homer is the greatest of poets and first of tragedy writers; but we must remain firm in our conviction that hymns to the gods and praises of famous men are the only poetry which ought to be admitted into our State. For if you go beyond this and allow the honeyed muse to enter, either in epic or lyric verse, not law and the reason of mankind, which by common consent have ever been deemed best, but pleasure and pain will be the rulers in our State.

That is most true, he said.

And now since we have reverted to the subject of poetry, let this our defence serve to show the reasonableness of our former judgement in sending away out of our State an art having the tendencies which we have described; for reason constrained us. But that she may not impute to us any harshness or want of politeness, let us tell her that there is an ancient quarrel between philosophy and poetry; of which there are many proofs, such as the saying of 'the yelping hound howling at her lord,' or of one 'mighty in the vain talk of fools,' and 'the mob of sages circumventing Zeus,' and the 'subtle thinkers who are beggars after all'; and there are innumerable other signs of ancient enmity between them. Notwithstanding this, let us assure our sweet friend and the sister arts of imitation, that if she will only prove her title to exist in a well-ordered State we shall be delighted to receive her—we are very conscious of her charms; but we may not on that account betray the truth. I dare say, Glaucon, that you are as much charmed by her as I am, especially when she appears in Homer?

Yes, indeed, I am greatly charmed.

Shall I propose, then, that she be allowed to return from exile, but upon this condition only—that she makes a defence of herself in lyrical or some other metre?

Certainly.

And we may further grant to those of her defenders who are lovers of poetry and yet not poets the permission to speak in prose on her behalf: let them show not only that she is pleasant but also useful to States and to human life, and we will listen in a kindly spirit; for if this can be proved we shall surely be the gainers—I mean, if there is a use in poetry as well as a delight?

Certainly, he said, we shall be the gainers.

If her defence fails, then, my dear friend, like other persons who are enamoured of something, but put a restraint upon themselves when they think their desires are opposed to their interests, so too must we after the manner of lovers give her up, though not without a struggle. We too are inspired by that love of poetry which the education of noble States has implanted in us, and therefore we would have her appear at her best and truest; but so long as she is unable to make good her defence, this argument of ours shall be a charm to us, which we will repeat to ourselves while we listen to her strains; that we may not fall away into the childish love of her which captivates the many. At all events we are well aware that poetry being such as we have described is not to be regarded seriously as attaining to the truth; and he who listens to her, fearing for the safety of the city which is within him, should be on his guard against her seductions and make our words his law.

Yes, he said, I quite agree with you.

Yes, I said, my dear Glaucon, for great is the issue at stake, greater than appears, whether a man is to be good or bad. And what will any one be profited if under the influence of honour or money or power, aye, or under the excitement of poetry, he neglect justice and virtue?

Yes, he said; I have been convinced by the argument, as I believe that any one else would have been.

2

ARISTOTLE

(384–322 B.C.)

*Tragedy in the Poetics**

Aristotle agrees with Plato that art is imitation, but does not agree with him that it is removed from truth. In the Poetics *Aristotle uses the example of tragedy to counter Plato's major criticism of art. For Aristotle, art captures the universal truths by imitating select men in action. Art does arouse the emotions, but, for Aristotle, in order to cleanse them, thus producing better men, not ungovernable aesthetes. Plato would simply avoid all that plays on the emotions as likely to excite further emotion; Aristotle claims that driving the emotions to their limits in artistic experiences purges them from man. Plato's theory is one of starvation of emotion; Aristotle's is one of satiation until the relief of those passions through reason is the only alternative.*

The Poetics *has been called by many a handbook for playwrighting, but this does not seem to be Aristotle's sole intention. Certainly Aristotle did not think that by simply following established rules a great play could be written. Instead, Aristotle admits that man is an imaginative animal whose passions and emotions are constantly activated by the creations of his mind. The* Poetics *considers man's aesthetic experiences and the most fruitful ways to channel them for understanding the universals in human life.*

* Aristotle, *De Arte Poetica*, I. Bywater, trans. (1911), with omissions.

The Origins of the Poetic Arts

THE objects the imitator represents are actions, with agents who are necessarily either good men or bad—the diversities of human character being nearly always derivative from this primary distinction, since the line between virtue and vice is one dividing the whole of mankind. It follows, therefore, that the agents represented must be either above our own level of goodness, or beneath it, or just such as we are. It is clear that each of the above-mentioned arts will admit of these differences, and that it will become a separate art by representing objects with this point of difference. Even in dancing, flute-playing, and lyre-playing such diversities are possible.

This difference it is that distinguishes Tragedy and Comedy also; the one would represent personages as worse, and the other as better, than the men of the present day.

A third difference in these arts is in the manner in which each kind of object is represented. Given both the same means and the same kind of object for imitation, one may either (1) speak at one moment in narrative and at another in an assumed character, as Homer does; or (2) one may remain the same throughout, without any such change; or (3) actors may represent the whole story dramatically, as though they were actually doing the things described.

As we said at the beginning, therefore, the differences in the imitation of these arts come under three heads, their means, their objects, and their manner.

It is clear that the general origin of poetry was due to two causes, each of them part of human nature. Imitation is natural to man from childhood, one of his advantages over the other animals being this, that he is the most imitative creature in the world, and learns at first by imitation. And it is also natural for all to delight in works of imitation. The truth of this second point is shown by experience: though the objects themselves may be painful to see, we delight to view the most realistic representations of them in art, figures for example of loathsome animals and of dead bodies. The explanation is to be found in a further fact: to be learning something is the greatest of pleasures not only to the philosopher but also to the rest of mankind, however small their capacity for it; the reason of the delight in seeing the picture is that one is at the same time learning—gathering the meaning of things, *e.g.* that the man there is so-and-so; for if one has not seen the thing before, one's pleasure will not be in the picture as an imitation of it, but will be due to the execution or coloring or some similar cause. Imitation, then, being natural to men—as also are music and rhythm, the meters being obviously species of rhythm—it was from spontaneous beginnings, and by a series of improvements for the most part gradual on their first efforts, that they created poetry out of their improvizations.

Poetry, however, soon broke up into two kinds according to the differences of character in the individual poets; for the more serious among them would represent noble actions, and those of noble personages, and the meaner sort the actions of the ignoble. The latter class produced satires at first, just as others did hymns and eulogies. Homer's position is peculiar: just as he was in the serious style the poet of poets, standing alone not only through literary excellence, but also through the dramatic character of his imitations, so too he was the first to outline for us the general forms of Comedy by producing not a dramatic satire, but a dramatic picture of the Ridiculous. As soon, however, as Tragedy and Comedy appeared in the field, those naturally drawn to the one line of poetry became writers of comedies, and those naturally drawn to the other, writers of tragedies, because these new modes of art were grander and of more esteem than the old.

Tragedy certainly began in improvizations—as did also Comedy; the one originating with the authors of the Dithyramb, the others with those of the phallic songs, which still survive as institutions in many of our cities. And its advance after that was little by little, through their improving on whatever they had before them at each stage. It was in fact only after a long series of changes that the movement of Tragedy stopped on its attaining to its natural form. (1) The number of actors was first increased to two by Aeschylus, who curtailed the business of the Chorus, and made the dialogue, or spoken portion, take the leading part in the play. (2) A third actor and scenery were due to Sophocles. (3) Tragedy acquired also its magnitude. Descarding short stories and a ludicrous diction, through its passing out of its satiric stage, it assumed, though only at a late point in its progress, a tone of dignity; and its metre changed then from trochaic to iambic. The reason for their original use of the trochaic tetrameter was that their poetry was satiric and more connected with dancing than it now is. As soon, however, as a spoken part came in, nature herself found the appropriate metre. The iambic, we know, is the most speakable of metres, as is shown by the fact that we very often fall into it in conversation, whereas we rarely talk hexameters, and only when we depart from the speaking tone of voice. (4) Another change was a plurality of episodes or acts.

As for Comedy, it is (as has been observed) an imitation of men worse than the average; worse, however, not as regards the full range of badness, but only as regards one particular kind, the Ridiculous, which is a species of the Ugly. The Ridiculous may be defined as a mistake or deformity not productive of pain or harm to others; the comic mask for instance, that excites laughter, is something ugly and distorted without causing pain.

Epic poetry has been seen to agree with Tragedy to this extent, that of being an imitation of serious subjects in a grand kind of verse. It differs from it, however, (1) in that it has a single metre and is narrative; and (2) in its length—which is due to its action having no fixed limit of time, whereas Tragedy endeavors to keep as far as possible within a single circuit of the sun, or something near that. This, I say, is another point of difference between them, though at first the practice in this respect was just the same in tragedies as in epic poems. They differ also (3) in their constituent parts, some being common to both and others peculiar to Tragedy—hence a judge of good and bad in Tragedy is a judge of that in epic poetry also. All the parts of an epic are included in Tragedy; but those of Tragedy are not all of them to be found in the Epic.

The Elements of Tragedy

A Tragedy, then, is the imitation of an action that is serious and also, as having magnitude complete in itself; in language with pleasurable accessories, each kind brought in separately in the parts of the work; in a dramatic, not in a narrative form; with incidents arousing pity and fear, wherewith to accomplish its catharsis of such emotions. Here by 'language with pleasurable accessories' I mean that which has rhythm and melody; and by 'the kinds separately' I mean that some portions are worked out with verse only, and others in turn with song.

Since the imitation is achieved through action, it follows that in the first place the stage-appearance of the actors must be some part of the whole; and in the second Melody and Diction, these two being the means of the imitation. Here by 'Diction' I mean merely this, the composition of the verses; and by 'Melody,' what is too completely understood to require explanation. But further: what is represented also is an action; and the action involves agents, who must necessarily have their distinctive qualities both of character and thought, since it is from these that we ascribe certain qualities to their actions. For thought and character are two natural causes of action, and it is because of these that all men fail or succeed. Now the action (that which was done) is represented in the play by the Fable or Plot. The Fable, in our present sense of the term, is simply this, the combination of the incidents, or things done in the story; whereas Character is what makes us ascribe certain moral qualities to the agents; and Thought is shown in all they say when proving a particular point or, it may be, enunciating a general truth.

There are six parts consequently of every tragedy, which give it its quality. These are (1) Fable or Plot, (2) Character, (3) Diction, (4) Thought, (5) Spectacle or Stage-appearance, and (6) Melody; two of them (3, 6) arising from the means, one (5) from the manner, and three (1, 2, 4) from the objects of the dramatic imitation; and there is nothing else besides these six. Of these elements, then, not a few of the dramatists have made due use, as every play, one may say, admits of Spectacle (Stage-appearance), Character, Fable, Diction, Melody, and Thought.

The most important of the six is the combination of the incidents of the story. Tragedy is essentially an imitation not of persons but of action and life, of happiness and misery. All human happiness or misery takes the form of action; the end for which we live is a certain kind of activity, not a quality. Character gives us qualities, but it is in our actions—what we do—that we are happy or the reverse. In a play accordingly they do not act in order to portray the Characters; they include the Characters for the sake of the action. So that it is the action in it, *i.e.* its Fable or Plot, that is the end and purpose of the tragedy; and the end is everywhere the chief thing. Besides this, a tragedy is impossible without action, but there may be one without Character.

We maintain, therefore, that the first essential, the life and soul, so to speak, of Tragedy is the Plot; and that Character comes second. Third comes the element of Thought, *i.e.* the power of saying what can be said, or what is appropriate to the occasion. Fourth among the literary elements is the Diction of the personages, *i.e.*, as before explained, the expression of their thoughts in words, which is practically the same thing with verse as with prose. As for the two remaining parts, the Melody is the greatest of the pleasurable accessories of Tragedy. The Spectacle or Stage appearance, though an attraction, is the least artistic of all the parts, and has least to do with the art of poetry. The tragic effect is quite possible without a public performance and actors; and besides, arranging the Stage-appearance is more a matter for the costumier than the poet.

The Plot After these definitions let us now consider the proper construction of the Fable or Plot, as that is at once the first and the most important thing in Tragedy. We have laid it down that a Tragedy is an imitation of an action that is complete in itself, as a whole of some magnitude; for a whole may be of no magnitude to speak of. Now a whole is that which has beginning, middle, and end. A beginning is that which does not necessarily follow anything else, while something by nature follows or results from it; an end is that which naturally follows something else, either as its necessary or usual consequent, but nothing follows it; and a middle, that which by nature follows and is followed by something. A well-constructed Plot, therefore, cannot either begin or end at random; beginning and end in it must be of the forms just described.

Furthermore, everything beautiful, whether it be a living creature or any whole made up of parts, must not only present a certain order in its arrangement of parts, but also be of a certain definite magnitude. Beauty is a matter of size and order, and therefore impossible either (1) in a very minute creature, or (2) in a creature of vast size since, in that case, instead of the object being seen all at once, the unity and wholeness of it is lost to the beholder. Just in the same way, then, as a beautiful whole made up of parts, or a beautiful living creature, must be of some size, but a size to be taken in by the eye, so a story or Plot must be of some length, but of a length to be taken in by the memory.

The Unity of a Plot does not consist, as some suppose, in its having one man as its single hero. An infinity of things happen to one man, some of which it is impossible to reduce to unity; and in like manner there are many actions of one man which cannot be made to form one action. The truth is that, just as in the other imitative arts one imitation is always of one thing, so in poetry the story, as an imitation of action, must represent one action, a complete whole, with its several incidents so closely connected that the transposal or withdrawal of any one of them will disjoin and dislocate the whole. For that which makes no perceptible difference by its presence or absence is no real part of the whole.

Poetry gives General Truths

From what we have said it will be seen that the poet's function is to describe, not the thing that has happened, but a kind of thing that might happen, *i.e.* what is possible according to probability or necessity. The distinction between historian and poet is not in the one writing prose and the other verse—you might put the work of Herodotus into verse, and it would still be a species of history; it consists really in this, that the one describes the thing that has been, and the other a kind of thing that might be. Hence poetry is something more philosophic and of graver import than history, because it tends to give general truths, whereas history gives particular facts. By a "general truth" I mean what such or such a kind of man will probably or necessarily say or do—which is the aim of poetry, though it affixes proper names to the characters.

It is evident from the above that the poet must be a maker of stories rather than of verses, inasmuch as he is a poet by virtue of the imitative element of his work, and it is actions that he imitates. And if he should come to take a subject from actual history, he is none the less a poet for that; since some historic occurrences may very well be in the probable and possible order of things; and it is in that aspect of them that he is their poet.

Tragic Plot and Character

Tragedy, however, is an imitation not only of a complete action, but also of incidents arousing pity and fear. Such incidents have the very greatest effect on the mind when they occur unexpectedly and at the same time in consequence of one another; there is more of the marvellous in them than if they happened of themselves or by mere chance. Even matters of chance seem most marvellous if there is an appearance of design as it were in them. A Plot, therefore, of this sort is necessarily finer than others.

The next points after what we have said above will be these: (1) What is the poet to aim at, and what is he to avoid, in constructing his Plots? and (2) What are the conditions on which the tragic effect depends?

We assume that, for the finest form of Tragedy, the Plot must imitate actions arousing fear and pity, since that is the distinctive function of this kind of imitation. It follows, therefore, that there are three forms of Plot to be avoided. (1) A good man must not be seen passing from happiness to misery, or (2) a bad man from misery to happiness. The first situation is not fear-inspiring or piteous, but simply odious to us. The second is the most untragic that can be; it has none of the requisites of Tragedy; it does not appeal either to the human feeling in us, or to our pity, or to our fears. Nor, on the other hand, should (3) an extremely bad man be seen falling from happiness into misery. Such a story may arouse the human feeling in us, but it will not move us to either pity or fear; pity is occasioned by undeserved misfortune, and fear by misfortune of one like ourselves; so that there will be nothing either piteous or fear-inspiring in the situation.

There remains, then, the intermediate kind of personage, a man not pre-eminently virtuous and just, whose misfortune, however, is brought upon him not by vice and depravity but by some fault; a man of great reputation and prosperity, like Oedipus, Thyestes, and the men of note of similar families. The perfect Plot, accordingly, must have a single, and not (as some tell us) a double issue; the change in the hero's fortunes must be not from misery to happiness, but on the contrary from happiness to misery; and the cause of it must lie not in any depravity, but in some great fault on his part; the man himself being either such as we have described, or better, not worse, than that.

The tragic fear and pity may be aroused by the Stage-appearance or Spectacle; but they may also be aroused by the very structure and incidents of the play—which is the better way and shows the better poet. The Plot in fact should be so framed that, even without seeing the things take place, he who simply hears the account of them shall be filled with horror and pity at the incidents; which is just the effect that the mere recital of the story in *Oedipus* would have on one. To produce this same effect by means of the Stage-appearance is less artistic, and requires extraneous aid. Those, however, who make use of the Stage-appearance to put before us that which is merely monstrous and not productive of fear, are wholly out of touch with Tragedy; not every kind of pleasure should be required of a tragedy, but only its own proper pleasure.

The tragic pleasure is that of pity and fear, and the poet has to produce it by a work of imitation; it is clear, therefore, that this quality should be included in the incidents of his story. Let us see, then, what kinds of incident strike one as horrible, or rather as piteous. In a deed of this description the parties must necessarily be either friends, or enemies, or indifferent to one another. Now when enemy does it to enemy, there is nothing to move us to pity either in his doing or in his meditating the deed, except so far as the actual pain of the sufferer is concerned; and the same is true when the parties are indifferent to one another. Whenever the tragic deed, however, is done within the family—when murder or the like is done or meditated by brother on brother, by son on father, by mother on son, or son on mother—these are the situations the poet should seek after. The traditional stories, accordingly, must be kept as they are, *e.g.* the murder of Clytemnestra by Orestes.

On the construction of the Plot, and the kind of Plot required for Tragedy, enough has now been said.

Concerning "Character" there are four points to aim at. First and foremost, that the character should be worthy. There will be an element of character in the play, if (as has been observed) what a person says or does reveals a certain moral purpose; and there will be a worthy element of character, if the purpose so revealed is worthy. This is possible in every type of personage, even in a woman or a slave, though the one is perhaps an inferior, and the other wholly insignificant. The second point is to make the characters appropriate. The Character before us may be, say, manly; but it is not appropriate in a female Character to be manly, or clever. The third is to make them lifelike, which is not the same as their being worthy and appropriate, in our sense of the term. The fourth is to make them consistent and the same throughout; even if inconsistency be part of the man portrayed as presenting that form of character, he should still be consistently inconsistent.

As Tragedy is an imitation of personages better than the ordinary man, we in our way should follow the example of good portrait-painters, who reproduce the distinctive features of a man, and at the same time, without losing the likeness, make him handsomer than he is. The poet in like manner, in portraying men quick or slow to anger, or with similar infirmities of character, must know how to represent them as such, and at the same time as men of worth, as Agathon and Homer have represented Achilles.

The Plot and Characters having been discussed, it remains to consider the Diction and Thought. As for the Thought, we may assume what is said of it in our Art of Rhetoric, as it belongs more properly to that department of inquiry. The Thought of the personages is shown in everything to be effected by their language—in every effort to prove or disprove, to arouse emotion (pity, fear, anger, and the like), or to maximize or minimize things.

As regards the Diction, one subject for inquiry under this head is the various modes of speech; *e.g.* the difference between command and prayer, simple statement and threat, question and answer, and so forth. The theory of such matters, however, belongs to Elocution and the professors of that art. Whether the poet knows these things or not, his art as a poet is never seriously criticized on that account. So we may leave this topic as appertaining to another art, and not to that of poetry.

Let this, then, suffice as an account of Tragedy, the art imitating by means of action on the stage.

3

W. H. AUDEN
(1907–   )

*The Christian Tragic Hero**

In this essay on Moby Dick *Auden attempts to characterize tragedy within the framework of Christian values. He compares it to Greek (classical) tragedy and concludes that the Greek form of fated tragedy does not fit the Christian conception of man's nature. The Christian sin of pride, Auden argues, is not identical with the Greek* hubris *(arrogance). The Christian man knows that he is weak but thinks that he can overcome himself. The Greek knows that he is strong but then thinks himself invincible. Christian tragedy revolves around choices, the Greek around the unavoidable. However, is this Christian art form tragic?*

* From *New York Times Book Review* (December 16, 1945). © 1945 by the New York Times Company. Reprinted by permission.

"MOBY DICK" is at once an heroic epic like the "Iliad," an heroic tragedy like the "Oresteia," an heroic quest like the legend of the "Golden Fleece," and an allegorical religious quest like "Pilgrim's Progress"; it is also a nineteenth-century American novel. Even if it were not the great book it is, it would therefore be of unusual interest to the critic who would compare the values believed in and the attitudes held at different stages in Western civilization. I propose in this article to consider only one of them, the concept of the Tragic Hero in Greece and in Christendom. Most of the characteristics one observes in Melville's hero can also be seen in, say, the heroes of Shakespeare's tragedies, but Melville's choral asides make them more explicit in his own case.

To sum them up in advance, the conclusions I shall try to demonstrate are these: first, Greek tragedy is the tragedy of necessity; i.e., the feeling aroused in the spectator is "What a pity it had to be this way"; Christian tragedy is the tragedy of possibility, "What a pity it was this way when it might have been otherwise"; secondly, the hubris which is the flaw in the Greek hero's character is the illusion of a man who knows himself strong and believes that nothing can shake that strength, while the corresponding Christian sin of pride is the illusion of a man who knows himself weak but believes he can by his own efforts transcend that weakness and become strong.

In using the term Christian I am not trying to suggest that Melville or Shakespeare or any other author necessarily believed the Christian dogmas, but that their conception of man's nature is, historically, derived from them.

Greek Tragedy Examined

As an example of Greek tragedy let us take "Oedipus Rex." As a young man, Oedipus learns from a prophecy that he is fated to murder his father and marry his mother. Believing that his foster parents are his real parents he leaves Carthage. He meets an old man on the road; they quarrel about who shall give way to the other, and Oedipus kills him. He comes to Thebes, saves it from a monster, and is rewarded by the hand of its Queen, Jocasta. Thebes is stricken with plague, and the Oracle declares the cause to be the undetected presence of a criminal. Oedipus undertakes an investigation and discovers that the criminal is himself. In expiation of his crime he puts out his eyes, and Jocasta hangs herself.

A modern reader, accustomed to the tragedy of possibility, instinctively asks, "Where and when did he make the wrong choice?" and as instinctively answers, "He should not have listened to the prophesy in the first place, or, having done, then he should never have struck the old man or anyone else, and should never have married Jocasta or anyone else." But such thoughts would never have occurred to Sophocles or his audience. Macbeth and Captain Ahab are wrong to listen to the prophecies about them, because they are equivocal, and each reads into his a possibility he is wrong to desire; the prophesy Oedipus hears is not only unequivocal but something he is right to wish to avoid. When he kills the old man he feels no guilt, neither is he expected to feel any, and when he married Jocasta there is nothing the matter with the relation as such. It is only when it turns out that, as a matter of fact, the former was his father and the latter is his mother that guilt begins.

The tragedy is that what had to happen happened, and if one asks what was wrong with Oedipus, that such a terrible fate should be assigned to him, one can only say that it is a punishment for a hubris which was necessarily his before he learnt of the prophesy at all; i.e., had he not such a character, the prophesy would never have been made.

Other Greek heroes are faced with the tragic choice between two evils: Agamemnon must either sacrifice his daughter or fail in his duty to the Greek army; Antigone must be false either to her loyalty to her brother or to her loyalty to her city.

The tragic situation, of learning that one is a criminal or of being forced to become one, is not created by the flaw in the hero's character, but is sent him by the gods as a punishment for having such a flaw.

The pessimistic conclusion that underlies Greek tragedy seems to be this: that if one is a hero, i.e., an exceptional individual, one must be guilty of hubris and be punished by a tragic fate; the only alternative and not one a person can choose for himself is to be a member of the chorus, i.e., one of the average mass; to be both exceptional and good is impossible.

How does "Moby Dick" compare with this?

The Tragedy of Captain Ahab

The hero, Captain Ahab, far from being exceptionally fortunate, is at the beginning, what in a Greek Tragedy he could only be at the end, exceptionally unfortunate. He is already the victim of what the modern newspaper, which is Greek in this respect, would call a tragedy; a whale has bitten off his leg. What to the Greeks could only have been a punishment for sin is here a temptation to sin, an opportunity to choose; by making the wrong choice and continuing to make it, Ahab punishes himself. To say that a character is tempted means that it is confronted by possibility, that it is not a fixed state but a process of becoming: the possibilities are not infinite; i.e., Ahab cannot become Starbuck or Pip or Ishmael or anyone else except Ahab, but the possibilities are eternal; the past is irrevocable but always redeemable now.

Thus we can at every moment answer the question, "What should Ahab do now?" Before the story opens he has suffered and made his first wrong choice. He was not wrong to make Moby Dick into a symbol of all the inexplicable suffering in the world; on the contrary, the capacity to see the universal in the particular is the mark of human greatness, and it is only Flask, the Philistine trimmer, who says, "A whale is only a whale"; he was wrong, however, to insist on his own explanation, that the motive behind the whale's act and behind all suffering is personal malevolence. Once he has done so, he can still be saved, but he has made his salvation a much harder task, for he is now required to forgive the whale personally, in contrast, for instance, to Captain Boomer, who, like Ahab, has been deprived of a limb by Moby Dick, but in his pragmatic English way explains the whale's ferocity as mere clumsiness which is easier to forgive than malice.

In Greek tragedy are two kinds of characters, the exceptional hero and the average chorus, and neither can become the other; in Christian tragedy there is not only an infinite variety of possible characters, varying all the way from Ahab, the captain, who defiantly insists on being absolutely unique, down to Pip, the cabin boy, who is too afraid to claim even his own name, but overshadowing them all is the possibility of each becoming both exceptional and good; this ultimate possibility for hero and chorus alike is stated in Father Mapple's sermon, and it is to become a saint—i.e., the individual who of his own free will surrenders his will to the will of God. In this surrender he does not become a ventriloquist's doll, for the God who acts through him can only do so by his consent; there always remain two wills, and the saint, therefore (unlike the late Greek conception of the undramatic Sage who is good by necessity because he knows), never ceases to be tempted to obey his own desires.

Of this possibility Ahab's career is at every point a negative parody.

The saint doesn't ask to be one, he is called to become one, and assents to the call. The outward sign that Ahab is so called, is the suffering which is suddenly intruded into his life. What he is called to become, we do not, of course, know for certain—all we know for certain is that he rejected it—but we can guess that he was called to give up hunting whales—i.e., the normal cannibalistic life of this world, a life which is permitted, for instance, to Queequeg (who, though sinless, is not a saint, but the innocent man before the fall) but no longer to Ahab once he has been made uniquely conscious of the suffering it inflicts. Of the others, less is required: of Starbuck, that he face evil instead of superstitiously avoiding it, of Stubb that he face his fears instead of whistling in the dark; but of Ahab alone is it required, because he alone has the necessary heroic passion, to become a real and not a merely respectable Quaker.

Ahab is not deaf; he hears the call and refuses it with all the passion with which he might have accepted it; like the saint he wills one thing, to kill Moby Dick. For this he leaves his wife and child; for this his first act in the book is to throw away his pipe, his last physical addiction, his last relation with the element of earth; for this he destroys the ship's quadrant, its relation to the element of air so that the Pequod can only know the universe through compass and line in terms of the dualistic antagonism of fire and water.

The saint, knowing his will to be weak, may express his external resolve by a temporal or bodily ritual act, but his vow and his act concern his own will alone. Ahab attempts to use ritual as a magical means of compelling the will of others, as when he forces the crew to swear on their harpoons, and finally even to compel lifeless things, as when he baptizes a harpoon itself.

Just as the saint never ceases to be tempted to forsake his calling, so vice versa, Ahab is never free from the possibility of renouncing his refusal. Divine grace offers itself, now in the nostalgic beauty of fine weather, now as Gabriel, the mad idolator of the whale, an unlovely reflection of himself, and finally, in its strongest and least disguised form, as the cry for help of a friend in distress when the Pequod meets the Rachel, and it is only after he has refused this last offer that his doom becomes necessary. Melville portrays this decisive change with great subtlety. For it is at this point that Ahab places the idiot Pip in his cabin and, in a grotesque parody of the saint as the servant of servants, takes for himself the humble position of lookout on the mast which is the negative image of the martyr's cross. Instead of gaining a martyr's crown, however, his hat, the badge of his authority, is snatched from his head by the Jovian eagle, and from this moment Fedallah, the slave, the projection of Ahab's will, seems suddenly to have taken charge of his creator, or rather his summoner. Fedallah is clearly intended by Melville, I think, to represent the demonic, i.e., that which (Unlike Ahab, who is tempted by suffering) tempts itself and denies for the sake of denying, and about which, therefore, nothing historic can be said; we are only told his religion.

So Ahab, refusing life, goes unrepentant, like all of Shakespeare's tragic heroes, to the unnecessary death he has chosen, dragging with him all his companions, and the only survivor is, as in Greek tragedy, the Chorus, the spectator, Ishmael. But Ishmael is not, like the Greek Chorus, the eternal average man, for he isn't a character at all. To be a character one must will and act, and Ishmael has no will, only consciousness; he does not act, he only knows, and what he knows is good and evil, i.e., possibility. He cannot die because he has not yet begun to live, and he ends the book as a baby reborn from the sea in Queequeg's coffin, thrust back into life as an orphan with his first choice still to make.

4

PRESTON ROBERTS

(1921–   )

*Bringing Pathos Into Focus**

The modern theater and its relationship to historical types of tragedy is the subject of Roberts' analysis. Modern plays have a meaning and characteristic structure which are not included in the techniques and criticisms of classical and Christian drama. Pre-occupation with the pathetic, what Roberts calls the "less than tragic and incapable of redemption," is the mark of the modern play. The action moves from bad to worse. Certainly there is little of the purging catharsis of the classical play. How does the audience feel after perceiving the pathos of Willy Loman's existence? Roberts maintains that we are left with a sense of despair and poignance. What, then, is the value of contemporary theater? Roberts' claim is that it captures an image of man so important that it takes priority over the classical and Christian points of view. It captures the value conflicts of man, Roberts says, and through this unique achievement shows us the limitations of all other dramatic forms.

* From *Motive Magazine* (December, 1953). By permission of the Editor.

THE modern theatre is one of the great theatres in Western cultural history, just as historic in its own setting as the ancient Greek, the Elizabethan, or the French Neo-Classic theatres were in theirs. It is becoming clear that modern plays have a characteristic movement and structure all their own, an inner world of events and meaning just as serious as those which we associate with Greek or Christian drama.

However, modern plays are so close to us in time and we are so close to them in spirit that it is difficult to say which modern plays are the perfection of their type or what kind of serious drama it is of which they are exemplary. We may quite rightly feel that Shakespeare's *Hamlet* is the model for much of modern drama and that Ibsen's *Rosmersholm* was the first real example of it. But no one modern play stands out as the perfection of its type in the way Sophocles' *Oedipus the King* serves as the classic example of a Greek tragedy or Shakespeare's *King Lear* as the classic example of Christian drama. Nor can we identify the inner movement and structure of a modern play with anything like the precision which Aristotle achieved with reference to Greek plays in his *Poetics* more than two thousand years ago. We may rightly think that modern plays characteristically deal with man's emotional insecurity rather than with his intellectual finiteness or his moral guilt and religious sin. But there have been many kinds of modern drama—romantic, realistic, naturalistic, Marxist, Freudian, and existentialist. It is hard to see them under a single rubris or to understand the genus of which they are the species. It is still more difficult to say whether modern plays are more or less moving and profound as serious drama than the more conventionally Greek or Christian plays. We have to recognize that we are deeply moved by them, and that we do take them very seriously. But it is hard to say whether we are moved by them too little or too much or whether we take them more or less seriously than we should.

Nonetheless, we now stand deep within, if not near the bitter end, of the modern period in literary history. We must therefore take our courage in both hands and make some attempt, however weak and imperfect, to see what distinguishes modern plays from more traditional forms of drama, and to say what we should think of them in relation to their ancient Greek and Christian prototypes.

Tennessee Williams' *A Streetcar Named Desire* and Arthur Miller's *Death of a Salesman* may not be the best of modern plays. James Joyce's *Exiles* and Jean-Paul Sartre's *No Exit* certainly make better reading, and the plays of Ibsen and Shaw probably make still better theatre. But *A Streetcar Named Desire* and *Death of a Salesman* make both good reading and good theatre. Moreover, they are rightly characteristic modern plays, if not exactly the perfection of their type. Whereas *A Streetcar Named Desire* is primarily the story of a sick and lost individual, a modern tragedy composed in a psychological or Freudian mode, *Death of a Salesman* is basically a modern tragedy fashioned in a sociological or Marxist pattern, the story of a sick and lost society. They may thereby serve as representative, if not as exhaustive or the best, examples of modern drama.

Pathos as the Distinguishing Character of Modern Drama

The first and most distinguished mark of modern plays is their pathos. Just as Greek plays like *Oedipus the King* were distinguished by their preoccupation with what is simply and purely tragic about life and just as Christian plays like *King Lear* have been distinguished by their concern with what is redemptive or more than tragic in life, just so modern plays like *A Streetcar Named Desire* and *Death of a Salesman* would appear to be distinguished by their absorption in what is pathetic or less than tragic and incapable of redemption in experience.

They seem to be peculiarly concerned with those aspects of experience which lie below the conscious mind or active will, whether it be Darwin's instinctual struggle for survival, Pavlov's conditioned reflex, Freud's repressed unconscious, Marx's latent class conflicts, or Dewey's habit, inertia, and fatigue. They characteristically deal with senseless agencies and compulsive forces at work deep inside and far outside human nature, underground aspects of existence whose operations the human spirit cannot readily observe, understand, enjoy, or control.

It is the preoccupation with what is pathetic in life which endows modern plays with their distinctive inner movement and structure. They may begin with a sense of meaningfulness and hope, but they end in a sense of meaninglessness and futility. Their protagonists are usually rather sick and driven figures long before the play begins, stripped of almost every meaning and value except mere life itself. At the start of the action, they are confronted with an initial situation which appears to present a possible way out of their pathetic misery. However, in the course of events, they exhibit themselves to be completely incapable of responding to any such new way of life. Instead of taking hold of what is possible, they cling to what is impossible—some memory they can never re-enact or some dream they are always powerless to be or do. Some kind of sickness, psychologically within or sociologically without, drives them relentlessly this way and that and down and down until they move from normality to madness and destroy themselves or are destroyed by others in senseless acts of violence.

The movement or change in character in a modern play is from bad to worse or from one form of misery to another. The structure of the incidents or plot is the expression of a remorselessly efficient causality. What appears at the beginning to be their last chance, indeed their only real chance, does not turn out to have been a real chance at all in the end. The final emotional effect upon us as the audience or as readers is therefore one of mingled poignance and despair: Poignance because the protagonist has become such a shadow of his former self or potential self; and despair because there has been no one meaningful way for him to live and so many meaningless ways for him to die.

A Streetcar Named Desire

For example, Blanche DuBois, the protagonist in *A Streetcar Named Desire*, is a very sick and lost woman long before the play begins. As the elder and more attractive daughter of an old, aristocratic Southern family, she has been driven to solve the problem of her life by defying the harsh, yet living and solid, realities of the new South in the name of the soft, but dead and ephemeral, appearances of the old. In the hopeless process of so doing, she has simply lost one thing after another—the ancestral plantation estate called Belle Reve through foreclosure, her boyish and gifted husband through suicide, her position as a schoolteacher in the little Southern town of Laurel, Mississippi, through an attempt to seduce one of her more sensitive and intelligent pupils, and her status as a respectable member of any small Southern community through still other expressions of her growing nymphomania.

About all that is left of Blanche as the play opens is a faded, haunted, and weary remnant of herself, her former and potential self. At the start of the action, her appearance and behavior are, pathetically enough, more like those of a lowly prostitute or a cheap coquette than of the grand Southern belle or lady who figures so prominently in her memories and dreams.

In the course of the action within the play itself, Blanche is given what appears to be her last and only real chance to rescue her life from such pathetic ineffectuality. During a prolonged visit at the shabby New Orleans flat of her younger and less attractive, but married, pregnant, and well-adjusted sister, she is introduced to a more meaningful way of solving her life's problems. Stella's more creative way is based upon acceptance rather than defiance of the new South. However, Blanche proves herself to be completely incapable of responding to this more creative way of life by virtue of the sickness with which her past and present insecurities burden her. In fact, everything she says and does makes any normal way of life, not to speak of a more creative one, less and less possible for her.

In the first part of the play, faint memories of their early childhood together at Belle Reve and vague dreams of an eventual rescue by some young and wealthy Southern gentleman drive Blanche to reject her sister's husband, Stanley Kowalski, in a highly defensive way. He is a Polish worker and—to say the least—no gentleman. Instead of welcoming the strength and vitality of the marriage between Stella and Stanley as enabling her to make a fresh start, Blanche attempts to weaken the relationship by accusing Stella of that kind of purely physical love for her husband of which Blanche herself has long since been a helpless victim. She also proposes that Stella leave Stanley in order to set up a little shop somewhere with her. In so doing, she only succeeds in arousing Stanley's suspicions that she actually has made a good thing out of selling Belle Reve, is a real threat to his wife and home, and is a lost woman in many more interesting ways than meet the eye.

In the middle part of the play, after Stella has refused to leave Stanley in spite of her sister's hysterical objections to him, Blanche's tortured memories of her dead husband make her emotionally uneasy before the advances of Mitch, the one eligible bachelor among the friends of Stanley and Stella who is at once a part of the old and the new South. Although Mitch is very much tied to his mother's apron strings and not everything Blanche might desire in a suitor, she does need him just as desperately as he needs her. However, the inner ambivalences on Blanche's part here, conjoined with the outer consequences of having provoked Stanley in the first part of the action, quickly destroy her last chance of deliverance from pathetic misery. Instead of being rescued by Mitch, she suffers the humiliation of being exposed and then raped by Stanley the night Stella is away at the hospital having her baby.

In the last part of the play, Blanche's compulsive fantasy of a romantic rescue by Shep Huntleigh, a young Dallas millionaire, takes over her entire sensibility and cuts her off from all possibility of salvation. She ends in the arms of a fate worse than rape and indistinguishable from death—the arms of a doctor and nurse from a public mental institution. Through no intellectual error in judgment or willful fault of her own, Blanche DuBois has been driven from her initial neurosis to her final psychosis. In the process, she has lost a moral struggle she could not possibly have won. As a sick and lost woman, she may have had a past but no real present or actual future.

Death of a Salesman

Just so, Willy Loman, the protagonist in *Death of a Salesman,* is a very sick and lost man long before that play begins. Willy Loman is a salesman. As a member of the vast lower middle class in an urban and industrial America, he has been driven to solve the problem of his life by defying the dark realities of his lot as a salesman in the name of the bright appearances of a younger, more rural, and less class-conscious America. He has remembered the early pioneers and the first capitalists who made good with or without effort. He has dreamt of rising to the top and beating the system, either directly through his own efforts or vicariously through the lives of his sons, Biff and Happy.

In the hopeless process of doing so, he too has simply lost one thing after another—from his yard and garden which encroaching apartment houses have snuffed out to the love and respect of his elder and favorite son, Biff, who has become a bum because of inability to fulfill his father's dream. As the play begins, Willy Loman is an almost completely broken man, shattered in body, mind, and spirit. The idea of suicide has not merely occurred to him; he has actually attempted to take his own life, not just once, but several times.

In the course of the action, Willy is given what appears to be his last and only real chance to rescue his life from such pathetic ineffectuality. This apparent chance is presented to him by the return of his prodigal son, Biff, who has come home to have it out with his father and to discover who and what he and his father really are. Biff attempts to deliver his father from his pathetic misery by suggesting a new way of life based upon defiance of or indifference to the old dream of making good or beating the system.

However, Willy proves himself to be completely incapable of responding to his son's new way of life by virtue of the sickness with which past and present insecurities have beset him. In fact, everything he says and does makes his son's new way of life less and less possible for him. In the first part of the play, he forces both himself and his son into making one last, desperate attempt to rise to the top. In so doing, he only succeeds in losing his own job and driving his son into a position where he will have to leave home forever. In the last part of the play, Willy is compelled to face up to the facts for the first time in his life—the fact that he is worth more dead than alive and the fact that suicide is the only way left for him to make good and beat the system.

In summary, what is most distinctively modern about Blanche DuBois and Willy Loman as protagonists is that they are defeated by their emotional insecurity or sickness rather than by their ignorance or intellectual finiteness or by any kind of moral guilt or religious sin. They fail in their moral struggle simply because they are incapable of responding to the good, not because they do not or cannot know what the good is or because they refuse to do the good which they do know.

The Course of Action in Modern Plays Compared to Greek and Christian Types

What is particularly modern about the plots in which their characters are implicated is that the course of the action moves from a bad to a worse state of affairs rather than from good to bad or from bad to good fortune. What is characteristically modern about the emotional effect they provide in us as the audience or readers is the sense of poignance and despair rather than the Greek sense of pity and fear or of the Christian sense of judgment and forgiveness.

We feel poignance rather than pity or judgment because the protagonist is defeated by an emotional quirk or block rather than by an intellectual error in judgment or willful pride. We feel despair rather than fear or forgiveness because what appeared to be the protagonist's last and only real chance turns out to have been no real chance at all.

Traditional plays of the Greek and Christian types have very different kinds of movement and structure and very different kinds of emotional effect. In Greek plays, like *Oedipus the King,* the protagonist is defeated by his ignorance or intellectual finiteness, not by his emotional insecurity or sickness. The plot moves from good to bad fortune and from happiness to misery, not from bad to worse fortune and from one form of unhappy misery to another. The final emotional effect is one of fear and pity, not one of poignance and despair. We feel pity because the protagonist suffers in excess of what he morally and religiously deserves. We feel fear because there have been no rational means of escape from his predicament.

For example, Oedipus is defeated by his ignorance of the facts that he has murdered his father, Laius, and married his mother, Jocasta. These facts of parricide and incest are facts he has to know to avoid tragedy. However, these are precisely the facts he does not know and cannot know by virtue of his intellectual finiteness. In terms of what he does or can know, Oedipus does the perfectly right, just, and noble thing throughout the action. Namely, he simply persists inflexibly in his search for the murderer of Laius, regardless of the consequences to himself.

What is so completely and purely tragic about his fate is that the best course of action of which he can possibly think turns out to be exactly the course of action which seals his doom, destroys that which he most loved, and accomplishes the opposite of what he nobly intended. The pattern of incidents or plot in which the character of Oedipus is implicated therefore moves from initial good fortune to final bad fortune and from initial happiness to final misery.

Such a character and such a plot do not provoke emotions of poignance and despair because the protagonist has been able to remain true to his own essential nature throughout the course of the action and can accept or defy his fate with the untarnished integrity of his soul at the play's end. As Aristotle said, the story of Oedipus arouses emotions of pity and fear: pity because Oedipus suffers more than mere lack of knowledge deserves; and fear because there have been no rational means of escape from the terrible consequences of such ignorance.

In Christian plays like *King Lear,* the protagonist is defeated by his guilt and sin, and not just by his sickness or his ignorance, and the plot eventually moves from a bad to a good state of affairs and from misery to happiness, not simply from good to bad or from bad to worse fortune.

For example, King Lear is defeated in his moral struggle by his spiritual pride, not just by his emotional insecurity or by his intellectual finiteness. This pride expresses itself at the very beginning of the action when he insists upon identifying his status as a king with his role as a father and refuses to distinguish between the pleasing, but merely apparent, virtue of his two faithless daughters, Goneril and Regan, and the painful but real virtue of his one faithful daughter, Cordelia. He therefore asks for and deserves much of the dire suffering he receives. However, the ultimate consequences of his pride are not just pathetic or just tragic but redemptive as well.

In the course of the action, King Lear is rescued from his spiritual pride by processes of judgment and forgiveness operating both inside and outside his own nature. He moves from false, illusory, and complacent happiness born of pride, through the meaningful suffering which comes of judgment, to the final happiness of finding his life in the very process of losing it. The emotional effect provoked by the story of King Lear is thereby a sense of judgment and forgiveness, not just a modern sense of poignance and despair or a Greek sense of pity and fear. We feel judgment because King Lear has suffered what he morally and religiously deserved. We feel forgiveness because King Lear has been enabled to forgive his daughter, Cordelia, even as he has been forgiven by her.

The second distinguishing mark of modern plays is that the Greek concern for what is purely tragic about life and the Christian concern for what is redemptive or more than tragic in life are used as foils to the modern concern for what is pathetic or less than tragic and incapable of redemption in experience. More specifically, the kinds of movement and structure characteristic of Greek and Christian plays are used as foils to the kinds of movement and structure peculiar to modern plays. The pathos of modern plays is thereby rendered all the more pathetic by the invocation of tragic and redemptive motifs which turn out to be in excess of or irrelevant to the facts.

For example, Blanche DuBois is endowed with what appear to be both Christian and Greek qualities as a protagonist. In the first part of the play when she is giving the marriage between Stella and Stanley such an inexcusable hard time, she is made to appear far more arrogant in her spiritual pride than neurotic in her anxiety. Just so, in the middle part of the play where she converses with Mitch, she is represented as being far more blind in the Greek sense than presumptuous in the Christian sense or sick in the modern sense. However, in the course of the action, both our initial hope for the downfall of her self-righteousness and our later desire that her blinded nobility may not suffer in excess of what it deserves are transformed by our final recognition of the nature and extent of her sickness. It is then that we come to see that both her pride and her ignorance are expressions of her sickness.

Her final movement from neurosis to psychosis is thereby rendered all the more sad by the fact that we had been led to hope that some kind of judgment and forgiveness might rescue her from her pride. Just so, her end is rendered all the more desparate by the fact that we had been led to hope that some kind of movement from ignorance to knowledge might enable her to defy or accept circumstances with the unbroken integrity of her spirit.

Similarly, in *Death of a Salesman,* we are led to believe that Willy Loman is more blind than simply driven in the first part of the play and that he is more proud than just blind or driven in the second part of the play. When his wife Linda speaks to her sons of the greatness of Willy's spirit in the face of impossible odds both inside and outside his own true nature, we feel his suffering nobility no less than his piteous abnormality. We therefore hope that he may not suffer in excess of what his essential nobility deserves.

When Biff tries to tell his father that he is a fake and has failed him no less deeply than he, Biff, has failed his father, we feel Willy's moral guilt and religious sin no less than his intellectual finiteness or his emotional insecurity. We therefore hope that some kind of judgment and forgiveness may rescue him from his pride. However, when all is said and done, it becomes clear that Willy's blindness in the Greek sense and Willy's pride in the Christian sense have been, both of them, foils to Willy's sickness in the modern sense.

In Defense of Modern Plays

If it is difficult to say what distinguishes modern plays from the more traditional forms of serious drama, it is still more difficult to say what we should think of them in relation to their Greek and Christian prototypes. However, there would appear to be at least three positive things which must be said in their defense.

First of all, from a purely historical standpoint, we have to recognize that modern plays are portraying an aspect of existence which both Greek and Christian plays tended to ignore or deny. That is, modern plays are bringing pathos into the focus of dramatic interest and attention for the first time, a type or level of experience which Greek and Christian plays ignored as being less than tragic or incapable of redemption and denied as being unworthy of serious dramatic representation. As such, modern plays enjoy the rare distinction of bringing to full expression the third basic kind of subject matter characteristic of serious drama in the West, a subject matter which is just as great in its own terms and its own setting as the materials of the Greek and Christian drama were in theirs.

The historic uniqueness of modern plays—and the greatness this fact of historic uniqueness alone represents—can scarcely be exaggerated. To discover something relatively new so late in Western cultural history is in itself no small accomplishment. To hold high what has traditionally been held low is a still more remarkable achievement.

In the second place, from a more critical and less purely historical viewpoint, we have to recognize that the pathetic aspect of experience stressed by modern plays is not only historically unique but classically serious as well.

That is, modern plays are not simply portraying an aspect of experience never fully portrayed before. They are doing this, to be sure. They are also doing more. They are portraying this aspect of experience convincingly by means of a spare and disciplined dramatic form of their own discovery as well. They are demonstrating that what is pathetic or less than tragic and beyond rescue in life is just as important, dramatically speaking, as what is tragic or less than tragic. They are showing that sickness in the modern sense is no less capable of arousing our sympathy than ignorance in the Greek sense or guilt and sin in the Christian sense. They are disclosing that it is no less moving for characters to move from bad to worse and from one form of misery to another than it is for characters to move from good to bad fortune or from misery to happiness.

In short, modern plays are exhibiting themselves to be the perfection of an aesthetically moving kind of dramatic form or structure, not simply the purveyors of an historically unique kind of dramatic subject matter or material.

In the third place, from a constructive as well as from a simply historical or critical point of view, modern plays would appear to be just as meaningful and true to life as they are historically unique in subject matter and aesthetically moving in dramatic form. That is, they seem to be capturing one of the ultimate images of man's life, an image so ultimate in nature that all past and future images must now stand subject to it.

In other words, we have to add the modern theme of man's pathetic ineffectuality to the Greek theme of man's suffering nobility and the Christian theme of man's idolatrous impatience if we are to comprehend the whole of life. In fact, the modern image of man's emotional insecurity would appear to be revealing that we can no longer properly see what the Greeks meant by man's finiteness or fully understand what Christians have meant by man's spiritual pride apart from some basic reference to what the moderns mean by man's piteous abnormality.

A still more radical way of saying the same thing would be to say that Greek and Christian plays can never mean quite the same thing to us again and can never mean quite as much to us now that we have seen and read modern plays. In short, modern plays have enabled us to see the limitations, no less than the scope, of more traditional forms of drama.

Nonetheless, it would appear to be just as possible for us to take modern plays too seriously as not to take them seriously enough. Traditionally Greek and Christian plays remain just as historically unique, just as aesthetically moving, and just as meaningful and true to life as modern plays. Modern readers and critics who attempt to make Greek and Christian plays over in the modern image, who refuse to admit that ignorance and pride can be as dramatically moving as sickness, or who are wont to deny that finiteness and pretension are just as ultimate factors in the human situation as emotional insecurity, are just as wrong as Greek or Christian readers and critics who try to ignore or deny what is uniquely moving and profound about modern plays.

That is, it is just as wrong to deny any metaphysical status or ontological quality to blindness and pride as it is to deny these things to sickness. We must take modern plays seriously, but not too seriously.

I would like to make a brief prediction concerning the drama of the period upon whose threshold we would now appear to stand: namely, that the drama of the future will seek to bring Greek, Christian, and modern images into a more meaningful relationship to one another. The plays of the future will not simply identify these images, as if they were little more than three ways of saying the same thing.

5

LUDWIG WITTGENSTEIN

(1889–1951)

*Lecture on Aesthetics**

Beyond any doubt, Wittgenstein has exerted great influence on the style and form of most contemporary philosophy in the English-speaking world. Wittgenstein's philosophical ideas cannot be easily summarized. His work is more a method for investigating philosophical problems than a systematic series of answers to those problems. He claims that he sets forth no theories in philosophy. It is rather difficult, for that reason and because most of his work is found in relatively short comments, to state Wittgenstein's position. Clearly he is concerned with language and its many uses, and the contexts in which language is the key to understanding philosophical difficulties. Philosophy, he says, "leaves everything as it is." It does not add new information to the perplexing problems of life; it attempts to clarify those problems by carefully describing the language at work in them.

This selection is taken from a lecture on aesthetics and is not written by *Wittgenstein, but is a compilation of his students' notes edited by Cyril Barrett. One of the major ideas in Wittgenstein's later works, and a significant part of this lecture, is his idea of forms of life. In his* Philosophical Investigations *he tells us that, "To imagine a language is to imagine a form of life." A form of life is one of the things typical of a human being; it encompasses his responses to his environment. Language plays a dominant role in expressing and determining our form of life. Wittgenstein tells us that to use properly aesthetic language (judgments of art), one must begin with a description of a way of life. Aesthetic words play roles in the language in our culture and in the culture of various periods of history. To understand their use it is necessary to describe the circumstances in which they are appropriate expressions, to know the culture, to have that form of life.*

Wittgenstein's way of doing philosophy is engaging. You cannot sit back and read him. He demands your involvement. Consider the kinds of examples he asks one to consider, i.e., "Why it is impossible to get a decent picture of your friend even if you pay £1,000?" You must constantly stop and rethink the point which at first seems so evident. Wittgenstein's analysis of aesthetic problems revolves around the activities of judgment, not just aesthetic words such as "beautiful," "moving," etc. "We don't start from certain words, but from certain occasions or activities," he believes. Apply what Wittgenstein says about the appreciation of art in general to tragedy in particular.

* From Cyril Barrett, *Wittgenstein Lectures and Conversations on Aesthetics, Psychology and Religious Belief* (Berkeley, California: University of California Press, 1967), pp. 1–11. Reprinted by permission of the Regents of the University of California.

Misunderstandings in the Use of Aesthetic Language

1. The subject (Aesthetics) is very big and entirely misunderstood as far as I can see. The use of such a word as 'beautiful' is even more apt to be misunderstood if you look at the linguistic form of sentences in which it occurs than most other words. 'Beautiful' [and 'good'—R] is an adjective, so you are inclined to say: "This has a certain quality, that of being beautiful".

2. We are going from one subject-matter of philosophy to another, from one group of words to another group of words.

3. An intelligent way of dividing up a book on philosophy would be into parts of speech, kinds of words. Where in fact you would have to distinguish far more parts of speech than an ordinary grammar does. You would talk for hours and hours on the verbs 'seeing', 'feeling', etc., verbs describing personal experience. We get a peculiar kind of confusion or confusions which comes up with all these words. You would have another chapter on numerals—here there would be another kind of confusion: a chapter on 'all', 'any', 'some', etc.—another kind of confusion: a chapter on 'you', 'I', etc.—another kind: a chapter on 'beautiful', 'good'—another kind. We get into a new group of confusions; language plays us entirely new tricks.

4. I have often compared language to a tool chest, containing a hammer, chisel, matches, nails, screws, glue. It is not a chance that all these things have been put together—but there are important differences between the different tools—they are used in a family of ways —though nothing could be more different than glue and a chisel. There is constant surprise at the new tricks language plays on us when we get into a new field.

5. One thing we always do when discussing a word is to ask how we were taught it. Doing this on the one hand destroys a variety of misconceptions, on the other hand gives you a primitive language in which the word is used. Although this language is not what you talk when you are twenty, you get a rough approximation to what kind of language game is going to be played. Cf. How did we learn 'I dreamt so and so'? The interesting point is that we didn't learn it by being shown a dream. If you ask yourself how a child learns 'beautiful', 'fine', etc., you find it learns them roughly as interjections. ('Beautiful' is an odd word to talk about because it's hardly ever used.) A child generally applies a word like 'good' first to food. One thing that is immensely important in teaching is exaggerated gestures and facial expressions. The word is taught as a substitute for a facial expression or a gesture. The gestures, tones of voice, etc., in this case are expressions of approval. What *makes* the word an interjection of approval?* It is the game it appears in, not the form of words. (If I had to say what is the main mistake made by philosophers of the present generation, including Moore, I would say that it is that when language is looked at, what is looked at is a form of words and not the use made of the forms of words.) Language is a characteristic part of a large group of activities —talking, writing, travelling on a bus, meeting a man, etc. We are concentrating, not on the words 'good' or 'beautiful', which are entirely

* And not of disapproval or of surprise, for example?—R

uncharacteristic, generally just subject and predicate ('This is beautiful'), but on the occasions on which they are said—on the enormously complicated situation in which the aesthetic expression has a place, in which the expression itself has almost a negligible place.

Aesthetic Judgements as Giving a Character to a Piece of Art

6. If you came to a foreign tribe, whose language you didn't know at all and you wished to know what words corresponded to 'good', 'fine', etc., what would you look for? You would look for smiles, gestures, food, toys. ([Reply to objection:] If you went to Mars and men were spheres with sticks coming out, you wouldn't know what to look for. Or if you went to a tribe where noises made with the mouth were just breathing or making music, and language was made with the ears. Cf. "When you see trees swaying about they are talking to one another." ("Everything has a soul.") You compare the branches with arms. Certainly we must interpret the gestures of the tribe on the analogy of ours.) How far this takes us from normal aesthetics [and ethics—T]. We don't start from certain words, but from certain occasions or activities.

7. A characteristic thing about our language is that a large number of words used under these circumstances are adjectives—'fine', 'lovely', etc. But you see that this is by no means necessary. You saw that they were first used as interjections. Would it matter if instead of saying "This is lovely", I just said "Ah!" and smiled, or just rubbed my stomach? As far as these primitive languages go, problems about what these words are about, what their real subject is, [which is called 'beautiful' or 'good'.—R.] don't come up at all.

8. It is remarkable that in real life, when aesthetic judgments are made, aesthetic adjectives such as 'beautiful', 'fine', etc., play hardly any role at all. Are aesthetic adjectives used in a musical criticism? You say: "Look at this transition", or [Rhees] "The passage here is incoherent". Or you say, in a poetical criticism, [Taylor]: "His use of images is precise". The words you use are more akin to 'right' and 'correct' (as these words are used in ordinary speech) than to 'beautiful' and 'lovely'.

9. Words such as 'lovely' are first used as interjections. Later they are used on very few occasions. We might say of a piece of music that it is lovely, by this not praising it but giving it a character. (A lot of people, of course, who can't express themselves properly use the word very frequently. As they use it, it is used as an interjection.) I might ask: "For what melody would I most like to use the word 'lovely'?" I might choose between calling a melody 'lovely' and calling it 'youthful'. It is stupid to call a piece of music 'Spring Melody' or 'Spring Symphony'. But the word 'springy' wouldn't be absurd at all, any more than 'stately' or 'pompous'.

10. If I were a good draughtsman, I could convey an innumerable number of expressions by four strokes—

Such words as 'pompous' and 'stately' could be expressed by faces. Doing this, our descriptions would be much more flexible and various than they are as expressed by adjectives. If I say of a piece of Schubert's that it is melancholy, that is like giving it a face (I don't express approval or disapproval). I could instead use gestures or [Rhees] dancing. In fact, if we want to be exact, we do use a gesture or a facial expression.

11. [*Rhees*: What rule are we using or referring to when we say: "This is the correct way"? If a music teacher says a piece *should* be played this way and plays it, what is he appealing to?]

12. Take the question: "How should poetry be read? What is the correct way of reading it?" If you are talking about blank verse the right way of reading it might be stressing it correctly—you discuss how far you should stress the rhythm and how far you should hide it. A man says it ought to be read *this* way and reads it out to you. You say: "Oh yes. Now it makes sense." There are cases of poetry which should almost be scanned—where the metre is as clear as crystal—others where the metre is entirely in the background. I had an experience with the 18th century poet Klopstock. I found that the way to read him was to stress his metre abnormally. Klopstock put ᵕ — ᵕ (etc.) in front of his poems. When I read his poems in this new way, I said: "Ah-ha, now I know why he did this." What had happened? I had read this kind of stuff and had been moderately bored, but when I read it in this particular way, intensely, I smiled, said: "This is *grand*," etc. But I might not have said anything. The important fact was that I read it again and again. When I read these poems I made gestures and facial expressions which were what would be called gestures of approval. But the important thing was that I read the poems entirely differently, more intensely, and said to others: "Look! This is how they should be read." Aesthetic adjectives played hardly any rôle.

13. What does a person who knows a good suit say when trying on a suit at the tailor's? "That's the right length", "That's too short", "That's too narrow". Words of approval play no rôle, although he will look pleased when the coat suits him. Instead of "That's too short" I might say "Look!" or instead of "Right" I might say "Leave it as it is". A good cutter may not use any words at all, but just make a chalk mark and later alter it. How do I show my approval of a suit? Chiefly by wearing it often, liking it when it is seen, etc.

14. (If I give you the light and shadow on a body in a picture I can thereby give you the shape of it. But if I give you the highlights in a picture you don't know what the shape is.)

15. In the case of the word 'correct' you have a variety of related cases. There is first the case in which you learn the rules. The cutter learns how long a coat is to be, how wide the sleeve must be, etc. He learns rules—he is drilled—as in music you are drilled in harmony and counterpoint. Suppose I went in for tailoring and I first learned all the rules, I might have, on the whole, two sorts of attitude. (1) Lewy says: "This is too short." I say: "No. It is right. It is according to the rules." (2) I develop a feeling for the rules. I interpret the rules. I might say: "No. It isn't right. It isn't according to the rules." Here I would be

making an aesthetic judgement about the thing which is according to the rules in sense (1). On the other hand, if I hadn't learnt the rules, I wouldn't be able to make the aesthetic judgement. In learning the rules you get a more and more refined judgement. Learning the rules actually changes your judgement. (Although, if you haven't learnt Harmony and haven't a good ear, you may nevertheless detect any disharmony in a sequence of chords.)

16. You could regard the rules laid down for the measurement of a coat as an expression of what certain people want. People separated on the point of what a coat should measure: there were some who didn't care if it was broad or narrow, etc.; there were others who cared an enormous lot. The rules of harmony, you can say, expressed the way people wanted chords to follow—their wishes crystallized in these rules (the word 'wishes' is much too vague). All the greatest composers wrote in accordance with them. ([Reply to objection:] You can say that every composer changed the rules, but the variation was very slight; not all the rules were changed. The music was still good by a great many of the old rules.—This though shouldn't come in here.)

Aesthetic Judgement as Appreciation

17. In what we call the Arts a person who has judgement developes. (A person who has a judgement doesn't mean a person who says 'Marvellous!' at certain things.) If we talk of aesthetic judgements, we think, among a thousand things, of the Arts. When we make an aesthetic judgement about a thing, we do not just gape at it and say: "Oh! How marvellous!" We distinguish between a person who knows what he is talking about and a person who doesn't. If a person is to admire English poetry, he must know English. Suppose that a Russian who doesn't know English is overwhelmed by a sonnet admitted to be good. We would say that he does not know what is in it at all. Similarly, of a person who doesn't know metres but who is overwhelmed, we would say that he doesn't know what's in it. In music this is more pronounced. Suppose there is a person who admires and enjoys what is admitted to be good but can't remember the simplest tunes, doesn't know when the bass comes in, etc. We say he hasn't seen what's in it. We use the phrase 'A man is musical' not so as to call a man musical if he says "Ah!" when a piece of music is played, any more than we call a dog musical if it wags its tail when music is played.

18. The word we ought to talk about is 'appreciated'. What does appreciation consist in?

19. If a man goes through an endless number of patterns in a tailor's, [and] says: "No. This is slightly too dark. This is slightly too loud", etc., he is what we call an appreciator of material. That he is an appreciator is not shown by the interjections he uses, but by the way he chooses, selects, etc. Similarly in music: "Does this harmonize? No. The bass is not quite loud enough. Here I just want something different. . . ." This is what we call an appreciation.

20. It is not only difficult to describe what appreciation consists in, but impossible. To describe what it consists in we would have to describe the whole environment.

21. I know exactly what happens when a person who knows a lot about suits goes to the tailor, also I know what happens when a person who knows nothing about suits goes—what he says, how he acts, etc. There is an extraordinary number of different cases of appreciation. And, of course, what I know is nothing compared to what one could know. I would have—to say what appreciation is—e.g. to explain such an enormous wart as arts and crafts, such a particular kind of disease. Also I would have to explain what our photographers do today—and why it is impossible to get a decent picture of your friend even if you pay £1,000.

22. You can get a picture of what you may call a very high culture, e.g., German music in the last century and the century before, and what happens when this deteriorates. A picture of what happens in Architecture when you get imitations—or when thousands of people are interested in the minutest details. A picture of what happens when a dining-room table is chosen more or less at random, when no one knows where it came from.

23. We talked of correctness. A good cutter won't use any words except words like 'Too long', 'All right'. When we talk of a Symphony of Beethoven we don't talk of correctness. Entirely different things enter. One wouldn't talk of appreciating the *tremendous* things in Art. In certain styles in Architecture a door is correct, and the thing is you appreciate it. But in the case of a Gothic Cathedral what we do is not at all to find it correct—it plays an entirely different rôle with us. The entire *game* is different. It is as different as to judge a human being and on the one hand to say 'He behaves well' and on the other hand 'He made a great impression on me'.

24. 'Correctly', 'charmingly', 'finely', etc. play an entirely different rôle. Cf. the famous address of Buffon—a terrific man—on style in writing; making ever so many distinctions which I only understand vaguely but which he didn't mean vaguely—all kinds of nuances like 'grand', 'charming', 'nice'.

Expressions of Judgement and the Culture of a Period of History

25. The words we call expressions of aesthetic judgement play a very complicated rôle, but a very definite rôle, in what we call a culture of a period. To describe their use or to describe what you mean by a cultured taste, you have to describe a culture. What we now call a cultured taste perhaps didn't exist in the Middle Ages. An entirely different game is played in different ages.

26. What belongs to a language game is a whole culture. In describing musical taste you have to describe whether children give concerts, whether women do or whether men only give them, etc., etc. In aristocratic circles in Vienna people had [such and such] a taste, then it came into bourgeois circles and women joined choirs, etc. This is an example of tradition in music.

27. [*Rhees*: Is there tradition in Negro art? Could a European appreciate Negro art?]

28. What would tradition in Negro Art be? That women wear cut-grass skirts? etc., etc. I don't know. I don't know how Frank Dobson's

appreciation of Negro Art compares with an educated Negro's. If you say he appreciates it, I don't yet know what this means. He may fill his room with objects of Negro Art. Does he just say: "Ah!"? Or does he do what the best-Negro musicians do? Or does he agree or disagree with so and so about it? You may call this appreciation. Entirely different to an educated Negro's. Though an educated Negro may also have Negro objects of art in his room. The Negro's and Frank Dobson's are different appreciations altogether. You do something different with them. Suppose Negroes dress in their own way and I say I appreciate a good Negro tunic—does this mean I would have one made, or that I would say (as at the tailor's): "No . . . this is too long", or does it mean I say: "How charming!"?

Can We Appreciate the Art of Other Periods?

29. Suppose Lewy has what is called a cultured taste in painting. This is something entirely different to what was called a cultured taste in the fifteenth century. An entirely different game was played. He does something entirely different with it to what a man did then.

30. There are lots of people, well-offish, who have been to good schools, who can afford to travel about and see the Louvre, etc., and who know a lot about and can talk fluently about dozens of painters. There is another person who has seen very few paintings, but who looks intensely at one or two paintings which make a profound impression on him. Another person who is broad, neither deep nor wide. Another person who is very narrow, concentrated and circumscribed. Are these different kinds of appreciation? They may all be called 'appreciation'.

31. You talk in entirely different terms of the Coronation robe of Edward II and of a dress suit. What did *they* do and say about Coronation robes? Was the Coronation robe made by a tailor? Perhaps it was designed by Italian artists who had their own traditions; never seen by Edward II until he put it on. Questions like 'What standards were there?', etc. are all relevant to the question 'Could you criticize the robe as they criticized it?' You appreciate it in an entirely different way; your attitude to it is entirely different to that of a person living at the time it was designed. On the other hand 'This is a fine Coronation robe' might have been said by a man at the time in exactly the same way as a man says it now.

32. I draw your attention to differences and say: "Look how different these differences are!" "Look what is in common to the different cases", "Look what is common to Aesthetic judgements". An immensely complicated family of cases is left, with the highlight—the expression of admiration, a smile or a gesture, etc.

33. [Rhees asked Wittgenstein some question about his 'theory' of deterioration.]

Do you think I have a theory? Do you think I'm saying what deterioration is? What I do is describe different things called deterioration. I might approve deterioration—"All very well your fine musical culture; I'm very glad children don't learn harmony now." [*Rhees*: Doesn't what you say imply a preference for using 'deterioration' in certain ways?]

All right, if you like, but this by the way—no, it is no matter. My example of deterioration is an example of something I know, perhaps something I dislike—I don't know. 'Deterioration' applies to a tiny bit I may know.

34. Our dress is in a way simpler than dress in the 18th century and more a dress adapted to certain violent activities, such as bicycling, walking, etc. Suppose we notice a similar change in Architecture and in hairdressing, etc. Suppose I talked of the deterioration of the style of living. If someone asks: "What do you mean by deterioration?" I describe, give examples. You use 'deterioration' on the one hand to describe a particular kind of development, on the other hand to express disapproval. I may join it up with the things I like; you with the things you dislike. But the word may be used without any affective element; you use it to describe a particular kind of thing that happened. It was more like using a technical term—possibly, though not at all necessarily, with a derogatory element in it. You may say in protest, when I talk of deterioration: "But this was very good." I say: "All right. But this wasn't what I was talking about. I used it to describe a particular kind of development."

To Understand the Use of Aesthetic Words Is to Describe a Form of Life

35. In order to get clear about aesthetic words you have to describe ways of living. We think we have to talk about aesthetic judgements like 'This is beautiful', but we find that if we have to talk about aesthetic judgements we don't find these words at all, but a word used something like a gesture, accompanying a complicated activity.

36. [*Lewy*: If my landlady says a picture is lovely and I say it is hideous, we don't contradict one another.]

In a sense [and in *certain examples*—R] you do contradict one another. She dusts it carefully, looks at it often, etc. You want to throw it in the fire. This is just the stupid kind of example which is given in philosophy, as if things like 'This is hideous', 'This is lovely' were the only kinds of things ever said. But it is only one thing amongst a vast realm of other things—one special case. Suppose the landlady says: "This is hideous", and you say: "This is lovely"—all right, that's that.

Further Reading

Beardsley, Monroe. *Aesthetics.* New York: Harcourt, Brace and World, 1958.

Dewey, John. *Art as Experience.* New York: Capricorn Books, 1934.

Friedman, Maurice. *To Deny Our Nothingness.* New York: Dell Publishing, 1967.

Hofstradter and Kuhns. *Philosophies of Art and Beauty.* New York: Modern Library, 1964.

Kant, Immanuel. *Observations on the Feeling of the Beautiful and Sublime.* Trans. J. T. Goldwaitt. Berkeley: University of California Press, 1960.

Levich, Marvin. *Aesthetics and the Philosophy of Criticism.* New York: Random House, 1963.

Myers, Henry Alonzo. *Tragedy: a View of Life.* Ithaca: Cornell University Press, 1956.

Sewell, Richard. *The Vision of Tragedy.* New Haven: Yale University Press, 1959.

PART VIII

SCIENCE AND TRUTH

INTRODUCTORY READINGS

Aldous Huxley

Joseph Priestley

INQUIRY

SELECTED SOURCES

Bacon

Whewell

Hanson

Whorf

James

Bridgman

Wiener

Aldous Huxley

Science in the Brave New World*

THE ROOM INTO WHICH THE THREE WERE USHERED WAS THE CONtroller's study.

"His fordship will be down in a moment." The Gamma butler left them to themselves.

Helmholtz laughed aloud.

"It's more like a caffeine-solution party than a trial," he said, and let himself fall into the most luxurious of the pneumatic armchairs. "Cheer up, Bernard," he added, catching sight of his friend's green unhappy face. But Bernard would not be cheered; without answering, without even looking at Helmholtz, he went and sat down on the most uncomfortable chair in the room, carefully chosen in the obscure hope of somehow deprecating the wrath of the higher powers.

The Savage meanwhile wandered restlessly round the room, peering with a vague superficial inquisitiveness at the books in the shelves, at the sound-track rolls and the reading machine bobbins in their numbered pigeon-holes. On the table under the window lay a massive volume bound in limp black leather-surrogate, and stamped with large golden T's. He picked it up and opened it. MY LIFE AND WORK, BY OUR FORD. The book had been published at Detroit by the Society for the Propagation of Fordian Knowledge. Idly he turned the pages, read a sentence here, a paragraph there, and had just come to the conclusion that the book didn't interest him, when the door opened, and the Resident World Controller for Western Europe walked briskly into the room.

* Aldous Huxley, *Brave New World* (New York: Harper & Row, 1946, pp. 260–275. From Chapter 16 in *Brave New World* by Aldous Huxley. Copyright 1932, 1960 by Aldous Huxley. Reprinted by permission of Harper & Row, Publishers.

Mustapha Mond shook hands with all three of them; but it was to the Savage that he addressed himself. "So you don't much like civilization, Mr. Savage," he said.

The Savage looked at him. He had been prepared to lie, to bluster, to remain sullenly unresponsive; but, reassured by the good-humoured intelligence of the Controller's face, he decided to tell the truth, straightforwardly. "No." He shook his head.

Bernard started and looked horrified. What would the Controller think? To be labelled as the friend of a man who said that he didn't like civilization—said it openly and, of all people, to the Controller—it was terrible. "But, John," he began. A look from Mustapha Mond reduced him to an abject silence.

"Of course," the Savage went on to admit, "there are some very nice things. All that music in the air, for instance . . ."

"Sometimes a thousand twangling instruments will hum about my ears and sometimes voices."

The Savage's face lit up with a sudden pleasure. "Have you read it too?" he asked. "I thought nobody knew about that book here, in England."

"Almost nobody. I'm one of the very few. It's prohibited, you see. But as I make the laws here, I can also break them. With impunity, Mr. Marx," he added, turning to Bernard. "Which I'm afraid you *can't* do."

Bernard sank into a yet more hopeless misery.

"But why is it prohibited?" asked the Savage. In the excitement of meeting a man who had read Shakespeare he had momentarily forgotten everything else.

The Controller shrugged his shoulders. "Because it's old; that's the chief reason. We haven't any use for old things here."

"Even when they're beautiful?"

"Particularly when they're beautiful. Beauty's attractive, and we don't want people to be attracted by old things. We want them to like the new ones."

"But the new ones are so stupid and horrible. Those plays, where there's nothing but helicopters flying about and you *feel* the people kissing." He made a grimace. "Goats and monkeys!" Only in Othello's words could he find an adequate vehicle for his contempt and hatred.

"Nice tame animals, anyhow," the Controller murmured parenthetically.

"Why don't you let them see *Othello* instead?"

"I've told you; it's old. Besides, they couldn't understand it."

Yes, that was true. He remembered how Helmholtz had laughed at *Romeo and Juliet*. "Well then," he said, after a pause, "something new that's like *Othello*, and that they could understand."

"That's what we've all been wanting to write," said Helmholtz, breaking a long silence.

"And it's what you never will write," said the Controller. "Because, if it were really like *Othello* nobody could understand it, however new it might be. And if it were new, it couldn't possibly be like *Othello*."

"Why not?"

"Yes, why not?" Helmholtz repeated. He too was forgetting the unpleasant realities of the situation. Green with anxiety and apprehension, only Bernard remembered them; the others ignored him. "Why not?"

"Because our world is not the same as Othello's world. You can't make flivvers without steel—and you can't make tragedies without social instability. The world's stable now. People are happy; they get what they want, and they never want what they can't get. They're well off; they're safe; they're never ill; they're not afraid of death; they're blissfully ignorant of passion and old age; they're plagued with no mothers or fathers; they've got no wives, or children, or lovers to feel strongly about; they're so conditioned that they practically can't help behaving as they ought to behave. And if anything should go wrong, there's *soma*. Which you go and chuck out of the window in the name of liberty, Mr. Savage. *Liberty!*" He laughed. "Expecting Deltas to know what liberty is! And now expecting them to understand *Othello!* My good boy!"

The Savage was silent for a little. "All the same," he insisted obstinately, "*Othello's* good, *Othello's* better than those feelies."

"Of course it is," the Controller agreed. "But that's the price we have to pay for stability. You've got to choose between happiness and what people used to call high art. We've sacrificed the high art. We have the feelies and the scent organ instead."

"But they don't mean anything."

"They mean themselves; they mean a lot of agreeable sensations to the audience."

"But they're . . . they're told by an idiot."

The Controller laughed. "You're not being very polite to your friend, Mr. Watson. One of our most distinguished Emotional Engineers . . ."

"But he's right," said Helmholtz gloomily. "Because it *is* idiotic. Writing when there's nothing to say . . ."

"Precisely. But that requires the most enormous ingenuity. You're making flivvers out of the absolute minimum of steel—works of art out of practically nothing but pure sensation."

The Savage shook his head. "It all seems to me quite horrible."

"Of course it does. Actual happiness always looks pretty squalid in comparison with the over-compensations for misery. And, of course, stability isn't nearly so spectacular as instability. And being contented has none of the glamour of a good fight against misfortune, none of the picturesqueness of a struggle with temptation, or a fatal overthrow by passion or doubt. Happiness is never grand."

"I suppose not," said the Savage after a silence. "But need it be quite so bad as those twins?" He passed his hand over his eyes as though he were trying to wipe away the remembered image of those long rows of identical midgets at the assembling tables, those queued-up twin-herds at the entrance to the Brentford monorail station, those human maggots swarming round Linda's bed of death, the endlessly repeated face of his assailants. He looked at his bandaged left hand and shuddered. "Horrible!"

"But how useful! I see you don't like our Bokanovsky Groups; but, I assure you, they're the foundation on which everything else is built. They're the gyroscope that stabilizes the rocket plane of state on its unswerving course." The deep voice thrillingly vibrated; the gesticulating hand implied all space and the onrush of the irresistible machine. Mustapha Mond's oratory was almost up to synthetic standards.

"I was wondering," said the Savage, "why you had them at all—seeing that you can get whatever you want out of those bottles. Why don't you make everybody an Alpha Double Plus while you're about it?"

Mustapha Mond laughed. "Because we have no wish to have our throats cut," he answered. "We believe in happiness and stability. A society of Alphas couldn't fail to be unstable and miserable. Imagine a factory staffed by Alphas—that is to say by separate and unrelated individuals of good heredity and conditioned so as to be capable (within limits) of making a free choice and assuming responsibilities. Imagine it!" he repeated.

The Savage tried to imagine it, not very successfully.

"It's an absurdity. An Alpha-decanted, Alpha-conditioned man would go mad if he had to do Epsilon Semi-Moron work—go mad, or start smashing things up. Alphas can be completely socialized—but only on condition that you make them do Alpha work. Only an Epsilon can be expected to make Epsilon sacrifices, for the good reason that for him they aren't sacrifices; they're the line of least resistance. His conditioning has laid down rails along which he's got to run. He can't help himself; he's foredoomed. Even after decanting, he's still inside a bottle—an invisible bottle of infantile and embryonic fixations. Each one of us, of course," the Controller meditatively continued, "goes through life inside a bottle. But if we happen to be Alphas, our bottles are, relatively speaking, enormous. We should suffer acutely if we were confined in a narrower space. You cannot pour upper-caste champagne-surrogate into lower-caste bottles. It's obvious theoretically. But it has also been proved in actual practice. The result of the Cyprus experiment was convincing."

"What was that?" asked the Savage.

Mustapha Mond smiled. "Well, you can call it an experiment in rebottling if you like. It began in A.F. 473. The Controllers had the island of Cyprus cleared of all its existing inhabitants and re-colonized with a specially prepared batch of twenty-two thousand Alphas. All agricultural and industrial equipment was handed over to them and they were left to manage their own affairs. The result exactly fulfilled all the theoretical predictions. The land wasn't properly worked; there were strikes in all the factories; the laws were set at naught, orders disobeyed; all the people detailed for a spell of low-grade work were perpetually intriguing for high-grade jobs, and all the people with high-grade jobs were counter-intriguing at all costs to stay where they were. Within six years they were having a first-class civil war. When nineteen out of the twenty-two thousand had been killed, the survivors unanimously petitioned the World Controllers to resume the government of the island. Which they did. And that was the end of the only society of Alphas that the world has ever seen."

The Savage sighed, profoundly.

"The optimum population," said Mustapha Mond, "is modelled on the iceberg—eight-ninths below the water line, one-ninth above."

"And they're happy below the water line?"

"Happier than above it. Happier than your friend here, for example." He pointed.

"In spite of that awful work?"

"Awful? *They* don't find it so. On the contrary, they like it. It's light, it's childishly simple. No strain on the mind or the muscles. Seven and a half hours of mild, unexhausting labour, and then the *soma* ration and games and unrestricted copulation and the feelies. What more can they ask for? True," he added, "they might ask for shorter hours. And of course we could give them shorter hours. Technically, it would be perfectly simple to reduce all lower-caste working hours to three or four a day. But would they be any the happier for that? No, they wouldn't. The experiment was tried, more than a century and a half ago. The whole of Ireland was put on to the four-hour day. What was the result? Unrest and a large increase in the consumption of *soma;* that was all. Those three and a half hours of extra leisure were so far from being a source of happiness, that people felt constrained to take a holiday from them. The Inventions Office is stuffed with plans for labour-saving processes. Thousands of them." Mustapha Mond made a lavish gesture. "And why don't we put them into execution? For the sake of the labourers; it would be sheer cruelty to afflict them with excessive leisure. It's the same with agriculture. We could synthesize every morsel of food, if we wanted to. But we don't. We prefer to keep a third of the population on the land. For their own sakes—because it takes *longer* to get food out of the land than out of a factory. Besides, we have our stability to think of. We don't want to change. Every change is a menace to stability. That's another reason why we're so chary of applying new inventions. Every discovery in pure science is potentially subversive; even science must sometimes be treated as a possible enemy. Yes, even science."

Science? The Savage frowned. He knew the word. But what it exactly signified he could not say. Shakespeare and the old men of the pueblo had never mentioned science, and from Linda he had only gathered the vaguest hints: science was something you made helicopters with, something that caused you to laugh at the Corn Dances, something that prevented you from being wrinkled and losing your teeth. He made a desperate effort to take the Controller's meaning.

"Yes," Mustapha Mond was saying, "that's another item in the cost of stability. It isn't only art that's incompatible with happiness; it's also science. Science is dangerous; we have to keep it most carefully chained and muzzled."

"What?" said Helmholtz, in astonishment. "But we're always saying that science is everything. It's a hypnopædic platitude."

"Three times a week between thirteen and seventeen," put in Bernard.

"And all the science propaganda we do at the College . . ."

"Yes; but what sort of science?" asked Mustapha Mond sarcastically. "You've had no scientific training, so you can't judge. I was a pretty good physicist in my time. Too good—good enough to realize that all our science is just a cookery book, with an orthodox theory of cooking that nobody's allowed to question, and a list of recipes that mustn't be added to except by special permission from the head cook. I'm the head cook now. But I was an inquisitive young scullion once. I started doing a bit of cooking on my own. Unorthodox cooking, illicit cooking. A bit of real science, in fact." He was silent.

"What happened?" asked Helmholtz Watson.

The Controller sighed. "Very nearly what's going to happen to you young men. I was on the point of being sent to an island."

The words galvanized Bernard into a violent and unseemly activity. "Send *me* to an island?" He jumped up, ran across the room, and stood gesticulating in front of the Controller. "You can't send *me*. I haven't done anything. It was the others. I swear it was the others." He pointed accusingly to Helmholtz and the Savage. "Oh, please don't send me to Iceland. I promise I'll do what I ought to do. Give me another chance. Please give me another chance." The tears began to flow. "I tell you, it's their fault," he sobbed. "And not to Iceland. Oh, please, your fordship, please . . ." And in a paroxysm of abjection he threw himself on his knees before the Controller. Mustapha Mond tried to make him get up; but Bernard persisted in his grovelling; the stream of words poured out inexhaustibly. In the end the Controller had to ring for his fourth secretary.

"Bring three men," he ordered, "and take Mr. Marx into a bedroom. Give him a good *soma* vaporization and then put him to bed and leave him."

The fourth secretary went out and returned with three green-uniformed twin footmen. Still shouting and sobbing, Bernard was carried out.

"One would think he was going to have his throat cut," said the Controller, as the door closed. "Whereas, if he had the smallest sense, he'd understand that his punishment is really a reward. He's being sent to an island. That's to say, he's being sent to a place where he'll meet the most interesting set of men and women to be found anywhere in the world. All the people who, for one reason or another, have got too self-consciously individual to fit into community-life. All the people who aren't satisfied with orthodoxy, who've got independent ideas of their own. Every one, in a word, who's any one. I almost envy you, Mr. Watson."

Helmholtz laughed. "Then why aren't you on an island yourself?"

"Because, finally, I preferred this," the Controller answered. "I was given the choice: to be sent to an island, where I could have got on with my pure science, or to be taken on to the Controllers' Council with the prospect of succeeding in due course to an actual Controllership. I chose this and let the science go." After a little silence, "Sometimes," he added, "I rather regret the science. Happiness is a hard master—particularly other people's happiness. A much harder master, if one isn't conditioned to accept it unquestioningly, than truth." He sighed, fell silent again, then continued in a brisker tone, "Well, duty's duty. One can't consult one's own preferences. I'm interested in truth, I like science. But truth's a menace, science is a public danger. As dangerous as it's been beneficent. It has given us the stablest equilibrium in history. China's was hopelessly insecure by comparison; even the primitive matriarchies weren't steadier than we are. Thanks, I repeat, to science. But we can't allow science to undo its own good work. That's why we so carefully limit the scope of its researches—that's why I almost got sent to an island. We don't allow it to deal with any but the most immediate problems of the moment. All other enquiries are most sedulously discouraged. It's curious," he went on after a little pause, "to read what people in the time of Our Ford used to write about scientific progress. They seemed to have imagined that it could be allowed to go on indefinitely, regardless of everything else. Knowledge was the highest good, truth the supreme value; all the rest was secondary and subordinate. True, ideas were beginning to change even then. Our Ford himself did a great deal to shift the emphasis from truth and beauty to comfort and happiness. Mass production demanded the shift. Universal happiness keeps the wheels steadily turning; truth and beauty can't. And, of course, whenever the masses seized political power, then it was happiness rather than truth and beauty that mattered. Still, in spite of everything, unrestricted scientific research was still permitted. People still went on talking about truth and beauty as though they were the sovereign goods. Right up to the time of the Nine Years' War. *That* made them change their tune all right. What's the point of truth or beauty or knowledge when the anthrax bombs are popping all around you? That was when science first began to be controlled—after the Nine Years' War. People were ready to have even their appetites controlled then. Anything for a quiet life. We've gone on controlling ever since. It hasn't been very good for truth, of course. But it's been very good for happiness. One can't have something for nothing. Happiness has got to be paid for. You're paying for it, Mr. Watson—paying because you happen to be too much interested in beauty. I was too much interested in truth; I paid too."

"But *you* didn't go to an island," said the Savage, breaking a long silence.

The Controller smiled. "That's how I paid. By choosing to serve happiness. Other people's—not mine. It's lucky," he added, after a pause, "that there are such a lot of islands in the world. I don't know what we should do without them. Put you all in the lethal chamber, I suppose. By the way, Mr. Watson, would you like a tropical climate? The Marquesas, for example; or Samoa? Or something rather more bracing?"

Helmholtz rose from his pneumatic chair. "I should like a thoroughly bad climate," he answered. "I believe one would write better if the climate were bad. If there were a lot of wind and storms, for example . . ."

The Controller nodded his approbation. "I like your spirit, Mr. Watson. I like it very much indeed. As much as I officially disapprove of it." He smiled. "What about the Falkland Islands?"

"Yes, I think that will do," Helmholtz answered. "And now, if you don't mind, I'll go and see how poor Bernard's getting on."

Joseph Priestley

The Discovery of Dephlogisticated Air (Oxygen)*

PRESENTLY, AFTER MY RETURN FROM ABROAD, I WENT TO WORK UPON the *mercurius calcinatus*, which I had procured from Mr. Cadet; and, with a very moderate degree of heat, I got from about one-fourth of an ounce of it, an ounce-measure of air, which I observed to be not readily imbibed, either by the substance itself from which it had been expelled (for I suffered them to continue a long time together before I transferred the air to any other place) or by water, in which I suffered this air to stand a considerable time before I made any experiment upon it.

In this air, as I had expected, a candle burned with a vivid flame; but what I observed new at this time (November 19), and which surprised me no less than the fact I had discovered before, was, that, whereas a few moments agitation in water will deprive the modified nitrous air of its property of admitting a candle to burn in it; yet, after more than ten times as much agitation as would be sufficient to produce this alteration in the nitrous air, no sensible change was produced in this. A candle still burned in it with a strong flame; and it did not, in the least, diminish common air, which I have observed that nitrous air, in this state, in some measure does.

But I was much more surprised, when, after two days, in which this air had continued in contact with water (by which it was diminished about one-twentieth of its bulk) I agitated it violently in water about five minutes, and found that a candle still burned in it as well as in common air. The same degree of agitation would have made phlogisticated nitrous air fit for respiration indeed, but it would certainly have extinguished a candle.

* From Joseph Priestley, *Experiments and Observations on Different Kinds of Air*, Vol. II (1775).

These facts fully convinced me, that there must be a very material difference between the constitution of air from *mercurius calcinatus*, and that of phlogisticated nitrous air, notwithstanding their resemblance in some particulars. But though I did not doubt that the air from *mercurius calcinatus* was fit for respiration, after being agitated in water, as every kind of air without exception, on which I have tried the experiment, had been, I still did not suspect that it was respirable in the first instance; so far was I from having any idea of this air being, what it really was, much superior, in this respect, to the air of the atmosphere.

In this ignorance of the real nature of this kind of air, I continued from this time (November) to the 1st of March following; having, in the meantime, been intent upon my experiments on the vitriolic acid air above recited, and the various modifications of air produced by spirit of nitre, an account of which will follow. But in the course of this month, I not only ascertained the nature of this kind of air, though very gradually, but was led to it by the complete discovery of the constitution of the air we breathe.

Till this 1st of March, 1775, I had so little suspicion of the air from *mercurius calcinatus*, &c., being wholesome, that I had not even thought of applying it to the test of nitrous air; but thinking (as my reader must imagine I frequently must have done) on the candle burning in it after long agitation in water, it occurred to me at last to make the experiment; and putting one measure of nitrous air to two measures of this air, I found, not only that it was diminished, but that it was diminished quite as much as common air, and that the redness of the mixture was likewise equal to that of a similar mixture of nitrous and common air.

After this I had no doubt but that the air from *mercurius calcinatus* was fit for respiration, and that it had all the other properties of genuine common air. But I did not take notice of what I might have observed, if I had not been so fully possessed by the notion of there being no air better than common air, that the redness was really deeper, and the diminution something greater than common air would have admitted.

Moreover, this advance in the way of truth, in reality, threw me back into error, making me give up the hypothesis I had first formed, viz. that the *mercurius calcinatus* had extracted spirit of nitre from the air; for I now concluded, that all the constituent parts of the air were equally, and in their proper proportion, imbibed in the preparation of this substance, and also in the process of making red lead. For at the same time that I made the above mentioned experiment on the air from *mercurius calcinatus*, I likewise observed that the air which I had extracted from red lead, after the fixed air was washed out of it, was of the same nature, being diminished by nitrous air like common air: but, at the same time, I was puzzled to find that air from the red precipitate was diminished in the same manner, though the process for making this substance is quite different from that of making the two others. But to this circumstance I happened not to give much attention.

I wish my reader be not quite tired with the frequent repetition of the word surprise, and others of similar import; but I must go on in that style a little longer. For the next day I was more surprised than ever I had been before, with finding that, after the above-mentioned mixture of nitrous air and the air from *mercurius calcinatus,* had stood all night, (in which time the whole diminution must have taken place; and, consequently, had it been common air, it must have been made perfectly noxious, and entirely unfit for respiration or inflammation) a candle burned in it, and even better than in common air.

I cannot, at this distance of time, recollect what it was that I had in view in making this experiment; but I know I had no expectation of the real issue of it. Having acquired a considerable degree of readiness in making experiments of this kind, a very slight and evanescent motive would be sufficient to induce me to do it. If, however, I had not happened, for some other purpose, to have had a lighted candle before me I should probably never have made the trial; and the whole train of my future experiments relating to this kind of air might have been prevented.

Still, however, having no conception of the real cause of this phenomenon, I considered it as something very extraordinary; but as a property that was peculiar to air that was extracted from these substances, and adventitious; and I always spoke of the air to my acquaintance as being substantially the same thing with common air.

I particularly remember my telling Dr. Price, that I was myself perfectly satisfied of its being common air, as it appeared to be so by the test of nitrous air; though, for the satisfaction of others, I wanted a mouse to make the proof quite complete.

On the 8th of this month I procured a mouse, and put it into a glass vessel, containing two ounce-measures of the air from *mercurius calcinatus.* Had it been common air, a full-grown mouse, as this was, would have lived in it about a quarter of an hour. In this air, however, my mouse lived a full half hour; and though it was taken out seemingly dead, it appeared to have been only exceedingly chilled; for, upon being held to fire, it presently revived, and appeared not to have received any harm from the experiment.

By this I was confirmed in my conclusion, that the air extracted from *mercurius calcinatus,* &c., was, at least, as good as common air; but I did not certainly conclude that it was any better; because, though one mouse would live only a quarter of an hour in a given quantity of air, I knew it was not impossible but that another mouse might have lived in it half an hour; so little accuracy is there in this method of ascertaining the goodness of air; and indeed I have never had recourse to it for my own satisfaction, since the discovery of that most ready, accurate, and elegant test that nitrous air furnishes. But in this case I had a view to publishing the most generally satisfactory account of my experiments that the nature of the thing would admit of.

This experiment with the mouse, when I had reflected upon it some time, gave me so much suspicion that the air into which I had put it was better than common air, that I was induced, the day after, to apply the test of nitrous air to a small part of that very quantity of air which the mouse had breathed so long; so that, had it been common air, I was satisfied it must have been very nearly, if not altogether, as noxious as possible, so as not to be affected by nitrous air; when, to my surprise again, I found that though it had been breathed so long, it was still better than common air. For after mixing it with nitrous air, in the usual proportion of two to one, it was diminished in the proportion of four and one-half to three and one-half; that is, the nitrous air had made it two-ninths less than before, and this in a very short space of time; whereas I had never found that, in the longest time, any common air was reduced more than one-fifth of its bulk by any proportion of nitrous air, nor more than one-fourth by any phlogistic process whatever. Thinking of this extraordinary fact upon my pillow, the next morning I put another measure of nitrous air to the same mixture, and, to my utter astonishment, found that it was farther diminished to almost one-half of its original quantity. I then put a third measure to it; but this did not diminish it any farther; but, however, left it one measure less than it was even after the mouse had been taken out of it.

Being now fully satisfied that this air, even after the mouse had breathed it half an hour, was much better than common air; and having a quantity of it still left, sufficient for the experiment, viz. an ounce-measure and a half, I put the mouse into it; when I observed that it seemed to feel no shock upon being put into it, evident signs of which would have been visible, if the air had not been very wholesome; but that it remained perfectly at its ease another full half hour, when I took it out quite lively and vigorous. Measuring the air the next day, I found it to be reduced from one and one-half to two-thirds of an ounce-measure. And after this, if I remember well (for in my register of the day I only find it noted, that it was considerably diminished by nitrous air), it was nearly as good as common air. It was evident, indeed, from the mouse having been taken out quite vigorous, that the air could not have been rendered very noxious.

For my farther satisfaction I procured another mouse, and putting it into less than two ounce-measures of air extracted from *mercurius calcinatus* and air from red precipitate (which, having found them to be of the same quality, I had mixed together) it lived three-quarters of an hour. But not having had the precaution to set the vessel in a warm place, I suspect that the mouse died of cold. However, as it had lived three times as long as it could probably have lived in the same quantity of common air, and I did not expect much accuracy from this kind of a test, I did not think it necessary to make any more experiments with mice.

Being now fully satisfied of the superior goodness of this kind of air, I proceeded to measure that degree of purity, with as much accuracy as I could, by the test of nitrous air; and I began with putting one measure of nitrous air to two measures of this air, as if I had been examining common air; and now I observed that the diminution was evidently greater than common air would have suffered by the same treatment. A second measure of nitrous air reduced it to two-thirds of its original quantity, and a third measure to one-half. Suspecting that the diminution could not proceed much farther, I then added only half a measure of nitrous air, by which it was diminished still more; but not much, and another half-measure made it more than half of its original quantity; so that, in this case, two measures of this air took more than two measures of nitrous air, and yet remained less than half of what it was. Five measures brought it pretty exactly to its original dimensions.

At the same time, air from the red precipitate was diminished in the same proportion as that from *mercurius calcinatus*, five measures of nitrous air being received by two measures of this without any increase of dimensions. Now as common air takes about one-half of its bulk of nitrous air, before it begins to receive any addition to its dimensions from more nitrous air, and this air took more than four half-measures before it ceased to be diminished by more nitrous air, and even five half-measures made no addition to its original dimensions, I conclude that it was between four and five times as good as common air. It will be seen that I have since procured air better than this, even between five and six times as good as the best common air that I have ever met with.

INQUIRY

Thus the world is divided into Scientists, who practice the art of infallibility, and non-scientists, sometimes contemptuously called "laymen," who are taken in by it.

ANTHONY STANDEN
Science is a Sacred Cow

Surveyors are spiderlike contraptions with retrorockets to lower them gently on the moon's airless surface. They have "arms" for picking up rocks and TV "eyes" for analyzing specimens clenched in their claws.*

The Fictional Aura of Science

This description of a moon surveyor is almost humorous. It is typical of the writing in so-called scientific articles in magazines and newspapers that aim to "enlighten" the public on recent developments in various scientific fields, medicine to space technology. A kind of fictional aura has descended upon the whole framework of science in the eyes of the general public. The translator of science to the average man is the reporter, editor, or freelance writer, publishing in the popular mass media; and unfortunately most of what we come to know as science reads like Jules Verne or H. G. Wells. The methodology of science and the concepts involved in theoretical reasoning, the presuppositions of science and the scientific concept of truth, of prime interest to philosophers, seldom enter into the popular scientific report.

Astronomer Richard C. Hall of Flagstaff, Arizona, comments on the above description: "We may ask whether the quotes were left off 'claws' because the writer became convinced of the bestial qualities of the Surveyor."† Hall maintains that the popular press has isolated many of us from the real workings of science by techniques of journalism designed to increase the gap between layman and scientist; the techniques make the scientist appear more like a wizard

* U.S. News and World Report (April 15, 1965).

† Richard C. Hall, unpublished paper.

than a dedicated researcher into the relationship between facts of physical existence. (Similar ideas are expressed by C. P. Snow in his book *The Two Cultures*.)

Consider an example from *Time Magazine* cited by Hall. *Time* gives us a verbal picture of a superhuman computer: "The scheduled maneuvers were perfectly calculated by one of the unsung heroes of the mission: an IBM 7094 Mode II computer. . . . (It) has been taught all the incredible complications of orbital calculations."* Actually, the basis of all "orbital calculations" is Kepler's three simple laws of orbital motion; and the problem of a satellite in orbit around the earth, the two-body problem, is one of the most elemental in physics. The implication of the article, of course, is that science is far too difficult for the average man to comprehend. It alienates us from science instead of educating us. For most of us, science, though admittedly a major factor in our lives, is also a mysterious factor. We might begin to wonder if it is just such a misinformed attitude about science that leads to the restriction of its uses in the *Brave New World*.

Our concern in this chapter is to examine philosophically the methodology of science, its claims and its presuppositions. Consider the account given by Joseph Priestley of his experiments with "dephlogisticated air," oxygen. Here we have an account by a scientist of his process of discovery. Can a well-defined method or procedure of science be determined from Priestley's report? Most of us have been told since elementary school that scientists proceed according to well-defined plans. It is claimed that *the* scientific method is a series of concise steps, memorized by the novice and used with the guarantee of reaching truth in the matter under consideration. Lionel Ruby, in his book *The Art of Making Sense*, organizes the so-called scientific method into eight steps. He tells us that scientific inquiry begins when a situation generates our interest, when we feel the need to know why something happens or does not happen. Second, the problem must be precisely formulated. The third step, Ruby tells us, is the observation of relevant facts based on the use of previous knowledge. (What makes a fact relevant? Is a theory or hypothesis needed before judgments of relevance can be made?) Then an explanatory hypothesis is to be formulated, and deductions from the hypothesis are to be made; that is, the implications of accepting a particular hypothesis are explored and tested by observation and/or experiment. The final step of the method, according to Ruby, is that the scientist must conclude that his hypothesis is confirmed or not confirmed on the basis of the evidence he has collected.†

Can we trace such a step procedure in Priestley's work? If we could, would it be conclusive evidence of its success? Notice that, although the claim is to a precise formulation of a method of thinking, the actual plan is rather vague. We should wonder what

* *Time*, Vol. 86, No. 26, p. 33.
† Lionel Ruby, *The Art of Making Sense* (Philadelphia: Lippincott, 1954), pp. 220–221.

generates the interest of a certain scientist in a problem, while the majority of his colleagues are satisfied with current answers or do not even recognize the situation as problematic in the first place. Does nature change and thereby create new problems, or is the only change in the way men look at the same old events? How important is the crisis situation to discovery in science? Are experiments crucial in establishing hypotheses? What do we mean when we say that a particular hypothesis is established by the evidence? Are we only saying something about our language? Have we said anything about the physical world?

Francis Bacon, in his classic *Novum Organum,* maintains that the "true way" of "searching into and discovering truth" is to proceed gradually from the facts of nature to wider and wider generalizations, until the general axioms of nature are inductively derived. Theory, hypotheses, and conjectures play no role in Bacon's method of scientific discovery. He arrives at this idea of scientific method because he also holds a particular philosophy of nature. Nature, for Bacon, is an open book which the unprejudiced cannot misread. Bacon originally called his method *interpretatio naturae,* which meant something like "reading out nature for those who cannot read themselves." Galileo may have had a similar idea when he wrote, "Philosophy (philosophy then meant all ways of knowing and especially what we now call science) is written in that vast book which stands open before our eyes, I mean the universe;" he adds, "but it cannot be read until we have learnt the language and become familiar with the characters in which it is written."*

Bacon's philosophy of science was aimed at establishing the best way of preparing oneself to read the book of nature. Of major importance in his method is ridding the mind of its biases and concepts. One must divest himself of all preconceptions and allow himself to become familiar with the raw facts of nature. But is this possible? Are ideal scientists men with no preconceptions about nature? With no notions of what to expect?

What do we mean by "a fact"? We say such things as: "That's a fact!"; "The facts of the case are . . ."; "I don't care what your opinion is, I just want the facts." When we use the word "fact" we seem to imply that what we are dealing with is separate from our theories, ideas, opinions. We suggest that "facts" are things which our opinions do not change, immutable objects, independent of our thinking about them. But what makes something a fact?

Benjamin Whorf's studies of the Hopi Indian language in "Science and Linguistics" provide us with a useful example. According to Whorf, Hopi languge provides no dimensions for time, and time words cannot be pluralized, nor do they permit simultaneity (all major concepts in Western science). Action verbs apparently are not distinguishable in tenses. If a science were to be constructed in Hopi, Whorf claims that it would be based on ideas foreign to our

* Stuart Hampshire, ed., *The Age of Reason* (New York: New American Library, 1956), p. 33.

sciences—"Intensity" and "Variation"—instead of our ideas of velocity and rate (among others). When called upon to report a chemical reaction, a Hopi would talk about its intensity, while a Western chemist would generally speak of its velocity. At first we might think that both the Hopi and Western chemist were reporting the same observations and simply using different words. But velocity has no place in a language without related time concepts. The Hopi does not *see* the velocity of a chemical reaction, and no analogies to moving objects, such as running horses, will serve to introduce the concept of velocity into a language with no place for it. All movement is satisfactorily described for the Hopi in terms of intensities. What then are the facts? Is the Hopi wrong, the Western chemist correct? Do the facts of velocity only apply to the situation when observed by someone who speaks the language of velocity? Whorf's conclusion is that "all observers are not led by the same physical evidence to the same picture of the universe unless their linguistic backgrounds are similar or can in some way be calibrated."*

Facts and Language

The facts which we take to be immovable apparently depend to some degree upon the language we use to express them. Do we see facts? Or do we see objects, witness events? What would a fact look like? Could you take a picture of a fact? If facts are not picturable or observable, then they must be linguistic. Reading the book of Nature, as Bacon would have it, cannot just be a matter of looking around. Learning the facts is not achieved by standing in the woods and letting your senses become stimulated. The facts of science do not arise miraculously from experience. Many are in direct opposition to common experience. Bacon, we are told, fought the acceptance of the Copernican (sun-centered solar system) point of view because it was not compatible with common sense. The Copernican theory, which called for placing the sun in a category exclusive of the planets and for putting the earth in a category with the bright moving objects in the sky, clearly was not in line with Bacon's experience. After all, he could not even imagine standing on one of those bright moving objects, and the sun undoubtedly circled the earth everyday. Yet the facts are Copernican.

If science is not just a matter of cataloguing experiences and drawing generalizations from them, what is its method of discovering truths of nature, and what is our criterion for saying some statement is a truth of nature? William Whewell maintains that knowledge involves both subjective conjectures and empirical (physical) data: "Without Thought there could be no connexion; without Things there could be no reality."† For Whewell, a scientist begins with ideas which are clear and appropriate to the problem he confronts, not generalizations of data. The scientist invents an hypothesis by means of which he is able to order and structure his data. The

* See Selected Sources.

† William Whewell, *History of Scientific Ideas* (London: John W. Parker and Son, 1858), Vol. I, p. 25.

mental ability of the scientist to conceive a new way of looking at things is a key to discovery. This involves a switch to a new point of view. Copernicus, Darwin, Einstein and other leaders of scientific revolutions have been able to produce radical changes. Where do scientists get their new ideas? What is the source of new hypotheses? Is science only a natural outgrowth of its past? Is an act of creative genius involved in seeing everyday things in new and problematical ways?

Writing about Kepler, the great early astronomer, Albert Einstein says that, "It seems that the human mind has first to construct forms independently before we can find them in things . . . knowledge cannot spring from experience alone but only from the comparison of the inventions of the intellect with observed fact."* Can this analysis be applied also to Priestley's experiments? What does Priestley mean when he talks of "this advance in the way of truth?" If scientific discovery is more than a matter of reporting, if it calls for subjective conjectures and concepts, how does it attain what we call truth?

What is True is What Works

Pragmatists have an answer which is quite appealing, especially to many scientists. William James tells us to "grant an idea or belief to be true"; then ask yourself, "What concrete difference will its being true make in any one's actual life . . . what, in short, is the truth's cash-value in experience?"† In other words, what is true is what works. If we get satisfactory results from the implementation of some idea, we consider it true. If we get unsatisfactory results we take it to be false. The subject, the individual, plays a dominant role in pragmatic thinking. Something may be true only for me. Pragmatic thinking also stresses the transitory nature of truth: "We have to live to-day by what truth we can get to-day, and be ready to-morrow to call it falsehood."‡

But if what scientists discover is not *truth* once and for all, what is the relationship between "true" hypotheses and reality? And how do we distinguish a real scientist from a pseudo-scientist if not by reference to the reality they are supposedly discussing?

P. W. Bridgman coins the term "operationalism" to characterize what he feels to be the proper approach of a scientist to his work. For Bridgman, the meaning of scientific terms is found in the way they are applied to concrete processes, objects or events in the scientist's experiences. The truth of statements is a relative matter and can never be considered completed. Bridgman cites Einstein's theory of relativity as the generating influence of operationalism. Einstein showed that absolute concepts in science were meaningful only within prescribed co-ordinate systems and that when they were

* Albert Einstein, *Essays in Science* (New York: The Wisdom Library, 1934), p. 27.

† See Selected Sources.

‡ See Selected Sources.

applied outside of those systems they ceased to be meaningful; they had no function. Concepts ought to be defined according to those operations which must be performed when they are used. We can understand a concept, Bridgman argues, only if we know to what physical operations it applies. This approach is drastically different from traditional ideas concerning the truth of concepts, which were defined in terms of properties.

Define a concept such as space. Do you find that you are inclined to do so by listing properties which something must have in order to be space? Or do you tend to talk of the operations of measurement, etc., involved in determining spatial relations? Bridgman's position is that if concepts are defined only by the operations used in applying them, and not by their properties, science comes closer to dealing with the actual experiential world, and not just with words. Think again of Priestley's experiments. Was he describing reality, or was he defining his terms operationally? Is it possible to restrict oneself only to operational definitions?

A large and ever increasing number of terms in science seems to have meaning only within the framework of certain theories. Terms like "electron," "gene," and "neutino" are examples. Do we want to know if such things exist, or is it enough to know that they play vital parts in successful explanatory theories? Are we distressed when evidence of their existence is not up to the standards we have for everyday objects? Does it seem less real to talk of electrons and sub-nuclear particles than to talk of tables and chairs? None of us thinks that unicorns exist, because we can find no specimens of unicorns.

If we could not demonstrate visibly that sub-atomic particles exist, would it matter to science? Our first reaction is "Yes," but consider their history. Dalton, Gay-Lussac and Avogadro, early founders of chemistry, worked with atomic and molecular theories despite the fact that they could not produce an atom. Apparently, the ability to point to such entities does not settle the question of their existence as it usually does with everyday objects. In his book *The Nature of the Physical World,* Sir Arthur Eddington, astronomer and philosopher, compares "electrons" to the nonsense words of Lewis Carroll's "Jabberwocky" poem: "It would not be a bad reminder of the essential unknownness of the fundamental entities of physics to translate it [the language of physics] into 'Jabberwocky'; provided all numbers—all metrical attributes—are unchanged, it does not suffer in the least."* What then is the relationship of sense data and reality to physics and other sciences? Bertrand Russell makes a relevant comment: "Physical things are those series of appearances whose matter obeys the laws of physics."†

* Sir Arthur Eddington, *The Nature of the Physical World* (Ann Arbor: University of Michigan Press, 1958), pp. 291–292.

† Bertrand Russell, "The Relation of Sense-data to Physics" (1912). Reprinted in Dante and Morgenbesser, *Philosophy of Science* (Cleveland: World Publishing Company, 1960), pp. 33–54.

Real Science is Adventure

In the *Brave New World,* we are told by Mustapha Mond that science is dangerous, that it is incompatible with happiness, that it is subversive. Real science, he tells us, is not cookbook; it is adventure. Is he suggesting that science, as distinct from technology, embodies a set of presuppositions, value commitments, which are inconsistent with those of the Brave New World, perhaps inconsistent with any society where the happiness of the members is the primary objective? What are these values of science? To what are scientists committed philosophically which causes them in turn to be restricted to islands in the Brave New World?

Many philosophers and scientists have talked of the faith of science, an underlying conviction about scientific endeavors. Norbert Wiener characterizes it as the belief that nature will not work against the efforts of the scientists to find order and that failure can be attributed only to human causes. Albert Einstein writes:

> Scientific research can reduce superstition by encouraging people to think and survey things in terms of cause and effect. Certain it is that a conviction akin to religious feeling, of rationality or intelligibility of the world, lies behind all scientific work of a higher order.*

In another instance he writes "The Lord may be subtle, but he isn't plain mean."

Value Considerations in Science

Upon close examination, many basic scientific tenets are value-loaded. Philosophers have taken great pains to demonstrate that such basic notions as cause and effect are not demonstrable in the physical world. Induction seems to be based on an idea of the uniformity of nature, but that idea is at best only an inductive generalization. In short, despite the pretense to pure objective thinking, much of the foundation of science is philosophical and value-loaded. Norbert Wiener makes the comment in *The Human Use of Human Beings* that unless science can exist in an atmosphere of naiveté free of political demands, the faith necessary for the scientific way of life cannot exist.†

If science is value-based, does it also have value-oriented responsibilities within the framework of society? Are scientists responsible for the consequences of the application of their discoveries? Are there moral and social responsibilities to be borne by science when usage of its discoveries causes death, mutilation and destruction? Who bears the responsibility after the discovery has left the laboratory? These questions are of prime interest to moral philosophers and to sociologists and psychologists. They also play a major role in recent commentary about science on the world's campuses. Where should the scientist stop? Does it matter if one scientist refuses to go beyond a certain point, when others are always willing and able to carry on his work?

* Einstein, *op. cit.,* p. 11.

† Norbert Wiener, *The Human Use of Human Beings* (Garden City, N.Y.: Doubleday, 1954), pp. 187–193.

Norbert Wiener makes an appeal for value considerations in science. "We had better be quite sure that the purpose put into the machine is the purpose which we really desire and not merely a colorful imitation of it." Suppose, like the Brave New World, we take the happiness of the majority of men as our purpose. Are we then bound to think of science in the same way as the Brave New World does? As Mond puts it, "Universal happiness keeps the wheels steadily turning; truth and beauty can't." Is the Brave New World such a bad idea?

1

FRANCIS BACON

(1561–1626)

*Aphorisms Concerning the Interpretation of Nature and the Kingdom of Man**

Bacon attacks the rationalist tradition of the Middle Ages (the notion that the basic truths of the universe can be discovered simply by reflection). Knowledge, Bacon claims, must be based on unprejudiced empirical data. Before one can learn from nature, the mind must be freed from the traps of dogma and superstition. "Idols of the mind" are what Bacon calls the ways of thinking incorrectly about nature. Bacon argues that these idols must be torn down and replaced by an inductive method of deriving truths of nature. We must free ourselves from egocentric concerns and the theories of nature which men have constructed and allow nature to impart its secrets to us. Once having learned the secrets of nature, we are in a position to master it. Reliable knowledge is to be found by organizing the facts of nature in gradual inductive steps.

Bacon's philosophy then has two distinct parts: a negative analysis of the "four idols of the mind" which distort truth, and a positive attempt to establish a new method of gaining knowledge by beginning with the particulars of experience and generalizing to more and more inclusive theories.

* Francis Bacon, *Novum Organum* (1620), Bk. 1, with omissions.

1. Man, being the servant and interpreter of nature, can do and understand so much and so much only as he has observed in fact or in thought of the course of nature: beyond this he neither knows anything nor can do anything.

3. Human knowledge and human power meet in one; for where the cause is not known the effect cannot be produced. Nature to be commanded must be obeyed; and that which in contemplation is as the cause is in operation as the rule.

12. The logic now in use serves rather to fix and give stability to the errors which have their foundation in commonly received notions, than to help the search after truth. So it does more harm than good.

15. There is no soundness in our notions whether logical or physical. Substance, Quality, Action, Passion, Essence itself, are not sound notions: much less are Heavy, Light, Dense, Rare, Moist, Dry, Generation, Corruption, Attraction, Repulsion, Element, Matter, Form, and the like; but all are fantastical and ill defined.

16. Our notions of less general species as Man, Dog, Dove, and of the immediate perceptions of the sense, as Hot, Cold, Black, White, do not materially mislead us; yet even these are sometimes confused by the flux and alteration of matter and the mixing of one thing with another. All the others which men have hitherto adopted are but wanderings, not being abstracted and formed from things by proper methods.

18. The discoveries which have hitherto been made in the sciences are such as lie close to vulgar notions, scarcely beneath the surface. In order to penetrate into the inner and further recesses of nature, it is necessary that both notions and axioms be derived from things by a more sure and guarded way; and that a method of intellectual operation be introduced altogether better and more certain.

Ways of Discovering Truth

19. There are and can be only two ways of searching into and discovering truth. The one flies from the senses and particulars to the most general axioms, and from these principles, the truth of which it takes for settled and immovable, proceeds to judgment and to the discovery of middle axioms. And this way is now in fashion. The other derives axioms from the senses and particulars, rising by a gradual and unbroken ascent, so that it arrives at the most general axioms last of all. This is the true way, but as yet untried.

20. The understanding left to itself takes the same course (namely, the former) which it takes in accordance with logical order. For the mind longs to spring up to positions of higher generality, that it may find rest there; and so after a little while wearies of experiment. But this evil is increased by logic, because of the order and solemnity of its disputations.

21. The understanding left to itself, in a sober, patient, and grave mind, especially if it be not hindered by received doctrines, tries a little that other way, which is the right one, but with little progress; since the understanding, unless directed and assisted, is a thing unequal, and quite unfit to contend with the obscurity of things.

22. Both ways set out from the senses and particulars, and rest in the highest generalities; but the difference between them is infinite. For the one just glances at experiment and particulars in passing, the other dwells duly and orderly among them. The one, again, begins at once by establishing certain abstract and useless generalities, the other rises by gradual steps to that which is prior and better known in the order of nature.

23. There is a great difference between the *Idols* of the human mind and the *Ideas* of the divine. That is to say, between certain empty dogmas, and the true signatures and marks set upon the works of creation as they are found in nature.

Anticipation and Interpretation of Nature

26. The conclusions of human reason as ordinarily applied in matter of nature, I call for the sake of distinction *Anticipations of Nature* (as a thing rash or premature). That reason which is elicited from facts by a just and methodical process, I call *Interpretation of Nature.*

27. Anticipations are a ground sufficiently firm for consent; for even if men went mad all after the same fashion, they might agree one with another well enough.

28. For the winning of assent, indeed, anticipations are far more powerful than interpretations; because being collected from a few instances, and those for the most part of familiar occurrence, they straightway touch the understanding and fill the imagination; whereas interpretations on the other hand, being gathered here and there from very various and widely dispersed facts, cannot suddenly strike the understanding; and therefore they must needs, in respect of the opinions of the time, seem harsh and out of tune; much as the mysteries of faith do.

36. One method of delivery alone remains to us; which is simply this: we must lead men to the particulars themselves, and their series and order; while men on their side must force themselves for awhile to lay their notions by and begin to familiarize themselves with facts.

37. The doctrine of those who have denied that certainty could be attained at all, has some agreement with my way of proceeding at the first setting out; but they end in being infinitely separated and opposed. For the holders of that doctrine assert simply that nothing can be known; I also assert that not much can be known in nature by the way which is now in use. But then they go on to destroy the authority of the senses and understanding; whereas I proceed to devise and supply helps for the same.

38. The idols and false notions which are now in possession of the human understanding, and have taken deep root therein, not only so beset men's minds that truth can hardly find entrance, but even after entrance obtained, they will again in the very instauration of the sciences meet and trouble us, unless men being forewarned of the danger fortify themselves as far as may be against their assaults.

The Idols of the Mind

39. There are four classes of idols which beset men's minds. To these for distinction's sake I have assigned names,—calling the first class *Idols of the Tribe;* the second, *Idols of the Cave;* the third, *Idols of the Market-place;* the fourth, *Idols of the Theater.*

40. The formation of ideas and axioms by true induction is no doubt the proper remedy to be applied for the keeping off and clearing away of idols. To point them out, however, is of great use, for the doctrine of idols is to the interpretation of nature what the doctrine of the refutation of sophisms is to common logic.

Idols of the Tribe

41. The Idols of the Tribe have their foundation in human nature itself, and in the tribe or race of men. For it is a false assertion that the sense of man is the measure of things. On the contrary, all perceptions, as well of the sense as of the mind, are according to the measure of the individual and not according to the measure of the universe. And the human understanding is like a false mirror, which, receiving rays irregularly, distorts and discolors the nature of things by mingling its own nature with it.

Idols of the Cave

42. The Idols of the Cave are the idols of the individual man. For everyone (besides the errors common to human nature in general) has a cave or den of his own, which refracts and discolors the light of nature; owing either to his own proper and peculiar nature or to his education and conversation with others; or to the reading of books, and the authority of those whom he esteems and admires; or to the differences of impressions, accordingly as they take place in a mind preoccupied and predisposed or in a mind indifferent and settled; or the like. So that the spirit of man (according as it is meted out to different individuals) is in fact a thing variable and full of perturbation, and governed as it were by chance. Whence it was well observed by Heraclitus that men look for sciences in their own lesser worlds, and not in the greater or common world.

Idols of the Market-Place

43. There are also idols formed by the intercourse and association of men with each other, which I call Idols of the Market-place, on account of the commerce and consort of men there. For it is by discourse that men associate; and words are imposed according to the apprehension of the vulgar. And therefore the ill and unfit choice of words wonderfully obstructs the understanding. Nor do the definitions or explanations wherewith in some things learned men are wont to guard and defend themselves, by any means set the matter right. But words plainly force and overrule the understanding, and throw all into confusion, and lead men away into numberless empty controversies and idle fancies.

Idols of the Theater

44. Lastly, there are idols which have immigrated into men's minds from the various dogmas of philosophies, and also from wrong laws of demonstration. These I call Idols of the Theater; because in my judgment all the received systems are but so many stage-plays, representing worlds of their own creation after an unreal and scenic fashion. Nor is it only of the systems now in vogue, or only of the ancient sects and philosophies, that I speak: for many more plays of the same kind may yet be composed and in like artificial manner set forth; seeing that errors the most widely different have nevertheless causes for the most

part alike. Neither again do I mean this only of entire systems, but also of many principles and axioms in science, which by tradition, credulity, and negligence have come to be received.

46. The human understanding when it has once adopted an opinion (either as being the received opinion or as being agreeable to itself) draws all things else to support and agree with it. And though there be a greater number and weight of instances to be found on the other side, yet these it either neglects and despises, or else by some distinction sets aside and rejects; in order that by this great and pernicious predetermination the authority of its former conclusions may remain inviolate. And therefore it was a good answer that was made by one who when they showed him hanging in a temple a picture of those who had paid their vows as having escaped shipwreck and would have him say whether he did not now acknowledge the power of the gods,— "Aye," asked he again, "but where are they painted that were drowned after their vows?" And such is the way of all superstition, whether in astrology, dreams, omens, divine judgments, or the like; wherein men, having a delight in such vanities, mark the events where they are fulfilled, but where they fail, though this happen much oftener, neglect and pass them by. But with far more subtlety does this mischief insinuate itself into philosophy and the sciences; in which the first conclusion colors and brings into conformity with itself all that come after, though far sounder and better. Besides, independently of that delight and vanity which I have described, it is the peculiar and perpetual error of the human intellect to be more moved and excited by affirmatives than by negatives; whereas it ought properly to hold itself indifferently disposed towards both alike. Indeed in the establishment of any true axiom, the negative instance is the more forcible of the two.

48. The human understanding is unique; it cannot stop or rest, and still presses onward, but in vain. Therefore it is that we cannot conceive of any end or limit to the world; but always as of necessity it occurs to us that there is something beyond. Neither again can it be conceived how eternity has flowed down to the present day: for that distinction which is commonly received of infinity in time past and in time to come can by no means hold; for it would thence follow that one infinity is greater than another, and that infinity is wasting away and tending to become finite. The like subtlety arises touching the infinite divisibility of lines, from the same inability of thought to stop. But this inability interferes more mischievously in the discovery of causes: for although the most general principles in nature ought to be held merely positive, as they are discovered, and cannot with truth be referred to a cause; nevertheless the human understanding being unable to rest still seeks something prior in the order of nature. And then it is that in struggling towards that which is further off it falls back upon that which is more nigh at hand,—namely, on final causes; which have relation clearly to the nature of man rather than to the nature of the universe, and from this source have strangely defined philosophy. But

he is no less an unskilled and shallow philosopher who seeks causes of that which is most general, than he who in things subordinate and subaltern omits to do so.

50. But by far the greatest hindrance and aberration of the human understanding proceeds from the dullness, incompetency, and deceptions of the senses; in that things which strike the sense outweigh things which do not immediately strike it, though they be more important. Hence it is that speculation commonly ceases where sight ceases, insomuch that of things invisible there is little or no observation. Hence all the working of the spirits inclosed in tangible bodies lies hid and unobserved of men. So also all the more subtle changes of form in the parts of coarser substances (which they commonly call alteration, though it is in truth local motion through exceedingly small spaces) is in like manner unobserved. And yet unless these two things just mentioned be searched out and brought to light, nothing great can be achieved in nature, as far as the production of works is concerned. So again the essential nature of our common air, and of all bodies less dense than air (which are very many), is almost unknown. For the sense by itself is a thing infirm and erring; neither can instruments for enlarging or sharpening the senses do much: but all the truer kind of interpretation of nature is effected by instances and experiments fit and apposite; wherein the sense decides touching the experiment only, and the experiment touching the point in nature and the thing itself.

The Idols Imposed by Words

59. The *Idols of the Market-place* are the most troublesome of all: idols which have crept into the understanding through the alliances of words and names. For men believe that their reason governs words; but it is also true that words react on the understanding; and this it is that has rendered philosophy and the sciences sophistical and inactive. Now words, being commonly framed and applied according to the capacity of the vulgar, follow those lines of division which are most obvious to the vulgar understanding. And whenever an understanding of greater acuteness or a more diligent observation would alter those lines to suit the true divisions of nature, words stand in the way and resist the change. Whence it comes to pass that the high and formal discussions of learned men end oftentimes in disputes about words and names; with which (according to the use and wisdom of the mathematicians) it would be more prudent to begin, and so by means of definitions reduce them to order. Yet even definitions cannot cure this evil in dealing with natural and material things; since the definitions themselves consist of words, and those words beget others: so that it is necessary to recur to individual instances, and those in due series and order; as I shall say presently when I come to the method and scheme for the formation of notions and axioms.

60. The idols imposed by words on the understanding are of two kinds. They are either names of things which do not exist (for as there are things left unnamed through lack of observation, so likewise are there names which result from fantastic suppositions and to which

nothing in reality corresponds), or they are names of things which exist, but yet confused and ill-defined, and hastily and irregularly derived from realities. Of the former kind are Fortune, the Prime Mover, Planetary Orbits, Elements of Fire, and like fictions which owe their origin to false and idle theories. And this class of idols is more easily expelled, because to get rid of them it is only necessary that all theories should be steadily rejected and dismissed as obsolete.

But the other class, which springs out of a faulty and unskillful abstraction, is intricate and deeply rooted. Let us take for example such a word as *humid,* and see how far the several things which the word is used to signify agree with each other; and we shall find the word *humid* to be nothing else than a mark loosely and confusedly applied to denote a variety of actions which will not bear to be reduced to any constant meaning. For it both signifies that which easily spreads itself round any other body; and that which in itself is indeterminate and cannot solidize; and that which readily yields in every direction; and that which easily divides and scatters itself; and that which easily unites and collects itself; and that which readily flows and is put in motion; and that which readily clings to another body and wets it; and that which is easily reduced to a liquid, or being solid easily melts. Accordingly when you come to apply the word,—if you take it in one sense, flame is humid; if in another, air is not humid; if in another, fine dust is humid; if in another, glass is humid. So that it is easy to see that the notion is taken by abstraction only from water and common and ordinary liquids, without any due verification.

There are however in words certain degrees of distortion and error. One of the least faulty kinds is that of names of substances, especially of lowest species and well-deduced (for the notion of *chalk* and of *mud* is good, of *earth* bad); a more faulty kind is that of actions, as *to generate, to corrupt, to alter;* the most faulty is of qualities (except such as are the immediate objects of the sense) as *heavy, light, rare, dense,* and the like. Yet in all these cases some notions are of necessity a little better than others, in proportion to the greater variety of subjects that fall within the range of the human sense.

2

WILLIAM WHEWELL

(1794–1866)

*On the Process of Discovery**

For Whewell, induction is not just a process of collecting facts and generalizing from them. Facts make no sense in themselves and must be organized through conceptions invented by the scientist. Knowledge has two elements, the formal subjective conceptions of the mind and the objective particulars of experience. The process of scientific discovery, for Whewell, takes place in three steps. The elements of knowledge are classified, the facts are "colligated" by means of a conception, and finally the colligation is verified by reference to experience. Whewell argues that the wisdom (sagacity) of the discovering scientist is not a learned skill. He suggests that conjecture and hypothesis is the most common ground upon which science develops.

Compare Whewell's analysis to Bacon's. It is not without reason that Whewell entitled his work Novum Organum Renovatum, *a renovation of Bacon's classic,* Novum Organum. *The two differ most sharply on the question of the value of hypothetical, or conjectural, thinking in discovering truth. They both use the term "induction" to characterize their methods, but do they mean the same thing?*

* William Whewell *Novum Organum Renovatum* (London: John W. Parker and Son, 1858), selections from pp. 79–120.

Of the Colligation of Facts

APHORISM [I]

Science begins with common observation of facts; but even at this stage, requires that the observations be precise. Hence the sciences which depend upon space and number were the earliest formed. After common observation, come Scientific Observation and Experiment.

APHORISM [II]

The Conceptions by which Facts are bound together, are suggested by the sagacity of discoverers. This sagacity cannot be taught. It commonly succeeds by guessing; and this success seems to consist in framing several tentative hypotheses and selecting the right one. But a supply of appropriate hypotheses cannot be constructed by rule, nor without inventive talent.

APHORISM [III]

The truth of tentative hypotheses must be tested by their application to facts. The discoverer must be ready, carefully to try his hypotheses in this manner, and to reject them if they will not bear the test, in spite of indolence and vanity. . . .

Of Certain Characteristics of Scientific Induction

APHORISM [IV]

The process of scientific discovery is cautious and rigorous, not by abstaining from hypotheses, but by rigorously comparing hypotheses with facts, and by resolutely rejecting all which the comparison does not confirm.

APHORISM [V]

Hypotheses may be useful, though involving much that is superfluous, and even erroneous: for they may supply the true bond of connexion of the facts; and the superfluity and errour may afterwards be pared away.

APHORISM [VI]

It is a test of true theories not only to account for, but to predict phenomena.

APHORISM [VII]

Induction is a term applied to describe the process of a true Colligation of Facts by means of an exact and appropriate Conception. An Induction is also employed to denote the proposition which results from this process.

APHORISM [VIII]

The Consilience of Inductions takes place when an Induction, obtained from one class of facts, coincides with an Induction, obtained from another different class. This Consilience is a test of the Theory in which it occurs.

APHORISM [IX]

An Induction is not the mere sum of the Facts which are colligated. The Facts are not only brought together, but seen in a new point of view. A new mental Element is super-induced; and a peculiar constitution and discipline of mind are requisite in order to make this Induction.

APHORISM [X]

Although in Every Induction a new conception is super-induced upon the Facts; yet this once effectually done, the novelty of the conception is overlooked, and the conception is considered as a part of the fact. . . .

Of the Logic of Induction

APHORISM [XI]

The Logic of Induction consists in stating the Facts and the Inference in such a manner, that the Evidence of the Inference is manifest; just as the Logic of Deduction consists in stating the Premises and the Conclusion in such a manner that the Evidence of the Conclusion is manifest.

APHORISM [XII]

The Logic of Deduction is exhibited by means of a certain Formula; namely, a Syllogism; and every train of deductive reasoning, to be demonstrative, must be capable of resolution into a series of such Formulæ legitimately constructed. In like manner, the Logic of Induction may be exhibited by means of certain Formulæ; and every train of inductive inference, to be sound, must be capable of resolution into a scheme of such Formulæ, legitimately constructed.

APHORISM [XIII]

The inductive act of thought by which several Facts are colligated into one Proposition, may be expressed by saying: The several Facts are exactly expressed as one Fact, if, and only if, we adopt the Conceptions and the Assertion of the Proposition.

APHORISM [XIV]

The One Fact, thus inductively attained from several Facts, may be combined with other Facts, and colligated with them by a new act of Induction. This process may be indefinitely repeated: and these successive processes are the Steps of Induction, or of Generalization, from the lowest to the highest.

APHORISM [XV]

The relation of the successive Steps of Induction may be exhibited by means of an Inductive Table, in which the several Facts are indicated, and tied together by a Bracket, and the Inductive Inference placed on the other side of the Bracket; and this arrangement repeated, so as to form a genealogical Table of each Induction, from the lowest to the highest.

APHORISM [XVI]

The Logic of Induction is the Criterion of Truth inferred from Facts, as the Logic of Deduction is the Criterion of Truth deduced from necessary Principles. The Inductive Table enables us to apply such a Criterion; for we can determine whether each Induction is verified and justified by the Facts which its Bracket includes; and if each induction in particular be sound, the highest, which merely combines them all, must necessarily be sound also.

APHORISM [XVII]

The distinction of Fact and Theory is only relative. Events and phenomena, considered as Particulars which may be colligated by Induction, are Facts; considered as Generalities already obtained by colligation of other Facts, they are Theories. The same event or phenomenon is a Fact or a Theory, according as it is considered as standing on one side or the other of the Inductive Bracket. . . .

Of Laws of Phenomena and of Causes

APHORISM [XVIII]

Inductive truths are of two kinds, Laws of Phenomena, and Theories of Causes. It is necessary to begin in every science with the Laws of Phenomena; but it is impossible that we should be satisfied to stop short of a Theory of Causes. In Physical Astronomy, Physical Optics, Geology, and other sciences, we have instances showing that we can make a great advance in inquiries after true Theories of Causes.

In the first attempts at acquiring an exact and connected knowledge of the appearances and operations which nature presents, men went no further than to learn *what* takes place, not *why* it occurs. They discovered an Order which the phenomena follow, Rules which they obey; but they did not come in sight of the Powers by which these rules are determined, the Causes of which this order is the effect. Thus, for example, they found that many of the celestial motions took place as if the sun and stars were carried round by the revolutions of certain celestial spheres; but what causes kept these spheres in constant motion, they were never able to explain. In like manner in modern times, Kepler discovered that the planets describe ellipses, before Newton explained why they select this particular curve, and describe it in a particular manner. The laws of reflection, refraction, dispersion, and other properties of light have long been known; the causes of these laws are at present under discussion. And the same might be said of many other sciences. The discovery of *the Laws of Phenomena* is, in all cases, the first step in exact knowledge; these Laws may often for a long period constitute the whole of our science; and it is always a matter requiring great talents and great efforts, to advance to a knowledge of the *Causes* of the phenomena.

Hence the larger part of our knowledge of nature, at least of the certain portion of it, consists of the knowledge of the Laws of Phenomena. In Astronomy indeed, besides knowing the rules which guide the appearances, and resolving them into the real motions from which they arise, we can refer these motions to the forces which produce them. In Optics, we have become acquainted with a vast number of laws by which varied and beautiful phenomena are governed; and perhaps we may assume, since the evidence of the Undulatory Theory has been so fully developed, that we know also the Causes of the Phenomena. But in a large class of sciences, while we have learnt many Laws of Phenomena, the causes by which these are produced are still unknown or disputed. Are we to ascribe to the operation of a fluid or fluids, and if so, in what manner, the facts of heat, magnetism, electricity, galvanism? What are the forces by which the elements of chemical compounds are held together? What are the forces, of a higher order, as we cannot help believing, by which the course of vital action in organized bodies is kept up? In these and other cases, we have extensive departments of science; but we are as yet unable to trace the effects to their causes; and our science, so far as it is positive and certain, consists entirely of the laws of phenomena.

In those cases in which we have a division of the science which teaches us the doctrine of the causes, as well as one which states the rules which the effects follow, I have, in the *History,* distinguished the two portions of the science by certain terms. I have thus spoken of *Formal* Astronomy and *Physical* Astronomy. The latter phrase has long been commonly employed to describe that department of Astronomy which deals with those forces by which the heavenly bodies are guided in their motions; the former adjective appears well suited to describe a collection of rules depending on those ideas of space, time, position, number, which are, as we have already said, the *forms* of our apprehension of phenomena. The laws of phenomena may be considered as *formulæ,* expressing results in terms of those ideas. In like manner, I have spoken of Formal Optics and Physical Optics; the latter division including all speculations concerning the machinery by which the effects are produced. Formal Acoustics and Physical Acoustics may be distinguished in like manner, although these two portions of science have been a good deal mixed together by most of those who have treated of them. Formal Thermotics, the knowledge of the laws of the phenomena of heat, ought in like manner to lead to Physical Thermotics, or the Theory of Heat with reference to the cause by which its effects are produced;—a branch of science which as yet can hardly be said to exist.

What *kinds of cause* are we to admit in science? This is an important, and by no means an easy question. In order to answer it, we must consider in what manner our progress in the knowledge of causes has hitherto been made. By far the most conspicuous instance of success in such researches, is the discovery of the causes of the motions of the heavenly bodies. In this case, after the formal laws of the motions,—their conditions as to space and time,—had become known, men were enabled to go a step further; to reduce them to the familiar and general cause of motion—mechanical force; and to determine the laws which this force follows. That this was a step in addition to the knowledge previously possessed, and that it was a real and peculiar truth, will not be contested. And a step in any other subject which should be analogous to this in astronomy;—a discovery of causes and forces as certain and clear as the discovery of universal gravitation;—would undoubtedly be a vast advance upon a body of science consisting only of the laws of phenomena.

3

NORWOOD RUSSELL HANSON

(1924–1966)

*Retroductive Inference**

Hanson has been one of the primary contributors to the contemporary philosophy of science. His book, Patterns of Discovery, *has had a far-reaching effect upon reconsiderations of the process of discovery in science. This article is an attempt to distinguish two popular approaches to discovery in terms of their inferential and conceptual nature. The hypothetico-deductive method (called "HD" by Hanson) and the retroductive method ("RD") appear in completed form to be very much alike. The HD method is involved in conclusion-deducing, as is mathematics, but it is also a hypothesis-testing method. An hypothesis is linked to already confirmed premises; a conclusion is drawn and tested. If the observational consequences deduced from the premise cluster are confirmed, the hypothesis is said to be also confirmed to that extent. The RD scientific method centers on the attempted explanation of anomalies, events which appear unfamiliar or not explainable within the traditional framework. The RD scientist, as Hanson characterizes him, starts with the anomaly and seeks a set of premises which can account for it. It is an explanatory technique as opposed to the HD testing method. Formally these methods look alike, with premises and a conclusion, but Hanson argues that there is a major conceptual, not just psychological, difference which distinguishes these two ways of science. His examples from the history of astronomy provide interesting devices for testing his contention.*

* From *Philosophy of Science, The Delaware Seminar,* Bernard Baumrin, ed. (1961–1962), Vol. 1, pp. 21–37. Used by permission of the publishers, Interscience Publishers, Division of John Wiley & Sons, New York.

THE history of philosophy has in part been a history of attempts to describe scientific argument. In the *Posterior Analytics,* Aristotle writes of how naturalists argue from finite observations to general laws. Critics, like Sextus Empiricus, challenged Aristotle's account as unsound. A spectrum of views concerning scientific reasoning gradually proliferated. From Bacon through Reichenbach it was urged that all scientific argument reduces to induction by simple enumeration. From Mill through Braithwaite, scientists were seen to proceed by the hypothetico-deductive method (henceforth "HD"). Still others have esposed something called "retroduction" (RD) as the analysis of how scientists reason. Peirce, and Aristotle himself, opted for this view.

One objective of this paper will be to demonstrate that the differences between these philosophical accounts are not "merely psychological," but genuinely conceptual. Perhaps neither the HD nor the RD account has any application for the analysis of scientific argumentation. Or maybe both apply, but never at once. However this may be, it is not the case that the HD and the RD accounts constitute conceptually *equivalent* characterizations of any one scientific argument.

Our second objective is to distinguish yet again how people *do* argue from abstract questions about the form of argument. The delineation of the moves through which scientists reason while problem solving is as much the business of philosophy of science as is the *post factum* formal reconstruction of that argument for abstract logical purposes.

If these two objectives can be achieved, an historical point may then be made. The distinction drawn by 19th century astronomers between the Orthodox Problem of Perturbations and the Inverse Problem of Perturbations exemplifies the contrast we shall draw between the HD and RD accounts. Part of the conceptual excitement of the 19th century may be lost to logicians and historians who remain insensitive to this distinction.

Hypothetico-Deductive Inference

The insight of the HD analysis consists in distinguishing the rational activity of the natural scientist from that of the mathematician, a distinction which Popper, Reichenbach, Braithwaite, Bergmann, and Carnap draw better and more finely than earlier inductive logicians like Hume, Mill, Jevons, Venn, and Johnson. The mathematician argues "typically" when he entertains certain premises solely to "unpack" them. His concern is neither with their contingent truth nor falsity, nor with that of the conclusions unpackable therefrom. It is the *unpacking relationship* which alone interests the formal scientist. The natural scientist, however, cares not only about consistency within a universe of discourse; he is concerned also with the contingent truth of claims about the universe in which we live. That a statement follows from *some* premise cluster may be a necessary condition for its descriptive utility. But it is not sufficient. False conclusions can follow validly from contingently false premises, or from logically false ones.

If each premise is contingently true, and if the deduction is valid, the conclusion will have "about" the same probability as has the premise cluster. There is thus a formal connection between a conclusion's probability and the joint probability of its premises. But problems seldom come to the scientist thus. Rarely is he given a list of claims and charged to draw up another list of their consequences. Usually he encounters some anomaly, and desires an explanation. It cannot follow from any *obvious* premise cluster else it would not be anomalous. So, one proceeds to cluster *some* established truths with hypotheses to see whether they may not jointly entail the anomaly. But now estimate the probability: the anomaly's description is assumed correct. The available premises obtain. From the joint probability of the anomaly plus these obvious premises one now estimates the probability of an hypothesis which, when conjoined with the premises, entails the anomaly.

The HD account is concerned not only with *conclusion deducing*, but with *hypothesis testing*. Hypotheses are tested by linking them with already confirmed statements to form a premise cluster. From this cluster, observational consequences are generated. If these are confirmed, the hypothesis is to that extent confirmed. But if further consequences turn out false, the probability of the hypothesis diminishes.

Much scientific reasoning and argumentation displays this HD pattern. Whenever the extension of a partially confirmed theory is in question, one generates further observational consequences of the theory and checks them against the facts. Indeed, detecting flaws in apparatus, and deviations in measuring instruments—as well as the theoretical discovery of "unexpected" phenomena—consists largely in deductively decomposing the premise clusters of theoretical science. This sets out the "logical expectations" of a given theory, and hence highlights any deviation from these expectations. The very identification of an event as "anomalous" depends on this HD elaboration of familiar premise clusters.*

Retroductive Inference

The HD theorist attends thus to the scientist's inferences from contingent premise clusters to observationally vulnerable conclusions. The RD account focuses rather on the explanation of anomalies. RD enthusiasts think scientific argumentation to consist first in the recognition of anomalies, and then in the hunt for some premise cluster which, if confirmed, would explain the anomaly. This premise cluster will contain initial conditions and an hypothesis, the form of which "reveals itself" by its initial absence from the cluster. Thus, that the law of Universal Gravitation had an inverse square *form* seemed clear to the young Newton from the logical gap left in the cluster of known mechanical laws when he assumed that such laws were sufficient to explain *all* mechanical phenomena—the tides, hydrodynamics, ballistics, celestial motions, etc. A further hypothesis was needed. But although it was not discovered until 1687, Newton perceived its form "lurking" in the very statement of his problem in 1665. So while the HD account pictures the scientist with a ready-made theory and a store of initial conditions in hand, generating from these testable observation statements, the RD account pictures him as possessing only the initial conditions and an upsetting anomaly, by reflections upon which he seeks an hypothesis to explain the anomaly and to found a new theory. Again, the HD account focuses on *hypothesis testing;* the RD account is concerned with *anomaly explaining*.

Some signal events in history have involved reasoning of this RD kind. The discovery of Neptune, and of the neutrino, are characterizable thus. Just as the discovery of Pluto, and of the antiproton, seem

* There are other "less active" interpretations of the HD account. No matter. Even if every HD theorist were perfectly clear in setting out his views as *ex post facto* abstract logical analyses of scientific argumentation (which is not the case), this paper would still be making a distinction of import.

better described in HD terms. Here one runs out the consequences of an accepted theory and tests them. In the RD case, some facts surprisingly fail to confirm the consequences of an accepted theory; one then argues from these to some new hypothesis which may resolve the anomaly.

That the HD and RD Accounts Are but Psychologically Different

HD and RD enthusiasts both recognize that their formal criteria for success in argument are *precisely the same.* Thus, imagine that one scientist argues from premises *A*, *B*, *C* and hypothesis *H*, to conclusion *D* (which, although originally unexpected, ultimately is confirmed in fact). Another encounters the anomalous fact that *D*, and conjoins this with *A*, *B*, and *C* so as to "corner an hypothesis *H* which, when bracketed with *A*, *B*, and *C*, will "explain" *D*. Both scientists have been arguing; both have been using their heads. Differently. But the criterion for their having succeeded with their different tasks will be simply this: that *D* follows from *A*, *B*, *C*, and *H*. If either the first or the second scientist was mistaken in thinking *D* to be entailed by *A*, *B*, *C*, and *H*, then his reasoning fails.

But if the *logical* criteria for success or failure of reasoning in either case are the *same,* then whatever distinguishes these two scientific arguments must be nonlogical, and therefore (so the position develops) *merely psychological.* This is the strong form of the thesis that, though the aspects of scientific thinking distinguished by the HD and RD accounts may be interesting to psychologists, they contain nothing of importance for philosophers and logicians. My first objective is to attack that conclusion.

The "Direction" of Arguments

Consider a logic teacher presenting a problem to his class. One orthodox assignment might be this: "Here are three premises, *A*, *B*, and *C*. From these alone generate the theorem, *D*." The teacher is here charging his students to find what follows from premises written "at the top of the page." This is related to the traveler's puzzlement when he asks, "here I am, river to the left, mountains to the right, canyon ahead; *where do I go from here?*"

Contrast with this the different assignment a logic teacher might give: "Here is a theorem *D*. Find any three premises *A*, *B*, and *C* from which *D* is generable." Here, he gives his students *D* written, as it were, "at the bottom of a page." He asks them to work back from this to three premises which, if written at the top of the page, will be that from which D follows. Analogously, the traveler's question would be "*would I be able to return here from over there?* or there? or there?"

These two queries of the traveler will be answered, and appraised, by the same geographical criterion; "is there a geographical route connecting point *A* with point *B*?" Whether one is at *A* asking if he can get from there to *B*, or asking while at *B* whether he could return from some other point *A* *back* to *B*—the ultimate geographical issue is only whether some traversable route connects *A* and *B*.

Similarly, the criteria for assessing the logic students' answers are the same whether the teacher asks his question in terms of premise unpacking, or in terms of premise hunting. "Is there a logical route connecting *A*, *B*, *C* with *D*?" Whether one is at *D* and looking for some *A*, *B*, *C*, *H* from which he could get back to *D*, or whether one begins at *A*, *B*, *C*, *H* and asks whether he can make it to *D*—that these are different is not relevant in strict logic. The question of the existence of a route, logical or geographical, is independent of whether the route is traversed from one end to the other, or from the other end to the one: from *A*, *B*, *C*, *H*, to *D* or from *D* to *A*, *B*, *C*, *H*.

The Form of an Argument vs. Arguing According to Form

It is often supposed that when considering the *form* of an argument one should consider it as if it were *mathematical.* It is imagined that the ways logicians and mathematicians argue illuminates the issue of logical form. This is false. Mathematicians no less than other reasonable men argue sometimes from premises to conclusions, and sometimes from anomaly to its explanation independently of any *general* metamathematical question of whether some logical route connects the beginning point of the argument with its terminus. The actual arguments of mathematicians are just like ours. They have an arrow built into them; they progress from a starting point to a finish line.

The *logical form* of an argument, however, does not progress at all. It is static, time-independent, problem-neutral—above the battles of natural science and formal science alike. Hence, if deducing is what logicians and mathematicians *do* when arguing from premises to conclusions, then "deductive" cannot distinguish the formal characteristics of one kind of argument as against others, i.e., probabilistic, analogical, etc. If deduction is what someone does during the *de facto* business of reasoning, the alternative ways of proceeding with one's reasoning might be different and might have different names, e.g., "hypothetico-deduction," "retroduction," etc. This may be so even though from a *strictly* formal standpoint nothing may distinguish such procedures.

More on the Direction of a Scientific Argument

Just as arguing from premises at the top of a page down to a conclusion differs from working from a conclusion "up" to premises at the top, even when the logical form of each will be identical to that of the other —so also, arguing from initial conditions plus hypothesis, *A*, *B*, *C*, *H*, down to an observation statement *D* is different from working "up" from an anomaly *D* to some *H* which, when conjoined with initial conditions *A*, *B*, *C* will entail, and hence explain, the anomaly. This, although the logical structure of each procedure is the same as that of the other. The only question here is "does some logical route connect *A*, *B*, *C*, and *H* with *D*?"

The HD Procedure Consists in Arguing from the Top of a Page Down

The HD account centers on hypothesis testing. It stresses the generating of observation statements *D* from premises *A*, *B*, *C*, and *H*. When the *D*'s square with the facts, *H* is, insofar, confirmed. The typical description gives *A*, *B*, *C*, as known, *H* as conjectured, while D_1, D_2, D_3,

. . . have yet to be "unpacked" from this premise cluster. The analogy between what the mathematician does during some of his problem solving and what the scientist is taken to do by the HD philosopher, is instructive. The natural scientist does not know in advance *what* observation statements D_1, D_2, D_3 may be generable from *A*, *B*, *C*, and *H*. This is what makes this HD procedure an indirect test of *H* (*after* it has been formulated and conjoined with *A*, *B*, *and C*). In both mathematics and natural science, arguments often exfoliate deductively; they proceed from the "top of the page" down to the *D*-statements. This does not identify the two procedures, however. The formal scientist is not concerned with the empirical truth of *A*, *B*, *C*, or *H* or of the conclusions drawn therefrom. That a conclusion *D* is validly generable from premises *A*, *B*, *C*, *H*, contingent truth or falsity aside, will be his one concern. A natural scientist proceeding in the HD manner, however, will begin with initial conditions *A*, *B*, and *C* established as true. The status of *H* remains unknown. After *D* is deduced from this set and discovered to describe the facts, *H* may be said to have become "probabilified." The natural scientist's concern is to determine whether a given *H* can thus be raised to the same degree of acceptability as the initial condition *A*, *B*, and *C*. This he settles by enlarging and diversifying the set of observation statements D_1, D_2, D_3, . . . The regular confirmation of which will systematically raise *H*'s probability. This distinguishes the epistemic context within which the mathematician and natural scientist work. Still, vis-à-vis the *direction* of argument, the mathematician and the natural scientist will both on occasion argue from the top of the page down, and this is traditionally described as "deducing."

The RD Procedure Consists in Arguing from the Bottom of a Page Up

When wearing his RD cap, the natural scientist begins his inquiry in puzzlement. After unpacking a well-established theory, replete with hypothesis *H*, into the expected observation statements *D*, he discovers that nature is not described by some of these latter. His normal expectations (and those of the theory) are thus thwarted. He has no reason to doubt initial conditions *A*, *B*, and *C*; their independent verification is what made them initial conditions. But he is astonished to note that the *orthodox* hypothesis *H* does not, when conjoined with *A*, *B*, *C*, generate descriptions of the facts. Thus the question: "Given the anomaly *D*, and the initial conditions *A*, *B*, *C*—from the hypothesis *H'* * does *D* follow when *H'* is bracketed with *A*, *B*, and *C*?"

Again, the Formal Criteria Are Identical

Consider the two schemata on page 588.

Notice that the solid arrows represent the *actual* order of the scientist's argument. The "beginning" in the one case is *H* plus *A*, *B*, *C*, which set is then unpacked into the heretofore-unformulated D_1,D_2, D_3. In the other case, the occasion for the inquiry is the anomaly *D*: the rational moves from that point are towards a premise cluster *A*, *B*, *C*, *H* which can "explain" the anomaly. The dotted arrow, however, repre-

* *I.e.*, any hypothesis other than *H*.

HD characterization	RD characterization

$$\begin{bmatrix} A, B, C \text{ (initial conditions)} \\ \text{plus} \\ H \text{ (hypothesis)} \end{bmatrix}$$

$D_1, D_2, D_3 \ldots$ (anomalies—descriptions of unexpected observations; these are incompatible with the expected HD unpacking of currently accepted hypotheses)

$D_1, D_2, D_3 \ldots$ (observation statements, as yet untested)

$$\begin{bmatrix} A, B, C \text{ (well-established} \\ \text{conditions of inquiry)} \\ \text{plus} \\ H_1, \text{ or } H_2, \text{ or } H_3 \ldots \end{bmatrix}$$

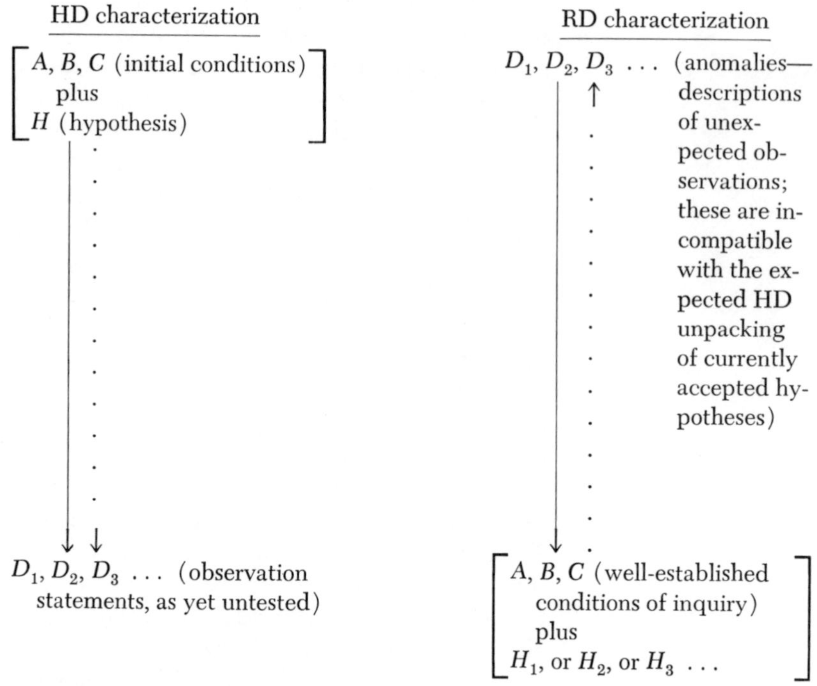

sents the *logical* order of the progressions. It points the same way in both cases—towards D_1, D_2, D_3; hence the logical criteria for appraising the validity of arguments of either form above are identical. Here then are two argument-schemata which, vis-à-vis logical structure, are the *same* argument, but, vis-à-vis their *de facto* development within the problem-solving context, are clearly different. The HD "starts from" initial conditions and an hypothesis and terminates in low-level observationally testable statements. The other "begins with" statements of actual observations—one unexpected on an HD basis—and terminates in a statement of initial conditions A, B, C, and some heretofore-unformulated hypothesis H.

Consider again the claim that this difference can be no more than psychological since both argument schemata are identical in logical form. This cannot be correct: the same conceptual probe leads to quite different reactions. That probe consists just in this: that from consistent premises, A, B, C, and H, any two resulting theorems, D_1 and D_2, must themselves be consistent. Whereas, it is not in general the ease that any two sets of premises, A, B, C and H, and A', B', C', and H'— either of which may resolve some anomaly D—will themselves be mutually consistent.

Thus consider the premise sets, A, B, C, *and* the claim "John is a bachelor." If these four premises are consistent, everything, D, which follows from them will also be mutually consistent, e.g., "John is unmarried," "John is male," "John is an adult," etc. But begin now from the low-level claim, D: "John is male." This *can* be shown to follow from A, B, C and "John is a bachelor." But it also follows from A, B, C, *and* "John is a married uncle." These two premise sets, however, are not consistent with each other. Since conceptually different answers result from this probe, the two characterizations must therefore be conceptually different and not merely psychologically so.

Here it might be objected, "Yes, 'John is a bachelor' and 'John is a married uncle' *are* inconsistent, and any premise sets in which they are imbedded will also be inconsistent. But these two premise sets are not inconsistent with respect to what is required in order to generate the single conclusion 'John is male.' Indeed, they could not be so, by the principle that if p entails q (and q is not necessary) then $\sim p$ cannot also entail q. The only analysis is this: that when $(r \cdot p)$ obtains and $p \rightarrow q$, then q will follow—and it will follow also from $(\sim r \cdot p)$ and $p \rightarrow q$. Hence a single anomaly D (i.e., q) can follow from two mutually incompatible premise sets only when the incompatibility plays no immediate role in the deduction."

This is an extremely potent objection. But it leaves the conceptual issue unscathed. It remains that A, B, C, H and R, if consistent, will entail only compatible conclusions D_1, D_2, D_3 . . . , etc. But an anomaly, D_3, might be explained not only by *different* premise sets—$A\ B\ C\ H\ R$ and $M\ N\ L\ O\ P$—but also by *incompatible* premise sets—$A\ B\ C\ H\ R$ and $A\ B\ C\ H\ \sim R$—where R and $\sim R$ are admittedly redundant to the derivation. Redundant or not, the conceptual distinction persists and rules out the "mere psychology" interpretation.

Moreover, in distinguishing premise sets *as embedded in scientific theories,* no premises are wholly redundant in the degenerate logical sense. For, although R and $\sim R$ may be redundant for this *one* accounting of D_3, they will not be redundant in general (as would a tautology) in the business of distinguishing the whole theories in which these arguments occur. Thus, in the wave theory of light, R may signify that a light ray *decelerates* on entering a denser medium, whereas in the particulate theory $\sim R$ will signify that the light *accelerates* on entering a denser medium. But neither R nor $\sim R$ will be needed immediately in the deduction of D—e.g., the proposition that the sines of the angles of incidence and refraction stand in ratio to each other. Nonetheless, *explaining* this latter phenomenon will involve reference ultimately not just to the premise set A, B, C, and H (which may be identical in both the wave theory and the particle theory): the explanations will sooner or later involve A, B, C, H, and R, on the one hand and A, B, C, H, and $\sim R$, on the other. So the conceptual difference remains, and is not trivialized by the redundancy move just noted.

Some Illustrations from the History of Science

Suppose someone urged that, so far as conceptual differences go, nothing distinguishes the "Classical Problem of Perturbations" and the "Inverse Problem of Perturbations." Such a person would not be taken seriously either by astronomers or by historians. I wish to describe these different approaches to perturbation theory, and to mark the analogies between them and the contrasts already drawn.

The Classical Problem of Perturbations may be characterized thus: Suppose we know the dynamical elements of some planet A (e.g., its mass, mean angular velocity, mean period of revolution, mean distance from the sun, orbital eccentricity, perihelial precession, etc.). And suppose also that we know the dynamical elements of some other planet *B*. Assuming the truth of the law of universal gravitation (*H* in this case), we can easily calculate the perturbation on *B* caused by *A* and *vice versa*. These calculations readily convert into predictions of the future positions of both planets. These are confirmed or disconfirmed by future observations. Should the observations confirm the predictions, they will indirectly reconfirm the law of gravitation, and reassure us also that the dynamical elements of both *A* and *B* have been properly described.

The Classical Problem of Perturbations thus reads remarkably like an HD reconstruction. So, knowing, as we do, the dynamical elements of the earth and Mars, we can predict the future positions of both by adding correction terms in the form of perturbation readjustments to the appropriate celestial theory. Indeed, by the systematic use of the HD method the discrepancies in unadjusted theories are regularly discovered, and the need for correction terms at the observational level clearly perceived. Nor is this HD technique *merely* a way of generating the detailed consequences of specific hypotheses. Nor is it merely ancillary to scientific theorizing; it is probably the only way of coming to perceive the need for further correction terms. The HD description is more accurate than any other in characterizing advances like the discovery of Halley's comet, of Pluto, of the antiproton and the antineutron. So, nothing in this paper is calculated to minimize the services rendered by cerebrations of the HD variety.

The Inverse Problem of Perturbations

Other discoveries—of the planet Neptune, the neutrino, and the positive electron—are different from what has been discussed. The Inverse Problem of Perturbations is a case in point; it may be characterized thus: Suppose we know the dynamical elements of some planet *B*, and that we know from "unadjusted" celestial dynamics that the observed positions of *B* do not correspond to those predicted. *B* is perturbed from its expected path. The problem is now one of reasoning from this anomaly, these perturbations, to an hypothesis about some as-yet-undetected planet *A* whose specially designed dynamical elements would explain the observed perturbations. Explanation will have been achieved if *B*'s observed perturbations logically follow from the hypothesis that *A*, with its tailor-made properties, exists. [This is precisely the argument which prepared us for the neutrino. Anomaly: Unlike α particles ejected from a spontaneously decaying radioactive source, the β particles display ranges, and hence energies covering a wide spectrum. But this conflicts with the accepted principle of the conservation of energy, since if the radioactive source is homogeneous, and all β particles have the same properties, then that some should have more energy than others suggests that in these "others" energy is not being conserved. Hypothesis: if β particles were always ejected *along with* some other as-yet-undetected particle (neutral charge, no rest mass, etc.) then each emitted particle-pair (β *and* neutrino) would have an aggregate energy equal to that of every other particle-pair. Emitted β particles do not leave a "star" of tracks, as do α particles, because these "neutrinos" are consuming different amounts of energy in each pair-emission: a fact which cannot show up in a Wilson chamber. *Therefore* neutrinos exist!] The existence of planet *A* will explain *B*'s perturbations, if from this "existence hypothesis" *B*'s perturbations can be shown to follow. And then we should be able to predict *B*'s *future* perturbations on the basis of this same hypothesis. The HD procedure and the RD procedure are therefore indissolubly linked. They are even, indeed, conceptually linked. They are two stages of a three-stage rational process consisting in (*1*) unpacking the perhaps heretofore unformulated observational consequences of a given theory, or of a typical premise set within that theory, and (*2*) noting that one of these observational consequences, anomalously, does not square with the facts. The hunt is then on for some new hypothesis which, when conjoined with the orthodox premises *will* entail the anomaly, (*3*) unpacking in orthodox HD fashion this new premise set (containing the new hypothesis) into *other* as yet unformulated observational consequences: this is a further indirect test of the new anomaly explainer.

One of the great misunderstandings within the history of 19th century astronomy arose from this failure to distinguish arguing of the RD type from that of the HD type. My example is concerned with an exchange of letters between John Couch Adams and Professor George Airy, the distinguished Astronomer Royal.

Without engaging the vexed question of assigning ultimate priority, there can be little doubt that Adams' calculations in 1845 were sufficient for detecting the then-unknown planet which was perturbing Uranus. Adams' work was unknown to Leverrier when he took up this problem. But it is significant that both these astronomers, independently, concerned themselves with the Inverse Problem of Perturbations. Both of them recognized that they were departing from the usual perturbational problems of theoretical celestial mechanics.

As early as 1841 Adams formulated the problem of Uranus' orbit as follows: Given the anomalous motions of Uranus, from assuming the existence of what kind of planet, having what elements, could Uranus' observed positions be reconciled with orthodox Newtonian theory? *From* the anomaly, in other words, Adams envisages a rational process proceeding through the laws of celestial mechanics to some additional existence hypothesis which, if confirmed, would "explain" the Uranus' observed positions—rendering them thereby non-anomalous. Adams explicitly distinguishes this formulation of his problem from quite another one, namely the *arbitrary* assumption of some planets' existence—some planet having properties conjured up *de novo*. From this hypothesis of such a planet (plus associated initial conditions) to reason one's way in accordance with unadjusted Newtonian theory to observation statements—this is not Adams' idea of his own procedure. For even if this arbitrary hypothesis does explain the observed positions, it remains a different undertaking. Again, from the point of view of logical form, no distinction can be drawn between these two procedures: The inverse problem of perturbations and the orthodox problem of perturbations are thus indistinguishable in strict logic. But Adams sharply distinguishes the two as being different in *kind*. And no contemporary astronomer would be satisfied with being told by a philosopher that only a psychological difference demarcates the inverse from the orthodox problem of perturbations.

In one of his haughty letters to Adams, the Astronomer Royal thanks him for his detailed calculations and for having deduced the consequences of his *hypothesis* of a trans-Uranic premise. This convinced Adams that Airy had not really understood his work. For Adams did not arbitrarily select some hypothesis out of the air and unpack it into observation statements (some of which "accidentally" fit the facts). He began rather with incontrovertible observational facts (however "anomalous" in terms of the accepted theory) and slowly reasoned his way from these *back* to an hypothesis *H* which, almost as soon as it was formulated was seen *not* to be arbitrary in that it easily generated the anomaly.

Leverrier also sharply distinguishes the inverse from the orthodox problem of perturbations and definitely identifies his undertaking as being of the former variety. (Cf. Hanson, "Leverrier: The Zenith and Nadir of Newtonian Mechanics," in *Isis,* Vol. 53, Part 3, No. 173, Sept. 1962, pp. 359–378.)

Now this is a moment in the history of 19th century science which, I submit, could be misunderstood by one who minimized the *conceptual* differences between the HD description of scientific discoveries and the RD descriptions. These are not all-or-nothing exclusive accounts. You cannot recognize anomalies without the HD unpacking of accepted hypotheses. And you can't get new hypotheses for future HD unpacking without an RD type hunt for new hypotheses. Some HD theorists, by focusing only on logical form, which move has the consequence of conflating the HD and RD accounts, take all significant scientific *reasoning* in fact to be of the HD variety. A rationale of quite a different kind is often in evidence in the head work leading to discoveries such as that of the positive electron, the neutrino, and Neptune. To set out the conceptual structure of all of these examples as if they were instances of the same thing—and this the proponents of the HD analysis sometimes certainly do—would be to afford but a very incomplete understanding of the place of reason in the world of scientific discovery.

Long before this moment the following counter-claim will have been formulated: The HD philosopher had never purported to *describe* the process of scientific thinking. Since his interests are fundamentally *logical,* his concern is only to distinguish—in an *ex post facto* logical manner—arguments within formal science from arguments within natural science. Since the distinction between statements which are, within a given language, certifiably true or false, and hypotheses which are at most *probably* true or false, is a *logical* distinction—and since the HD theorist is concerned *only* with this distinction—his is not a descriptive undertaking, but a logical one.

This is unobjectionable. But many HD philosophers have gone further. They have characterized the HD account not simply in *ex post facto* terms, but as somehow relevant to the way in which scientists *actually proceed,* and the way in which science *actually develops.* Insofar as this is done it is an incomplete account; two stages of a irreducible trinity of processes. Moreover, *whether or not* HD theorists are concerned with the distinction we have drawn here, whether or not my exegesis of their views is correct, there *is* such a distinction to be drawn. And insofar as HD philosophers have denied that such a distinction can be drawn on anything but psychological grounds, it has been my objective here to deny precisely that.

4

BENJAMIN LEE WHORF
(1897–1941)

*Science and Linguistics**

Whorf was a pioneer in the field of comparative linguistics. His thesis, derived from a study of many different types of language, is that there is an essential relationship between language and the way we think; that our language, in fact, is the shaper of even our so-called most private thoughts. Whorf makes two major points about science and linguistics. He claims, first, that all higher levels of thinking are language-dependent and, second, that the structure of the language used determines the way in which one understands his environment. People who speak different languages see the universe differently and make entirely different claims and evaluations of it. Whorf proposes what he calls a new principle of relativity: "All observers are not led by the same physical evidence to the same picture of the universe, unless their linguistic backgrounds are similar, or can in some way be calibrated." Some languages cannot be systematically standardized, and the sciences which necessarily would result within these diverse patterns of thought would also be non-calibratable.

* From *Technology Review* (April, 1940), pp. 229–231, and 247–248. Used by kind permission of the editor of *Technology Review*.

EVERY normal person in the world, past infancy in years, can and does talk. By virtue of that fact, every person—civilized or uncivilized—carries through life certain naïve but deeply rooted ideas about talking and its relation to thinking. Because of their firm connection with speech habits that have become unconscious and automatic, these notions tend to be rather intolerant of opposition. They are by no means entirely personal and haphazard; their basis is definitely systematic, so that we are justified in calling them a system of natural logic—a term that seems to me preferable to the term common sense, often used for the same thing.

According to natural logic, the fact that every person has talked fluently since infancy makes every man his own authority on the process by which he formulates and communicates. He has merely to consult a common substratum of logic or reason which he and everyone else are supposed to possess. Natural logic says that talking is merely an incidental process concerned strictly with communication, not with formulation of ideas. Talking, or the use of language, is supposed only to "express" what is essentially already formulated nonlinguistically. Formulation is an independent process, called thought or thinking, and is supposed to be largely indifferent to the nature of particular languages. Languages have grammars, which are assumed to be merely norms of conventional and social correctness, but the use of language is supposed to be guided not so much by them as by correct, rational, or intelligent THINKING.

Thought, in this view, does not depend on grammar but on laws of logic or reason which are supposed to be the same for all observers of the universe—to represent a rationale in the universe that can be "found" independently by all intelligent observers, whether they speak Chinese or Choctaw. In our own culture, the formulations of mathematics and of formal logic have acquired the reputation of dealing with this order of things: i.e., with the realm and laws of pure thought. Natural logic holds that different languages are essentially parallel methods for expressing this one-and-the-same rationale of thought and, hence, differ really in but minor ways which may seem important only because they are seen at close range. It holds that mathematics, symbolic logic, philosophy, and so on are systems contrasted with language which deal directly with this realm of thought, not that they are themselves specialized extensions of language. The attitude of natural logic is well shown in an old quip about a German grammarian who devoted his whole life to the study of the dative case. From the point of view of natural logic, the dative case and grammar in general are an extremely minor issue. A different attitude is said to have been held by the ancient Arabians: Two princes, so the story goes, quarreled over the honor of putting on the shoes of the most learned grammarian of the realm: whereupon their father, the caliph, is said to have remarked that it was the glory of his kingdom that great grammarians were honored even above kings.

The familiar saying that the exception proves the rule contains a good deal of wisdom, though from the standpoint of formal logic it became an absurdity as soon as "prove" no longer meant "put on trial." The old saw began to be profound psychology from the time it ceased to have standing in logic. What it might well suggest to us today is that, if a rule has absolutely no exceptions, it is not recognized as a rule or as anything else; it is then part of the background of experience of which we tend to remain unconscious. Never having experienced anything in contrast to it, we cannot isolate it and formulate it as a rule until we so enlarge our experience and expand our base of reference that we encounter an interruption of its regularity. The situation is somewhat analogous to that of not missing the water till the well runs dry, or not realizing that we need air till we are choking.

For instance, if a race of people had the physiological defect of being able to see only the color blue, they would hardly be able to formulate the rule that they saw only blue. The term blue would convey no meaning to them, their language would lack color terms, and their words denoting their various sensations of blue would answer to, and translate, our words "light, dark, white, black," and so on, not our word "blue." In order to formulate the rule of norm of seeing only blue, they would need exceptional moments in which they saw other colors. The phenomenon of gravitation forms a rule without exceptions; needless to say, the untutored person is utterly unaware of any law of gravitation, for it would never enter his head to conceive of a universe in which bodies behaved otherwise than they do at the earth's surface. Like the color blue with our hypothetical race, the law of gravitation is a part of the untutored individual's background, not something he isolates from that background. The law could not be formulated until bodies that always fell were seen in terms of a wider astronomical world in which bodies moved in orbits or went this way and that.

Similarly, whenever we turn our heads, the image of the scene passes across our retinas exactly as it would if the scene turned around us. But this effect is background, and we do not recognize it; we do not see a room turn around us but are conscious only of having turned our heads in a stationary room. If we observe critically while turning the head or eyes quickly, we shall see, no motion it is true, yet a blurring of the scene between two clear views. Normally we are quite unconscious of this continual blurring but seem to be looking about in an unblurred world. Whenever we walk past a tree or house, its image on the retina changes just as if the tree or house were turning on an axis; yet we do not see trees or houses turn as we travel about at ordinary speeds. Sometimes ill-fitting glasses will reveal queer movements in the scene as we look about, but normally we do not see the relative motion of the environment when we move; our psychic makeup is somehow adjusted to disregard whole realms of phenomena that are so all-pervasive as to be irrelevant to our daily lives and needs.

Fallacies of Natural Logic

Natural logic contains two fallacies: First, it does not see that the phenomena of a language are to its own speakers largely of a background character and so are outside the critical consciousness and control of the speaker who is expounding natural logic. Hence, when anyone, as a natural logician, is talking about reason, logic, and the laws of correct thinking, he is apt to be simply marching in step with purely grammatical facts that have somewhat of a background character in his own language or family of languages but are by no means universal in all languages and in no sense a common substratum of reason. Second, natural logic confuses agreement about subject matter, attained through use of language, with knowledge of the linguistic process by which agreement is attained: i.e., with the province of the despised (and to its notion superfluous) grammarian. Two fluent speakers, of English let us say, quickly reach a point of assent about the subject matter of their speech; they agree about what their language refers to. One of them, *A*, can give directions that will be carried out by the other, *B*, to *A*'s complete satisfaction. Because they thus understand each other so perfectly, *A* and *B*, as natural logicians, suppose they must of course know how it is all done. They think, e.g., that it is simply a matter of choosing words to express thoughts. If you ask *A* to explain how he got *B*'s agreement so readily, he will simply repeat to you, with more or less elaboration or abbreviation, what he said to *B*. He has no notion of the process involved. The amazingly complex system of linguistic patterns and classifications, which *A* and *B* must have in common before they can adjust to each other at all, is all background to *A* and *B*.

These background phenomena are the province of the grammarian—or of the linguist, to give him his more modern name as a scientist. The word linguist in common, and especially newspaper, parlance means something entirely different, namely, a person who can quickly attain agreement about subject matter with different people speaking a number of different languages. Such a person is better termed a polyglot or a multilingual. Scientific linguists have long understood that ability to speak a language fluently does not necessarily confer a linguistic knowledge of it, i.e., understanding of its background phenomena and its systematic processes and structure, any more than ability to play a good game of billiards confers or requires any knowledge of the laws of mechanics that operate upon the billiard table.

The situation here is not unlike that in any other field of science. All real scientists have their eyes primarily on background phenomena that cut very little ice, as such, in our daily lives; and yet their studies have a way of bringing out a close relation between these unsuspected realms of fact and such decidedly foreground activities as transporting goods, preparing food, treating the sick, or growing potatoes, which in time may become very much modified, simply because of pure scientific investigation in no way concerned with these brute matters themselves. Linguistics presents a quite similar case; the background phenomena with which it deals are involved in all our foreground activities of talking and of reaching agreement, in all reasoning and arguing of cases, in all law, arbitration, conciliation, contracts, treaties, public opinion, weighing of scientific theories, formulation of scientific results. Whenever agreement or assent is arrived at in human affairs, and whether or not mathematics or other specialized symbolisms are made part of the procedure, THIS AGREEMENT IS REACHED BY LINGUISTIC PROCESSES, OR ELSE IT IS NOT REACHED.

As we have seen, an overt knowledge of the linguistic processes by which agreement is attained is not necessary to reaching some sort of agreement, but it is certainly no bar thereto; the more complicated and difficult the matter, the more such knowledge is a distinct aid, till the point may be reached—I suspect the modern world has about arrived at it—when the knowledge becomes not only an aid but a necessity. The situation may be likened to that of navigation. Every boat that sails is in the lap of planetary forces; yet a boy can pilot his small craft around a harbor without benefit of geography, astronomy, mathematics, or international politics. To the captain of an ocean liner, however, some knowledge of all these subjects is essential.

The Principle of Linguistic Relativity

When linguists became able to examine critically and scientifically a large number of languages of widely different patterns, their base of reference was expanded; they experienced an interruption of phenomena hitherto held universal, and a whole new order of significances came into their ken. It was found that the background linguistic system (in other words, the grammar) of each language is not merely a reproducing instrument for voicing ideas but rather is itself the shaper of ideas, the program and guide for the individual's mental activity, for his analysis of impressions, for his synthesis of his mental stock in trade. Formulation of ideas is not an independent process, strictly rational in the old sense, but is part of a particular grammar, and differs, from slightly to greatly, between different grammars. We dissect along lines laid down by our native languages. The categories and types that we isolate from the world of phenomena we do not find there because they stare every observer in the face; on the contrary, the world is presented in a kaleidoscopic flux of impressions which has to be organized by our minds—and this means largely by the linguistic systems in our minds. We cut nature up, organize it into concepts, and ascribe significances as we do, largely because we are parties to an agreement to organize it in this way—an agreement that holds throughout our speech community and is codified in the patterns of our language. The agreement is, of course, an implicit and unstated one, BUT ITS TERMS ARE ABSOLUTELY OBLIGATORY; we cannot talk at all except by subscribing to the organization and classification of data which the agreement decrees.

This fact is very significant for modern science, for it means that no individual is free to describe nature with absolute impartiality but is constrained to certain modes of interpretation even while he thinks himself most free. The person most nearly free in such respects would be a linguist familiar with very many widely different linguistic systems. As yet no linguist is in any such position. We are thus introduced to a new principle of relativity, which holds that all observers are not led by the same physical evidence to the same picture of the universe, unless their linguistic backgrounds are similar, or can in some way be calibrated.

This rather startling conclusion is not so apparent if we compare only our modern European languages, with perhaps Latin and Greek thrown in for good measure. Among these tongues there is a unanimity of major patterns which at first seems to bear out natural logic. But this unanimity exists only because these tongues are all Indo-European dialects cut to the same basic plan, being historically transmitted from what was long ago one speech community; because the modern dialects have long shared in building up a common culture; and because much of this culture, on the more intellectual side, is derived from the linguistic backgrounds of Latin and Greek. Thus this group of languages satisfies the special case of the clause beginning "unless" in the statement of the linguistic relativity principle at the end of the preceding paragraph. From this condition follows the unanimity of description of the world in the community of modern scientists. But it must be emphasized that "all modern Indo-European-speaking observers" is not the same thing as "all observers." That modern Chinese or Turkish scientists describe the world in the same terms as Western scientists means, of course, only that they have taken over bodily the entire

Western system of rationalizations, not that they have corroborated that system from their native posts of observation.

When Semitic, Chinese, Tibetan, or African languages are contrasted with our own, the divergence in analysis of the world becomes more apparent; and, when we bring in the native languages of the Americas, where speech communities for many millenniums have gone their ways independently of each other and of the Old World, the fact that languages dissect nature in many different ways becomes patent. The relativity of all conceptual systems, ours included, and their dependence upon language stand revealed. That American Indians speaking only their native tongues are never called upon to act as scientific observers is in no wise to the point. To exclude the evidence which their languages offer as to what the human mind can do is like expecting botanists to study nothing but food plants and hothouse roses and then tell us what the plant world is like!

Let us consider a few examples. In English we divide most of our words into two classes, which have different grammatical and logical properties. Class 1 we call nouns, e.g., "house, man;" class 2, verbs, e.g., "hit, run." Many words of one class can act secondarily as of the other class, e.g., "a hit, a run," or "to man (the boat)," but, on the primary level, the division between the classes is absolute. Our language thus gives us a bipolar division of nature. But nature herself is not thus polarized. If it be said that "strike, turn, run," are verbs because they denote temporary or short-lasting events, i.e., actions, why then is "fist" a noun? It also is a temporary event. Why are "lightning, spark, wave, eddy, pulsation, flame, storm, phase, cycle, spasm, noise, emotion" nouns? They are temporary events. If "man" and "house" are nouns because they are long-lasting and stable events, i.e., things, what then are "keep, adhere, extend, project, continue, persist, grow, dwell," and so on doing among the verbs? If it be objected that "possess, adhere" are verbs because they are stable relationships rather than stable percepts, why then should "equilibrium, pressure, current, peace, group, nation, society, tribe, sister," or any kinship term be among the nouns? It will be found that an "event" to us means "what our language classes as a verb" or something analogized therefrom. And it will be found that it is not possible to define "event, thing, object, relationship," and so on, from nature, but that to define them always involves a circuitous return to the grammatical categories of the definer's language.

The Example of the Hopi Language

In the Hopi language, "lightning, wave, flame, meteor, puff of smoke, pulsation" are verbs—events of necessarily brief duration cannot be anything but verbs. "Cloud" and "storm" are at about the lower limit or duration for nouns. Hopi, you see, actually has a classification of events (or linguistic isolates) by duration type, something strange to our modes of thought. On the other hand, in Nootka, a language of Vancouver Island, all words seem to us to be verbs, but really there are no classes 1 and 2; we have, as it were, a monistic view of nature that gives us only one class of word for all kinds of events. "A house occurs" or "it houses" is the way of saying "house," exactly like "a flame occurs" or "it burns." These terms seem to us like verbs because they are inflected for durational and temporal nuances, so that the suffixes of the word for house event make it mean long-lasting house, temporary house, future house, house that used to be, what started out to be a house, and so on.

Hopi has one noun that covers every thing or being that flies, with the exception of birds, which class is denoted by another noun. The former noun may be said to denote the class (*FC–B*)—flying class minus bird. The Hopi actually call insect, airplane, and aviator all by the same word, and feel no difficulty about it. The situation, of course, decides any possible confusion among very disparate members of a broad linguistic class, such as this class (*FC–B*). This class seems to us too large and inclusive, but so would our class "snow" to an Eskimo. We have the same word for falling snow, snow on the ground, snow packed hard like ice, slushy snow, wind-driven flying snow—whatever the situation may be. To an Eskimo, this all-inclusive word would be almost unthinkable; he would say that falling snow, slushy snow, and so on, are sensuously and operationally different, different things to contend with; he uses different words for them and for other kinds of snow. The Aztecs go even farther than we in the opposite direction, with "cold," "ice," and "snow" all represented by the same basic word with different terminations; "ice" is the noun form; "cold," the adjectival form; and for "snow," "ice mist."

What surprises most is to find that various grand generalizations of the Western world, such as time, velocity, and matter, are not essential to the construction of a consistent picture of the universe. The psychic experiences that we class under these headings are, of course, not destroyed; rather, categories derived from other kinds of experiences take over the rulership of the cosmology and seem to function just as well. Hopi may be called a timeless language. It recognizes psychological time, which is much like Bergson's "duration," but this "time" is quite unlike the mathematical time, *T*, used by our physicists. Among the peculiar properties of Hopi time are that it varies with each observer, does not permit of simultaneity, and has zero dimensions; i.e., it cannot be given a number greater than one. The Hopi do not say, "I stayed five days," but "I left on the fifth day." A word referring to this kind of time, like the word day, can have no plural. The puzzle picture [shown here] will give mental exercise to anyone who would like to figure out how the Hopi verb gets along without tenses. Actually, the only practical use of our tenses, in one-verb sentences, is to distinguish among five typical situations, which are symbolized in the picture. The timeless Hopi verb does not distinguish between the present, past, and future of the event itself but must always indicate what type of validity the SPEAKER intends the statement to have: (a) report of an event (situations 1, 2, 3 in the picture); (b) expectation of an event (situation 4); (c) generalization or law about events (situation 5). Situation 1, where the speaker and listener are in contact with the same objective field, is divided by our language into the two conditions, 1*a* and 1*b*, which it calls present and past, respectively.

This division is unnecessary for a language which assures one that the statement is a report.

Hopi grammar, by means of its forms called aspects and modes, also makes it easy to distinguish among momentary, continued, and repeated occurrences, and to indicate the actual sequence of reported events. Thus the universe can be described without recourse to a concept of dimensional time. How would a physics constructed along these lines work, with no *T* (time) in its equations? Perfectly, as far as I

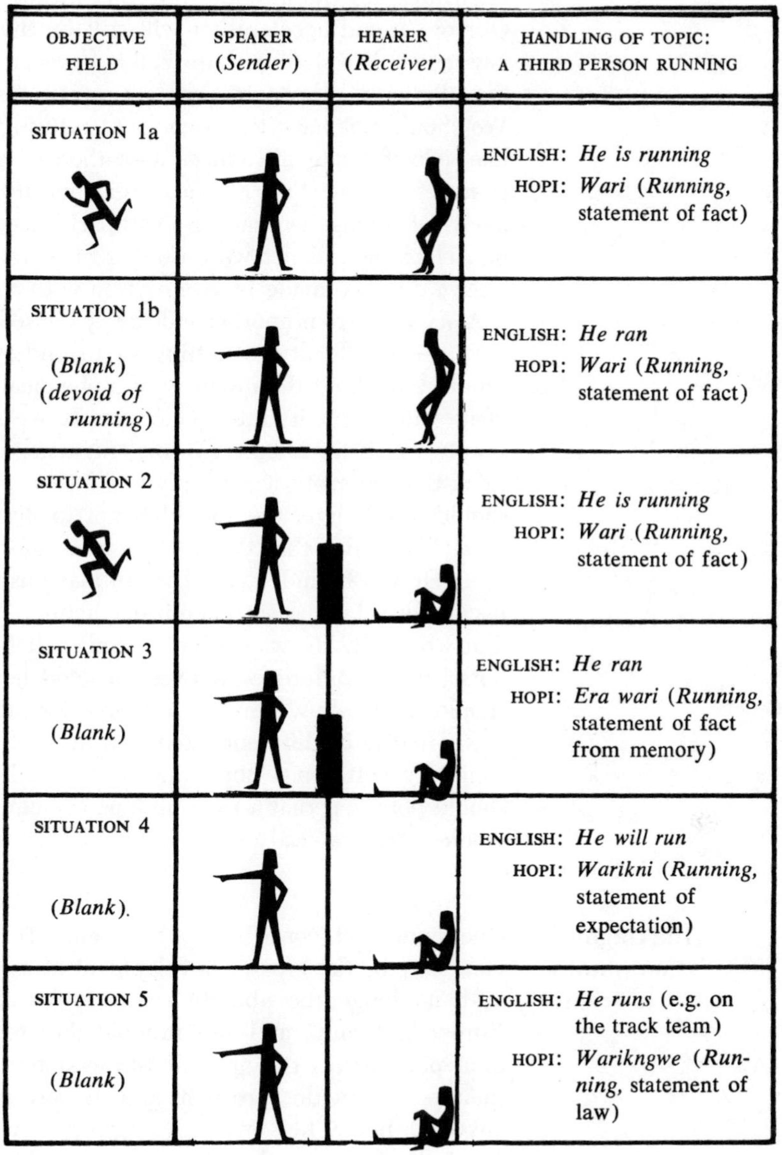
OBJECTIVE FIELD
SPEAKER (*Sender*)
HEARER (*Receiver*)
HANDLING OF TOPIC: A THIRD PERSON RUNNING
SITUATION 1a
ENGLISH: *He is running*
HOPI: *Wari* (*Running,* statement of fact)
SITUATION 1b
(*Blank*) (*devoid of running*)
ENGLISH: *He ran*
HOPI: *Wari* (*Running,* statement of fact)
SITUATION 2
ENGLISH: *He is running*
HOPI: *Wari* (*Running,* statement of fact)
SITUATION 3
(*Blank*)
ENGLISH: *He ran*
HOPI: *Era wari* (*Running,* statement of fact from memory)
SITUATION 4
(*Blank*).
ENGLISH: *He will run*
HOPI: *Warikni* (*Running,* statement of expectation)
SITUATION 5
(*Blank*)
ENGLISH: *He runs* (e.g. on the track team)
HOPI: *Warikngwe* (*Running,* statement of law)

Contrast between a "temporal" language (English) and a "timeless" language (Hopi). What are to English differences of time are to Hopi differences in the kind of validity.

can see, though of course it would require different ideology and perhaps different mathematics. Of course *V* (velocity) would have to go too. The Hopi language has no word really equivalent to our "speed" or "rapid." What translates these terms is usually a word meaning intense or very, accompanying any verb of motion. Here is a clue to the nature of our new physics. We may have to introduce a new term *I*, intensity. Every thing and event will have an *I*, whether we regard the thing or event as moving or as just enduring or being. Perhaps the *I* of an electric charge will turn out to be its voltage, or potential. We shall use clocks to measure some intensities, or, rather, some RELATIVE intensities, for the absolute intensity of anything will be meaningless. Our old friend acceleration will still be there but doubtless under a new name. We shall perhaps call it *V*, meaning not velocity but variation. Perhaps all growths and accumulations will be regarded as *V*'s. We should not have the concept of rate in the temporal sense, since, like velocity, rate introduces a mathematical and linguistic time. Of course we know that all measurements are ratios, but the measurements of intensities made by comparison with the standard intensity of a clock or a planet we do not treat as ratios, any more than we so treat a distance made by comparison with a yardstick.

A scientist from another culture that used time and velocity would have great difficulty in getting us to understand these concepts. We should talk about the intensity of a chemical reaction; he would speak of its velocity or its rate, which words we should at first think were simply words for intensity in his language. Likewise, he at first would think that intensity was simply our own word for velocity. At first we should agree, later we should begin to disagree, and it might dawn upon both sides that different systems of rationalization were being used. He would find it very hard to make us understand what he really meant by velocity of a chemical reaction. We should have no words that would fit. He would try to explain it by likening it to a running horse, to the difference between a good horse and a lazy horse. We should try to show him, with a superior laugh, that his analogy also was a matter of different intensities, aside from which there was little similarity between a horse and a chemical reaction in a beaker. We should point out that a running horse is moving relative to the ground, whereas the material in the beaker is at rest.

The Linguistic Contribution to Science

One significant contribution to science from the linguistic point of view may be the greater development of our sense of perspective. We shall no longer be able to see a few recent dialects of the Indo-European family, and the rationalizing techniques elaborated from their patterns, as the apex of the evolution of the human mind, nor their present wide spread as due to any survival from fitness or to anything but a few events of history—events that could be called fortunate only from the parochial point of view of the favored parties. They, and our own thought processes with them, can no longer be envisioned as spanning the gamut of reason and knowledge but only as one constellation in a galactic expanse. A fair realization of the incredible degree of diversity of linguistic system that ranges over the globe leaves one with an inescapable feeling that the human spirit is inconceivably old; that the few thousand years of history covered by our written records are no more than the thickness of a pencil mark on the scale that measures our past experience on this planet; that the events of these recent millenniums spell nothing in any evolutionary wise, that the race has taken no sudden spurt, achieved no commanding synthesis during recent millenniums, but has only played a little with a few of the linguistic formulations and views of nature bequeathed from an inexpressibly longer past. Yet neither this feeling nor the sense of precarious dependence of all we know upon linguistic tools which themselves are largely unknown need be discouraging to science but should, rather, foster that humility which accompanies the true scientific spirit, and thus forbid that arrogance of the mind which hinders real scientific curiosity and detachment.

5

WILLIAM JAMES

(1842–1910)

*Pragmatism's Conception of Truth**

"Pragmatism is a method only," is James's statement. It equates truth with the "cash-value" of an idea, the practical results of taking it as true. Truth is something that happens to ideas, James argues, not a property of an idea. Ask, "What concrete difference will its being true make in anyone's actual life?" and you will see how truth is related to practical behavior. Ideas become true; events make them true. What about verifying the truth of ideas? In the general tradition of philosophy, an idea was thought to be verified when the idea and what it was said to represent in the physical world corresponded. For James, verification of our ideas is a part of a process of living: "The possession of true thoughts means . . . the possession of invaluable instruments of action." Successful experience is the verification of our ideas. Truths are relative to the personal interests of individuals.

* William James, *Pragmatism* (New York: Longmans, Green, 1907), pp. 197–223.

TRUTH, as any dictionary will tell you, is a property of certain of our ideas. It means their "agreement," as falsity means their "disagreement," with "reality." Pragmatists and intellectualists both accept this definition as a matter of course. They begin to quarrel only after the question is raised as to what may precisely be meant by the term "agreement," and what by the term "reality," when reality is taken as something for our ideas to agree with.

True Ideas as Copies of Reality

In answering these questions the pragmatists are more analytic and painstaking, the intellectualists more offhand and irreflective. The popular notion is that a true idea must copy its reality. Like other popular views, this one follows the analogy of the most usual experience. Our true ideas of sensible things do indeed copy them. Shut your eyes and think of yonder clock on the wall, and you get just such a true picture or copy of its dial. But your idea of its "works" (unless you are a clockmaker) is much less of a copy, yet it passes muster, for it in no way clashes with the reality. Even though it should shrink to the mere word "works," that word still serves you truly; and when you speak of the "time-keeping function" of the clock, or of its spring's "elasticity," it is hard to see exactly what your ideas can copy.

You perceive that there is a problem here. Where our ideas cannot copy definitely their object, what does agreement with that object mean? Some idealists seem to say that they are true whenever they are what God means that we ought to think about that subject. Others hold the copy-view all through, and speak as if our ideas possessed truth just in proportion as they approach to being copies of the Absolute's eternal way of thinking.

These views, you see, invite pragmatistic discussion. But the great assumption of the intellectualists is that truth means essentially an inert static relation. When you've got your true idea of anything, there's an end of the matter. You're in possession; you *know;* you have fulfilled your thinking destiny. You are where you ought to be mentally; you have obeyed your categorical imperative; and nothing more need follow on that climax of your rational destiny. Epistemologically you are in stable equilibrium.

The Pragmatic View

Pragmatism, on the other hand, asks its usual question. "Grant an idea or belief to be true," it says, "what concrete difference will its being true make in any one's actual life? How will the truth be realized? What experiences will be different from those which would obtain if the belief were false? What, in short, is the truth's cash-value in experiential terms?"

The moment pragmatism asks this question, it sees the answer: *True ideas are those that we can assimilate, validate, corroborate and verify. False ideas are those that we cannot.* That is the practical difference it makes to us to have true ideas; that, therefore, is the meaning of truth, for it is all that truth is known-as.

This thesis is what I have to defend. The truth of an idea is not a stagnant property inherent in it. Truth *happens* to an idea. It *becomes* true, is *made* true by events. Its verity *is* in fact an event, a process: the process namely of its verifying itself, its veri-*fication.* Its validity is the process of its valid-*ation.*

But what do the words verification and validation themselves pragmatically mean? They again signify certain practical consequences of the verified and validated idea. It is hard to find any one phrase that characterizes these consequences better than the ordinary agreement-formula—just such consequences being what we have in mind whenever we say that our ideas "agree" with reality. They lead us, namely, through the acts and other ideas which they instigate, into or up to, or towards, other parts of experience with which we feel all the while—such feeling being among our potentialities—that the original ideas remain in agreement. The connexions and transitions come to us from point to point as being progressive, harmonious, satisfactory. This function of agreeable leading is what we mean by an idea's verification. Such an account is vague and it sounds at first quite trivial, but it has results which it will take the rest of my hour to explain.

Let me begin by reminding you of the fact that the possession of true thoughts means everywhere the possession of invaluable instruments of action; and that our duty to gain truth, so far from being a blank command from out of the blue, or a "stunt" self-imposed by our intellect, can account for itself by excellent practical reasons.

Truth as a Means to Other Satisfactions

The importance to human life of having true beliefs about matters of fact is a thing too notorious. We live in a world of realities that can be infinitely useful or infinitely harmful. Ideas that tell us which of them to expect count as the true ideas in all this primary sphere of verification, and the pursuit of such ideas is a primary human duty. The possession of truth, so far from being here an end in itself, is only a preliminary means towards other vital satisfactions. If I am lost in the woods and starved, and find what looks like a cow-path, it is of the utmost importance that I should think of a human habitation at the end of it, for if I do so and follow it, I save myself. The true thought is useful here because the house which is its object is useful. The practical value of true ideas is thus primarily derived from the practical importance of their objects to us. Their objects are, indeed, not important at all times. I may on another occasion have no use for the house; and then my idea of it, however verifiable, will be practically irrelevant, and had better remain latent. Yet since almost any object may some day become temporarily important, the advantage of having a general stock of *extra* truths, of ideas that shall be true of merely possible situations, is obvious. We store such extra truths away in our memories, and with the overflow we fill our books of reference. Whenever such an extra truth becomes practically relevant to one of our emergencies, it passes from cold-storage to do work in the world and our belief in its grows active. You can say of it then either that "it is useful because it is true" or that "it is true because it is useful." Both these phrases mean exactly the same thing, namely that here is an idea that gets fulfilled and can be verified. True is the name for whatever idea starts the verification-process, useful is the name for its completed function in experience. True ideas would never have been singled out as such, would never have acquired a class-name, least of all a name suggesting value, unless they had been useful from the outset in this way.

From this simple cue pragmatism gets her general notion of truth as something essentially bound up with the way in which one moment in our experience may lead us towards other moments which it will be worth while to have been led to. Primarily, and on the common-sense level, the truth of a state of mind means this function of *a leading that is worth while*. When a moment in our experience, of any kind whatever, inspires us with a thought that is true, that means that sooner or later we dip by that thought's guidance into the particulars of experience again and make advantageous connexion with them. This is a vague enough statement, but I beg you to retain it, for it is essential.

Our experience meanwhile is all shot through with regularities. One bit of it can warn us to get ready for another bit, can "intend" or be "significant of" that remoter object. The object's advent is the significance's verification. Truth, in these cases, meaning nothing but eventual verification, is manifestly incompatible with waywardness on our part. Woe to him whose beliefs play fast and loose with the order which realities follow in his experience; they will lead him nowhere or else make false connexions.

By "realities" or "objects" here, we mean either things of common sense, sensibly present, or else common-sense relations, such as dates, places, distances, kinds, activities. Following our mental image of a house along the cow-path, we actually come to see the house; we get the image's full verification. *Such simply and fully verified leadings are certainly the originals and prototypes of the truth-process.* Experience offers indeed other forms of truth-process, but they are all conceivable as being primary verifications arrested, multiplied or substituted one for another.

Take, for instance, yonder object on the wall. You and I consider it to be a "clock," although no one of us has seen the hidden works that make it one. We let our notion pass for true without attempting to verify. If truths mean verification-process essentially, ought we then to call such unverified truths as this abortive? No, for they form the overwhelmingly large number of the truths we live by. Indirect as well as direct verifications pass muster. Where circumstantial evidence is sufficient, we can go without eye-witnessing. Just as we here assume Japan to exist without ever having been there, because it *works* to do so, everything we know conspiring with the belief, and nothing interfering, so we assume that thing to be a clock. We *use* it as a clock, regulating the length of our lecture by it. The verification of the assumption here means its leading to no frustration or contradiction. Verifi*ability* of wheels and weights and pendulum is as good as verification. For one truth-process completed there are a million in our lives that function in this state of nascency. They turn us *towards* direct verification; lead us into the *surroundings* of the objects they envisage; and then, if everything runs on harmoniously, we are so sure that verification is possible that we omit it, and are usually justified by all that happens.

Truth lives, in fact, for the most part on a credit system. Our thoughts and beliefs "pass," so long as nothing challenges them, just as bank-notes pass so long as nobody refuses them. But this all points to direct face-to-face verifications somewhere, without which the fabric of truth collapses like a financial system with no cash-basis whatever. You accept my verification of one thing, I yours of another. We trade on each other's truth. But beliefs verified concretely by *somebody* are the posts of the whole superstructure.

Another great reason—beside economy of time—for waiving complete verification in the usual business of life is that all things exist in kinds and not singly. Our world is found once for all to have that peculiarity. So that when we have once directly verified our ideas about one specimen of a kind, we consider ourselves free to apply them to other specimens without verification. A mind that habitually discerns the kind of thing before it, and acts by the law of the kind immediately, without pausing to verify, will be a "true" mind in ninety-nine out of a hundred emergencies, proved so by its conduct fitting everything it meets, and getting no refutation.

Indirectly or only potentially verifying processes may thus be true as well as full verification-processes. They work as true processes would work, give us the same advantages, and claim our recognition for the same reasons. All this on the common-sense level of matters of fact, which we are alone considering.

Relations Among Purely Mental Ideas

But matters of fact are not only stock in trade. *Relations among purely mental ideas* form another sphere where true and false beliefs obtain, and here the beliefs are absolute, or unconditional. When they are true they bear the name either of definitions or of principles. It is either a principle or a definition that 1 and 1 make 2, that 2 and 1 make 3, and so on; that white differs less from gray than it does from black; that when the cause begins to act the effect also commences. Such propositions hold of all possible "ones," of all conceivable "whites" and "grays" and "causes." The objects here are mental objects. Their relations are perceptually obvious at a glance, and no sense-verification is necessary. Moreover, once true, always true, of those same mental objects. Truth here has an "eternal" character. If you can find a concrete thing anywhere that is "one" or "white" or "gray" or an "effect," then your principles will everlastingly apply to it. It is but a case of ascertaining the kind, and then applying the law of its kind to the particular object. You are sure to get truth if you can but name the kind rightly, for your mental relations hold good of everything of that kind without exception. If you then, nevertheless, failed to get truth concretely, you would say that you had classed your real objects wrongly.

In this realm of mental relations, truth again is an affair of leading. We relate one abstract idea with another, framing in the end great systems of logical and mathematical truth, under the respective terms of which the sensible facts of experience eventually arrange themselves, so that our eternal truths hold good of realities also. This marriage of fact and theory is endlessly fertile. What we say is here already true in advance of special verification, *if we have subsumed our objects rightly*. Our ready-made ideal framework for all sorts of possible objects follows from the very structure of our thinking. We can no more play fast and loose with these abstract relations than we can do so with our sense-experiences. They coerce us; we must treat them consistently, whether or not we like the results. The rules of addition apply to our debts as rigorously as to our assets. The hundredth decimal of π, the ratio of the circumference to its diameter, is predetermined ideally now, though no one may have computed it. If we should ever need the figure in our dealings with an actual circle we should need to have it given rightly, calculated by the usual rules; for it is the kind of truth that those rules elsewhere calculate.

Between the coercions of the sensible order and those of the ideal order, our mind is thus wedged tightly. Our ideas must agree with realities, be such realities concrete or abstract, be they facts or be they principles, under penalty of endless inconsistency and frustration.

So far, intellectualists can raise no protest. They can only say that we have barely touched the skin of the matter.

Truth and Verification

Realities mean, then, either concrete facts, or abstract kinds of thing and relations perceived intuitively between them. They furthermore and thirdly mean, as things that new ideas of ours must no less take account of, the whole body of other truths already in our possession. But what now does "agreement" with such three-fold realities mean?—to use again the definition that is current.

Here it is that pragmatism and intellectualism begin to part company. Primarily, no doubt, to agree means to copy, but we saw that the mere word "clock" would do instead of a mental picture of its works, and that of many realities our ideas can only be symbols and not copies. "Past time," "power," "spontaneity"—how can our mind copy such realities?

To "agree" in the widest sense with a reality *can only mean to be guided either straight up to it or into its surroundings, or to be put into such working touch with it as to handle either it or something connected with it better than if we disagreed.* Better either intellectually or practically! And often agreement will only mean the negative fact and nothing contradictory from the quarter of that reality comes to interfere with the way in which our ideas guide us elsewhere. To copy a reality is, indeed, one very important way of agreeing with it, but it is far from being essential. The essential thing is the process of being guided. Any idea that helps us to *deal,* whether practically or intellectually, with either the reality or its belongings, that doesn't entangle our progress in frustrations, that *fits,* in fact, and adapts our life to the reality's whole setting, will agree sufficiently to meet the requirement. It will hold true of that reality.

Thus, *names* are just as "true" or "false" as definite mental pictures are. They set up similar verification-processes, and lead to fully equivalent practical results.

All human thinking gets discursified; we exchange ideas; we lend and borrow verifications, get them from one another by means of social intercourse. All truth thus gets verbally built out, stored up, and made available for every one. Hence, we must *talk* consistently just as we must *think* consistently: for both in talk and thought we deal with kinds. Names are arbitrary, but once understood they must be kept to. We mustn't now call Abel "Cain" or Cain "Abel." If we do, we ungear ourselves from the whole book of Genesis, and from all its connexions with the universe of speech and fact down to the present time. We throw ourselves out of whatever truth that entire system of speech and fact may embody.

The overwhelming majority of our true ideas admit of no direct or fact-to-face verification—those of past history, for example, as of Cain and Abel. The stream of time can be remounted only verbally, or verified indirectly by the present prolongations or effects of what the past harbored. Yet if they agree with these verbalities and effects, we can know that our ideas of the past are true. *As true as past time itself was,* so true was Julius Caesar, so true were antediluvian monsters all in their proper dates and settings. That past time itself was, is guaranteed by its coherence with everything that's present. True as the present *is,* the past *was* also.

Agreement thus turns out to be essentially an affair of leading—leading that is useful because it is into quarters that contain objects that are important. True ideas lead us into useful verbal and conceptual quarters as well as directly up to useful sensible termini. They lead to consistency, stability and flowing human intercourse. They lead away from eccentricity and isolation, from foiled and barren thinking. The untrammelled flowing of the leading-process, its general freedom from clash and contradiction, passes for its indirect verification; but all roads lead to Rome, and in the end and eventually, all true processes must lead to the face of directly verifying sensible experiences *somewhere,* which somebody's ideas have copied.

Such is the large loose way in which the pragmatist interprets the word agreement. He treats it altogether practically. He lets it cover any process of conduction from a present idea to a future terminus, provided only it run prosperously. It is only thus that "scientific" ideas, flying as they do beyond common sense, can be said to agree with their realities. It is, as I have already said, *as if* reality were made of ether, atoms or electrons, but we mustn't think so literally. The term "energy" doesn't even pretend to stand for anything "objective." It is only a way of measuring the surface of phenomena so as to string their changes on a simple formula.

Yet in the choice of these man-made formulas we cannot be capricious with impunity any more than we can be capricious on the common-sense practical level. We must find a theory that will *work;* and that means something extremely difficult; for our theory must mediate between all previous truths and certain new experiences. It must derange common sense and previous belief as little as possible, and it must lead to some sensible terminus or other that can be verified exactly. To "work" means both these things; and the squeeze is so tight that there is little loose play for any hypothesis. Our theories are wedged and controlled as nothing else is. Yet sometimes alternative theoretic formulas are equally compatible with all the truths we know, and then we choose between them for subjective reasons. We choose the kind of theory to which we are already partial; we follow "elegance" or "economy." Clerk-Maxwell somewhere says it would be "poor scientific taste" to choose the more complicated of two equally well-evidenced conceptions; and you will all agree with him. Truth in science is what gives us the maximum possible sum of satisfactions, taste included, but consistency both with previous truth and with novel fact is always the most imperious claimant.

I have led you through a very sandy desert. But now, if I may be allowed so vulgar an expression, we begin to taste the milk in the cocoanut. Our rationalist critics here discharge their batteries upon us, and to reply to them will take us out from all this dryness into full sight of a momentous philosophical alternative.

Our account of truth is an account of truths in the plural, of processes of leading, realized *in rebus,* and having only this quality in common, that they *pay.* They pay by guiding us into or towards some part of a system that dips at numerous points into sense-percepts, which we may copy mentally or not, but with which at any rate we are now in the kind of commerce vaguely designated as verification. Truth for us is simply a collective name for verification-processes, just as health, wealth, strength, etc., are names for other processes connected with life, and also pursued because it pays to pursue them. Truth is *made,* just as health, wealth and strength are made, in the course of experience. . . .

The Rationalist and the Pragmatist

The most fateful point of difference between being a rationalist and being a pragmatist is now fully in sight. Experience is in mutation, and our psychological ascertainments of truth are in mutation—so much rationalism will allow; but never that either reality itself or truth itself is mutable. Reality stands complete and ready-made from all eternity, rationalism insists, and the agreement of our ideas with it is that unique unanalyzable virtue in them of which she has already told us. As that intrinsic excellence, their truth has nothing to do with our experiences. It adds nothing to the content of experience. It makes no difference to reality itself; it is supervenient, inert, static, a reflexion merely. It doesn't *exist,* it *holds* or *obtains,* it belongs to another dimension from that of either facts or fact-relations, belongs, in short, to the epistemological dimension—and with that big word rationalism closes the discussion.

Thus, just as pragmatism faces forward to the future, so does rationalism here again face backward to a past eternity. True to her inveterate habit, rationalism reverts to "principles," and thinks that when an abstraction once is named, we own an oracular solution.

The tremendous pregnancy in the way of consequences for life of this radical difference of outlook will only become apparent in my later lectures. I wish meanwhile to close this lecture by showing that rationalism's sublimity does not save it from inanity.

When, namely, you ask rationalists, instead of accusing pragmatism of desecrating the notion of truth, to define it themselves by saying exactly what *they* understand by it, the only positive attempts I can think of are these two:

1. "Truth is the system of propositions which have an unconditional claim to be recognized as valid."*

2. "Truth is a name for all those judgments which we find ourselves under obligation to make by a kind of imperative duty."†

The first thing that strikes one in such definitions is their unutterable triviality. They are absolutely true, of course, but absolutely insignifi-

* A. E. Taylor, *Philosophical Review,* vol. xiv, p. 288.

† H. Rickert, *Der Gegenstand der Erkenntnis,* chapter on "Die Urteilsnotwendigkeit."

cant until you handle them pragmatically. What do you mean by "claim" here, and what do you mean by "duty"? As summary names for the concrete reasons why thinking in true ways is overwhelmingly expedient and good for mortal men, it is all right to talk of claims on reality's part to be agreed with, and of obligations on our part to agree. We feel both the claims and the obligations, and we feel them for just those reasons.

But the rationalists who talk of claim and obligation *expressly say that they have nothing to do with our practical interests or personal reasons.* Our reasons for agreeing are psychological facts, they say, relative to each thinker, and to the accidents of his life. They are his evidence merely, they are no part of the life of truth itself. That life transacts itself in a purely logical or epistemological, as distinguished from a psychological, dimension, and its claims antedate and exceed all personal motivations whatsoever. Though neither man nor God should ever ascertain truth, the word would still have to be defined as that which *ought* to be ascertained and recognized.

There never was a more exquisite example of an idea abstracted from the concretes of experience and then used to oppose and negate what it was abstracted from.

Philosophy and common life abound in similar instances. The "sentimentalist fallacy" is to shed tears over abstract justice and generosity, beauty, etc., and never to know these qualities when you meet them in the street, because the circumstances make them vulgar. Thus I read in the privately printed biography of an eminently rationalistic mind: "It was strange that with such admiration for beauty in the abstract, my brother had no enthusiasm for fine architecture, for beautiful painting, or for flowers." And in almost the last philosophic work I have read, I find such passages as the following: "Justice is ideal, solely ideal. Reason conceives that it ought to exist, but experience shows that it cannot. . . . Truth, which ought to be, cannot be. . . Reason is deformed by experience. As soon as reason enters experience it becomes contrary to reason."

The rationalist's fallacy here is exactly like the sentimentalist's. Both extract a quality from the muddy particulars of experience, and find it so pure when extracted that they contrast it with each and all its muddy instances as an opposite and higher nature. All the while it is *their* nature. It is the nature of truths to be validated, verified. It pays for our ideas to be validated. Our obligation to seek truth is part of our general obligation to do what pays. The payments true ideas bring are the sole why of our duty to follow them. Identical whys exist in the case of wealth and health.

Truth as Conditional

Truth makes no other kind of claim and imposes no other kind of ought than health and wealth do. All these claims are conditional; the concrete benefits we gain are what we mean by calling the pursuit a duty. In the case of truth, untrue beliefs works as perniciously in the long run as true beliefs work beneficially. Talking abstractly, the quality "true" may thus be said to grow absolutely precious and the quality "untrue" absolutely damnable: the one may be called good, the other bad, unconditionally. We ought to think the true, we ought to shun the false, imperatively.

But if we treat all this abstraction literally and oppose it to its mother soil in experience, see what a preposterous position we work ourselves into.

We cannot then take a step forward in our actual thinking. When shall I acknowledge this truth and when that? Shall the acknowledgment be loud?—or silent? If sometimes loud, sometimes silent, which *now?* When may a truth go into cold-storage in the encyclopedia? and when shall it come out for battle? Must I constantly be repeating the truth "twice two are four" because of its eternal claim on recognition? or is it sometimes irrelevant? . . .

It is quite evident that our obligation to acknowledge truth, so far from being unconditional, is tremendously conditioned. Truth with a big T, and in the singular, claims abstractly to be recognized, of course; but concrete truths in the plural need be recognized only when their recognition is expedient. A truth must always be preferred to a falsehood when both relate to the situation; but when neither does, truth is as little of a duty as falsehood. . . .

With this admission that there are conditions that limit the application of the abstract imperative, *the pragmatistic treatment of truth sweeps back upon us in its fulness.* Our duty to agree with reality is seen to be grounded in a perfect jungle of concrete expediencies. . . .

Our critics certainly need more imagination of realities. I have honestly tried to stretch my own imagination and to read the best possible meaning into the rationalist conception, but I have to confess that it still completely baffles me. The notion of a reality calling on us to "agree" with it, and that for no reasons, but simply because its claim is "unconditional" or "transcendent," is one that I can make neither head nor tail of. I try to imagine myself as the sole reality in the world, and then to imagine what more I would "claim" if I were allowed to. If you suggest the possibility of my claiming that a mind should come into being from out of the void inane and stand and *copy* me, I can indeed imagine what the copying might mean, but I can conjure up no motive. What good it would do me to be copied, or what good it would do that mind to copy me, if further consequences are expressly and in principle ruled out as motives for the claim (as they are by our rationalist authorities) I cannot fathom. . . . Copying is one genuine mode of knowing (which for some strange reason our contemporary transcendentalists seem to be tumbling over each other to repudiate); but when we get beyond copying, and fall back on unnamed forms of agreeing that are expressly denied to be either copyings or leadings or fittings, or any other processes pragmatically definable, the *what* of the "agreement" claimed becomes as unintelligible as the why of it. Neither content nor motive can be imagined for it. It is an absolutely meaningless abstraction.

Surely in this field of truth it is the pragmatists and not the rationalists who are the more genuine defenders of the universe's rationality.

6

P. W. BRIDGMAN

(1882–1961)

*Operationalism and the Relative Character of Knowledge**

Bridgman received the Nobel Prize for physics in 1946 for research on phenomena under high pressure. He also was a major figure in the philosophy of science in this century. Bridgman is the formulator of the operational point of view in science. His major interest is in the problems of defining physical concepts so that they will be clear and exact. He works from his knowledge of the actual methods of physics, especially relativity theory and thermodynamics, and concludes that the only meaning of a physical concept lies in defining the operations of measurement performed by the concept on some physical object. This view goes counter to the traditional idea that concepts are defined in terms of the properties of the object they are said to involve. Bridgman tells us, "We mean by any concept nothing more than a set of operations." If concepts are operationally defined, then the scientist is not committed to a theory of nature as a whole, which might need to be revised in the future. Experience provides the sole verification for our use of concepts because they are solely defined in the language of experience, operations. All knowledge, for Bridgman, is relative to the operations used in definitions of the concepts.

* P. W. Bridgman, *The Logic of Modern Physics* (New York: Macmillan, 1927), pp. 1–32 with omission of section "Detailed Discussion of the Concept of Length." Reprinted with permission of The Macmillan Company.

WHATEVER may be one's opinion as to our permanent acceptance of the analytical details of Einstein's restricted and general theories of relativity, there can be no doubt that through these theories physics is permanently changed. It was a great shock to discover that classical concepts, accepted unquestioningly, were inadequate to meet the actual situation, and the shock of this discovery has resulted in a critical attitude toward our whole conceptual structure which must at least in part be permanent. Reflections on the situation after the event shows that it should not have needed the new experimental facts which led to relativity to convince us of the inadequacy of our previous concepts, but that a sufficiently shrewd analysis should have prepared us for at least the possibility of what Einstein did.

Looking now to the future, our ideas of what external nature is will always be subject to change as we gain new experimental knowledge, but there is a part of our attitude to nature which should not be subject to future change, namely that part which rests on the permanent basis of the character of our minds. It is precisely here, in an improved understanding of our mental relations to nature, that the permanent contribution of relativity is to be found. We should now make it our business to understand so thoroughly the character of our permanent mental relations to nature that another change in our attitude, such as that due to Einstein, shall be forever impossible. It was perhaps excusable that a revolution in mental attitude should occur once, because after all physics is a young science, and physicists have been very busy, but it would certainly be a reproach if such a revolution should ever prove necessary again.

New Kinds of Experience Always Possible

The first lesson of our recent experience with relativity is merely an intensification and emphasis of the lesson which all past experience has also taught, namely, that when experiment is pushed into new domains, we must be prepared for new facts, of an entirely different character from those of our former experience. This is taught not only by the discovery of those unsuspected properties of matter moving with high velocities, which inspired the theory of relativity, but also even more emphatically by the new facts in the quantum domain. To a certain extent of course, the recognition of all this does not involve a change of former attitude; the *fact* has always been for the physicist the one ultimate thing from which there is no appeal, and in the face of which the only possible attitude is a humility almost religious. The new feature in the present situation is an intensified conviction that in reality new orders of experience do exist, and that we may expect to meet them continually. We have already encountered new phenomena in going to high velocities, and in going to small scales of magnitude: we may similarly expect to find them, for example, in dealing with relations of cosmic magnitudes, or in dealing with the properties of matter of enormous densities, such as is supposed to exist in the stars.

Implied in this recognition of the possibility of new experience beyond our present range, is the recognition that no element of a physical situation, no matter how apparently irrelevant or trivial, may be dismissed as without effect on the final result until proved to be without effect by actual experiment.

The attitude of the physicist must therefore be one of pure empiricism. He recognizes no *a priori* principles which determine or limit the possibilities of new experience. Experience is determined only by experience. This practically means that we must give up the demand that all nature be embraced in any formula, either simple or complicated. It may perhaps turn out eventually that as a matter of fact nature can be embraced in a formula, but we must so organize our thinking as not to demand it as a necessity.

Einstein's Contribution in Changing Our Attitude Toward Concepts

Recognizing the essential unpredictability of experiment beyond our present range, the physicist, if he is to escape continually revising his attitude, must use in describing and correlating nature concepts of such a character that our present experience does not exact hostages of the future. Now here it seems to me is the greatest contribution of Einstein. Although he himself does not explicitly state or emphasize it, I believe that a study of what he has done will show that he has essentially modified our view of what the concepts useful in physics are and should be. Hitherto many of the concepts of physics have been defined in terms of their properties. An excellent example is afforded by Newton's concept of absolute time. The following quotation from the Scholium in Book I of the *Principia* is illuminating:

> I do not define Time, Space, Place or Motion, as being well known to all. Only I must observe that the vulgar conceive those quantities under no other notions but from the relation they bear to sensible objects. And thence arise certain prejudices, for the removing of which, it will be convenient to distinguish them into Absolute and Relative, True and Apparent, Mathematical and Common.
>
> (1) Absolute, True, and Mathematical Time, of itself, and from its own nature flows equably without regard to anything external, and by another name is called Duration.

Now there is no assurance whatever that there exists in nature anything with properties like those assumed in the definition, and physics, when reduced to concepts of this character, becomes as purely an abstract science and as far removed from reality as the abstract geometry of the mathematicians, built on postulates. It is a task for experiment to discover whether concepts so defined correspond to anything in nature, and we must always be prepared to find that the concepts correspond to nothing or only partially correspond. In particular, if we examine the definition of absolute time in the light of experiment, we find nothing in nature with such properties.

The new attitude toward a concept is entirely different. We may illustrate by considering the concept of length: what do we mean by the length of an object? We evidently know what we mean by length if we can tell what the length of any and every object is, and for the physicist nothing more is required. To find the length of an object, we have to perform certain physical operations. The concept of length is therefore fixed when the operations by which length is measured are fixed: that is, the concept of length involves as much as and nothing more than the set of operations by which length is determined. In general, we mean by any concept nothing more than a set of operations; *the concept is synonymous with the corresponding set of operations.* If the concept is physical, as of length, the operations are actual physical operations, namely, those by which length is measured; or if the concept is mental, as of mathematical continuity, the operations are mental operations, namely those by which we determine whether a given aggregate of magnitudes is continuous. It is not intended to imply that there is a hard and fast division between physical and mental concepts, or that one kind of concept does not always contain an element of the other; this classification of concept is not important for our future considerations.

We must demand that the set of operations equivalent to any concept be a unique set, for otherwise there are possibilities of ambiguity in practical applications which we cannot admit.

Applying this idea of "concept" to absolute time, we do not understand the meaning of absolute time unless we can tell how to determine the absolute time of any concrete event, i.e., unless we can measure absolute time. Now we merely have to examine any of the possible operations by which we measure time to see that all such operations are relative operations. Therefore the previous statement that absolute time does not exist is replaced by the statement that absolute time is meaningless. And in making this statement we are not saying something new about nature, but are merely bringing to light implications already contained in the physical operations used in measuring time.

It is evident that if we adopt this point of view toward concepts, namely that the proper definition of a concept is not in terms of its properties but in terms of actual operations, we need run no danger of having to revise our attitude toward nature. For if experience is always described in terms of experience, there must always be correspondence between experience and our description of it, and we need never be embarrassed, as we were in attempting to find in nature the prototype of Newton's absolute time. Furthermore, if we remember that the operations to which a physical concept are equivalent are actual physical operations, the concepts can be defined only in the range of actual experiment, and are undefined and meaningless in regions as yet untouched by experiment. It follows that strictly speaking we cannot make statements at all about regions as yet untouched, and that when we do make such statements, as we inevitably shall, we are making a conventionalized extrapolation, of the looseness of which we must be fully conscious, and the justification of which is in the experiment of the future.

There probably is no statement either in Einstein or other writers that the change described above in the use of "concept" has been self-consciously made, but that such is the case is proved, I believe, by an examination of the way concepts are now handled by Einstein and others. For of course the true meaning of a term is to be found by observing what a man does with it, not by what he says about it. We may show that this is the actual sense in which concept is coming to be used by examining in particular Einstein's treatment of simultaneity.

Before Einstein, the concept of simultaneity was defined in terms of properties. It was a property of two events, when described with respect to their relation in time, that one event was either before the other, or after it, or simultaneous with it. Simultaneity was a property of the two events alone and nothing else; either two events were simultaneous or they were not. The justification for using this term in this way was that it seemed to describe the behavior of actual things. But of course experience then was restricted to a narrow range. When the range of experience was broadened, as by going to high velocities, it was found that the concepts no longer applied, because there was no counterpart in experience for this absolute relation between two events. Einstein now subjected the concept of simultaneity to a critique, which consisted essentially in showing that the operations which enable two events to be described as simultaneous involve measurements on the two events made by an observer, so that "simultaneity" is, therefore, not an absolute property of the two events and nothing else, but must also involve the relation of the events to the observer. Until therefore we have experimental proof to the contrary, we must be prepared to find that the simultaneity of two events depends on their relation to the observer, and in particular on their velocity. Einstein, in thus analyzing what is involved in making a judgment of simultaneity, and in seizing on the act of the observer as the essence of the situation, is actually adopting a new point of view as to what the concepts of physics should be, namely, the operational view.

Of course Einstein actually went much further than this, and found precisely how the operations for judging simultaneity change when the observer moves, and obtained quantitative expressions for the effect of the motion of the observer on the relative time of two events. We may notice, parenthetically, that there is much freedom of choice in selecting the exact operations; those which Einstein chose were determined by convenience and simplicity with relation to light beams. Entirely apart from the precise quantitative relations of Einstein's theory, however, the important point for us is that if we had adopted the operational point of view, we would, before the discovery of the actual physical facts, have seen that simultaneity is essentially a relative concept, and would have left room in our thinking for the discovery of such effects as were later found. . .

The Relative Character of Knowledge

Two other consequences of the operational point of view must now be examined. First is the consequence that all our knowledge is relative. This may be understood in a general or a more particular sense. The general sense is illustrated in Haldane's book on the *Reign of Relativity.* Relativity in the general sense is the merest truism if the operational definition of concept is accepted, for experience is described in terms of concepts, and since our concepts are constructed of operations, all our knowledge must unescapably be relative to the operations selected. But knowledge is also relative in a narrower sense, as when we say there is no such thing as absolute rest (or motion) or absolute size, but rest and size are relative terms. Conclusions of this kind are involved in the specific character of the operations in terms of which rest or size are defined. An examination of the operations by which we determine whether a body is at rest or in motion shows that the operations are relative operations: rest or motion is determined with respect to some other body selected as the standard. In saying that there is no such thing as absolute rest or motion we are not making a statement about nature in the sense that might be supposed, but we are merely making a statement about the character of our descriptive processes. Similarly with regard to size: examination of the operations of the measuring process shows that size is measured relative to the fundamental measuring rod.

The "absolute" therefore disappears in the original meaning of the word. But the "absolute" may usefully return with an altered meaning, and we may say that a thing has absolute properties if the numerical magnitude is the same when measured with the same formal procedure by all observers. Whether a given property is absolute or not can be determined only by experiment, landing us in the paradoxical position that the absolute is absolute only relative to experiment. In some cases, the most superficial observation shows that a property is not absolute, as, for example, it is at once obvious that measured velocity changes with the motion of the observer. But in other cases the decision is more difficult. Thus Michelson thought he had an absolute procedure for measuring length, by referring to the wave length of the red cadmium line as standard; it required difficult and accurate experiment to show that this length varies with the motion of the observer. Even then, by changing the definition of the length of a moving object, we believe that length might be made to reassume its desired absolute character.

To stop the discussion at this point might leave the impression that this observation of the relative character of knowledge is of only a very tenuous and academic interest, since it appears to be concerned mostly with the character of our descriptive processes, and to say little about external nature. [What this means we leave to the metaphysician to decide.] But I believe there is a deeper significance to all this. It must be remembered that all our argument starts with the concepts as given. Now these concepts involve physical operations; in the discovery of what operations may be usefully employed in describing nature is buried almost all physical experience. In erecting our structure of physical science, we are building on the work of all the ages. There is then this purely physical significance in the statement that all motion is relative, namely that no operations of measuring motion have been found to be useful in describing simply the behavior of nature which are not operations relative to a single observer; in making this statement we are stating something about nature. It takes an enormous amount of real physical experience to discover relations of this sort. The discovery that the number obtained by counting the number of times a stick may be applied to an object can be simply used in describing natural phenomena was one of the most important and fundamental discoveries ever made by man.

Meaningless Questions

Another consequence of the operational character of our concepts, almost a corollary of that considered above, is that it is quite possible, nay even disquietingly easy, to invent expressions or to ask questions that are meaningless. It constitutes a great advance in our critical attitude toward nature to realize that a great many of the questions that we uncritically ask are without meaning. If a specific question has meaning, it must be possible to find operations by which an answer may be given to it. It will be found in many cases that the operations cannot exist, and the question therefore has no meaning. For instance, it means nothing to ask whether a star is at rest or not. Another example is a question proposed by Clifford, namely, whether it is not possible that as the solar system moves from one part of space to another the absolute scale of magnitude may be changing, but in such a way as to affect all things equally, so that the change of scale can never be detected. An examination of the operations by which length is measured in terms of measuring rods shows that the operations do not exist (because of the nature of our definition of length) for answering the question. The question can be given meaning only from the point of view of some imaginary superior being watching from an external point of vantage. But the operations by which such a being measures length are different from the operations of our definition of length, so that the question acquires meaning only by changing the significance of our terms—in the original sense the question means nothing.

To state that a certain question about nature is meaningless is to make a significant statement about nature itself, because the fundamental operations are determined by nature, and to state that nature cannot be described in terms of certain operations is a significant statement.

It must be recognized, however, that there is a sense in which no serious question is entirely without meaning, because doubtless the questioner had in mind some intention in asking the question. But to give meaning in this sense to a question, one must inquire into the meaning of the concepts as used by the questioner, and it will often be found that these concepts can be defined only in terms of fictitious properties, as Newton's absolute time was defined by its properties, so that the meaning to be ascribed to the question in this way has no connection with reality. I believe that it will enable us to make more significant and interesting statements, and therefore will be more useful, to adopt exclusively the operational view, and so admit the possibility of questions entirely without meaning.

This matter of meaningless questions is a very subtle thing which may poison much more of our thought than that dealing with purely physical phenomena. I believe that many of the questions asked about social and philosophical subjects will be found to be meaningless when examined from the point of view of operations. It would doubtless conduce greatly to clarity of thought if the operational mode of thinking were adopted in all fields of inquiry as well as in the physical. Just as in the physical domain, so in other domains, one is making a significant statement about his subject in stating that a certain question is meaningless.

In order to emphasize this matter of meaningless questions, I give here a list of questions, with which the reader may amuse himself by finding whether they have meaning or not.

1. Was there ever a time when matter did not exist?
2. May time have a beginning or an end?

3. Why does time flow?
4. May space be bounded?
5. May space or time be discontinuous?
6. May space have a fourth dimension, not directly detectible, but given indirectly by inference?
7. Are there parts of nature forever beyond our detection?
8. Is the sensation which I call blue really the *same* as that which my neighbor calls blue? Is it possible that a blue object may arouse in him the same sensation that a red object does in me and *vice versa?*
9. May there be missing integers in the series of natural numbers as we know them?
10. Is a universe possible in which $2 + 2 \neq 4$?
11. Why does negative electricity attract positive?
12. Why does nature obey laws?
13. Is a universe possible in which the laws are different?
14. If one part of our universe could be *completely* isolated from the rest, would it continue to obey the same laws?
15. Can we be sure that our logical processes are valid?

General Comments on the Operational Point of View

To adopt the operational point of view involves much more than a mere restriction of the sense in which we understand "concept," but means a farreaching change in all our habits of thought, in that we shall no longer permit ourselves to use as tools in our thinking concepts of which we cannot give an adequate account in terms of operations. In some respects thinking becomes simpler, because certain old generalizations and idealizations become incapable of use; for instance, many of the speculations of the early natural philosophers become simply unreadable. In other respects, however, thinking becomes much more difficult, because the operational implications of a concept are often very involved. For example, it is more difficult to grasp adequately all that is contained in the apparently simple concept of "time," and requires the continual correction of mental tendencies which we have long unquestioningly accepted.

Operational thinking will at first prove to be an unsocial virtue; one will find oneself perpetually unable to understand the simplest conversation of one's friends, and will make oneself universally unpopular by demanding the meaning of apparently the simplest terms of every argument. Possibly after every one has schooled himself to this better way, there will remain a permanent unsocial tendency, because doubtless much of our present conversation will then become unnecessary. The socially optimistic may venture to hope, however, that the ultimate effect will be to release one's energies for more stimulating and interesting interchange of ideas.

Not only will operational thinking reform the social art of conversation, but all our social relations will be liable to reform. Let any one examine in operational terms any popular present-day discussion of religious or moral questions to realize the magnitude of the reformation awaiting us. Wherever we temporize or compromise in applying our theories of conduct to practical life we may suspect a failure of operational thinking.

7

NORBERT WIENER

(1894–1964)

*Some Moral and Technical Consequences of Automation**

Wiener is best known as the developer of the science of cybernetics, which is concerned with the relationship between communication and control in human beings and machines. He also, however, was very interested in the application of cybernetic and automational developments to society. Wiener, in The Human Use of Human Beings, *presents the thesis that society is a vast series of channels for internal communication and that the integrity of those channels must be maintained for the welfare of man. Machines as well as men are integral parts of society. In this selection, Wiener discusses philosophic problems in the Age of Automation. Wiener examines the attitudes prevalent in the automated society and the values which lie at the base of our use of technology. He sees that the question of the use or misuse of the scientist's discoveries is a moral one. The moral problem, Wiener tells us, is similar to the question of slavery. The master must know beforehand exactly what he wants from the slave, for what purpose the slave is to be used, or the positions of master and slave are likely to become reversed.*

* From *Science*, 131 (May 6, 1960), pp. 1355–1358. Used by kind permission of *Science*.

Cybernetics

SOME thirteen years ago, a book of mine was published by the name of *Cybernetics*. In it I discussed the problems of control and communication in the living organism and the machine. I made a considerable number of predictions about the development of controlled machines and about the corresponding techniques of automatization, which I foresaw as having important consequences affecting the society of the future. Now, thirteen years later, it seems appropriate to take stock of the present position with respect to both cybernetic technique and the social consequences of this technique.

Before commencing on the detail of these matters, I should like to mention a certain attitude of the man in the street toward cybernetics and automatization. This attitude needs a critical discussion, and in my opinion it should be rejected in its entirety. This is the assumption that machines cannot possess any degree of originality. This frequently takes the form of a statement that nothing can come out of the machine which has not been put into it. This is often interpreted as asserting that a machine which man has made must remain continually subject to man, so that its operation is at any time open to human interference and to a change in policy. On the basis of such an attitude, many people have pooh-poohed the dangers of machine techniques, and they have flatly contradicted the early predictions of Samuel Butler that the machine might take over the control of mankind.

It is true that in the time of Samuel Butler the available machines were far less hazardous than machines are today, for they involved only power, not a certain degree of thinking and communication. However, the machine techniques of the present day have invaded the latter fields as well, so that the actual machine of today is very different from the image that Butler held, and we cannot transfer to these new devices the assumptions which seemed axiomatic a generation ago. I find myself facing a public which has formed its attitude toward the machine on the basis of an imperfect understanding of the structure and mode of operation of modern machines.

It is my thesis that machines can and do transcend some of the limitations of their designers, and that in doing so they may be both effective and dangerous. It may well be that in principle we cannot make any machine the elements of whose behavior we cannot comprehend sooner or later. This does not mean in any way that we shall be able to comprehend these elements in substantially less time than the time required for operation of the machine, or even within any given number of years or generations.

As is now generally admitted, over a limited range of operation, machines act far more rapidly than human beings and are far more precise in performing the details of their operations. This being the case, even when machines do not in any way transcend man's intelligence, they very well may, and often do, transcend man in the performance of tasks. An intelligent understanding of their mode of performance may be delayed long after the task which they have been set has been completed.

This means that though machines are theoretically subject to human criticism, such criticism may be ineffective until long after it is relevant. To be effective in warding off disastrous consequences, our understanding of our man-made machines should in general develop *pari passu* with the performance of the machine. By the very slowness of our human actions, our effective control of our machines may be nullified. By the time we are able to react to information conveyed by our senses and stop the car we are driving, it may already have run head on into a wall.

Game-playing

I shall come back to this point later in this article. For the present, let me discuss the technique of machines for a very specific purpose: that of playing games. In this matter I shall deal more particularly with the game of checkers, for which the International Business Machines Corporation has developed very effective game-playing machines.

Let me say once for all that we are not concerned here with the machines which operate on a perfect closed theory of the game they play. The game theory of von Neumann and Morgenstern may be suggestive as to the operation of actual game-playing machines, but it does not actually describe them.

In a game as complicated as checkers, if each player tries to choose his play in view of the best move his opponent can make, against the best response he can give, against the best response his opponent can give, and so on, he will have taken upon himself an impossible task. Not only is this humanly impossible but there is actually no reason to suppose that it is the best policy against the opponent by whom he is faced, whose limitations are equal to his own.

The von Neumann theory of games bears no very close relation to the theory by which game-playing machines operate. The latter corresponds much more closely to the methods of play used by expert but limited human chess players against other chess players. Such players depend on certain strategic evaluations, which are in essence not complete. While the von Neumann type of play is valid for games like ticktacktoe, with a complete theory, the very interest of chess and checkers lies in the fact that they do not possess a complete theory. Neither do war nor business competition nor any of the other forms of competitive activity in which we are really interested.

In a game like ticktacktoe, with a small number of moves, where each player is in a position to contemplate all possibilities and to establish a defense against the best possible moves of the other player, a complete theory of the von Neumann type is valid. In such a case, the game must inevitably end in a win for the first player, a win for the second player or a draw.

I question strongly whether this concept of the perfect game is a completely realistic one in the cases of actual, nontrivial games. Great generals like Napoleon and great admirals like Nelson have proceeded in a different manner. They have been aware not only of the limitations of their opponents in such matters as materiel and personnel but equally of their limitations in experience and in military know-how. It was by a realistic appraisal of the relative inexperience in naval operations of the continental powers as compared with the highly developed tactical and strategic competence of the British fleet that Nelson was able to display the boldness which pushed the continental forces off the seas. This he could not have done had he engaged in the long, relatively indecisive, and possibly losing, conflict to which his assumption of the best possible strategy on the part of his enemy would have doomed him.

In assessing not merely the materiel and personnel of his enemies but also the degree of judgment and the amount of skill in tactics and strategy to be expected of them, Nelson acted on the basis of their record in previous combats. Similarly, an important factor in Napoleon's conduct of his combat with the Austrians in Italy was his knowledge of the rigidity and mental limitation of Würmser.

This element of experience should receive adequate recognition in any realistic theory of games. It is quite legitimate for a chess player to play, not against an ideal, nonexisting, perfect antagonist, but rather against one whose habits he has been able to determine from the record. Thus, in the theory of games, at least two different intellectual efforts must be made. One is the short-term effort of playing with a determined policy for the individual game. The other is the examination of a record of many games. This record has been set by the player himself, by his opponent or even by players with whom he has not personally played. In terms of this record, he determines the relative advantages of different policies as proved over the past.

There is even a third stage of judgment required in a chess game. This is expressed at least in part by the length of the significant past. The development of theory in chess decreases the importance of games played at a different stage of the art. On the other hand, an astute chess theoretician may estimate in advance that a certain policy currently in fashion has become of little value, and that it may be best to return to earlier modes of play to anticipate the change in policy of the people whom he is likely to find as his opponents.

Thus, in determining policy in chess there are several different levels of consideration which correspond in a certain way to the different logical types of Bertrand Russell. There is the level of tactics, the level of strategy, the level of the general considerations which should have been weighed in determining this strategy, the level in which the length of the relevant past—the past within which these considerations may be valid—is taken into account, and so on. Each new level demands a study of a much larger past than the previous one.

I have compared these levels with the logical types of Russell concerning classes, classes of classes, classes of classes of classes and so on. It may be noted that Russell does not consider statements involving all types as significant. He brings out the futility of such questions as that concerning the barber who shaves all persons, and only those persons who do not shave themselves. Does he shave himself? On one type he does, on the next type he does not and so on indefinitely. All such questions involving an infinity of types may lead to unsolvable paradoxes. Similarly, the search for the best policy under all levels of sophistication is a futile one and must lead to nothing but confusion.

These considerations arise in the determination of policy by machines as well as in the determination of policy by persons. These are the questions which arise in the programming of programming. The lowest type of game-playing machine plays in terms of a certain rigid evaluation of plays. Quantities such as the value of pieces gained or lost, the command of the pieces, their mobility and so on can be given numerical weights on a certain empirical basis, and a weighting may be given on this basis to each next play conforming to the rules of the game. The play with the greatest weight may be chosen. Under these circumstances, the play of the machine will seem to its antagonist—who cannot help but evaluate the chess personality of the machine—a rigid one.

The next step is for the machine to take into consideration not merely the moves as they occurred in the individual game but the record of games previously played. On this basis, the machine may stop from time to time, not to play but to consider what (linear or nonlinear) weighting of the factors which it has been given to consider would correspond best to won games as opposed to lost (or drawn) games. On this basis, it continues to play with a new weighting. Such a machine would seem to its human opponent to have a far less rigid game personality, and tricks which would defeat it at an earlier stage may now fail to deceive it.

The present level of these learning machines is that they play a fair amateur game at chess but that in checkers they can show a marked superiority to the player who has programmed them after from ten to twenty playing hours of working and indoctrination. They thus most definitely escape from the completely effective control of the man who has made them. Rigid as the repertory of factors may be which they are in a position to take into consideration, they do unquestionably—and so say those who have played with them—show originality, not merely in their tactics, which may be quite unforeseen, but even in the detailed weighting of their strategy.

As I have said, checker-playing machines which learn have developed to the point at which they can defeat the programmer. However, they appear still to have one weakness. This lies in the end game. Here the machines are somewhat clumsy in determining the best way to give the *coup de grâce*. This is due to the fact that the existing machines have for the most part adopted a program in which the identical strategy is carried out at each stage of the game. In view of the similarity of values of pieces in checkers, this is quite natural for a large part of the play but ceases to be perfectly relevant when the board is relatively empty and the main problem is that of moving into position rather than that of direct attack. Within the frame of the methods I have described it is quite possible to have a second exploration to determine what the policy should be after the number of pieces of the opponent is so reduced that these new considerations become paramount.

Chess-playing machines have not, so far, been brought to the degree of perfection of checker-playing machines, although, as I have said, they can most certainly play a respectable amateur game. Probably the reason for this is similar to the reason for their relative efficiency in the end game of checkers. In chess, not only is the end game quite different in its proper strategy from the mid game but the opening game is also. The difference between checkers and chess in this respect is that the initial play of the pieces in checkers is not very different in character from the play which arises in the mid game, while in chess, pieces at the beginning have an arrangement of exceptionally low mobility, so that the problem of deploying them from this position is particularly difficult. This is the reason why opening play and development form a special branch of chess theory.

There are various ways in which the machine can take cognizance of these well-known facts and explore a separate waiting strategy for the opening. This does not mean that the type of game theory which I have here discussed is not applicable to chess but merely that it requires much more consideration before we can make a machine that can play master chess. Some of my friends who are engaged in these problems believe that this goal will be achieved in from ten to twenty-five years. Not being a chess expert, I do not venture to make any such predictions on my own initiative.

It is quite in the cards that learning machines will be used to program the pushing of the button in a new push-button war. Here we are considering a field in which automata of a nonlearning character are probably already in use. It is quite out of the question to program these machines on the basis of an actual experience in real war. For one thing, a sufficient exerience to give an adequate programming would probably see humanity already wiped out.

Moreover, the techniques of push-button war are bound to change so much that by the time an adequate experience could have been accumulated, the basis of the beginning would have radically changed. Therefore, the programming of such a learning machine would have to be based on some sort of war game, just as commanders and staff officials now learn an important part of the art of strategy in a similar manner. Here, however, if the rules for victory in a war game do not correspond to what we actually wish for our country, it is more than likely that such a machine may produce a policy which would win a nominal victory on points at the cost of every interest we have at heart, even that of national survival.

Man and Slave

The problem, and it is a moral problem, with which we are here faced is very close to one of the great problems of slavery. Let us grant that slavery is bad because it is cruel. It is, however, self-contradictory, and for a reason which is quite different. We wish a slave to be intelligent, to be able to assist us in the carrying out of our tasks. However, we also wish him to be subservient. Complete subservience and complete intelligence do not go together. How often in ancient times the clever Greek philosopher slave of a less intelligent Roman slaveholder must have dominated the actions of his master rather than obeyed his wishes! Similarly, if the machines become more and more efficient and operate at a higher and higher psychological level, the catastrophe foreseen by Butler of the dominance of the machine comes nearer and nearer.

The human brain is a far more efficient control apparatus than is the intelligent machine when we come to the higher areas of logic. It is a self-organizing system which depends on its capacity to modify itself into a new machine rather than on ironclad accuracy and speed in problem-solving. We have already made very successful machines of the lowest logical type, with a rigid policy. We are beginning to make machines of the second logical type, where the policy itself improves with learning. In the construction of operative machines, there is no specific foreseeable limit with respect to logical type, nor is it safe to make a pronouncement about the exact level at which the brain is superior to the machine. Yet for a long time at least there will always be some level at which the brain is better than the constructed machine, even though this level may shift upwards and upwards.

It may be seen that the result of a programming technique of automatization is to remove from the mind of the designer and operator an effective understanding of many of the stages by which the machine comes to its conclusions and of what the real tactical intentions of many of its operations may be. This is highly relevant to the problem of our being able to foresee undesired consequences outside the frame of the strategy of the game while the machine is still in action and while intervention on our part may prevent the occurrence of these consequences.

Here it is necessary to realize that human action is a feedback action. To avoid a disastrous consequence, it is not enough that some action on our part should be sufficient to change that course of the machine, because it is quite possible that we lack information on which to base consideration of such an action.

In neurophysiological language, ataxia can be quite as much of a deprivation as paralysis. A patient with locomotor ataxia may not suffer from any defect of his muscles or motor nerves, but if his muscles and tendons and organs do not tell him exactly what position he is in, and whether the tensions to which his organs are subjected will or will not lead to his falling, he will be unable to stand up. Similarly, when a machine constructed by us is capable of operating on its incoming data at a pace which we cannot keep, we may not know, until too late, when to turn it off. We all know the fable of the sorcerer's apprentice, in which the boy makes the broom carry water in his master's absence, so that it is on the point of drowning him when his master reappears. If the boy had had to seek a charm to stop the mischief in the *grimoires* of his master's library, he might have been drowned before he had discovered the relevant incantation. Similarly, if a bottle factory is programmed on the basis of maximum productivity, the owner may be made bankrupt by the enormous inventory of unsalable bottles manufactured before he learns he should have stopped production six months earlier.

The "Sorcerer's Apprentice" is only one of many tales based on the assumption that the agencies of magic are literal-minded. There is the story of the genie and the fisherman in the *Arabian Nights,* in which the fisherman breaks the seal of Solomon which has imprisoned the genie and finds the genie vowed to his own destruction; there is the tale of the "Monkey's Paw," by W. W. Jacobs, in which the sergeant major brings back from India a talisman which has the power to grant each of three people three wishes. Of the first recipient of this talisman we are told only that his third wish is for death. The sergeant major, the second person whose wishes are granted, finds his experiences too terrible to relate. His friend, who receives the talisman, wishes first for £200. Shortly thereafter, an official of the factory in which his son works comes to tell him that his son has been killed in the machinery and that, without any admission of responsibility, the company is sending him as consolation the sum of £200. His next wish is that his son should come back, and the ghost knocks at the door. His third wish is that the ghost should go away.

Disastrous results are to be expected not merely in the world of fairy tales but in the real world wherever two agencies essentially foreign to each other are coupled in the attempt to achieve a common purpose. If the communication between these two agencies as to the nature of this purpose is incomplete, it must only be expected that the results of this cooperation will be unsatisfactory. If we use, to achieve our purposes, a mechanical agency with whose operation we cannot efficiently interfere once we have started it, because the action is so fast and irrevocable that we have not the data to intervene before the action is complete, then we had better be quite sure that the purpose put into the machine is the purpose which we really desire and not merely a colorful imitation of it.

Time Scales

Up to this point I have been considering the quasi-moral problems caused by the simultaneous action of the machine and the human being in a joint enterprise. We have seen that one of the chief causes of the danger of disastrous consequences in the use of the learning machine is that man and machine operate on two distinct time scales, so that the machine is much faster than man and the two do not gear together without serious difficulties. Problems of the same sort arise whenever two control operators on very different time scales act together, irrespective of which system is the faster and which system is the slower. This leaves us the much more directly moral question: What are the moral problems when man as an individual operates in connection with the controlled process of a much slower time scale, such as a portion of political history or—our main subject of inquiry—the development of science?

Let it be noted that the development of science is a control and communication process for the long-term understanding and control of matter. In this process fifty years are as a day in the life of the individual. For this reason, the individual scientist must work as a part of a process whose time scale is so long that he himself can only contemplate a very limited sector of it. Here, too, communication between the two parts of a double machine is difficult and limited. Even when the individual believes that science contributes to the human ends which he has at heart, his belief needs a continual scanning and re-evaluation which is only partly possible. For the individual scientist, even the partial appraisal of this liaison between the man and the process requires an imaginative forward glance at history which is difficult, exacting and only limitedly achievable. And if we adhere simply to the creed of the scientist, that an incomplete knowledge of the world and of ourselves is better than no knowledge, we can still by no means always justify the naïve assumption that the faster we rush ahead to employ the new powers for action which are opened up to us, the better it will be. We must always exert the full strength of our imagination to examine where the full use of our new modalities may lead us.

Further Reading

Butterfield, Herbert. *The Origins of Modern Science*. New York: Free Press, 1957.

Feigl and Maxwell. *Current Issues in the Philosophy of Science*. New York: Holt, Rinehart and Winston, 1961.

Hanson, Norwood Russell. *Patterns of Discovery*. Cambridge: Cambridge University Press, 1958.

Kuhn, Thomas S. *The Structure of Scientific Revolutions*. Chicago: University of Chicago Press, 1962.

Mill, John Stuart. *Philosophy of Scientific Method*. New York: Hafner Publishing, 1950.

Nagel, Ernest. *The Structure of Science*. New York: Harcourt, Brace & World, 1961.

Popper, Karl. *Conjectures and Refutations*. New York: Basic Books, 1963.

Reichenbach, Hans. *The Rise of Scientific Philosophy*. Berkeley: University of California Press, 1951.

Smart, J. J. C. *Between Science and Philosophy*. New York: Random House, 1968.

Vygotsky, Lev Semenovich. *Thought and Language*. Cambridge: M. I. T. Press, 1962.

Whorf, Benjamin Lee. *Language, Thought & Reality*. Cambridge: M. I. T. Press, 1956.

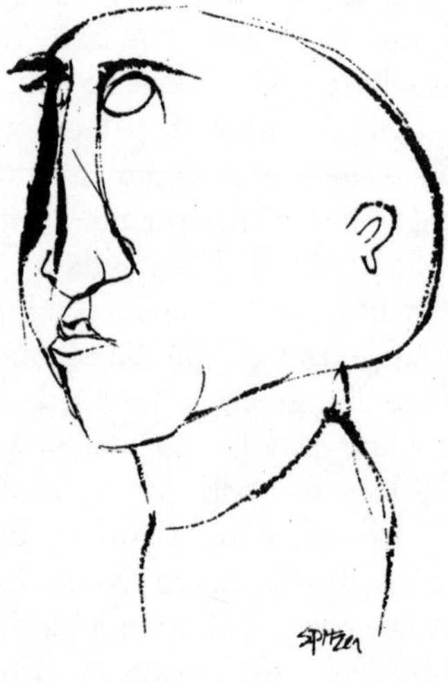